Third Edition

CULTURAL ～ ANTHROPOLOGY

MARVIN HARRIS

University of Florida

HarperCollins*Publishers*

A list of text, table, and illustration credits appears as a "Credits" section at the back of this book and is hereby made part of this copyright page.

Sponsoring Editor: Alan McClare
Project Editor: Donna DeBenedictis/Robert Cooper
Art Direction: Lucy Krikorian
Text Design: Robin Hoffmann/Brand X Studio
Cover Design: Kay Cannizzaro
Cover Photo: Courtesy of Kenneth Good
Title Page Photo: Robert Caputo/Stock Boston
Photo Research: Ilene Cherna Bellovin
Production Administrator: Beth Maglione
Compositor: Progressive Typographers
Printer and Binder: R. R. Donnelly & Sons Company

CULTURAL ANTHROPOLOGY, Third Edition

Library of Congress Cataloging-in-Publication Data
Harris, Marvin, 1927 –
    Cultural anthropology/Marvin Harris. —3rd ed.
        p.   cm.
    Includes bibliographical references (p.).
    Includes index.
    ISBN 0-06-042667-5
    1. Ethnology.   I. Title.
GN316.H36   1991
306 — dc20   90-5024
                                                                                CIP

ISBN   0-06-042667-5 (student edition)
ISBN   0-06-042702-7 (teacher edition)

91 92 93   9 8 7 6 5 4 3 2

BRIEF CONTENTS

꒰ ꒱

DETAILED CONTENTS

TO THE INSTRUCTOR

This new edition of *Cultural Anthropology* features four substantial changes: a new chapter on gender and culture (Chapter 13), much new material in 11 new or heavily revised sections, new boxed material emphasizing important points, and a major overhaul of the illustration program. This edition also benefits from a serious effort to make the book gender-neutral. The result, I think, is a much improved *Cultural Anthropology*.

Most of the content of this third edition of *Cultural Anthropology* has been critically examined by Nancy Scheper-Hughes under the auspices of the American Anthropological Association's Gender and Anthropology Project. I like to think of it as having been "gender-proofed." This does not mean that the new edition embodies all of the suggestions made by Scheper-Hughes and other feminist readers. I have not always heeded their advice, but I have at least thought long and hard about their points of view. Perhaps the most important and concentrated modification resulting from the gender-proofing process is a new chapter called "Gender and Culture" (Chapter 13). I had pre-

viously treated gender roles and gender hierarchies in the chapter called "Personality and Sex." Now, personality and culture has its own separate chapter as well.

I have also split the previous edition's Chapter 1 into an "Introduction" (new Chapter 1) and "The Nature of Culture" (new Chapter 2). The reason for this is that there was a sharp topical break between describing anthropology as a profession and the substantive treatment of the concept of culture. So there are now 18 chapters plus an appendix, as compared with 16 chapters plus an appendix in the previous edition. In terms of substantive coverage, however, there is really just one additional chapter.

Much new material based on 190 new and updated bibliographic entries appears throughout this edition. And there are 11 new or substantially modified sections not counting those that appear in the "Gender and Culture" chapter, as follows:

Are Religion and Science Necessarily in Conflict?

Phonetics

Phonemics

Measuring the Costs and Benefits of Rearing Children

The Contraception, Infanticide, Abortion Debate

Domestic Groups and the Avoidance of Incest

Causes of Matrilocality

Hawaii: On the Threshold of the State

The New Racism

The Drug Connection

Particularizing Approaches

Another preoccupation in this as in the previous editions has been readability. With the help of a gifted copyeditor, I have gone over the text word-by-word to make sure that what I want to say is being said in simple and straightforward prose. Readability has been further enhanced by the use of the following boxes:

*Why Major in Anthropology?

*Simultaneous Independent Inventions

*Etic and Behavioral Components of the Universal Pattern

Black English

Language and Logic

*Not All Hunter-Gatherers Are Alike

Reciprocity Among the !Kung

Modest Providers

Boastful Providers

*Principal Forms of Human Marriage

Song Duel

The Right Stuff

Ordered Anarchy

*Egalitarian Versus Hierarchical Redistribution

The Tragic Fate of the !Kung San

A World of Limited Good

*The Broken Fountain

*Culture or Poverty?

*A Yurok Woman's View of Menstrual Seclusion

Sexual Symbolism in Bangladesh

*The Body and Culture

Scapegoating the Windigo

Getting Drunk on Truk

*Meat and Politics in the Soviet Union

Peyote Religion

*Some Social Functions of Music, Song, and Dance

*Modern Times: Working for a Large Oil Company as a Customer Service Operator

Presidential Mandates?

The boxes with asterisks contain new material—mostly dramatic or pithy quotations, definitions, or points that I feel need to be stressed. Those without asterisks are boxes that incorporate quotes that were previously part of the regular text. These serve the additional function of enhancing readability by "unpacking" the sections in which they formerly appeared.

Visual impact has always been a concern of mine. For this edition all the visual materials have been carefully examined for quality and relevance and many new photos have been added.

Once again, it is time to express my appreciation to the people at HarperCollins for their assistance in trying to make this a textbook that serves your teaching needs in a lively, comprehensive, and up-to-date manner. I thank especially editors Alan McClare and Donna DeBenedictis, copyeditor Katherine Hieatt, and Ilene Cherna Bellovin, photo researcher.

In making revisions for this edition I was able to draw on the evaluations submitted by a fine group of scholars who teach introductory anthropology. They are Ann W. Brittain, University of Miami; James Garber, Southwest Texas State University; Michael P. Hoffman, University of Arkansas; Yvonne Jones, University of Louisville; Patrick McKim, California Polytechnic Institute, San Luis Obispo; Scott Rushforth, New Mexico State University; David N. Suggs, Kenyon College; and Arthur Tuden, University of Pittsburgh.

Barbara Bode of the University of Rhode Island kindly sent me her class's evaluations of the previous edition. (Christopher Bates: You made my day!) I also want to thank Daniel Cartledge for his help in putting the bibliography together, as well as Madeline Harris for her tender loving care.

Marvin Harris

TO THE STUDENT

Cultural Anthropology provides you, the student, with a global and comparative perspective for understanding the origin and prospects of the modern world. In the pages that follow you will learn mostly about the customs and beliefs of people who are alive today or who lived in the recent past — people who inhabit great cities and are citizens of superpowers, as well as people who live in tiny desert bands and remote jungle villages.

You are about to encounter an amazing variety of customs and beliefs. Some you may find amusing; others may shock you. But I have not written this book to compete with Ripley's *Believe-It-Or-Not*. We have a more serious task before us. My aim is to explain — to the limits of currently known facts and the latest scientific theories — why customs and beliefs differ from one society to another, and why, despite such differences, remarkable similarities exist in the way human beings live in even the most distant parts of the globe.

I have done everything I could think of to make this book as easy to read as possible. Yet the subject matter of cultural anthropology is vast and complex. If we are to have serious explanations of scholarly merit, mental concentration cannot be eliminated. I won't apologize. I think you will get a lot out of reading this book. It will tell you not only what cultural anthropology is all about, but something more important. It will tell you about your own customs and beliefs — how they originated, why they are maintained, and why they are changing. In other words, it will tell you a good deal about who you are and why you and your relatives, friends, and fellow citizens think and act in certain ways and not in others.

Although I have worked hard to make this edition both readable and informative, room for improvement undoubtedly exists. If you have any suggestions as to how further improvements can be made, please send them to me in care of HarperCollins and I will try to incorporate them in future editions.

Marvin Harris

Chapter 1

INTRODUCTION

Anthropology is the study of humankind—of ancient and modern people and their ways of living. Since this subject is very large and complex, different branches of anthropology focus on different aspects of the human experience. Some branches focus on how our species, known scientifically as *Homo sapiens*, evolved from earlier species. Others focus on how *H. sapiens* came to possess the uniquely human facility for language, how languages evolved and diversified, and how modern languages serve the needs of human communication. Still others focus on the learned traditions of human thought and behavior known as *cultures*. They study how ancient cultures evolved and diversified, and how and why modern cultures change or stay the same.

Within departments of anthropology at major universities in the United States the different perspectives of anthropology are usually represented by four fields of study: cultural anthropology (sometimes called *social anthropology*), archaeology, anthropological linguistics, and physical anthropology. (See Box 1.1.)

Cultural anthropology deals with the description and analysis of cultures — the socially learned traditions — of past and present ages. It has a subdiscipline, *ethnography*, that systematically describes contemporary cultures. Comparison of these descriptions provides the basis for hypotheses and theories about the causes of human life-styles (Figure 1.1d).

Archaeology and cultural anthropology share similar goals but differ in the methods they use and the cultures they study. Archaeology examines the material remains that cultures of the past leave behind on or below the Earth's surface. Without the findings of archaeology, we would not be able to understand the past, especially where people have left no written records. And without understanding the past we cannot understand the present (Figure 1.1a).

Anthropological linguistics is the study of the great variety of languages spoken by human beings. Anthropological linguists attempt to trace the history of all known families of languages. They are concerned with the way language influences and is influenced by other aspects of human life, and with the relationship between the evolution of language and the evolution of our species, *Homo sapiens*. They are also concerned with the relationship between the evolution of languages and the evolution of different cultures (Figure 1.1b).

Physical anthropology (also called *biological anthropology*) is the study of human origins and our biologically determined nature. Physical anthropologists seek to reconstruct the course of human evolution by studying the fossil remains of ancient humanlike species. Physical anthropologists also seek to describe the distribution of hereditary variations among contemporary populations and to sort out and measure the relative contributions to human life made by heredity, environment, and culture (Figure 1.1c).

This book is mainly concerned with the cultural anthropology. (See the author's *Cul-*

(a)

(b)

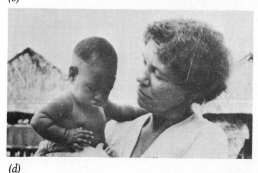

(d)

Figure 1.1 Anthropolgists at work.
(a) Jerald T. Milanich, archaeologist, Florida
Museum of Natural History, with prehistoric (A.D.
200–900) native American bird vessel. (b) Linguist
Francesca Merlin with the speakers of a previously
unknown language near Mt. Hagen, New Guinea.
(c) Physical anthropologist Donald Johanson fossil
hunting at Olduvai Gorge. (d) Ethnographer
Margaret Mead among the Manus Islanders.

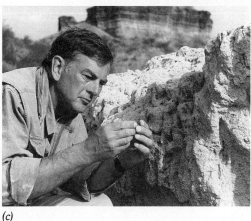

(c)

ture, People, Nature: An Introduction to General Anthropology, 5th edition, for a more comprehensive view of the other fields.)

Why Anthropology?

Many disciplines other than anthropology are
concerned with the study of human beings.
Biologists, geneticists, and physiologists study
our physical nature. In medicine alone,
hundreds of specialists investigate the human
body, and psychiatrists and psychologists, rank
upon rank, seek the essence of the human
mind and soul. Many other disciplines examine
our cultural, intellectual, and aesthetic behavior. These disciplines include sociology,
human geography, social psychology, history,
political science, economics, linguistics, theology, philosophy, musicology, art, literature,
and architecture. There are also many "area
specialists" who study the languages and life-

Box 1.1

AN ANTHROPOLOGICAL SCORECARD

Anthropologists frequently identify themselves with one or more specialized branches of the four major fields. The following is only a partial listing.

CULTURAL ANTHROPOLOGY

Ethnography   Describe contemporary cultures.

Applied Anthropology   Study and make proposals to solve practical problems and evaluate results.

Medical Anthropology   Study biological and cultural factors in health, disease, and the treatment of the sick.

Urban Anthropology   Study city life.

Development Anthropology   Study the causes of underdevelopment and development among the less developed nations.

ARCHAEOLOGY

Historic Archaeology   Study cultures of the recent past by means of a combination of written records and archaeological excavations.

Industrial Archaeology   Historic archaeology that focuses on industrial factories and facilities.

Contract Archaeology   Conduct archaeological surveys for environmental impact statements and protection of historic and prehistoric sites.

PHYSICAL (BIOLOGICAL) ANTHROPOLOGY

Primatology   Study social life and biology of monkeys, great apes, and other primates.

Human Paleontology   Search for and study fossil remains of early human species.

Forensic Anthropology   Identify victims of murders and accidents and provide expert testimony in court.

Population Genetics   Study hereditary differences in human populations.

LINGUISTICS

Historical Linguistics   Reconstruct the origins of specific languages and of families of languages.

Descriptive Linguistics   Study the grammar and syntax of languages.

Sociolinguistics   Study the actual use of language in the communication behavior of daily life.

styles of particular peoples, nations, or regions: "Latin Americanists," "Indianists," "Sinologists," and so on. What, then, is distinctive about anthropology?

The distinction of anthropology is that it is global and comparative. Other disciplines are concerned with only a particular segment of human experience or a particular time or phase of our cultural or biological development. But anthropologists never base their findings on the study of a single population, race, tribe, class, nation, time, or place. Anthropologists insist first and foremost that conclusions based on the study of one particular human group or civilization be checked against the evidence of other groups or civilizations. In this way anthropologists hope to transcend the biases of their own sex, class, tribe, race, nation, religion, or culture. In anthropological perspective, all peoples and cultures are equally worthy of study. Thus, anthropology is incompatible with the view of those who would have themselves and no one else represent humanity, stand at the pinnacle of progress, or be chosen by God or history to fashion the world in their own image.

Anthropologists believe that a sound knowledge of humankind can be achieved only by studying distant as well as near lands and ancient as well as modern times. By adopting this broad view of the totality of human experience, perhaps we humans can tear off the blinders put on us by our local life-styles and see ourselves as we really are.

"Anthropologists! Anthropologists!"

Because of its biological, archaeological, linguistic, cultural, comparative, and global perspective, anthropology can answer many fundamental questions about human existence. Anthropologists are making important contributions to understanding the significance of humankind's animal heritage and hence to the definition of what is distinctively human about human nature. Anthropology is strategically equipped to study the significance of race in the evolution of cultures and in the conduct of contemporary life. It also holds the key to understanding the origins of social inequality in the form of racism, sexism, exploitation, poverty, and international underdevelopment.

Why Study Anthropology?

Most anthropologists make their livings by teaching in universities, colleges, and junior colleges, and by carrying out university-based research. But a substantial and increasing proportion of anthropologists finds employment in nonacademic settings. Museums — especially museums of natural history, archaeology museums, and museums of art and folklore — have long relied on the expertise of anthropologists. In recent years, anthropologists have been welcome in a greater variety of public and private positions: in government agencies concerned with welfare, drug abuse, mental health, environmental impact, housing, education, foreign aid, and agricultural development; in the private sector as personnel and ethnic relations consultants and as management consultants for multinational firms; and as staff members of hospitals and foundations (see Box 1.2).

In recognition of the growing importance of these nonacademic roles for anthropologists, many university departments of anthro-

---

Box 1.2

WHY MAJOR IN ANTHROPOLOGY?

Anthropology is one of the few major fields to combine fascinating coursework and practical career training in one academic package.

Anthropology — the study of "who we are and how we came to be that way" — not only provides a sound liberal arts education but also gives students a needed edge in today's fiercely competitive world of careers and jobs.

In these times of narrow specialization, anthropological study is refreshingly broad. Topics range from tribal New Guinea politics to chimpanzee "language" to issues in providing health care for urban America's ethnic poor. As a result, anthropology majors frequently adopt outlooks on life that are as broad as the discipline itself.

This focus on comprehensive breadth is especially valuable to men and women seeking careers in corporate America in realms of strategic planning, decision making, and programs management. Anthropology's scope and intellectual roominess can prepare students to make objective, far-

sighted decisions at the professional level in any career field.

Moreover, your training in anthropology will help sensitize you to the mosaic of ethnic differences found on planet Earth. You will study the world's societies — groups from the Pacific, North and South America, Asia, Africa, Europe, and the USSR — as well as our own nation's Hispanic, Laotian, Japanese, Native American, and other ethnic-minority groups. Exposure to inter-ethnic ways of thinking and feeling will help you understand the diverse contending motivations at work in today's global economy.

To the career-minded student, few concepts are as useful, at all levels of the corporate pyramid, as the anthropological concept of *culture.* Understand the inner assumptions and unvoiced axioms of the people you work with — glimpse the world as their culture teaches them to picture it — and you will be able to relate across "class" lines and across ethnic boundaries as if you had a natural gift for bridging communication gaps.

Source: Givens 1989.

---

pology have started or expanded programs in *applied anthropology.* These programs supplement traditional anthropological studies with training in statistics, computer languages, and other skills suitable for solving practical problems in human relationships under a variety of natural and cultural conditions.

Despite the expanding opportunities in applied fields, the study of anthropology remains valuable not so much for the opportunities it presents for employment but for its contribution to the basic understanding of human variations and relationships. Just as the majority of students of mathematics do not become mathematicians, so too the majority of students of anthropology do not become anthropologists. For human-relation fields such as law, medicine, nursing, education, government, psychology, economics, and business administration, anthropology has a role to play that is as basic as mathematics. Only by becoming sensitive to and learning to cope with the cultural dimensions of human existence can one hope to be optimally effective in any of these fields.

In the words of Frederica De Laguna, "Anthropology is the only discipline that offers a conceptual schema for the whole context of human experience. . . . It is like the carrying frame onto which may be fitted all the several subjects of a liberal education, and by organiz-

ing the load, making it more wieldy and capable of being carried" (1968:475).*

Summary

Anthropology is the study of humankind. Its four major branches are cultural or social anthropology, anthropological linguistics, physical (or biological) anthropology, and archaeology. Its distinctive approach lies in its global, comparative, and multidimensional perspective.

* See the first page of the bibliography for an explanation of the system of citations used in this book.

Chapter 2

THE NATURE OF
CULTURE

❧~❧~❧

This chapter defines what is meant by culture,
relates the concept of culture to that of society, and
identifies certain general processes and components
of society and culture. The general processes and
components set forth in this chapter will be used
throughout the rest of the book to describe and
explain social and cultural differences and similarities.

Definitions of Culture and Society

When anthropologists speak of culture, they do not mean the literary and artistic achievements and standards of "cultured" elites. For anthropologists, plumbers and farmers are as cultured as art collectors and concert-goers, and studying the lives of ordinary people is just as important as studying the lives of famous and influential people. When anthropologists speak of culture, they mean the total socially acquired life-style of a group of people including patterned, repetitive ways of thinking, feeling, and acting.

The definition of culture as consisting of patterns of acting (behavior) as well as patterns of thought and feeling follows the precedent set by Sir Edward Burnett Tylor, the founder of academic anthropology in the English-speaking world and author of the first general anthropology textbook:

> Culture . . . taken in its wide ethnographic sense is that complex whole which includes knowledge, belief, art, morals, law, custom, and any other capabilities and habits acquired by man as a member of society. The condition of culture among the various societies of mankind, in so far as it is capable of being investigated on general principles, is a subject apt for the study of laws of human thought and action. [1871:1]

Many anthropologists prefer to view culture as a purely mental phenomenon consisting of the ideas that people share concerning how one should think and act. As such, culture has been compared to a computer program — to a kind of "software" that tells people what to do under various circumstances. But there is a danger here of mistaking the relationship between ideas and behavior. When the rate of cultural change is high, as it is in most parts of the world today, behavior often changes before ideas change, and one can speak of behavior programming a people's ideas as readily as ideas programming their behavior. For example, prior to the 1970s, women who had husbands and school-age children in the United States believed that wives should depend on their husbands for the family income. Driven by rising prices and a desire to enjoy a higher standard of living, however, many married women with school-age children violated this "program" and went to work anyway. Today the majority of married women are in the labor force, with the highest participation rates found among women with school-age children, and it is generally regarded as fitting and proper for women to do this (see Chapter 18 for a more detailed look at how and why the program governing marriage and the family in the United States changed).

What does the term *society* designate? As used in this book, society means an organized group of people who share a habitat and who depend on each other for their survival and well-being. Each society has an overall culture. But the situation is more complex since human societies, especially those with the state as their form of political organization, often contain subgroups that possess more or less distinctive life-styles. In referring to patterns of culture characteristic of such groups, anthropologists often use the term *subculture*. This term indicates that the culture of a society is not uniform for all its members. Thus, even small societies may have male and female subcultures, while in larger and more complex societies one encounters subcultures associated with ethnic, religious, and class distinctions.

Finally, the term *sociocultural* should be noted. This term is short for "social and cultural" and is useful as a reminder that society and culture form a unit or a system.

Enculturation and Cultural Relativism

The culture of a society tends to be similar in many respects from one generation to the next. In part this continuity in life-ways is main-

tained by the process known as *enculturation*. Enculturation is a partially conscious and partially unconscious learning experience whereby the older generation invites, induces, and compels the younger generation to adopt traditional ways of thinking and behaving (Figure 2.1). Thus, Chinese children use chopsticks instead of forks, speak a tonal language, and dislike milk because they have been enculturated into Chinese culture rather than into the culture of the United States. Enculturation is primarily based on the control that the older generation exercises over the means of rewarding and punishing children. Each generation is programmed not only to replicate the behavior of the previous generation but to reward behavior that conforms to the patterns of its own enculturation experience and to punish, or at least not reward, behavior that does not so conform (Figure 2.2).

The concept of enculturation (despite its limitations, as discussed below) occupies a central position in the distinctive outlook of modern anthropology. Failure to comprehend the role of enculturation in the maintenance of each group's patterns of behavior and thought lies at the heart of the phenomenon known as *ethnocentrism*. Ethnocentrism is the belief that one's own patterns of behavior are always natural, good, beautiful, or important, and that strangers, to the extent that they live differently, live by savage, inhuman, disgusting, or irrational standards. People who are intolerant of cultural differences usually ignore the following fact: Had they been enculturated within another group, most of those supposedly savage, inhuman, disgusting, and irrational life-styles would now be their own. Recognizing the fallacy of ethnocentrism leads to tolerance for and curiosity about cultural differences.

Anthropologists place great emphasis on *cultural relativism*, which means that they are

(a)

(b)

Figure 2.1 *How, what, and when we eat: Culture at work.*
(a) *Midday meal, Rangoon, Burma. Food is good to touch as well as to eat.* (b) *Fast food, America's most notable contribution to world cuisine.* (c) *The correct way to eat in China.*

(c)

committed to trying to understand how the world looks to people in different cultures without letting their own preferences and beliefs get in the way. Cultural relativism does not mean that anthropologists are equally tolerant of all cultures. Like everybody else, anthropologists make ethical judgments about the value of different kinds of cultural patterns. One need not regard cannibalism, warfare, human sacrifice, and poverty as worthy cultural achievements in order to carry out an objective study of these phenomena. Nor is there anything wrong with setting out to study certain cultural patterns because one wants to change them. Scientific objectivity does not arise from having no biases—everyone is biased—but from taking care not to let one's biases influence the result of research (Jorgensen 1971).

Limitations of the Enculturation Concept

Under present world conditions it is easy to see that enculturation cannot account for a considerable portion of the life-styles of existing social groups. Clearly, replication of cultural patterns

(a)

(b)

Figure 2.2   Passing culture on.
In Bali (a) a man reads to his grandchildren from a script on narrow bamboo strips. (b) In India, a Sikh father teaches his daughter how to rap a turban. (c) In Mission Viejo, California, young people learn to culturally approved manner of eating artichokes (d) Navajo rug makers are made, not born.

(c)

(d)

(a)

*Figure 2.3 Culture, people, and the sun.
The relationship between people and the sun is
mediated by culture. Sunbathing (a) is a modern
invention. On the beach at Villerville in 1908 (b),
only "mad dogs and Englishmen went out in the
midday sun" without their parasols. As the rising
incidence of skin cancer attests, sunbathing can
indeed be hazardous to your health.*

(b)

from one generation to the next is never complete (Figure 2.3). Old patterns are not always faithfully repeated in successive generations, and new patterns are continually being added (Figure 2.4). Recently, the rate of innovation and nonreplication in the industrial societies has reached proportions alarming to adults who were programmed to expect that their children's behavior would duplicate their own. This lack of cross-generational continuity has been called the *generation gap*. As explained by Margaret Mead:

> Today, nowhere in the world are there elders who know what the children know; no matter how remote and simple the societies are in which the children live. In the past there were always some elders who knew more than any children in terms of their experience of having grown up

within a cultural system. Today there are none. It is not only that parents are no longer guides, but that there are no guides, whether one seeks them in one's own country or abroad. There are no elders who know what those who have been reared within the last twenty years know about the world into which they were born. [1970:77–78]

Clearly, enculturation cannot account for the generation gap and for other consequences of rapid cultural change such as the shift from manufacturing jobs to service and information jobs in the United States (Harris 1987). Enculturation, in other words, can account for the continuity of culture; but it cannot account for the evolution of culture.

Even with respect to the continuity of culture, enculturation has important limitations.

(a)

(b)

Figure 2.4   The limitation of enculturation.
(a) Michael Jackson's generation cannot be said to
have been musically enculturated by (b) Frank
Sinatra's.

Every replicated pattern is not the result of the programming that one generation experiences at the hands of another. Many patterns are replicated because successive generations adjust to similar conditions in social life in similar ways. Sometimes the programming received may even be at variance with actual patterns; people may be enculturated to behave in one way but be obliged by conditions beyond their control to behave in another way. For example, enculturation is responsible for replicating the patterns of behavior associated with driving a car. Another replicated pattern consists of stalled traffic. Are automobile drivers programmed to make traffic jams? On the contrary, they are programmed to keep moving and to go around obstacles. Yet traffic jams are a highly patterned cultural phenomenon (Figure 2.5).

Poverty requires a similar analysis, as we will see in a later chapter (Chapter 12). Many poor people find themselves living in houses, eating food, working, and raising families according to patterns that replicate their parents' subculture, not because their parents wanted them to follow these patterns, but because they confront long-lasting political and economic conditions that perpetuate their poverty.

Diffusion

Whereas enculturation refers to the passing of cultural traits from one generation to the next, *diffusion* refers to the passing of cultural traits from one culture and society to another (Figure 2.6). This process is so common that the majority of traits found in any society can be said to have originated in some other society. One can say, for example, that much of the government, religion, law, diet, and language of the United States was "borrowed" or diffused from other cultures. Thus the Judeo-Christian religions come from the Middle East; parliamentary democracy comes from Western Europe; the food grains in our diet — rice, wheat, corn — come from ancient and distant civilizations; and the English language comes from the amalgam of several different European tongues (see page 61).

Early in this century (see Appendix), diffusion was regarded by many anthropologists as the most powerful explanation for sociocultural differences and similarities. The lingering effects of this approach can still be seen in popular attempts to explain the similarities among major civilizations as the result of the derivation of one from another — Polynesia from Peru, or vice versa; lowland Mesoamerica from highland Mesoamerica (Mesoamerica is Mexico plus Central America), or vice versa; China from Europe, or vice versa; the New World (the Americas) from the Old, and so forth. In recent years, however, diffusion has lost ground as an explanatory principle.

It is true that in general, the closer two societies are to each other, the greater will be the cultural resemblance between them, but these resemblances cannot simply be attributed to some automatic tendency for traits to diffuse. It must be kept in mind that societies close together in space are likely to occupy similar environments; hence the similarities between them may be caused by the effects of similar environmental conditions (Harner 1970). Moreover, there are numerous cases of societies in close contact for hundreds of years that maintain radically different ways of life. For example, the Incas of Peru (see page 206) had an imperial government, while the nearby forest societies lacked centralized leadership of

(a)

Figure 2.5   Traffic jams
(a) *New York;* (b) *Mexico City.*

(b)

(a)

(b)

(c)

Figure 2.6   Can you reconstruct the diffusionary history of the objects and activities shown in these scenes?
(a) Headman in Arnhemland, Australia, summoning his clanspeople to a meeting with a radio whose battery is recharged by solar energy; (b) Mongolian metropolis; (c) Brazilian woodsman.

any kind. Other well-known cases are the African Ituri forest hunters and their Bantu agriculturalist neighbors, and the "apartment house" Pueblos and their marauding, nomadic Apache neighbors in the southwest United States. Resistance to diffusion, in other words, is as common as acceptance. If this were not the case, there would be no struggle between Catholics and Protestants in Northern Ireland, Mexicans would speak English (or U.S. citizens Spanish), and Jews would accept the divinity of Jesus Christ (or Christians would reject it). Furthermore, even if one accepts diffusion as an explanation, there still remains the question of why the diffused item originated in the first place. Finally, diffusion cannot account for many remarkable instances in which people who are known never to have had any contact with each other invented similar tools and techniques, and developed remarkably similar forms of marriage and religious beliefs. The most dramatic examples of such *independent inventions* consist of discoveries and inventions that not only occur independently but at approximately the same time (see Box 2.1).

In sum, diffusion is no more satisfactory as a mode of explanation of similar cultural traits than is enculturation. If nothing but diffusion and enculturation were involved in determining human social life, then we should expect all cultures to be the same and to stay the same; this is clearly not the case.

It must not be concluded, however, that diffusion plays *no* role in sociocultural evolution. The nearness of one culture to another often does influence the rate and direction of change as well as shape the specific details of sociocultural life, even if it does not shape the general features of the two cultures. For example, the custom of smoking tobacco originated among the native peoples of the Western Hemisphere and after 1492 spread to the re-

motest regions of the globe. This could not have happened if the Americans had remained cut off from the other continents. Yet contact alone obviously does not tell the whole story, since hundreds of other native American traits, like living in wigwams or hunting with bow and arrow, were not taken up even by the colonists who lived next door to native Americans.

Mental and Behavioral Aspects of Culture

By talking with people, anthropologists learn about a vast inner mental world of thought and feeling. This inner world exists on different levels of consciousness. First, there are patterns that exist far below consciousness. The rules of grammar are an example of such "deep structures." Second, there are patterns that exist closer to consciousness and that are readily formulated when the proper questions are asked. People can usually formulate values and norms, and proper codes of conduct for activities such as weaning babies, courting mates, choosing leaders, treating diseases, entertaining guests, categorizing kin, worshiping God, and thousands of additional commonplace behaviors. But such rules, plans, and values may not ordinarily be formalized or completely conscious. Third, there are equally numerous, fully conscious, explicit, and formal rules of conduct and statements of values, plans, goals, and aspirations that may be discussed during the course of ordinary conversations, written in law codes, or announced at public gatherings (e.g., rules about littering, making bank deposits, playing football, trespassing, and so on). Finally, to make matters more complex, cultures have rules not only for behavior but for breaking rules for behavior — as when one

---

Box 2.1

SIMULTANEOUS INDEPENDENT INVENTIONS

When the culture process has reached a point where an invention or discovery becomes possible, that invention or discovery becomes inevitable. . . .

The discovery of sun spots was made independently by at least four men in a single year: by Galileo, Fabricius, Scheiner, and Harriott, in 1611. The parallax of a star was first measured by Bessel, Struve, and Henderson, working independently, in 1838. Oxygen was discovered independently by Scheele and Priestly in 1774. The invention of the self-exciting dynamo was claimed by Hjorth, Varley, Siemens, Wheatstone, and Ladd in 1866–67, and by Wilde between 1863–67. The solution of the problem of respiration was made independently by Priestly, Scheele, Lavoisier, Spallanzani, and Davy, in a single year: 1777. Invention of the telescope and the thermometer each is claimed by eight or nine persons independently and at approximately the same time. "Even the south pole, never before trodden by the foot of human beings, was at last reached twice in one summer." The great work of Mendel in genetics lay unnoticed for many years. But when it was eventually re-discovered, it was done not by one [person] but by three—de Vries, Correns, and Tschermak—and in a single year, 1900. One could go on indefinitely. When the growing, interactive culture process reaches a certain point, an invention or discovery takes place.

The simultaneity of multiple inventions or discoveries is sometimes striking and remarkable. Accusations of plagiarism are not infrequent; bitter rivalries are waged over priorities. "The right to the monopoly of the manufacture of the telephone was long in litigation; the ultimate decision rested on an *interval of hours* between the recording of concurrent descriptions by Alexander Bell and Elisha Gray."

Source: White 1949:208–210.

---

parks in front of a sign that says "No Parking" and gambles on not getting a ticket (Figure 2.7).

But conversations are not the only source of anthropological knowledge about culture. In addition, anthropologists observe, measure, photograph, and take notes about what people do during their daily, weekly, or annual rounds of activities. They watch births take place, attend funerals, go along on hunting expeditions, watch marriage ceremonies, and attend thousands of other events and activities as they unfold. These actual events and activities constitute the behavioral aspect of culture. The method of observing these events and activities at close hand on a daily basis over a long period is known as *participant observation.*

(a)

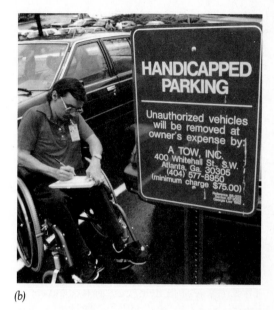

(b)

(c)

Figure 2.7   *Rules for breaking rules.*
Cultural behavior cannot be predicted from a
knowledge of a simple set of rules. In (b), a
handicapped driver is taking down the license
number of a car that has parked against the rule.

(d)

Emic and Etic Aspects of Culture

The distinction between mental and behavioral events does not resolve the question of what constitutes an adequate description of a culture as a whole. The problem is that both the thoughts and behavior of the participants can be viewed from two different perspectives: from that of the participants themselves, and from that of the observers. In both instances, scientific, objective accounts of the mental and behavioral fields are possible. In the first instance the observers employ concepts and distinctions that are meaningful and appropriate to the participants; in the second instance they employ concepts and distinctions that are meaningful and appropriate to the observers. The first way of studying culture is called *emics* [pronounced ē-miks] and the second way is called *etics* [pronounced et-iks] (see Chapter 4 for the derivation of these terms from *phonemics* and *phonetics*). The test of the adequacy of emic descriptions and analyses is whether they correspond with a view of the world that natives accept as real, meaningful, or appropriate. In carrying out emic research, anthropologists attempt to acquire a knowledge of the categories and rules one must know in order to think and act as a native. They attempt to learn, for example, what rule lies behind the use of the same kin term for mother and mother's sister among the Bathonga, or when it is appropriate to shame house guests among the Kwakiutl, or when to ask a boy or a girl out for a date among U.S. teenagers.

The test of the adequacy of etic descriptions, however, is simply their ability to generate scientific theories about the causes of sociocultural differences and similarities. Rather than employ concepts that are necessarily real, meaningful, and appropriate from the native point of view, the anthropologist now uses categories and rules derived from the vocabulary of science, which are often unfamiliar to the native. Etic studies often involve the measurement and juxtaposition of activities and events that native informants find inappropriate or meaningless (Headland 1990).

Emics, Etics, and Cattle Sex Ratios

The following example demonstrates the importance of the difference between emics and etics in nonlinguistic aspects of culture. In the Trivandrum district of the state of Kerala in southern India, farmers insist that they would never deliberately shorten the life of one of their animals — that they would never kill it or starve it to death — thereby affirming the standard Hindu prohibition against the slaughter of cattle. Yet among Kerala farmers the mortality rate of male calves is almost twice as high as the mortality rate of female calves. In fact, male cattle 0–1 year of age are outnumbered by female cattle of the same group in a ratio of 67:100. The farmers themselves are aware that male calves are more likely to die than female calves, but they attribute the difference to the relative "weakness" of the males. "The males get sick more often," they say. When asked to explain why male calves get sick more often, some farmers suggest that the males eat less than the females. Finally, some farmers even admit that the male calves eat less because they are not allowed to stay at the mother's teats for more than a few seconds. But none could (or would) say that since there is little demand for traction animals in Kerala, male cattle are culled and female cattle are reared. The emics of the situation are that no one knowingly or willingly would shorten the life of a calf. (Of course, at some level of consciousness the farmers may very well know what they are doing and are simply reluctant to tell other people about it — see Harris 1987b.) Again and again farmers affirm that every calf has the "right to live" regardless of its sex. But the etics of the situation are that cattle sex ratios are systematically adjusted to the needs of the local ecology and economy through preferential male "bovicide." Although the unwanted calves are not slaughtered, many are more or less starved to death. In other parts of India, where different ecological and economic conditions prevail, etic "bovicide" is practiced more against female rather than male cattle, resulting in some states in an adult cattle sex ratio of over 200 oxen for every 100 cows (see Chapter 15 for more discussion on the emics and etics of cattle in India).

The comparison of etic and emic versions of culture gives rise to some of the most important and intriguing problems in anthropology.

The Universal Pattern

In order to compare one culture with another, the anthropologist has to collect and organize cultural data in relation to cross-culturally recurrent aspects or parts of the social and cultural whole. The structure of these recurrent aspects or parts is called the *universal pattern*.

Anthropologists agree that every human society has provisions for behavior and thoughts related to making a living from the environment, having children, organizing the exchange of goods and labor, living in domestic groups and larger communities, and for the creative, expressive, playful, aesthetic, moral, and intellectual aspects of human life. However, there is no agreement on how many subdivisions of these categories should be recognized or on what priority they should be given

when it comes to the conduct of research. A universal pattern consisting of three major divisions — infrastructure, structure, and superstructure — will be used in this book (Box 2.2).

1. **Infrastructure.** Consists of the etic and behavioral activities by which each society satisfies minimal requirements for subsistence — the *mode of production* — and by which each society regulates population growth — the *mode of reproduction*.

2. **Structure.** Consists of the economic and political etic and behavioral activities by which every society organizes itself into groups that allocate, regulate, and exchange goods and labor. Depending on whether the focus of organization is on domestic groups or on the internal and external relationships of the whole society, one may speak of *domestic economies* or *political economies* as universal components on the structural level.

3. **Superstructure.** Consists of behavior and thought devoted to artistic, playful, religious, and intellectual endeavors plus all the mental and emic aspects of a culture's infrastructure and structure.

The Diversity of Anthropological Theories

The kinds of research that anthropologists carry out and the kinds of conclusions they stress are greatly influenced by the basic assumptions they make about the causes of cultural evolution. Basic assumptions made by anthropologists of different theoretical persuasions are called *research strategies*, or *paradigms*.

Box 2.2

THE ETIC AND BEHAVIORAL COMPONENTS OF THE UNIVERSAL PATTERN

INFRASTRUCTURE

Mode of Production The technology and the practices employed for expanding or limiting basic subsistence production, especially the production of food and other forms of energy, given the restrictions and opportunities provided by a specific technology interacting with a specific habitat.

> Technology of subsistence
> Techno-environmental relationships
> Ecosystems
> Work patterns

Mode of Reproduction The technology and the practices employed for expanding, limiting, and maintaining population size.

> Demography
> Mating patterns
> Fertility, natality, mortality
> Nurturance of infants
> Medical control of demographic
>   patterns
> Contraception, abortion, infanticide

STRUCTURE

Domestic Economy The organization of reproduction and basic production, exchange, and consumption within camps, houses, apartments, or other domestic settings.

> Family structure
> Domestic division of labor
> Domestic socialization, enculturation,
>   education
> Age and sex roles
> Domestic discipline hierarchies,
>   sanctions

Political Economy The organization of reproduction, production, exchange, and consumption within and between bands, villages, chiefdoms, states, and empires.

> Political organizations, factions, clubs,
>   associations, corporations
> Division of labor, taxation, tribute
> Political socialization, enculturation,
>   education
> Class, caste, urban, rural hierarchies
> Discipline, police/military control
> War

SUPERSTRUCTURE

Behavioral Superstructure

> Art, music, dance, literature,
>   advertising
> Religious rituals
> Sports, games, hobbies
> Science

No textbook can conceivably be written so as to represent all the current research strategies with bias toward none and equal coverage for all. In the chapters to come the author has made a conscious effort to include alternative viewpoints on controversial issues. Inevitably, however, the author's own research strategy dominates the presentation. The point of view followed throughout is known as *cultural materialism*. This is a research strategy which holds that the primary task of cultural anthropology is to give causal explanations for the differences and similarities in thought and behavior found among human groups. Cultural materialism makes the assumption that this task can best be carried out by studying the material constraints to which human existence is subjected. These constraints arise from the need to produce food, shelter, tools, and machines, and to reproduce human populations within limits set by biology, technology, and the environment. They are called *material* constraints or conditions in order to distinguish them from constraints or conditions imposed by ideas and other mental or spiritual aspects of a society's superstructure, such as values, religion, and art. For cultural materialists, the most likely causes of variation in the mental or spiritual aspects of human life are the variations in a society's infrastructure.

This does not mean that the mental and spiritual aspects of cultures are regarded as being somehow less significant or less important than production, reproduction, and ecology. A human society can no more survive without ideas and values than it can survive without tools and shelter. Indeed, moral values, religious beliefs, and aesthetic standards are in one sense the most significant and most distinctively human attributes. Their importance is not an issue. What is an issue is how we can best explain — if we can explain at all —

why a particular human population has one set of values, beliefs, and aesthetic standards while others have different sets of values, beliefs, and aesthetic standards. (See the Appendix for a discussion of alternative approaches in anthropology.)

Summary

A culture consists of the socially acquired ways of thinking, feeling, and acting of the members of a particular society. Cultures maintain their continuity by means of the process of enculturation. In studying cultural differences, it is important to guard against the habit of mind called ethnocentrism, which arises from a failure to appreciate the far-reaching effects of enculturation on human life. Enculturation, however, cannot explain how and why cultures change. Moreover, not all cultural recurrences in different generations result from enculturation. Some result from reactions to similar conditions or situations.

Whereas enculturation denotes the process by which culture is transmitted from one generation to the next, diffusion denotes the process by which culture is transmitted from one society to another. Diffusion, like enculturation, is not automatic and cannot stand alone as an explanatory principle. Neighboring societies can have both highly similar as well as highly dissimilar cultures.

Culture, as defined in this book, consists of patterns of bodily activity as well as of thoughts that take place inside people's heads. In studying human cultures one must make explicit whether it is the native participant's point of view or the observer's point of view that is being expressed. These are the emic and etic points of view, respectively. Both mental and behavioral aspects of culture can be approached from either the emic or etic point of view. Emic and etic versions of reality often differ markedly. However, there is usually some degree of correspondence between them. In addition to emic, etic, mental, and behavioral aspects, all cultures share a universal pattern. The universal pattern as defined in this book consists of three main components: infrastructure, structure, and superstructure. These in turn consist respectively of the modes of production and reproduction; domestic and political economy; and the creative, expressive, aesthetic, and intellectual aspects of human life. The definition of these categories is essential to organizing research, and differs according to the research strategy one adopts.

Within anthropology there are many alternative research strategies; the one followed in this book is cultural materialism. The aim of this strategy is to discover, by emphasizing the influence of material conditions, the causes of the differences and similarities in thought and behavior that characterize particular human populations.

Chapter 3

GENES, EVOLUTION, AND CULTURE

❧

This chapter discusses the relationship between biological evolutionary processes and the development of a cultural "takeoff" unique to human beings. Culture is shown to be encoded in the brain and not in the genes, the units of biological heredity. The theories of scientific creationists are examined and their attacks against evolutionism in biology and anthropology are refuted.

The human capacity for culture is a product of biological evolutionary processes. The most powerful evolutionary process is known as *natural selection*. Natural selection takes place as a result of the potentially infinite reproductive powers of life and the actual finite nature of the space and energy upon which life depends. Natural selection acts upon the units of hereditary instructions, or *genes*, located in the reproductive cells of each organism. It does so by increasing or decreasing the frequency of genetic variants. The main source of genetic variants is *mutations* — "errors" that occur during the process by which genes replicate themselves. Some genetic variants increase the fitness of the individuals possessing them; others decrease the fitness of the individuals possessing them. *Fitness* here means nothing more than the number of offspring in which a particular genetic variant appears in successive generations. Genes that lead to higher fitness are said to be "selected for"; genes that lead to lower fitness are said to be "selected against."

Fitness is associated with many different kinds of factors. It may be related to the organism's ability to resist disease, to gain or hold space more securely, or to obtain energy in larger or more dependable amounts. It may be related to the increased efficiency and dependability of some aspect of the reproductive process itself.

Through differential reproductive success, natural selection can drastically alter the frequency of *genotypes* (i.e., types of genes) after a few tens of generations. An example of the power of natural selection to raise the frequency of a rare gene is the evolution of penicillin-resistant strains of bacteria. The genes conferring resistance are present in normal populations of bacteria, but in only a small percentage of individuals. As a result of the differential reproductive success of such individuals, however, the resistant strain of bacteria soon becomes the most common genotype.

Natural Selection Versus the Struggle for Survival

During the nineteenth century, Social Darwinists envisioned Malthus's "struggle for survival" as the mainspring of both biological and cultural evolution (see Appendix, page 399). Natural selection was pictured incorrectly as the preying upon and destruction of one another by organisms of the same species. Although within-species killing sometimes does play a role in biological evolution, the factors promoting differential reproductive success are in the main not related to an organism's ability to destroy other members of its own population.

Today, biologists recognize that natural selection favors cooperation and altruism within species as often as it favors competition. In social species the perpetuation of an individual's genes often depends as much on the reproductive success of its close relatives as on its own survival and reproduction. Many social insects, for example, even have sterile "castes" that assure their own genetic success by "altruistically" rearing the progeny of their fertile siblings.

Natural Selection and Behavior

Natural selection not only shapes the anatomy and physiology of organisms; it can also shape their behavioral characteristics. Specific genes determine, for example, whether species of fruit flies will fly upward or downward when threatened by a predator; the laying of eggs by a wasp in a particular kind of caterpillar; the mating rituals of fish; the web building of spiders; the specialized behavior of insect castes; and countless other drives and instincts characteristic of animal species.

It is important to understand how such behavior gets established. Organisms make "errors" in their behavior that express "errors" in their genes. In the Galápagos Islands, for example, there are species of iguana that swim and dive in the surf for food. These lizards are descended from species genetically

"programmed" to hunt on land. But "errors" developed in the program that allowed some individuals to venture closer to the sea. The deviant genes were selected for probably because they increased the food resources the sea-venturing iguanas could eat. By being selected for over the course of many generations, the sea-venturing iguanas became programmed for swimming and diving rather than for hunting on land. The sequence here may be described schematically as:

old genotype → genetic "error"
           → behavioral deviation
           → selection
           → new genotype

The Evolution of Learning

While it is very useful for organisms to be equipped with a species-specific program of behavioral responses encoded in their genes, there is another type of behavior that has certain advantages over genetic programming. This is behavior that is programmed as a result of learning. Learning permits organisms to adjust to and to take more effective advantage of a wider variety of opportunities for achieving reproductive success than is possible through genetic programming. For example, seagulls learn to recognize and to follow fishing boats; they learn the location of fast-food restaurants, town dumps, and other sources of garbage; and they thereby greatly improve their fitness *without changing their genotype*, as schematized in the following sequence:

old genotype → learned responses
           → selection
           → old genotype

In fact, one might say it is essential for seagull fitness that the acquisition of these new behavioral responses *not* be linked to variation in the genotype. A seagull genetically programmed to stay on the shoreline would not be able to take advantage of the opportunities presented by following fishing boats out to sea or by waiting for McDonald's patrons to spill their french fries in the parking lot.

The ability to learn has been selected for in many higher animal species precisely because learning is a more flexible and rapid method of achieving reproductive success than genetic evolution. Learning permits a whole population to adjust to or take advantage of novel opportunities in a single generation without having to wait for the appearance and spread of genetic mutations.

Nonhuman Culture

Selection for increased learning capacity set the stage for the emergence of culture as an important source of *learned behavioral repertories* (i.e., routine patterns of behavior that can be activated on appropriate occasions). This capacity has a neurological base; it depends on the evolution of larger and more complex brains and of more "intelligent" species.

Many nonhuman species are intelligent enough to possess rudimentary traditions. Songbirds, for example, have traditional songs that vary from one population to another within a given species; many animals follow paths to waterholes or feeding grounds laid down over generations; others migrate to traditional nesting sites.

The most elaborate examples of nonhuman culture have been found, not unexpectedly, among our species's closest relatives, the monkeys and great apes.

Primatologists of the Primate Research Institute of Kyoto University have found a wide variety of traditions among local troops of monkeys. The males of certain troops, for example, take turns looking after the infants while the infants' mothers are feeding. Such babysitting is characteristic only of the troops at Takasaki-yama and Takahashi. Other cultural differences have been noted too. When the monkeys of Takasaki-yami eat the fruit of the *muku* tree, they throw away the hard stone inside or swallow it and excrete it in their feces. But the monkeys of Arishi-yama break the stone with their teeth and eat the pulpy interior. Some troops eat shellfish; others do not. Cultural differences have also been noted with respect to the characteristic distance the monkeys maintain among themselves during feeding and with respect to the order of males, females, and juveniles in line of march when certain troops move through the forest.

The scientists at the Primate Research Institute have even been able to observe the actual spread of learned behavioral innovations from individual to individual. To attract monkeys near the shore for easier observation, scientists put sweet potatoes out on the beach. One day a young female began to wash the sand from the sweet potatoes by plunging them in a small brook that ran through the beach. This washing behavior spread throughout the group and gradually replaced the former rubbing habit. Nine years later, 80 or 90 percent of the animals were washing their sweet potatoes, some in the brook, others in the sea (Figure 3.1). When wheat was spread on the beach, the monkeys of Koshima at first had a hard time separating the kernels from the sand. Soon, however, the same young female invented a process for desanding the wheat, and this behavior was also taken over by others. The process was to plunge the wheat into the water (Figure 3.2): The wheat floats and the sand drops to the bottom (Itani 1961; Itani and Nishimura 1973; Miyadi 1967).

Figure 3.1 Japanese Monkey Culture.
A female monkey of Koshima troop washing a sweet potato.

Rudimentary Cultures Among the Great Apes

Over a period of many years, Jane Goodall (1986) and her associates have studied the behavior of a single population of free-ranging chimpanzees in the Gombe National Park in Tanzania (Figure 3.3). One of their most remarkable discoveries is that the chimpanzees "fish" for ants and termites (Figure 3.4). "Ter-

miting" involves first breaking off a twig or a vine, stripping it of leaves and side branches, and then locating a suitable termite nest. Such a nest is as hard as concrete and impenetrable except for certain thinly covered tunnel entrances. The chimpanzee scratches away the thin covering and inserts the twig. The termites inside bite the end of the twig, and the chimpanzee pulls it out and licks off the termites clinging to it. Especially impressive is the

(a)

(b)

Figure 3.2 Japanese Monkeys Washing Wheat.
(a) Members of Koshima troop separating wheat from sand by placing mixture in water. (b) Central figure carrying the mixture in its left hand. Two monkeys in foreground are floating the wheat and picking it up.

Figure 3.3   Jane Goodall
Making friends with a young chimpanzee in Gombe
National Park, Tanzania.

fact that the chimpanzees will prepare the twig
first and then carry it in their mouths from nest
to nest while looking for a suitable tunnel entrance (Van Lawick-Goodall 1968). "Anting"
is an interesting variation on this theme. The
Gombe chimps "fish" for a species of aggressive nomadic driver ant that can inflict a painful

Figure 3.4   Chimpanzee Termiting.
A stick carefully stripped of leaves is inserted into the
nest. The chimpanzee licks off the termites that cling to
the stick when it is withdrawn.

bite. On finding the temporary subterranean nest of these ants, the chimps make a tool out of a green twig and insert it into the nest entrance. Hundreds of fierce ants swarm up the twig to repel the invader:

> The chimpanzee watches their progress and when the ants have almost reached its hand, the tool is quickly withdrawn. In a split second the opposite hand rapidly sweeps the length of the tool . . . catching the ants in a jumbled mass between thumb and forefinger. These are then popped into the open, waiting mouth in one bite and chewed furiously. [McGrew 1977:278]

The chimpanzees also manufacture "sponges" for sopping up water from a hollow in a tree. They strip a handful of leaves from a twig, put the leaves in their mouths, chew briefly, put the mass of leaves in the water, let them soak, put the leaves to their mouths, and suck the water off. They employ a similar sponge to dry their fur, to wipe off sticky substances, and to clean the bottoms of their babies. Gombe chimpanzees also use sticks as levers and digging tools to pry ant nests off trees and to widen the entrance of subterranean beehives.

In other locations, observers have watched chimpanzees in their native habitats pound or hammer tough-skinned fruits, seeds, and nuts with sticks and stones. One chimp in the Budongo Forest, Uganda, used a leaf on a twig to fan away flies (Sugiyama 1969).

Chimpanzees appear to go further than other primates in using weapons and projectiles. They hurl stones, feces, and sticks with considerable accuracy. Under semicontrolled conditions they have been observed to wield long clubs with deadly aim. One investigator (Kortlant 1967) built a stuffed leopard whose head and tail could be moved mechanically. He

set the leopard down in open country inhabited by chimpanzees, and when the chimpanzees came into view, he animated the leopard's parts. The chimps attacked the leopard with heavy sticks, tore it apart, and dragged the remnants off into the bush.

There appear to be no specific genes that are responsible for chimpanzee termiting, anting, and the other behaviors noted above. True, in order for such behavior to occur, genetically determined capacities for learning, for manipulating objects, and for eating insects must be present in the young chimpanzee. But these general biological capacities and predispositions cannot explain termiting and anting. If there were nothing but groups of young chimpanzees, twigs, and termite nests, termiting and anting would be unlikely to occur. The missing ingredient would be the information about termiting and anting stored in the brains of adult chimpanzees.

Among the Gombe Stream chimpanzees, the young do not begin termiting until they are 18 to 22 months old. At first their behavior is clumsy and inefficient, and they do not become proficient until they are about 3 years old. Van Lawick-Goodall witnessed many instances of infants watching intently as the adults termited. Novices often retrieved discarded termiting sticks and attempted to use them on their own. Anting, with its risk of being bitten, takes longer to learn. The youngest chimp to achieve proficiency was about 4 years old (McGrew 1977:282). The conclusion that anting is a cultural trait is strengthened by the fact that chimps at other sites do not exploit driver ants even though this species is widely distributed throughout Africa. At the same time, other groups of chimps do exploit other species of ants, and in ways that differ from the Gombe tradition. For example, chimps in the Mahali mountains, 170 kilometers south of Gombe, insert twigs and bark into the nests of tree-dwelling ants, which are ignored by the Gombe chimps (Nishida 1973).

Why Is Culture So Rudimentary Among Nonhumans?

The development of traditions of tool manufacture and tool use would be of great value to any intelligent species. Why then have such traditions remained so rudimentary among all species except our own and those immediately ancestral to us? The answer has to do with the need for combining advanced intelligence with an appropriate configuration of limbs, fingers, and thumbs.

Although primates are "brainy" enough to make and use tools, their anatomy and normal mode of existence disincline them to develop extensive tool-using traditions. Among monkeys and apes, the hand has not been used much for manipulating tools because the forelimbs are essential for walking and climbing. That is probably why the most common tool-using behavior among many different species of monkeys and apes is the repelling of intruders with a barrage of nuts, pinecones, branches, fruits, feces, or stones. Throwing such objects requires only a momentary loss of the ability to run away or climb if danger threatens.

In the Beginning Was the Foot

The separation of the ancestral line leading to human beings from the line leading to chimpanzees, our closest nonhuman relatives, probably occurred between 5 and 8 million years ago. By 2.5 million years ago (Cichon 1985; Pilbeam 1985, 1986) there were at least two kinds of *hominids* (members of the human family), one called the *Australopithecines*, which became extinct, and the other called *Homo habilis*, which was a remote but direct ancestor of our species (Figure 3.5). We know they were hominids because their limbs and bodies were already completely adapted to walking upright —there are even 3-million-year-old australopithecine footprints to prove it (Figure 3.6)! Hominids therefore were not initially selected for their braininess but for their peculiar upright gait. Why this gait, called *bipedalism*, was selected for is still a matter of debate, but it is clear that once hands were no longer needed for walking or running, tool use could expand far beyond tool use by monkeys and apes. Bipedal creatures could manufacture and carry tools such as clubs, digging sticks, and stone hammers and knives without lessening their ability to explore, move about, and flee from danger.

Some 2 million years ago, *Homo habilis* was succeeded by a larger and brainier human ancestor known as *Homo erectus*. Despite its considerably bigger brain, however, *H. erectus* does not appear to have had a markedly advanced capacity for complex mental tasks. For almost 1.3 million years, the tools manufactured by *H. erectus* changed very little while its brain size increased only slightly, or not at all. About 200,000 years ago the pace of both biological and cultural evolution quickened, leading to the appearance in Africa of the first anatomically modern *Homo sapiens* between 150,000 and 100,000 years before the present (Figure 3.7).

Cultural Takeoff

About 40,000 years ago, the relationship between cultural and biological evolution underwent a profound change. Although there was

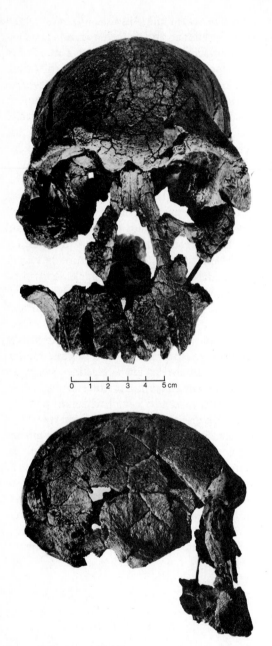

0   1   2   3   4   5 cm

Figure 3.5   Homo Habilis.

Figure 3.6   Earliest Hominid Footprints.
These footprints were discovered at Laetoli by Mary
Leakey. Human foot is shown for comparison.

no increase in the average size of the human brain, the complexity and rate of change of human sociocultural systems increased by many orders of magnitude. It is clear that a kind of takeoff had occurred whereby culture began to evolve more rapidly than our kind's genotypes. Cultural takeoff means that to understand the last 40,000 years of the evolution of culture, primary emphasis must be given to cultural rather than biological processes. Natural selection and organic evolution lie at the base of culture, but once the capacity for culture became fully developed, a vast number of cultural differences and similarities could arise and disappear entirely independent of changes in genotypes (M. Harris 1989).

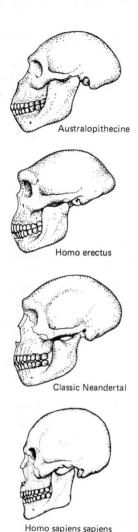

Australopithecine

Homo erectus

Classic Neandertal

Homo sapiens sapiens

Figure 3.7   The Evolution of the Hominids.

Language and Cultural Takeoff

Closely linked with cultural takeoff is the uniquely human capacity for language and for language-assisted systems of thought. While other primates use complex signal systems to facilitate social life, human languages are qualitatively different from all other animal communication systems. The unique features of human languages undoubtedly arose from genetic changes related to the increasing dependence of the earliest hominids on traditions of tool use and other social activities that are facilitated by exchanging and pooling goods and information.

One way to sum up the special characteristics of human language is to say that we have achieved "semantic universality" (Greenberg 1968). A communication system that has *semantic universality* can convey information about aspects, domains, properties, places, or events in the past, present, or future, whether actual or possible, real or imaginary, near or far. The features of human languages that make semantic universality possible will be discussed in the next chapter.

In recent years, a revolutionary series of experiments has revealed that the gap between human and ape language capacities is not as great as had previously been supposed. Yet these same experiments have shown that innate species-specific factors prevent this gap from being closed. Many futile attempts had been made to teach chimpanzees to speak in human fashion. After six years of intensive training, however, the chimpanzee Viki learned to say only "mama," "papa," and "cup." When it was found that the vocal tract of apes cannot make the sounds necessary for human speech, attention shifted toward trying to teach apes to use sign languages and to read and write (Figure 3.8). Washoe, a female chimpanzee, learned 160 different standard signs of Ameslan (American Sign Language). Washoe used these signs productively. She first learned the sign for "open" with a particular door and later spontaneously extended its use beyond the initial training context to all closed doors,

Figure 3.8   Nim Chimpsky Signing "Me Hat" To Herbert Terrace.

then to closed containers such as the refrigerator, cupboards, drawers, briefcases, boxes, and jars. When Susan, a research assistant, stepped on Washoe's doll, Washoe had many ways to tell her what was on her mind: "Up Susan; Susan up; mine please up; gimme baby; please shoe; more mine; up please; please up; more up; baby down; shoe up; baby up; please move up" (Gardner and Gardner 1971, 1975).

David Premack (1971, 1976) used a set of plastic chips to teach a chimpanzee named Sarah the meaning of a set of 130 symbols with which the two could communicate. Premack could ask Sarah rather abstract questions, such as "What is an apple the same as?" Sarah could respond by selecting the chips that stood for "red," "round," "stem," and "less desirable than grapes." Premack made a special effort to incorporate certain rudimentary grammatical rules into his human-chimp language. Sarah could respond appropriately to the plastic-chip command: "Sarah put the banana in the pail and the apple in the dish." (Sarah herself, how-

ever, did not make such complex demands of Premack.)

A male pygmy chimpanzee named Kanzi has learned to understand English words and short sentences without specific training (Rumbaugh 1988). Kanzi hears the words through headphones, and his caregivers do not know which words are being tested, so they cannot give the animal cues. Kanzi has also learned (with training) to manipulate keyboard symbols (Figure 3.9) to make requests, and he seems to use some simple grammatical ordering rules.

Both Washoe and Lucy, a chimpanzee raised by Roger Fouts, learned to generalize the sign for "dirty" from the sign for "feces." Lucy applied it to Fouts when he refused her requests! Lucy also invented the combinations "cry hurt food" to name radishes and "candy fruit" for watermelon.

Figure 3.9   Kanzi Communicates with a Keyboard. Kanzi, a pygmy chimp with the most advanced linguistic skill yet acquired by a nonhuman primate, answers questions and makes requests by punching symbols on a specially designed computer keyboard.

Koko, a female gorilla trained by Francine Patterson (1981), holds the record thus far of 300 Ameslan words (Figure 3.10). Koko signed "finger bracelet" for ring; "white tiger" for zebra; "eye hat" for mask. Koko has also begun to talk about her inner feelings, signaling happiness, sadness, fear, and shame (Hill 1978:98–99).

A remarkable achievement of these studies is that they have demonstrated that signing chimpanzees can pass on their signing skills to nonsigning chimpanzees without human mediation. Loulis, a 10-month-old chimp, was presented to Washoe, who adopted the infant and promptly began to sign to him. By 36 months, Loulis was using 28 signs that he had learned from Washoe. After about five years of learning to sign from Washoe and two other signing chimps, but not from humans, Loulis had acquired the use of 55 signs.

Even more remarkable is that Washoe, Loulis, and other signing chimps regularly used their sign language to communicate with each other even when humans were not present. These "conversations," as recorded on videotape, occurred from 118 to 649 times a month (Fouts and Fouts 1985).

It is clear, however, that a vast gap still remains between the language performance of humans and apes. Despite all the effort being expended on teaching apes to communicate, none has acquired the linguistic skills we take for granted in 3-year-old children (Terrace 1979). What all these experiments have shown is that it is entirely plausible to conceive of natural selection giving rise to the human capacity for semantic universality by selecting for intellectual skills already present in rudimentary form among our apelike hominid ancestors (Bickerton 1984; Parker 1985:622).

Figure 3.10   Koko
Koko is giving the sign "Pour-Drink" to her teacher, Francine Patterson.

Scientific Raciology

The position adopted in this book is that the causes of sociocultural similarities and differences are primarily cultural rather than biological. We will see that plausible and testable cultural theories can be constructed to account for many recurrent and variable aspects of human social life.

In the nineteenth century almost all educated Westerners were firm adherents of the doctrines of *scientific raciology*. They believed that Asians, Africans, and native Americans could achieve industrial civilization only slowly and imperfectly. Nineteenth-century scientists insisted that they had scientific proof that whites were intellectually superior and that an unbridgeable biological gulf separated them from the rest of humanity (Haller 1971). They conceded the possibility of an occasional native American, Asian, or African "genius," but they insisted that the average hereditary capabilities of the races were drastically different. These raciological theories were based on the fact that in the nineteenth century, Europeans had fought, tricked, and traded their way to control over almost the entire human species. The apparent inability of Asians, Africans, and native Americans to resist the encroachment of European armies, businesspeople, missionaries, and administrators was interpreted as living proof that the Europeans were biologically superior.

The racial explanation of European political domination was a convenient excuse for colonialism and for the exploitation and enslavement of people unable to defend themselves against technologically advanced European armaments. Today a few informed scientists would wish to attribute the temporary technological superiority of Europe and North America to genetic factors. Europe has not always had the most advanced technology. At various stages in the evolution of culture, non-Europeans in Asia or Africa have temporarily held the lead. Moreover, with the breakup of the great colonial empires, it would be extremely foolhardy for the advanced industrial nations to imagine that their genetic heritage will protect them from the rising political and economic power of the Third World.

Today the emergence of Japan as the Asian economic match of the United States and Western Europe discourages anyone from believing that the achievement of advanced technology can be attributed to genes that are more common in one race than in another (Figure 3.11). The problem with genetic interpreta-

tions of history and of cultural evolution is that they cannot account for the ups and downs of different regions and races except by adding or subtracting hypothetical genes for this or hypothetical genes for that.

To take another example, in the nineteenth century the British believed that the Irish were an inferior "race." To account for the economic success of the Irish in the New World, a racist would have to assume that the genes had suddenly changed or that there was something special about the genes of those who emigrated. Such explanations are scientifically undesirable because they depend on the appearance and disappearance of genes for economic success that no one has ever identified and that may not exist. Cultural explanations of the ups and downs of different human populations are scientifically preferable to racial explanations because they depend on factors such as rainfall, soil conditions, and population density, which are far more concrete and visible than hypothetical genes for technological ingenuity and economic success. The explanation for the rise of Japan as a great industrial power would become *unnecessarily* complicated, and hence scientifically undesirable, if in addition to cultural and ecological factors one were to posit the sudden appearance of Japanese genes for transistors and Toyotas.

The same criticism can be made of genetic explanations for traits such as matrilineality, patrilineality, and cognatic descent groups; nuclear and polygamous families; kinship terminologies; reciprocity; redistribution; feudalism; capitalism; and almost all the other cultural variations to be discussed in this book. To suppose that there are genes for each of these traits is contradicted by established facts concerning the processes of enculturation and diffusion. We know that adopted children who are brought up in cultures different from their parents' cultures acquire the culture of their foster

Figure 3.11   Nissan Motors Robotized Assembly Line.
Japan has taken the lead in automation. On this assembly line, robots are doing spot welding. The robots are frequently given names by the workers—usually the names of female film stars.

parents. And we know that traits originating in one culture can spread around the world to all cultures far too fast to be based on genetic change. Infants reared apart from their parents always acquire the cultures of the people among whom they are reared. Children of English-speaking American whites reared by Chinese parents grow up speaking perfect Chinese. They handle their chopsticks with precision and have no urge to eat at McDonald's. Children of Chinese reared in white American households speak the standard English dialect of their foster parents, are inept at using chopsticks, and do not yearn for bird's nest soup or Peking duck. Moreover, people

everywhere have a demonstrated ability to acquire every conceivable aspect of the world's cultural inventory. Native Americans brought up in Brazil incorporate complex African rhythms into their religious performances; American blacks who attend the proper schools become stars in classical European opera. Jews brought up in Germany prefer German cooking; Jews brought up in Yemen prefer Middle Eastern dishes. Under the influence of fundamentalist Christian missionaries, the sexually uninhibited people of Polynesia began to dress their women in long skirts and to follow rules of strict premarital chastity. Native Australians reared in Sydney show no inclination to hunt kangaroo or mutilate their genitals; they do not experience uncontrollable urges to sing about witchetty-grubs and the Emu ancestors (see page 296).

The evidence of enculturation and diffusion on every continent and among every major race and population proves that the overwhelming bulk of the response repertoire of any human population can be acquired by any other human population through learning processes and without the slightest exchange or mutation of genes. (See the Appendix for additional discussion of scientific raciology in the history of theories of culture.)

Sociobiology

Sociobiology is a research strategy that attempts to explain some sociocultural differences and similarities in terms of natural selection. It is based on a refinement of natural selection known as the principle of *inclusive fitness*. This principle states that natural selection favors traits that spread an individual's genes by increasing not only the number of an individual's offspring, but the number of offspring of close relatives, such as brothers and sisters, who carry many of the same genes. What controls biological evolution, therefore, is whether a trait increases the inclusive total of an individual's genes in succeeding generations and not merely the number of one's own children.

Inclusive fitness has been used to account for certain social traits in nonhuman species that traditional versions of natural selection were unable to explain. For example, it accounts for the evolution of sterile castes among social insects such as bees and ants. By not having children of its own and by feeding and caring for its fertile brothers and sisters, each sterile individual increases its inclusive fitness.

Other "altruistic" traits of social species can also be explained in this manner (Barash 1977; Wilson 1975).

Although sociobiology is a strategy that emphasizes the basic importance of genetic factors as determinants of human social life, its advocates do not necessarily accept the theories of scientists who believe that races and classes differ in intellectual capacity and in other important behavioral traits because they have different genotypes. Most sociobiologists, in fact, stress the unity of the human *biogram* —the basic genetic heritage that defines human nature. They have shown little interest in studying the possibility that each race has its own biogram. One must be careful, therefore, not to lump sociobiologists indiscriminately with scientific raciologists and political racists.

Sociobiologists do not deny that the bulk of human social responses are socially learned and therefore not directly under genetic control. Sociobiologist E. O. Wilson (1977:133) writes: "The evidence is strong that almost but probably not quite all differences among cultures are based on learning and socialization rather than on genes." Sociobiologist Richard Alexander (1976:6) also states: "I hypothesize that the vast bulk of cultural variations among peoples alive today will eventually be shown to have virtually nothing to do with their genetic differences." Few if any sociobiologists are interested in linking variations in human social behavior to the variable frequencies with which genes occur in different human populations.

It must be granted that the sociobiologists' interest in identifying the constants of human nature can lead to an understanding of the outer "envelope" —to use a metaphor proposed by E. O. Wilson (Harris and Wilson 1978) —constraining the directions that cultural evolution can take. Virtually all anthropologists agree that there is a human nature corresponding to the genetic heritage of *Homo sapiens.* But most anthropologists differ from sociobiologists in attributing few cultural practices, such as warfare or male supremacy, directly to the expression of human nature. Moreover, it is clear that human nature can account only for the universals of culture, not for the enormous range of variations at any particular moment in history. (See the Appendix for further discussion of sociobiology.)

When our species achieved semantic universality and crossed the threshold of cultural takeoff, it completed a transition to a level of existence as momentous as the creation of matter out of energy, or of life out of matter. *Homo sapiens* is not just another animal to be studied like ants or beavers; we are the only animal on earth (and for at least a dozen light years around in the heavens as well) whose primary mode of evolving new ways of coping with the problems of survival and reproduction depends overwhelmingly on cultural selection rather than on natural selection. Culture is encoded not in the genes, but in the brain (Lewontin, Rose, and Kamin 1984). Therefore, few cultural differences and similarities can be explained by the principle of inclusive fitness.

Scientific Creationism

"Scientific creationists" are religious fundamentalists who deny the validity of anthropological views of biological and cultural evolution and who seek to compel the public schools either to stop teaching evolution or to give equal time to their own views. They seek to achieve this aim by labeling evolutionism as "theory, not fact," and arguing that since evolutionism is merely a "theory," why should not other theories be taught alongside it? This rea-

soning is partly valid. All scientific "facts," "theories," and "laws" are held provisionally and are subject to being overturned by new evidence, so it cannot be denied that evolutionism is "theory, not fact." But the theories scientists teach are those that have withstood rigorous testing and are supported by the greatest amount of evidence. Creationist theory is not acceptable as science because it has not withstood rigorous testing and is contradicted by an enormous amount of evidence. No student should be prevented from reading about scientifically discredited theories, but no teacher should be compelled to teach every theory that has ever been discredited. (There are still people who believe that the Earth is flat. Should their views be given equal time in an astronomy class?)

Scientific creationists claim that the entire universe — including all the galaxies, stars, planets, minerals, plants, and animals — was created in six 24-hour days. These six days of creation allegedly took place no more than 10,000 years ago. They claim that humans and every kind of animal now extinct, such as dinosaurs, were alive at the same time. All species ate only plants and were capable of living forever. Even wolves and tigers had to be vegetarians, for no animals could die. But 8,000 years ago the entire earth was flooded to a height of over 17,000 feet in 40 days. At the end of one year, all this water flowed into ocean basins that had not previously existed. All present-day land-animal species were saved from this flood by being taken on board a wooden barge that alone survived the catastrophic winds and waves sweeping the entire globe (Godfrey 1981; Morris 1974a, 1974b).

According to the Institute for Creationist Research, most of the Earth's water was contained in a vapor "canopy" in the upper atmosphere and in underground reservoirs. The flood was initiated by the volcanic eruption of the underground waters, which caused turbulence in the atmosphere and "broke the water canopy." Almost every land animal died. The creatures killed by the flood were then washed into lower elevations, buried by sediments, and fossilized. The first to be buried and fossilized were creatures that lived on the bottom of the sea — shells and other invertebrates; fish were buried next; then amphibians and reptiles (because they lived at "higher elevations"); finally mammals and birds ("because of their greater mobility"). The last to die were human beings — in fact, they were seldom buried by sediments but lay on top of the ground, where their bodies decayed rather than becoming fossilized — and that accounts for why there are few fossilized human bones mixed in with those of extinct animals. Moreover, everywhere smaller and lighter creatures succumbed first and were buried deepest, while stronger and larger creatures were supposedly buried in the higher sediments. Thus the flood produced the general order of fossils in the geological strata, from simple to complex and from small to large, with humans on top. It is this layering that the scientific establishment has mistaken for evidence of evolution, the creationists assert.

This entire scenario lacks scientific credibility. There is no physical evidence for the pre-floodwater vapor canopy, no geophysical reason why the supposed underground reservoirs should have suddenly erupted simultaneously all over the Earth, and no known geophysical processes that could account for the sudden formation of ocean basins into which the floodwaters conveniently drained at the end of just one year. Moreover, geological strata contain numerous formations that could not conceivably have been produced by raging floodwaters, such as desert sandstones complete with salt deposits indicative not of floods but of evaporation from ancient lakes; successive layers of intact coral reefs, each of which would have required tens of thousands of years of clear, calm waters to develop; and whole forests of fossilized trees standing bolt upright because they were buried not by raging floods but by successive deposits of volcanic ash, layer on layer, one atop another.

The creationists' attempt to explain why the deepest strata contain the simplest forms of life and why fossil vertebrates generally appear above fossil invertebrates, amphibians above fish, reptiles above amphibians, mammals above reptiles, and so forth, is logically inconsistent. Why should land mammals have survived the 40 days of rain and flood better than sharks, whose fossil remains are first found far below those of mammals? The same question applies to fossil reptiles, including aquatic dinosaurs and giant crocodiles and turtles. How could the land mammals, struggling up the face of the tallest mountains (against torrents of hot brine spewing down on them), survive while the sharks, aquatic dinosaurs, and crocodiles had drowned, sunk to the bottom, and been buried? Evolutionary theory of course has no difficulty in explaining the relative positions of invertebrates, fish, reptiles, mammals, and humans in the Earth's geological strata — that is the sequence in which they evolved.

What kind of evidence do the scientific creationists have for the alleged coexistence of modern human types with long-extinct species such as dinosaurs? The creationists have made films and written books about the so-called "manprints" and man tracks found in the Paluxy River near Glen Rose, Texas. These manprints and man tracks are the imaginative results of wishful thinking (see Box 3.1). As a result of field inspections carried out by a team of anthropologists (Cole and Godfrey 1985),

Box 3.1

THE PALUXY RIVER FOOTPRINTS

Figure 3.12   Paluxy River "Footprints."
Creationists have long regarded this as a
human footprint inside a brontosaurus foot-
print. It is neither one nor the other, but a
purely natural erosinal feature.

Scientists have explored the region around the Paluxy River near Glen Rose, Texas, since the 1930s, finding hundreds of dinosaur tracks [Figure 3.12]. The geology and paleontology of the area are well known. Scientific creationists claim human tracks are found among the dinosaur tracks, which if true would challenge the interpretations of evolutionists. Contrary to television and comic book portrayals of "cave men" with dinosaur neighbors, humans evolved millions of years after dinosaurs became extinct, and remains of dinosaurs and humans are never found together.

.What about the Paluxy River "man tracks" then? In some of the "man tracks" presented in creationist books, faint traces of side toes can be seen, suggesting that these footprints are really just eroded dinosaur tracks. These tracts show claw marks at the "heel" of the "human" print, another indication that the track is a misinterpreted dinosaur track. Also, in at least one footprint sequence, dinosaur tracks and human footprints alternate. Either people evolved very rapidly from dinosaurs and then back again, or the "human" tracks are just indistinct dinosaur tracks!

These dinosaur prints lack the anatomy of human footprints, although some creationists claim to be able to see "big toes," "balls," and "arches" in eroded holes in the river bank. If the whole bank is surveyed, however, it can be seen that there are hundreds of erosion holes and washed-out places. The irregular shapes are like inkblot tests: one can imagine all kinds of figures. The "human" prints imagined from these erosional features are carefully selected examples that are best described as wishful projections of the hopes of scientific creationists to see what they want to see.

Source: Scott 1984.

the widely distributed creationist film "Footprints in Stone" has been withdrawn from circulation (Taylor 1985), and it has been admitted that "certain of the prints once labeled human are taking on a completely different character" — that is, the character of dinosaur, not human, footprints (Morris 1985:ii).

According to the creationists, after the flood, people who had previously spoken the same tongue suddenly began to converse in mutually unintelligible languages. This unintelligibility caused humans to emigrate from their homeland to distant parts of the globe. But there is no evidence to support such an event, and in fact it is contradicted by all that is known about the history of languages. As we shall see (page 61), the science of historical linguistics has patiently reconstructed the ancestral forms of the major linguistic families of the globe. The languages we speak today evolved gradually from these ancestral protolanguages. They did not provoke the geographical dispersals and separations of ancient peoples but were rather the result of geographical dispersals and separations. This is a process that has been thoroughly studied and documented with the aid of written materials.

Creationists claim that the Old Stone Age lasted not the 2 million years (or more) that archaeologists contend but only 3,000, from the dispersal caused by the Tower of Babel to the reappearance of advanced civilizations outside of the Middle East. The creationists argue that if the Old Stone Age lasted for a million years, the population of the Earth would be much greater than it is today. "It is essentially incredible that there would have been 25,000 generations of humans, with a resulting population of only 3.5 billion," since the average family "had to have at least 2.5 children," creationists say. But as we shall see (page 91), a substantial anthropological literature demonstrates that prehistoric peoples maintained very low rates of population growth by means of abstinence, abortion, prolonged nursing, and direct and indirect forms of infanticide. There is thus no reason to believe that the average family would have had at least 2.5 children who lived to reproductive age.

The creationist theory that all civilizations can be traced back to the Middle East ignores the most important archaeological discoveries of the twentieth century — that pre-Columbian state societies in Mexico and Peru evolved from a hunter-gatherer base independently of significant Old World influences. Archaeologists have found step-by-step evidence for the processes by which native American plants and animals unknown in the Old World, such as llamas, alpacas, guinea pigs, potatoes, manioc, maize, and amaranth, were domesticated and integrated into prehistoric native American cultures (Weatherford 1989). It was these plants and animals that furnished the food-energy base necessary for the evolution of bands into villages, villages into chiefdoms, chiefdoms into states, and states into empires in pre-Columbian America.

Are Religion and Science Necessarily in Conflict?

At the close of the last century, leading philosophers, theologians, and scientists succeeded in bringing about a truce in the war between science and religion that had raged ever since Giordano Bruno was burned at the stake in the sixteenth century for saying that the Earth was not the center of the universe. Scientists and theologians of many faiths came to accept the idea that there was no need for conflict between them as long as religious beliefs that science could not empirically test were not said to be scientific theories. People of deep religious conviction have ever since found it perfectly compatible with their beliefs in God, Christ, Krishna, Allah, heaven, or immortality to accept basic scientific theories about the origin and evolution of the Earth, life, humankind, and culture. And scientists, some of whom hold the same faiths, have found it equally compatible with their research to let the empirically nontestable essence of modern-day world religions stand entirely free of scientific attack. But if creationists insist on attacking the evolutionary core of modern science, modern science has no choice but to strike back against the religious core of creationism (see Spuhler 1985 for a comprehensive survey of the creationist controversy).

Summary

The human capacity for culture is a product of natural selection. Natural selection alters genotypes through differential reproductive success. Natural selection is not synonymous with a struggle for survival between individuals. Fitness may result as often from cooperation and altruism. Both anatomical and behavioral traits can be shaped by natural selection and encoded in the genes. Behavior gets encoded through the sequence:

old genotype → genetic error
 → behavioral deviation
 → selection
 → new genotype

Learning is a process of behavioral change that is entirely different from the behavioral change induced by natural selection. Learning permits organisms to adjust to or take advantage of novel contingencies and opportunities independently of genetic changes:

old genotype → new behavior
 → selection
 → old genotype

Learning is the basis of cultural traditions. Although the capacity for acquiring traditions was shaped by natural selection and awaited the evolution of brainier species, culture is encoded in the brain, not in the genes. Cultural behavior such as tool making and tool use occurs in many nonhuman species, especially monkeys and great apes. Yet even among monkeys and great apes, tool-using traditions remain rudimentary. The reason for this is that monkeys and apes use their forelimbs for climbing and walking and hence cannot readily carry tools. Early hominids such as the australopithecines had ape-size brains but upright posture. The evolution of the human foot thus set the pattern for further evolution of the human brain and the unique degree of human dependence on culture. The increasing braininess of *Homo erectus* and *Homo sapiens* resulted in an increasing reliance on culture, and the increasing reliance on culture resulted in increasing braininess. This process accelerated dramatically about 40,000 years ago when culture "took off," and vast numbers of traditions evolved at a rapid rate without any significant changes in the size of the brain.

A vital ingredient in this takeoff was the development of the human capacity for semantic universality. As shown by numerous experiments, chimpanzees and gorillas can be taught to use several hundred signs. Compared with 3-year-old human infants, however, apes have only rudimentary capabilities for linguistic productivity.

In the nineteenth century the dominant political position of the European powers was interpreted as proof of the superiority of the white race. The main problem with such genetic interpretations of history and of cultural evolution is that they cannot account for the shifting locus of technological and political change except by postulating changes in the frequencies of genes. But the existence of these genes is purely hypothetical.

The basic independence of cultural differences and similarities from genetic determination is shown by the ability of individuals and whole populations to change their cultural repertories through enculturation and diffusion in one generation.

Sociobiology is a hereditarian research strategy that stands somewhat apart from scientific raciology. It is concerned with the effects of human nature on culture, and it seeks to explain cultural similarities and some cultural differences by means of the principle of inclusive fitness. This principle stresses mea-surement of the reproductive success of closely related individuals as the key to natural selection in social species.

In the known world, cultural takeoff has occurred only among human beings. This take-off was as momentous as the appearance of matter out of energy or of life out of matter. The great bulk of cultural variations, as even leading sociobiologists admit, cannot be explained by natural selection acting on human genes.

The theories of scientific creationism are not acceptable alternatives to evolutionism. They are either untestable or contradicted by the available evidence. Evolutionary theories have been rigorously tested and found to be compatible with the available evidence. If creationism is presented as untestable religious belief, then there can be no quarrel between creationism and evolutionism, but scientists are obliged to criticize creationism if it is set forth as a valid scientific theory.

Chapter 4

LANGUAGE

This chapter is intended as a brief introduction to anthropological linguistics. It begins with an analysis of the features of human languages that make possible semantic universality. Then the distinction between phonetic and phonemic units is set forth. The relationship between language and culture is explored, and, finally, the significance of consciousness for cultural change is illustrated by the processes of linguistic change.

Productivity

Human languages achieve semantic universality in part by possessing the feature known as *productivity* (Hockett and Ascher 1964). To every message that we send, we can always add another whose meaning cannot be predicted from the information in previous messages.

Nonhuman languages have only limited powers of productivity. C. R. Carpenter's (1940) classic study of gibbon language shows the limits of the productivity of nonhuman primate languages in natural settings. Carpenter found that gibbons have nine major types of calls. These calls convey socially useful information such as: "I am here," "I am angry," "Follow me," "Here is food," "Danger!" and "I am hurt." Because each call can be repeated at different volumes and durations, the gibbon system possesses a small amount of productivity. For example, the gibbon can say "Danger!" with different degrees of emphasis roughly equivalent to the series "Danger!" "Danger! Danger!" "Danger! Danger! Danger!" and so on. But this series exhibits little productivity

because the amount of information conveyed does not increase at the same rate that length of the message increases. A "danger" call repeated twenty times in succession is informationally not much different from "danger" repeated nineteen times. In contrast, the productivity of human language is extremely efficient. In order to convey more and more specific information in a particular domain, our messages do not have to keep getting longer. We can say: "Be careful, there's a strange movement over there," "I think I see a leopard," and "It's in that tree." Moreover, these unique powers of productivity are not constrained to the small set of subjects that gibbons and other primates "talk about." Rather, we are capable of producing an infinite number of messages about an infinite number of subjects.

Displacement

Another component of semantic universality is the feature known as *displacement* (Hockett and Ascher 1964). A message is displaced when either the sender or the receiver has no immediate direct sensory contact with the conditions or events to which the message refers. We have no difficulty, for example, in telling each other about events such as football games after they are over or about events such as meetings and appointments before they take place. Human language is capable of communicating an infinity of details about an infinity of displaced domains. This contrasts with all nonhuman communication systems. Among primates, for example, usually only the listener exhibits some degree of displacement, as when a "danger" message is understood at a distance. But the sender must be in sensory contact with the source of danger in order to give an appropriate warning. A gibbon does not say, "Danger! There may be a leopard on the other side of this hill." On the other hand, in human communication both sender and receiver are frequently displaced. We talk routinely about people, places, and things seen, heard, or felt in the past or future; or that others have told us about; or that enjoy a completely imaginary existence.

Displacement is the feature we usually have in mind when we refer to human language as having the capacity to convey "abstract information." Some of the greatest glories of human life — including poetry, literature, and science — depend on displacement, but so too do some of our species's most shameful achievements — lies and false promises. As St. James put it: "But the tongue can no man tame; it is an unruly evil, full of deadly poison. . . . Out of the same mouth proceedeth blessing and cursing" (James 3:6 – 11).

Humans are not the only liars, however. Birds, for example, often lead predators away from nests by feigning broken wings, and many animals "play dead." Until recently, this kind of deception was thought to occur only be-

tween members of different species. It is now known, however, that some birds give "false alarms" to their own kind in order to have a fruit tree all to themselves, and chimpanzees hide their facial expressions to prevent competing chimpanzees from detecting their fear (de Waal 1983).

Arbitrariness

Another striking feature of human languages is the unprecedented degree to which they are constructed out of sounds whose physical shape and meaning have not been programmed in our genes. Most infrahuman communication systems consist of genetically stereotyped signals whose meaning depends on genetically stereotyped decoding behavior. For example, in communicating its sexual receptivity, a female dog emits chemical signals whose interpretation is genetically programmed into all sexually mature male dogs. Primate call patterns, like those of Carpenter's gibbons, are somewhat less tied to specific genetic programs and are known to vary among local groups of the same species, but the basic signal repertory of primate communication systems is species-specific: The facial expressions, hand gestures, cries, whimpers, and shrieks of chimpanzees constitute a genetically controlled repertory that is shared by all chimpanzees.

This is not the case with human languages. True enough, the general capacity for human language is also species-specific; that is, the ability to acquire semantic universality is genetically determined. Nonetheless, the actual constituents of human language codes are virtually free of genetic constraints (not counting such things as the physiology of the ear and of the vocal tract). Take as an example the languages of England and France. There are no genes that make the English say "water," "dog," or "house." These words are arbitrary because (1) they do not occur in the language behavior of most human beings; (2) neighboring populations in France, with whom there is considerable gene flow, utilize "eau," "chien," and "maison" to convey similar meanings; and (3) all normal human infants drawn from any population will acquire these English or French words with equal facility depending on whether they are enculturated (see page 10) in England or in France.

There is another important sense in which human language is arbitrary. Human language code elements lack any physically regular relationship to the events and properties that they signify. That is, there is no inherent physical reason why "water" designates water. Many nonhuman communication systems, on the other hand, are based on code elements that resemble, are part of, or are analogous to the items they denote. Bees, for example, trace the location of sources of nectar by smelling the pollen grains that cling to the feet of their hive mates. Chimpanzees communicate threats of violence by breaking off branches and waving or throwing them. Although we humans also frequently communicate by means of similar *iconographic symbols* — like shaking our fists or pointing to a desired object — the elements in spoken language seldom bear anything other than an arbitrary relationship in their meaning. Even such words as "bow-wow" or "hiss" are arbitrary. "Ding-dong" may sound like a bell to speakers of English but not to Germans, for whom bells say "bim-bam."

Duality of Patterning

Human semantic universality is achieved by means of a remarkably small number of arbitrary sounds called *phonemes*. Phonemes are

sounds that native speakers perceive as being distinct — that is, as contrasting with other sounds. Phonemes are meaningless in isolation, but when they are combined into prescribed sequences, phonemes convey a definite meaning. The contrastive sounds in the utterance "cat" by themselves mean nothing, but combined they signify a small animal. In reverse order the same sounds signify a small nail or a sailing maneuver. Thus the basic elements in human language have *duality of patterning*: The same contrastive sounds combine and recombine to form different messages.

Theoretically, semantic universality could be achieved by a code that has duality of patterning based on only two distinctive elements. This is actually the case with the dots and dashes of Morse Code and with the binary 0 and 1 of digital computers. But a natural language having only two phonemes would require a much longer string of phonemes per average message than one having several phonemes. The smallest number of phonemes known in a natural language is thirteen, in Hawaiian. English has between thirty-five and forty (depending on which authority is cited). Once there are more than ten or so phonemes, there is no need to produce exceptionally long strings per message. A repertory of ten phonemes, for example, can be combined to produce 10,000 different words consisting of four phonemes each. Let us now take a closer look at how phonemes can be identified and how they are combined to form meaningful utterances.

Phonetics

Phonemes consist of etic sounds called *phones*. The study of etic sounds is called *phonetics*. In order to be effective as code elements, the phones of a language must be clearly distinguishable. One way to achieve a well-defined set of phones is to make each phone contrast as much as possible with every other phone. But when does one phone contrast with another? No two phones "naturally" contrast with each other. If we are able to distinguish one phoneme from another it is only because as native speakers we have learned to accept and recognize certain phones and not others as being contrastive. For example, the [t] in "ten" and the [d] in "den" are automatically regarded by speakers of English as contrastive sounds. (A symbol between brackets denotes a phone.) Yet these two sounds actually have many *phonetic* — that is, acoustical — features in common. It is culture, not nature, that makes them significantly different.

What is the critical difference between [t] and [d] for speakers of English? Let us examine the *articulatory features* — that is, the manner in which they are produced by the vocal tract (Figure 4.1). Notice that when you produce either sound, the tip of your tongue presses against the *alveolar ridge* just behind the top of your teeth. Notice also that when either sound is made, the flow of the column of air coming from the lungs is momentarily interrupted and then released only in order to form the rest of the sounds in the utterance. In what way, then, are they different? The major articulatory difference between [t] and [d] consists of the way the column of air passes through the vocal chords. The vibration of the vocal chords produces a *voiced* effect in the case of [d] but not in the case of [t]. Both [t] and [d] are described phonetically as *alveolar stops*, but [d] is a *voiced alveolar stop*, whereas [t] is an *unvoiced alveolar stop*. The use of a voiced and unvoiced alveolar stop to distinguish utterances such as "ten" – "den," "tock" – "dock," "to" – "do," or "train" – "drain" is an entirely arbitrary device that is characteristic of English but that is absent in many other languages.

Phonemics

The structure of a given language's *phonemic system* — its system of meaningful sound contrasts — is discovered by testing observed phonetic variations within the context of pairs of words that sound alike in all but one respect. The testing consists in part of asking native speakers whether they detect a change in meaning. That is what is achieved in the comparison between "ten" and "den." By asking native speakers to compare similar pairs of words, we can detect most of the phonemic contrasts in English. For example, another instance in which voicing sets up a phonemic contrast is found in "bat" — "pat." Here the initial sounds are also stops, but this time they are made by pressing both lips together, and are called *bilabial stops*. Again one of the stops, [b], is voiced, whereas the other, [p], is unvoiced. It is only the fact that these phones are contras-

Figure 4.1   Parts of oral passage.

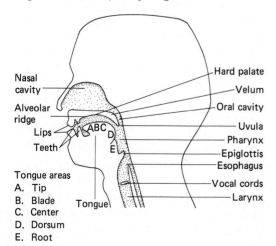

Nasal cavity

Alveolar ridge

Lips

Teeth

Tongue areas
A. Tip
B. Blade
C. Center
D. Dorsum
E. Root

Tongue

Hard palate

Velum

Oral cavity

Uvula

Pharynx

Epiglottis

Esophagus

Vocal cords

Larynx

tive from the native speaker's point of view that validates the classification of these two sounds as different phonemes. It is this fact that is generalized when the terms *emic* from *phonemic* and *etic* from *phonetic* (Headland 1990) are applied to other domains of culture (see page 20).

To the linguist's trained ear, many sound differences that escape the notice of the native speaker will appear as possible contenders for phonemic status. For example, the removal of the labial obstruction in the utterance "pat" is accompanied by a slight puff of air that is not found at the beginning of "bat." This phonetic feature is known as *aspiration* and can easily be detected by placing your hand close to your lips and pronouncing first "pat" and then "bat" several times in succession. A more precise phonetic description of the [p] in "pat," therefore, is that it is an *aspirated bilabial unvoiced stop*, for which the phonetic symbol is [pʰ]. Both aspirated and nonaspirated /p/s occur in English. (A symbol between slant lines indicates a phoneme.) Thus the bilabial stops in "sap," "flip," and "hip" are nonaspirated. Hence the question arises as to whether [p] and [pʰ] constitute separate phonemes. There are no meaningful English utterances in which the substitution of [p] for [pʰ] alters the meaning of an utterance. Instead, [p] and [pʰ] are in *complementary distribution*; that is, they occur regularly in different sound environments. Closely resemblant but nondistinctive sounds such as [p] and [pʰ] are called *allophones*. In a sense, every specific instance of any given phoneme is an allophone, since no two utterances are ever exactly the same in either articulation or acoustic effect. A given phoneme, then, designates a range or class of allophones.

Phones that regularly occur in one language may not occur at all in another. When the same phone does occur in two languages, it may be phonemic in one but not the other.

When similar phones are phonemic in two languages, they may have a different set of free and conditioned allophones.

In Chinese, for example, the nonphonemic aspirated and nonaspirated [t] of English "tick" and "stick" are phonemic. Also, Chinese uses "sing-song" tonal differences for phonemic contrasts in ways that English does not. On the other hand, in English the initial sound difference in "luck" and "rot" are phonemic, whereas in Chinese they are not (in an initial position). Hence "rots of ruck" sounds the same as "lots of luck" to a Chinese learning English.

Morphemes

The smallest units of language that have a definite meaning are called *morphemes*. Like each phoneme, each morpheme designates a class of basic units. In this case the constituents of the class are called *morphs*. Hence, just as phonemes are a class of allophones, so morphemes are a class of *allomorphs*. For example, the prefix "in-" as in "insane" and the prefix "un-" as in "unsafe" are morphs that belong to a morpheme meaning "not."

Morphemes may consist of single phonemes or of strings of phonemes in many different combinations and permutations. Some morphemes can occur as isolates, whereas some can occur only in conjunction with other morphemes. "Hello," "stop," and "sheep" are *free* morphemes because they can constitute the entirety of a well-formed message. ("Are those goats or sheep?" "Sheep.") But the past-forming /-ed/ of "talked" or "looked" and the /-er/ of "speaker" or "singer" are *bound* morphemes because they can never constitute well-formed messages on their own. Languages vary widely in their reliance on free or bound morphemes. Chinese, for example, has many free morphemes, while Turkish has many bound morphemes. Words are free morphemes or combinations of morphemes that can constitute well-formed messages. ("The" by this definition is not a word but a bound morpheme.)

Grammar: Rules Governing the Construction of Morphemes

Grammar consists of sets of unconscious rules for combining phonemes into morphemes and morphemes into appropriate sentences. Some linguists also include as part of grammar the rules for interpreting the meaning of words and the rules for speaking in ways that are appropriate in particular contexts. The existence of rules governing the formation of permitted sequences of phonemes can be seen in the reaction of speakers of English to common names in Polish such as Zbigniew Brzezinski. The rules of English, unlike the rules of Polish, do not permit sound combinations such as "zb." Similarly, speakers of English know by unconscious rule that the words "btop" and "ndak" cannot exist in English, since they involve prohibited sound combinations.

Grammar: Syntax

Similar unconscious rules govern the combination of morphemes into sentences. This branch of grammar is called *syntax*. Native speakers can distinguish between grammatical and nongrammatical sentences even when they have never heard particular combinations before. A classic example is:

  a. Colorless green ideas sleep furiously.
  b. Furiously sleep ideas green colorless.

Most speakers of English will recognize sentence *a* as a grammatical utterance but reject *b* as ungrammatical even when both seem equally nonsensical.

Native speakers can seldom state the rules governing the production of grammatical utterances. Even the difference between singular and plural nouns is hard to formulate as a conscious rule. Adding an *s* converts "cat" into "cats," "slap" into "slaps," "fat" into "fats"; but something else happens in "house" – "houses," "rose" – "roses," "nose" – "noses"; and something else again in "crag" – "crags," "flag" – "flags," and "hand" – "hands." (Three different allomorphs — /-s/, /-ez/, and /-z/ — are employed according to a complex rule that most native speakers of English cannot put into words.)

The set of unconscious structural rules, and the sharing of these rules by the members of a speech community, makes it possible for human beings to produce and interpret a potentially infinite number of messages, none of which need precisely replicate any other previous message. Noam Chomsky described this behavior as follows:

> Normal   linguistic   behavior . . . as speaker or reader or hearer, is quite generally with novel utterances, with utterances that have no physical or formal similarity to any of the utterances that have ever been produced in the past experience of the hearer or, for that matter, in the history of the language, as far as anyone knows. [1973:118]

Deep Structure

How is it possible for us to create so many different messages and still be understood? No one is quite sure of the answer to this question.

One of the most popular theories is that proposed by Chomsky. According to Chomsky, every utterance has a *surface structure* and a *deep structure*. Surface structures may appear dissimilar, yet deep structures may be identical. For example, "Meat and gravy are loved by lions" is superficially dissimilar to the sentence "Lions love meat and gravy." Yet both sentences take as their model a third sentence: "Lions love meat and lions love gravy." This third sentence more closely reflects the "deep structure," which can be transformed into various superficially different variations.

What is the deep structure of a sentence like "John knows a kinder person than Bill"? Note that the meaning of this sentence is ambiguous. Does John know a kinder person than Bill knows, or does John know a kinder person than Bill is? There must be two different deep structures that have gotten confused in the single ambiguous surface structure (Katz 1971:79–81).

Theoretically, a knowledge of the transformation rules should also lead to the identification of the deep structures that underlie apparently dissimilar ways of saying the same thing. Unfortunately, it has not yet proved feasible to identify all the transformation rules in any given language, and many linguists are convinced that there is a difference in meaning between deep structure sentences and their surface structure transforms (Silverstein 1972:376).

An essential feature of Chomsky's notion of grammar is that at the deepest levels, all human languages share an inborn species-specific structure. It is the existence of this inborn structure that makes it possible for children to learn to speak at an early age and that makes it possible to translate any human language into any other human language. Other authorities, however, doubt the existence of inborn grammar and attribute the acquisition of language skills by children to ordinary learning processes (Bickerton 1984).

Language Acquisition

How do children learn to speak a particular language? Recent studies show that the acquisition of language proceeds step by step from the acquisition of phonemes to simple morphemes and grammatical rules, to more and more complex vocabularies and structural rules. It has been found that children will not learn to speak if they merely hear others speak. A boy with normal hearing and comprehension, but with deaf parents who communicated in Ameslan, watched and listened to television every day. His parents hoped that he would learn English. Because the boy was asthmatic, he was kept at home and interacted only with people who communicated in sign language. By the age of 3 he was fluent in Ameslan but neither understood nor spoke English. This shows that in order to learn a language, children must be able to test out and improve their tentative knowledge of phonemes, morphemes, and grammar by interacting with other people. In other words, although human beings have a uniquely developed, species-specific capacity for language, we will not automatically begin to speak as soon as we hear others doing it. We learn our languages by using them to make requests and by responding to the requests that others make (Moscowitz 1978:94b).

Are There Superior and Inferior Languages?

European linguists of the nineteenth century were convinced that the languages of the world could be arranged in a hierarchical order. They invariably awarded the prize for efficiency, elegance, and beauty to Latin, the mastery of whose grammar was long a precondition for scholarly success in the West.

Beginning with the study of American Indian languages, however, anthropological linguists, led by Franz Boas, showed that the belief in the superiority of "civilized" grammars was untenable. It was found that grammatical rules run the full gamut from simple to complex systems among peoples on all levels of technological and political development. The conclusion of the great anthropological linguist Edward Sapir (1921:234) stands unchallenged: "When it comes to linguistic form, Plato walks with the Macedonian swineherd, Confucius with the head-hunting savages of Assam."

Other kinds of language differences have been cited as evidence that one language is more "primitive" than another. For example, there are numerous words for different types of parrots in native Brazilian Tupi languages, and yet no term for parrots in general. On the other hand, some languages seem to lack specific terms. For example, there are languages that have no specific words for numbers higher than five. Larger quantities are simply referred to as "many." But the extent to which discourse is specific or general reflects the culturally defined need to be specific or general, not the capacity of one's language to transmit messages about specific or general phenomena. Brazilian Indians have little need to distinguish parrots in general from other birds, but they must be able to distinguish one parrot from another, since each type is valued for its plumage. The ordinary individual in a small-scale society can name and identify 500 to 1000 separate plant species, but the ordinary modern urbanite can usually name only 50 to 100 such species. Paradoxically, urbanites usually have a more complex set of general terms, such as *plant, tree, shrub,* and *vine,* than band and vil-

lage peoples, for whom such generalities are of little practical use (Witowski and Brown 1978:445–446). English, which has terms for many special vehicles—*cart, stretcher, auto, sled, snowmobile*—lacks a general term for wheeled vehicles. Yet this does not prevent one from communicating about wheeled vehicles as distinguished from sleds and helicopters when the need arises. Similarly, the absence of higher-number terms usually means that there are few occasions when it is useful to specify large quantities precisely. When these occasions become more common, any language can cope with the problem of numeration by repeating the largest term or by inventing new ones.

It has been found that small-scale societies tend to have languages with fewer color terms than more complex societies. Some languages have separate terms only for brightness contrasts, such as those designated by black and white. With the evolution of more complex societies, languages tend to add color distinctions in a regular sequence: red → green or blue → brown → pink, orange, purple. The emergence of these distinct color terms is probably linked with increasing technological control over dyes and paints (Witowski and Brown 1978). Similarly, many languages use one term to designate "hand" and "arm" and one term for "leg" and "foot." It has been found that this lack of distinction correlates with languages spoken by peoples who live in the tropics and wear little clothing. Among peoples who live in colder climates and who wear special garments (gloves, boots, sleeves, pants, etc.) for different parts of the body, the parts of the limbs tend to be designated by distinctive terms (Witowski and Brown 1985).

These differences, in any event, are necessarily superficial. Semantic productivity is infinite in all known languages. When the social need arises, terms appropriate to industrial civilization can be developed by any language. This can be done either through the direct borrowing of the words of one language by another (*sputnik, blitzkrieg, garage*) or by the creation of new words based on new combinations of the existing stock of morphemes (*radiometric, railroad, newspaper*). No culture is ever at a loss for words — not for long, that is.

Language, Social Class, and Ethnicity

Another form in which the claim for language superiority appears is associated with the dialect variations characteristic of stratified societies (see page 201). One hears of the "substandard" grammar or "substandard" pronounciation of a particular ethnic group or social class. Such allegations have no basis in linguistic science except insofar as one is willing to accept all contemporary languages as corrupt and "substandard" versions of earlier languages.

When the dialect variant of a segment of a larger speech community is labeled "substandard," what is usually being dealt with is a political rather than a linguistic phenomenon (Hertzler 1965; Southworth 1974). The demotion of dialects to inferior status can be understood only as part of the general process by which ruling groups attempt to maintain their superordinate position (see Chapter 12). Linguistically, the phonemes and grammar of the poor and uneducated classes are as efficient as those of the rich, educated, and powerful classes.

This point should not be confused with the problem of functional vocabulary differences. Exploited and deprived groups often lack key specialized and technical words and concepts as a result of their limited educational experience. This constitutes a real handicap in competing for jobs, but has nothing to do with the question of the adequacy of the phonological and grammatical systems of working-class and ethnic dialects (Figure 4.2).

Well-intentioned educators often claim

Figure 4.2   Class and accent.
The language spoken by these youths in London (a) is as distinct from that spoken by the royal guests at the Ascot horse races (b) as the clothes worn by each class.

(a)

(b)

that the poor and ghetto children are reared in a "linguistically deprived" environment. In a detailed study of the actual speech behavior of blacks in northern ghettos, William Labov (1972a, 1972b) has shown that this belief reflects the ethnocentric prejudices of middle-class teachers and researchers rather than any deficit in the grammar or logical structure of the ghetto dialect. The nonstandard English of the black ghetto, black vernacular English, contains certain forms that are unacceptable in white, middle-class settings. Among the most common are negative inversion ("don't nobody know"), negative concord ("you ain't goin' to no heaven"), invariant "be" ("when they be sayin"), dummy "it" instead of "there" ("it ain't no heaven"), and copula deletion ("if you bad"). Yet the use of these forms in no way prevents or inhibits the expression of complex thoughts in concise and logically consistent patterns (Box 4.1).

The grammatical properties of nonstandard language are not haphazard and arbitrary variations. On the contrary, they conform to rules that produce regular differences with respect to the standard grammar. All the dialects of English possess equivalent means for expressing the same logical content (see Box 4.2).

Language, Thought, and Causality

A question that has been investigated by linguists for many years is the extent to which different word categories and grammars produce habitually incompatible modes of thought among peoples who belong to different language communities (Hymes 1971; Kay and Kempton 1984). At the center of this controversy is the comparison made by the anthro-

Box 4.1

BLACK ENGLISH

Soon as you die, your spirit leaves you. (And where does the spirit go?) Well, it all depends. (On what?) You know, like some people say if you're good an' shit, your spirit goin' t'heaven . . . 'm' if you bad, your spirit goin' to hell. Well, bullshit! Your spirit goin' to hell ayway, good or bad. (Why?) Why? I'll tell you why. 'Cause, you see, doesn' no body really know that it's a God, y'know, 'cause, I mean I have seen black gods, pink gods, white gods, all color gods, and don't nobody know it's really a God. An' when they be saying' if you good, you goin' t'heaven, tha's bullshit, 'cause you ain't goin' to no heaven. 'Cause it ain't no heaven for you to go to.

Source: Labov 1972a:214–215.

Box 4.2

LANGUAGE AND LOGIC

Whatever problems working-class children may have in handling logical operations are not to be blamed on the structure of their language. There is nothing in the vernacular which will interfere with the development of logical thought, for the logic of standard English cannot be distinguished from the logic of any other dialect of English by any test that we can find.

Source: Labov 1972a:229.

pological linguist Benjamin Whorf between native American languages and the *Indo-European family* of languages, a group that includes English, many of the languages of Europe, Hindu, Persian, and others. According to Whorf, when two language systems have radically different vocabularies and grammars, their respective speakers live in wholly different thought-worlds. Even such fundamental categories as space and time are said to be experienced differently as a result of the linguistic "molds" that constrain thought (Box 4.3).

According to Whorf, English sentences are constructed in such a way as to indicate that some substance or matter is part of an event that is located at a definite time and place. Both time and space can be measured and divided into units. In the native American Hopi language, however, events are not located with reference to time but, rather, to the categories of "being" as opposed to "becoming" (Figure 4.3). English encourages one to think of time as a divisible rod that starts in the past, passes through the present, and continues into the future—hence, the English language's past, present, and future tenses. Hopi grammar, however, merely distinguishes all events that have already become manifest from all those still in the process of becoming manifest; it has no equivalent of past, present, and future tenses. Does this mean that a Hopi cannot indicate that an event happened last month or that it is happening right now or that it will

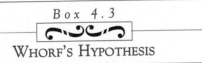

Box 4.3

WHORF'S HYPOTHESIS

The forms of a person's thoughts are controlled by inexorable laws of pattern of which he is unconscious. These patterns are the unperceived intricate systematization of his own language—shown readily enough by a candid comparison and contrast with other languages, especially those of a different linguistic family. His thinking itself is in a language—in English, in Sanskrit, in Chinese. And every language is a vast pattern-system, different from others, in which are culturally ordained the forms and categories by which the personality not only communicates, but also analyzes nature, notices or neglects types of relationship and phenomena, channels his reasoning, and builds the house of his consciousness.

Source: Benjamin Whorf, *Language, Thought and Reality,* p. 252. Copyright © 1956 by John Wiley & Sons, Inc.

Figure 4.3   A Hopi Indian caring for young corn.

happen tomorrow? Of course not. But Whorf's point is that the English tense system makes it easier to measure time, and he postulated some type of connection between the tense system of Indo-European languages and the inclination of Euro-Americans to read timetables, make time payments, and punch time clocks.

In rebuttal, other linguists have pointed out that the three-tense system that is supposed to color thinking about time really does not exist in English. First, there is no specific verb form indicating the future tense in English; one uses auxiliaries such as *will* and *shall*. Second, English speakers frequently use the present tense and even the past tense to talk about the future: "I'm *eating* at six this evening"; "If I *told* you, would you do anything?" This means that the use of tenses in English is a good deal more relaxed and ambiguous than high school grammars indicate. If one needed an opportunity to become confused about time, English provides no unusual obstacles (Haugen 1977).

A more important objection to Whorf's point of view is that it implicitly distorts the fundamental causal relationships between language and culture. No one would deny that the absence of calendars, clocks, and timetables must have given preindustrial societies such as the Hopi an orientation to time very different from that of industrial-age societies. But there is no evidence to support the view that industrialization is in any way facilitated or caused by having one kind of grammar rather than another.

An interest in calendars and other time-reckoning devices is a recurrent feature of social and political development associated with peoples whose languages are as diverse as those of the Egyptians and the Mayas. Indeed, the Chinese contributed as much to the invention of modern mechanical clocks as did the Europeans. On the other hand, a lack of concern with counting time is a characteristic of preindustrial peoples in general, from Patagonia to Baffin Land and from New Guinea to the Kalahari desert — peoples who speak a thousand different tongues.

As it is with time reckoning, so it is with other aspects of culture. The Aztecs, whose powerful state marks the high point of political development in aboriginal North America, spoke a language closely related to that of the hunting and food-gathering Utes. Religions as different as Hinduism, Christianity, and Buddhism have flourished among peoples who speak closely related Indo-European languages. Malayo-Polynesian, Bantu, and Arabic have served equally well as media for the spread of Islam, whereas Chinese, Russian, and Spanish have served equally well for the spread of Marxism. Industrial capitalism in Japan shares much with that in the United States, although the Japanese and English languages show few resemblances.

Obligatory Elitism and Sexism

Languages differ in having certain obligatory categories built into their grammatical rules. English requires us to specify number. Speakers of the Romance languages must indicate the sex (gender) of all nouns. Certain American Indian languages (for example, Kwakiutl) must indicate whether an object is near or far from the speaker and whether it is visible or invisible. These obligatory categories in all probability do not indicate any active psychological tendency to be obsessed with numbers, sex, or the location of people or objects.

It should not be concluded, however, that grammatical conventions are always trivial.

Certain obligatory grammatical categories do mirror social life quite faithfully. Consider the pronouns and verb forms for peers versus subordinates in the Romance languages. Because of the existence of a second-person "familiar" form in the conjugation of Romance verbs, the speaker of French or Spanish is frequently obligated to evaluate and express the relative social standing of persons engaged in a conversation. Today these second-person familiar forms (e.g., *tu hablas, tu parles*—in Spanish and French; roughly, "thou speaketh") are primarily applied to children, pets, very close friends, and loved ones. But another usage persists, especially in parts of Latin America, where landlords and officials apply the *tu* forms to servants, workers, and peasants as well as to children and pets. These forms clearly reflect an active consciousness of class and rank distinctions and bear a social significance that is far from trivial or merely conventional.

Similarly, certain obligatory categories in standard English seem to reflect a pervasive social bias in favor of male-centered viewpoints and activities. Many nouns and pronouns that refer to human beings lack gender—*child, everybody, everyone, person, citizen, American, human*, and so on. Teachers of standard English used to prescribe masculine rather than feminine pronouns to refer to these words. Thus it was considered "correct" to say: "Everyone must remember to take *his* toothbrush," even though the group being addressed consists of both males and females. Newspaper columnists were fond of writing: "The average American is in love with *his* car." And high school grammars used to insist that one must say: "All the boys and girls were puzzled but no one was willing to raise *his* hand" (Roberts 1964:382). Obviously a perfectly intelligible and sexually unbiased substitute is readily available in the plural possessive pronoun *their*. In fact, nowadays almost everybody uses *their* in their [sic] everyday conversation (Newmeyer 1978). The male-centered conventions of the English language may not be as benign and trivial as some male anthropologists once believed them to be (Lakoff 1973; Philips 1980:531). It seems likely, for example, that the use of *him* and *he* as pronouns for God reflects the fact that men are the traditional priests of Judaism and Christianity.

But as Franklin Southworth (1974) has shown in his study of changes in the use of obligatory forms of address in India, mere linguistic changes are easy to make—so easy, in fact, that they sometimes function as "masks for power" by creating the superficial impression of democratization. One must certainly guard against trying to change the world by mere word magic. Yet if a particular word or grammatical rule hurts and offends people, why continue to use it?

Linguistic Change

Like all other parts of culture, language is constantly undergoing change. These changes result from slight phonemic, morphemic, or grammatical variations. They are often identifiable at first as "dialect" differences, such as those that distinguish the speech of American Southerners from the speech of New Englanders. If groups of Southerners and New Englanders were to move off to separate islands and lose all linguistic contact with each other and their homelands, their speech would eventually cease to be mutually intelligible. The longer the separation, the less resemblance there would probably be among them.

The process of dialect formation and geographical isolation is responsible for much of the great diversity of languages. Many mutually unintelligible languages of today are "daughter" languages of a common "parent" language. This can be seen by the regular resemblances that languages display in their features. For example, English /t/ corresponds to German /z/, as in the following pairs of words (after Sturtevant 1964:64–66):

tail	*Zagel*	tin	*Zinn*
tame	*zahm*	to	*zu*
tap	*zapfen*	toe	*Zehe*
ten	*zehn*	tooth	*Zahn*

These correspondences result from the fact that both English and German are daughter languages of a common parent language known as Proto-West Germanic.

In the 2000 years that have elapsed since the Roman conquest of Western Europe, Latin has evolved into an entire family of languages, of which French, Italian, Portuguese, Rumanian, and Spanish are the principal representatives. If linguists did not know of the existence of Latin through the historical records, they would be obliged to postulate its existence on the basis of the sound correspondences among the Romance languages. It is obvious that every contemporary spoken language is nothing but a transformed version of a dialect of an earlier language, and even in the absence of written records, languages can be grouped together on the basis of their "descent" from a common ancestor. Thus, in a more remote period, Proto-West Germanic was undifferentiated from a large number of languages, including the ancestral forms of Latin, Hindi, Persian, Greek, Russian, and Gaelic — members of the Indo-European family of languages. Inferences based on the similarities among the Indo-European languages have led linguists to reconstruct the sound system of the parent lan-

guage from which they all ultimately derive. This language is called *Proto-Indo-European* (Figure 4.4).

Languages may also change without any geographical separation of different portions of a speech community. For example, within 1000 years, English changed from Old English to its modern form as a result of shifts in pronunciation and the borrowing of words from other languages. The two languages today are mutually unintelligible (see Box 4.4). As these changes illustrate, Modern English can be regarded as a "corruption" of Old English. Indeed, it bears repeating that all modern languages are "corruptions" of older languages. This does not prevent people from forming committees to save the "King's English" or to protect the "purity" of French. However, the expectation of linguistic change is so great that linguists have developed a technique for dating the separation of one language from another, called *glottochronology*. This technique is based on the assumption that due to borrowing and internal changes, about 14 percent of the most basic words in a language's vocabulary will be replaced every 1000 years.

Language and Consciousness

Language and language change illustrate the remarkable forms that can emerge in human culture without the conscious design of the participants. As pointed out by Alfred Kroeber:

> The unceasing processes of change in language are mainly unconscious or covert, or at least implicit. The results of the change may come to be recognized by speakers of the changing languages; the gradual act of change, and especially

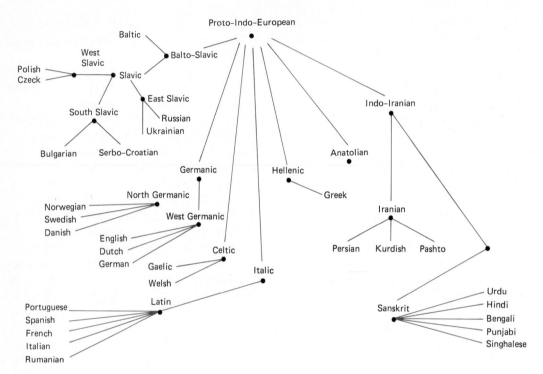

Figure 4.4 Proto–Indo-European family of languages.

the causes, mostly happen without the speaker being aware of them. . . . When a change has begun to creep in, it may be tacitly accepted or it may be observed and consciously resisted on the ground of being incorrect or vulgar or foreign. But the underlying motives of the objectors and the impulses of the innovator are likely to be equally unknown to themselves. [1948:245]

This aspect of language change can be generalized to changes in all of the other sectors of sociocultural systems. As stated long ago by Adam Fergusson, a great eighteenth-century Scottish philosopher, the forms of society

"even in what are termed enlightened ages are made with equal blindness toward the future." Cultural systems are "indeed the result of human action, but not the execution of any human design."

It is true that we are the only animals capable of talking about ourselves and of consciously analyzing our problems. We alone have conscious self-awareness, which many people regard as the most important attribute of human nature (C. Smith 1985). Yet something is usually overlooked when consciousness is celebrated as our species's crowning glory. What is often forgotten is that our minds are subject to restraints that do not affect the

---

BOX 4.4

THE KING'S ENGLISH A.D. 1066

Figure 4.5   Coronation of Harold II, king of the Anglo-Saxons, A.D. 1066.

On bissum eare . . . be he cyning waes, he for ut mid scrip-here to eanes Willelme; and ba hwile com Tosti eorl into Humbran mid 60 scripum. Eadwine eorl com mid land-fierde and darf hine ut; and ba butse-carlas hine forsocon, and he for to Scotlande mid 12 snaccum, and hine emette Harald se Norrena cyning mid 300 scipum, and Totsi him tobeag. And man cyode Harolde cyning hu hit waes baer edon and eworden, and he com mid miclum here Engliscra manna and emette hine aet Staengfordes brycge and hine ofslog, and bone eorl Tosti, and eallne bone here ehtlice ofercom.

In this year when he [Harold] was king, he went out with a fleet against William; and meanwhile Earl Tosti came into the Humber with sixty ships. Earl Edwin came with a land force and drove him out; and then the sailors forsook him [Tosti], and he went to Scotland with twelve small boats, and Harald, the Norwegian king, met him with three hundred ships, and Tosti submitted to him. And they told King Harold (Figure 4.5) what had been done and had befallen there, and he came with a large army of Englishmen and met him [the Norwegian king] at Stamford Bridge and slew him and Earl Tosti, and courageously overcame the whole army.

Source: The Anglo-Saxon Chronicle.

mental lives of other organisms. Since we live by culture, our minds are shaped and channeled by culture. Hence, the gift of semantic universality has many strings attached to it. Language does not necessarily give us freedom of thought; on the contrary, it often traps us into delusions and myths. Because we live by culture and because our minds are molded by culture, we have more to become aware of than other creatures. We alone must struggle to understand how culture controls what we do and what we think. Without this additional level of awareness, the human brain cannot be said to be fully conscious.

Summary

Human language is unique in possessing semantic universality, or the capacity to produce unlimited numbers of novel messages without loss of informational efficiency. In contrast to gibbon calls, for example, human language has unrestricted powers of productivity. One of the most important means of achieving this productivity is the arbitrariness of the elements that convey the information. Despite the importance of our genetic heritage for acquiring speech, the actual languages we speak depend entirely on enculturation; moreover, words in general lack any physical or iconographic resemblance to their referents.

Another important component in the achievement of semantic universality is duality of patterning. This refers to the use of arbitrary code elements in different combinations to produce different messages. The basic code elements of human languages are the phonemes, or classes of contrastive phones. A phoneme consists of a bundle of allophones that are contrastive with respect to the allophones of other phonemes. Different languages have widely different repertories of phones, phonemes, and allophones. None of these elements carries meaning in itself.

Duality of patterning is further exemplified by the combination of phonemes into morphemes, which are the minimal units of meaningful sound. Morphemes are classes of phonemes and contain variant forms called allomorphs. Morphemes are either free or bound, depending on whether they can occur alone and constitute well-formed utterances.

The ability to send and receive messages in a human language depends on the sharing of rules for combining phonemes into morphemes and morphemes into sentences. These rules are part of a language's grammar, and they are usually held unconsciously. On the phonemic level they specify the permitted and prohibited combinations of phonemes; on the morphemic level they specify the sequences of morphemes and allomorphs required for well-formed utterances. Such rules are called *syntax*. Knowledge of the rules of syntax makes it possible to produce completely novel utterances and yet be understood. A theory that accounts for this property of syntax states that there is a deep structure to which various superficially dissimilar utterances can be reduced. Novel sentences are transformations of these deep structures and can be understood by tracing them back to their underlying components.

All human languages are mutually translatable, and there is no evidence that some languages have more efficient grammars than others. Categories and vocabularies differ widely, but these differences do not indicate any inherent defect in a language or any intellectual inferiority on the part of the speakers. General and specific categorizations — as with numbers, plant classifications, and color terms — reflect the practical need for making general or specific distinctions under particular cultural and natural conditions.

The view that certain dialects of standard languages are "inferior" forms of speech reflects class and ethnic biases. Dialects such as black vernacular English do not in and of themselves inhibit clear and logical thought.

Attempts to show that differences in grammar determine how people think and behave in different cultures have not been successful. Few, if any, correlations other than vocabulary can be shown between language and the major forms of demographic, technological, economic, ecological, domestic, political, and religious adaptations. This does not mean that obligatory linguistic categories such as those concerned with sex, age, and class differences are trivial aspects of sociocultural life. These aspects of language must be regarded seriously and examined for their possibly harmful effects.

Languages, like all other aspects of culture, are constantly being changed as a result of both internal and external processes. All languages are "corruptions" of earlier parent languages. Glottochronology is based on the premise that not only do all languages change, but they change at a predictable rate.

The study of language change, as well as the study of the other aspects of linguistics, shows the predominance of unconscious factors in sociocultural life. Although semantic universality is a great and uniquely human gift, it does not automatically bestow on us full consciousness and genuine freedom of thought. To become fully conscious, we must strive to understand how culture controls what we think and do.

Chapter 5

PRODUCTION

This chapter begins the description and analysis of infrastructure. It focuses on the main varieties of food production systems. Using energy as a measure of input and output, it examines the interrelationships among food production, technology, and the natural environment.

Production is a consequence of the application of human labor and technology to natural resources. The most fundamental kind of production is that of energy. Human life and culture cannot exist unless societies appropriate and transform the energy available in the environment. The amount of energy produced and the method of production depend in turn on an interaction between the energy-producing technology that a culture possesses at a given time and the exploitable features of the habitat to which the culture has access, such as sunlight, soils, forests, rainfall, or mineral deposits. Since neither technology nor the features of the environment can be changed rapidly or limitlessly, a culture's mode of energy production exerts a powerful constraining force on a people's entire way of life.

The interaction between technology and environment during the process of energy production is also basic for an understanding of *human ecology* (sometimes called *cultural ecology*), the study of how human populations and their activities are affected by the inorganic and organic features of their environments, and of how these inorganic and organic characteristics are in turn affected by human populations and their activities (Moran 1982).

Evolution of Energy Production

During the time of the earliest hominids, all the energy utilized for the conduct of social life stemmed from food. Exactly when fire began to be used is not known. Some control over fire may have been achieved by *Homo erectus,* but full control of fire may not have been achieved before the appearance of *Homo sapiens* (Binford 1988; Binford and Stone 1986). Certainly by the time of cultural takeoff 40,000 years ago, fire was being used for cooking, warmth, protection against carnivores, and driving game animals over cliffs or into ambushes, and possibly for favoring the growth of desired plant species. By 10,000 years ago, animals began to provide energy in the form of muscle power harnessed to plows, sleds, and wheeled vehicles. At about the same time, considerable wood and charcoal fuel was expended to produce pottery. With the rise of states, wind energy for sailing ships and wood energy for melting and casting metals began to be used. The energy in falling water was not tapped extensively until the medieval period in Europe. It is only in the last 200 or 300 years that the fossil fuels — coal, oil, and gas — began to dominate human ecosystems.

New sources of energy have followed each other in a logical progression, with the mastery of later forms dependent on the mastery of the earlier ones. For example, in both the Old World and the New World the sequence of inventions that led to metallurgy depended on the prior achievement of high-temperature wood-fire ovens and furnaces for baking ceramics, and the development of this technique depended on learning how to make and control wood fires in cooking. Low-temperature metallurgical experience with copper and tin almost of necessity had to precede the use of iron and steel. Mastery of iron and steel in turn had to precede the development of the mining machines that made possible the use of coal, oil, and gas. Finally, the use of these fossil fuels spawned the Industrial Revolution, from which the technology for today's nuclear energy derives (Figure 5.1).

Figure 5.1   Chernobyl nuclear explosion.
Explosion of Soviet reactor near Kiev contaminated meat and milk as far away as Sweden. Nuclear energy may yet turn out to be the least efficient mode of energy production ever created.

These technological advances have steadily increased the average amount of energy available per human being from Paleolithic times to the present. The rise in energy does not necessarily mean that humankind's ability to control nature has grown steadily, nor does increased use of energy per capita necessarily bring a higher standard of living or less work per capita. Also, a distinction must be made between total amount of energy available and the efficiency with which that energy is produced and put to use.

Modes of Food Production

Hunting and gathering was the only mode of food production until about 10,000 years ago during the Paleolithic. Hunter-gatherers are typically organized into small groups called *bands*, numbering from about 20 to 50 people. Bands consist of individual families who make camp together for periods ranging from a few days to several years before moving on to other campsites. Band life is essentially migratory; shelters are temporary and possessions are few. One must be careful, however, not to overgeneralize, since hunter-gatherers inhabit a wide range of environments. The Eskimo, hunter-gatherers of the Arctic, necessarily have ecologies and cultures somewhat different from those of desert-dwelling groups. Moreover, some hunter-gatherers who inhabit environments rich in wild plants and animals live in permanent villages such as those found among the people of the northwest Pacific coast.

Typically, agricultural peoples live in more permanent settlements than hunter-gatherers. But again, not all agricultural societies are alike. There are many varieties of agriculture, each with its ecological and cultural implications. *Rainfall agriculture* utilizes naturally occurring

showers as a source of moisture; *irrigation agriculture* depends on artificially constructed dams and ditches to bring water to the fields. Several varieties of rainfall agriculture and irrigation agriculture, each with its own ecological and cultural implications, must also be distinguished.

If rainfall agriculture is to be practiced, the problem of replenishing the nutrients taken from the soil by successive crops must be solved. One of the most ancient methods for solving this problem, still widely practiced to this day, is known as *slash-and-burn*. A patch of forest is cut down and left to dry. Then the slash is set on fire and later the ashes, which contain a rich supply of nutrients, are spread over the area to be planted (Figure 5.2). In re-

Figure 5.2 Planting in a slash-and-burn garden. This Amahuaca woman is using a digging stick to plant corn in a recently burned garden.

gions of heavy rainfall, a slash-and-burn garden cannot be replanted for more than two or three seasons before the nutrients in the ashes become depleted. A new patch of forest is then cleared and burned. Slash-and-burn thus requires large amounts of land in fallow awaiting the regrowth of vegetation suitable for burning.

A totally different solution to the problem of maintaining soil fertility is to raise animals as well as crops and to use animal manure as fertilizer. This is known as *mixed farming*, and was once characteristic of the European and American small family farm. With the advent of the industrial era, soil fertility has come to depend primarily on chemical fertilizers, eliminating the need for raising animals and crops on the same farm.

In irrigation agriculture, soil fertility is less of a problem, since the irrigation water often contains silt and nutrients that are automatically deposited on the fields. But irrigation agriculture varies greatly in type and in scale (Hunt 1988). Some irrigation systems are confined to terraces on the walls of mountain valleys, as in the Philippines; others embrace the floodplains of great rivers such as the Nile and the Yellow River (Figure 5.3). One form of

Figure 5.3 Irrigation agriculture.
There are many different forms of irrigation, each with its own special influences on social life. (a) and (b) are two views of the system of Terraces on steep mountain slopes built by generations of Ifugao farmers in the Philippines. (c) Javenese rice Terraces are broader and less steep. (d) China has massive canals and dams for flood control and farming.

(a)

(b)

(c)

(d)

Figure 5.4   Middle eastern *oat*
Drawing water from an underground aqueduct.

irrigation involves mounding: Mud is scooped from shallow lakes and piled up to form ridges in which crops are planted, as in the so-called floating gardens of Mexico. In the Middle East huge underground aqueducts called *qats* conduct water from mountain streams to distant desert farmlands (Figure 5.4). Throughout much of India, irrigation water is pulled up by ox power from deep brick-lined wells; more recently, it is pumped up electrically through drilled pipes.

The Influence of the Environment

Any item of technology must interact with factors present in a particular environment. Similar kinds of technologies in different environments may lead to different energy outputs. For example, the productivity of irrigation farming varies according to the size and dependability of the water supply, the availability of flat terrain, and the amount of minerals in the water. Similarly, the productivity of slash-and-burn agriculture varies in relation to how much forest is available for burning and how quickly the forest can regenerate itself. It is thus really not possible to speak of technology in the abstract; rather, we must always refer to the interaction between technology and the conditions characteristic of a specific natural environment.

In industrial societies, the influence of environment often appears to be subordinate to the influence exerted by technology. But it is incorrect to believe that industrial societies have liberated themselves from the influence of the environment, or that our species now dominates or controls the environment. It is true that replicas of American suburbs have been built in the deserts of Saudi Arabia and the snowfields of Alaska and that they can also be constructed on the moon. But the energy and material involved in such achievements derive from the interactions between technology and environment carried out in mines, factories, and farms in various parts of the world, which are depleting irreplaceable reserves of oil, water, soil, forests, and metallic ores. Similarly, at all sites where modern technology extracts or processes natural resources or where any form of industrial construction or production takes place, the problem arises of disposing of industrial wastes, pollutants, and other biologically significant by-products (Figure 5.5). Efforts are now under way in many industrial nations to reduce air and water pollution and to prevent the depletion and poisoning of the environment. The costs of such efforts testify to the continuing importance of the inter-

(a)

(b)

Figure 5.5 The hidden costs of the industrial mode of production.

(a) *Times Beach, Missouri. Floodwaters spread soil contaminated with dioxin, previously concentrated near highways, all over residential neighborhoods. Clean-up crews collect samples for analysis. (b) Abandoned hazardous waste dump. Pit is 5 feet deep and covers 34,000 square feet.*

action between technology and environment. These costs will continue to mount, for this is only the very beginning of the industrial era. In the centuries to come, the inhabitants of specific regions may pay for industrialization in ways as yet uncalculated.

Carrying Capacity and the Law of Diminishing Returns

Factors such as abundance of game, quality of soils, amounts of rainfall, and extent of forests available for energy production set an upper limit on the amount of energy that can be extracted from a given environment by means of a given technology of energy production. The upper limit of energy production in turn limits the number of human beings who can live in that environment. This upper limit on population is called the environment's *carrying capacity.*

Extreme caution must be exercised before concluding that a particular culture can "easily" raise production by increasing the size of its labor force or by increasing the amount of time devoted to work. Carrying capacity is difficult to measure (Glossow 1978; Street 1969). Allegations of untapped environmental potential are often based on insufficiently long periods of observation. Many puzzling features of food production result from adjustments to recurrent but infrequent ecological crises, such as droughts, floods, frosts, hurricanes, and epidemics of animal and plant diseases, that require long periods of observation. Moreover, a basic principle of ecological analysis states that communities of organisms adjust to the minimum life-sustaining conditions in their habitats rather than to the average conditions. One formulation of this principle is known as *Liebig's law of the minimum*. This law states that growth is limited by the minimum availability of one necessary factor rather than by the abundance of all necessary factors. The short-time observer of human ecosystems is likely to see the average condition, not the extremes, and is likely to overlook the limiting factor.

Nonetheless, there is some evidence that food production among preindustrial peoples is often only about one-third of what it might be if full advantage were taken of the environment's carrying capacity by means of the existing technology (Sahlins 1972). In order to understand why this "underproduction" occurs, we must distinguish between the effect of exceeding carrying capacity and the effect of exceeding the *point of diminishing returns* (Figure 5.6). When carrying capacity is exceeded, production will begin to decline as a result of irreversible damage to the environment. The depletion of soils is an example of the consequence of exceeding carrying capacity. When the point of diminishing returns is ex-

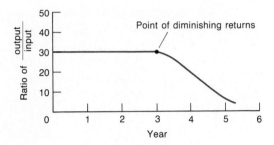

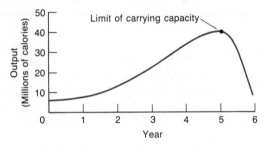

Figure 5.6   Production, carrying capacity, and diminishing returns.
Point of diminishing returns is reached in year 3, but limit of carrying capacity is reached in year 5. Production is intensified and continues to increase until year 5, then crashes.

ceeded, however, production may hold steady or may even continue to increase, even though there is less produced per unit of effort as a result of the growing scarcity or impoverishment of one or more environmental factors. The present condition of the ocean fisheries of the world is an example of exceeding the point of diminishing returns. Since 1970, the rate of return per unit of effort has declined by almost half, yet the total catch of fish has held steady (L. Brown 1978). A similar situation exists with respect to world agriculture and in the production of oil and gas (see below).

Except when they are under some form of political pressure, people will attempt to keep the ratio of output to input below the point of diminishing returns by limiting the expansion of their production efforts; no one willingly wants to work more for less. Thus, people may feel the need to change their routines and to institute cultural innovations long before carrying capacity is reached.

Expansion, Intensification, and Technological Change

If technology is held constant, production can be increased by putting more people to work or by having them work longer or faster. If this increase in input occurs without enlarging the area in which food production is taking place, *intensification* has occurred. If, however, there is a proportionate increase in the area throughout which food production takes place so that the input per hectare or square kilometer remains the same, then the system is *expanding* or growing but not being intensified.

Since all modes of production (indeed, all modes of activity of any sort) depend on finite resources, expansion cannot continue forever. Sooner or later any further increase in production will have to depend on intensification. And intensification, more or less rapidly, must lead to the point of diminishing returns caused by the depletion of nonrenewable resources, and a drop in efficiency. If the intensification is sustained, sooner or later production will collapse and fall to zero.

The all-important condition in this scenario, however, is that the technology is held constant. In human ecology, a common response to diminishing returns is to change the technology. Thus, as suggested in the work of Ester Boserup (1965), when hunters and gatherers deplete their environments and pass the point of diminishing returns, they are likely to

begin to adopt an agricultural mode of production; when slash-and-burn peoples pass the point of diminishing returns, they may begin to cultivate permanent fields using animal fertilizer; and when rainfall agriculturalists using permanent fields deplete their soils, they may shift to irrigation agriculture. The shift from preindustrial to industrial and petrochemical forms of agriculture can also be seen as a response to depletion and declining yield per unit of effort (Harris 1977).

Hunter-Gatherer Ecology

The !Kung San (the ! designates a sound that is not used in English, called a click) are a hunting-and-gathering people who live in the Kalahari Desert on both sides of the border between Botswana and Namibia in southern Africa (Lee 1979). Like most simple hunter-gatherers (see Box 5.1), the !Kung San move about a great deal from one camp to another in search of water, game, and wild plant foods. They build only temporary shelters and have a minimum of possessions, yet they are well nourished and moderately long-lived. The !Kung San men specialize in hunting while the !Kung San women specialize in gathering, although on occasion women bring small animals back to camp and men help in carrying heavy loads of nuts (Figure 5.7).

The number of people in a !Kung camp varies from 23 to 40, with an average camp size of 31 (20 adults and 11 children). During a four-week study period, Richard Lee calculated that 20 adults put in an average 2.4 days per week in hunting and gathering. On any particular day, the number of people hunting or gathering varied from zero to 16.

About 71 percent of the calories con-

NOT ALL HUNTER-GATHERERS ARE ALIKE

There are two main varieties of hunter-gatherer societies: simple and complex. The !Kung are an example of the simple variety and the Kwakiutl (see page 115) are an example of the complex variety. Complex hunter-gatherers share many features in common with sedentary agricultural peoples. The major differences between the two varieties of hunter-gatherers are:

Simple	Complex
Low population density	High population density
Not dependent on stored foods	Dependent on stored foods
Live in temporary camps most of the year	Live in villages most of the year
Weak distinctions of rank	Strong distinctions of rank

Sources: Keely 1988; Testart 1982; Woodburn 1982.

Figure 5.7 !Kung women returning to camp. They have been out gathering wild vegetables and are carrying digging sticks.

sumed by a !Kung camp are provided by women's gathering activities. Women range widely throughout the countryside, walking about 2 to 12 miles a day round trip for a total of about 1500 miles a year each. On an average trip each woman brings back a load of from 15 to 33 pounds of nuts, berries, fruits, leafy greens, and roots whose proportion vary from season to season.

Men hunt on the average only every three or four days and are successful only about 23 percent of the time they hunt. Hunting is therefore not an efficient source of energy for the !Kung. For every calorie (above basal metabolism) expended on hunting, only about 3 calories worth of meat were produced. Of the average total of about 2355 calories consumed per person per day, meat provides about 29 percent, nuts and vegetables the rest. One nut in particular, the mongongo, alone accounts for about 58 percent of the !Kung caloric intake and a large share of protein as well.

Studies of the !Kung and other hunter-gatherers who have survived into modern times have dispelled the notion that the hunting-gathering way of life necessarily condemns people to a miserable hand-to-mouth existence, with starvation avoided only by dint of unremitting daily effort. About 10 percent of the !Kung are over 60 years of age (as compared with 5 percent in agricultural countries such as Brazil and India), and medical examination shows them to be in good health.

Judged by the large quantity of meat and other sources of protein in their diet, their sound physical condition, and their abundant leisure, the !Kung San have a high standard of living. The key to this situation is that their population is low in relation to the resources they exploit. There is less than one person per square mile in their land and their production effort remains far below carrying capacity, with no appreciable intensification (except in recent years because of the appearance of neighboring peoples who possess livestock).

Optimal Foraging Theory

Despite their low level of food production, hunters and gatherers do not eat every edible species in their habitat. They pass up many edible plants and animals even when they encounter them while searching for food. Of some 262 species of animals known to the !Kung San, for example, only about 80 are eaten (Lee 1979:226). This pickiness also occurs among animals that, like human hunter-gatherers, must *forage* (i.e., search) for their food.

To account for this selective behavior, ecologists have developed a set of principles known as *optimal foraging theory* (Box 5.2). This theory predicts that hunters or collectors will pursue or harvest only those species that maximize the rate of caloric return for the time they spend foraging. There will always be at least one species that will be taken on encounter, namely, the one with the highest rate of caloric return for each hour of "handling time"—time spent in pursuing, killing, collecting, carrying, preparing, and cooking the

---

Box 5.2

AN INTUITIVE EXPLANATION OF OPTIMAL FORAGING THEORY

Imagine that you are in a forest in which some trees have a $1 bill and other trees have a $20 bill hanging from the topmost branch. Should you climb every money tree you come across or should you climb only the $20 trees? The answer depends on how many $20 money trees there are. If there are a lot of them, it would be a mistake to climb $1 trees. On the other hand, no matter how scarce $20 trees might be, if you happened to find one, you would always stop to climb it.

---

species after it is encountered. The foragers will take a second, third, or fourth species when they encounter it only if by doing so it raises the rate of caloric return for their total effort (Charnov 1976; Smith 1983). Foragers, of course, do not actually measure how many calories they expend or obtain. But through repeated trial and error, they achieve a rather precise knowledge of whether it is worth their while to take a particular species. (If lions and wolves can develop this selective behavior, so can humans!)

To illustrate, suppose that there are only three animal species in a particular forest: wild pigs, anteaters, and bats. Suppose further that in 4 hours of searching through this forest, a forager can expect to encounter one wild pig, and that the handling (pursuit, killing, cooking) of a wild pig costs 2 hours, while its caloric value is 20,000 calories. If the handling time for an anteater is also 2 hours, but its caloric return is only 10,000 calories, will the hunter stop to catch an anteater when he encounters one or will he hold out for a wild pig? In 4 hours of searching, if he takes wild pig and nothing but wild pig, the hunter's rate of caloric return will be:

$$\frac{20,000 \text{ cal}}{4 \text{ hr} + 2 \text{ hr}} = \frac{20,000 \text{ cal}}{6 \text{ hr}}$$

$$= \frac{3,333 \text{ cal}}{1 \text{ hr}}$$

If he also stops to take an anteater, his rate of return will be:

$$\frac{20,000 \text{ cal} + 10,000 \text{ cal}}{4 \text{ hr} + 2 \text{ hr} + 2 \text{ hr}} = \frac{30,000 \text{ cal}}{8 \text{ hr}}$$

$$= \frac{3,750 \text{ cal}}{1 \text{ hr}}$$

He should not pass up anteaters, since 3,750 is greater than 3,333. What about bats? Suppose that for bats, handling time is also 2 hours but caloric return is only 500 calories. Will he stop for a bat?

$$\frac{20,000 \text{ cal} + 10,000 \text{ cal} + 500 \text{ cal}}{4 \text{ hr} + 2 \text{ hr} + 2 \text{ hr} + 2 \text{ hr}}$$

$$= \frac{30,500 \text{ cal}}{10 \text{ hr}} = \frac{3,050 \text{ cal}}{1 \text{ hr}}$$

If he stopped for a bat instead of holding out for an anteater or a wild pig, he would be "wasting energy," since 3,750 is greater than 3,050.

Optimal foraging theory predicts, in other words, that foragers will continue to add items to their diet only as long as each new item increases (or does not diminish) the overall efficiency of their foraging activities. This prediction is especially interesting with regard to the question of how the abundance of a food item, such as an insect species, influences its position on or off the optimal diet list. Items that lower the overall rate of caloric return will not be added to the list no matter how abundant they become. Only the abundance of the higher-ranked items influences the breadth of the list. As a high-ranking item becomes scarce, items previously too inefficient to be on the list get added. The reason for this is that since more time must be spent before the high-ranking item is encountered, the average rate of return for the whole list shifts downward so that it is no longer a waste of energy to stop for items that have a lower rate of caloric return.

In a study of the actual rates of caloric return among the Aché Indians of eastern Paraguay (Figure 5.8), Kristen Hawkes and her associates found that only 16 species were taken on encounter during foraging expeditions (Hawkes et al. 1982). The average rate of return after encounter of the 16 resources ranged from 65,000 calories per hour for collared peccaries to 946 calories per hour for a species of palm fruit. As predicted, despite the fact that each item was decreasingly efficient measured in postencounter calories per hour, its inclusion in the diet raised the overall efficiency of the Aché foraging system. For example, if the Aché were to take only the top two species — collared peccaries and deer — their overall foraging efficiency would be only 148 calories per hour, since counterbalancing their high caloric return, these species are scarce and seldom encountered. Adding the third- and fourth-ranked items — pacas and coatis — increases overall foraging efficiency to 405 calories per hour. As each of the remaining less valuable species is added, the overall average rate of return continues to rise, but in smaller and smaller increments. The list ends at a species of palm fruit that yields 946 calories an hour. Pre-

(a)   (b)

Figure 5.8   Aché hunters.
(a) *Drawing bow;* (b) *returning from hunt with slain peccary.*

sumably, the Aché do not include additional species because they have found by trial and error that there are none available that would not lower their overall foraging efficiency (about 872 calories an hour for all 16 items).

Optimal foraging theory therefore offers an explanation for what must otherwise seem to be a capricious indifference on the part of many human societies to thousands of edible species of plants and animals in their habitats. It also presents a predictive framework for possible past and future changes in the list of prod-

ucts consumed by foragers based on fluctuations in the abundance of the more efficient food sources. If, for example, collared peccaries and deer were to become increasingly abundant, the Aché would soon find it to be a waste of energy to gather palm fruits; eventually, they would give up eating palm larvae, and if encounter rates with deer and collared peccaries rose to a point where stopping to take anything else lowered the overall rate of return, they would take nothing but deer and collared peccaries. Going the other way, if deer and collared peccaries became decreasingly abundant, the Aché would never cease to capture them on encounter, but they would no longer find it wasteful to stop and harvest resources that they now spurn, including certain kinds of insects.

Optimal foraging theory helps to explain why people on skimpy diets may nonetheless pass up items that are very abundant in their habitat, such as insects and earthworms. It is not the commonness or rarity of a food item that predicts whether it will be in the diet, but its contribution to the overall efficiency of food production. A word of caution is useful here, though: It should not be concluded that energetic efficiency is the only factor that determines the diet of human hunter-gatherers. Many other factors, such as protein, fat, mineral, and vitamin composition of foods, may also determine which species are favored. But energetic efficiency is always an important consideration and is the factor that has thus far been measured most successfully by anthropologists.

Figure 5.9   "Cooking" the garden.
A Tsembaga Maring woman during the burning phase of swidden cycle.

Slash-and-Burn Food Energy Systems

Roy Rappaport (1984) has made a careful study of the food energy system of the Tsembaga Maring, a clan living in semipermanent villages on the northern slopes of the central highlands of New Guinea. The Tsembaga, who number about 204, plant taro, yams, sweet potatoes, manioc, sugar cane, and several other crops in small gardens cleared and fertilized by the slash-and-burn method (Figure 5.9). Slash-and-burn is a more efficient method of meeting caloric needs than hunting, yielding 18 calories output for every 1 calorie of input. Thus the Tsembaga are able to satisfy their caloric needs with a remarkably small investment of working time — only 380 hours per year per food producer spent on raising crops. And at the same time the Tsembaga manage to feed almost ten times as many people as the !Kung and to live in semipermanent houses (except during routs caused by warfare).

But tropical slash-and-burn modes of production are constrained by environmental problems. First, there is the problem of forest regeneration. Because of leaching by heavy rains and because of the invasion of insects and weeds, the productivity of slash-and-burn gardens drops rapidly after two or three years of use, and additional land must be cleared to avoid a sharp reduction in labor efficiency and output (Clarke 1976; Janzen 1973). Optimum productivity is achieved when gardens are cleared from a substantial secondary growth of large trees. If gardens are cleared when the secondary growth is very immature, only a small amount of wood-ash fertilizer will be produced by burning. On the other hand, if the trees revert to climax-forest size, they will be very difficult to cut down. Optimum regeneration may take anywhere from 10 to 20 years or more, depending on local soils and climates (Moran 1982).

Thus, in the long run, slash-and-burn ecosystems use up a considerable amount of forest per capita, but in any particular year only 5 percent of the total territory may actually be in production (Boserup 1965:31). The Tsembaga, for example, plant only 42 acres in a given year. Nonetheless, about 864 acres in their territory have been gardened. This is about the amount of forest that the Tsembaga will need if their population remains at about 200 people and if they burn secondary-growth garden sites every 20 years. Rappaport estimates that the Tsembaga had at their disposal an amount of forest land sufficient to support another 84 people without permanently damaging the regenerative capacities of the forest. However, the bulk of this land lies above or below the optimum altitude levels for their major crops and thus would probably somewhat diminish efficiency if put into use. All slash-and-burn peoples confront the ultimate specter of "eating up their forest" (Condominas 1957) by shortening the fallow period to a point where grasses and weeds replace trees — at least this is what has happened to other New Guinea peoples not so far from the Tsembaga (Sorenson 1972; Sorenson and Kenmore 1974). However, even in regions that have enough trees to allow 10 to 20 years for regeneration, population density may remain very low as a result of other limiting factors (Carneiro 1960). Amazonia is such a region (although massive fires being set by modern farmers and ranchers pose an ever-growing threat to the survival of the traditional slash-and-burn village societies).

The Problem of Animal Food

Another problem with tropical slash-and-burn modes of production is the depletion of animal species. This problem is especially acute where the main staples are protein-deficient root crops such as sweet potatoes, plantains, yams, manioc, and taro. Natural tropical forests produce a vast amount of *plant* biomass per acre, but they are very poor producers of *animal* biomass as compared, for example, with grasslands and marine ecosystems (Richards 1973). The animals that inhabit tropical forests tend to be small, furtive, and arboreal. As human population density rises, these animals quickly become very scarce and hard to find. The total animal biomass — the weight of all the spiders, insects, worms, snakes, mammals, and so on — in a hectare of central Amazon rain forest is 45 kilograms. This compares with 304 kilograms in a dry East Africa thorn forest. In East African savannah grasslands, 627 kilograms of large herbivores are found per hectare, far outweighing all the large and small animals found per hectare in the Amazon (Fittkau and Klinge 1973:8). Although plant foods can provide nutritionally adequate diets if eaten in variety and in large quantities, meat is a more efficient source of essential nutrients than plant food, kilo for kilo. Hence one of the most important limiting factors in the growth of slash-and-burn energy systems is thought to be the availability of animal food (Gross 1975, 1981; Harris 1984). Whatever etic ecological and nutritional reason there may be for it, there is no doubt that the Tsembaga, like virtually every other human group, highly prize animal food, especially in the form of fatty meat. (Vegetarians who abstain from meat usually prize animal foods in the form of milk and yogurt.) The Tsembaga, whose population density is 67 persons per square mile, compared with less than 1 per square mile among the !Kung San, have depleted the wild animals in their territory. Among the Tsembaga, the flesh eaten on the majority of days ranges from nothing at all to less than 1 ounce. Fruits and vegetables constitute approximately 99 percent by weight of the usual daily intake. These figures do not include the sometimes considerable amount of meat that the Tsembaga consume on special festive occasions (Rappaport 1984:448).

The Tsembaga have compensated for the scarcity of game animals by stocking their land with a domesticated animal—the pig. The Tsembaga's pigs root for themselves during the day but come home to a meal of sweet potatoes and food scraps in the evening. An average Tsembaga pig weighs as much as an average Tsembaga human, and Rappaport estimates that each pig consumes almost as much garden produce as each person. When the Tsembaga pig herd is at its maximum, almost as much time and energy are devoted to feeding pigs as to feeding people. Like many New Guinea cultures, the Tsembaga allow their pig population to increase over a number of years, slaughtering pigs only on ceremonial occasions (Watson 1977). When the effort needed to care for the pigs becomes excessive, a pig feast is held, resulting in a sharp decline in the pig population (Figure 5.10). This feast may be related to the

Figure 5.10   Dispatching a pig.
Pigs have great ritual significance throughout New Guinea and Melanesia. The people in this scene are Fungai Maring, neighbors of the Tsembaga Maring.

cycle of reforestation in the Tsembaga's gardens and the regulation of war and peace between the Tsembaga and their neighbors (Morren 1984:173).

Irrigation Agriculture

Under favorable conditions, irrigation agriculture yields more calories per calorie of effort than any other preindustrial mode of food production. And among irrigation farmers, the Chinese have excelled for thousands of years.

A detailed study of the labor inputs and weight yield of agricultural production in pre-Communist times was carried out by the anthropologists Fei Hsiao-t'ung and Chang Chih-I (1947) in the village of Luts'un, Yunnan Province. Over 50 calories were obtained for each calorie of effort in the fields. The principal crops were rice (which accounted for 75 percent of the total), soybeans, corn, manioc, and potatoes. Because of the high productivity of their agriculture, the 700 people of Luts'un produced five times more food than they consumed. What happened to this *surplus*? It was diverted from the village to towns and cities; it was exchanged via markets and money for nonfarm goods and services; it was taxed away by the local, provincial, and central governments; it went into rent as payment for use of land; and it was used to raise large numbers of children and to sustain a high rate of population increase.

The high population density of parts of China and of other societies that practice irrigation agriculture results from the fact that if the amount of water flowing to the fields is expanded, increasing amounts of labor can be invested in production without substantial losses in the output-input ratio. Thus, instead of using the labor-saving potential of their technology to work less, irrigation agriculturists opt for intensifying their effort and increasing their output.

Energy and Pastoral Nomadism

Grains (such as wheat, barley, and corn) convert about 0.4 percent of photosynthetically active sunlight into human edible matter. If one feeds this grain to animals rather than to people and then eats the meat, 90 percent, on the average, of the energy available in the grains will be lost (National Research Council 1974). The loss in efficiency associated with the processing of plant food through the gut of domesticated animals accounts for the relatively infrequent occurrence of cultures whose mode of food production is that called *pastoral nomadism* (Figure 5.11). Full pastoral nomads are peoples who raise domesticated animals and who do not depend on hunting, gathering, or the planting of their own crops for a significant portion of their diet. Pastoral nomads typically occupy arid grasslands and steppes in which precipitation is too sparse or irregular to support rainfall agriculture, and where irrigation is not possible because of altitude or distance from major river valleys. By specializing in animal husbandry, pastoral nomads can move their herds about over long distances and take advantage of the best pasture.

However, pastoral peoples usually obtain grain supplements to their diet of milk, cheese, blood, and meat (the last always being a relatively small part of the daily fare) through trade with agricultural neighbors. Meat, cheese, milk, and other animal products are usually in short supply wherever preindustrial agricultural systems support dense populations. Pastoralists frequently attempt to improve their bargaining position by raiding the sedentary

Figure 5.11 Pastoral nomadism.
The huts of these inhabitants of Turkomenia, U.S.S.R., are made of camel skins, felt, and cane and are easily disassembled and transported to a new camp.

villagers and carrying off the grain harvest without paying for it. They can often do this with impunity, since their possession of animals such as camels and horses makes them highly mobile and militarily effective. Continued success in raiding may force the farming population to acknowledge the pastoralists as their overlords. Repeatedly in the history of the Old World, relatively small groups of pastoral nomads — the Mongols and the Arabs being the two most famous examples — have succeeded in gaining control of large civilizations that were based on irrigation agriculture. The inevitable outcome of these conquests, however, was that the conquerors were absorbed by the agricultural system as they attempted to feed the huge populations that had fallen under their control (Khazanov 1984; Lattimore 1962; Lees and Bates 1974; Salzman 1971).

Energy and the Evolution of Culture

According to Leslie White (1949:368–369), a basic law governs the evolution of cultures: "Other factors remaining constant, culture evolves as the amount of energy harnessed per year is increased, or as the efficiency of the means of putting energy to work is increased." The first part of this law seems to be supported by the per capita output of Chinese irrigation agriculture, as exemplified in Luts'un, and the per capita output of the !Kung and Tsembaga, as Table 5.1 shows.

The second part of White's law is not so clear. It is true that if one considers only human labor inputs, the ratio of output to input rises from 11 for the !Kung to 18 for the Tsembaga, to 54 for Luts'un (Harris

Table 5.1

PER CAPITA ENERGY PRODUCTION

	TOTAL OUTPUT IN CALORIES (IN THOUSANDS)	POPULATION	PER CAPITA OUTPUT IN CALORIES (IN THOUSANDS)
!Kung	23,400	35	670
Tsembaga	150,000	204	735
Luts'un	3,790,000	700	5,411

1971:204ff.). But these figures do not include the energy that the Tsembaga use in the combustion of trees to make their gardens, nor the considerable amount of energy that the Tsembaga "waste" in converting vegetable foods to pork. Nor do the figures for Luts'un include the considerable energetic cost of milling and cooking rice. As Timothy Bayliss-Smith (1977) has shown in an attempt to test White's law, South Sea communities drawn into participating in aspects of modern industrial modes of production produce much more food energy per capita, but their efficiency shows no clear upward trend. In fact, if we consider the total energy outputs and inputs of food production in fully industrial societies, the trend in efficiency of putting energy to work runs counter to White's prediction.

Industrial Food Energy Systems

It is difficult to estimate the output-input ratio of industrial agriculture because the amount of indirect labor put into food production exceeds the amount of direct labor (Figure 5.12).

Figure 5.12   Industrial farming.
Rice harvest near Yuba City, California. Are these farmers or engineers?

An Iowa corn farmer, for example, puts in 9 hours of work per acre, which yield 81 bushels of corn with an energy equivalent of 8,164,800 calories (Pimentel et al. 1973). This gives a nominal ratio of 5000 calories output for every calorie of input! But this is a misleading figure. First of all, three-quarters of all the croplands in the United States are devoted to the production of animal feeds, with a consequent 90 percent reduction in humanly consumable calories. Indeed, the livestock population of the United States consumes enough food calories to feed 1.3 billion people (Cloud 1973). Second, enormous amounts of human labor are embodied in the tractors, trucks, combines, oil and gas, pesticides, herbicides, and fertilizers used by the Iowa corn farmer.

A misunderstood aspect of industrial food energy systems is the difference between higher yields per acre and the ratio of energy input to output. As a result of more and more intensive modes of production, involving genetically improved crops and higher dosages of chemical fertilizers and pesticides, yields per acre have steadily improved (Jensen 1978). But this improvement has been made possible only as a result of a steady increase in the amount of fuel energy invested for each calorie of food energy produced. In the United States, 15 tons of machinery, 22 gallons of gasoline, 203 pounds of fertilizer, and 2 pounds of chemical insecticides and pesticides are invested per acre per year. This represents a cost of 2,890,000 calories of nonfood energy per acre per year (Pimentel et al. 1975), a cost that has increased steadily since the beginning of the century. Before 1910, more calories were obtained from agriculture than were invested in it. By 1970, it took 8 calories in the form of fossil fuels to produce 1 calorie of food. Today, vast quantities of energy are used simply to process and package food (Box 5.3). If the people of India

were to emulate the U.S. system of food production, their entire energy budget would have to be devoted to nothing but agriculture (Steinhart and Steinhart 1974). In the words of Howard Odum:*

> A whole generation of citizens thought that the carrying capacity of the earth was proportional to the amount of land under cultivation and higher efficiencies in using the energy of the sun had arrived. This is a sad hoax, for industrial man no longer eats potatoes made from solar energy; now he eats potatoes made of oil. [1970:15]

Summary

The comparative study of modes of production involves considering the quantitative and qualitative aspects of energy production and of ecological relationships. Most of the energy flowing through preindustrial energy systems consists of food energy. The technology of energy production cannot be altered at whim. It has evolved through successive stages of technical competence, in which the mastery of one set of tools and machines has been built on the mastery of an earlier set. Through technological advance, the energy available per capita has steadily increased. However, technology never exists in the abstract, but only in the particular instances where it interacts with a specific environment. There is no such thing as technology dominating or controlling the natural environment. Even in the most advanced industrial ecosystems, depletion and pollution of habitats add unavoidable costs to energy production and consumption. Technology interacting

* Howard Odum, *Environment, Power, and Society*, p. 15. Copyright © 1970 by John Wiley & Sons, Inc.

Box 5.3

Energy Input in Packaging and Processing Industrial Food

Energy Required to Produce Various Food Packages		Energy Inputs for Processing Various Products	
Package	kcal	Package	kcal/kg
Wooden berry basket	69	Instant coffee	18,948
Styrofoam tray (size 6)	215	Chocolate	18,591
Molded paper tray (size 6)	384	Breakfast cereals	15,675
Polyethylene pouch (16 oz, or 455 g)	559	Beet sugar (assumes 17% sugar in beets)	5,660
Steel can, aluminum top (12 oz)	568	Dehydrated foods (freeze-dried)	3,542
Small paper set-up box	722	Cane sugar (assumes 20% sugar in cane)	3,380
Steel can, steel top (16 oz)	1,006	Fruit and vegetables (frozen)	1,815
Glass jar (16 oz)	1,023	Fish (frozen)	1,815
Coca-Cola bottle, nonreturnable (16 oz)	1,471	Baked goods	1,485
Aluminum TV-dinner container	1,496	Meat	1,206
Aluminum can, pop-top (12 oz)	1,643	Ice cream	880
Plastic milk container, disposable (½ gal.)	2,159	Fruit and vegetables (canned)	575
Coca-Cola bottle, returnable (16 oz)	2,451	Flour (includes blending of flour)	484
Polyethylene bottle (1 qt)	2,494	Milk	354
Polypropylene bottle (1 qt)	2,752		
Glass milk container, returnable (½ gal)	4,455		

Source: Adapted from Pimentel and Pimentel 1985:38–39.

with environment determines carrying capacity, which is the upper limit of production, and hence the limit of the human population density possible without depletion and permanent damage.

When carrying capacity is exceeded, production will decline precipitously. The fact that a food energy system is operating as much as two-thirds below carrying capacity does not mean that ecological restraints are absent. Energy systems tend to stop growing before reaching the point of diminishing returns, which is defined as the point at which the ratio of output to input begins to fall, holding technology constant. A distinction must also be made between the effects of growth and the effects of intensification. Growth may continue for a long time without leading to a decline in the ratio of output to input. Intensification, however, which is defined as increased input in a fixed area, may lead to critical depletions, diminishing returns, and irreversible damage to the habitat's carrying capacity. All the factors in production must be approached from the perspective of Liebig's law, which states that extremes, not averages, set the limits for carrying capacity.

A common human cultural response to declining efficiency brought about by intensification is to alter technology and thereby adopt new modes of production.

Hunting-gathering was the universal mode of food production throughout over 90 percent of humankind's existence. As exemplified by the !Kung San, while hunter-gatherers' output-to-input efficiency is low, especially for the male-dominated activity of hunting, hunter-gatherers can enjoy high standards of living by maintaining low population densities and avoiding intensification. Energetic efficiency plays an important role in the selection of the species that hunter-gatherers use for food. According to optimal foraging theory, foragers stop to take only those species whose handling adds to or does not decrease the overall efficiency of their foraging effort.

Slash-and-burn agriculturalists such as the Tsembaga Maring produce their caloric needs with greater efficiency than the !Kung San, but they have depleted the game animals in their habitat and must rely on costly domesticated pigs for their animal proteins and fats. By using irrigation agriculture, the people of Luts'un produce a large surplus. Their output-input ratio for human effort is three times higher than the output-input ratio of the Tsembaga.

Pastoralism, another preindustrial mode of food production, is practiced only in areas unsuitable for agriculture, because feeding plant food to domesticated animals rather than consuming crops directly results in a 90 percent reduction in the efficiency of conversion of sunlight to human food.

As Leslie White predicted, there has been a steady increase in the amount of energy harnessed per capita as cultures have evolved. Energy efficiency has also increased as measured by the return for human labor input. But when sources of energy other than human calories are included in the calculation of efficiency, advances in technology are shown to have resulted in a decrease in the efficiency of food production, as demonstrated by the enormous energy inputs that characterize industrial agricultural systems.

Chapter 6

REPRODUCTION

This chapter completes the introduction to the study of infrastructure. It examines the relationship between production and reproduction from the perspective of the costs and benefits of child rearing. The culturally controlled practices that have the effect of raising or lowering rates of population growth in the absence of modern contraceptive methods are also discussed.

The Relation Between Production and Reproduction

Reproduction is a form of production — the "product" being new human beings. Under optimal conditions, human females can have between 20 and 25 live births during their fertile years (which last roughly from age 15 to 45). In all human societies women on the average have far fewer children than that. The record, 8.97 children per woman, is held by the Hutterites, a communitarian sect whose members live in western Canada (Lang and Göhlen 1985). If all children born live to reproduce, any number of births greater than 2 per woman would potentially result in population increase (holding death rates constant). Even small rates of population increase can result in enormous populations in a few generations. The !Kung, for example, have a population growth rate of 0.5 percent per year. If the world had started 10,000 years ago with a population of 2, and if that population had grown at 0.5 percent per year, the world population would now be 604,436,000,000,000,000,000,000. No such growth has occurred because, through various combinations of cultural and natural factors, reproduction has been kept within limits imposed by systems of production.

Much controversy surrounds the nature of the relationship between production and reproduction. Followers of Thomas Malthus, the founder of the science of demography (i.e., the science of population phenomena), have long held the view that the level of population is determined by the amount of food produced. Population, according to the Malthusians, would always rise to the limit of production; in fact, it would tend to rise faster than any conceivable rise in productivity, thereby dooming a large portion of humanity to perpetual poverty, hunger, and misery. However, from the evidence showing that many preindustrial societies maintain their level of production well below carrying capacity (see Chapter 5), it is clear that Malthus was wrong in at least one crucial respect. It is possible, moreover, to turn Malthus upside down and see the amount of food produced as being determined by the level of population growth. In this view, which has been advocated most forcefully by Ester Boserup (see page 75), food production tends to rise to the level demanded by population growth. As population expands, production is intensified and new modes of production evolve to satisfy the increased demand for food.

In light of modern anthropological research, the position that seems most correct is that production and reproduction are equally important in shaping the course of sociocultural evolution, and that to an equal extent each is the cause of the other. Reproduction generates *population pressure* (i.e., physiological and psychological costs such as malnutrition and illness) that leads to intensification, diminishing returns, and irreversible environmental depletions. Moreover, such pressures may be felt even while a population is not increasing, if standards of living are low and the means used to maintain population at a low level are themselves costly (as, for example, infanticide and primitive methods of abortion — see below). Thus, while production sets limits to population growth, population pressure provides the motivation to overcome such limits (Johnson and Earle 1987; Keely 1988).

Population pressure introduces an element of instability into all human cultures. This instability often interacts with natural sources of instability (called "perturbations"), such as changes in ocean currents and advances and retreats of continental glaciers, to bring about large-scale shifts in modes of production.

Preindustrial Population-Regulating Practices

Contrary to the Malthusian view, preindustrial cultures regulated the size of their families so as to minimize the costs and maximize the benefits of reproduction. In an age that lacked condoms, diaphragms, pills, spermicides, or knowledge of the human ovulatory cycle, how could such regulation occur? Four categories of practice that have the effect of regulating population growth were relied on: (1) care and treatment of fetus, infants, and children; (2) care and treatment of girls and women (and to a lesser extent of boys and men); (3) intensity and duration of lactation (i.e., the period of breast feeding); (4) variations in the frequency of coital intercourse. To say that such practices were relied on does not mean that they were relied on consciously, but that they formed part of etic behavioral practice, sometimes in direct opposition to emic rules.

TREATMENT OF FETUS AND CHILDREN

Maltreatment of fetus, infant, and young child is a common means of lowering reproductive costs. A subtle gradation leads from active attempts to *avoid* fetal death, infant death, and child death to active efforts to *promote* fetal death, infant death, and child death. Full support of the fetus involves supplementing the diets of pregnant women and reducing their work loads (MacCormack 1982:8). Indirect abortion begins when heavy work loads and meager diets are imposed on pregnant women. Direct abortion occurs with starvation diets for pregnant women and often involves trauma caused by squeezing the mother's abdomen with tight bands, jumping on her, or having her ingest toxic substances. In a study of 350 preindustrial societies, George Devereux (1967:98) found that direct abortion was "an absolutely universal phenomenon."

Some forms of infanticide are as widely practiced as abortion. Again, there is a subtle gradation from indirect to direct methods. Full support of the life of a newborn infant requires that it be fed to gain weight rapidly and that it be protected against extremes of temperature and from falls, burns, and other accidents. In-direct infanticide begins with inadequate feed-ing and careless and indifferent handling, espe-cially when the infant gets sick. Direct infanticide involves more or less rapid starva-tion, dehydration, exposure to the elements, suffocation, or blows to the head (Scrimshaw 1983). Often there is no sharp distinction be-tween abortion and infanticide. The Yano-mami (see page 187), for example, induce labor during the sixth or seventh month of preg-nancy and kill the fetus if it shows signs of life after expulsion. Similarly, there is often no clear distinction between infanticide and the direct or indirect removal of unwanted chil-dren 2 or 3 years old by more or less rapid starvation and neglect during illness. In this connection, it should be pointed out that many cultures do not regard children as human until certain ceremonies, such as naming or hair cut-ting, are performed. Infanticide and the in-duced death of small children seldom take place *after* such ceremonies have been per-formed (Minturn and Stashak 1982). Hence in the emic perspective, such deaths are rarely seen as homicides.

TREATMENT OF WOMEN

The treatment of women can raise or lower the age at which women begin to be capable of bearing children and the age at which they can no longer conceive. It can also affect the total number of pregnancies they are capable of sus-taining. Women who are nutritionally de-prived are not as fertile as women whose diets are adequate, although considerable contro-versy exists as to how severe the deprivations must be before significant declines in fertility occur (see Box 6.1). It is known that severe, famine-level nutritional deprivation can re-

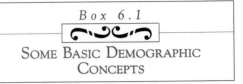

Box 6.1

SOME BASIC DEMOGRAPHIC CONCEPTS

Crude Birth Rate   The number of births per thousand people, in a given year.

Crude Death Rate   The number of deaths per thousand people, in a given year.

Fertility Rate   The number of live births per thousand women aged 15–44, in a given year.

Completed Fertility Rate   The average number of children born to women who have completed their reproductive years.

Fecundity   The physiological capacity to produce a live child.

Mortality   Death as a factor in population stability or change.

duce fertility by 50 percent (Bongaarts 1980:568). Rose Frisch (1984:184), however, maintains that a 10–15 percent weight loss is sufficient to delay menarche (first menses) and to disrupt the menstrual cycle. It should be kept in mind that this dispute concerns the effect of malnutrition on fertility. The effects of nutritional stress on mother, fetus, and in-fant are well established. Poor maternal nutri-tion increases the risk of premature births and of low birth weights, both of which increase fetal and infant mortality; poor maternal nutri-tion also diminishes the quantity if not the quality of breast milk, thus lowering the chances of infant survival still further (Hamil-ton et al. 1984:388). In turn, women who be-come pregnant and who recurrently provide mother's milk from a nutritionally depleted body also have elevated mortality rates (Fredrick and Adelstein 1973; Jelliffe and Jelliffe 1978; Trussell and Pebly 1984). These nutritional effects will all vary in interaction with the amount of psychological and physical stress imposed on pregnant and lactating women. Female life expectancy can be affected, in addition, by exposure to toxic, body-shock techniques of abortion, again in interaction with general nutritional status.

Extreme malnutrition and physical and mental stress can also affect male fecundity (see Box 6.1) by reducing libido (sexual desire) and sperm count. However, the abundance of sperm as compared with the ova and the female's birthing and nursing physiology renders the treatment of females far more important than the treatment of males in regulating reproduction. High sickness and mortality rates among males are readily counterbalanced by the widespread practice of polygyny (one husband with several wives — see page 135) and by the fact that one male can impregnate dozens of females.

LACTATION

Amenorrhea (disruption of the menstrual cycle) is a typical accompaniment of breast feeding. The effect is associated with the production of *prolactin*, a hormone that regulates mammary activity. Prolactin in turn inhibits the production of the hormones that regulate the ovulatory cycle. Several biocultural factors appear to control the duration of lactation amenorrhea. To begin with, there is the state of the mother's health and her diet. Additional variables include the intensity of suckling as determined by the age at which the infant is fed supplemental soft foods and by the scheduling

of suckling episodes. While the relative importance of these factors remains controversial (Bongaarts 1980, 1982; Frisch 1984), it is clear that under favorable conditions prolonged nursing can result in birth-spacing intervals of 3 or more years, with a degree of reliability comparable to that of modern mechanical and chemical contraceptives (Short 1984:36). But one must be on guard against the notion that any social group is free to adjust its fertility rate upward or downward merely by intensifying and prolonging lactation (Figure 6.1). Prolonged lactation cannot take place without suitably nourished mothers. Moreover, because human breast milk is deficient in iron, its

Figure 6.1 Breast feeding older children. San women breast-feed their children for 4 to 5 years per child.

use as the sole source of nourishment much beyond 6 months will cause anemia in the infant.

COITAL FREQUENCY AND SCHEDULING

Coital abstinence can be sustained long enough to reduce pregnancies, and delays in the onset of coital behavior can shorten the female's reproductive span (Nag 1983). The effects of lactational amenorrhea can be reinforced by coital abstinence while the mother continues to nurse her child. Also, various forms of nonreproductive sex can influence fertility rates: Homosexuality, masturbation, coitus interruptus (withdrawal before ejaculation), and noncoital heterosexual techniques for achieving orgasm can all play a role in regulating fertility. Age of marriage is another important population-regulating variable, but its significance depends on the existence of a taboo on extramarital sex and unwed motherhood. As we shall see (page 144), many societies do not regard couples who have not had children as being married. In such cases, age of marriage cannot influence the number of children a woman will have (Wilmsen 1982:4).

Type of marriage is also relevant to fertility. Polygyny, for example, assures that almost all females will engage in reproductive sex (in the absence of contraception). But polygyny is also effective in prolonging sexual abstinence and the latter's reinforcing effect on lactational amenorrhea. In addition, polygyny probably results in lower rates of coital intercourse per wife as husbands grow older (Bongaarts and Odile 1984:521–522).

It is clear from this summary that preindustrial societies have never lacked means for regulating their reproductive rates in response to the limits and possibilities of their modes of production.

The Influence of Disease and Other Natural Factors

Most of the great lethal epidemic diseases — smallpox, typhoid fever, flu, bubonic plague, and cholera — are primarily associated with dense urbanized populations rather than with dispersed hunter-gatherers or small village cultures. Even such diseases as malaria and yellow fever were probably less important among low-density populations who could avoid swampy mosquito breeding grounds. (Knowledge of the association between swamps and disease is very ancient, even though mosquitoes were not recognized as disease carriers.) Other diseases such as dysentery, measles, tuberculosis, whooping cough, scarlet fever, and the common cold were also probably less significant among hunter-gatherers and early farmers (Armelagos and McArdle 1975; Black 1975; Cockburn 1971; Wood 1975). The ability to recuperate from these infections is closely related to the general level of bodily health, which in turn is heavily influenced by diet, especially by balanced protein levels (Scrimshaw 1977). The role of disease as a long-term regulator of human population is thus to some extent a consequence of the success or failure of other population-regulating mechanisms. Only if these alternatives are ineffective and population density rises, productive efficiency drops, and diet deteriorates will some diseases figure as an important check on population growth (Post 1985).

There is some evidence to indicate that Paleolithic hunter-gatherers were healthier than late Neolithic agriculturalists and the peasant farmers of preindustrial state societies. Exactly when and where a deterioration occurred is the focus of much continuing research (Cohen and Armelagos 1984; Cohen 1989). It seems likely that for much of the

Upper Paleolithic, at least, "artificial" population controls rather than sickness were the principal factors governing rates of population growth (Handwerker 1983:20; 1986).

Obviously, it cannot be denied that a component in human birth and death rates reflects "natural" causes over which cultural practices have little influence. In addition to lethal disease, natural catastrophes such as droughts, floods, and earthquakes may raise death rates and lower birth rates in a manner that leaves little room for cultural intervention. And there are of course biological constraints on the number of children a human female can have, as well as natural limitations on the length of human life. But to a surprising degree, even when people are faced with severe crises and deprivations, cultural practices are relied on that let some die and others live (see page 101).

The Costs and Benefits of Rearing Children

The phrase *population pressure* implies that people are sensitive to the costs and benefits entailed in the process of reproduction. Costs of rearing children include the extra food consumed during pregnancy, the work forgone by pregnant women, the expenses involved in providing mother's milk and other foods during infancy and childhood, the burden of carrying infants and children from one place to another, and in more complex societies, expenditures for clothing, housing, medical care, and education. In addition, the birth process itself is dangerous and often places at risk the life of the mother.

Benefits of reproduction include the contribution that children make to food production, to family income in general, and to the care and economic security of their parents.

Children are also widely valued for their role in marital exchanges and intergroup alliances (see pages 144 and 150)—that is, in many cultures, groups exchange sons and daughters in order to obtain husbands and wives. These exchanges are used to arrange alliances against aggressors. Hence, where chronic warfare exists, larger groups are safer than smaller ones; they have more alliances as well as greater military strength. All this, of course, is not to deny that people have children for sentimental reasons as well.

Humans may have a genetically controlled propensity, shared with other primates, to find infants emotionally appealing and to derive emotional satisfaction from holding and fondling them and from watching and helping them play and learn. As children grow older, their respect and love for their parents may also be highly valued. But it is clear that this appreciation of infants and children, if it is innate, can be modified by culture so completely as to allow most people to have fewer children than they are biologically capable of producing and to enable others, such as monks, priests, nuns, and even some modern-day "yuppies," to have none at all.

Much recent evidence suggests that the rate at which the parental generation has children is largely determined by the extent to which having each additional child results in a net gain of benefits over costs for the average couple (Caldwell 1982; Harris and Ross 1987; Nardi 1983). Among hunter-gatherers, for example, the number of children is limited by the burden that infants present to mothers who must carry them several thousand kilometers each year on their foraging expeditions. According to Richard Lee, !Kung San mothers try to avoid having one child close upon another, in order to escape the burden of carrying two children at once. The benefits of additional children are further reduced among hunter-gatherers by the vulnerability of wild species of plants and animals to depletion. As band size increases, per capita food production tends to decline, since hunter-gatherers have no effective way of creating a concomitant increase in the population of the wild plants and animals they use for food. Finally, the children of hunter-gatherers do not produce more than they consume until relatively late in childhood. For these reasons, population densities among hunter-gatherers seldom rise above one person per square mile. If contemporary hunter-gatherers are at all representative of prehistoric times, *Homo sapiens* must have been a very rare creature at the time of cultural takeoff. Perhaps there were only 5 million people in the entire world in those times (Dumond 1975; Hassan 1978:78) and certainly no more than 15 million (Mark Cohen 1977:54), compared with 4.5 billion today. Whether one takes the upper or lower estimate, there is no doubt that for tens of thousands of years the rate of growth of the human population was very slow (see Table 6.1).

With the advent of agriculture and domesticated animals the balance of reproductive costs and benefits shifted in favor of having more children. Children no longer had to be carried about over long distances and they could perform many useful economic chores at an early age. Also, since the rate of reproduction of domesticated plants and animals could be controlled, a considerable amount of intensification and hence population growth could be achieved without a decline in per capita output. After weaning, children in many agricultural societies rapidly begin to "pay for themselves." They contribute to the production of their own food, clothing, and housing, and under favorable conditions they may begin to produce surpluses above their own subsistence needs as early as 6 years of age. This transition is hastened with successive births, since senior siblings and other children assume much of the cost of grooming and caring for their juniors.

Measuring the Costs and Benefits of Rearing Children

A number of attempts have been made to measure the economic value of children in contemporary peasant communities. For example, in

Table 6.1
RATE OF GROWTH OF THE HUMAN POPULATION

PERIOD	WORLD POPULATION AT END OF PERIOD	PERCENTAGE ANNUAL RATE OF GROWTH DURING PERIOD
Paleolithic	5,000,000	0.0015
Mesolithic	8,500,000	0.0330
Neolithic	75,000,000	0.1000
Ancient empires	225,000,000	0.5000

Sources: Hassan 1981; Spengler 1974.

village Java, boys of 12 – 14 years contribute 33 hours of economically valuable work per week and girls 9 – 11 contribute about 38 hours a week of the same. Altogether, children contribute about half of all work performed by household members (Figure 6.2). Much household labor involves making handicrafts, working in petty trade, and processing various foods for sale. Similar findings are reported for Nepal (Nag et al. 1978; White 1976).

Costs are more difficult to measure, but Javenese children themselves do most of the work needed to rear and maintain their siblings, freeing mothers for income-producing tasks. In any event, larger households are more efficient income-producing units in rural Java, because a smaller proportion of total labor time is required for maintenance. Given these conditions, women have about five births and four

Figure 6.3   Child workers, Bangladesh.

Figure 6.2   Child worker.
A Javanese boy earning his keep.

surviving children, which "seems an entirely appropriate response" (White 1982:605). (It is nonetheless a response that yields an alarming 2 percent per annum increase in Java's population).

Meade Cain (1977:225) has quantified both benefits and costs for male children in a rural Bangladesh village (Figure 6.3). Cain describes his findings:

> Male children become net producers at the latest by the age of 12. Furthermore, male children work long enough hours at high enough rates of productivity to compensate for consumption during their earlier periods of dependence by the age of 15. Therefore, in general . . . parents . . . realize a net economic return on male children for the period when they are subordinate members of the parental household.

Thus, contrary to the popular perception that people in less developed countries have large numbers of children simply because they do not know how to avoid conception, there is much evidence that more children and larger households mean a higher, not a lower, standard of living in the short run. In explaining why they did not wish to join any family planning programs, the men of Manupur village in the Punjab explained: "Why pay 2,500 rupees for an extra hand? Why not have a son?" (Mamdani 1973:77). But it should be emphasized that high fertility may simply give large families a more favorable standard of living relative to that of smaller families in a situation in which the average standard of living for the whole farming sector is stagnant or even deteriorating (Weil 1986).

With the expansion of urban, industrial, technical, and white-collar employment opportunities, the net return from child rearing can be increased by investing in fewer but better-educated offspring. In Rampur village, close to the Indian capital of New Delhi, the number of children per woman declined as wage opportunities increased outside the village (Das Gupta 1978). Tractors, tube wells, and pumps reduced the demand for child labor. In addition, parents wanted their children to get more education to prepare for higher-quality jobs in New Delhi. Similarly in Sri Lanka (Tilakaratne 1978), employers of wage labor have come to prefer adult males rather than children who are able to work only part time as a result of having to attend school. More white-collar jobs are becoming available for which children are unsuited because they have not achieved the required levels of literacy and mathematical skills. Even families headed by manual workers desire to have children participate in white-collar, high-status jobs and to give them more schooling. Marriage to an edu-

cated and well-employed man or woman has become the ideal, and this can be done only by postponing marriage, which in turn decreases the number of children per woman.

In Indian villages located near the city of Bangalore, three factors accounted for the trend against child labor: (1) Land holdings had become fragmented and too small to absorb the labor of additional children in agriculture; (2) new nonfarm employment opportunities requiring arithmetic skills and literacy had opened up; (3) educational facilities had been introduced or improved within the villages (Caldwell et al. 1983). Similarly, on returning to the village of Manupur in the Punjab (see above, this page, Nag and Kak (1984) found a sharp increase in the number of couples practicing contraception and a sharp reduction in the number of sons regarded as desirable. These changes resulted from shifts in the mode of production, which lowered the demand for child labor. Shortening or eliminating fallow, for example, has led to the disappearance of grazing land within the village, so that young boys can no longer make themselves useful tending cattle. The loss of cattle and the increased reliance on chemical fuels and fertilizer have also done away with the childhood task of collecting cow dung (Figure 6.4); to be used for fertilizer and fuel (see page 313); with the introduction of industrial herbicides, children are no longer needed for weeding. Furthermore, there has been a substantial rise in the proportion of Manupur workers employed in industrial, commercial, and government sectors. Meanwhile, the mechanization of farm operations, the expanded use of credit, and the need to keep account books have made Manupur parents consciously eager to expand their children's educational horizons. Secondary school enrollment increased in a decade from 63 percent to 81 percent for boys and from 29 to 63

Figure 6.4   Manupur, Punjab, India.
Collection of cow dung by children to make cow-dung cakes for use as cooking fuel is becoming less important as families become more prosperous and the land is farmed more intensively.

percent for girls. Parents now want at least one son to have a white-collar job so that the family will not be entirely dependent on agriculture, and many parents want both sons and daughters to attend college.

The Contraception, Abortion, and Infanticide Debate

An important implication of the existence of powerful cultural practices for raising or lowering fertility and mortality rates is that human reproduction is not an act that can be described as taking place at a specific moment, such as the moment of the union between an ovum and a sperm. Human reproduction is a social process that begins long before conception and that continues long after birth. For human reproduction to take place, prospective parents must have adequate material and psychological support, the pregnant woman and her fetus must be nourished and protected, the nursing mother and her infant must be fed and cared for, and a commitment must be made by the parents and many other individuals to find the resources necessary to rear the newborn from infancy and childhood to adulthood.

As we have just seen, the decision to make the social effort necessary to give birth to and rear children is heavily influenced by the balance of costs and benefits confronting prospective parents. We can be confident that when the balance is adverse, some form of birth or death control will be activated at some point in the reproductive process. The kinds of birth or death control measures employed, however, vary from one culture to another. To a degree that is shocking to modern sensibilities, preindustrial and underdeveloped societies employ reproduction-regulating measures that achieve their effect *after* the birth of a child. The existence of these postpartum reproduction-regulating practices can be obscured by the failure to distinguish between emic and etic viewpoints. Yet the recognition of postpartum etic death control practices is essential to understanding the controversy concerning contraception, abortion, and infanticide. Much evidence exists that if reproduction is not limited before or during pregnancy, then it will be limited after pregnancy by direct or indirect infanticide or pedicide (the killing of young children). Attempts to discourage contraception, medical abortion, and other modern prepartum reproductive controls may inadvertently increase reliance on postpartum homicidal practices. It is with this possibility in mind that the case of indirect infanticide in Northeast Brazil is presented in the next section.

INDIRECT INFANTICIDE IN NORTHEAST BRAZIL

Northeast Brazil is a region subjected to periodic droughts, chronic malnutrition, and widespread poverty. Its infant mortality rate is about 200 deaths per thousand births in the first year of life (compared with a rate of less than 10 in developed countries). A study carried out by Nancy Scheper-Hughes (1984) in this region reveals that at least some of the infant and child deaths reported by a sample of 72 women are best described as forms of indirect infanticide. Out of a total of 686 pregnancies (an average of 9.5 per woman!), 85 were terminated by in-

duced or spontaneous abortions, and there were 16 stillbirths. Out of 588 live births, 251 died before 5 years of age, an average of 3.5 infant and child deaths per woman. These deaths were concentrated at the beginning and end of the women's fertile years, a pattern that Scheper-Hughes attributes to the inexperience of mothers with their firstborn and to their economic, physical, and psychological inability to cope with the needs of the lastborn. (A more likely explanation for the higher mortality of the firstborn is that they were conceived while their mothers were still in their teens and were therefore still growing, which increases the probability that their babies would be born underweight and vulnerable to disease [Frisancho et al. 1983].) Some women indicated that the lastborn had been unwanted and that "it was a blessing that God decided to take them in their infancy" (Scheper-Hughes 1984:539).

More important than birth order in determining a mother's tendency to withdraw support from a particular infant was the mother's "perception of the child's innate constitution and temperament as they relate to 'readiness or fitness for life.'" Mothers expressed a preference for "quick, sharp, active, verbal, and developmentally precocious children" (ibid.). Children with the opposite traits were not given medical assistance when they became ill, and they were not fed as well as their sisters and brothers. Mothers spoke of children who "'wanted to die', whose will and drive toward life was not sufficiently strong or developed" (ibid.). These unwanted children tend to die during one of the crises of childhood: infections of the umbilical cord, infant diarrhea, or teething. The women regard some childhood diseases as incurable, but the diagnostic symptoms of these diseases are so broad that almost any childhood disorder can be interpreted as a sign that the child is doomed to

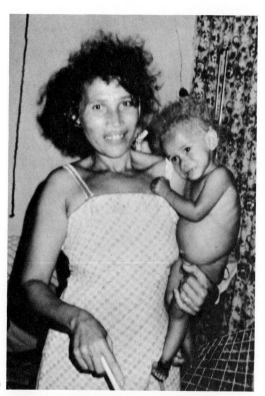

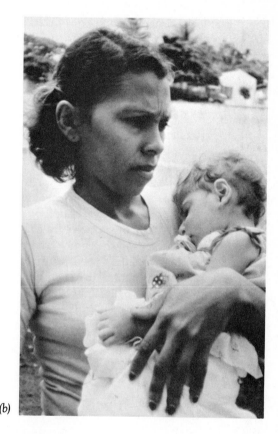

(a)

(b)

Figure 6.5   Doomed infant, northeast Brazil.
(a) *The mother says that her 16-month-old son has an "aversion" to life and will not live much longer. The color of his hair and lack of teeth show that he is suffering from advanced protein-calorie malnutrition.* (b) *Baby has anemia and is listless and malnourished. The mother says she is conforming to God's will that the child should soon be an angel.*

die: fits and convulsions, lethargy and passivity, retarded verbal or motor function, or a "ghost-like" or "animal-like" appearance (Figure 6.5). Writes Scheper-Hughes (ibid.:541): "I do not know what exactly prompts a folk diagnosis of this kind, but I suspect that its flexibility allows mothers a great deal of latitude in deciding which of their children are not favored for survival as 'normal' children."

When a child marked with one of these fatal diseases dies, mothers do not display grief.

They say there was no remedy, that even if you treat the disease, the child "will never be right"; that it is "best to leave them to die"; and that no one wants to take care of such a child. As Scheper-Hughes points out, the folk (emic) symptoms of fatal childhood diseases in Northeast Brazil correspond to etic symptoms of "malnutrition and parasitic infections interacting with physical and psychological neglect." To the extent that mothers practice indirect (or direct) infanticide through neglect, they are reacting to life-threatening conditions that are not of their own making: shortage of food, contaminated water supplies, unchecked infectious diseases, lack of day-care for children of working mothers, absence of affordable medical care, and the other stigmas and penalties of extreme poverty. While recognizing that mothers hasten the deaths of their unwanted children by rationing infant and child care, we must not fall into the trap of "blaming the victims." These women do not have access to modern forms of contraception or to medical abortion, and they are themselves too poorly nourished to limit their pregnancies by prolonged lactation. Moreover, abstinence is difficult for them because of their need to attract male support and companionship. In Scheper-Hughes's words, because of the indignities and inhumanities forced upon them, these women must at times "make choices and decisions that no woman and mother should have to make" (1984:541).

Industrial Modes of Reproduction

Shifts in the costs and benefits of rearing children lie behind the "demographic transition" that took place in Europe, the United States, and Japan during the nineteenth century (Handwerker 1983, 1986). This transition involved a drop in both birth rates and death rates and a slowing of the rate of population growth (Figure 6.6).

    With industrialization, the cost of rearing children rose rapidly, especially after the introduction of child labor laws and compulsory education statutes. The skills required for earning a living took longer to acquire; hence, parents had to wait longer before they could receive any economic benefits from their children. At the same time, the whole pattern of

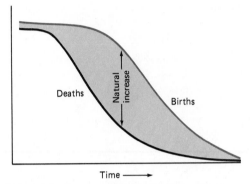

Figure 6.6 Demographic transition.
Rapid fall in death rate followed by slower fall of birth rate causes temporary increase in population growth until demographic transition is completed.

how people earned their livings changed. Work ceased to be something done by family members on the family farm or in the family shop. Rather, people earned wages as individuals in factories and offices. What the family did together was to consume; its only product was children. The return flow of benefits from rearing children came to hinge more and more on their willingness to help out in the medical and financial crises that beset older people. But longer life spans and spiraling medical costs make it increasingly unrealistic for parents to expect such help from their children. Thus the industrial nations have been obliged to substitute old age and medical insurance and old age homes for the preindustrial system in which children took care of their aged parents.

    To meet the rise in the cost of rearing children in industrial societies, wives as well as husbands must participate in the wage-earning labor force. As long as this situation continues, more and more men and women decide to have only one child or none, and more and more individuals find that the traditional forms of

marriage, family, sex, and emotional togetherness are incompatible with the maintenance of
middle-class status (Harris and Ross 1987).

Summary

Production sets limits to reproduction. Contrary to the position advocated by Thomas
Malthus, populations do not normally rise to
the maximum limit of production, nor are they
usually checked by starvation and other catastrophes. Instead, they are usually maintained
well below carrying capacity. Reproduction
leads to population pressure, which leads to
intensification, depletions, and changes in the
modes of production.

Variations in reproductive rates cannot be
explained by the universal desire to have children. Rather, reproductive rates reflect the
variable costs and benefits of rearing children
under different modes of production. Hunter-
gatherer reproduction rates are influenced by
the need for women to avoid carrying more
than one infant at a time over long distances, as
well as by the limited intensifiability of hunter-
gatherer modes of production. Sedentary agriculturalists rear more children because agriculture can be intensified, the burden of carrying
infants and toddlers is reduced, children more
rapidly "pay for themselves," and senior children can take care of juniors.

Findings from contemporary peasant societies lend support to the cost-benefit approach
to reproductive rates. In Java, children contribute about half of all the work of household
members. In Bangladesh, male children by age
12 produce more than they consume, and in 3
more years make up for all previous expenses
incurred on their behalf. Moreover, contrary
to the popular impression that the poorest
peasant households have the most children,

there is often a positive correlation between
large numbers of children and wealthier families.

With the expansion of urban, industrial,
technical, and white-collar employment, the
benefits of raising fewer but "costlier" children
outweigh the advantages of rearing many but
"cheaper" children. In India and Sri Lanka, the
number of children per woman has declined as
children cease to have important roles in agriculture and as the offspring of peasants find
advancement through white-collar jobs and
business opportunities that require high levels
of education. These shifts in the costs of rearing children in relation to new modes of production are similar to the shifts that brought
about the "demographic transition" in nineteenth-century Europe and the United States.

Thus, again contrary to Malthusian
theory, preindustrial cultures regulated the size
of their families so as to minimize the costs and
maximize the benefits of reproduction. While
they lacked a modern technology of contraception or abortion, they were nonetheless
never at a loss for means of controlling birth
and death rates. Four principal categories of
practice were used: care and treatment of fetus,
infants, and children; care and treatment of
girls and women; intensity and duration of lactation; and variations in the frequency of heterosexual coitus. Subtle gradations exist between abortion, infanticide, and induced child
mortality. While much controversy surrounds
the question of whether poor nutrition reduces the ability of women to conceive, there is
no doubt that poor nutrition jeopardizes the
life of mother, fetus, and child. The amenorrhea associated with lactation is a more benign
form of fertility regulation widely practiced by
preindustrial people. Finally, various forms of
nonreproductive sex and degree of sexual abstinence can raise or lower reproductive rates.

While there is a "natural" component in human death rates, the influence of natural variables is always conditioned to some extent by cultural practices. Moreover, the influence of disease on death rates in small-scale band and village societies should not be exaggerated. To a surprising extent, even when people are faced with epidemics, droughts, famine, and other natural catastrophes, cultural practices are relied on to let some live and others die. A vivid example of such practices can be seen in Northeast Brazil: Impoverished mothers who lack access to modern contraception or medical abortion contribute to the extremely high rates of infant and child mortality through the selective neglect and indirect infanticide of their unwanted offspring. Care must be taken not to "blame the victims": Lacking the means of rearing all their children, these mothers have no way to avoid a tragic choice.

It is clear, therefore, that human reproduction is a complex social process that begins long before conception and continues long after birth.

Chapter 7

ECONOMIC ORGANIZATION

In this chapter the focus shifts from infrastructure to structure. Beginning with a definition of economy as the organizational aspect of production and exchange, the chapter goes on to identify types of economies by the way in which they exert control over work and ownership (or the relations of production). The principal kinds of exchange are indicated, and their relationship to infrastructural conditions is explored. Money is defined, and the distinction between price-market and non-price-market economies is emphasized. The chapter concludes by examining the relationship between, on the one hand, changes in the division of labor and in time allocated to work; and on the other, the evolution of modes of production and reproduction.

Definition of Economy

In a narrow sense, *economy* refers to the allocation of scarce means to competing ends. Most professional economists hold that human beings in general tend to "economize" — that is, to allocate scarce means so as to maximize the achievement of ends while minimizing the expenditure of means. In a broader sense, however, an economy refers to the activities responsible for providing a society with its goods and services: "An economy is a set of institutionalized activities which combine natural resources, human labor, and technology to acquire, produce, and distribute material goods and specialist services in a structured, repetitive fashion" (Dalton 1969:97). The two definitions of economy are not necessarily incompatible. Anthropologists stress the fact that the specific motivations for producing, exchanging, and consuming goods and services are shaped by cultural traditions. Different cultures value different goods and services, and tolerate or prohibit different kinds of relationships among the people who produce, exchange, and consume. For example, as we will see in a moment, some cultures emphasize cooperative acquisition and sharing of wealth, whereas others stress competitive acquisition and retention of wealth. Some cultures emphasize communal property; others place great importance on private property. It is obvious, therefore, that "economizing" has different premises and different consequences in different cultural contexts.

Infrastructural Versus Structural Aspects of Economies

With respect to the broader definition of *economy*, it is useful to maintain a distinction between those aspects that we have treated as modes of production (Chapter 5) and hence as parts of infrastructure, and those aspects that we can more conveniently examine as part of the structural level of sociocultural systems. As we have seen, modes of production are characterized by the way in which a given technology is applied to a specific environment to produce the energy on which social life depends. The features of economy that we will discuss here are organizational in nature. Sometimes called the *relations of production*, they include such matters as division of labor, exchange and distribution of products and services, control over labor, and ownership or differential access to technology and natural resources.

What is the justification for distinguishing between economy as infrastructure and economy as structure? The answer is that by doing so, anthropologists study the extent to which the evolution of the organizational features of economy are predictable from a knowledge of modes of production and reproduction. Many aspects of the structural level of sociocultural systems, including economic organizations, have evolved in response to the opportunities and constraints presented by the basic elements of production and reproduction, given specific kinds of technologies and environments. It is true that production and reproduction cannot proceed without the organizational components of the economy. And it is also true that these organizational components in turn impose limits on production and reproduction. As we shall see, however, major transformations in the economic organization of social life do not occur randomly, but in response to infrastructural preconditions characteristic of particular modes of production and reproduction.

Exchange

Most of what is produced by human labor is distributed by means of exchange. (The exceptions consist of instances of direct consumption by the producers themselves.) *Exchange* refers to the panhuman pattern of giving and receiving valuable objects and services. The joint provisioning of children by adult men and women is a form of giving and receiving that is important for the definition of what it means to be human. Human beings could not survive infancy without receiving valuable objects and services from their parents. However, patterns of exchange differ markedly from one culture to another. Following the work of the economist Karl Polanyi, anthropologists have come to distinguish three main types of exchange: *reciprocal, redistributive,* and *market.*

Reciprocal Exchange

One of the most striking features of the economic life of hunter-gatherers and small-scale agricultural societies is the prominence of exchanges that are conducted according to the principle known as *reciprocity* (Figure 7.1). In reciprocal exchanges the flow of products and services is not contingent on any definite counterflow. The partners in the exchange take according to need and give back according to no set rules of time or quantity.

Richard Lee has written a succinct description of reciprocity as it occurs among the !Kung. According to Lee, anywhere from 1 to 16 of the 20 adults in the !Kung band leave camp every morning to spend the day collecting or hunting. They return in the evening with whatever food they have managed to find. Everything brought back to camp is shared equally, regardless of whether the recipients have spent the day sleeping or hunting. Eventually all the adults will have gathered or hunted and given as well as received food. But wide discrepancies in the balance of giving and receiving may exist between individuals over a long period without becoming the subject of any special talk or action (see Box 7.1).

Some form of reciprocal exchange occurs

Figure 7.1   *Reciprocity at a Yanomami funeral feast.*
Close relatives of the deceased are about to distribute a basketful of boiled plantains and smoked meats to the rest of the village.

Box 7.1

RECIPROCITY AMONG THE !KUNG

Not only do families pool that day's production, but the entire camp—residents and visitors alike—shares equally in the total quantity of food available. The evening meal of any one family is made up of portions of food from each of the other families resident. Foodstuffs are distributed raw or are prepared by the collectors and then distributed. There is a constant flow of nuts, berries, roots and melons from one family fireplace to another until each person resident has received an equitable portion. The following morning a different combination of foragers moves out of camp and when they return late in the day, the distribution of foodstuffs is repeated.

Source: Lee 1969:58.

in all cultures, especially among relatives and friends. In the United States and Canada, for example, husbands and wives, friends, and brothers, sisters, and other kin regulate and adjust their economic lives to a minor degree according to informal, uncalculated, give-and-take transactions. Teenagers do not pay cash for their meals at home or the use of the family car. Wives do not bill their husbands for cooking a meal. Friends give each other birthday gifts and Christmas presents. These exchanges, however, constitute only a small portion of the total acts of exchange among North Americans. The great majority of exchanges in modern cultures involve rigidly defined counterflows that must take place by a certain time.

RECIPROCITY AND THE FREELOADER

As we know from the experience of taking from parents or from giving a birthday or holiday gift and not receiving one in return, the failure of an individual to reciprocate in some

degree will eventually lead to bad feelings even between close relatives and friends or husbands and wives. No one likes a "freeloader." In economies dominated by reciprocity, a grossly asymmetrical exchange does not go unnoticed. Some individuals will come to enjoy reputations as diligent gatherers or outstanding hunters, whereas others acquire reputations as shirkers or malingerers. No specific mechanisms exist for obliging the debtors to even up the score, yet there are subtle sanctions against becoming a complete freeloader. Such behavior generates a steady undercurrent of disapproval. Freeloaders are eventually subject to collective punishment. They may meet with violence because they are suspected of being bewitched or of bewitching others through the practice of sorcery (see page 176).

What is distinctive about reciprocal exchange, therefore, is not that products and services are simply given away without any thought or expectation of return, but rather that there is (1) no immediate return, (2) no systematic calculation of the value of the services and products exchanged, and (3) an overt denial that a balance is being calculated or that the balance must come out even.

No culture can rely exclusively on purely altruistic sentiments to get its goods and services produced and distributed. But in simple band and prestate village societies, goods and services are produced and exchanged in such a way as to keep the notion of material balance, debt, or obligation in an emically subordinate position. This is accomplished by expressing the necessity for reciprocal exchanges as kinship obligations. These kinship obligations (see Chapter 8) establish reciprocal expectations with respect to food, clothing, shelter, and other goods.

Kinship-embedded reciprocal exchanges constitute only a small portion of modern exchange systems, whereas among hunter-gatherers and small-scale agriculturalists, almost all exchanges take place between kin for whom the giving, taking, and using of goods has sentimental and personal meaning.

RECIPROCITY AND TRADE

Even hunters and gatherers, however, want valuables such as salt, flint, obsidian, red ochre, reeds, and honey that are produced or controlled by groups with whom they have no kinship ties. Among band and village peoples, economic dealings between nonkin are based on the assumption that every individual will try to get the best of an exchange through chicanery

and theft. As a result, trading expeditions are likely to be hazardous in the extreme and to bear a resemblance to war parties.

One interesting mechanism for facilitating trade between distant groups is known as *silent trade*. The objects to be exchanged are set out in a clearing, and the first group retreats out of sight. The other group comes out of hiding, inspects the wares, lays down what it regards as a fair exchange of its own products, and retreats again. The first group returns and, if satisfied, removes the traded objects. If not, it leaves the wares untouched as a signal that the balance is not yet even. In this fashion the Mbuti of the Ituri Forest trade meat for bananas with the Bantu agriculturalists, and the Vedda of Sri Lanka trade honey for iron tools with the Sinhalese.

More-developed trade relations occur between agricultural villages. Conditions for the development of trade markets seem to have been especially favorable in Melanesia. In New Guinea, people regularly trade fish for pigs and vegetables (Figure 7.2). Among the Kapauku of western New Guinea (today, West Irian, Indonesia), full-fledged price markets involving shell and bead money (see page 119) may have existed before the advent of European control (Figure 7.3). Generally speaking, however, marketing and money as a regular mode of trade is associated with the evolution of the state (see Chapter 11) and with the enforcement of order by means of police and soldiers.

Perhaps the most common solution to the problem of trading without kinship ties or state-supervised markets is the establishment of special *trade partnerships*. In this arrangement, members of different bands or villages regard one another as metaphorical kin. The members of trading expeditions deal exclusively with their trade partners, who greet them as "brothers" and give them food and

Figure 7.2 *New Guinea market.*
Man (left) is giving yams in exchange for fish (right).

shelter. Trade partners try to deal with one another in conformity with the principle of reciprocity, deny an interest in getting the best of the bargain, and offer wares as if they were gifts (Heider 1969).

THE KULA

The classic example of trade partnerships is described in Bronislaw Malinowski's *Argonauts of the Western Pacific*. The argonauts in question are the Trobriand Islanders, who

Figure 7.3 *Kapauku of western New Guinea*
The men (wearing penis sheaths) are counting shell money.

trade with neighboring islands by means of daring canoe voyages across the open sea (Figure 7.4). The entire complex associated with this trade is known as the *Kula*. According to the men who take these risky voyages, the purpose of the Kula trade is to exchange shell ornaments with their trade partners. The ornaments, known to the Trobrianders as *vaygu'a*, consist of armbands and necklaces. In trading with the Dobuans, who live to the southeast, the Trobrianders give armbands and receive necklaces. In trading with the people who live to the southwest, the Trobrianders give necklaces and receive armbands in return. The armbands and necklaces are then traded in oppo-

site directions from island to island, finally passing through their points of origin from the direction opposite to the one in which they were first traded.

Participation in the Kula trade is a major ambition of youth and a consuming passion of senior men. The *vaygu'a* have been compared with heirlooms or crown jewels. The older they are and the more complex their history, the more valuable they become in the eyes of the Trobrianders. Like many other examples of special-purpose exchange media (see page 119), Kula valuables are seldom used to "buy" anything. They are, however, given as gifts in marriage and as rewards to canoe builders (Scoditti

Figure 7.4   Kula canoe.
These large canoes are used by the Trobrianders for long-distance voyages.

1983). Most of the time the ornaments are simply used for the purpose of obtaining other armbands and necklaces. To trade *vaygu'a*, men establish more or less permanent partnerships with each other on distant islands. These partnerships are usually handed down from one kinsman to another, and young men are given a start in the Kula trade by inheriting or receiving an armband or a necklace from a relative. When the expedition reaches shore, the trade partners greet one another and exchange preliminary gifts. Later, the Trobrianders deliver the precious ornaments, accompanied by ritual speeches and formal acts concerned with establishing the honorable, giftlike character of the exchange. As in the case of reciprocal transactions within the family, the trade partner may not be immediately able to provide a shell whose value is equivalent to the one just received. Although the voyager may have to return home empty-handed except for some preliminary gifts, he does not complain. He expects his trade partner to work hard to make up for the delay by presenting him with even more valuable shells at their next meeting.

Why all this effort in order to obtain a few baubles of sentimental or aesthetic value? As is often the case, the etic aspects of the Kula are different from the emic aspects. The boats that take part in the Kula expedition carry trade items of great practical value in the life of the various island peoples who participate in the Kula ring. While the trade partners fondle and admire their priceless heirlooms, members of the expedition trade for practical items: coconuts, sago palm flour, fish, yams, baskets, mats, wooden swords and clubs, green stone for tools, mussel shells for knives, creepers and lianas for lashings. These items can be bargained over with impunity. Although Trobrianders deny it, the *vaygu'a* are valuable not only for their qualities as heirlooms, but for

their truly priceless gift of trade (Irwin 1983:71ff.; Scoditti 1983:265).

Kula is also better understood as part of the Trobriand and the neighboring island's system of achieving or validating political rank. Those who come into possession of the most valuable shells are usually extremely able leaders who are accomplished navigators and, in former times, bold warriors (Campbell 1983:203). This accounts for the fact that in modern times Kula has persisted even though the amount of practical items traded has declined.

Finally, why the clockwise and counterclockwise circulation of the shells? This feature accords with the notion that Kula is an institution for establishing peaceful interisland relationships to facilitate trade. By preventing partners from trading armbands for armbands or necklaces for necklaces, Kula assures the involvement of a large number of islands in the trade network. (Only limited numbers of long-distance canoe trips are possible.)

Redistributive Exchange

As we shall see in Chapter 11, the evolution of economic and political systems results largely from the development of coercive forms of exchange that supplement or almost entirely replace reciprocal exchange. Coercive forms of exchange did not appear in sudden full-blown opposition to reciprocal forms. Rather, they probably first arose through what seemed to be merely an extension of familiar reciprocal forms.

The exchange system known as *redistribution* can best be understood as such an extension. In redistribution exchange, the labor products of several different individuals are brought to a central place, sorted by type, counted, and then given away to producers and nonproducers alike. Considerable organizational effort is required if large quantities of goods are to be brought to the same place at the same time and given away in definite shares. This coordination is usually achieved by individuals who act as *redistributors*. Typically, redistributors consciously attempt to increase and intensify production, for which they gain prestige in the eyes of their peers.

Egalitarian and stratified forms of redistribution must be distinguished. As an *egalitarian* system of exchange, redistribution is carried out by a redistributor who has worked harder than anyone else producing the items to be given away, who takes the smallest portion or none at all, and who, after it is all over, possesses no greater material wealth than anyone else. In its egalitarian form, therefore, redistribution appears to be merely an extreme example of reciprocity; the generous provider gives everything away and for the moment gets nothing in return, except the admiration of those who benefit from the transaction.

In the *stratified* form, however, the redistributor withholds his or her own labor from the production process, retains the largest share, and ends up with more material wealth than anyone else.

Redistributive exchange, like reciprocal exchange, is usually embedded in a complex set of kinship relations and rituals that may obscure the etic significance of the exchange behavior. Redistribution often takes the form of a feast held to celebrate some important event such as a harvest, the end of a ritual taboo, the construction of a house, a death, a birth, or a marriage. A common feature of Melanesian redistributive feasts is that the guests gorge themselves with food, stagger off into the bush, stick their fingers down their throats, vomit, and then return to eating with renewed zest.

Another common feature of redistributive feasting is the boastful and competitive attitude of the redistributors and their kin with respect to other individuals or groups who have given feasts. This contrasts markedly with reciprocal exchange. Let us take a closer look at this contrast.

Reciprocity Versus Redistribution

Boastfulness and acknowledgment of generosity are incompatible with the basic etiquette of reciprocal exchanges. Among the Semai of Central Malaya, no one even says "thank you" for the meat received from another hunter (Figure 7.5). Having struggled all day to lug the

Figure 7.5 Semai hunter
Among the Semai, reciprocity prevails.

carcass of a pig home through the jungle heat, the hunter allows his prize to be cut up into exactly equal portions, which are then given away to the entire group. As Robert Dentan explains, to express gratitude for the portion received indicates that you are the kind of ungenerous person who calculates how much you give and take: "In this context saying thank you is very rude, for it suggests first that one has calculated the amount of a gift and second, that one did not expect the donor to be so generous" (1968:49). To call attention to one's generosity is to indicate that others are in debt to you and that you expect them to repay you. It is repugnant to egalitarian peoples even to suggest that they have been treated generously. Richard Lee tells how he learned about this aspect of reciprocity through a revealing incident. To please the !Kung with whom he was staying, he decided to buy a large ox and have it slaughtered as a Christmas present. He spent days searching the neighboring Bantu agricultural villages looking for the largest and fattest ox in the region. Finally, he bought what appeared to be a perfect specimen. But one !Kung after another took him aside and assured him that he had been duped into buying an absolutely worthless animal. "Of course, we will eat it," they said, "but it won't fill us up—we will eat and go home to bed with stomachs rumbling." Yet when Lee's ox was slaughtered, it turned out to be covered with a thick layer of fat. Lee eventually succeeded in getting his informants to explain why they had claimed that his gift was valueless, even though they certainly knew better than he what lay under the animal's skin (see Box 7.2).

In flagrant violation of these prescriptions for modesty in reciprocal exchanges, redistributive exchange systems involve public proclamations that the host is a generous person and a great provider. This boasting is one of the most conspicuous features of the *potlatches* en-

Box 7.2
MODEST PROVIDERS

Yes, when a young man kills much meat he comes to think of himself as a chief or a big man, and he thinks of the rest of us as his servants or inferiors. We can't accept this, we refuse one who boasts, for someday his pride will make him kill somebody. So we always speak of his meat as worthless. This way we cool his heart and make him gentle.

Source: Lee 1968:62.

gaged in by the native Americans who inhabit the Northwest Coast of the United States and Canada (Figure 7.6). In descriptions made famous by Ruth Benedict in *Patterns of Culture*, the Kwakiutl redistributor emerges as a virtual megalomaniac (see Box 7.3).

In the potlatch the guests continue to behave somewhat as Lee's !Kung do. They grumble and complain and are careful never to appear satisfied or impressed. Nonetheless, there has been a careful public counting of all the gifts displayed and distributed (Figure 7.7). Both hosts and guests believe that the only way to throw off the obligations incurred in accepting these gifts is to hold a counter potlatch in which the tables are reversed.

The Infrastructural Basis of Redistribution and Reciprocity

Why do the !Kung esteem hunters who never draw attention to their own generosity, whereas the Kwakiutl and other redistributor

Figure 7.6   *Kwakiutl of the northwest, ca. 1900.*
The signs over the doors read: "Boston. He is the Head chief of Arweete. He is true Indian. Honest. He don't owe no trouble to white man." and "Cheap. He is one of the head chief of all tribes in this country. White man can get information."

Box 7.3

BOASTFUL PROVIDERS

I am the great chief who makes people ashamed.
I am the great chief who makes people ashamed.

Our chief brings shame to the faces.
Our chief brings jealousy to the faces.
Our chief makes people cover their faces by
   what he is continually doing in this world.
Giving again and again, [fish] oil feasts to all
   the tribes.

I am the only great tree, I the chief!
I am the only great tree, I the chief!

You are my subordinates, tribes.
You sit in the middle of the rear of the house,
   tribes.

I am the first to give you property, tribes.
I am your Eagle, tribes!

Bring your counter of property, tribes, that he
   may try in vain to count the property that is
   to be given away by the great copper maker,
   the chief.

Source: Adapted from Boas, Ethnology of the Kwakiutl, 2 vols. *35th Annual Report of the Bureau of American Ethnology. Washington, D.C., 1921.*

Figure 7.7   Potlatch.
Spokesman for Kwakiutl chief making speech next to
blankets about to be given away.

societies esteem leaders who can boast about how much they give away? One theory is that reciprocity reflects an adjustment to modes of production in which intensification would rapidly lead to diminishing returns and environmental depletions. Hunters and gatherers seldom have an opportunity to intensify production without rapidly reaching the point of diminishing returns. Intensification poses a grave threat to such peoples in the form of faunal overkills. To encourage the !Kung hunter to be boastful is to endanger the group's survival. In addition, reciprocity is advantageous for most hunter-gatherers because there is a great deal of chance variation in the success of individuals and families from one day to the

next. As Richard Gould (1982:76) has observed: "The greater the degree of risk, the greater the extent of sharing."

Agricultural villages generally have greater leeway for increasing production by investing more labor. They can raise their standards of consumption if they work harder, and yet not immediately jeopardize their energy efficiency by depleting their habitats. And agriculture is usually a more dependable, less risky mode of production than hunting and gathering.

The Kwakiutl are not agriculturalists; they derived most of their food from the annual upriver runs of salmon and candlefish. But by using their aboriginal dip nets, the Kwakiutl and their neighbors could not affect the overall rate of reproduction of these species. Hence, their mode of production was highly intensifiable. Moreover, while there were fluctuations in the size of the annual migrations of these fish from one year to the next (Langdon 1979), there were few risks involved from day to day. Thus, it was ecologically feasible for the Kwakiutl to try to intensify production by using prestige and the privilege of boasting to reward those who worked harder or who got others to work harder (Isaac 1988; Mitchell and Donald 1988).

THE ORIGIN OF DESTRUCTIVE POTLATCHES

Potlatching came under scientific scrutiny long after the people of the Pacific Northwest had entered into trade and wage-labor relations with Russian, English, Canadian, and American nationals. Declining populations and a sudden influx of wealth had combined to make the potlatches increasingly competitive and destructive by the time Franz Boas began to study them in the 1880s (Rohner 1969). At this period the entire tribe was in residence at the Fort Rupert trading station of the Hudson's Bay Company, and the attempt on the part of one potlatch giver to outdo another had become an all-consuming passion. Blankets, boxes of fish oil, and other valuables were deliberately being destroyed by burning or by throwing them into the sea. On one occasion, described in *Patterns of Culture*, an entire house burned to the ground when too much fish oil was poured on the fire. Potlatches that ended in this fashion were regarded as great victories for the potlatch givers.

It seems likely that before the coming of the Europeans, Kwakiutl potlatch feasts were less destructive and more like Melanesian feasts (see page 196). Although rivalrous feasts are wasteful, the net increment in total production may exceed the loss due to gorging and spoilage. Moreover, after the visitors have eaten to their satisfaction, there still remains much food, which they carry back home with them.

The fact that guests come from distant villages leads to additional important ecological and economic advantages. It has been suggested that feasting rivalry between groups raises productivity throughout a region more than if each village feasts only its own producers. Second, as has been suggested for the Northwest Coast region, rivalrous intervillage redistributions may overcome the effects of localized, naturally induced production failures. Failure of the salmon runs at a particular stream could threaten the survival of certain villages, while neighbors on other streams continue to catch their usual quotas. Under such circumstances, the impoverished villagers would want to attend as many potlatches as they could and carry back as many vital supplies as they could get their host to part with by reminding them of how big their own pot-

latches had been in previous years. Intervillage potlatches thus may have been a form of savings in which the prestige acquired at one's own feast served as a tally. The tally was redeemed when the guests turned hosts. If a village was unable year after year to give its own potlatches, it lost its prestige credit (Piddocke 1965; Suttles 1960).

When an impoverished and unprestigious group could no longer hold its own potlatches, the people abandoned their defeated redistributor-chief and took up residence among relatives in more productive villages. Thus the boasting and the giving away and displaying of wealth led to the recruitment of additional labor power into the work force gathered about a particularly effective redistributor. This helps to explain why Northwest Coast peoples lavished so much effort on the production of their world-famous totem poles. These poles bore the redistributor-chief's "crests" in the guise of carved mythic figures; title to the crests was claimed on the basis of outstanding potlatch achievements. The larger the pole, the greater the potlatch power and the more the members of poor villages would be tempted to change their residence and gather around another chief.

With the coming of the Europeans, however, there was a shift toward more destructive forms of redistribution. The impact of European diseases reduced the population of the Kwakiutl from about 10,000 in 1836 to about 2,000 by the end of the century. At the same time, trading companies, canneries, lumber mills, and gold-mining camps pumped an unprecedented amount of wealth into the aboriginal economy. The percentage of people available to celebrate the glory of the potlatcher dropped. Many villages were abandoned; hence rivalry intensified for the allegiance of the survivors.

A final and perhaps the most important factor in the development of destructive potlatches was the change in the technology and intensity of warfare. The earliest contacts in the late eighteenth century between the Europeans and the native Americans of the Northwest Pacific Coast centered on the fur trade. In return for sea otter skins, the Europeans gave guns to the Kwakiutl and to the Kwakiutl's traditional enemies. This had a double effect. On the one hand, warfare became more deadly; and on the other, it forced local groups to fight one another for control of trade in order to get the ammunition on which success in warfare now depended. Small wonder, therefore, that as population declined, the potlatch chiefs were willing to throw away or destroy wealth that was militarily unimportant in order to attract manpower for warfare and fur trade (Ferguson 1984).

STRATIFIED REDISTRIBUTION

A subtle line separates egalitarian from stratified forms of redistribution. In the egalitarian form, contributions to the central pool are voluntary, and the workers either get back all or most of what they put into it or receive items of comparable value. In the stratified form, the workers must contribute to the central pool or suffer penalties, and they may not get back anything. Again, in the egalitarian form, the redistributor lacks the power to coerce followers into intensifying production and must depend on their goodwill; in the stratified form, the redistributor has that power and the workers must depend on that person's goodwill. The processes responsible for the evolution of one form of redistribution into another will be discussed in Chapter 11. Here, we will only note that fully developed forms of stratified redistribution imply the existence of a class of rulers who have the power to compel others to do their bidding. The expression of this power in the realm of production and exchange results in the economic subordination of the labor force and in its partial or total loss of control over access to natural resources and technology and over the place, time, and duration of work.

Price-Market Exchange: Buying and Selling

Marketplaces occur in rudimentary form wherever groups of nonkin and strangers assemble and trade one item for another. Among hunter-gatherers and simple agriculturalists, marketplace trading usually involves the barter of one valuable consumable item for another: fish for yams, coconuts for axes, and so forth. In this type of market, before the development of all-purpose money (see the next section), only a limited range of goods or services is exchanged. The great bulk of exchange transactions takes place outside the marketplace and continues to involve various forms of reciprocity and redistribution. With the development of all-purpose money, however, price-market exchanges come to dominate all other forms of exchange. In a price market, the price of the goods and services exchanged is determined by buyers competing with buyers and sellers competing with sellers. Virtually everything that is produced or consumed comes to have a price, and buying and selling becomes a major cultural preoccupation or even obsession (Figure 7.8).

It is possible to engage in reciprocal exchange using money, as when a friend gives a loan and does not specify when it must be repaid. Redistributive exchange can be carried

Figure 7.8   Hunting and gatherng in a price-market economy.

out with money, as in the collection of taxes and the disbursement of welfare payments. Buying and selling on a price market, however, is a distinctive mode of exchange, since it involves the specification of the precise time, quantity, and type of payment. Furthermore, unlike either reciprocity or redistribution, once the money payment is concluded, no further obligation or responsibility exists between buyer and seller. They can walk away from each other and never meet again. Price-market exchanges, therefore, are noteworthy for the anonymity and impersonality of the exchange process, and stand in contrast to the personal and kin-based exchanges of reciprocal and redistributive economies. Now let us take a closer look at the nature of that strange entity we call money.

MONEY

The idea and practice of endowing a material object with the capacity of measuring the social value of other material objects, animals, people, and labor occurs almost universally. Such standard-of-value "stuffs" are widely exchanged for goods and services. Throughout much of Africa, for example, a young man gives cattle to his father-in-law and gets a wife in return (see page 145). In many parts of Melanesia, shells are exchanged for stone implements, pottery, and other valuable artifacts. Elsewhere, beads, feathers, shark teeth, dog teeth, or pig tusks are exchanged for other valuable items and are given as compensation for death or injury and for personal services rendered by magicians, canoe builders, and other specialists. With rare exceptions, however, these "money stuffs" lack some of the major characteristics of the money stuffs found in price-market economies. In price-market economies money is commercial or market money, an all-purpose medium of exchange. It has the following features:

1. **Portability.** It comes in sizes and shapes convenient for being carried about from one transaction to the next.

2. **Divisibility.** Its various forms and values are explicit multiples of each other.

3. **Convertibility.** A transaction completed by a higher-valued unit can be made as well by its lower-valued multiples.

4. **Generality.** Virtually all goods and services have a money value.

5. **Anonymity.** For most purchases, anyone with the market price can conclude a transaction.

6. **Legality.** The nature and quantity of money in circulation is controlled by a government.

Although special-purpose valuables may have some of these features, only all-purpose money has every one of them. Where reciprocity, egalitarian redistribution, and trade-partner relations are the dominant modes of exchange, money in the modern dollar sense does not and cannot exist.

For example, cattle that are exchanged for wives are not the kind of currency you would want to take to the supermarket checkout counter, being neither very portable nor readily divisible. As employed in *bride-price* (see page 145), cattle are frequently not convertible; that is, a large, beautiful, fat bull with a local reputation cannot readily be substituted for by two small but undistinguished animals. Furthermore, cattle lack generality, since only wives can be "purchased" with them, and they lack anonymity because any stranger who shows up with the right amount of cattle will find that he cannot simply take the woman and leave the cattle. Cattle are exchanged for women only between kinship groups who have an interest in establishing or reinforcing pre-existing social relationships. Finally, cattle are put into circulation by each individual household as a result of productive effort that is unregulated by any central authority.

In other instances, special-purpose money stuff bears a greater resemblance to all-purpose money. For example, the inhabitants of Rossell Island, which lies off the east coast of New Guinea, use a type of shell money that has sometimes been confused with all-purpose money.

The shells have portability and they occur in some forty named units that rise from low to medium to high value. Shells of low value can be used to purchase food, pottery, tools, and other ordinary goods. But these shells cannot be used for the important exchanges that occur at pig redistributions, weddings, and funerals.

In order for these exchanges to take place, "payment" has to be made with the higher-ranking shells. The most valuable shells are owned and traded by "big men" (see page 195). No amount of low-value shells could buy a high-ranking one. Moreover, the high-ranking shells do not circulate. Instead, their owners take them back after the pig feast, marriage, or funeral and substitute a number of lower-ranking shells whose value is roughly commensurate with that of the higher-ranking shells. While each higher-ranking shell is divisible in the sense of having a value that can be expressed in terms of lower-ranking shells, the lower-ranking shells are not acceptable for important exchanges unless they are backed or validated by a "big man's" high-value shells (Lick 1983:511).

CAPITALISM

Price-market exchange reaches its highest development when it is embedded in the form of political economy known as capitalism. In capitalist societies, buying and selling by means of all-purpose money extends to land, resources, and housing. Labor has a price called wages, and money itself has a price called interest (*Polanyi*). Of course, there is no such thing as a completely free market in which price is set wholly by supply and demand and in which everything can be sold. By comparison with other forms of political economy, however, capitalism is aptly described as a political economy in which money can buy anything. This being so, everyone tries to acquire as much money as possible, and the object of production itself is not merely to provide valuable goods and services but to increase one's possession of money—that is, to make a profit and accumulate capital (Figure 7.9). The rate of cap-

Figure 7.9   Tokyo stock exchange.

italist production depends on the rate at which profits can be made, and this in turn depends on the rate at which people purchase, use, wear out, and destroy goods and services. Hence, an enormous effort is expended on extolling the virtues and benefits of products in order to convince consumers that they should make additional purchases. Prestige is awarded not to the person who works hardest or gives away the greatest amount of wealth, but rather to the person who has the most possessions and who consumes at the highest rate.

In theory, socialist and communist political economies are supposed to replace price-market consumerism and the capitalist money obsession with egalitarian forms of redistribution and reciprocal exchanges. All contemporary socialist societies, however, operate with price-market money economies, and many of them are as possession-oriented as capitalist societies. It is also questionable whether any of them has achieved the classlessness that is the

prerequisite for truly egalitarian forms of redistribution (see Chapter 12).

Capitalism inevitably leads to marked inequalities in wealth based on differential ownership or control over resources and the infrastructure of production. As in all stratified economies, the rich use political means to keep the poor from confiscating their wealth and privileges. Some anthropologists, however, see many of the features of capitalism present in societies that lack state-administered laws and police-military means of control. Let us turn, therefore, to the question of the extent to which capitalism is foreshadowed in band and village societies.

"PRIMITIVE CAPITALISM"?
THE KAPAUKU CASE

There is no doubt that, in general, band and village societies lack the essential features of capitalism because, as we have seen, their exchange systems are based on reciprocal and redistributive exchanges rather than on price-market exchanges. In some cases, however, egalitarian reciprocal and redistributive systems may have certain features strongly reminiscent of contemporary capitalism.

The Kapauku Papuans of West Irian, Indonesia, are a case in point (see Figure 7.3). According to Leopold Pospisil (1963), the Kapauku have an economy that is best described as "primitive capitalism." All Kapauku agricultural land is said to be owned individually; money sales are the regular means of exchange; money, in the form of shells and glass beads, can be used to buy food, domesticated animals, crops, and land; money can also be used as payment for labor. Rent (see next page) for leased land and interest on loans are also said to occur.

A closer look at the land tenure situation, however, reveals fundamental differences between the political economy of Kapauku and capitalist peasant societies (see page 223). To begin with, there is no landowning class. Instead, access to land is controlled by kinship groups known as *sublineages* (see page 160). No individual is without membership in such a group. These sublineages control communal tracts of land, which Pospisil calls "territories."

It is only within sublineage territories that one may speak of private titles, and the economic significance of these titles is minimal on several counts. (1) The price of land is so low that all the gardens under production have a market value in shell money less than the value of ten female pigs. (2) Prohibition against trespass does not apply to sublineage kin. (3) Although even brothers will ask each other for land payments, credit is freely extended among all sublineage members. The most common form of credit with respect to land consists

merely of giving land on loan, and in expectation that the favor will shortly be returned. (4) Each sublineage is under the leadership of a *headman* (see Chapter 10) whose authority depends on his generosity, especially toward the members of his own sublineage. A rich headman does not refuse to lend his kinsmen whatever they need to gain access to the environment, since "a selfish individual who hoards money and fails to be generous, never sees the time when his word is taken seriously and his advice and decisions followed, no matter how rich he may become" (Pospisil 1963:49).

Obviously, therefore, the wealth of the headman does not bestow the power associated with capitalist ownership. In Brazil or India, tenants or sharecroppers can be barred from access to land and water regardless of their landlord's "reputation." In the United States, under the rules of capitalist landownership, it is of no significance to the sheriff and the police officers when they evict farmers that the bank is being "selfish."

Pospisil states that differences in wealth are correlated with striking differences in consumption of food and that Kapauku children from poor homes are undernourished while neighbors are well fed. However, the neighbors are not members of the same sublineage: As Pospisil notes, sublineage kinsmen "exhibit mutual affection and a strong sense of belonging and unity" and "any kind of friction within the group is regarded as deplorable" (1963:39). It is true that certain sublineages are poorer than others. Sickness and misfortune of various sorts frequently lead to inequalities in physical well-being among the kinship units, but such misfortunes do not lead to the formation of a poverty class as they do under capitalism. Without central political controls, marked economic inequalities cannot be perpetuated for long, because the rich cannot defend themselves against the demand of the poor that they be given credit, money, land, or whatever is necessary to end their poverty. Under aboriginal conditions, some Kapauku villagers might have starved while neighbors ate well, but it is extremely unlikely that those who starved did so because they lacked access to land, money, or credit.

A stingy egalitarian redistributor is a contradiction in terms, for the simple reason that there are no police to protect such people from the murderous intentions of those whom they refuse to help. As Pospisil tells it:

> Selfish and greedy individuals, who have amassed huge personal properties, but who have failed to comply with the Kapauku requirement of "generosity" toward their less fortunate tribesmen may be, and actually frequently are, put to death. . . . Even in regions such as the Kamu Valley, where such an execution is not a penalty for greediness, a nongenerous wealthy man is ostracized, reprimanded, and thereby finally induced to change his ways. [1963:49]

Landownership

Ownership of land and resources is one of the most important aspects of political control. It is as much political as economic because unequal access to the environment implies some form of coercion applied by political superiors against political inferiors.

As we have just seen, certain forms of land and resource ownership do occur in egalitarian societies. Ownership of garden lands, for example, is often claimed by kin groups in village communities, but everybody belongs to such kin groups, and hence adults cannot be pre-

vented from using the resources they need to make a living. Landownership by landlords, rulers, or the government, however, means that individuals who lack title or tenure may be barred from using land even if it leads to death through starvation.

As we will see in Chapter 11, ownership of land and resources results from infrastructural processes that select for more dense and more productive populations. Landownership is a stimulus to production because it forces food producers to work longer and harder than they would if they had free access to resources. Landownership raises production mainly through the extraction of rent from the food producers. *Rent* is a payment in kind or in money for the opportunity to live or work on the owner's land. This payment automatically compels tenants to increase their work input. By raising or lowering rents, the landlord exercises a fairly direct measure of control over work input and production.

Because the extraction of rent is evolutionarily associated with an increase in food production, some anthropologists regard the payment of rent as indicative of the existence of *surplus* food—an amount greater than what is needed for immediate consumption by the producers. But it is important to note that the "surplus" food the landowner takes away as rent need not be a *superfluous* quantity from the producers' standpoint. The producers usually can very well use the full amount of their output to ease the costs of rearing children or to raise their own standard of living. If they surrender their produce, it is usually because they lack the power to withhold it. In this sense, all rent is an aspect of politics, because without the power to enforce property titles, rent would seldom be paid. Thus, there is a close resemblance between rent and taxation: Both depend on the existence of coercive power in the form of police and weapons that can be called into action if the taxpayer or tenant refuses to pay.

In certain highly centralized societies, as in the ancient Inca Empire (see page 206), there is no distinction between rent and taxes, since there is no landlord class. Instead, the government bureaucracy has a monopoly over the means of extracting wealth from commoner food producers. States and empires also exercise direct control over production by setting regional or community quotas for particular crops and by conscripting armies of commoners to work on construction projects. Compulsory labor conscription, known as *corvée*, is merely another form of taxation. As we will see in Chapter 11, all these coercive forms of extracting wealth from food producers probably arose from egalitarian forms of redistribution as a consequence of intensification and population pressure.

The Division of Labor

One of the most important organizational features of every economy is the assignment of different tasks to different people. This is called the *division of labor*. All economies, for example, assign different kinds of work to children and adults and to males and females. In most hunting and simple agricultural economies, men hunt large animals, fish, collect honey, and burn and clear forests. Women and children collect shellfish, plants, and small animals; they weed, harvest, and process grains and tubers. Men do most of the craft work in stone, wood, and metals; women spin fibers, weave cloth, and make pottery and baskets. In more advanced economies, men usually do the plowing and the herding of large animals. In almost all societies women do most of the cooking of plant foods, water carrying, cleaning, and other household chores, plus taking care of infants and small children. In general, in preindustrial societies, men perform the activities that require greater muscular effort and freedom of movement (Burton and White 1987; Murdock and Provost 1973).

It seems likely that the division between male and female tasks in hunter-gatherer and simple agricultural economies adds to the efficiency of food production. Because of their heavier musculature, men can bend stronger bows, hurl spears further, and wield bigger clubs (see page 252). Training men rather than women in the use of these weapons has another advantage: Since the weapons of war are essentially the weapons of the hunt, investment in the training of men to be hunters simultaneously trains them to be warriors. Women are seldom trained to be warriors (see page 252). It is consistent with this pattern, therefore, that men also specialize in craft production involving stone, metal, and wood, since these are the materials out of which the weapons of war and the hunt are fashioned (Murdock and Provost 1973).

While the muscle-strength differences between men and women can be reduced by training, the remaining advantage for males—20 to 30 percent—is sufficient to make the difference between life and death in certain kinds of economies. In India, for example, every ounce of human muscle power is needed to carry out plowing operations with oxen and crude plows. Males carry out the most physically demanding tasks not to keep women down but to keep production up (Maclachlan 1983).

The impact of various forms of the sexual division of labor on sex and gender roles will be discussed in Chapter 13. Little of this explanation applies to the sexual division of labor in industrial societies, where the use of machines cancels out most of the muscular advantage that men have over women (see page 252).

One of the most pronounced trends in cultural evolution is the increasing amount of specialization that accompanies the expansion of production and the growth of population. In hunter-gatherer and other small-scale societies, virtually every adult male does the same kind of work and virtually every adult female does the same kind of work. As per capita production increases, more and more adults become craft specialists, first part time, then full time. Concomitant with the rise of the state, substantial numbers of people cease to work directly in food production but devote themselves full time to such crafts as pottery, weaving, metallurgy, canoe building, and trading. Others become scribes, priests, rulers, warriors, and servants. The tendency toward increasing specialization is even stronger in industrial societies. The U.S. Bureau of Labor Statistics, for example, keeps track of 80,000 different kinds of jobs. Clearly the process of specialization depends on high rates of production and reproduction. Of course, specialization itself increases the efficiency of production, but it cannot do so unless the basic mode of energy production is capable of being intensified. Only advanced forms of agriculture can support an economy organized around full-time specialists.

Patterns of Work

The flip side of the lack of specialization in hunter-gatherer and simple agricultural societies is that each adult performs many different tasks from day to day, in contrast to the standardized routines of factory or office em-

ployees. Moreover, the decision to switch from one task to another — from setting traps to making arrows or collecting honey, for example — is largely voluntary and arrived at either individually or by group consensus. It would probably be correct, therefore, to say that people in small-scale prestate societies did not experience work as a tedious aspect of life. Indeed, recent experimental reforms of factory work patterns are designed to let workers do many jobs instead of just one and to include them in "quality circles" that make decisions about how tasks are performed. These experiments represent attempts to recapture some of the enviable characteristics of work in small-scale, unspecialized economies.

In societies with hunter-gatherers and simple agricultural infrastructures, people do not spend as much time at work as in intensive agriculture societies. The !Kung San, for example, put in an average of only about 20 hours per week in hunting. The basic reason for this is that their mode of production is not intensifiable. If they worked more hours per week, they would not only find it progressively more difficult to capture their prey, but they would run the risk of depleting the animal population below the point of recovery. In a sense, the !Kung San benefit from being at the mercy of the natural rates of increase of the plants and animals in their habitat; their mode of production obliges them to work less than intensive agriculturalists or modern factory workers.

In Table 7.1 the amount of time spent on work among the !Kung is compared with that in two other societies — the Machiguenga, slash-and-burn agriculturalists of the eastern Andes in Peru and Kali Loro, an irrigation rice-growing peasant village of Java. The average work time is considerably greater for both sexes in Kali Loro, the society that has the most advanced technology. The basic reason for this

Table 7.1
HOURS OF WORK PER DAY

	!KUNG		MACHIGUENGA		KALI LORO	
	MEN	WOMEN	MEN	WOMEN	MEN	WOMEN
Food production and preparation	3.09	1.80	4.60	4.20	5.49	4.70
Crafts	1.07	0.73	1.40	2.10	0.50	2.32
Trade/wage work	0.00	0.00	1.60	0.00	1.88	1.88
Housework/child care	2.20	3.20	0.00	1.10	0.50	2.07
Total	6.36	5.73	7.60	7.40	8.37	10.97

Sources: Carlstein 1983; Johnson 1975; Lee 1979; White 1976.

Figure 7.10 Machiguenga at work.
As in most slash-and-burn economies, Machiguenga men do the heavy work of felling trees and clearing the forest for new plantings. Here, a Machiguenga uses the felled trees to build a house.

is that, as previously discussed, irrigation agriculture is highly intensifiable (page 83). In addition, Kali Loro is part of a stratified state society, in which there are political and economic controls such as taxation, rent, and price markets, which compel or induce people to work more hours than would be necessary if they could keep for their own use all the goods and services they produce.

Work occupies an ever-greater part of daily life among industrial wage earners. To the basic eight-hour day, add one hour for commuting, a half-hour for shopping for food and other items (including transportation), a half-hour for cooking, a half-hour for housework and repairs, and a half-hour for child care (including transportation of children and babysitters). These are minimal estimates; for many modern-day Americans, the time devoted to any activity could be doubled. (See Gross 1984 for a comprehensive review of time allocation studies.) The total—11 hours—is on a par with the work time of the Javanese peasant women. True, this schedule is kept only on workdays, but on the weekend, the time devoted to all the other forms of work greatly

Figure 7.11   Labor-saving devices that don't save work.
The first assembly line. Ford's Highland Park, Michigan, magneto assembly line saved 15 minutes per unit and initiated the era of mass production in 1913. But the workers worked harder than ever.

increases, and many people have second jobs, as well. When politicians boast about how much progress has been made in obtaining leisure for the working class, they have in mind the standard established in nineteenth-century Europe, when factory workers put in 12 hours a day or more, rather than the standards observed by the Machiguenga or the !Kung (Figures 7.10, 7.11, and 7.12).

Figure 7.12   All work and no play in a Japanese camera factory.
Workers get 10 minutes per day for exercise and 10 minutes per day for a "tea break."

Summary

All cultures have an economy—a set of institutions that combines technology, labor, and natural resources to produce and distribute goods and services. The organizational aspects of economy are distinguished from its infrastructural aspects in order to explore the relationship between infrastructure and structure. Modes of exchange, for example, express different degrees of intensifiability and population growth.

Exchange is an integral part of all economies, but there are several different ways of organizing the flow of goods and services from producers to consumers.

Modern-day price markets and buying and selling are not universal traits. The idea that money can buy everything (or almost everything) has been alien to most of the human beings who have ever lived. Two other modes of exchange—reciprocity and redistribution—once played a more important economic role than price markets.

In reciprocal exchange, the time and quantity of the counterflow is not specified. This kind of exchange can be effective only when it is embedded in kinship or close personal relationships. Daily food distribution among the !Kung San is an example of reciprocal exchange. Control over the counterflow in reciprocal exchange is achieved by communal pressure against freeloaders and shirkers. Reciprocity lingers on in price-market societies within kinship groups and is familiar to many of us as gift-giving to relatives and friends.

In the absence of price markets and police-military supervision, trade poses a special problem to people accustomed to reciprocal exchange. Silent barter is one solution. Another is to create trading partners who treat each other as kin. The Kula is a classic example of how barter for necessities is carried out under the cloak of reciprocal exchanges.

Redistributive exchange involves the collection of goods in a central place and its disbursement by a redistributor to the producers. In the transition from egalitarian to stratified forms of redistribution, production and exchange cross the line separating voluntary from coerced forms of economic behavior. In the egalitarian form of redistribution, the redistributor depends on the goodwill of the producers; in the stratified form, the producers depend on the goodwill of the redistributor. Redistribution is characterized by the counting of shares contributed and shares disbursed. Unlike reciprocity, redistribution leads to boasting and overt competition for the prestigious status of great provider. The Kwakiutl potlatch is a classic example of the relationships between redistribution and bragging behavior. The predominance of redistribution over reciprocity is related to the intensifiability of various modes of production. Where production can be intensified without depletions, rivalrous redistributions may serve adaptive ecological functions, such as providing an extra margin of safety in lean years and equalizing regional production. The development of destructive potlatches among the Kwakiutl may have been caused by factors stemming from contact with Europeans, such as the intensification of warfare, trade for guns and ammunition, and depopulation.

Price-market exchange depends on the development of all-purpose money as defined by the criteria of portability, divisibility, convertibility, generality, anonymity, and legality. Although some of these features are possessed by limited-purpose standards of value, as in the case of Rossell Island shell money, all-purpose money and price markets imply the existence of state forms of control.

The highest development of the price-market mode of exchange is associated with the political economy of capitalism, in which virtually all goods and services can be bought and sold. Since capitalist production depends on consumerism, prestige is awarded to those who own or consume the greatest amount of goods and services. Price-market exchanges are embedded in a political economy of control made necessary by the inequalities in access to resources and the conflict between the poor and the wealthy. The Kapauku illustrate why price-market institutions and capitalism cannot exist in the absence of such controls.

The relationship between political forms of control and modes of production and exchange focuses in many societies on the question of landownership. Rent, corvée labor, and taxation all reflect differential access to nature and technology. Thus we see why the comparative study of economics must involve the study of the institutions in which economizing is embedded.

The division of labor is a hallmark of human social life. Sex and age are universally used to assign different economic tasks. In preindustrial societies, men carry out activities that require greater strength. Their monopoly over the weapons of the hunt is also probably related to their role as combatants in warfare. Women in preindustrial societies specialize in tasks centered on food gathering and child care. The infrastructural basis for this widespread sexual division of labor, however, ceases to exist in industrial societies.

Changes in infrastructure—higher energy outputs and bigger populations—are also responsible for changes in the numbers of full-time specialists in advanced agricultural and industrial economies as compared with hunter-gatherers and simple agriculturalists. Parallel with an increase in specialization, work becomes less voluntary, less spontaneous, and more coerced and routinized. Paradoxically, despite the greater amounts of energy harnessed per capita per year, most advanced agriculturalists and factory and office workers labor longer hours than people like the !Kung or the Machiguenga.

Chapter 8

DOMESTIC LIFE

In this chapter we continue the comparative study of the structural parts of sociocultural systems and examine the major forms of domestic groups. We will inquire whether all domestic groups are built up from a single form of family and whether there is a genetic basis for the exchanges of personnel that link domestic groups together. This chapter is primarily descriptive, but some theoretical explanations that are treated more fully in later chapters are discussed here in a preliminary way. We must know the extent of variation in domestic groups before we can tackle the problem of explaining why some varieties occur in one culture and not in another.

Domestic Life

All societies have activities and thoughts that can usefully be lumped under the category of the domestic sphere of life. The focus of the domestic sphere is a dwelling space, shelter, residence, or domicile, in which certain universally recurrent activities take place. It is not possible to give a simple checklist of what these activities are. In many cultures, domestic activities include preparation and consumption of food; cleaning, grooming, and disciplining the young; sleeping; and adult sexual intercourse. However, there is no culture in which these activities are carried out exclusively within domestic settings. For example, sexual intercourse among band and village peoples more often takes place in the bush or forest than in the house where sleeping occurs. In other instances, sleeping itself takes place primarily away from the setting in which eating occurs, and in still other instances, domiciles may lack resident children, as when childless adults live alone or when children are sent off to school. The combinations of activities that character-ize human domestic life are so varied that it is difficult to find any single underlying common denominator for all of them. This in itself, however, is an important fact, since no other species exhibits such an enormous range of different behaviors associated with patterns of eating, shelter, sleep, sex, and rearing of infants and children.

The Nuclear Family

Can a particular kind of group be found in all domestic settings? Many anthropologists believe there is such a group, and refer to it as the *nuclear family*: husband, wife, and children (Figure 8.1). Ralph Linton held the view that father, mother, child are the "bedrock underlying all other family structures," and he predicted that "the last man will spend his last hours searching for his wife and child" (1959:52). George Peter Murdock found the nuclear family in each of 250 societies. He concluded that it was universal. According to Murdock (1949), the nuclear family fulfills vital

Figure 8.1 Japanese nuclear families.
All dressed up for a day at a shrine in the Meiji
area of Tokyo.

tive role, and given the anatomical and physiological differences between men and women, the sexual division of labor makes subsistence more efficient.

The nuclear family thus provides for heterosexual sex, reproduction, enculturation, and economic support more effectively than any other institution, according to this view.

It is important to investigate the validity of these claims at some length. The idea that the nuclear family is universal or nearly universal lends support to the view that nonnuclear family domestic units are inferior, pathological, or contrary to human nature. In actuality, however, no one knows the limits within which human domestic arrangements must be confined in order to satisfy human nature and effectively carry out some or all of the four functions listed above.

functions that cannot be carried out as efficiently by other groups. The functions identified by Murdock are (1) sex, (2) reproduction, (3) education, and (4) subsistence.

1. The nuclear family satisfies sexual needs and diminishes the disruptive force of sexual competition.
2. The nuclear family guarantees the protection of the female during her long pregnancy and during the months and years of lactation.
3. The nuclear family is essential for enculturation. Only the coresident adult man and woman possess knowledge adequate for the enculturation of children of both sexes.
4. Given the behavioral specialties imposed on the human female by her reproduc-

Alternatives to the Nuclear Family

Even though nuclear families can be found in the overwhelming majority of human cultures, it has long been obvious that every culture has alternative forms of domestic organization and that these frequently are more important, involving a higher proportion of the population, than the nuclear family. Moreover, the four functions listed above, as already suggested, can readily be carried out in the context of alternative institutions that may lie entirely outside the domestic sphere.

In the case of the nuclear family in modern industrial cultures, this is evident with respect to enculturation and education. Enculturation and education in contemporary life are increasingly carried out in special nondomestic buildings — schools — under the auspices of nonkinspeople — teachers.

Many village and band societies also separate their children and adolescents from the nuclear family and the entire domestic scene in order to teach them the lore and ritual of the ancestors, sexual competence, or the military arts. Among the Nyakyusa of southern Tanzania, for example, 6- or 7-year-old boys begin to put up reed shelters or playhouses on the outskirts of their village. These playhouses are gradually improved upon and enlarged, eventually leading to the construction of a whole new village. Between the ages of 5 and 11, Nyakyusa boys sleep in their parents' house, but during adolescence they are permitted to visit only during daylight hours. Sleeping now takes place in the new village, although the mother still does the cooking. The founding of a new village is complete when the young men take

wives who cook for them and begin to give birth to the next generation (Wilson 1963).

Another famous variation on this pattern is found among the Masai of East Africa, where unmarried men of the same *age-set*, or ritually defined generation, establish special villages or camps from which they launch war parties and cattle-stealing raids. It is the mothers and sisters of these men who cook and keep house for them (Figure 8.2).

The common English upper-class practice of sending sons aged 6 or older to boarding schools should also be noted. Like the Masai, the English aristocracy refused to let the burden of maintaining the continuity of their society rest on the educational resources of the nuclear household.

In many societies, married men spend a good deal of time in special *men's houses*. Food is handed in to them by wives and children,

Figure 8.2   Masai age-set.
Masai warriors look fierce during an initiation ceremony.

who are themselves forbidden to enter. Men also sleep and work in these "clubhouses," although they may on occasion bed down with their wives and children.

Among the Fur of the Sudan, husbands usually sleep apart from their wives in houses of their own and take their meals at an exclusive men's mess. One of the most interesting cases of the separation of cooking and eating occurs among the Ashanti of West Africa. Ashanti men eat their meals with their sisters, mothers, and maternal nephews and nieces, not with their wives and children. But it is the wives who do the cooking. Every evening in

Ashanti land there is a steady traffic of children taking their mother's cooking to their father's sister's house (see Barnes 1960; Bender 1967).

Finally, there is at least one famous case — the Nayar of Kerala — in which "husband" and "wife" do not live together at all. Many Nayar women "married" ritual husbands and then stayed with their brothers and sisters (Figure 8.3). Their mates were men who visited overnight. Children born of these matings were brought up in households dominated by their mother's brother and never knew their father. We will return in a moment for a closer look at the Nayar.

(a)

Figure 8.3   Nayar of Kerala.
(a) *Nayar villagers along the Kerala waterways.* (b) *Nayar women beating the outer shells of coconuts. The softened fibers will be woven into mats.*

(b)

Polygamy and the Nuclear Family

Next we must consider whether the combination father-mother-child has the same functional significance where either father or mother is married to and is living with more than one spouse at a time. This is an important question because plural marriage — *polygamy* — occurs to some extent in at least 90 percent of all cultures (see Box 8.1).

In one form, called *polygyny* (Figure 8.4), a husband is shared by several wives; in another, much less common form called *polyandry* (Figure 8.5), a wife is shared by several husbands. Is there a nuclear family when there are plural husbands or wives? G. P. Murdock suggested that nuclear families do exist in such situations. The man or woman simply belongs to more than one nuclear family at a time. But this overlooks the fact that plural marriages create domestic situations that are behaviorally and mentally very different from those created by *monogamous* (one husband, one wife) marriages.

Polygamous sexual arrangements, for example, are obviously quite different from those characteristic of monogamous marriages. The mode of reproduction is also different, especially with polygyny, because the spacing of births is easier to control when husbands have several wives. Also, distinctive patterns of nursing and infant care arise when the mother sleeps alone with her children while the father sleeps with a different wife each night (see page 271). From the perspective of child rearing, there are special psychological effects associated with a father who divides his time among several mothers and who relates to his children through a hierarchy of wives. The monogamous U.S. or Canadian nuclear family places the focus of adult attention on a small group of full siblings. In a polygynous household, a dozen or more half-siblings must share the affection of the same man. Furthermore, the presence of co-wives or co-husbands changes the burden of child care a particular parent must bear. For example, industrial-age parents are troubled by the question of what to do with children when both parents go to work or visit friends. Polygynous families, however, have a built-in solution to the baby-sitting problem in the form of co-wives.

Turning finally to economic functions, the minimal polygamous economic unit often consists of the entire coresident production team and not each separate husband-wife pair. Domestic tasks — nursing, grooming, cleaning, fetching water, cooking, and so on — often cannot be satisfactorily performed by a single wife. In polygynous societies, one of the main motivations for marrying a second wife is to

Box 8.1

PRINCIPAL FORMS OF HUMAN MARRIAGE

Monogamy Marriage with one spouse exclusively and for life.

Serial Monogamy Marriage with one spouse at a time but with remarriage after death or divorce.

Polygamy Marriage with more than one spouse at a time.

Polygyny Marriage with more than one wife at a time.

Polyandry Marriage with more than one husband at a time.

Figure 8.4 Polygyny.
(a) Polygynous household, Senegal. Islamic law permits this man to take one more wife to fill his quota of four, providing he can take good care of her. (b) Sitting Bull. This famous Sioux chief is shown with two of his wives and three of his children. Polygyny was widespread among native American peoples. The photo was taken in 1882 at Fort Randall, South Dakota.

(a)

(b)

Figure 8.5 Polyandry. This Tibetan woman (wearing the veil) is being married to the two men on the left, who are brothers.

spread the work load and increase domestic output. It seems inappropriate, therefore, to equate nuclear families in monogamous households with husband-wife-child units in polygamous households.

The Extended Family

In a significant proportion of the societies studied by anthropologists, domestic life is dominated by groupings larger than simple nuclear or polygamous families. Probably the majority of existing cultures still carry on their domestic routines in the context of some form of *extended family* — that is, a domestic group consisting of siblings, their spouses and their children, and/or parents and married children (Figure 8.6). Extended families may also be polygynous. A common form of extended family in Africa, for example, consists of two or more brothers, each with two or three wives, living with their adult sons, each of whom has one or two wives. Among the Bathonga of southern Mozambique, domestic life fell under the control of the senior males of the polygynous ex-

tended family's senior generation. These prestigious and powerful men in effect formed a board of directors of a family-style corporation. They were responsible for making decisions about the domestic group's holdings in land, cattle, and buildings; they organized the subsistence effort of the coresident labor force, especially of the women and children, by assigning fields, crops, and seasonal work tasks. They tried to increase the size of their cattle herds and supplies of food and beer, obtain more wives, and increase the size and strength of the entire unit. The younger brothers, sons, and grandsons in the Bathonga extended families could reach adulthood, marry, build a hut, carry out subsistence tasks, and have children only as members of the larger group, subject to the policies and priorities established by the senior males (Junod 1912). Within the Bathonga extended family households, there really was no unit equivalent to a nuclear family, and this is true of extended families in many other cultures, whether they are monogamous or polygamous.

In traditional Chinese extended families, for example, marriage is usually monogamous

Figure 8.6   Extended family, United States.
The demand for labor was high on this Minnesota farm in 1895.

(Figure 8.7). A senior couple manages the domestic labor force and arranges marriages. Women brought into the household as wives for the senior couple's sons are placed under the direct control of their mother-in-law. She supervises their cleaning, cooking, and raising of children. Where there are several daughters-in-law, cooking chores are often rotated, so that on any given day a maximum contingent of the domestic labor force can be sent to work in the family's fields (Cohen 1976). The degree to which the nuclear family is submerged and effaced by these arrangements is brought out by a custom formerly found in certain Taiwanese households: "Adopt a daughter; marry a sister." In order to obtain control over their son's wife, the senior couple adopts a daughter. They bring this girl into the household at a very early age and train her to be hard-working and obedient. Later they oblige their son to marry this stepsister, thereby preventing the formation of an economically independent nuclear family within their midst, while at the same time conforming to the socially imposed incest prohibitions (Wolf 1968).

Among the Rajputs of northern India, extended families take similar stern measures to maintain the subordination of each married pair. A young man and his wife are even forbidden to talk to each other in the presence of senior persons, meaning in effect that they "may converse only surreptitiously at night" (Minturn and Hitchcock 1963:241). Here the husband is not supposed to show an open concern for his wife's welfare; if she is ill, that is a matter for her mother-in-law or father-in-law to take care of: "The mother feeds her son even after he is married . . . [and] runs the family as long as she wishes to assume the responsibility."

As a final brief example of how extended families modify the nuclear family relations,

Figure 8.7 Taiwan marriage.
Groom's extended family assembled for wedding ceremony.

there is Max Gluckman's (1955:60) wry comment on the Barotse of Zambia: "If a man becomes too devoted to his wife he is assumed to be the victim of witchcraft."

Why do so many societies have extended families? Probably because nuclear families frequently lack sufficient manpower and womanpower to carry out both domestic and subsistence tasks effectively. Extended families provide a larger labor pool and can carry out a greater variety of simultaneous activities (Pasternak et al. 1976).

One-Parent Domestic Groups

Millions of children throughout the world are reared in domestic groups in which only one parent is present. This may result from divorce or death of one of the parents, but it also may result from inability or unwillingness to marry. The most common form of nonnuclear one-parent domestic arrangement is for the mother to be present and the father to be absent. Such households are called *matrifocal*. The mother accepts a series of men as mates, usually one at a time, but sometimes polyandrously. The man and woman are usually coresident for brief periods, but over the years there may be long intervals during which the mother does not have a resident mate.

At one extreme, associated with very rich or very poor women, mother and children may live alone. At the other extreme, mother and her children may live together with her sisters and her mother and constitute a large extended family in which adult males play only temporary roles as visitors or lovers.

Matrifocal households are best known from studies carried out in the West Indies (Blake 1961; M. G. Smith 1966; R. T. Smith 1973), in Latin America (Adams 1968; Lewis 1961, 1964), and among U.S. inner-city blacks (Furstenberg et al. 1975; Gonzalez 1970; Stack 1974; N. Tanner 1974). However, the worldwide incidence of matrifocality has been obscured by the tendency to regard such domestic units as aberrant or pathological (Moynihan 1965). In describing domestic groups, social scientists frequently concentrate on the emically preferred form and neglect etic and behavioral actualities. Mother-child domestic groups often result from poverty and hence are associated with many social ills and are regarded as undesirable, but there is no evidence that such domestic arrangements are inherently any more or less pathological, unstable, or contrary to "human nature" than the nuclear family.

Matrifocal extended family households shade imperceptibly into matrilocal extended family households. Among the matrilocal Nayar, for example, mother's mates never resided with mother and children (see Figure 8.3). Moreover, unlike matrifocal households, Nayar households contained several generations of males related through females. It was one of the senior males — that is, a mother's brother — who was the head of the household, not a grandmother, as in the case of the extended matrifocal family.

What Is Marriage?

One of the problems with the proposition that the nuclear family is the basic building block of all domestic groups is that it rests on the assumption that widely different forms of mat-

ings can all be called "marriage." Yet in order to cover the extraordinary diversity of mating behavior characteristic of the human species, the definition of marriage has to be made so broad as to be confusing. Among the many ingenious attempts to define marriage as a universally occurring relationship, the definition proposed by Kathleen Gough, who has studied among the Nayar, merits special attention. But it must be read more than once!

> Marriage is a relationship established between a woman and one or more persons, which provides that a child born to the woman under circumstances not prohibited by the rules of the relationship, is accorded full birth-status rights common to normal members of his [or her] society or social stratum. [1968:68]

According to Gough, for most if not all societies, this definition identifies a relationship "distinguished by the people themselves from all other kinds of relationships." Yet Gough's definition seems oddly at variance with English dictionary and native Western notions of marriage. First of all, it makes no reference to rights and duties of sexual access or to sexual performance. Moreover, it does not necessarily involve a relationship between men and women since it merely refers to a woman and "one or more" other persons of unspecified sex.

Gough does not mention sexual rights and duties because of the case of the Nayar. In order to bear children in a socially acceptable manner, pubescent Nayar girls had to go through a four-day ceremony that linked them with a "ritual husband." Completion of this ceremony was a necessary prerequisite for the beginning of a Nayar woman's sexual and reproductive career. Ideally, the Nayar strove to find a ritual husband among the men of the higher-ranking Namboodri Brahman caste. The males of this caste were interested in having sex with Nayar women, but they refused to regard the children of Nayar women as their heirs. So after the ritual marriage, Nayar women stayed home with their sisters and brothers and were visited by both Namboodri Brahman and Nayar men. Gough regards the existence of the ritual husbands as proof of the universality of marriage (although not of the nuclear family), since only children born to ritually married Nayar women were "legitimate," even though the fathers were unknown.

But what can be the reason for defining marriage as a relationship between a woman and "persons" rather than between "women and men"? There are many instances among African societies—the Dahomey case is best known—in which women "marry" women. This is accomplished by having a woman, who herself is already usually married to a man, pay bride-price (see page 145) for a bride. The female bride-price payer becomes a "female husband." She starts a family of her own by letting her "wife" become pregnant through relationships with designated males. The offspring of these unions fall under the control of the "female father" rather than of the biological *genitors* (see page 153).

Wide as it is, Gough's definition ignores certain mating relationships that take place between males. For example, among the Kwakiutl, a man who desires to acquire the privileges associated with a particular chief can "marry" the chief's male heir. If the chief has no heirs, a man may "marry" the chief's right or left side, or a leg or an arm.

In Euramerican culture, enduring mating relationships between coresident homosexual men or between coresident homosexual women are also often spoken of as marriage. It has thus been suggested that all reference to the sex of the people involved in the relationship should be omitted in the definition of marriage in order to accommodate such cases (Dillingham and Isaac 1975). Yet the task of understanding varieties of domestic organization is made more difficult when all these different forms of mating are crammed into the single concept of marriage. Part of the problem is that when matings in Western culture are denied the designation "marriage," there is an unjust tendency to regard them as less honorable or less authentic relationships. And so anthropologists are reluctant to stigmatize woman-woman or man-man matings, or Nayar or matrifocal visiting mate arrangements, by saying they are not marriages. But whatever we call them, it is clear that they cover an enormous behavioral and mental range. There is no scientific evidence that any one of them is more or less "natural."

Since the term *marriage* is too useful to drop altogether, a more narrow definition seems appropriate: *Marriage* denotes the behavior, sentiments, and rules concerned with coresident heterosexual mating and reproduction in domestic contexts.

To avoid offending people by using *marriage* exclusively for coresident heterosexual domestic mates, a simple expedient is available. Let such other relationships be designated as "noncoresident marriages," "man-man marriages," "woman-woman marriages," or by any other appropriate specific nomenclature. It is clear that these matings have different demographic, economic, and ideological implications, so nothing is to be gained by arguing about whether they are "real" marriages.

Legitimacy

The essence of the marital relationship, according to some anthropologists, is embodied in that portion of Gough's definition dealing with the assignment of "birth-status rights" to children. Children born to a married woman "under circumstances not prohibited by the rules of the relationship" (e.g., adultery) are legal or legitimate children. Children born to unmarried women are illegitimate. As Bronislaw Malinowski put it: "Marriage is the licensing of parenthood."

But many societies do not distinguish between legitimate or legal child rearing and illegitimate or illegal child rearing. It is true that women are universally discouraged from attempting to rear or dispose of their newborn infants according to their own whim, but many societies have several different sets of rules defining permissible modes of conception and child rearing. Some of these alternatives may be esteemed more highly than others, but the less esteemed alternatives do not necessarily place children in a status analogous to that of Western illegitimacy (Scheffler 1973:754–755). For example, among Brazilians living in small towns there are four kinds of relationships between a man and a woman, all of which provide children with full birth rights: church marriage, civil marriage, simultaneous church and civil marriage, and consensual marriage. For a Brazilian woman the most esteemed way to have children is through simultaneous church and civil marriage. This mode legally entitles her to a portion of her husband's property upon his death. It also provides the added security of knowing that her husband cannot desert her and enter into a civil or religious marriage elsewhere. The least desirable mode is the consensual marriage, because the woman can make no property claims against her con-

sort, nor can she readily prevent him from deserting her. Yet the children of a consensual arrangement can make property claims against both father and mother while suffering no deprivation of birth rights in the form of legal disadvantages or social disapproval as long as the father acknowledges paternity.

Among the Dahomey, Herskovits (1938) reported thirteen different kinds of marriage determined largely by bride-price arrangements. Children enjoyed different birth rights depending on the type of marriage. In some marriages the child was placed under the control of the father's domestic group, and in others under the control of a domestic group headed by a female "father" (see above). The point is not that a child is legitimate or illegitimate, but rather that there are specific types of rights, obligations, and groupings that emanate from different modes of sexual and reproductive relations. Most of the world's people are not concerned with the question of whether a child is legitimate, but with the question of who will have the right of controlling the child's destiny. No society grants women complete "freedom of conception," but the restrictions placed on motherhood and the occasions for punishment and disapproval vary enormously.

Where the domestic scene is dominated by large extended families and where there are no strong restrictions on premarital sex, the pregnancy of a young unmarried woman is rarely the occasion for much concern. Under certain circumstances, an "unwed mother" may even be congratulated rather than condemned. Among the Kadar of northern Nigeria, as reported by M. G. Smith (1968), most marriages result from infant betrothals. These matches are arranged by the fathers of the bride and groom when the girl is 3 to 6 years old. Ten years or more may elapse before the bride goes to live with her betrothed. During this time, a Kadar girl is not unlikely to become pregnant. This will disturb no one, even if the biological father is a man other than her future husband:

> Kadar set no value on premarital chastity. It is fairly common for unmarried girls to be impregnated or to give birth to children by youths other than their betrothed. Offspring of such premarital pregnancies are members of the patrilineage . . . of the girl's betrothed and are welcomed as proof of the bride's fertility. [1968:113]

Analogous situations are quite common among other societies whose domestic groups value children above chastity.

Functions of Marriage

Every society has rules that define the conditions under which sexual relations, pregnancy, birth, and child rearing may take place, and that allocate privileges and duties in connection with these conditions. And every society has its own sometimes unique combination of rules and rules for breaking rules in this domain. It would be futile to define marriage by any one ingredient in these rules — such as legitimation of children — even if such an ingredient could be shown to be universal. This point can be illustrated by enumerating some of the variable regulatory functions associated with institutions commonly identified as marriage. The following list incorporates suggestions made by Edmund Leach (1968). Marriage *sometimes*

1. Establishes the legal father of a woman's children

2. Establishes the legal mother of a man's children

3. Gives the husband or his extended family control over the wife's sexual services

4. Gives the wife or her extended family control over the husband's sexual services

5. Gives the husband or his extended family control over the wife's labor power

6. Gives the wife or her extended family control over the husband's labor power

7. Gives the husband or his extended family control over the wife's property

8. Gives the wife or her extended family control over the husband's property

9. Establishes a joint fund of property for the benefit of children

10. Establishes a socially significant relationship between the husband's and the wife's domestic groups

As Leach remarks, this list could be greatly extended, but the point is "that in no single society can marriage serve to establish all these types of rights simultaneously, nor is there any one of these rights which is invariably established by marriage in every known society" (1968:76).

Marriage in Extended Families

In extended families, marriage must be seen primarily in the context of group interests. Individuals serve the interest of the extended family. The larger domestic group never loses interest in or totally surrenders its rights to the productive, the reproductive, and the sexual functions of spouses and children. Marriage under these circumstances is aptly described as an "alliance" between groups. This alliance influences present and future matings involving other members of both groups.

Among many societies, the corporate nature of marriage is revealed by the exchange of personnel or of valuable goods between the respective domestic groups in which bride and groom were born. The simplest form of such transactions is called *sister exchange* and involves the reciprocal "giving away" of the groom's sisters in compensation for the loss of a woman from each group.

Among many peoples around the world, corporate interests are expressed in the institution known as *bride-price* (Figure 8.8). The wife-receiver gives valuable items to the wife-giver. Of course, bride-price is not equivalent to the selling and buying of automobiles or refrigerators in modern industrial price-market societies (see page 118). The wife-receivers do not "own" their woman in any total sense; they must take good care of her, or her brothers and "fathers" (i.e., her father and father's brothers) will demand that she be returned to them. The amount of bride-price is not fixed; it fluctuates from one marriage to another. (In Africa the traditional measure of "bride-wealth" was cattle, although other valuables such as iron tools were also used. Nowadays, cash payments are increasingly common.) Among the Bathonga, a family that had many daughter-sisters was in a favorable position. By exchanging women for cattle, the family could exchange cattle back for women: the more cattle, the more mother-wives; and the more mother-wives, the larger the reproductive and productive labor force and the greater the corporate material welfare and influence of the extended family.

Sometimes the transfer of wealth from one group to another is carried out in installments:

Figure 8.8 *Bride-price.*
Among the Kapauku, the bride-price consists of shell money.

so much on initial agreement, more when the woman goes to live with her husband, and another, usually final, payment when she has her first child. Failure to have a child often voids the marriage; the woman goes home to her brothers and fathers, and the husband's family gets its bride-price back.

A common alternative to bride-price is known as *bride-service* (sometimes called *suitor-service*). The groom or husband compensates his in-laws by working for them for several months or years before taking his bride away to live and work with him and his extended family. Bride-service may be involved in the conditions under which matrilocal residence tends to occur, as we will see in Chapter 9. If the suitor lingers on and never takes his bride home, he may be participating in an etic shift from patrilocal to matrilocal residence.

Bride-price and suitor-service tend to occur where production is being increased, land is plentiful, and the labor of additional women and children is seen as scarce and as being in the best interests of the corporate group (Bossen 1988; Goody 1976). Where the corporate group is not interested in or not capable of expanding production or in increasing its numbers, wives may be regarded as a burden. Instead of paying bride-price to the family of the bride, the groom's family may demand a reverse payment, called *dowry* (Figure 8.9). As

we shall see in Chapter 9, when this payment consists of money or movable property instead of land, it is usually associated with a low or oppressed status for women (Schlegel and Barry 1986:145; Schlegel and Eloul 1988).

The opposite of bride-price is not dowry but *groom-price*, in which the groom goes to work for the bride's family and the bride's family compensates the groom's family for the loss of his productive and reproductive powers. This form of marriage compensation is extremely rare — only one well-documented case is known (Nash 1974).

Domestic Groups and the Avoidance of Incest

All these exchanges point to the existence of a profound paradox in the way human beings find mates. Marriage between members of the same domestic group is widely prohibited. Husband and wife must come from separate domestic groups. The members of the domestic group must "marry out" — that is, marry *exogamously*; they cannot "marry in" — that is, marry *endogamously*.

Certain forms of endogamy are universally prohibited. No culture tolerates father-daughter and mother-son marriages. Sister-brother marriage is also widely prohibited, but it occurred, especially between half-siblings, among the ruling classes of highly stratified societies such as those of the Inca and ancient Egypt (Bixler 1982). In the emics of Western civilization, sister-brother, father-daughter, and mother-son sex relations and marriages are called *incest*. Why are these sex relations and marriages so widely prohibited?

Explanations of nuclear family incest prohibition fall into two major types: (1) those that

Figure 8.9 Dowry.
This Arab bride is exhibiting her wealth.

stress an instinctual component and (2) those that emphasize the social and cultural advantages of exogamy.

INSTINCT

Advocates of genetic theories of incest avoidance long ago recognized that it was unlikely that genes contained definite instructions for shutting down sex drives in the presence of siblings, children, and parents. Following the lead of Edward Westermark (1894), they propose, instead, that there is an innate tendency for members of the opposite sex to find each other sexually uninspiring if they have been brought up in close physical proximity to each other during infancy and childhood (Shepher 1983; Spiro 1954). Westermark's principle is much in favor among sociobiologists because it provides a way out of the dilemma posed by the relatively high rates at which brother-sister incest may sometimes take place, as in ancient Egypt (Figure 8.10). If the brother and sister were brought up apart from each other in different houses or by different nurses and caretakers, then, according to the Westermark principle, they might very well find each other sexually attractive enough to mate (Bixler 1981, 1982; Wilson 1978:38–39).

Behind the Westermark theory and other genetic explanations of incest avoidance is the assumption that close inbreeding results in an increased likelihood that individuals who carry defective genes will mate with each other and give birth to children who suffer from pathological conditions that lower their rate of reproduction. Also, simply by lowering the amount of genetic diversity in a population, inbreeding might have an adverse effect on its ability to adapt to new diseases or other novel environmental hazards. So, those individuals

Figure 8.10 Cleopatra.
Eleven generations of close inbreeding involving step-siblings had no obvious deleterious consequences.

who find themselves "turned off" through the Westermark effect would have avoided inbreeding, reproduced at a higher rate, and gradually replaced those who were "turned on" by their close kin.

There are several soft spots in this part of the argument. It is true that in large modern populations incest leads to a high rate of still-births and congenitally diseased and impaired children (Adams and Neil 1967; Stern 1973:497). But the same results need not occur from close inbreeding practiced in small pre-agricultural societies. Inbreeding in small pre-agricultural societies leads to the gradual elimination of harmful recessive genes because such societies have little tolerance for infants and children who are congenitally handicapped and impaired. Lack of support for such children eliminates the harmful genetic variations from future generations, and results in populations that carry a much smaller "load" of harmful gene variants than modern populations (Livingstone 1969, 1981).

To test the Westermark theory, one cannot point to the mere occurrence of incest avoidance. One has to show that sexual ardor cools when people grow up together, independent of any existing norms that call for incest avoidance. Since this cannot be done experimentally without controlling the lives of human subjects, advocates of the theory lean heavily on two famous case studies that allegedly demonstrate the predicted loss of sexual ardor. The first of these concerns Taiwanese adopt-a-daughter-marry-a-sister marriage (see page 139). Studies have shown that these marriages, in which husband and wife grow up together at close quarters, lead to fewer children, greater adultery, and higher divorce rates than normal marriages, in which future wives and husbands grow up in separate households (Wolf and Haung 1980). But these observations scarcely confirm Westermark's theory. The Taiwanese explicitly recognize that adopt-a-daughter-marry-a-sister is an inferior, even humiliating, form of marriage. Normally, to seal a marriage bond, the families of bride and groom exchange considerable wealth as a sign of their support for the newlyweds. But these exchanges are smaller or absent altogether in adopt-a-daughter-marry-a-sister. This makes it impossible to prove that sexual disinterest rather than chagrin and disappointment over being treated like second-class citizens is the source of the couple's infertility.

The second case used to confirm Westermark's theory concerns an alleged lack of sexual interest displayed by boys and girls who attended the same classes from nursery school to age 6 in the Israeli cooperative community known as a kibbutz (Figure 8.11). Allegedly these boys and girls were so thoroughly "turned off" that among marriages contracted by people who were reared in a kibbutz, not one involved men or women who had been reared together from birth to age 6 (Shepher 1983). This seems impressive, but there is a fatal flaw. Out of a total of 2,516 marriages, there were 200 in which both partners were reared in the same kibbutz, although they were not in

Figure 8.11 Kibbutz boys and girls.
Does childhood familiarity lead to sexual avoidance?

the same class for six years. Given the fact that all kibbutz youth were inducted into the army and commingled with tens of thousands of potential mates from outside their kibbutz before they got married, the rate of 200 marriages from within the same kibbutz is far more than could be expected by chance. One must now ask, of the 200 marriages from within the same kibbutz, what was the chance that not a single one would be between a boy and a girl who had attended the same classes? Since girls were generally three years younger than the boys they married, only a very few marriages between people who were reared for six years in the same class could be expected. Actually, it turns out that five marriages did occur between boys and girls who had been reared together for part of the first six years of their lives. Since Westermark's theory does not predict how long it takes for reared-together boys and girls to lose their interest in each other, these five marriages actually disconfirm the theory (Hartung 1985).

The proposal that there is an instinctual sexual aversion within the nuclear family is also contradicted by evidence of strong sexual attraction between father and daughter and between mother and son. Freudian psychoanalysis indicates that children and parents of the opposite sex have a strong desire to have sexual encounters with each other. Indeed, in the case of the father-daughter relationship, at least, these wishes are acted on more frequently than is popularly believed. Social workers, for example, estimate that tens of thousands of cases of incest occur in the United States annually, of which the great majority are of the father-daughter variety (Cicchetti and Carlson 1989; Glaser and Frosh 1988). Finally, the instinct theory of incest avoidance is hard to reconcile with the widespread occurrence of endogamous practices that are carried out simultaneously and in support of exogamic arrange-

ments. Members of exogamous extended families, for example, frequently are involved in marriage systems that encourage them to mate with one kind of first cousin (*cross cousin*) but not another (*parallel cousin*, see page 157). The difference between these two forms of inbreeding cannot be explained satisfactorily by natural selection (but see Alexander 1977). Furthermore, the widespread preference for some form of cousin marriage itself weighs against the conclusion that exogamy expresses an instinct established by the harmful effects of inbreeding.

SOCIAL AND CULTURAL ADVANTAGES OF EXOGAMY

Nuclear family incest avoidance and other forms of exogamy among domestic groups can be explained quite effectively in terms of demographic, economic, and ecological advantages (Leavitt 1989). These advantages are not necessarily the same for all societies. It is known, for example, that band societies rely on marriage exchanges to establish long-distance networks of kinspeople. Bands that formed a completely closed breeding unit would be denied the mobility and territorial flexibility essential to their subsistence strategy. Territorially restricted, endogamous bands of 20 to 30 people would also run a high risk of extinction as a result of sexual imbalances caused by an unlucky run of male births and adult female deaths, which would place the burden for the group's reproduction on one or two aging females. Exogamy is thus essential for the effective utilization of a small population's productive and reproductive potential. Once a band begins to obtain mates from other bands, the prevalence of reciprocal economic relations leads to the expectation that the receivers will reciprocate. The taboos on mother-son, father-daughter, and brother-sister marriages can therefore be interpreted as a defense of these reciprocal exchange relationships against the ever-present temptation for parents to keep their children for themselves, or for brothers and sisters to keep each other for themselves.

In this connection it is frequently overlooked that sexual encounters between father-daughter and mother-son constitute a form of adultery. Mother-son incest is an especially threatening variety of adultery in societies that have strong male supremacist institutions. Not only is the wife "double-dealing" against her husband, but the son is "double-dealing" against his father. This may explain why the least common and emically most feared and abhorred form of incest is that between mother and son. It follows that father-daughter incest will be somewhat more common, since husbands enjoy double standards of sexual behavior more often than wives and are less vulnerable to punishment for adultery. Finally, the same consideration suggests an explanation for the relatively high frequency of brother-sister matings and their legitimizations as marriages in elite classes — they do not conflict with father-mother adultery rules.

After the evolution of the state, exogamic alliances between domestic groups continued to have important infrastructural consequences. Among peasants, exogamy also increases the total productive and reproductive strength of the intermarried groups. It permits the exploitation of resources over a larger area than the nuclear or extended families could manage on an individual basis; it facilitates trade; and it raises the upper limit of the size of groups that can be formed to carry out seasonal activities that require large labor inputs (e.g., communal game drives, harvests, and so on). Furthermore, where intergroup warfare poses

a threat to group survival, the ability to mobilize large numbers of warriors is decisive. Hence, in militaristic, highly male-centered village cultures, sisters and daughters are frequently used as pawns in the establishment of alliances. These alliances do not necessarily eliminate warfare between intermarrying groups, but they make it less common, as might be expected from the presence of sisters and daughters in the enemy's ranks (Kang 1979; Podolefsky 1984; Tefft 1975).

Among elite classes and castes, endogamy often combines with extended family exogamy to maintain wealth and power within the ruling stratum (see page 207). But as already noted, even the nuclear family may become endogamous when there is an extreme concentration of political, economic, and military power. With the evolution of price-market forms of exchange, the extended family tends to be replaced by nuclear family domestic units. Domestic group alliances lose some of their previous adaptive importance and the traditional functions of the incest avoidance must be reinterpreted. Incest has been decriminalized in Sweden, and there is an effort to do likewise in the United States (Y. Cohen 1978; De Mott 1980). Some scientists argue that incest prohibitions will eventually disappear because there are many alternative ways of establishing intergroup relationships in modern states, such as price markets and compulsory public education (Leavitt 1989). Yet given the scientific knowledge that nuclear family incest is genetically risky in populations carrying a heavy load of harmful recessives, the repeal of anti-incest legislation seems unlikely and unwise.

The possibility that incest avoidance is genetically programmed in *Homo sapiens* has received some support from field studies of monkey and ape mating behavior. As among humans, father-daughter, mother-son, and brother-sister matings are uncommon among our nearest animal relatives. However, to some extent the avoidance of sex by these pairs can be explained in terms of male dominance and sexual rivalry. There is no experimental evidence suggesting an aversion to incest per se among monkeys and apes. Moreover, if such an instinctual aversion exists, its significance for human nature remains in doubt (see Demarest 1977).

Preferential Marriages

The widespread occurrence of exogamy implies that the corporate interests of domestic groups must be protected by rules that stipulate who is to marry whom. Having given a woman away in marriage, most groups expect either material wealth or women in exchange. Consider two domestic groups, A and B, each with a core of resident brothers. If A gives a woman to B, B may immediately reciprocate by giving a woman to A. This reciprocity is often achieved by a direct exchange of the groom's sister. But the reciprocity may take a more indirect form. B may return a daughter of the union between the B man and the A woman. The bride in such a marriage will be her husband's father's sister's daughter, and the groom will be his wife's mother's brother's son. (The same result would be achieved by a marriage between a man and his mother's brother's daughter.) Bride and groom are each other's cross cousins (see page 157). If A and B have a rule that such marriages are to occur whenever possible, then they are said to have *preferential cross-cousin marriage*.

Reciprocity in marriage is sometimes achieved by several intermarrying domestic groups that exchange women in cycles and are called *circulating connubia*. For example, A → B → C → A; or A ↔ B and C ↔ D in one generation and A ↔ D and B ↔ C in the next, and then back to A ↔ B and C ↔ D. These exchanges are enforced by preferential marriage with appropriate kinds of cousins, nephews, nieces, and other kin.

Another common manifestation of corporate domestic interest in marriage is the practice of supplying replacements for inmarrying women who die prematurely. To maintain reciprocity or to fulfill a marriage contract for which bride-price has been paid, the brother of a deceased woman may permit the widower to marry one or more of the deceased wife's sisters. This custom is known as the *sororate*. Closely related to this practice is the preferential marriage known as the *levirate*, in which the services of a man's widows are retained within the domestic unit by having them marry one of his brothers. If the widows are old, these services may be minimal, and the levirate then functions to provide security for women who would otherwise not be able to remarry.

Thus the organization of domestic life in preindustrial societies everywhere reflects the fact that husbands and wives usually originate in different domestic groups that continue to maintain a sentimental and practical interest in the marriage partners and their children.

Summary

The structural level of sociocultural systems is made up in part by interrelated domestic groups. Such groups can usually be identified by their attachment to a living space or domicile in which activities such as eating, sleeping, marital sex, and nurturance and discipline of the young take place. However, there is no single or minimal pattern of domestic activities. Similarly, the nuclear family cannot be regarded as the minimal building block of all domestic groups. While nuclear families occur in almost every society, they are not always the dominant domestic group, and their sexual, reproductive, and productive functions can readily be satisfied by alternative domestic and nondomestic institutions. In polygamous and extended families, the father-mother-child subset may not enjoy any practical existence apart from the set of other relatives and their multiple spouses. Although children need to be nurtured and protected, no one knows the limits within which human domestic arrangements must be confined in order to satisfy human nature. One of the most important facts about human domestic arrangements is that no single pattern can be shown to be more "natural" than any other.

Human mating patterns also exhibit an enormous degree of variation. While something similar to what is called marriage occurs all over the world, it is difficult to specify the mental and behavioral essence of the marital relationship. Man-man, woman-woman, female father, and childless marriages make it difficult to give a minimal definition of marriage without hurting someone's feelings. Even coresidence may not be essential, as the Nayar and other single-parent households demonstrate. And if we restrict the definition of marriage to coresident heterosexual matings that result in reproduction, there is a staggering variety of rights and duties associated with the productive, sexual, and reproductive functions of the marriage partners and their offspring.

In order to understand coresident heterosexual reproductive marriage in extended families, marriage must be seen as a relationship between corporate groups as much as between cohabiting mates. The divergent interests of these corporate groups are reconciled by means of reciprocal exchanges that take the form of sister exchange, bride-price, suitor-service, dowry, and groom-price. The common principle underlying these exchanges, except

for dowry, is that in giving a man or woman away to another extended family, the domestic corporation does not renounce its interest in the offspring of the mated pair and expects compensation for the loss of a valuable worker.

Most domestic groups are exogamous. This can be seen as a result of instinctual programming or social and cultural adaptation. The discussion of exogamy necessarily centers on the incest prohibitions within the nuclear family. Father-daughter, sister-brother, and mother-son matings and marriages are almost universally forbidden. The chief exception is brother-sister marriages, which occur in several highly stratified societies among the ruling elites. The instinct theory of incest avoidance stresses evidence from Taiwan and Israel, which suggests that children reared together develop a sexual aversion to each other. These cases do not prove what they intend to prove, however.

A purely cultural theory of incest avoidance can be built out of the need for bands and domestic groups to defend their capacity to engage in reciprocal marriage exchanges by preventing parents from keeping their children for themselves. In the future, the perpetuation of the incest taboos may be related exclusively to the increasing genetic dangers associated with close inbreeding in populations carrying a large load of harmful genes.

Exogamy and incest avoidance form only a small part of the spectrum of preferred and prohibited marriages that reflect the pervasive corporate interests of domestic groups. Preferences for certain kinds of marriage exchanges create circulating connubia in which reciprocity between domestic groups may be direct or indirect. Such preferences may be expressed as a rule requiring marriage with a particular kind of cousin. Preferential marriage rules such as the levirate and sororate also exemplify the corporate nature of the marriage bond.

Chapter 9

KINSHIP, LOCALITY, AND DESCENT

This chapter continues the discussion of domestic organization. It examines the principal mental and emic components of domestic groups and relates them to the etic and behavioral aspects of those groups. It also sets forth some of the theories that relate the mental and behavioral variations in domestic organization to infrastructural conditions.

Kinship

The study of domestic life in hundreds of cultures all over the world has led anthropologists to conclude that two ideas are involved in the organization of domestic life everywhere. The first of these is the idea of *affinity*, or of relationships through marriage. The second is the idea of *descent*, or parentage. People who are related to each other through descent or a combination of affinity and descent are relatives, or *kin*. The domain of ideas constituted by the beliefs and expectations kin share about one another is called *kinship*. The study of kinship, therefore, must begin with the mental and emic components of domestic life.

Descent*

Kinship relations are often confused with biological relations. But the emic meaning of de-

* British social anthropologists restrict the term *descent* to relationships extending over more than two generations and use *filiation* to denote descent relationships within the nuclear family (Fortes 1969).

scent is not the biological meaning of descent. As we have discussed previously, marriage may explicitly establish "parentage" with respect to children who are biologically unrelated to their culturally defined "father." Even where a culture insists that descent must be based on actual biological fatherhood, domestic arrangements may make it difficult to identify the biological father. For these reasons, anthropologists distinguish between the culturally defined "father" and the *genitor*, the actual biological father. A similar distinction is necessary in the case of "mother." Although the culturally defined mother is usually the *genetrix*, the widespread practice of adoption also creates many discrepancies between emic and etic motherhood.

Theories of reproduction and heredity vary from culture to culture, "but so far as we know, no human society is without such a theory" (Scheffler 1973:749). Descent, then, is the belief that certain persons play an important role in the creation, birth, and nurturance of certain children. As Daniel Craig (1979) has suggested, descent implies the preservation of some aspect of the substance or spirit of people in future generations and thus is a symbolic

153

form of immortality. Perhaps that is why one form or another of parentage and descent are universally believed in.

In Western folk traditions, married pairs are linked to children on the basis of the belief that male and female make equally important contributions to the child's being. The male's semen is regarded as analogous to seed, and the woman's womb is analogous to the earth in which the seed is planted. Blood, the most important life-sustaining and life-defining fluid, supposedly varies according to parentage. Each child's body is thought of as being filled with blood obtained from mother and father. As a result of this imagery, "blood relatives" are distinguished from relatives who are linked only through marriage. This led nineteenth-century anthropologists to use the ethnocentric term *consanguine* (of the same blood) to denote relations of descent. People persist in talking about "blood relatives" even though it is known that closely related individuals may have different blood types, distantly or unrelated individuals may have the same blood type, and the closeness of a relationship is measured by the proportion of shared DNA and not by shared blood.

Descent need not depend on the idea of blood inheritance, nor need it involve equal contributions from both father and mother. The Ashanti believe that blood is contributed only by the mother and that it determines only a child's physical characteristics, while a child's spiritual disposition and temperament are the product of the father's semen. The Alorese of Indonesia believe that the child is formed by a mixture of seminal and menstrual fluids, which accumulate for two months before beginning to solidify. Many other cultures share this idea of a slow growth of fetus as a result of repeated additions of semen during pregnancy. For the polyandrous Tamil of the Malabar Coast of India, the semen of several different males is believed to contribute to the growth of the same fetus.

The Eskimo believe that pregnancy results when a spirit child climbs up a woman's bootstraps and is nourished by semen. The Trobrianders profess a famous dogma denying any procreative role to semen. Here also, a woman becomes pregnant when a spirit child climbs into her vagina. The only physical function of the Trobriand male is to widen the passageway into the womb. The Trobriand "father," nonetheless, has an essential social role, since no self-respecting spirit child would climb into a Trobriand girl who was not married.

A similar denial of the male's procreative role occurs throughout Australia; among the Murngin, for example, there was the belief that the spirit children live deep below the surface of certain sacred water holes. For conception to take place, one of these spirits appears in the future father's dreams. In the dream the spirit child introduces itself and asks its father to point out the woman who is to become its mother. Later, when this woman passes near the sacred water hole, the spirit child swims out in the form of a fish and enters her womb.

Despite the many different kinds of theories about the nature of procreative roles, there is worldwide acknowledgment of some special contributory action linking both husband and wife to the reproductive process, although they may be linked quite unevenly and with vastly different expectations concerning rights and obligations.

Descent Rules

By reckoning descent relationships, individuals are apportioned different duties, rights, and privileges with respect to other people and

Figure 9.1   American kindred.
Thanksgiving is an occasion for both siblings and cousins to get together.

Figure 9.2   How to read kinship diagrams.

△	Male
○	Female
=	Is married to
		Is descended from
⌐_⌐	Is the sibling of
◬	Ego whose genealogy is being shown

with regard to many different aspects of social life. A person's name, family, residence, rank, property, ethnic and national status (see Figure 9.1) may depend on *ascriptions* through descent independent of any *achievements* other than getting born and staying alive. (Ascribed statuses and achieved statuses are found in all cultures.)

Anthropologists distinguish two great classes of descent rules: the cognatic and the unilineal. *Cognatic descent rules* are those in which both male and female parentage are used to establish any of the above-mentioned duties, rights, and privileges. *Unilineal descent rules* restrict parental links exclusively to males or exclusively to females (see Figure 9.2 on the symbols used in kinship diagrams.) The most common form of cognatic rule is *bilateral de-*

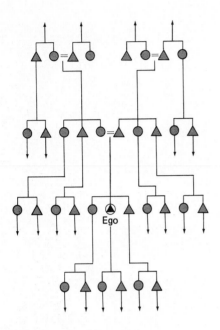

Figure 9.3   Bilateral descent.
Everyone on the diagram has a descent relationship with ego.

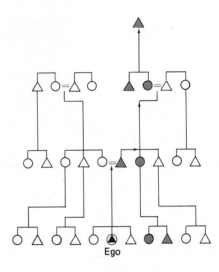

Figure 9.4   Ambilineal descent.
Ego traces descent through both males and females, but not equally and not simultaneously.

scent, the reckoning of kinship evenly and symmetrically along maternal and paternal lines in ascending and descending generations through individuals of both sexes (Figure 9.3).

The second main variety of cognatic rule is called *ambilineal descent* (Figure 9.4). Here the descent lines traced by ego (Box 9.1) ignore the sex of the parental links, but the lines do not lead in all directions evenly. As in bilateral descent, ego traces descent through males and females, but the line twists back and forth, including some female ancestors or descendants but excluding others and including some male ancestors or descendants and excluding others. In other words, ego does not reckon descent simultaneously and equally through mothers, fathers, and grandparents.

There are also two main varieties of unilineal descent: *patrilineality* and *matrilineality*. When descent is reckoned patrilineally, ego follows the ascending and descending genealogical lines through males only (Figure 9.5). Note that this does not mean that only males have descent relationships; in each generation there are relatives of both sexes. However, in the passage from one generation to another

Box 9.1

EGO

Anthropologists employ the word *ego* to denote the "I" from whose point of view kinship relations are being reckoned. It is sometimes necessary to state whether the reference person is a male ego or a female ego.

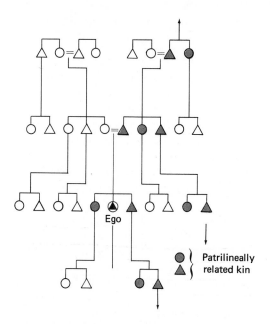

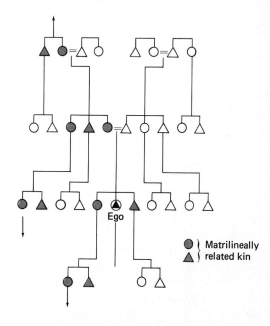

Figure 9.5 *Patrilineal descent.*
Descent is traced exclusively through males.

Figure 9.6 *Matrilineal descent.*
Descent is traced exclusively through females.

only the male links are relevant; children of females are dropped from the descent reckoning.

When descent is reckoned matrilineally, ego follows the ascending and descending lines through females only (Figure 9.6). Once again, it should be noted that males as well as females can be related matrilineally; it is only in the passage from one generation to another that the children of males are dropped from the descent reckoning.

One of the most important logical consequences of unilineal descent is that it segregates the children of siblings of the opposite sex into distinct categories. This effect is especially important in the case of cousins. Note that with patrilineal descent, ego's father's sister's son and daughter do not share common descent with ego, whereas ego's father's brother's son

and daughter do share common descent with ego. In the case of matrilineal descent, the same kind of distinction results with respect to ego's "cousins" on the mother's side. Children whose parents are related to each other as brother and sister are known as *cross cousins;* children whose parents are related to each other as brother and brother or sister and sister are known as *parallel cousins* (Figure 9.7).

Anthropologists distinguish an additional variety of descent rule, called *double descent,* in which ego simultaneously reckons descent matrilineally through mother and patrilineally through father. This differs from unilineal descent, in which descent is reckoned only through males or only through females but not both together. And it differs from bilateral descent, in which descent is reckoned bilaterally through mother and father.

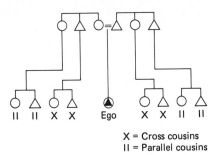

X = Cross cousins
II = Parallel cousins

Figure 9.7   Cross cousins and parallel cousins.

Many other combinations of these descent rules may also occur. In all cultures, for example, there is some degree of bilateral descent in the reckoning of rights and obligations. If a society observes patrilineal descent in the grouping of people into landowning domestic groups, this does not mean that ego and mother's brother's daughter do not regard each other as having special rights and obligations. Modern Euramerican culture is strongly bilateral in kin group composition and inheritance of wealth and property; yet family names are *patronymic* — that is, they follow patrilineal descent lines. The point is that several varieties of descent may occur simultaneously within a given society if the descent rules are pertinent to different spheres of thought and behavior.

Each of the above descent rules provides the logical basis for mentally aligning people into emic kinship groups. These groups exert great influence on the way people think and behave in both domestic and extradomestic situations. An important point to bear in mind about kinship groups is that they need not consist of coresident relatives — that is, they need not be domestic groups. We proceed now to a description of the principal varieties of kinship groups.

Cognatic Descent Groups: Bilateral Variety

Bilateral descent applied to an indefinitely wide span of kin and to an indefinite number of generations leads to the concept of groups known as *kindreds* (Figure 9.8). When modern-day Americans and Europeans use the word *family* and have in mind more than just their nuclear families, they are referring to their kindreds. The main characteristic of the kindred is that the span and depth of bilateral reckoning is open-ended. Relatives within ego's kindred can be judged as "near" or "far" depending on the number of genealogical links that separate them, but there is no definite or uniform principle for making such judgments

Figure 9.8   Kindreds.
Children have kindreds that are different from those of either parent.

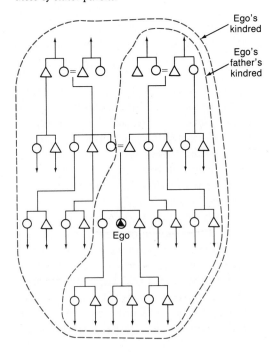

Ego's kindred

Ego's father's kindred

or for terminating the extension of the kinship circle. An important consequence of this feature, as shown in Figure 9.8, is that egos and their siblings are identified with a kindred whose membership cannot be the same for any other persons (except for ego's *double cousins* —cousins whose parents are two brothers who have exchanged sisters). This means that it is impossible for coresident domestic groups to consist of kindreds and very difficult for kindreds to maintain corporate interests in land and people.

Cognatic Descent Groups: Ambilineal Variety

The open-ended, ego-centered characteristics of the bilateral kindred can be overcome by specifying one or more ancestors from whom descent is traced through males and/or females. The resultant group logically has a membership that is the same regardless of which ego carries out the reckoning. This is the *cognatic lineage* (the terms *ramage* and *sept* are also used) (Figure 9.9).

The cognatic lineage is based on the assumption that all members of the descent group are capable of specifying the precise genealogical links relating them to the lineage founder. A common alternative, as in the ambilineal "clans" of Scotland, is for the descent from the lineage founder to be *stipulated* rather than *demonstrated*. This can be done easily enough if the name of the founder gets passed on ambilineally over many generations. After a while many of the persons who carry the name will belong to the group simply by virtue of the name rather than because they can trace their genealogical relationship all the way back to the founding ancestor. An appropriate desig-

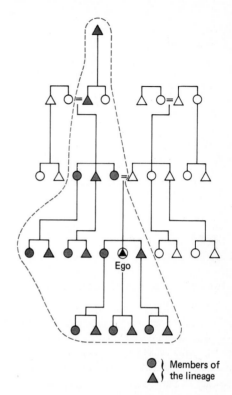

Figure 9.9 *Cognatic lineage.*
Descent is traced to an apical ancestor through males and/or females.

nation for such groups is *cognatic clan*. (In recent times, some members of Scots clans have different surnames as a result of patronymy and must demonstrate descent; see Neville 1979.)

Unilineal Descent Groups

When unilineal descent is systematically demonstrated with respect to a particular ancestor, the resultant kin group is called a *patrilineage* (Figure 9.10) or a *matrilineage*. All lineages contain the same set of people regardless of the

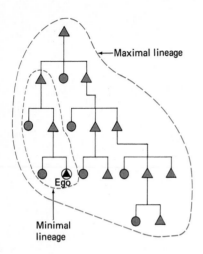

Figure 9.10   Patrilineages.
Everyone on the diagram belongs to the same
maximal lineage.

genealogical perspective from which they are
viewed. This makes them ideally suited to be
coresident domestic groups and to hold joint
interests in persons and property. Because of
exogamy, however, both sexes cannot remain
coresident beyond childhood. Some lineages
include all the generations and collateral descendants of the first ancestor. These are *maximal* lineages. Lineages that contain only three
generations are *minimal* lineages (see Figure
9.10).

When unilineal descent from a specific ancestor is stipulated rather than demonstrated,
the group that results is known as either a *pa-
triclan* or a *matriclan* (the terms *patrisib* and
matrisib are also in use). There are many bor-
derline cases, however, in which it is difficult to
decide whether one is dealing with a lineage or
a clan.

Just as lineages may contain lineages, clans
may contain clans, which are usually called
subclans. Finally, it should be noted that clans
may also contain lineages.

Postmarital Locality Patterns

In order to understand the processes responsible for different varieties of domestic groups
and different ideologies of descent, we must
discuss one additional aspect of domestic organization. There is considerable agreement
among anthropologists that an important de-
terminant of descent rules is the pattern of
residence after marriage. The principal postmarital locality practices are described in Box
9.2.

Postmarital residence practices influence
descent rules because they determine who will
enter, leave, or stay in a domestic group (Murdock 1949; Naroll 1973). They thus provide
domestic groups with distinctive cores of relatives that correspond to the inclusions and ex-
clusions produced by the movements of married couples. These movements themselves are
influenced by the demographic, technological,
economic, and ecological conditions in which
people find themselves. Thus, in many societies descent rules and other kinship principles
can be seen as organizing and justifying domestic group structures in relation to particular
infrastructural conditions.

Causes of Bilateral Descent

Bilateral descent is associated with various
combinations of neolocality, ambilocality, and
bilocality. These locality practices in turn usually reflect a high degree of mobility and flexibility among nuclear families. Mobility and
flexibility, as we have seen (Chapter 5), are useful for hunters and gatherers, and are an in-
trinsic feature of band organization. The !Kung
San, for example, are primarily bilateral, and
this reflects in turn a predominant bilocal post-

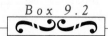

Box 9.2

PRINCIPAL VARIETIES OF POSTMARITAL RESIDENCE

NAME OF PATTERN	PLACE WHERE MARRIED COUPLE RESIDES
Neolocality	Apart from either husband's or wife's kin
Bilocality	Alternately shifting from husband's kin to wife's kin
Ambilocality	Some couples with husband's kin, others with wife's kin
Patrilocality	With husband's father
Matrilocality	With wife's mother
Avunculocality	With husband's mother's brother
Amitalocality	With wife's father's sister
Uxorilocality	With the wife's kin (several of the above may be combined with uxorilocality)
Virilocality	With the husband's kin (several of the above may be combined with virilocality)

---

marital residence pattern. !Kung San camps contain a core of siblings of both sexes, plus their spouses and children and an assortment of more distant bilateral and affinal kin. Each year, in addition to much short-time visiting, about 13 percent of the population makes a more or less permanent residential shift from one camp to another, and about 35 percent divide their time equally among two or three different camps (Lee 1979:54). This mobility and flexibility is advantageous for people who must rely on hunting and gathering for their livelihood.

In the United States and Canada bilaterality is associated with a similar flexibility and mobility of nuclear families. Bilaterality in this case reflects a neolocal pattern that is advantageous with respect to wage-labor opportunities and the substitution of price-market money exchanges for kinship-mediated forms of exchange. Whereas the !Kung San always live with relatives and depend on kindreds and ex-

tended families for their subsistence, European and American nuclear families often live far away from any relatives whatsoever and interact with their kindreds primarily at holidays, weddings, and funerals.

Determinants of Cognatic Lineages and Clans

Cognatic lineages and cognatic clans are associated with *ambilocality*. This is a form of postmarital residence in which the married couple elects to stay on a relatively permanent basis with the wife's or the husband's domestic group. Ambilocality differs from European and American neolocality since residence is established with a definite group of kin. Ambilocality also differs from the bilocality of hunting-and-gathering societies in that the shifting from one domestic group to another occurs less frequently. This implies a relatively more sedentary form of village life and also a somewhat greater potential for developing exclusive "corporate" interests in people and property. Yet all cognatic descent groups, whether bilateral or ambilineal, have less potential for corporate unity than unilineal descent groups, a point to which we return in a moment.

One example of how cognatic lineages work has already been discussed. Such lineages occurred among the Pacific Northwest Coast potlatchers (see Chapter 7). The Kwakiutl potlatch chiefs sought to attract and to hold as large a labor force as they possibly could. (The more people a village put to work during a salmon run, the more fish they would catch.)

The core of each village consisted of a chieftain and his followers, usually demonstrably related to him through ambilineal descent and constituting a cognatic lineage known as a *numaym*. The chieftain claimed hereditary privileges and noble rank on the basis of ambilineal reckoning from his noble forebears. Validation of this status depended on his ability to recruit and hold an adequate following in the face of competition from like-minded neighbor chieftains. This importance placed on individual choice and the uncertainty surrounding the group's corporate estate is typical of cognatic lineages in other cultures as well.

Determinants of Unilineal Lineages and Clans

Although there is no basis for reviving nineteenth-century notions of universal stages in the evolution of kinship (see Appendix), certain well-substantiated general evolutionary trends do exist. Hunting-and-gathering societies tend to have cognatic descent groups and/or bilocal residence because their basic ecologi-

cal adjustment demands that local groups remain open, flexible, and nonterritorial. With the development of horticulture and more settled village life, the identification between domestic groups or villages and definite territories increased and became more exclusive. Population density increased and warfare became more intense, for reasons to be discussed (Chapter 10), contributing to the need for emphasizing exclusive group unity and solidarity (Ember et al. 1974). Under these conditions, unilineal descent groups with well-defined localized membership cores, a heightened sense of solidarity, and an ideology of exclusive rights over resources and people became the predominant form of kinship group. Using a sample of 797 agricultural societies, Michael Harner (1970) has shown that a very close statistical association exists between an increased reliance on agriculture as opposed to hunting and gathering and the replacement of cognatic descent groups by unilineal descent groups. Horticultural village societies that are organized unilineally outnumber those that are organized cognatically 380 to 111 in Harner's sample. Moreover, almost all the unilineal societies display signs of increased population pressure, as indicated by the depletion of wild plant and food resources.

Unilineal descent groups are closely associated with one or the other variety of unilocal residence — that is, patrilineality with patrilocality and matrilineality with matrilocality. In addition, there is a close correlation between avunculocality and matrilineality. With patrilineality, fathers, brothers, and sons form the core of the domestic group; and with matrilocality, mothers, sisters, and daughters form the core of the domestic group. The connections between these locality practices and descent rules should be clear, although the reason for the connection between avunculocality and matrilineality is more complex. With avuncu-

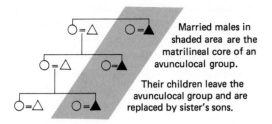

Married males in shaded area are the matrilineal core of an avunculocal group.

Their children leave the avunculocal group and are replaced by sister's sons.

Figure 9.11   Avunculocality.

locality, mother's brothers and sister's sons form the core of the domestic unit. Sister's son is born in her husband's mother's brother's household, but as a juvenile or adult, sister's son leaves this household and takes up residence with his own mother's brother (Figure 9.11). The way in which avunculocality works and the reason for its association with matrilineality will become clearer in a moment, as we examine the infrastructural causes of matrilocality and patrilocality.

Causes of Patrilocality

The overwhelming majority of known societies have male-centered residence and descent patterns. Seventy-one percent of 1179 societies classified by George Murdock (1967) are either patrilocal or virilocal; and in the same sample, societies that have patrilineal kin groups outnumber societies that have matrilineal kin groups 558 to 164. Patrilocality and patrilineality are the statistically "normal" mode of domestic organization. They have been predominant not only, as was once thought, in societies that have plows and draft animals or that practice pastoral nomadism, but in simple horticultural and slash-and-burn societies as well (Divale 1974).

It is difficult to escape the conclusion that the underlying reason for the prevalence of

patrilocality among village societies is that co-operation among males is in some sense more crucial than cooperation among females. Men, for example, are more effective in hand-to-hand combat than women, and women are less mobile than men during pregnancy and when nursing infants. As a consequence, men generally monopolize the weapons of war and the hunt, leading to male control over trade and politics. The practice of intense small-scale warfare between neighboring villages may be a crucial factor in promoting a widespread complex of male-centered and male-dominated institutions (Divale and Harris 1976). We will return to the issue of sex and gender hierarchies in Chapter 13.

Causes of Matrilocality

It is generally agreed that matrilineal descent groups will not form independently — that is, in the absence of matrilineal neighbors — unless matrilocality is the postmarital residence practice. But why matrilocality? One theory holds that when women's role in food production became more important, as in horticultural societies, domestic groups would tend to be structured around a core of females. This theory, however, must be rejected, because there is no greater association between horticulture and matrilocality than between horticulture and patrilocality (Divale 1974; Ember and Ember 1971). Moreover, it is difficult to see why field labor would require a degree of cooperation so high that only women from the same domestic groups could carry it out efficiently, nor why it would require all brothers and sons to be expelled from the natal domestic group (Burton and White 1987; Sanday 1973).

A more plausible theory is that matrilocality is selected when males are obliged to absent themselves from their wives and homes for prolonged periods. This occurs when warfare, hunting, and trade change from quick, short-distance forays to long-distance expeditions lasting several months. If patrilocal males leave a village for extended periods, they leave behind their patrilineal kin and group's corporate interests in property and people to be looked after solely by their wives. The allegiance of their wives, however, is to another patrilineal kin group. A patrilocal group's women are drawn from different kin groups and have little basis for cooperating among themselves when they are unsupervised by the male managers of the corporate domestic units into which they have married. There is no one home, so to speak, "to mind the store." Matrilocality solves this problem because it structures the domestic unit around a permanent core of resident mothers, daughters, and sisters who have been trained to cooperate with each other from birth and who identify the "minding of the store" with their own material and sentimental interests. Thus matrilocal domestic groups are less likely to be disrupted by the prolonged absence of their adult males.

In order for the transition from patri- to matrilocality to take place, a man merely needs to refuse to let his sister follow the patrilocal rule, denying her in marriage unless the husband agrees to live with her family rather than she with his. Women for their part would not be passive pawns in this arrangement since they would benefit from being able to live with their own parents and sisters rather than their husbands' parents and brothers. The prestige and power of women in matrilocal societies is generally greater than in patrilocal societies (see page 246).

The ability to launch and successfully complete long-distance expeditions implies that neighboring villages will not attack each other when the men are away. This is best as-sured by forming the expeditions around a core of males drawn from several neighboring villages or different households within a given village. Among patrilocal, patrilineal villages, the belligerent territorial teams consist of patrilineally related kin who constitute competitive "fraternal interest groups." These groups make shifting alliances with neighboring villages, exchange sisters, and raid each other. Most combat takes place between villages that are about a day's walk from each other. Matrilocal, matrilineal cultures, on the other hand, are bonded not by the exchange of women but by the inmarrying of males from different domestic groups. Scattering fathers and brothers into several different households in different villages prevents the formation of competitive and disruptive fraternal interest groups.

Thus matrilocal, matrilineal societies such as the Iroquois of New York and the Huron of Ontario enjoy a high degree of internal peace. But most such matrilineal societies have a history of intense warfare directed outward against powerful enemies (Gramby 1977; Trigger 1978). The Nayar, for example, were a soldier caste in the service of the kings of Malabar. Among the matrilocal Mundurucu of the Amazon, conflict between villages was unheard of and interpersonal aggression was suppressed. But the Mundurucu launched raids against enemies hundreds of miles away, and unrelenting hostility and violence characterized their relations with the "outside world" (Murphy 1956). We will encounter other examples of warlike matrilineal societies in Chapter 10.

Causes of Avunculocality

In matrilocal, matrilineal societies, males are reluctant to relinquish control over their own sons to the members of their wives' kin groups, and they are not easily reconciled to the fact that it is their sons rather than their daughters who must move away from them at marriage. Because of this contradiction, matrilocal, matrilineal systems tend to revert to patrilocal, patrilineal systems if the forces responsible for keeping males away from their natal villages and domestic groups are removed or moderated.

One way to solve this contradiction is to loosen the male's marital obligations (already weak in matrilocal societies) to the point where he need not live with his wife at all. This is the path followed by the Nayar. As we have seen, Nayar men had no home other than their natal domestic unit; they were untroubled by what happened to their children — whom they were scarcely able to identify — and they had no difficulty keeping their sisters and their nephews and nieces under proper fraternal and avuncular control.

But a more common solution to the tension between male interests and matrilineality is the development of avunculocal patterns of residence. It is a remarkable fact that there are more matrilineal descent groups that are avunculocal than matrilineal descent groups that are matrilocal (see Table 9.1).

Under avunculocality a male eventually goes to live with his mother's brothers in their matrilineal domestic unit; his wife joins him there. Upon maturity, a male ego's son will in turn depart for ego's wife's brother's domestic unit (ego's daughter, however, may remain resident if she marries her father's sister's son). Thus the male core of an avunculocal domestic unit consists of a group of brothers and their sister's sons. The function of this arrangement seems to be to maintain a male fraternal interest group in the residential core of the matrilineal descent group as a means of coping with the development of internal tensions including the outbreak of internal warfare (Keegan and Maclachlan 1989).

The logical opposite of avunculocality — namely, *amitalocality* (amita = aunt) — exists if brother's daughters and father's sisters constitute the residential core of a patrilineal domestic unit. Most instances of amitalocality involve patrilocal, patrilineal descent groups that practice matrilateral cross-cousin marriage. Such groups contain male ego's paternal aunts. But these women will not constitute the residential core of the domestic unit, since it is they and not their husbands who depart from their natal domiciles to reside with their spouses (cf. Ottenheimer 1984).

A rather thin line separates avunculocality

Table 9.1

RELATIONSHIP BETWEEN RESIDENCE AND DESCENT IN THE ETHNOGRAPHIC ATLAS

	POSTMARITAL RESIDENCE				
KIN GROUPS	MATRILOCAL OR UXORILOCAL	AVUNCULOCAL	PATRILOCAL OR VIRILOCAL	OTHER	TOTAL
Patrilineal	1	0	563	25	588
Matrilineal	53	62	30	19	164

Sources: Divale and Harris 1976; Murdock 1967.

from patrilocality. If the resident group of brothers decides to permit one or more of its sons to remain with them after marriage, the residential core will begin to resemble an ambilocal domestic group. If more sons than nephews are retained in residence, the locality basis for a reassertion of patrilineal descent will be present.

After a society has adopted matrilocality and developed matrilineal descent groups, changes in the original conditions may lead to a restoration of the patrilocal, patrilineal pattern. At any given moment, many societies are probably in a transitional state between one form of residence and another and one form of kinship ideology and another. Since the changes in residence and descent may not proceed in perfect tandem at any given moment — that is, descent changes may lag behind residence changes — one should expect to encounter combinations of residence with the "wrong" descent rule. For example, a few patrilocal societies and quite a large number of virilocal societies have matrilineal descent, and one or two uxorilocal societies have patrilineal descent (see Table 9.1). But there is evidence for a very powerful strain toward consistency in the alignment among domestic groups; their ecological, military, and economic adaptations; and their ideologies of descent.

Kinship Terminologies

Another aspect of domestic ideology that participates in the same strain toward functional consistency is kinship terminology. Every culture has a special set of terms (such as *father, mother, cousin*) for designating types of kin. The terms plus the rules for using them constitute a culture's *kin terminological system*.

Lewis Henry Morgan was the first anthropologist to realize that despite the thousands of different languages over the face of the globe, and despite the immense number of different kinship terms in these languages, there are only a handful of basic types of kin terminological systems. These systems can best be defined by the way in which terms are applied to an abbreviated genealogical grid consisting of two generations, including ego's siblings of the same and opposite sex and ego's cross and parallel cousins. Here we will examine only three of the best-known systems in order to illustrate the nature of the causal and functional relationships that link alternative kinship terminologies to the other aspects of domestic organizations. (It should be emphasized that these are basic terminological *types*. Actual instances often vary in details.)

ESKIMO TERMINOLOGY

The kind of kin terminological systems with which most North Americans are familiar is known as *Eskimo*, shown in Figure 9.12. Two important features of this system are these: First, none of the terms applied to ego's nuclear relatives — 1, 2, 6, 5 — is applied outside the nuclear family; and second, there is no distinction between maternal and paternal sides. This means that there is no distinction between cross and parallel cousins or between cross and parallel aunts or uncles. These features reflect the fact that societies using Eskimo terminology generally lack corporate descent groups. In the absence of such groups, the nuclear family tends to stand out as a separate and functionally dominant productive and reproductive unit. For this reason, its members are given a terminological identity separate from all other kin types. On the other hand, the lumping of

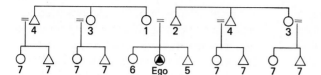

Figure 9.12   *Eskimo terminology.*

all cousins under a single term (7) reflects the strength of bilateral as opposed to unilineal descent. The influence of bilateral descent is also reflected in the failure to distinguish terminologically between aunts and uncles on the mother's side and those on the father's side. The theoretical predictions concerning Eskimo terminology are strongly confirmed by the tabulations of Murdock's *Ethnographic Atlas* (1967). Of the 71 societies having Eskimo terminology, only 4 have large extended families and only 13 have unilineal descent groups. In 54 of the 71 Eskimo terminology societies, descent groups are entirely absent or are represented only by kindreds.

As the name implies, *Eskimo* is frequently found among hunters and gatherers. This is because any factors that isolate the nuclear family increase the probability that an Eskimo terminology will occur. As we have seen, among hunting-and-gathering groups, the determining factors are low population densities and the need for maximum geographical mobility in relationship to fluctuations in the availability of game and other resources. In industrial societies the same terminological pattern reflects the intrusion of price-market institutions into the domestic routine and the high level of wage-induced social and geographic mobility.

HAWAIIAN TERMINOLOGY

Another common kin terminological system is known as *Hawaiian*. This is the easiest system to portray, since it has the fewest number of terms (Figure 9.13). In some versions even the distinction between the sexes is dropped, leaving one term for the members of ego's generation and another for the members of ego's parents' generation. The most remarkable feature of Hawaiian terminology, as compared with Eskimo, is the application of the same terms to people inside and outside the nuclear family. Hawaiian is thus compatible with situations where the nuclear family is submerged within a domestic context dominated by extended families and other corporate descent groups. In Murdock's *Ethnographic Atlas*, 21 percent of the Hawaiian terminology societies do indeed have large extended families. In addition, well over 50 percent of Hawaiian terminology societies have some form of corporate descent group other than extended families.

Theoretically, most of these descent

Figure 9.13   *Hawaiian terminology.*

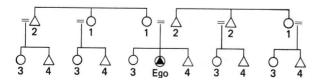

groups should be cognatic rather than unilineal. The reason for this prediction is that the merging of relatives on the maternal side with those on the paternal side indicates an indifference toward unilineality, and an indifference toward unilineality is logically consistent with ambilineal or bilateral descent.

Data from Murdock's ethnographic sample only partially support this prediction: There are, indeed, many more Hawaiian terminology societies that have cognatic as opposed to unilineal descent, but there are many exceptions for which as yet no generally accepted explanation is available.

IROQUOIS

In the presence of unilineal kin groups, there is a worldwide tendency to distinguish parallel from cross cousins, as previously noted. This pattern is widely associated with a similar distinction in the first ascending generation, whereby father's brothers are distinguished from mother's brothers and father's sisters are distinguished from mother's sisters.

An *Iroquois* terminology exists where — in addition to these distinctions between cross and parallel cousins and cross and parallel aunts and uncles — mother's sister is terminologically merged with mother, father's brother is terminologically merged with father, and parallel cousins are terminologically merged with ego's brothers and sisters (Figure 9.14).

This pattern of merging occurs in large part as a result of the shared membership of siblings in corporate unilineal descent groups and of the marriage alliances based on cross-cousin marriage between such groups. In Murdock's ethnographic sample there are 166 societies having Iroquois terminology. Of these, 119 have some form of unilineal descent group (70 percent).

We have only skimmed the surface of a few of the many fascinating and important problems in the field of kinship terminology (Figure 9.15). But perhaps enough has been said to establish at least one point: Kin terminological systems possess a remarkable logical coherence. Yet like so many other aspects of culture, kin terminological systems are never the planned product of any inventive genius. Most people are unaware that such systems even exist. Clearly, the major features of these systems represent recurrent unconscious adjustments to the prevailing conditions of domestic life. Yet there are many details of kin terminologies, as well as of other kinship phenomena, that are as yet not well understood.

Summary

To study kinship is to study the ideologies that justify and normalize the corporate structure of domestic groups. The basis of kinship is the tracing of relationships through marriage and descent. Descent is the belief that certain persons play a special role in the conception, birth, or nurturance of certain children. Many different folk theories of descent exist, none of which corresponds precisely to modern-day

Figure 9.14 Iroquois terminology.

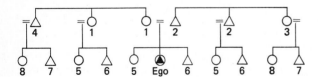

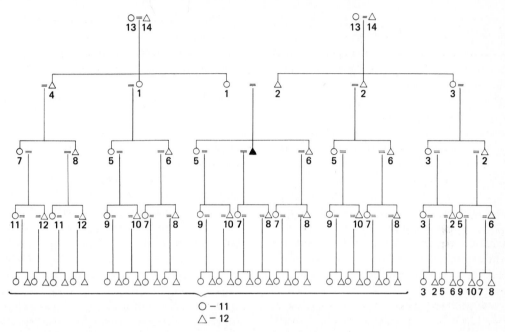

Figure 9.15 *For the kinship enthusiast: Crow terminology, male ego.*
Many cultures have terminological systems in which the influence of lineality overwhelms generational criteria. These systems occur in both matrilineal and patrilineal versions. The matrilineal variety is known as Crow. These Crow systems involve the distinction between patrilateral and matrilateral cross cousins. Not only are these cousins distinguished from each other, but the patrilateral cross cousins are equated with father's sister, and father. There is also the curious fact that the matrilateral cross cousins are equated with ego's daughter and son.

scientific understandings of procreation and reproduction.

The principal varieties of cognatic descent rules are the bilateral and the ambilineal; these are associated with kindreds on the one hand, and with cognatic lineages and clans on the other. The principal varieties of unilineal descent are matrilineality and patrilineality. These are associated, respectively, with patri- and matrilineages or patri- and matriclans.

An important key to understanding alternative modes of descent and domestic organization is the pattern of postmarital residence. Bi-

lateral descent and bilateral descent groups are associated with neolocality, bilocality, and ambilocality. More specifically, the flexible and mobile forms of band organization are facilitated by bilocality, whereas the greater isolation of nuclear families in price-market economies gives rise to neolocality. Cognatic lineages and clans, on the other hand, give functional expression to ambilocality.

Unilineal domestic groups reflect unilocal patterns of residence. These in turn imply well-defined membership cores and an emphasis on exclusive rights over resources and people. There is a strong correlation between patrilocality and patrilineality on the one hand, and among matrilineality, matrilocality, and avunculocality on the other. Patrilocal and patrilineal groups are far more common than matrilineal or avunculocal groups. A reason for this is that warfare, hunting, and trading activities among village societies are monopolized by males. These activities, in turn, are facilitated by stressing the coresidence of fathers, brothers, and sons and the formation of fraternal interest groups. Under conditions of increasing population density and pressure on resources, local groups may find it adaptive to engage in long-distance war-trade-hunting expeditions. Such expeditions are facilitated by breaking up the fraternal interest groups and structuring domestic life around a residential core of mothers, sisters, and daughters or, in other words, by developing a matrilocal, matrilineal organization. Since males in matrilineal, matrilocal societies continue to dominate military and political institutions, they are inclined to reinject the patrilineal principle into domestic life and to moderate the effects of matrilocality on their control over their sons and daughters. This accounts for the fact that as many matrilineal societies are avunculocal as are matrilocal.

Thus the principal function of alternative rules of descent may be described as the establishment and maintenance of networks of cooperative and interdependent kinspeople aggregated into ecologically effective and militarily secure domestic production and reproduction units. In order for such units to act effectively and reliably, they must share an organizational ideology that interprets and validates the structure of the group and the behavior of its members. This interpretation of kinship rules can also be applied to the principal varieties of kin terminological systems. Such systems tend to classify relatives in conformity with the major features of domestic organization, locality practices, and descent rules. Eskimo terminology, for example, is functionally associated with domestic organizations in which nuclear families tend to be mobile and isolated; Hawaiian terminology is functionally associated with cognatic lineages and cognatic clans; and Iroquois terminology, with its emphasis on the distinction between cross and parallel cousins, is functionally associated with unilinear descent groups.

Chapter 10

LAW, ORDER, AND WAR
IN PRESTATE SOCIETIES

In this chapter we continue our discussion of the
structural level of sociocultural systems. The focus
now shifts from the structure of domestic groups to
the regulation of interpersonal relationships and the
maintenance of political cohesion and law and order
within and between band and village societies. The
chapter will show that conflict resolution through
warfare is present in both band and village societies,
and will discuss theories of why this is so.

Law and Order in Band and Village Societies

People in every society have conflicting interests (Figure 10.1). Even in band-level societies, old and young, sick and healthy, men and women do not want the same thing at the same time. Moreover, in every society people want something that others possess and are reluctant to give away. Every culture, therefore, must have structural provisions for resolving conflicts of interest in an orderly fashion and for preventing conflicts from escalating into disruptive confrontations. There are marked qualitative and quantitative differences, however, between the kinds of conflicting interests found in band and simple village societies and those found in more complex societies. There are also marked differences in the methods employed to prevent disruptive confrontations.

Hunter-gatherer societies such as the Eskimo, the !Kung San of the Kalahari, and the native Australians enjoy a high degree of personal security without having any rulers or law and order specialists. They have no kings, queens, dictators, presidents, governors, or mayors; police forces, soldiers, sailors, or marines; CIA, FBI, treasury agents, or federal marshals. They have no written law codes and no formal law courts; no lawyers, bailiffs, judges, district attorneys, juries, or court clerks; and no patrol cars, paddy wagons, jails, or penitentiaries. How do people get along without these law enforcement specialists and facilities, and why are modern societies so dependent on them?

The basic reasons for the differences are (1) the small size of band and simple village societies, (2) the central importance of domestic groups and kinship in their social organization, and (3) the absence of marked inequalities in access to technology and resources. Small size means that everyone knows everyone else personally; therefore, stingy, aggressive, and disruptive individuals can be identified by the group and exposed to the pressure of public opinion. The centrality of domestic group and kinship relations means that reciprocity can be the chief mode of exchange and that the collective interests of the domestic unit can be recog-

Figure 10.1   Yanomamo Club Fight.
Egalitarian people are not without problems of law and order.

nized by all its members. Finally, equality of access to technology and natural resources means that food and other forms of wealth cannot be withheld by a wealthy few while others endure shortages and hardships.

"Primitive Communism"?

Among band-level societies, all adults usually have access to the rivers, lakes, beaches, oceans, all the plants and animals, and the soil and the subsoil. Insofar as these are basic to the extrac-

tion of life-sustaining energy and materials, they are communal "property."

Anthropologists have reported the existence of nuclear family and even individual ownership of hunting-and-gathering territories among native American band-level societies in Canada, but these ownership patterns were associated with the fur trade and did not exist aboriginally (Knight 1974; Leacock 1973; Speck 1915). In other cases, reports of family territories fail to distinguish between ideological claims and actual behavior. The fact that a nuclear family regards a particular area as its "own" must be weighed against the conditions under which others can use the area and the consequences of trespass. If permission to use the area is always freely granted and if use without permission results merely in some muttering or name-calling, the modern notion of "ownership" may be the wrong concept to use. This, as we have seen (page 122), was the case with the "ownership" of Kapauku garden lands.

Among the !Kung San, water holes and hunting-and-gathering territories are emically "owned" by the residential core of particular bands. But since neighboring bands contain many intermarried kin, there is a great deal of sharing of access to resources as a result of mutual visiting. Neighbors who ask for permission to visit and to exploit the resources of a particular camp are seldom refused. Even people who come from distant bands and who lack close kin ties with the hosts are usually given permission to stay, especially for short periods, since it is understood that the hosts may return the visit at some future date (Lee 1979:337).

The prevalence of communal ownership of land, however, does not mean that hunter-gatherer bands lack private property altogether. There is little support for the theory of "primitive communism," which holds that there was a universal stage in the development of culture marked by the complete absence of private property (see Epstein 1968). Many material objects of band-level societies are effectively controlled ("owned") by specific individuals, especially items the user has produced. The members of even the most egalitarian societies usually believe that weapons, clothing, containers, ornaments, tools, and other "personal effects" ought not to be taken away or used without the consent of the "owner." However, the chance is remote that theft or misappropriation of such objects will lead to serious conflict (Woodburn 1982).

First of all, the accumulation of material possessions is rigidly limited by the recurrent need to break camp and travel long distances on foot. In addition, most utilitarian items may be borrowed without difficulty when the owner is not using them. If there are not enough such items to go around (arrows, projectile points, nets, bark or gourd containers), easy access to the raw materials and mastery of the requisite skills provide the have-nots with the chance of making their own. Moreover, among societies having no more than a few hundred people, thieves cannot be anonymous. If stealing becomes habitual, a coalition of the injured parties will eventually take action. If you want something, better to ask for it openly: Most such requests are readily obliged, since reciprocity is the prevailing mode of exchange. Finally, it should be pointed out that, contrary to the experience of the successful modern bank robber, no one can make a living from stealing bows and arrows or feather headdresses, since there is no regular market at which such items can be exchanged for food (see page 118).

Mobilizing Public Opinion: Song Duels

The most important requirement for the control of disputes in band societies is the temporary insulation of the disputants from the corporate response of their respective kin. As long as the disputants feel they have the backing of their kin, they will continue to press their claims and counterclaims. The members of kin groups, however, never react mechanically. They are eager not to be caught in a situation in which they are opposed by a majority of people. Public opinion, in other words, influences the support disputants can expect from their kin.

What matters is not so much who is morally right or wrong, or who is lying or telling the truth; the important thing is to mobilize public opinion on one side or the other decisively enough to prevent the outbreak of large-scale feuding.

A classic example of how such mobilization can be achieved independently of abstract principles of justice is the song contest of the central and eastern Eskimo (Figure 10.2). Here, it frequently happens that one man claims that another man has stolen his wife. The counter-claim is that she was not stolen but left voluntarily because her husband "was not man enough" to take good care of her. The issue is settled at a large public meeting that might be likened to a court. But no testimony is taken in support of either of the two versions of why the wife has left her husband. Instead, the "disputants" take turns singing insulting songs at each other. The "court" responds to each performance with differential degrees of laughter. Eventually one of the singers gets flustered, and the hooting and hollering raised against him becomes total—even his relatives have a hard time not laughing (Box 10.1).

The Eskimo have no police-military specialists to see to it that the "decision" is enforced. Yet, chances are that the man who has lost the song duel will give in, since he can no longer count on anyone to back him up if he chooses to escalate the dispute. Nonetheless, the defeated man may decide to go it alone.

Wife stealing does occasionally lead to

Figure 10.2   Song Contest.
Eskimo "disputants" in "court" in eastern Greenland.

Box 10.1

SONG DUEL

Something was whispered
Of a man and wife
Who could not agree
And what was it all about?
A wife who in rightful anger
Tore her husband's furs,
Took their boat
And rowed away with her son.
Ay-ay, all who listen,
What do you think of him
Who is great in his anger
But faint in strength,
Blubbering helplessly?

He got what he deserved
Though it was he who proudly
Started this quarrel with stupid words.

Source: Rasmussen 1929:231–232.

murder. When this happens, the man who has lost public support may survive on the strength of his own vigilance and fighting skill. He will probably have to kill again, however, and with each transgression the coalition against him becomes larger and more determined, until finally he falls victim to an ambush.

Mobilizing Public Opinion: Witchcraft Accusations

Among band and simple village societies, part-time magico-religious specialists known as *shamans* frequently play an important role in mobilizing public opinion and in eliminating persistent sources of conflict. Most cultures reject the idea that misfortune can result from natural causes. If animals suddenly become scarce or if several people fall sick, it is assumed that somebody is practicing witchcraft. It is the shaman's job to identify the culprit. Normally this is done through the art of *divination*. Putting themselves into trances with the aid of drugs, tobacco smoke, or monotonous drumming, shamans discover the name of the culprit. The people demand vengeance, and the culprit is ambushed and murdered.

The chances are that the murdered individual never attempted to carry out any witchcraft at all! In other words, the witches are probably wholly "innocent" of the crime with which they have been charged. Nonetheless, the shaman's witchcraft accusations usually conserve rather than destroy the group's feeling of unity.

Consider the case reported by Gertrude Dole (1966) for the Kuikuru—an egalitarian, village-dwelling group of Brazilian Indians (Figure 10.3). Fires had occurred in two houses. The shaman went into a trance and discovered that the fires had been caused by a man who had left the village some years previously and had never returned. This man had only one male relative, who was also no longer living in the village. Before the accused witch had left the village, he had become engaged to a young girl. The shaman's brother had wanted to marry the girl, but the girl's mother was opposed to the betrothal:

> During the course of the divining ceremony, the shaman carried on dialogues with various interested members of the community. When he finally disclosed the identity of the culprit, it created considerable anxiety. One after another, several individuals stood apart in the plaza and spoke in long monologues. . . . In the

Figure 10.3   Kuikuru Shaman.
The shaman is leaving the village with his assistants
on the way to a nearby lake to recover the lost soul
of a patient lying ill in the house seen in the
background. The shaman intends to dive to the
bottom of the lake and wrest the soul away from the
evil spirit who stole it from the patient, and then
implant it back into the patient's body.

heat of the excitement, the shaman's
brother left with a few companions to kill
the man suspected of witchcraft. [1966:76]

The ethnographer points out that among
the Kuikuru a change of residence from one
village to another usually indicates that there is

trouble brewing and that, in effect, the individual has been ostracized. (The Kuikuru suspected Dole and her anthropologist husband
of having been "kicked out" of their own society.) Thus the man accused of sorcery was not a
randomly chosen figure but one who fulfilled
several well-defined criteria: (1) a history of disputes and quarrels within the village, (2) a motivation for continuing to do harm (the broken
engagement), and (3) a weak kinship backing.

Thus the shaman's accusation was not
based on a spur-of-the-moment decision:
There had been a long incubation period during which the shaman in or out of trance
sounded out his fellow villagers on their attitudes toward the accused. As Dole indicates,
the supernatural authority of the shaman
allows him to make public indictments. But
shamans are not free to do any kind of mischief
that pops into their heads, as in late-night
movie versions of the sinister medicine man
turning the "natives" against the friendly European explorers. Rather, they are largely constrained by public opinion. Although the act of
divination appears to put the shaman in charge
of the judicial process, the shaman actually
"deduces, formulates, and expresses the will of
the people" (Dole 1966:76). Shamans abuse
their supernatural gifts if they accuse people
who are well liked and who enjoy strong kin
group support. If they persist in making such
mistakes, they themselves will be ostracized
and eventually murdered.

The peculiar thing about witchcraft as a
means of social control is that its practitioners,
if they exist at all, can seldom be detected. The
number of persons falsely accused of witchcraft
probably far exceeds the number who are justly
accused. It is clear, therefore, that nonpractice
of witchcraft is no safeguard against an accusation of witchcraft. How then do you protect
yourself from such false accusations? By acting

in an amiable, open, generous manner; by avoiding quarrels; and by doing everything possible not to lose the support of your kin groups. Thus, the occasional killing of a supposed sorcerer results in much more than the mere elimination of a few actual or potential antisocial individuals. These violent incidents convince everyone of the importance of not being mistaken for an evildoer. As a result, as among the Kuikuru, people are made more amiable, cordial, generous, and willing to cooperate:

> The norm of being amiable deters individuals from accusing one another of delicts [crimes], hence in the absence of effective political or kin-group control, interpersonal relations have become a kind of game, in which almost the only restrictive rule is not to show hostility to one another for fear of being suspected of witchcraft. [Dole 1966:74]

This system is not "fail-safe." Many cases are known of witchcraft systems that seem to have broken down, involving the community in a series of destructive retaliatory accusations and murders. In general, the incidence of witchcraft accusations varies with the amount of community dissension and frustration (Mair 1969; Nadel 1952). When a traditional culture is upset by exposure to new diseases, increased competition for land, and recruitment for wage labor, an epoch of increased dissension and frustration can be expected. This period is often characterized by frenzied activity among those who are skilled in tracking down and exposing the malevolent effects of witches. For example, the breakup of feudal society in Europe was accompanied by two centuries of intensified witch hunting. Similar "witch crazes" occurred among native populations in Africa and the Americas as a result of encounters with European and American slave raiders and settlers during colonial times.

Headmanship

To the extent that political leadership can be said to exist at all among band and simple village societies, it is exercised by headmen (or far less commonly, headwomen). The headman, unlike such specialists as king, president, or dictator, is a relatively powerless figure incapable of compelling obedience. He lacks sufficient force to do so. When he gives a command, he is never certain of being able to punish physically those who disobey. (Hence if he wants to stay in "office," he gives few direct commands.) In contrast, the political power of genuine rulers depends on their ability to expel or exterminate any readily foreseeable combination of nonconforming individuals and groups. Genuine rulers control access to basic resources and to the tools and weapons for hurting or killing people.

Among the Eskimo, leadership is especially diffuse, being closely related to success in hunting. A group will follow an outstanding hunter and defer to his opinion with respect to choice of hunting spots. But in all other matters, the "leader's" opinion carries no more weight than any other man's.

Similarly, among the !Kung San, each band has its recognized "leaders," most of whom are males. Such leaders may speak out more than others and are listened to with a bit more deference than is usual, but they "have no formal authority" and "can only persuade, but never enforce their will on others" (Lee 1979:333–334;1982). When Richard Lee asked the !Kung San whether they had "headmen" in the sense of powerful chiefs, he was told: "Of course we have headmen! In fact we are all headmen . . . each one of us is headman over himself" (ibid.:348).

A similar pattern of leadership is reported for the Semai of Malaya. Despite recent attempts by outsiders to bolster up the power of Semai leaders, the headman is merely the most prestigious figure among a group of peers. In the words of Robert Dentan, who carried out fieldwork among these egalitarian shifting horticulturalists:

> [The headman] keeps the peace by conciliation rather than coercion. He must be personally respected. . . . Otherwise people will drift away from him or gradually stop paying attention to him. Moreover, the Semai recognizes only two or three occasions on which he can assert his authority: dealing as a representative of his people with non-Semai; mediating a quarrel, if invited by the quarreling parties to do so but not otherwise; and . . . selecting and apportioning land for fields. Furthermore, most of the time a good headman gauges his general feeling about an issue and bases his decision on that, so that he is more a spokesman for public opinion than a molder of it. [1968:68]

Somewhat confusingly, the term *chief* is often used to designate the kind of leadership embodied in the concept of headman. But the context usually clarifies the kind of leadership involved. For example, Claude Lévi-Strauss refers to the Nambikwara Indians of Brazil as having "chiefs," yet he states firmly:

> It should be said at once that the chief cannot seek support either in clearly defined powers or in publicly recognized authority. . . . One or two malcontents

may throw the chief's whole programme out of joint. Should this happen, the chief has no powers of coercion. He can disembarrass himself of undesirable elements only in so far as all the others are of the same mind as himself. [1963b:303]

Headmanship is likely to be a frustrating and irksome position. The cumulative impression given by descriptions of leadership among Brazilian Indian groups, such as the Mehinacu of Brazil's Xingu National Park (see Box 10.2), is that of a zealous scoutmaster on an overnight cookout. The first one up in the morning, the headman tries to rouse his companions by standing in the middle of the village plaza and shouting. The headman seems to cajole, harangue, and plead from morning to night. If a task needs to be done, it is the headman who starts doing it, and it is the headman who works at it harder than anyone else. Moreover, the headman must set an example not only for hard work but for generosity. After a fishing or hunting expedition, he is expected to give away more of the catch than anyone else; if trade goods are obtained, he must be careful not to keep the best pieces for himself (Figure 10.4).

It is pertinent at this point to recall the plight of the ungenerous Kapauku headman (Chapter 7). Even the most generous headman in good standing cannot force obedience to his decisions:

> If the principals are not willing to comply, the authority [i.e., the headman] becomes emotional and starts to shout reproaches; he makes long speeches in which evidence, rules, decisions, and threats form inducements. Indeed, the authority may go as far as to start *wainai* (the mad dance), or change his tactics suddenly and weep bitterly about the misconduct of the defendant and the fact that he refuses to

Box 10.2

THE RIGHT STUFF

The most significant qualifications for Mehinacu chieftainship are learned skills and personal attributes. The chief, for example, is expected to excel at public speaking. Each evening he should stand in the center of the plaza and exhort his fellow tribesmen to be good citizens. He must call upon them to work hard in their gardens, to take frequent baths, not to sleep during the day, not to be angry with each other, and not to have sexual relations too frequently. . . . In addition to being a skilled orator, the chief is expected to be a generous man. This means that when he returns from a successful fishing trip, he will bring most of his catch out to the men's houses where it is cooked and shared by the men of the tribe. His wife must be generous, bringing manioc cakes and pepper to the men whenever they call for it. Further, the chief must be willing to part with possessions. When one of the men catches a harpy eagle, for example, the chief must buy it from him with a valuable shell belt in the name of the entire tribe. . . . A chief should also be a man who never becomes angry in public. . . . In his public speeches he should never criticize any of his fellow tribesmen, no matter how badly they may have affronted the chief or the tribe as a whole.

Source: Gregor 1969:88–89.

Figure 10.4   Mehinacu Chieftainship.
In front of the men's house, the chief is redistributing presents given to him by the ethnographer.

obey. Some native authorities are so skilled in the art of persuasion that they can produce genuine tears which almost always break the resistance of the unwilling party. [Pospisil 1968:221]

One wonders whether the Kapauku headman sheds tears more because he is frustrated than because he is skilled.

Blood Feud

As previously indicated (page 174), the ever-present danger confronting societies that lack genuine rulers is that their kinship groups tend to react as units to real or alleged aggression against one of their members. In this way disputes involving individuals may escalate. The worst danger arises from disputes that lead to homicide. The members of rulerless societies believe that the only proper reaction to a murder is to kill the murderer or any convenient member of the murderer's kin group. Yet the absence of centralized political authority does not mean that blood feuds cannot be brought under control.

Mechanisms for preventing homicide from flaring into a protracted feud include the transference of substantial amounts of prized possessions from the slayer's kin group to the victim's kin group. This practice is especially common and effective among pastoral peoples, whose animals are a concentrated form of material wealth and for whom bride-price is a regular aspect of kin group exogamy.

For example, among the Nuer, a pastoral and farming people who live amid the marshy grasslands of the Upper Nile in the Sudan, there is no centralized political leadership (see Box 10.3). The Nuer settle their feuds (or at

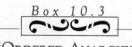

The lack of governmental organs among the Nuer, the absence of legal institutions of developed leadership, and generally, of organized political life is remarkable. . . . The ordered anarchy in which they live accords well with their character, for it is impossible to live among Nuer and conceive of rulers ruling over them. . . . The Nuer is a product of hard and egalitarian upbringing, is deeply democratic, and is easily roused to violence. This turbulent spirit finds any restraint irksome and no man recognizes a superior. Wealth makes no difference. A man with many cattle is envied but not treated differently from a man with few cattle. Birth makes no difference. . . . There is no master or servant in their society but only equals who regard themselves as God's noblest creation. . . . Among themselves even the suspicion of an order riles a man . . . he will not submit to any authority which clashes with his own interest and he does not consider himself bound to anyone.

Source: Evans-Pritchard 1940:181–182.

least deescalate them) by transferring 40 or more head of cattle to the victim's affines and kin. If a man has been killed, these animals will be used to "buy" a wife whose sons will fill the void left by his death. The dead man's closest kin are obliged to resist the offer of cattle, demanding instead a life for a life. However, more distant kin do their best to convince the others to accept the compensation. In this effort they are aided by certain semisacred arbitration specialists. The latter, known as *leopard skin chiefs* (Figure 10.5), are usually men whose kin groups are not represented locally and who can hence more readily act as neutral intermediaries.

The leopard skin chief is the only one who can ritually cleanse a murderer. If a homicide takes place, the killer flees at once to the leopard skin chief's house, which is a sanctuary respected by all Nuer. Nonetheless, the leopard skin chief lacks even the rudiments of political power; the most that he can do to the reluctant members of the slain man's relatives is to threaten them with various supernatural curses. Yet the determination to prevent a feud is so great that the injured relatives eventually accept the cattle as compensation (Verdon 1982).

Figure 10.5   Leopard Skin Chief.

Nonkin Associations: Sodalities

Although relations of affinity and descent dominate the political life of band and simple village peoples, nonkin forms of political organization also occur to a limited extent. Such groups are called *sodalities*. A common form of sodality is the exclusive men's or women's association or "club." These usually involve men and women drawn from different domestic groups who cooperate in secret ritual or craft performances. We will discuss these organizations in the chapter devoted to gender roles (Chapter 13). Age-grade associations are another common form of sodality, already mentioned with respect to the Masai warrior camps (page 133). Among the Samburu, another group of East African pastoralists, all men initiated into manhood over a span of about 12 to 14 years comprised an age set whose members had a special feeling of solidarity that cut across domestic and lineage kin groups. The age-set members advanced as a group from junior to senior status. As juniors they were responsible for military combat and as seniors they were responsible for initiating and training the up-coming age sets (Bernardi, 1985; Kertzer 1978; Spencer 1965).

A classic case of sodality is the native North American military associations that developed on the Great Plains after the introduction of the horse. Among the Crow and the Cheyenne, these associations tried to outdo one another in acts of daring during combat and in horse-stealing expeditions. Although the members of each club did not fight as a unit, they met in their respective tepees to reminisce and sing about their exploits, and they wore distinctive insignia and clothing. Gretel and Perttie Pelto (1976:324) have aptly compared them to organizations like the Veterans of Foreign Wars and the American Legion because their main function was to celebrate military exploits and to uphold the honor and prestige of the "tribe." However, on the occasion of a long march to a new territory or large-scale collective hunts, the military clubs took turns supervising and policing the general population. For example, they prevented over-eager hunters from stampeding the buffalo herds, and they suppressed rowdy behavior at ceremonials by fining or banishing disruptive individuals. But these were simply seasonal functions, since it was only during the spring and summer that large numbers of unrelated people could congregate together at the same camp.

Warfare Among Hunters and Gatherers

War is defined as armed combat between groups of people who constitute separate territorial teams or political communities (Otterbein 1973). Some anthropologists believe that warfare was universally practiced, even among Paleolithic (Old Stone Age) hunters and gatherers (Lizot 1979:151). Others hold that warfare was uncommon until the advent of state societies. It has been said that warfare was absent among the following hunter-gatherers: the Andaman Islanders, the Shoshoni, the Yahgan, and the Mission Indians of California (Lesser 1968; MacLeish 1972). Even these groups, however, may have practiced warfare at some time in the past. On the other hand, William Divale (1972) lists 37 hunting-and-gathering cultures in which warfare is known to have been practiced. Some anthropologists attribute these cases to the shocks of contact with state-level colonial systems. Warfare was probably practiced by some Paleolithic hunters and gatherers, but on a small scale and infrequently.

The archaeological evidence for warfare in the Paleolithic is inconclusive. Mutilated skulls found in Paleolithic caves have been interpreted as indicating prehistoric head-hunting and cannibalism, but no one really knows how the individuals died. Even if cannibalism was practiced, the cannibalized individuals were not necessarily enemies. Eating the brains of deceased kin is a form of mortuary ritual (see page 352).

Good archaeological evidence for cannibalism in conjunction with warfare is confined to the Neolithic (New Stone Age). At Fonte-brégova Cave (6000 – 5000 B.P.) in southeastern France, the remains of at least six individuals were butchered and eaten in a manner that cannot be distinguished from the way in which animal bones were butchered and eaten (Villa et al. 1986).

Warfare probably increased in intensity during the Neolithic among village-organized farming cultures. Some of the earliest Neolithic towns in the Middle East contained watchtowers and fortification walls.

Among nonsedentary hunters and gatherers, warfare involved a higher degree of individualized combat directed toward the adjustment of real or imagined personal injuries and deprivations. Although the combat teams may have had a temporary territorial base, the organization of battle and the consequences of victory or defeat reflected the loose association between people and territory. The victors did not gain territory by routing their enemies. Warfare among village-dwelling cultivators, however, frequently involves a total team effort in which definite territories are fought over and in which defeat may result in the rout of a whole community from its fields, dwellings, and natural resources.

The slippery line between warfare and personal retribution among hunters and gatherers is well illustrated in the example of armed conflict among the Tiwi of Bathurst and Melville Islands, northern Australia (Figure 10.6). As recounted by C. W. Hart and Arnold Pilling (1960), a number of men from the Tiklauila and Rangwila bands developed personal grievances against a number of men who were residing with the Mandiimbula band. The aggrieved individuals, together with their relatives, put on the white paint of war, armed themselves, and set off, some 30 strong, to do battle with the Mandiimbula:

Figure 10.6   Tiwi Warrior.
Tiwi man dressed in traditional dance body paint and feathers.

> On arrival at the place where the latter, duly warned of its approach, had gathered, the war partly announced its presence. Both sides then exchanged a few insults and agreed to meet formally in an open space where there was plenty of room. [1960:84]

During the night, individuals from both groups visited each other, renewing acquaintances. In the morning the two armies lined up at the opposite sides of the battlefield. Hostilities were begun by elders shouting insults and accusations at particular individuals in the "enemy" ranks. Although some of the old men urged that a general attack be launched, their grievances turned out to be directed not at the Mandiimbula band but at one or at most two or three individuals: "Hence when spears began to be thrown, they were thrown by individuals for reasons based on individual disputes" (Hart and Pilling 1960:84). Marksmanship was poor because it was the old men who did most of the spear-throwing:

Not infrequently the person hit was some innocent noncombatant or one of the screaming old women who weaved through the fighting men, yelling obscenities at everybody, and whose reflexes for dodging spears were not as fast as those of the men. . . . As soon as somebody was wounded . . . fighting stopped immediately until the implications of this new incident could be assessed by both sides. [ibid.]

Although hunters and gatherers seldom try to annihilate each other and often retire from the field after one or two casualties have occurred, the cumulative effect may be quite considerable. Remember that the average !Kung San band has only about 30 people in it. If such a band engages in war only twice per generation, and each time with the loss of only one adult male, casualties due to warfare would account for more than 10 percent of all adult male deaths. This is an extremely high figure when one realizes that less than 1 percent of all male deaths in Europe and the United States during the twentieth century have been battlefield casualties. In contrast, Lloyd Warner estimated that 28 percent of the adult male deaths among the Murngin, a hunting-and-gathering culture of northern Australia, were due to battlefield casualties (Livingston 1968).

Warfare Among Village Agriculturalists

Although village peoples were not the first to practice warfare, they did expand the scale and ferocity of military engagements. Village houses, food-processing equipment, crops in the field, domestic animals, secondary-growth forests, and prime garden lands represent capi-

tal investments closely identified with the arduous labor inputs of specific groups of individuals. The defense of this investment laid the basis for the development of stable, exclusive territorial identities. Villages often oppose each other as traditional enemies, repeatedly attack and plunder each other, and often expropriate each other's territories. Archaeologically, the onset of territoriality is suggested by the practice of burying deceased villagers beneath the houses they occupied during life (Flannery 1972). Ethnologically, the intensification of local identities is suggested by the development of unilineal systems of reckoning descent. As we saw (page 162), development of the concern with descent and inheritance is closely related to the degree to which agricultural populations cease to depend on hunting and gathering for their food supply.

Warfare among village cultivators is likely to be more costly in terms of battle casualties than among seminomadic hunters and gatherers. Among the Dani of West Irian, New Guinea, warfare has an open-field, ritualistic phase (which resembles the encounters described for the Tiwi) in which casualties are light. But there are also sneak attacks resulting in a hundred fatalities at a time and in the destruction and expulsion of whole villages. Karl G. Heider (1972) estimates that the Dani lost about 5 percent of their population per year to warfare and that 29 percent of the men and 3 percent of the women died as a result of battle injuries incurred primarily in raids and ambushes. Among the Yanomamo (Figure 10.7) of Brazil and Venezuela, who are reputed to have one of the world's "fiercest" and most warlike cultures, sneak raids and ambushes account for about 33 percent of adult male deaths from all causes and about 7 percent of adult female deaths from all causes (Chagnon 1974:160–161).

Figure 10.7   Yanomamo Warriors.
Preparations for battle include body painting and "line-ups."

Why War?

Because the population densities of band and simple village societies are generally very low, it often seems as if there is no infrastructural basis for warfare among such societies. The apparent absence of material motivations for warfare has given support to popular theories that attribute prestate warfare to an innate tendency for humans to be aggressive (Box 10.4). A variation on this theme is that band and village societies go to war not to gain any material advantage but because men regard it as an enjoyable sport. These theories are unsatisfactory. Although humans may have aggressive tendencies, there is no reason that such tendencies cannot be suppressed, controlled, or expressed in ways other than by armed combat. War is a particular form of organized activity that has developed during cultural evolution just as have other structural features, such as trade, the division of labor, and domestic groups. Just as there is no instinct for trade, for domestic organization, or for the division of labor, so there is no instinct for war. War is fought only to the extent that it is advantageous for some of the combatants.

The theory that warfare is engaged in because it is an enjoyable sport is contradicted by the fact that the most common reason cited by band and village warriors for going to war is to avenge deaths incurred in previous wars or

Box 10.4

AGGRESSION AND WAR

Our biological nature and evolutionary background may help us understand certain aspects of war. As a species, unquestionably we are capable of aggression on an unparalleled scale. But the capacity for collective violence does not explain the occurrence of war. Even if aggression is a universal trait, war is not. Warlike societies fight only occasionally, and many societies have no war at all. It is the circumstances of social life that explain this variation. But the image of humanity, warped by bloodlust, inevitably marching off to kill, is a powerful myth and an important prop of militarism in our society. Despite its lack of scientific credibility, there will remain those hard-headed "realists" who continue to believe in it, congratulating themselves for their "courage to face the truth," resolutely oblivious to the myth behind their reality.

Source: Ferguson 1984:12.

it not for the substantial material rewards that await the winners.

As we saw in Chapter 6, it is the adverse costs of rearing children that lead to low-population density and low rates of population growth among band and village societies. Therefore, the fact that population densities are low does not mean that band and village societies are not threatened by depletions of vital resources or by diminishing returns. Warfare in such societies almost always involves the prospect of safeguarding or improving a threatened standard of living by gaining access to vital resources, healthier habitats, or trade routes (Balee 1984; Biolsi 1984; J. Ross 1984). Warfare is thus best understood as a deadly form of competition between autonomous groups for scarce resources (R. Cohen 1984a; Ferguson 1988).

Game Animals and Warfare: The Yanomamo

The Yanomamo provide an important test of the theory that warfare has an infrastructural basis even among band and village groups that have very low population densities. The Yanomamo, with a population density of less than one person per square mile, derive their main source of food calories, with little effort, from the plaintains and banana trees that grow in their forest gardens. Like the Tsembaga Maring (page 80), they burn the forest to get these gardens started, but bananas and plantains are perennials that provide high yields per unit of labor input for many consecutive years. Since the Yanomamo live in the midst of the world's greatest tropical forest, the little burning they do scarcely threatens to "eat up the trees (Carneiro 1980)." A typical Yanomamo village has

deaths caused by enemy sorcerers. Combat is seldom entered into light-heartedly; the warriors need to psych themselves up with ritual dancing and singing, and often set out only after they have subdued their fears with psychotropic drugs. While some sports such as boxing and auto racing are also quite dangerous, they do not involve the same degree of mortal risk to which armed combatants expose themselves. Moreover, it is doubtful whether such dangerous sports would be practiced were

fewer than 100 people in it. A group this small could easily grow enough bananas or plantains in nearby garden sites without ever having to move (Figure 10.8). Yet the Yanomamo villages constantly break up into factions that move off into new territories.

Despite the apparent abundance of resources, the high level of Yanomamo warfare is probably caused by resource depletion and population pressure. The resource in question is meat. The Yanomamo lack domesticated sources of meat and must obtain their animal foods from hunting and collecting. Moreover, unlike many other inhabitants of the Amazon Basin, the Yanomamo traditionally did not have access to big-river fish and other aquatic animals that elsewhere provided high-quality animal foods sufficient to supply villages inhabited by over 1000 people.

It is possible for human beings to remain healthy on diets that lack animal foods; however, meat, fish, and other animal products contain compact packages of proteins, fats, minerals, and vitamins that make them extremely valuable and efficient sources of nutrients (see page 304 for a discussion of meat eating).

The theory relating meat to warfare among the Yanomamo is this: As Yanomamo villages grow, intensive hunting diminishes or threatens to diminish the availability of game nearby. Meat from large animals grows scarce and people eat more small animals, insects, and larva. The point of diminishing returns is

Figure 10.8   Yanomamo Village
This scene is more representative of everyday life among the Yanomamo, despite their warlike reputation. Note the plantains, the staple food of the Yanomamo, hanging from the rafters.

reached. Increased tensions within and between villages lead to the breaking apart of villages before they permanently deplete the animal resources. Tensions also lead to the escalation of raiding, which disperses the Yanomamo villages over a wide territory, and this also protects vital resources by creating no-man's-lands, which function as game preserves (Harris 1984).

Some anthropologists with firsthand knowledge of the Yanomamo have rejected this theory. They point to the fact that there are no clinical signs of protein deficiencies among the Yanomamo. Also they have shown that in at least one village, whose population is 35, daily per capita overall protein intake was 75 grams per day per adult, which is far higher than the minimum 35 grams recommended by the Food and Agricultural Organization. They have also shown that Yanomamo villages with low levels of protein intake (36 grams) seem to engage in warfare just as frequently as those that have high protein intake (75 grams) per adult. Finally, they point out that the other groups in the Amazon enjoy as much as 107 grams of animal protein per capita and still go to war frequently (Chagnon and Hames 1979; Lizot 1977, 1979). Kenneth Good (1987, 1989), however, has shown that obtaining adequate supplies of meat is a constant preoccupation among the Yanomamo, and that meat is actually consumed only once or twice a week on the average. Good also points out that the efficiency of hunting declines in areas close to villages, necessitating frequent long-distance hunts, some of which take the whole village on protracted treks. Were it not for these long sojourns away from the village, game near the village would soon be completely wiped out (ibid.).

Eric Ross (1979) has observed, moreover, that the average daily amount of animal protein consumed is a misleading figure. Because of fluctuations in the number and size of animals captured, there are actually many days during which there is little or no meat available. On days when a large animal such as a tapir is caught, the consumption rate may rise to 250 or more grams per adult; but for weeks at a time, the consumption rate may not rise above 30 grams per adult per day.

The absence of clinical signs of protein deficiency is not an argument against the theory, but rather supports the general point that band and village peoples can enjoy high standards of health as long as they control population growth (see page 77), and that warfare protects the Yanomamo from diminishing returns and the effects of depletions. The fact that villages with high and low protein intake have the same level of warfare also does not test the theory, because warfare necessarily pits villages at different stages of growth against each other. Hence, Yanomamo groups with little immediate infrastructural basis to go to war may have no choice but to engage in counter-raids against large groups that are depleting their game reserves and raiding their less populous neighbors in order to expand their hunting territory. The theory in question stresses that warfare is a regional phenomenon involving regional adjustments of population and resources.

The preponderance of evidence strongly supports the view that Amazonian fauna are a fragile resource, readily depleted with consequent adverse costs and benefits and/or a decline in per capita meat consumption. Michael Baksh (1985), for example, has quantitatively documented the effect of the nucleation of dispersed Machiguenga homesteads (see page 126) into a village of 250 people in eastern Peru. Baksh concludes that faunal resources in the vicinity of the village have been declining significantly in availability, that in the attempt to maintain previous levels of intake men are working harder, that there is more travel to distant hunting and fishing locations, and that faunal resources are limited in availability and encourage the existence of small, mobile groups.

> Men frequently arrive home empty-handed, or perhaps with a few grubs, some wild fruits, palm nuts, or manufacturing materials. A successful day-long or overnight trip might yield a small monkey or a few birds. One tapir and six peccary were obtained . . . over a 17 month period. [Ibid.:150–151]

Michael Paolisso and Ross Sackett (1982:1) report "an extreme scarcity of high quality protein" among the (non-Amazonian) Yukpa of western Venezuela. Despite the fact that the Yukpa use shotguns for hunting (or because of it), daily animal protein consumption has fallen from some higher amount to a mere 4.8 to 11.3 grams per capita per day, as measured by different dietary and consumption methods (personal communication, Michael Paolisso).

Similarly, William Vickers (1980:17) reports that as the population of a Siona-Sicoya village in northeastern Ecuador grew from 132 persons in 1973 to 160 in 1979, yield per hunt fell by 44 percent, time spent in hunting increased by 12 percent, and caloric efficiency fell by 50 percent. These adverse effects were particularly strong in relation to the preferred larger animal targets. (On the basis of an inconclusive brief visit, Vickers [1988] has modified his previous conclusion.)

This evidence suggests that Yanomamo warfare is best understood as a means of keeping population growth rates down as a precondition for assuring the capture and consumption of high-quality game animals. But more

data on the regional consequences of warfare on population growth and resource depletion are needed for a proper test of this theory (see Sponsel 1986 and Ferguson 1988 for additional sources).

Warfare and the Regulation of Population Growth

It may seem obvious that since people kill each other in warfare, warfare restrains population growth. But the matter is not so simple. Groups such as the Yanomamo cannot control the growth of their populations merely by killing each other at the rates reported above. The problem is that the individuals who are killed in battle are mostly males. Male deaths due to warfare among the Yanomamo have no long-run effect on the size of the population because, like most war-making preindustrial societies, the Yanomamo are polygynous. Any woman whose husband is killed is immediately remarried to another man. The reported female death rate from battle casualties is almost everywhere below 10 percent (see Polgar 1972:206), not enough to produce by itself a substantial lowering of population growth. Similar conclusions about the ineffectuality of combat deaths as a population control device have been reached with respect to warfare in industrial contexts. Catastrophes such as World War II "have no effect on the population growth or size" (Livingstone 1968:5). This can be seen vividly in the case of the Vietnam War — during the decade 1960–1970, population continued to increase at a phenomenal 3 percent per year.

Among band and village peoples, however, warfare may achieve its major effect as a regulator of population growth through an indirect consequence. William Divale has shown that there is a strong correlation between the practice of warfare and high levels of female mortality in the age groups from birth through 14 years (Divale and Harris 1976; 1978a, 1978b Divale et al. 1978; see Hirschfeld et al. 1978; Howe 1978). This is revealed by the ratio of males to females in the 0–14 age bracket among band and village societies actively engaged in warfare when they were first censused (Table 10.1).

It is generally accepted that slightly more boys than girls are born on a worldwide basis and that the average sex ratio at birth is about 105 males to 100 females. This imbalance, however, is much smaller than that found in the war-making village societies. The discrepancy may be accounted for by a higher rate of death among female infants, children, and juveniles than among their male counterparts. The higher rate of female mortality probably reflects the practice of direct and indirect neglect and infanticide against females more often than against males (see page 100 for a discussion of indirect infanticide). There is a strong correlation between societies which admit that they practice infanticide and those which were actively engaged in warfare when they were first censused; in these societies, at least, it is clear that female infanticide was more common than male infanticide.

Perhaps the reason for the killing and neglect of female children is that success in prein-dustrial warfare depends on the size of the male combat teams. When weapons are muscle-powered clubs, spears, and bows and arrows, victory will belong to the group that has the biggest and most aggressive males. Since there are ecological limits to the number of people who can be reared by band and village societies, war-making band and village societies tend to rear more males than females. The favoring of male over female children reduces the rate of growth of regional populations and, whether or not intended, may help to explain why warfare is so widely practiced by prestate peoples. According to this theory, slowing of regional population growth could not be achieved without warfare, since without the war-induced motivation to prefer male children to female children, each group would tend to rear all its female children and expand its population at its neighbor's expense. Warfare tends to equalize these costs, or at least to spread them among all the bands and villages in the region in the form of both high rates of female mortality produced by infanticide and neglect, and high rates of male mortality produced by combat. Although this system seems cruel and wasteful, the preindustrial alternatives for keeping population below the point of diminishing returns were equally cruel and wasteful, if not more so—abortion, malnutrition, and disease. The reader is warned that this theory remains highly controversial.

Table 10.1

SEX RATIOS AND WARFARE

	YOUNG MALES PER 100 FEMALES
Warfare present	128
Stopped 5–25 years before census	113
Stopped over 25 years before census	109

Source: Divale and Harris 1976.

Summary

Orderly relationships between the individuals and domestic groups in band and village societies are maintained without governments and law enforcement specialists. This is possible because of the small size of such societies, predominance of kinship and reciprocity, and egalitarian access to vital resources. Public opinion is the chief source of law and order in these societies.

There is an absence of individual or nuclear family ownership of land among hunting-and-gathering bands and most village peoples. However, even in the most egalitarian societies there is private ownership of some items. The prevalence of the reciprocal mode of exchange and the absence of anonymous price markets render theft unnecessary and impractical.

The major threat to law and order among band and village societies stems from the tendency of domestic and kinship groups to escalate conflicts in support of real or imagined injuries to one of their members. Such support does not depend on abstract principles of right and wrong, but on the probable outcome of a particular course of action in the face of public opinion. The Eskimo song duel illustrates how public opinion can be tested and used to end conflicts between individuals who belong to different domestic and kinship groups.

Witchcraft accusations are another means of giving public opinion an opportunity to identify and punish persistent violators of the rules of reciprocity and other troublemakers. Shamans act as the mouthpiece of the community, but their position is precarious, and they themselves are frequently identified as the source of misfortune and conflict. As among the Kuikuru, the fear of being accused of witchcraft encourages people to be amiable and generous. However, under stressful conditions witchcraft accusations may build to epidemic proportions and become a threat to the maintenance of law and order.

Headmanship reflects the pervasive egalitarian nature of the institutions of law and order in band and village societies. Headmen can do little more than harangue and plead with people for support. They lack physical or material means of enforcing their decisions; their success rests on their ability to intuit public opinion. As exemplified by the Nuer, avoidance of blood feud can be facilitated by the payment of compensation and by appeal to ritual "chiefs," who lack political and economic power.

Other instances of nonkin political organization take the form of voluntary associations or sodalities such as men's and women's clubs, secret societies, and age-grade sets. However, all these nonkin modes of political organization remain rather rudimentary and are overshadowed by the pervasive networks of kinship alliances based on marriage and descent, which constitute the "glue" of band and village societies.

Although both hunter-gatherers and village farmers engage in warfare, there is reason to believe that warfare was less frequent in the Paleolithic than in the Neolithic and that village farmers are more likely to attempt to rout each other.

Warfare cannot be explained as a consequence of aggression or as an enjoyable sport. Warfare is a particular form of organized activity and represents only one of the many ways in which cultures handle aggression. The causes of war in band and village societies are rooted in problems associated with production and reproduction, and almost always involve attempts to improve or preserve cost-benefit ratios and standards of living. Even where population densities are very low, as among the Yanomamo, problems of depleted and declining efficiency may exist. It cannot be said that the Yanomamo suffer from a shortage of protein, yet there is evidence that as their villages grow in size, the quality and quantity of animal resources decline and the cost of obtaining high-quality diets increases.

It also seems likely that warfare in some prestate contexts helped to restrain population growth and thus to protect resources from depletion. Warfare could have this effect through the encouragement of female infanticide and neglect. Evidence for this ecological interpretation of warfare consists of cross-cultural studies that correlate unbalanced sex ratios with active warfare. This theory is controversial, however.

Chapter 11

THE POLITICAL ECONOMY OF THE STATE

In this chapter we contrast the forms of political life characteristic of band and village societies with those of chiefdoms and states. We will examine a plausible theory of how the great transformations took place from bands and villages to chiefdoms and states. We will also discuss the role of coercive physical force and of more subtle forms of thought control in the maintenance of inequality and the status quo in ancient and modern states.

Bigmanship

As we have seen (page 179), headmen often function as intensifiers of production and as redistributors. They also get their relatives to work harder, and they collect and then give away the extra product. A village may have several headmen. Where technological and ecological conditions encourage intensification, a considerable degree of rivalry may develop among headmen living in the same village. They vie with one another to hold the most lavish feasts and to redistribute the greatest amount of valuables. Often, the most successful redistributors earn the reputation of being "big men."

Anthropologist Douglas Oliver (1955) carried out a classic study of "bigmanship" during his fieldwork among the Siuai on Bougainville in the Solomon Islands. Among the Siuai a "big man" is called a *mumi*, and to achieve *mumi* status is every youth's highest ambition (Figure 11.1). A young man proves himself capable of becoming a *mumi* by working hard and by carefully restricting his consumption of meat and coconuts. Eventually, he impresses his wife, children, and near relatives with the seriousness of his intentions, and they vow to help him prepare for his first feast. If the feast is a success, his circle of supporters widens and he sets to work readying an even greater display of

Figure 11.1 *Solomon Island Chiefs.*
They prefer to be called chiefs rather than mumis, *as of old.*

195

generosity. He aims next at the construction of a men's clubhouse in which his male followers can lounge about and in which guests can be entertained and fed. Another feast is held at the consecration of the clubhouse, and if this is also a success, the circle of people willing to work for him grows still larger and he will begin to be spoken of as a *mumi*. Larger and larger feasts mean that the *mumi*'s demands on his supporters become more irksome. Although they grumble about how hard they have to work, they remain loyal as long as their *mumi* continues to maintain or increase his renown as a "great provider."

Finally, the time comes for the new *mumi* to challenge the others who have risen before him. This is done at a *muminai* feast, where a tally is kept of all the pigs, coconut pies, and sago-almond puddings given away by the host *mumi* and his followers to the guest *mumi* and his followers. If the guest *mumi* cannot reciprocate in a year or so with a feast at least as lavish as that of his challengers, he suffers a great social humiliation and his fall from mumihood is immediate. In deciding on whom to challenge, a *mumi* must be very careful. He tries to choose a guest whose downfall will increase his own reputation, but he must avoid one whose capacity to retaliate exceeds his own.

At the end of a successful feast, the greatest of *mumis* still faces a lifetime of personal toil and dependence on the moods and inclinations of his followers. Mumihood does not confer the power to coerce others into doing one's bidding, nor does it elevate one's standard of living above anyone else's. In fact, since giving things away is the essence of *mumihood*, great *mumis* may even consume less meat and other delicacies than an ordinary, undistinguished Siuai. Among the Kaoka, another Solomon Island group reported on by H. Ian Hogbin

(1964:66), there is the saying: "The giver of the feast takes the bones and the stale cakes; the meat and the fat go to the others." At one great feast attended by 1100 people, the host *mumi*, whose name was Soni, gave away 32 pigs plus a large quantity of sago-almond puddings. Soni and his closest followers, however, went hungry. "We shall eat Soni's renown," his followers said.

Big Men and Warfare

Formerly, the *mumis* were as famous for their ability to get men to fight for them as they were for their ability to get men to work for them. Warfare had been suppressed by the colonial authorities long before Oliver carried out his study, but the memory of *mumi* war leaders was still vivid among the Siuai. As one old man put it:

> In the older times there were greater *mumi* than there are today. Then they were fierce and relentless war leaders. They laid waste to the countryside and their clubhouses were lined with the skulls of people they had slain. [Oliver 1955:411]

In singing praises of their *mumis*, the generation of pacified Siuai called them "warriors" and "killers of men and pigs" (ibid.:399).

> Thunderer, Earth-shaker
> Maker of many feasts,
> How empty of gong sounds will all the places
>   be when you leave us!
> Warrior, Handsome Flower,
> Killer of men and pigs,
> Who will bring renown to our places
> When you leave us.

Oliver's informants told him that *mumis* had more authority in the days when warfare was still being practiced. Some *mumi* war leaders even kept one or two prisoners who were treated like slaves and forced to work in the *mumi*'s family gardens. And people could not talk "loud and slanderously against their *mumis* without fear of punishment." This fits theoretical expectations, since the ability to redistribute meat and other valuables goes hand in hand with the ability to attract a following of warriors, equip them for combat, and reward them with spoils of battle. Rivalry between Bougainville's war-making *mumis* appeared to have been leading toward an islandwide political organization when the first European voyagers arrived. According to Oliver (ibid.:420): "For certain periods of time many neighboring villages fought together so consistently that there emerged a pattern of war-making regions, each more or less internally peaceful and each containing one outstanding *mumi* whose war activities provided internal 'social cohesion.'" These *mumis* enjoyed regional fame, but their prerogatives remained rudimentary. This is shown by the fact that the *mumis* had to provide their warriors with prostitutes brought into the clubhouses and with gifts of pork and other delicacies. Said one old warrior:

> If the *mumi* didn't furnish us with women, we were angry. . . . All night long we would copulate and still want more. It was the same with eating. The clubhouse used to be filled with food, and we ate and ate and never had enough. Those were wonderful times. [ibid.:415]

Furthermore, the *mumi* who wanted to lead a war party had to be prepared personally to pay an indemnity for any of his men who were killed in battle and to furnish a pig for each man's funeral feast.

Chiefs and Chiefdoms: Trobrianders and Cherokee

Headmen are the leaders of autonomous villages or bands. Chiefs are the leaders of more or less permanently allied groups of bands and villages called chiefdoms. The principal difference between autonomous bands and villages and chiefdoms is that chiefdoms consist of several communities or settlements. Chiefs have more power than headmen, but headmen who are successful redistributors are hard to distinguish from the leaders of small chiefdoms. Whereas headmen must achieve and constantly validate their status by recurrent feasts, chiefs inherit their office and hold it even if they are temporarily unable to provide their followers with generous redistributions. Chiefs tend to live better than commoners; unlike headmen, they do not always keep only "the bones and the stale cakes" for themselves. Yet in the long run, chiefs too must validate their titles by waging successful war, obtaining trade goods, and giving away food and other valuables to their followers.

THE TROBRIAND ISLANDERS

The difference between headmen and chiefs can be illustrated with the case of the Trobriand Islanders. Trobriander society was divided into several matrilineal clans and subclans of unequal rank and privilege through which access to garden lands was inherited. Bronislaw Malinowski (1920) reported that the Trobrianders were keen on fighting and that they conducted systematic and relentless wars, venturing across the open ocean in their canoes to trade — or, if need be, to fight — with the people of islands over 100 miles away. Unlike the Siuai *mumis*, the Trobriand chiefs occupied hereditary offices and could be deposed only through defeat in war. One of these, whom Malinowski considered to be the "paramount chief" of all the Trobrianders, held sway over more than a dozen villages, containing several thousand people all told. Chieftainships were hereditary within the wealthiest and largest subclans, and the Trobrianders attributed these inequalities to wars of conquest carried out long ago. Only the chiefs could wear certain shell ornaments as the insignia of high rank, and it was forbidden for any commoner to stand or sit in a position that put a chief's head at a lower elevation than anyone else's. Malinowski (1922) tells of seeing all the people present in the village of Bwoytalu drop from their verandas as if blown down by a hurricane at the sound of a drawn-out cry announcing the arrival of an important chief.

The Trobriand chief's power rested ultimately on his ability to play the role of "great provider," which depended on customary and sentimental ties of kinship and marriage rather than on the control of weapons and resources. Residence among the Trobriand commoners was normally avunculocal (see page 164). Adolescent boys lived in bachelor huts until they got married. They then took their brides to live in their mother's brother's household, where they jointly worked the garden lands of the husband's matrilineage. In recognition of the existence of matrilineal descent, at harvest time brothers acknowledged that a portion of the produce of the matrilineal lands was owed to their sisters and sent them presents of baskets filled with yams, their staple crop. The Trobriand chief relied on this custom to validate his title. He married the sisters of the headmen

of a large number of sublineages. Some chiefs acquired several dozen wives, each of whom was entitled to an obligatory gift of yams from her brothers. These yams were delivered to the chief's village and displayed on special yam racks. Some of the yams were then distributed in elaborate feasts at which the chief validated his position as a "great provider," while the remainder were used to feed canoe-building specialists, artisans, magicians, and family servants who thereby became partially dependent on the chief's power. In former times the yam stores also furnished the base for launching long-distance Kula trading expeditions (see page 111) among friendly groups and raids against enemies (Brunton 1975; Geoffry 1983; Malinowski 1935).

THE CHEROKEE

The political organization of the Cherokee of Tennessee (and of other southeastern woodland native Americans) bears striking resemblance to the Trobrianders' redistribution-warfare-trade-chief complex (Figure 11.2). The Cherokee, like the Trobrianders, were matrilineal, and they waged external warfare over long distances. At the center of the principal settlements was a large, circular, "council house" where the council of chiefs discussed issues involving several villages and where redistributive feasts were held. The council of chiefs had a supreme chief who was the central figure in the Cherokee redistributive network. At harvest time a large crib, identified as the "chief's granary," was erected in each field. "To this each family carries and deposits a certain quantity according to his ability or inclination, or none at all if he so chooses." The chief's granaries functioned as "a public treasury . . . to fly to for succor" in the case of crop failure, as a source of food "to accommo-

Figure 11.2   Cherokee Chief.
Black Coat, painted by George Catlin at Fort
Gibson in 1834.

date strangers, or travellers," and as a military store "when they go forth on hostile expeditions." Although every citizen enjoyed "the right of free and public access," commoners had to acknowledge that the store really belonged to the supreme chief who had "an exclusive right and ability . . . to distribute comfort and blessings to the necessitous" (Bartram in Renfrew 1973:234).

Limitations of Chiefly Power: The Tikopia

Even though the Trobrianders feared and respected their "greatly provider" war chiefs, they were still a long way from a state society.

Living on islands, the Trobrianders were not free to spread out, and their population density had risen in Malinowski's time to 60 persons per square mile. Nonetheless, the chiefs could not control enough of the production system to acquire great power. Perhaps one reason for this is that Trobriand agriculture lacked cereal grains. Since yams rot after three or four months (unlike rice or maize), the Trobriand "great provider" could not manipulate people through dispensing food year-round, nor could he support a permanent police-military garrison out of his stores. Another important factor was the open resources of the lagoons and ocean from which the Trobrianders derived their protein supply. The Trobriand chief could not cut off access to these resources and hence could not exercise permanent coercive political control over subordinates.

Another illustration of the constraints on the power of chiefs is found on Tikopia, one of the smallest of the Solomon Islands (Figure 11.3). Here the chiefs' pretensions were even greater than those of the Trobriand chief, but their actual power was considerably less. The Tikopian chiefs claimed that they "owned" all the land and sea resources, yet the size of the redistributive network and of the harvests under their control made such claims unenforceable. Tikopian chiefs enjoyed few privileges. Nominally they claimed control of their cognatic kin group's gardens, but in practice they could not restrict their kin from any unused sites. Labor for their own gardens was in scarce supply, and they themselves worked like any "commoner" in the fields. To validate their positions, they were obliged to give large feasts, which in turn rested on the voluntary labor and food contributions of their kin. Ties of kinship tended to efface the abstract prerequisites and etiquette of higher rank. Raymond Firth describes how a man from a commoner family, who in the kin terminology of the Ti-

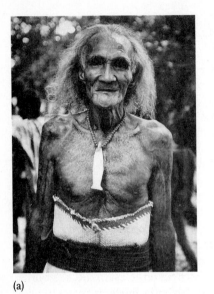

(a)

(b)

Figure 11.3   *Tikopia Chief and His "HONOR GUARD."*
(a) *Tikopia chief and* (b) *his hut. The two men standing outside the hut are the chief's "honor guard," but note the unpretentious residence.*

kopians was classified as a "brother," could exchange bawdy insults with the island's highest-ranking chief:

> On one occasion I was walking with the Ariki [chief] Kafika . . . when we passed the orchard of Pae Sao . . . all the principals present were "brothers" through various ties, and with one accord they fell upon each other with obscene chaff. Epithets of "Big testicles!" "You are the enormous testicles!" flew back and forth to the accompaniment of hilarious laughter. I was somewhat surprised at the vigor of the badinage for the Ariki Kafika, as the most respected chief of the island, has a great deal of sanctity attached to him. . . . However, this did not save him and he took it in good part. [1957:176–177]

Similar remarks pertain to the Cherokee chief. Outside the council, "he associates with the people as a common man, converses with them, and they with him in perfect ease and familiarity" (Bartram in Renfrew 1973:233).

The Origins of States

Under certain conditions, large chiefdoms evolved into states. The *state* is a form of politically centralized society whose governing elites have the power to compel subordinates to pay taxes, render services, and obey the law (Carneiro 1981:69; Johnson and Earle 1987). Three infrastructural conditions led to the transformation of chiefdoms into the *first* states.

1. **Population increase.** Villages grew to several thousand people, and/or regional population densities rose in excess of 20 to 30 people per square mile.

2. **Intensive agriculture.** The staple was a grain such as rice, wheat, barley, or maize, which provided a surplus above immediate needs at harvest and could be stored for long periods at low cost without becoming inedible.

3. **Circumscription.** The emigration of dissatisfied factions was blocked by similarly developed chiefdoms in adjacent territories or by features of the environment that required emigrants to adopt a new and less efficient mode of production and to suffer a decline in their standard of living. Most of the earliest states were circumscribed by their dependence on modes of production associated with fertile river valleys surrounded by arid or semi-arid plains or mountains. But circumscription can also be caused by the transformation of low-yielding into higher-yielding habitats as a result of a long-term investment in the mounding, ditching, draining, and irrigating of a chiefdom's territory.

The significance of circumscription, whatever its precise form, is that factions of discontented members of a chiefdom cannot escape from their elite overlords without suffering a sharp decline in their standard of living. Given these infrastructural conditions, certain changes in a chiefdom's political and economic structure become likely as well. First, the larger and denser the population and the greater the harvest surplus, the greater the ability of the elites to support craft specialists, palace guards, and a standing professional army. Second, the more powerful the elite, the greater its ability to engage in long-distance warfare and trade, and to conquer, incorporate, and exploit new populations and territories. Third, the more powerful the elite, the more stratified its redistribution (see Box 11.1) of trade wealth and harvest surplus. And fourth, the wider the territorial scope of political control and the larger

---

Box 11.1

EGALITARIAN VERSUS HIERARCHICAL FORMS OF REDISTRIBUTION

The realization that there is a crucial difference between headmen and chiefs who generously give away as much as they get, and chiefs and kings who selfishly keep more than they give away has led some anthropologists to deny that kings or powerful chiefs engaged in redistribution. Robert Carneiro (1981:61), for example, writes that the chief who rewards his elite followers "through the shrewd and self-interested disbursement of taxes . . . is no longer a redistributor" but "an appropriator or a concentrator." The originators of the concept of redistribution, however, did not restrict its use to egalitarian exchanges. Furthermore, in the interest of conceptualizing the process by which political-economic-military power became concentrated in the hands of elites, it is important to stress the continuity between the egalitarian and hierarchical forms of exchange in order to show how the latter evolved out of the former. This is best achieved by recognizing a spectrum of redistributive systems ranging from the scrupulously egalitarian to the ruthlessly hierarchical.

the investment in the mode of production, the less opportunity there is to flee and the less there is to be gained. Soon contributions to the central store cease to be voluntary, they become taxes; access to the farmlands and natural resources cease to be rights, they become dispensations; food producers cease being the chief's followers, they become peasants; redistributors cease being chiefs, they become kings; and chiefdoms cease being chiefdoms, they become states.

As the governing elites compel subordinates to pay taxes and tribute, provide military or labor services, and obey laws, the entire process of intensification, expansion, conquest, stratification, and centralization of control is continuously increased or "amplified" through a form of change known as "positive feedback" (Box 11.2). Where modes of production could sustain sufficient numbers of peasants and warriors, this feedback process recur-

rently resulted in states conquering states and in the emergence of preindustrial empires involving vast territories inhabited by millions of people (Carneiro 1981, 1988; R. Cohen 1984a; Fried 1978; Haas 1982; Hommon 1986; Kirch 1984; MacNeish 1981; Price 1979; Service 1975, 1978; see Feinman and Neitzel 1984).

Once the first states came into existence, they themselves constituted barriers against the flight of people who sought to preserve egalitarian systems. Moreover, with states as neighbors, egalitarian peoples found themselves increasingly drawn into warfare and were compelled to increase production and to give their redistributor-war chiefs more and more power in order to prevail against the expansionist tendencies of their neighbors. Thus, most states of the world were produced by a great diversity of specific historical and ecological conditions (Fried 1967), but once states come into existence, they tend to spread, engulf, and overwhelm nonstate peoples (Carneiro 1978; R. Cohen 1984a).

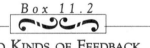

Box 11.2

TWO KINDS OF FEEDBACK

Negative   Changes are checked when certain limits are reached. Initial conditions tend to be restored. *Example:* Household temperature stays slightly above or slightly below the level set on a thermostat.

Positive   Changes are not checked. Each successive change increases or amplifies the tendency to change. *Example:* A microphone picks up the sound of its own loudspeaker and sends the signal back through its amplifier, which sends a stronger signal to the loudspeaker, resulting in a louder and louder sound.

Hawaii: On the Threshold of the State

When visited by Captain James Cook in A.D. 1778, the Hawaiian Islands were divided into four intensely hierarchical polities, each containing between 10,000 and 100,000 persons and each on the threshold (if not past it) of becoming a full-fledged state. Each was divided into named districts containing populations that ranged from about 4,000 to 25,000 people. The districts were in turn divided into many elongated territorial units called *ahupua'a*, which extended inland from the coast to the higher elevations of the island's interiors, and were each inhabited by an average of 200 persons. These inhabitants were of the commoner class, the *maka'ainana*—fishermen, farmers, and craftsworkers. Each *ahupua'a* was administered by officials of chiefly ranks, called *konohiki*, who were the local agents for the powerful district chiefs, called *ali'i*. These *ali'i* based their claims to high chiefly status on genealogies that extended upward for ten generations. (Such genealogies, however, were constantly adjusted and negotiated to accord with achieved political military status.) The chiefly class was topped off by a paramount figure called the *ali'i nui*, who was responsible for assigning privileges and administrative posts to the *ali'i*. In practice, the *ali'i* were in ceaseless turmoil over their relative rank, and the issue was decided by wars of conquest rather then genealogical reckoning. Up until the time of contact, no *ali'i nui* had managed to gain firm control over all of the districts on an island.

At the infrastructural level, the populous, incipient states of Hawaii were based on irrigation agriculture. Taro, sweet potatoes, and yams were the principal crops; both pigs and dogs were kept for meat. Hierarchical, taxlike forms of redistribution siphoned both food and craft items from the *maka'ainana* to the *ali'i*. It was the *konohiki*'s main responsibility to see to it that the commoners in his charge produced enough to satisfy the demands of the *ali'i*. The *ali'i* in turn used these "gifts" to reward his warriors, priests, allies, and the *konohiki* (Earle 1977).

Recent archaeological research demonstrates that the Hawaiian polities evolved out of an egalitarian system similar to that in Tikopia, as a result of the positive feedback among population increase, environmental depletions (deforestation and soil erosion), intensification of production (irrigation and pig husbandry), increased trade, escalating warfare, and competition for elite status. Three phases to this pro-

cess have been identified (Hommon 1986; Kirch 1984; Earle 1989):

Phase I: A.D. 500–1400. Initial colonization and population growth. Settlements are on best coastal sites. No irrigation is needed. Settlements are kinship-organized.

Phase II: 1400–1600. Expansion into less desirable island sites. Use of floodwater irrigation, mulching, and reduction of fallow periods.

Phase III: 1600–1778. Expansion of irrigation systems, use of marginal lands, deforestation, depletion of faunal resources, and soil erosion. Conquest, usurpation, and rebellion.

Would the Hawaiian polities have achieved a more stable and centralized state if their political history had not been interrupted by the landings of Europeans on their shores? (Actually, as a result of that contact, a unified Hawaiian kingdom was established in 1810, but this cannot be regarded as a pristine state.) According to the theory presented above, the answer is "no." All of the conditions for state formation were present, with one exception: The Hawaiian chiefs had no storageable grains. They did have storehouses that were used to sustain their followers. Indeed, David Malo, a nineteenth-century Hawaiian chief, noted that the storehouses of the Hawaiian kings were designed as a means of keeping people contented, so that they would not desert him: "As the rat will not desert the pantry, so the people will not desert the king while they think there is food in his storehouse" (quoted in D'Altroy and Earle 1985:192). But lacking maize, rice, wheat, or any of the other staple grains that provided the nutritional and energetic basis for the emergence of pristine states everywhere else, the Hawaiian storehouses were unable to sustain large numbers of followers, especially during times of drought and warfare-induced food shortage. Thus, no *ali'i nui* was able to achieve an enduring advantage over his rivals.

An African Kingdom: Bunyoro

The difference between a chiefdom and a state can be illustrated with the case of the Bunyoro, a kingdom located in Uganda and studied by John Beattie (1960). Bunyoro had a population of about 100,000 people and an area of 5,000 square miles. Supreme power over the Bunyoro territory and its inhabitants was vested in the Mukama, senior member of a royal lineage that reckoned its descent back to the beginning of time (Figure 11.4). The use of all natural resources, but especially of farming land, was a dispensation specifically granted by the Mukama to a dozen or more "chiefs" or to commoner peasants under their respective control. In return for these dispensations, quantities of food, handicrafts, and labor services were funneled up through the power hierarchy into the Mukama's headquarters. The Mukama in turn directed the use of these goods and services on behalf of state enterprises. The basic redistributive pattern was still plainly in evidence:

> In the traditional system the king was seen both as the supreme receiver of goods and services, and as the supreme giver. . . . The great chiefs, who themselves received tribute from their dependents, were required to hand over to the Mukama a part of the produce of their estates in the form of crops, cattle, beer or women. . . . But everyone must give to the king, not only the chiefs. . . . The Mukama's role as

Figure 11.4   Mukama of Bunyoro. This is a king, not a chief.

> giver was accordingly no less stressed. Many of his special names emphasize his magnanimity and he was traditionally expected to give extensively in the form both of feasts and of gifts to individuals. [Beattie 1960:34]

However great the Mukama's reputation for generosity, it is clear that he did not give away as much as he received. He certainly did not follow the Solomon Island *mumis* and keep only the stale cakes and bones for himself. Moreover, much of what he gave away did not flow back down to the peasant producers; instead, it remained in the hands of his genealogically close kin, who constituted a clearly demarcated aristocratic class. Part of what the Mukama took away from the peasants was bestowed on nonkin who performed extraordinary services on behalf of the state, especially in connection with military exploits. Another part was used to support a permanent palace guard and resident staff who attended to the Mukama's personal needs and performed religious rites deemed essential for the welfare of the Mukama and the nation. The Mukama's staff included custodian of spears, custodian of royal graves, custodian of the royal drums, custodian of royal crowns, "putters-on" of the royal crowns, custodians of royal thrones (stools) and other regalia, cooks, bath attendants, herdsmen, potters, bark-cloth makers, musicians, and others. Many of these officials had several assistants.

In addition, there was a loosely defined category of advisers, diviners, and other retainers who hung around the court, attached to the Mukama's household as dependents, in the hope of being appointed to a chieftainship. To this must be added the Mukama's extensive harem, his many children, and the polygynous households of his brothers and of other royal personages. To keep his power intact, the Mukama and portions of his court made frequent trips "throughout the Bunyoro territory," staying at local palaces maintained at the expense of his chiefs and commoners.

Feudalism

As Beattie points out, there are many analogies between the Bunyoro state and the "feudal" system existing in England at the time of the Norman invasion (1066). As in early medieval England, Bunyoro stratification involved a pledge of loyalty on the part of the district chiefs (lords) in return for grants of land and of the labor power of the peasants (serfs) who lived on these lands. The English king, like the Mukama, could call on these chiefs to furnish weapons, supplies, and warriors whenever an internal or external threat to the king's sovereignty arose. The survival of the English feudal royal lineage, as in Bunyoro, was made possible by the ability of the king to muster larger coalitions of lords and their military forces than could be achieved by any combination of disloyal lords. But there are important differences in demographic scale and in the ruler's role as redistributor that must also be noted. While redistribution was continued through a system of royal taxation and tribute, the police-military function of the English king was more important than among the Bunyoro. The English sovereign was not the "great provider"; he was, instead, the "great protector." With a population numbering over a million people and with agricultural and handicraft production organized on the basis of self-sustaining independent local estates, redistribution was wholly asymmetrical. It was not necessary for William the Conqueror (Figure 11.5) to cultivate an image of generosity among the mass of peasants throughout his kingdom. Although he was careful to be generous to the lords who supported him, the display of generosity to the peasants was no longer important. A vast gulf had opened between the styles of life of peasants and overlords. And the maintenance of these differences no longer rested mainly on the special contribution the overlords made to production, but largely on their ability to deprive the peasants of subsistence and of life itself. But on the European medieval manorial estates, feudal lords were well advised not to push the exploitation (see page 220) of their peasants beyond certain limits, lest they destroy the basis of their own existence.

In comparing African with European political development, we must remember that

Figure 11.5   William I (1027–1087), the Conqueror.
He invaded England from Normandy and defeated the English at the Battle of Hastings in 1066.

there were two periods of feudalism in Western and Northern Europe. The first, about which little is known, preceded the growth of the Roman Empire and was cut off by the Roman conquest. The second followed the collapse of the Roman Empire. Although the latter period provides the standard model of feudalism, the Bunyoro type of polity is actually a much more widely distributed form and probably closely resembles the political systems the Romans encountered and overran in their conquest of Western Europe (see Bloch 1964; Champion et al. 1984:315; Piggott 1966; Renfrew 1973).

Because of the Roman Empire, the feudalism of medieval Europe rested on a technology far in advance of the technology found in even the most populous kingdoms south of the Sa-

hara. The product taxed away by the Bunyoro ruling class was small compared with what was taxed away by the English feudal aristocracy. Architecture, metallurgy, textiles, and armaments were far more advanced in medieval Europe.

A Native American Empire: The Inca

Alternative evolutionary steps led to state systems that were larger and more centralized than those of medieval Europe. In several regions, there arose state systems in which scores of former small states were incorporated into highly centralized superstates or empires. In the New World, the largest and most powerful of these systems was the Inca Empire.

At its prime the Inca Empire stretched 1500 miles from northern Chile to southern Colombia and contained possibly as many as 6 million inhabitants. Because of government intervention in the basic mode of production, agriculture was organized not in terms of feudal estates, but rather in terms of villages, districts, and provinces. Each such unit was under the supervision not of a feudal lord who had sworn loyalty to another lord slightly his superior and who was free to use his lands and peasants as he saw fit, but of appointed government officials responsible for planning public works and delivering government-established quotas of laborers, food, and other material (Morris 1976). Village lands were divided into three parts, the largest of which was probably the source of the workers' own subsistence; harvests from the second and third parts were turned over to religious and government agents, who stored them in granaries (D'Altroy and Earle 1985).

The distribution of these supplies was entirely under the control of the central administration. Likewise, when labor power was needed to build roads, bridges, canals, fortresses, or other public works, government recruiters went directly into the villages. Because of the size of the administrative network and the density of population, huge numbers of workers could be placed at the disposal of the Inca engineers. In the construction of Cuzco's fortress of Sacsahuaman (Figure 11.6), probably the greatest masonry structure in the New World, 30,000 people were employed in cutting, quarrying, hauling, and erecting huge monoliths, some weighing as much as 200 tons. Labor contingents of this size were rare in medieval Europe but were common in ancient Egypt, the Middle East, and China.

Figure 11.6 Sacsahuaman.
The principal fortress of the Inca Empire, near Cugco, Peru.

Control over the entire empire was concentrated in the hands of the Inca. He was the first-born of the first-born, a descendant of the god of the sun and a celestial being of unparalleled holiness. This god-on-earth enjoyed power and luxury undreamed of by the poor Mehinacu chief in his plaintive daily quest for respect and obedience. Ordinary people could not approach the Inca face-to-face. His private audiences were conducted from behind a screen, and all who approached him did so with a burden on their backs. When traveling he reclined on an ornate palanquin carried by special crews of bearers (Mason 1957:184). A small army of sweepers, water carriers, woodcutters, cooks, wardrobemen, treasurers, gardeners, and hunters attended the domestic needs of the Inca in his palace in Cuzco, the capital of the empire. If members of this staff offended the Inca, their entire village was destroyed.

The Inca ate his meals from gold and silver dishes in rooms whose walls were covered with precious metals. His clothing was made of the softest vicuña wool, and he gave away each change of clothing to members of the royal family, never wearing the same garment twice. The Inca enjoyed the services of a large number of concubines who were methodically culled from the empire's most beautiful girls. His wife, however, to conserve the holy line of descent from the god of the sun, had to be his own full or half sister. When the Inca died, his wife, concubines, and many other retainers were strangled during a great drunken dance in order that he suffer no loss of comfort in the afterlife. Each Inca's body was eviscerated, wrapped in cloth, and mummified. Women with fans stood in constant attendance on these mummies, ready to drive away flies and to take care of the other things mummies need to stay happy.

The State and the Control
of Thought

Large populations, anonymity, use of market money, and vast differences in wealth make the maintenance of law and order in state societies more difficult to achieve than in bands, villages, and chiefdoms. This accounts for the great elaboration of police and paramilitary forces and the other state-level institutions and specialists concerned with crime and punishment (Figure 11.7). Although every state ultimately stands prepared to crush criminals and political subversives by imprisoning, maiming, or killing them, most of the daily burdens of maintaining law and order against discontented individuals and groups is borne by institutions

Figure 11.7 Stratification: The King of Morocco. Social inequality cannot endure without the use or threat of force.

that seek to confuse, distract, and demoralize potential troublemakers before they have to be subdued by physical force. Therefore, every state, ancient and modern, has specialists who perform ideological services in support of the status quo. These services are often rendered in a manner and in contexts that seem unrelated to economic or political issues.

The main thought-control apparatus of preindustrial states consists of magico-religious institutions. The elaborate religions of the Inca, Aztecs, ancient Egyptians, and other preindustrial civilizations sanctified the privileges and powers of the ruling elite. They upheld the doctrine of the divine descent of the Inca and the pharaoh, and taught that the entire balance and continuity of the universe required the subordination of commoners to persons of noble and divine birth. Among the Aztecs, the priests were convinced and sought to convince others that the gods must be nourished with human blood, and they personally pulled out the beating hearts of the state's prisoners of war on top of Tenochtitlán's pyramids (see page 300). In many states, religion has been used to condition large masses of people to accept relative deprivation as necessity, to look forward to material rewards in the afterlife rather than in the present one, and to be grateful for small favors from superiors lest ingratitude call down a fiery retribution in this life or in a hell to come.

To deliver messages of this sort and demonstrate the truths they are based on, state societies invest a large portion of national wealth in monumental architecture. From the pyramids of Egypt or Teotihuacán in Mexico to the Gothic cathedrals of medieval Europe, state-subsidized monumentality in religious structures makes the individual feel powerless and insignificant. Great public edifices — whether seeming to float, as in the case of the Gothic

*Figure 11.8   The Great Pyramid of Khufu.
Awe-inspiring proof of the divinity of Egypt's kings.*

cathedral of Amiens, or to press down with the infinite heaviness of the pyramids of Khufu (Figure 11.8) — teach the futility of discontent and the invincibility of those who rule, as well as the glory of heaven and the gods. This is not to say that they teach nothing else. As we shall see (page 306), religion is also often implicated in revolutionary movements.

Thought Control in Modern Contexts

A considerable amount of conformity is achieved not by frightening or threatening people, but by inviting them to identify with the governing elite and to enjoy vicariously the pomp of state occasions. Public spectacles such as religious processions, coronations, and victory parades work against the alienating effects of poverty and exploitation. During Roman times, the strategy for controlling the masses included letting them watch gladiatorial con-

tests and other circus spectaculars. In the movies, television, radio, organized sports, space shuttles, and lunar landings, modern state systems possess powerful techniques for distracting and amusing their citizenry. Through modern media the consciousness of millions of listeners, readers, and watchers is often manipulated along rather precisely determined paths by government-subsidized specialists (Parenti 1986; Kottak 1990). "Entertainment" delivered through the air or by cable directly into the shantytown house or tenement apartment is perhaps the most effective form of "Roman circus" yet devised.

State-supported universal education is another means of thought control. Teachers and schools obviously serve the instrumental needs of complex industrial civilizations by training each generation to provide the skills and services necessary for survival and well-being. But teachers and schools also devote a great deal of time to civics, history, citizenship, and social studies. These subjects are loaded with implicit or explicit assumptions about culture, people, and nature indicating the superiority of the political-economic system in which they are taught. In China and other highly centralized communist countries, no attempt is made to disguise the fact that one of the principal functions of universal education is political indoctrination. Western capitalist democracies are less open in acknowledging that their educational systems are also instruments of political control. Teachers and students are often unaware of the extent to which their books, curricula, and classroom presentations are designed to uphold the status quo. Yet school boards, boards of regents, library committees, and legislative committees openly call for conformity (Bowles and Gintis 1976; Ramirez and Meyer 1980).

Jules Henry, who went from studying Indians in Brazil to studying high schools in St. Louis, has contributed to the understanding of some of the ways by which universal education molds the pattern of national conformity. In his *Culture Against Man*, Henry shows how even in the midst of spelling and singing lessons, there can be basic training in support of the competitive "free enterprise system." Children are taught to fear failure; they are also taught to be competitive. Hence they soon come to look upon each other as the main source of failure, and they become afraid of each other. As Henry (1963:305) observes: "School is indeed a training for later life not because it teaches the 3R's (more or less), but because it instills the essential cultural nightmare—fear of failure, envy of success."

Children from economically deprived families are taught to blame themselves for being poor (Kluegel and Smith 1981). In addition, the economically deprived portion of the population is taught to believe that the electoral process guarantees redress against abuse by the rich and powerful through legislation aimed at redistributing wealth. Finally, most of the population is kept ignorant of the actual workings of the political-economic system and of the disproportionate power exercised by lobbies representing corporations and other special-interest groups. Henry concludes that U.S. schools, despite their ostensible dedication to creative inquiry, punish the child who has intellectually creative ideas with respect to social and cultural life:

> Learning social studies is, to no small extent, whether in elementary school or the university, learning to be stupid. Most of us accomplish this task before we enter high school. But the child with a socially creative imagination will not be encouraged to play among new social systems,

values, relationships; nor is there much likelihood of it, if for no other reason than that the social studies teachers will perceive such a child as a poor student. Furthermore such a child will simply be unable to fathom the absurdities that seem transparent *truth* to the teacher. . . . Learning to be an idiot is part of growing up or, as Camus put it, learning to be absurd. Thus the child who finds it impossible to learn to think the absurd truth . . . usually comes to think himself stupid. [1963:287–288]

The State and Physical Coercion

Although thought control can be an effective supplementary means of mantaining political control, there are limits to the lies and deceptions that governments can get away with. If people are experiencing stagnant or declining standards of living, no amount of propaganda and false promises can prevent them from becoming restless and dissatisfied. As discontent mounts, the ruling elites must either increase the use of direct force or make way for a restructuring of the political economy. In China, recent popular dissatisfaction with the ruling class has been met with both more thought control and an increase in direct physical repression (Figure 11.9). The great upheavals in the Soviet Union and Eastern Europe at the end of the 1980s also dramatically illustrate what can happen when ruling classes fail to deliver on their promises of a better life. No amount of thought control could hide the daily reality of long lines to buy food, the shoddy quality of manufactured goods, the endless red tape, the shortages of housing and electricity, and the widespread industrial pollution characteristic of life behind the Iron Curtain (Figure 11.10).

Figure 11.9   *Free Speech Versus Tanks on Tienanmen Square, Beijing, China. The tanks won.*

Figure 11.10   *People Against Dictatorship in Bucharest. The people won.*

Western parliamentary democracies rely more on thought control than on physical coercion to maintain law and order, but in the final analysis they too depend on guns and jails to maintain law and order. Natural disasters such as Hurricane Hugo and blackouts such as occurred in New York City in 1977 (Figure 11.11) quickly led to extensive looting and disorder, proving that thought control is not enough and that large numbers of ordinary citizens do not believe in the system and are held in check only by the threat of physical punishment (Curvin and Porter 1978; Weisman 1978).

The Fate of Prestate Bands and Villages

The career of state-level societies has been characterized by continuous expansion into and encroachment on the lands and freedoms of prestate peoples. For advanced chiefdoms the appearance of soldiers, traders, missionaries, and colonists often resulted in a successful transition to state-level organization. But over the vast regions of the globe inhabited by dispersed bands and villages, the spread of the state has resulted in the annihilation or total distortion of the way of life of thousands of once free and proud peoples. These devastating changes are aptly described as *genocide* — the extinction of whole populations — or as *ethnocide* — the systematic extinction of cultures.

The spread of European states into the Americas had a devastating effect on the inhabitants of the New World. Many methods were employed to rid the land of its original inhabitants in order to make room for the farms and industries needed to support Europe's over-

(a)   (b)

Figure 11.11 *The breakdown of law and order.*
(a) *Looting in the aftermath of New York City's blackout.* (b) *National Guard troops patrol the streets of Charleston, South Carolina, after hurricane Hugo to prevent looting.*

flowing population. Native American peoples were exterminated during unequal military engagements that pitted guns against arrows; others were killed off by new urban diseases brought by the colonists — smallpox, measles, and the common cold — against which people who lived in small, dispersed settlements lacked immunity (Crosby 1986:196ff.; Dobyns 1983; Wirsing 1985). Against the cultures of the natives there were other weapons. Their modes of production were destroyed by slavery, debt peonage, and wage labor; their political life was destroyed by the creation of chiefs and tribal councils who were puppets and convenient means of control for state administrators (Fried 1975); and their religious beliefs and rituals were demeaned and suppressed by missionaries who were eager to save their souls but not their lands and freedom (Josephy 1982; Ribeiro 1971; Walker 1972; Wilkinson 1987).

These genocidal attacks were not confined to North and South America. They were also carried out in Australia, on the islands of the Pacific, and in Siberia. Nor are they merely events that took place a long time ago and about which nothing can now be done: They are still going on in the remote vastness of the Amazon Basin and other regions of South America, where the last remaining New World free and independent band and village peoples have been cornered by the remorseless spread of colonists, traders, oil companies, teachers, ranchers, and missionaries (Bodley 1989; Davis 1977).

The tragic plight of some of the Aché Indians of eastern Paraguay is a case in point (see page 78). As documented by Mark Münzel (1973), these independent foragers were systematically hunted, rounded up, and forced to live on small reservations in order to make room for ranchers and farmers. Aché children were separated from their parents and sold to settlers as servants. The manhunters shot anyone who showed signs of resistance, raped the women, and sold the children. In March and April of 1972, about 171 "wild" Aché were captured and deliberately taken to the Aché reservation, where it was known that an influenza epidemic was already raging. By July, 55 Achés on the reservation had died (Münzel 1973:55).

More recently, the !Kung San, who have figured so prominently in these pages (pages 75, 108, 125), have become the target of immense statal forces, which have changed their way of life and which threaten their physical survival. Many !Kung San men were lured into service for the South African army in its war against the guerillas who sought to establish an independent state in Namibia. According to South African sources, the Sans' "acute sense of direction, tracking ability, knowledge of the bush, and far sight make them perfect guerilla fighters" (Lee and Hurlich 1982:338). South African patrols put the San out front to detect mines. Meanwhile, San women and children were rounded up and placed in military bush camps (see Box 11.3).

It is probable but not inevitable that none of the prestate societies will survive (see Box

---

Box 11.3

THE TRAGIC FATE OF THE !KUNG SAN

Deep in the dense Caprivi bush a colony of Bushmen are being taught a new culture and a new way of life by the White man. More than a thousand Bushmen have already discarded the bow and arrow for the R1 rifle and their wives are making clothes out of cotton instead of skin.

Gone are their days of hunting animals for food and living off the yield. They now have . . . salads with salt and pepper while the men wear boots and their ladies dress in the latest fashions. Their children go to schools and sing in choirs.

A handful of South African soldiers started the Colony some time ago, attracting the children of the veld to a secret Army Base where they are teaching them the modern way of life. "The most difficult thing to teach them is to use a toilet," the Commander of the Base said. Money and trade is something completely new to them but they are fast learning the White man's way of bickering.

In their small community they now have a store, hospital, school and various other training centres.

The men are being trained as soldiers while their womenfolk learn how to knit, sew and cook.

Source: Lee and Hurlich 1982:335–336.

Box 11.4

WE WILL NOT SEE THEIR LIKE AGAIN

The last of the tribal cultures are in serious jeopardy. When they are gone, we will not see their like again. The nonindustrialized statal cultures have joined forces with the industrialized states to eliminate them. The reason for this lies in the contrasting natures of statal and tribal cultures: the former are larger, more powerful, and expansionistic. Tribal cultures, representing an earlier cultural form, are denigrated as "savage" and viewed as an anachronism in the "modern world." The statal cultures have exercised their power by dividing all land on this planet among themselves. . . . This is as true for the Third World—where concerted efforts are made to destroy the last vestiges of tribalism as a threat to national unity—as it has been for the Western World.

Source: Gerald Weiss 1977a:890.

11.4). Yet anthropologists must not be defeatists and must strive to prevent that from happening. Observes Gerald Weiss:

No biologist would claim that evolution in the organic realm makes either necessary or desirable the disappearance of earlier forms, so no anthropologist should be content to remain a passive observer of the extinction of the Tribal World. [1977a:891]

Summary

Headmen, chiefs, and kings are found in three different forms of political organization: autonomous bands and villages, chiefdoms, and states. The "big man" is a rivalrous form of headmanship marked by competitive redistributions that expand and intensify production. As illustrated by the *mumis* of the Solomon Islands, bigmanship is a temporary status requiring constant validation through displays of generosity that leave the big man poor in possessions but rich in prestige and authority. Since they are highly respected, big men are well suited to act as leaders of war parties, long-distance trading expeditions, and other collective activities that require leadership among egalitarian peoples.

Chiefdoms consist of several more or less permanently allied communities. Like big men, chiefs also play the role of great provider, expand and intensify production, give feasts, and organize long-distance warfare and trading expeditions. However, as illustrated by the Trobriand, Cherokee, and Tikopian chiefdoms, chiefs enjoy hereditary status, tend to live somewhat better than the average commoner, and can be deposed only through defeat in warfare. The power of chiefs is limited by their ability to support a permanent group of police-military specialists and to deprive significant numbers of their followers of access to the means of making a living. In the transition from band and village organizations through chiefdoms to states, there is a continuous series of cumulative changes in the balance of power between elites and commoners that makes it difficult to say at exactly what point in the process we have chiefdoms rather than an alliance of villages, or states rather than a powerful chiefdom. The polities of the Hawaiian Islands illustrate the incipient phases of pristine state formation.

Dense populations, intensifiable modes of production, trade, storage grains, circumscription, and intense warfare underlie the emergence of pristine states. Secondary states, however, arose under a variety of conditions related to the spread of pristine states.

The difference between chiefdoms and states is illustrated by the case of the Bunyoro. The Mukama was a great provider for himself and his closest supporters but not for the majority of the Bunyoro peasants. The Mukama, unlike the Trobriand chief, maintained a permanent court of personal retainers and a palace guard. There are many resemblances between the Bunyoro and the feudal kingdoms of early medieval Europe, but the power of the early English kings was greater and depended less on the image of the great provider than on that of the great protector.

The most developed and highly stratified form of statehood is that of empire. As illustrated by the Inca of Peru, the leaders of ancient empires possessed vast amounts of power and were unapproachable by ordinary citizens. Production was supervised by a whole army of administrators and tax collectors. While the Inca was concerned with the welfare of his people, they viewed him as a god to whom they owed everything, rather than as a headman or chief who owed everything to them.

Since all state societies are based on marked inequalities between rich and poor and rulers and ruled, maintenance of law and order presents a critical challenge. In the final analysis it is the police and the military, with their control over the means of physical coercion, that keep the poor and the exploited in line. However, all states find it more expedient to maintain law and order by controlling people's thoughts. This is done in a variety of ways, ranging from state religions to public rites and spectacles and universal education.

The plight of the remaining prestate band and village societies must not be overlooked. As in the case of the Aché, civilization and modernization often lead to slavery, disease, and poverty for such people. The fate of the !Kung San illustrates the precarious future faced by the remaining prestate societies.

Chapter 12

STRATIFIED GROUPS

This chapter examines the principal varieties of
stratified groups found in state-level societies. We
will see that people who live in such societies think
and behave in ways that are determined to a great
extent by their membership in stratified groups and
by their positions in a stratification hierarchy. The
values and behavior of such groups are in turn
often related to a struggle for access to the structural
and infrastructural sources of wealth and power.

Class and Power

All state-level societies are organized into a hierarchy of groups known as classes. A *class* is a group of people who have a similar relationship to the apparatus of control in state-level societies and who possess similar amounts of power (or lack of power). To be powerful in human affairs is to be able to get people to obey one's requests and commands. In practice, this kind of power depends on the ability to provide or take away essential goods and services, and this in turn ultimately depends on one's degree of control over access to energy, resources, and technology—especially the technology of armed coercion (Figure 12.1).

The power of particular human beings cannot be measured simply by adding up the amount of energy they regulate or channel. If that were the case, the most powerful people in the world would be the technicians who turn the switches at nuclear power plants, or airline pilots who open the throttle on four engines, each of which has the power of 40,000 horses. Military field officers in the armed forces, with their enormous capacity for killing and maiming, are not necessarily powerful people. The crucial question in all such cases is this: Who controls the technicians, pilots, and generals, and makes them turn their "switches" on or off?

All state societies necessarily have at least two classes arranged hierarchically—rulers

Figure 12.1 Poverty and power.
This man is not only poor, he is also relatively powerless.

217

and ruled. But where there are more than two classes, they are not necessarily all arranged hierarchically with respect to each other. For example, fishermen and neighboring farmers are usefully regarded as two separate classes because they relate to the ruling class in distinctive ways; have different patterns of ownership, rent, and taxation; and exploit entirely different sectors of the environment. Yet neither has a clear-cut power advantage or disadvantage with respect to the other. Similarly, anthropologists often speak of an urban as opposed to a rural lower class, although the quantitative power differentials between the two may be minimal.

Sex, Age, and Class

Sex hierarchies are conventionally distinguished from class hierarchies. We will do the same and postpone the discussion of sex hierarchies (more accurately, gender hierarchies) to Chapter 13. This distinction rests on the fact that class hierarchies include both sexes, whereas sex hierarchies refer to the domination of one sex by another within and across classes. This does not mean that sex hierarchies are less important or less severe, but merely that their analysis is best carried out in the context of a discussion of general gender roles rather than in the context of state forms of stratification.

Age groups also are often associated with unequal distributions of power within both state and prestate societies. Indeed, hierarchical differences between mature adults and juveniles and infants are virtually universal. Moreover, the treatment of children by adults sometimes involves highly exploitative and physically and mentally punitive practices.

One might argue that age hierarchies are fundamentally different from class and sex hierarchies because the maltreatment and exploitation of children is always "for their own good." Superordinate groups of all sorts, however, usually say this of the subordinate groups under their control. The fact that some degree of subordination of juveniles and infants is necessary for enculturation and population survival does not mean that such hierarchies are fundamentally different from class and sex hierarchies. Brutal treatment of children can result in permanent damage to their health and well-being or even in their death. The resemblance between age hierarchies and class hierarchies is also strong where old people constitute a despised and powerless group. In some societies senior citizens are victims of punitive physical and psychological treatment comparable to that meted out to criminals and enemies of the state. Descriptions of class structure, therefore, must never lose sight of the differences in power and life-style associated with sex and age groups within each class.

Emics, Etics, and Class Consciousness

Class is an aspect of culture in which there are sharp differences between emic and etic points of view (Berreman 1981:18). Many social scientists accept class distinction as real and important only when it is consciously perceived and acted upon by the people involved. They hold that in order for a group to be considered a class, its members must have a consciousness of their own identity, exhibit a common sense of solidarity, and engage in organized attempts to promote and protect collective interests (Fallers 1977; T. Parsons 1970). Moreover, some social scientists (see Bendix, Reinhardt, and Lipset 1966) believe that classes exist only when persons with similar forms and quantities of social power organize into collective organizations such as political parties or labor unions. Other social scientists, however, believe that the most important features of class hierarchies are the actual concentrations of power in certain groups and the powerlessness of others, regardless of any conscious or even unconscious awareness of these differences on the part of the people concerned, and regardless of the existence of collective organizations (Roberts and Brintnall 1982:195–217).

From an etic and behavioral viewpoint, a class can exist even when the members of the class deny that they constitute a class, and even when instead of collective organizations they have organizations that compete, such as rival business corporations or rival unions. The reason for this is that subordinate classes that lack class consciousness are obviously not exempt from the domination of ruling classes. Similarly, members of ruling classes need not form permanent, hereditary, monolithic, conspiratorial organizations in order to protect and enhance their own interests. A struggle for power within the ruling class does not necessarily result in a fundamentally altered balance of power between the classes. The struggle for control of the English crown, the Chinese dynasties, the Soviet Party apparatus (Figure 12.2), and multinational corporations all testify to the fact that the members of a ruling class may fight among themselves at the same time that they dominate or exploit subordinates.

Of course, there is no disputing the importance of a people's belief about the shape and origin of their stratification system. Consciousness of a common plight among the members of a downtrodden and exploited class may very well lead to the outbreak of organized

(a)

Figure 12.2   The Soviet ruling class.
(a) *Old style atop Lenin's tomb;* (b) *new style. The outcome of Mikhail Gorbachev's attempt to democratize the Soviet Union's class structure remains in doubt. Here Gorbachev, accompanied by his wife, Raisa, mingles with the crowd.*

(b)

class warfare. Consciousness is thus an element in the struggle between classes, but it is not the exclusive cause of class differences.

Economic Exploitation

The control over large amounts of power by one class relative to another permits the members of the more powerful class to exploit the members of the weaker class. There is no generally accepted meaning of the term *exploitation*, but the basic conditions responsible for economic exploitation can be identified by reference to our earlier discussion of reciprocity and redistribution (Chapter 7). When balanced reciprocity prevails or when the redistributors keep only "the bones and stale cakes" for themselves, there is no economic exploitation (page 197). But when there is unbalanced reciprocity or when the redistributors start keeping the "meat and fat" for themselves, exploitation may soon develop.

In the theories of Karl Marx, all wage laborers are exploited because the value of what they produce is always greater than what they are paid. Similarly, some anthropologists take the view that exploitation begins as soon as there is a structured flow of goods and services between two groups (Newcomer 1977; Ruyle 1973, 1975). Against this view it can be argued that the activities of employers and of stratified redistributors may result in an improvement in the well-being of the subordinate class, and that without entrepreneurial or ruling class leadership everyone would be worse off (Dalton 1972, 1974). One cannot say, therefore, that every inequality in power and in consumption standards necessarily involves exploitation. If as a result of the rewards given to or taken by the ruling class, the economic welfare of all classes steadily improves, it would seem inappropriate to speak of the people responsible for that improvement as exploiters.

Exploitation may be said to exist when the following four conditions exist: (1) The subordinate class experiences deprivations with respect to basic necessities such as food, water, air, sunlight, leisure, medical care, housing, and transport; (2) the ruling class enjoys an abundance of luxuries; (3) the luxuries enjoyed by the ruling class depend on the labor of the subordinate class; and (4) the deprivations experienced by the subordinate class are caused by the failure of the ruling class to apply its power to the production of necessities instead of luxuries and to redistribute these necessities to the subordinate class (Boulding 1973). These conditions constitute an etic and behavioral definition of exploitation.

Because of the relationship between exploitation and human suffering, the study of exploitation is an important responsibility of social scientists who are concerned with the survival and well-being of our species. We must see to it that the study of exploitation is conducted empirically and with due regard to mental and emic as well as to etic and behavioral components (Brown 1985).

Peasant Classes

The majority of people alive today are members of one or another kind of peasant class. Peasants are the subordinate food-producing classes of state societies who use preindustrial technologies of food production. The kind of rent or taxes extracted from peasants defines the essential features of their structured inferiority. Many different types of rent and taxes are extracted from peasants, but "peasants of all times and places are structured inferiors" (Dalton 1972:406).

Each major type of peasant is the subject of a vast research literature. Anthropologists have studied peasants more than they have studied village peoples or hunters and gatherers (Pelto and Pelto 1973). Three major types of peasant classes can be distinguished.

1. **Feudal peasants.** These peasants are subject to the control of a decentralized hereditary ruling class whose members provide military assistance to one another but do not interfere in one another's territorial domains. Feudal peasants, or "serfs," inherit the opportunity to utilize a particular parcel of land; hence they are said to be "bound" to the land. For the privilege of raising their own food, feudal peasants render unto the lord rent in kind or in money. Rent may also take the form of labor service in the lord's kitchens, stables, or fields.

   Some anthropologists, following the lead of historians of European feudalism, describe feudal relationships as a more or less fair exchange of mutual obligations, duties, privileges, and rights between lord and serf. George Dalton (1969:390–391), for example, lists the following services and payments to peasants by feudal lords during European feudalism:

   Granting peasants the right to use land for subsistence and cash crops

   Military protection (e.g., against invaders)

   Police protection (e.g., against robbery)

   Juridicial services to settle disputes

   Feasts to peasants at Christmas and Easter; also harvest gifts

   Food given to peasants on days when they work the lord's fields

   Emergency provision of food during disaster

Dalton denies that feudal peasants are exploited, because it is not known whether "the peasant paid out to the lord much more than he received back." Other anthropologists point out that the reason feudal peasants are "structured inferiors" is that the feudal ruling class deprives them of access to the land and its life-sustaining resources, which is antithetical to the principle of reciprocity and egalitarian redistribution. The counterflow of goods and services listed by Dalton merely perpetuates the peasants' structured inferiority. The one gift that would alter that relationship— the gift of land, free of rent or taxes—is never given.

History suggests that the structured inferiority of feudal peasants is seldom acceptable to the peasants. Over and over again the world has been convulsed by revolutions in which peasants struggled in the hope of restoring free access to land (Wolf 1969; Scott 1985).

Many feudal peasantries owe their existence to military conquest, and this further emphasizes the exploitative nature of the landlord-serf relationship. For example, the Spanish crown rewarded Cortés, Pizarro, and the other *conquistadores* with lordships over large slices of the territories they had conquered in Mexico and Peru. The heavy tax and labor demands placed on the conquered native Americans thereafter contributed to a precipitous decline in their numbers (Dobyns 1983; C. Smith 1970).

2. **Agromanagerial state peasantries.** Where the state is strongly centralized, as in ancient Peru, Egypt, Mesopotamia, and China, peasants may be directly

subject to state control in addition to, or in the absence of, control by a local landlord class. Unlike the feudal peasants, agromanagerial peasants are subject to frequent conscription for labor brigades drawn from villages throughout the realm to build roads, dams, irrigation canals, palaces, temples, and monuments. In return, the state makes an effort to feed its peasants in case of food shortages caused by droughts or other calamities. The pervasive bureaucratic control over production and life-styles in the ancient agromanagerial states has often been compared to the treatment of peasants in modern socialist and communist societies such as China, Albania (Figure 12.3a), Vietnam, and Cambodia. The state in these countries is all-powerful, setting production quotas, controlling prices, and extracting taxes in kind and in labor. Much depends, of course, on the extent to which the peasants can exchange their lot with that of party bosses and bureaucrats, and vice versa. In Communist China (Figure 12.3b), effort was made

(a)

Figure 12.3   Peasants.
(a) *Albanian communist peasants.* (b) *Chinese peasants. Some of the 25,000 workers employed in the construction of the Shih Man Tan Reservoir on the Huai River are shown with their earth-moving equipment.* (c) *A Peruvian couple plowing and planting potatoes.*

(b)

(c)

under Mao Tse-tung to destroy the class nature of peasant identity and to merge all labor — intellectual, industrial, and agricultural — into a single working class. But some analysts hold that the political economy of China under Mao amounted to little more than a restoration of the despotic agromanagerial state socialism that had existed for thousands of years under the Chou, Han, and Ming dynasties (Wittfogel 1960, 1979). As a result of economic reforms in post-Mao China and other communist societies, peasant farmers have been given more freedom to buy and sell on open markets and have come to resemble capitalist peasants.

3. **Capitalist peasants.** In Africa, Latin America (Figure 12.3c), India, Southeast Asia, and Eastern Europe, feudal and agromanagerial types of peasantries have been replaced by peasants who enjoy increased opportunities to buy and sell land, labor, and food in competitive price markets. The varieties of structured inferiority within this group defy any simple taxonomy. Some capitalist peasants are subordinate to large land-owners; others are subordinate to banks that hold mortgages and promissory notes. When the crops in production enter the international market, holdings are of the large, or *latifundia*, type, and the real landowners tend to be the commercial banks. Elsewhere, in more isolated or unproductive regions, holdings may be very small, giving rise to postage-stamp farms known as *minifundia* and to the phenomenon Sol Tax (1953) aptly called "penny capitalism."

Capitalist peasants correspond to what Dalton calls "early modernized peasants." They display the following features:

Marketable land tenure

Predominance of production for cash sale

Growing sensitivity to national commodity and labor price markets

Beginnings of technological modernization

Although many capitalist peasants own their own land, they do not escape payment of rent or its equivalent. Many communities of landowning peasants constitute labor reserves for larger and more heavily capitalized plantations and farmers. Penny capitalists are frequently obliged to work for wages paid by these cash-crop enterprises. Penny capitalist peasants cannot obtain enough income to satisfy subsistence requirements from the sale of their products in the local market.

The Image of Limited Good

A recurrent question concerning the plight of contemporary peasant communities is the extent to which they are victims of their own values. It has often been noted, for example, that peasants are very distrustful of innovations and cling to their old ways of doing things. Based on his study of the village of Tzintzuntzan, in the state of Michoacan, Mexico, George Foster (1967) has developed a general theory of peasant life based on the concept of the "image of limited good." According to Foster, the people of Tzintzuntzan believe, as do many peasants throughout the world, that life is a dreary struggle, that very few people can achieve "success," and that they can improve themselves only at the expense of other people. If someone tries something new and succeeds at it, the rest of the community resents it, becomes jealous, and snubs the "progressive" individual. Many peasants, therefore, are afraid to change their way of life because they do not want to stir up the envy and hostility of friends and relatives.

Although there is no doubt that an image of limited good exists in many peasant villages in Mexico and elsewhere, the role it plays in preventing economic development is not clear. Foster provides much evidence for doubting the importance of the image of limited good in Tzintzuntzan (Figure 12.4). He tells the story of how a community development project sponsored by the United Nations achieved success initially, only to end in disasters that had little to do with the values held by the villagers. Also, most of the community's cash income was derived by working as migrant laborers in the United States. To get across the border, the migrants must bribe, scheme, and suffer great hardships. Yet 50 percent of them had succeeded in getting through, "many of them ten times or more" (Foster 1967:277).

As Foster suggests, the "image of limited good" is not a crippling illusion but rather a realistic appraisal of the facts of life in a society where economic success or failure is capricious and hinged to forces wholly beyond one's control or comprehension (see Box 12.1).

With the passage of time it has become clear that many of the heavily staffed development schemes in Mexico have been less successful than development efforts made by the people themselves with capital accumulated from working as migrants. James Acheson (1972), who studied a community near Tzintzuntzan, has argued that without realistic economic opportunities, development will not

Figure 12.4   Image of limited good.
Peasant women of Tzintzuntzan with their homemade pottery.

occur. If opportunities present themselves, some individuals will always take advantage of them, regardless of the image of limited good: "It is one thing to say that Tarascans [the people of the region of Tzintzuntzan] are suspicious, distrustful, and uncooperative; it is another to assume that this lack of cooperation precludes all possibility for positive economic change" (Acheson 1972:1165; see Acheson 1974; Foster 1974).

Box 12.1

A WORLD OF LIMITED GOOD

For the underlying fundamental truth is that in an economy like Tzintzuntzan's, hard work and thrift are moral qualities of only the slightest functional value. Because of the limitations on land and technology, additional hard work does not produce a signficant increment in income. It is pointless to talk to thrift in a subsistence economy, because usually there is no surplus with which to be thrifty. Foresight, with careful planning for the future, is also a virtue of dubious value in a world in which the best-laid plans must rest on a foundation of chance and capriciousness.

Source: George Foster 1967:150–151.

Class and Life-Style

Classes differ from one another not only in amount of power per capita but also in broad areas of patterned thought and behavior called *life-style.* Peasants, urban industrial wage workers, middle-class suburbanites, and upper-class industrialists have different life-styles (Figure 12.5). Cultural contrasts between classes are as great as contrasts between life in an Eskimo igloo and life in a Mbuti village of the Ituri forest.

Classes, in other words, have their own *subcultures* made up of distinctive work patterns, architecture, home furnishings, diet, dress, domestic routines, sex and mating practices, magico-religious rituals, art, and ideology. In many instances, different classes even have accents that make it difficult for them to talk to one another. Because of exposure of body parts to sun, wind, and callus-producing

Figure 12.5   Class and life-style.
(a) *Hunts Point, Bronx, New York.* (b) *Hampton Beach, New Hampshire.*

(a)   *(b)*

friction, working-class people tend to look different from their "superiors." Further distinctions are the result of dietary specialties — the fat and the rich were once synonymous. Throughout almost the entire evolutionary career of stratified societies, class identity has been as explicit and unambiguous as the distinction between male and female. The Chinese Han dynasty peasant, the Inca commoner, or the Russian serf could not expect to survive to maturity without knowing how to recognize members of the "superior" classes. Doubt was removed in many cases by state-enforced standards of dress: Only the Chinese nobility could wear silk clothing, only the European feudal overlords could carry daggers and swords, and only the Inca rulers could wear gold ornaments. Violators were put to death. In the presence of their "superiors," commoners still perform definite rituals of subordination, among which lowering the head, removing the hat, averting the eyes, kneeling, bowing, crawling, and maintaining silence unless spoken to occur almost universally.

Throughout much of the world, class identity continues to be sharp and unambiguous. Among most contemporary nations, differences in class-linked life-styles show little prospect of diminishing or disappearing, and the Soviet Union is no exception (Matthews 1978). Indeed, given the increase in luxury goods and services available to contemporary elites, contrasts in life-styles between the rich and powerful and the people of peasant villages or urban shantytowns (Figure 12.6) may be reaching an all-time high. During the recent epochs of industrial advance, governing classes throughout the world have gone from palanquins to Mercedes to private jets, while their subordinates find themselves without even a donkey or a pair of oxen. The elites now have their medical needs taken care of at the world's

Figure 12.6 Caracas shantytown.
Squatters in Latin American cities often enjoy the best views, since apartment houses were not built on hilltops because of lack of water. But this means that the squatters have to carry their water up the hill in cans.

best medical centers, while vast numbers of less fortunate people have never even heard of the germ theory of disease and will never be treated by modern medical techniques. Elites attend the best universities, while half of the people in the world remain illiterate.

"The Culture of Poverty"

In studying the problems of people living in urban slums and shantytowns, Oscar Lewis thought he had found evidence for a distinct set of values and practices that he called the "culture of poverty." Although not exactly comparable point by point, the concepts of the culture of poverty and of the image of limited good resemble each other in many respects, and represent similar attempts to explain the perpetuation of poverty by focusing on the traditions and values of the underprivileged groups — and they are both wrong for similar reasons. Lewis (1966) pictures the poor in such cities as Mexico City, New York, and Lima (Figure 12.7) as tending to be fearful, suspicious, and apathetic toward the major institutions of the larger society; as hating the police and being mistrustful of government; and as "inclined to be cynical of the church." They also have "a strong present-time orientation with relatively little disposition to defer gratification and plan for the future." This implies that poor people are less willing to save money and are more interested in "getting mine now" in the form of stereos, color television, the latest-style clothing, and gaudy automobiles. It also implies that the poor "blow" their earnings by getting drunk or going on buying sprees. Like George Foster, Lewis recognizes

Figure 12.7   Shantytown, Lima, Peru.

that in some measure the culture of poverty is partly a rational response to the objective conditions of powerlessness and poverty: "an adaptation and a reaction of the poor to their marginal position in a class-stratified society" (Lewis 1966:21). But he also states that once the culture of poverty comes into existence, it tends to perpetuate itself:

> By the time slum children are six or seven they have usually absorbed the basic attitudes and values of their subculture. Thereafter they are psychologically unready to take full advantage of changing conditions or improving opportunities that may develop in their lifetime. [ibid.]

Lewis proposes that only 20 percent of the urban poor actually have the culture of poverty, implying that 80 percent fall into the category of those whose poverty results from infrastructural and structural conditions, rather than from the traditions and values of a culture of poverty. The concept of the culture of poverty has been criticized on the grounds that values said to be distinctive of the urban poor are actually shared by the middle class. For example, being suspicious of government, politicians, and organized religion is not an exclusive poverty-class trait, nor is the tendency to spend above one's means. There is little evidence that the middle class as a whole lives within its income more effectively than poor people do. But when the poor mismanage their incomes, the consequences are much more serious. If the male head of a poor family yields to the temptation to buy nonessential items, his children may go hungry or his wife may be deprived of medical attention. But these consequences result from being poor, not from any demonstrable difference in the capacity to defer gratification.

The stereotype of the improvident poor masks an implicit belief that the impoverished segments of society ought to be more thrifty and more patient than the members of the middle class. It is conscience-saving to be able to attribute poverty to values for which the poor themselves can be held responsible (Leeds 1970; Murray 1984; Piven and Cloward 1971; Ryan 1982; Valentine 1970).

"Now Whose Fault Is That?"

The tendency to blame the poor for being poor is not confined to relatively affluent members of the middle class. The poor or near-poor themselves are often the staunchest supporters of the view that people who really want to work can always find work. This attitude forms part of a larger world view in which there is little comprehension of the structural conditions that make poverty inevitable for some. What must be seen as a system is viewed purely in terms of individual faults, individual motives, and individual choices. Hence the poor turn against the poor and blame one another for their plight.

In a study of a Newfoundland community called Squid Cove, Cato Wadel (1973) has shown how a structural problem of unemployment caused by factors entirely beyond the control of the local community can be interpreted in such a way as to set neighbor against neighbor. The men of Squid Cove earn their livings from logging, fishing, and construction (Figure 12.8). Mechanization in logging, depletion of the fishing grounds, and upgrading of construction skills have left most of the men without a steady, year-round means of making a living. A certain number of men, especially those who have large families and who are past their physical prime, place themselves on the

Figure 12.8   Newfoundland village. Fishermen mending their nets. Hard work is a traditional part of life in this rugged habitat.

able-bodied welfare rolls. In doing so they must be prepared to wage a desperate struggle to preserve their self-esteem against the tendency of their neighbors to regard them as shirkers who "don't do nothin' for the money they get." What makes the plight of the Squid Cove welfare recipients especially poignant is that Newfoundlanders have long been noted for their intense work ethic. Many welfare recipients formerly worked at extremely arduous unskilled jobs. For example, Wadel's principal informant, George, was a logger for 29 years. George stopped logging because he injured a disk in his spine. The injury was sufficient to prevent him from competing for the better-paying unskilled jobs, but insufficient to place him on the welfare roles as a disabled worker. George says he is willing to work, provided the job is not too heavy and does not require him to leave the house he owns in Squid Cove. "I'm willin' to work but there's no work around. . . . Now whose fault is that?" he asks. Others disagree. In Squid Cove, welfare is thought of as something "we," the taxpayers, give to "them," the unemployed. There is no generally accepted feeling that it is the responsibility of the government or the society to secure appropriate work; the responsibility for finding a job falls on the individual and no one else:

> For a welfare recipient to say outright that if work is not available, it is only proper for the government to provide adequate assistance, is not approved. Recipients thus have to be careful not to talk about their "rights." . . . On the other hand, if a recipient does not complain at all, this might be taken as a sign that he is satisfied with being on welfare, that he, in fact, is unwilling to work. Whatever the recipient does, complain or not, he is likely to be sanctioned. [Wadel 1973:38]

In explaining why he chose to study the plight of people on welfare, Cato Wadel writes: "From what has been said so far, it should be clear that I am not much in doubt about 'whose fault it is'":

> It is not the fault of the unemployed individual. If this study were summarized into a simple and clear statement, it would be that it is unemployment itself which produces behavior on the part of the unemployed which makes people blame the unemployment on the individual, and *not* the other way around: that a special attitude or personal defect produces unemployment. [ibid.:127]

Poverty in Naples

Thomas Belmonte lived for a year in a slum neighborhood in Naples, Italy, a city known as the "Calcutta of Europe." Belmonte describes the neighborhood, Fontana del Re (see Figure 12.9, Box 12.2), as being inhabited by a subproletariat, or underclass, who lacked steady employment and who produced so little that they could not even be said to be exploited because there was nothing to be taken away from them. There were people like Gabriele, who collected metal junk and broke it into pieces with the help of his four children but who also ran a little store during the day and drove a taxi for prostitutes at night. Others were part-time sailors, waiters, bartenders, dockworkers, scavengers, and movers. Some groomed dogs, others were jacks-of-all-trades. Some were full-time smugglers, dope dealers, pickpockets, purse-snatchers, and burglars. There were also dressmakers, flower vendors, beggars, and old women who added to their small pensions "by selling contraband cigarettes and condoms,

Figure 12.9 Poverty in Naples.
The infamous one-room hovels of the Bassi, usually without ventilation, running water, separate toilets, or heating, are home for tens of thousands of Neapolitan families.

Box 12.2

❧❧❧

THE BROKEN FOUNTAIN

At Fontana del Re in a corner strewn now with rubble, beneath the bruised, shattered visage of a lion, the eroded figure of a sculpted stone sea shell recedes into a wall.

"This was our fountain," they told me. "Oh you should have seen it, Tommaso. The water played night and day. In summer, the children scampered about in it. At night, falling asleep, you heard it, and it was like music." The young men told me it was they who had destroyed it. As children, many years before, with iron rods, they had gone every day to hammer and smash it, until they were satisfied and there was nothing left to break.

Thereafter, whenever I passed that ruined corner, I tried to imagine what the fountain had once been like, and thought and wondered and sorrowed the more as I understood how it came to be broken.

Source: Belmonte 1989:144.

and greasy sandwiches and wine so bad it burned a hole through your gut." The children of Fontana del Re did odd jobs that earned them about 33 cents an hour. Pepe, the 11-year-old son of a cobbler, had a job in a TV repair shop; his face and chest were scarred from defective tubes that blew up when he tested them. Several neighborhood children made daily forays to pry open the trunks of parked cars. Other children carried trays of espresso to offices and shops.

The people of Fontana del Re have many of Oscar Lewis's culture of poverty traits. But Belmonte traces most of these traits to being penniless and lacking steady employment (Box 12.3).

Minorities and Majorities

In addition to classes, most state societies are also stratified into so-called racial, ethnic, and cultural groups (R. Cohen 1978a and b). These groups, often called *minorities* or *majorities*, differ from classes in three ways: (1) They have distinctive life-styles that can be traced to the cultural traditions of another society, (2) their membership often spans different classes, and (3) their members are conscious of their existence as a group set apart from the rest of the population (Figure 12.10).

The separation into racial, ethnic, or cultural minorities is based on whether the criteria of group membership are primarily physical appearance, common origin in another country or region, or possession of a distinctive life-style. In reality, however, all three criteria occur in a bewildering number of combinations (Sanjek 1977). Racial and cultural differences and common ancestry are often claimed by or attributed to groups that lack them, giving rise to sharp discrepancies between emic and etic versions of group identity.

Racial, ethnic, and cultural *minorities* are groups that are subordinate or whose position is vulnerable to subordination. The term *majority* refers to the higher-ranking and more secure racial, ethnic, or cultural groups. The two terms are unsatisfactory because "majorities" such as the whites in South Africa are sometimes vastly outnumbered by the "minorities" whom they oppress and exploit (Figure

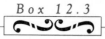

Box 12.3

CULTURE OR POVERTY?

The poor hesitate to plan for the future because they are hard-put to stay afloat in the present, and not because of a "present-time orientation." They have no trouble recalling the high and low points of their past. Their avoidance of banks relates to a realistic fear of inlation and a realistic mistrust of the literate officialdom. They do not patronize department stores because they prefer to cultivate their own, more prsonalized networks of local credit, marketing, and exchange. In direct contradiction to Lewis's formulation, the poor of Naples purchase vital supplies wisely and in bulk. They place numerous cultural controls on consumption, wasting nothing. They are habituated to delaying gratifications in terms of clothing, housing, plumbing, heating, travel, transportation, and entertainment. If in good times they alow themselves the one luxury of channeling surplus funds into good, abundant food, I think it ethnocentric to label them irrational or immature, since this is how they sublimate a historically inherited and confirmed terror of hunger.

Confronted by a scarcity of opportunities, they become resigned, to preserve their sanity, and do not think to transcend their condition so long as they remain in underdeveloped Naples. . . . They have a culture that is simultaneously against poverty, adapted to the stresses of poverty, and mangled by poverty. But they have a culture which is also fashioned out of a great mediterranean tradition, in the crucible of a great Mediterranean city. Their culture reflects their various and ingenious strategies for survival and their low position in a hierarchy; in other words, it is a class culture as well as a regional one. . . .

The Neapolitan urban poor are fashion-wise, street-wise, and urbane. They are not provincial. They live close to the gates of power in the wards of a great city, but unlike proletarians they are not integrated into the political and ideological currents of mass culture. They inhabit a world connected and apart from the main a dense and crowded urban world, submerged; a crude, loud, pushy world where the moral order is exposed as a fraud which conceals the hstorical ascendancy of cunning and force.

Source: Belmonte 1989:141–143.

(a)

Figure 12.10 Ethnic festivals—Celebrating ties among past, present, and future generations. (a) An Irish parade in New York City. (b) Celebrating Chinese New Year. (c) Attending a Jewish parade in New York City. (d) An Italian religious festival in Boston. Ethnicity is based on beliefs about descent.

(c)

(b)

(d)

Figure 12.11   The long road to freedom.
Nelson Mandela emerges from 27 years of impris-
onment to continue the struggle against apartheid in
South Africa.

12.11). No satisfactory substitute for these terms has been devised, however (Simpson and Yinger 1985).

The most important point to bear in mind about minorities and majorities is that they are invariably locked into a more or less open form of political, social, and economic struggle to protect or raise their position in the stratification system (Abruzzi 1982; Berreman 1981; Despres 1975; Schermerhorn 1978; Sowell 1983; Wagley and Harris 1958). Depending on their respective numbers, their special cultural strengths and weaknesses, and their initial advantages or disadvantages during the formation of the stratification system, their status as a group may rise or fall in the hierarchy. Thus, although many minorities are subject to excruciating forms of discrimination, segregation, and exploitation, others may actually enjoy fairly high, although not dominant, positions.

Assimilation Versus Pluralism

Some minorities are almost completely endogamous, and of these many are endogamous by "choice." The Jews, Amish, Chinese, and Greeks in the United States, the Hindus in Guyana, the Muslims in India, and the Japanese in Brazil are examples of groups for whom endogamy is a practice valued as much by the minority as by the rest of the population. Other minorities, such as the blacks of the United States and the coloreds of South Africa, have no strong motivation to be endogamous but find intermarriage blocked largely by the hostility of the rest of the population. Still other minorities neither possess internal barriers to exogamy nor encounter external resistance. Such groups (e.g., the Germans or Scots in the United States and the Italians in Brazil) usually move toward *assimilation*—the loss of separate identity as a minority group.

Where endogamy prevails, either by choice of the minority or by imposition of the "majority," a *pluralistic* condition may endure for centuries or even millennia. Assimilation may also fail to take place even when a certain amount of intermarriage occurs if there is a form of descent rule, as in the United States, that assigns the mixed offspring to the minority or if the rate of intermarriage is not very high relative to the rate of population increase.

What accounts for these variations? The attempt to explain why a minority will develop along pluralistic rather than assimilationist lines requires a broad evolutionary and comparative approach. The most important fact to consider is this: Minorities enter a particular state society under disadvantageous circumstances. They enter as migrants seeking employment as "guest workers," or relief from exploitative class systems in their native lands. Many are defeated peoples who have been overrun during wars of conquest and expansion, or who have been transferred from colonial outposts as indentured servants or slaves.

Each minority has a unique *adaptive capacity* to survive and prosper in the particular adverse situation in which it finds itself. This capacity is based on its prior experiences, history, language, and culture. If the class structure of the majority's social system is marked by individualized competition for upward mobility and a corresponding lack of class identity or class solidarity, the minority may derive advantages from the practice of endogamy, settlement in restricted regions or neighborhoods, and pursuit of pluralistic goals.

The reasons for the development of pluralistic goals are as diverse as the adaptive capacities in the world inventory of minorities and the structure of state societies in which they live. Some groups appear to be more likely than others to benefit from the preservation of their traditional culture patterns because these patterns have a high adaptive capacity. Jews, for example, long excluded from land-based means of earning a living in Europe, arrived in the rapidly urbanizing society of the late nineteenth-century United States "pre-adapted" to compete for upward mobility in urban occupations requiring high levels of literacy. Contemporary Japanese migrants to Brazil bring with them special skills related to intensive agriculture and truck farming. Chinese migrants in many parts of the world achieve outstanding success by adhering to traditional family-based patterns of business activity.

The emphasis on differences in language, religion, and other aspects of life-styles can increase the minority's sense of solidarity and may help its members to compete in impersonalized, competitive societies. Jewish, Chinese, Japanese, Greek, Syrian, Hindu, or Muslim merchants and businesspeople, for example,

frequently enjoy important commercial advantages in highly competitive situations. Based on his study of the relations between Afro-Americans and Hindus in Guyana, Leo Despres (1975) suggests that ethnic, cultural, and racial identities confer competitive advantages with respect to environmental resources. The Hindu segment of Guyana society, for example, has a firmer grip on the land than the black segment.

In many situations, however, strong minority solidarity carries with it the danger of overexposure and reaction. In maintaining and increasing their own solidarity, minorities run the risk of increasing the sense of alienation from the larger population and hence of becoming the scapegoats of genocidal policies. The fate of the Jews in Germany and Poland, the Hindu Indians in east and southern Africa, the Chinese in Indonesia, and the Muslims and Sikhs in India are some of the better-known examples of "successful" minority adaptations that were followed by mass slaughter and/or expulsion.

Castes in India

Indian castes are closed, endogamous, and stratified descent groups. They bear many resemblances to classes and racial, ethnic, and cultural minorities. No sharp line can be drawn between the castes of India and such groups as the Jews or blacks in the United States or the Inca elite. However, some features of the Indian caste hierarchy are unique and deserve special attention.

The unique features of Indian castes have to do with the fact that the caste hierarchy is an integral part of Hinduism, the religion of most of the people of India. (This does not mean that one must be a Hindu in order to belong to a caste. There are also Muslim and Christian castes in India.) It is a matter of religious conviction in India that all people are not spiritually equal and that the gods have established a hierarchy of groups. This hierarchy consists of the four major *varnas,* or grades of being. According to the earliest traditions (e.g., the Hymns of Rigveda), the four *varnas* correspond to the physical parts of Purusa, who gave rise to the human race through dismemberment. His mouth became the *Brahmans* (priests), his arms the *Kshatriyas* (warriors), his thighs the *Vaishyas* (merchants and craftsmen), and his feet the *Shudras* (menial workers) (Gould 1971). According to Hindu scripture, an individual's *varna* is determined by a descent rule— that is, it corresponds to the *varna* of one's parents and is unalterable during one's lifetime.

The basis of all Hindu morality is the idea that each *varna* has its appropriate rules of behavior, or "path of duty" *(dharma).* At the death of the body, the soul meets its fate in the form of a transmigration into a higher or lower being *(karma).* Those who follow the *dharma* will find themselves at a higher point on Purusa's body during their next life. Deviation from the *dharma* will result in reincarnation in the body of an outcaste or even an animal (Long 1987).

One of the most important aspects of the *dharma* is the practice of certain taboos regarding marriage, eating, and physical proximity. Marriage below one's *varna* is generally regarded as a defilement and pollution, acceptance of food cooked or handled by persons below one's *varna* is also a defilement and pollution, and any bodily contact between Brahman and Shudra is forbidden (Figure 12.12). In some parts of India there were not only untouchables but unseeables — people who could come out only at night.

Figure 12.12   Untouchables.
Caste in India must be seen from the bottom up to be understood.

Although the general outlines of this system are agreed upon throughout Hindu India (Long 1987; Maloney 1987a and b), there are enormous regional and local differences in the finer details of the ideology and practice of caste relationships. The principal source of these complications is the fact that it is not the *varna* but thousands of internally stratified subdivisions known as *jatis* (or subcastes) that constitute the real functional endogamous units. Moreover, even *jatis* of the same name (e.g., "washermen," "shoemakers," "herders," and so on) further divide into local endogamous subgroups and exogamous lineages (Klass 1979).

Caste from the Top Down and Bottom Up

There are two very different views of the Hindu caste system. The view that predominates among Westerners is that which conforms largely to the emics of the top-ranking Brahman caste. According to this view, each caste and subcaste has a hereditary occupation that guarantees its members basic subsistence and job security. The lower castes render vital services to the upper castes. Hence the upper castes know they cannot get along without the lower castes and do not abuse them. And in times of crisis, the upper castes will extend emergency assistance in the form of food or loans. Moreover, since the Hindu religion gives everyone a convincing explanation of why some are inferior and others superior, members of lower castes do not resent being regarded as a source of pollution and defilement and have no interest in changing the status of their castes in the local or regional hierarchy (Dumont 1970).

The other view — the view from the bottom up — makes the Indian caste system hard to distinguish from the racial, ethnic, and cultural minorities with which Westerners are familiar. Critics of the top-down view point out that whites in the United States once insisted that the Bible justified slavery and that blacks were well treated, contented with their lot in life, and not interested in changing their status. According to Joan Mencher, who has worked and lived among the untouchable castes of southern India, the error in the top-down view is just as great in India as in the United States. Mencher reports that the lowest castes are not satisfied with their station in life and do not believe they are treated fairly by their caste superiors. As for the security allegedly provided

by the monopoly of such professionals as smiths, washermen, barbers, potters, and so on, such occupations taken together never engaged more than 10 to 15 percent of the total Hindu population (most people are farmers). Caste professions never provided basic subsistence for the majority of the members of most castes. Among the Chamars, for example, who are known as leatherworkers, only a small portion of the caste engages in leatherwork. In the countryside almost all Chamars are a source of cheap agricultural labor. When questioned about their low station in life, many of Mencher's low-caste informants explained that they had to be dependent on the other castes since they had no land of their own. Did landowners in times of extreme need or crisis actually give free food and assistance to their low-caste dependents? "To my informants, both young and old, this sounds like a fairytale" (Mencher 1974b; see also Khare 1984).

Anthropological studies of actual village life in India have yielded a picture of caste relationships drastically opposed to the ideals posited in Hindu theology (Carrol 1977). One of the most important discoveries is that local *jatis* recurrently try to raise their ritual status. Such attempts usually take place as part of a general process by which local ritual status is adjusted to actual local economic and political power. There may be low-ranking subcastes that passively accept their lot in life as a result of their *karma* assignment; such groups, however, tend to be wholly lacking in the potential for economic and political mobility. "But let opportunities for political and economic advance appear barely possible and such resignation is likely to vanish more quickly than one might imagine" (Orans 1968:878).

One of the symptoms of this underlying propensity for *jatis* to redefine their ritual position to conform with their political and economic potential is a widespread lack of agreement over the shape of local ritual hierarchies as seen by inhabitants of the same village, town, or region. This is true of even the lowest "untouchables" (Barber 1968; Khare 1984). Kathleen Gough (1959) indicates that in villages of South India, the middle reaches of the caste hierarchy may have as many as 15 castes whose relative ritual ranks are ambiguous or in dispute. Different individuals and families even in the same caste give different versions of the rank-order of these groups. Elsewhere, even the claims of Brahman subcastes to ritual superiority are openly contested (Srinivas 1955). The conflict among *jatis* concerning their ritual position may involve prolonged litigation in the local courts and if not resolved may, under certain circumstances, lead to much violence and bloodshed (see Berreman 1975; Cohn 1955).

Contrary to the view that these features of caste are a response to the recent "modernization" of India, Karen Leonard (1978) has shown that similarly fluid and flexible individual, family, and subcaste strategies date back at least to the eighteenth century. According to Leonard, the internal organization and external relationships of the Kayastks, originally a caste of scribes and record keepers, shifted continuously to adapt to changing economic, political, and demographic circumstances. Kayastks attempted to better their lot in life as individuals, as families, and as subcastes according to changing opportunities. Marriage patterns and descent rules were constantly modified to provide maximum advantages with respect to government and commercial employment, and even the rule of endogamy was broken when alliances with other subcastes became useful: "Adaptability, rather than conformity to accepted Brahmanical or scholarly notions about caste, has always characterized

the Kayastk marriage networks and kin groups" (Leonard 1978:294).

In comparing Indian castes with minorities in other parts of the world, we should emphasize that substantial cultural differences are frequently associated with each local *jati*. Subcastes may speak different languages or dialects, follow different kinds of descent and locality rules, have different forms of marriage, worship different gods, eat different foods, and altogether present a greater contrast in lifestyle than that which exists between New Yorkers and the Zuni Indians. Moreover, many castes of India are associated with racial differences comparable to the contrast between whites and blacks in the United States. In view of all these resemblances, it might very well be argued that we could dispense with either the term *caste* or the term *minority*.

The stratification system of India is noteworthy not merely for the presence of endogamous descent groups possessing real or imagined racial and cultural specialties: Every state-level society has such groups. It is, rather, the extraordinary profusion of such groups that merits our attention. Nonetheless, the caste system of India is fundamentally similar to that of other countries that have closed classes and numerous ethnic and racial minorities. Like the blacks in the United States or the Catholics in Northern Ireland, low castes in India

resist the status accorded them, with its concomitant disabilities and discrimination, and strive for higher accorded status and its attendant advantages. High castes attempt to prevent such striving and the implied threat to their position. In this conflict of interest lies the explosive potential of all caste societies. [Berreman 1966:318]

Summary

All state societies are organized into stratified groups such as classes, minorities, and castes. Stratified groups consist of people who relate to the apparatus of control in similar ways and who possess similar amounts of power over the allocation of wealth, privileges, resources, and technology. *Power*, in this context, means control over energy or the ability to move and shape people and things. All state societies have at least two classes—rulers and ruled. Theoretically, ruling classes may voluntarily act in the best interests of commoners, but only if ruling-class power is not thereby diminished.

Sex and age hierarchies are also important forms of stratification, but they are not confined to state societies. Class differences involve both differential access to power and profound differences in life-styles. The understanding of class and all other forms of social stratification is made difficult by the failure to separate emic and etic versions of stratification hierarchies. From an etic and behavioral point of view, classes can exist even if there is no emic recognition of their existence and even if segments of the same class compete. Ruling classes need not form permanent, hereditary, monolithic, conspiratorial organizations. Their membership can change rapidly and they may actively deny that they constitute a ruling class. Similarly, subordinate classes need not be conscious of their identity and may exist only in an etic and behavioral sense.

Understanding the phenomenon of exploitation also depends on the distinction between emic and etic perspectives. It cannot be maintained that the mere existence of differential power, wealth, and privilege guarantees the existence of exploitation, nor that exploitation exists only when or as soon as people feel exploited. Etic criteria for exploitation focus on the acquisition of luxuries among elites based on the deprivation of necessities among commoners and perpetuation or intensification of misery and poverty.

The majority of the people in the world today are members of peasant classes. Peasants are structured inferiors who farm with preindustrial technologies and pay rent or taxes. Three major varieties of peasants can be distinguished: feudal, agromanagerial, and capitalist. Their structured inferiority depends in the first case on their inability to acquire land; in the second, on the existence of a powerful managerial elite that sets production and labor quotas; and in the third, on the operation of a price market in land and labor controlled by big landlords, corporations, and banks.

Among peasant classes, an "image of limited good" is widespread. However, there are also contradictory values and attitudes that lead to innovations under appropriate structural and infrastructural conditions. In Tzintzuntzan, despite the image of limited good, men struggled for a chance to work as migrant laborers, and both men and women participated in a series of ill-fated development experiments in the hope of bettering their lives.

For urban subordinate classes, the counterpart of the image of limited good is the culture of poverty. This concept focuses on the values and the traditions of the urban poor as an explanation for poverty. However, many of the values in the culture of poverty, such as distrust of authority, consumerism, and improvidence, are also found in more affluent classes. The irrelevance of the emphasis people place on the value of work for understanding the genesis of poverty classes can be seen in the case of Squid Cove. Newfoundlanders are well known for their work ethic, yet when mechanization and resource depletion left them without year-round jobs, they had no alternative but to accept welfare assistance. The broken fountain of Naples tells a similar story.

Systems of class stratification differ widely in the amount of upward mobility they permit. If classes were exogamous and if children of the very rich were disinherited, mobility would be much higher.

Racial, ethnic, and cultural minorities and majorities are present in virtually all state societies. These groups differ from classes in having distinctive life-styles derived from another society, internal class differences, and a high degree of group consciousness. Minorities and majorities struggle for access to and control over the sources of wealth and power, aided or hindered by their adaptive strengths and weaknesses in relation to specific arenas of competition. It is the specific nature of this struggle in the history of each minority-majority relationship that determines whether assimilation or pluralism will be emphasized by the minority and/or the majority. Advantages and disadvantages are associated with both options. Neither assimilationist nor pluralist commitments may suffice to overcome the effects of segregation, discrimination, and exploitation. It can be argued that racial and ethnic chauvinism benefits the ruling class more than the ordinary members of either the minority or majority.

Social scientists usually identify a third type of stratified group known as castes. Castes are epitomized by the case of Hindu India. Traditional views of Indian castes have been dominated by top-down idealizations in which the lower castes are represented as voluntarily accepting their subordinate status. Bottom-up studies show that Indian castes struggle for upward mobility in a flexible and adaptive fashion, and that they closely resemble cultural, ethnic, and racial minorities in other societies.

Chapter 13

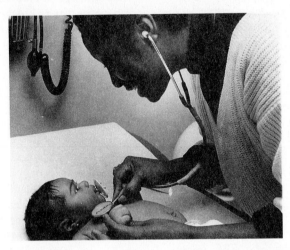

GENDER AND CULTURE

In this chapter we consider the influence of sexual differences on the structural aspects of sociocultural systems. *Male* and *female* are examined as culturally constructed genders, and the political economy of sex and gender hierarchies is examined along with the question of male-bias in anthropology. A theory to account for variations in gender hierarchies is set forth.

Sex Versus Gender

The etic sexual identity of human beings can be established by examining an individual's chromosomes, interior and exterior sex organs, and secondary sexual characteristics such as body build, size of breasts, and fat deposits. While all societies recognize a distinction between male and female based on some of these features, the emic definition of being male or female, or some other sex, varies considerably from one society to another. Anthropologists therefore prefer to use the term *gender* to denote the variable emic meanings associated with culturally defined sexual identities, and the phrase *gender roles* (instead of sex roles) when referring to the expected patterns of thought and behavior that are associated with gender identities (Gilmore 1990; Jacobs and Roberts 1989; Ortner and Whitehead 1981).

Margaret Mead's (1950) study of three New Guinea tribes — the Arapesh, Mundugumor, and Tchambuli — is the classic anthropological work on the spectrum of gender roles. Mead discovered that among the Arapesh, both men and women are expected to behave in a mild, sympathetic, and cooperative manner, reminiscent of what Americans expect from an ideal mother. Among the Mundugumor, men and women are expected to be equally fierce and aggressive. Among the Tchambuli, the women shave their heads, are prone to hearty laughter, show comradely solidarity, and are aggressively efficient as food providers; Tchambuli men, on the other hand, are preoccupied with art, spend a great deal of time on their hairdos, and are always gossiping about the opposite sex. Although Mead's interpretations have been challenged as too subjective (Errington and Gewertz 1987) there is no doubt that marked contrasts in gender roles do exist in different cultures.

Gender Ideologies

In many cultures, males believe they are spiritually superior to females and that females are dangerous and polluting, weak and untrustworthy. For example, one of the most wide-

*Figure 13.1   Interior of men's house, New Guinea.
The men use the masks to terrify the women and
children.*

spread of all gender ideologies has as its explicit
aim the retention of a male monopoly on
knowledge of the myths and rituals of human
origins and of the nature of supernatural
beings. This complex involves secret male initiation rites; male residence in a separate men's
house (Figure 13.1) from which women and
children are excluded; masked male dancers
who impersonate the gods and other spiritual
beings; the bull roarer, which is said to be the
voice of the gods and which is whirled about in

the bush or under cover of darkness to frighten
the women and uninitiated boys (see page 297);
storage of the masks, bull roarer, and other
sacred paraphernalia in the men's house; threat
of death or actual execution of any woman who
admits to knowing the secrets of the cult; and
threat of death or execution of any man who
reveals the secrets to women or uninitiated
boys (Gregor 1985:94ff.).

Ecclesiastical types of religions (see page
299) are also characterized by a pervasive functional interconnection between male-dominated rituals and myths on the one hand, and
male political-religious supremacy on the
other. The established high priests of Rome,
Greece, Mesopotamia, Egypt, ancient Israel,
and the entire Muslim and Hindu world were
or are men. High-ranking priestesses with autonomous control over their own temples, as
in Minoan Crete, are the exception, even when
the ecclesiastical cults include female deities.
Males traditionally dominated the ecclesiastical
organization of all the major world religions.
All three chief religions of Western civilization — Christianity, Judaism, and Islam —
stressed the priority of the male principle in the
formation of the world. They identified the
creator god as "He," and to the extent that they
recognized female deities, as in Catholicism,
traditionally assigned them a secondary role in
myth and ritual. They all held that men were
created first, and women second, out of a piece
of a man (Figure 13.2).

The Relativity of Gender Ideologies

How much of the male claim to spiritual superiority is believed by women? To begin with, as
we have seen in Chapter 12, one must be skeptical that any subjugated group really accepts

Figure 13.2 Re-created Creation.
(a) *Michaelangelo's* Creation, *from the Sistine Chapel. God, depicted as a male, creates Adam first.* (b) *Redrawing of the creation scene, with female God touching Eve.*

the reasons that the subjugators give to justify their claim to superior status. In addition, much new evidence suggests that women have their own gender ideologies, which have not been properly recorded because earlier generations of ethnographers were primarily males, and neglected or were unable to obtain the woman's point of view.

For example, the seclusion of menstruating women among the Yurok Indians of Northern California has consistently been interpreted by male ethnographers as a demonstration of the need to protect men from the pollution of menstrual blood. Only recently has it become clear that Yurok women had a completely different sense of what they were doing (Buckley 1982; Child and Child 1985). Rather than feeling that they were being confined for the benefit of Yurok men, they felt that they were enjoying a privileged opportunity to get away from the chores of everyday life, to meditate on their life goals, and to gather spiritual strength (Box 13.1). Similarly, while

Box 13.1

A YUROK WOMAN'S VIEW OF MENSTRUAL SECLUSION

A menstruating woman should isolate herself because this is the time when she is at the height of her powers. Thus, the time should not be wasted in mundane tasks and social distractions, nor should one's concentration be broken by concerns with the opposite sex. Rather, all of one's energies should be applied in concentrated meditation on the nature of one's life, "to find out the purpose of your life," and toward the "accumulation" of spiritual energy. The menstrual shelter, or room, is "like the men's sweathouse," a place where you "go into yourself and make yourself stronger."

Source: Buckley 1982:48–49.

men may have one idea about which sex is more valuable, women may have quite a different idea.

Among the !Kung, who are generally regarded as having complementary and egalitarian gender roles, one woman at least felt that men were dependent on women far more than women were dependent on men. Men would die without women, she said (Box 13.2).

As for the exclusion of women from male-centered rituals, women do not necessarily resent being excluded, because they do not attach much importance to what the men are doing with their bull roarers and masked dancing. Dorothy Counts tells how an old blind woman among the Kaliai of Papua New Guinea turned down the "honor" of being invited to remain in the village while the men performed their secret ceremonies. She left with the other women as she had always done, to feast and make lewd fun of the men's "secrets" (1985:61).

Male-Bias: Trobriands Revisited

There is much evidence, supplied principally by women ethnographers (Kaberry 1970; Matthews 1985; Sacks 1971; Sanday 1981), that the power of women has often been substantially underestimated or misconstrued by male anthropologists, who until recently were the main sources of cross-cultural data on gender roles. Even one of the greatest ethnographers, Bronislaw Malinowski, could fall short of providing a balanced view of gender roles in his classic study of the Trobriand Islanders. As discussed in Chapter 11, at harvest time in the Trobriands, brothers give their sisters' husbands gifts of yams. These yams provide much of the material basis for the political power of the Trobriand chiefs. Malinowski viewed the harvest gift as a kind of annual tribute from the wife's family to her husband, and therefore as a means of enhancing and consolidating male power. Annette Weiner has shown, however, that the harvest yams are given in the name of the wife and are actually as much a means of bolstering the value of being a woman as a means of conferring power on men. Malinowski overlooked the fact that the gift of yams had to be reciprocated, and that the counter-gift had to go not to a man's wife's brother but to a man's wife. In return for the yams received in his wife's name, the Trobriand husband had to provide her with a distinct form of wealth consisting of women's skirts and bundles of pandanus and banana leaves used for making skirts. Much of a husband's economic activity is devoted to trading pigs and other valuables in order to supply his wife with large quantities of

Box 13.2

A !Kung Woman's Point of View

Women are strong; women are important. Zhun/twa [!Kung San] men say that women are the chiefs, the rich ones, the wise ones. Because women possess something very important, something that enables men to live: their genitals. A woman can bring a man life even if he is almost dead. She can give him sex and make him alive again. If she were to refuse, he would die! If there were no women around, their semen would kill men. Did you know that? If there were only men, they would all die. Women make it possible for them to live.

Source: The words of Nisa, a !Kung San woman, as recorded by Marjorie Shostak (1981:288).

Figure 13.3   Trobriand Island sagli.
Women dominate the gift-giving display that is part of mortuary rituals.

women's wealth. The skirts and bundles of leaves are publicly displayed and given away at huge funeral ceremonies known as *sagali* (which Malinowski knew about but did not see fit to describe in detail). Weiner (1976:118) states that the *sagali* is one of the most important public events in Trobriand life (Figure 13.3):

> Nothing is so dramatic as women standing at a *sagali* surrounded by thousands of bundles. Nor can anything be more impressive than watching the deportment of women as they attend to the distribution. When women walk to the center [of the plaza] to throw down their wealth, they carry themselves with a pride as characteristic as that of any Melanesian bigman.

Failure of a husband to equip his wife with sufficient women's wealth to make a good showing at the *sagali* adversely affects his own prospects for becoming a big man. His brothers-in-law may reduce or eliminate their yam harvest gift if their sister cannot display and give away large quantities of bundles and skirts to relatives of the deceased. In Weiner's account, not only are men more dependent on women for their power than in Malinowski's account, but also women emerge as having far more influence in their own right. She concludes that all too often anthropologists "have allowed 'politics by men' to structure our thinking about other societies . . . leading us to believe erroneously that if women are not dominant in the political sphere of interaction, their power, at best, remains peripheral" (1976:228).

The distribution of power between the sexes is seldom simply a matter of women being completely at the mercy of men (or vice versa).

As the Trobriand study shows, male anthropologists in the past may not have grasped the more subtle aspects of gender hierarchies. Yet by emphasizing the ability of subordinates to manipulate the system in their favor, we must not fall into the trap of minimizing the real power differences embodied in many gender hierarchies. It is well known that slaves can sometimes outwit masters, that privates can frustrate generals, and that children can get parents to wait on them like servants. The ability to buffer the effects of institutionalized inequality is not the same as institutionalized equality.

Gender Hierarchy

Despite varying definitions of masculine and feminine, males tend in the majority of societies to be assigned more aggressive and violent roles than females (Schengel 1972). From our previous discussions (Chapters 10 and 11) of the evolution of political organization, it is clear that males often preempt the major centers of public power and control. Headmen rather than headwomen dominate both egalitarian and stratified forms of trade and redistribution. The same male preeminence is evidenced by the Semai and Mehinacu headmen; the Solomon Island *mumis* and the New Guinea big men (but see Counts 1985); the Nuer leopard skin chief; the Kwakiutl, Trobriand, and Tikopian chiefs; the Bunyoro Mukama; the Inca, the pharaohs, and the emperors of China and Japan. If queens reigned, it was always as temporary holders of power that belonged to the males of the lineage. Nothing more dramatically exposes the political subordination of women than the fact that in 1989 women comprised only 12.7 percent of the members of the world's legislative bodies. Fewer than 5 percent

of heads of state are women (*New York Times* 1989).

It was formerly believed that political control by women, or *matriarchy* (the opposite of *patriarchy*, or political control by men) occurred as a regular stage in the evolution of social organization. Today, virtually all anthropologists doubt the existence of matriarchies at any phase of cultural evolution (Rosaldo and Lamphere 1974:3). Claims for the existence of such societies often exaggerate the political significance of matrilineal descent and matrilocal residence. Ruby Rohrlich-Leavitt (1977:57), for example, argues that in Minoan Crete "women participated at least equally with men in political decision making, while in religion and social life they were supreme." This contention, however, is based on inferences from archaeological data that can be given contradictory interpretations (Ehrenberg 1989:109–118). It seems likely that Minoan Crete was matrilineal and that women enjoyed a relatively high political status. However, the basis of Crete's economy was maritime trade and it was men, not women, who dominated this activity. Rohrlich-Leavitt contends that the Cretan matriarchy was made possible by the absence of both warfare and a male military complex. However, it seems likely that military activities were focused on naval encounters that have left little archaeologically retrievable evidence (Reed 1984).

The Iroquois of New York state are another society that has been offered as an example of a matriarchy. According to Daniel McCall (1980), women dominated both domestic and political affairs in this matrilineal, matrilocal society prior to the coming of the Europeans and the intensification of warfare (but see Albers 1989:140–142). But McCall admits that after the arrival of the Europeans, male war chiefs dominated the tribal councils.

The question of Iroquois matriarchy therefore depends on their not being very warlike in former times. This seems doubtful because of the high correlation between matrilineal-matrilocal chiefdoms and intense external warfare (see page 163). There is no doubt, however, that Iroquois women wielded a great deal of power in political as well as domestic affairs (see page 250).

The absence of matriarchies is an important fact about gender hierarchies. But its significance should not be exaggerated. It does not mean that males universally dominate females, for there are many societies in which gender roles do not involve marked inequalities.

Gender and Exploitation

When males enjoy power advantages over women with respect to access to strategic resources (Josephides 1985), ideas about female pollution, whether shared by women or not, will in all likelihood be associated with significant deprivations and disadvantages (Goodale 1971). While the work of reinterpreting gender roles from a female point of view is pressed forward, one should not lose sight of the existence of real exploitation of women by men, in both pre-state and state societies.

The linking of negative stereotypes with various disadvantages has been stressed by Shirley Lindenbaum with respect to two strongly male-biased societies in which she has done fieldwork. In Bangladesh, Lindenbaum encountered an elaborate ideology of male supremacy expressed in symbols and rituals (see Box 13.3). She found similar beliefs and rituals among the Foré of highland New Guinea. In both instances, women were subject to important material deprivations. Among the Foré,

pregnant women were secluded in special huts, not to celebrate and concentrate female powers but to limit them.

> Her seclusion there is a sign of the half-wild condition brought on by the natural functions of her own body. Other women bring the food, for if she visited her gardens during this period of isolation she would blight all domesticated crops. Nor should she send food to her husband: ingesting food she had touched would make him feel weak, catch a cold, age prematurely. [Lindenbaum 1979:129]

If a Foré woman gives birth to a deformed or stillborn child, the woman is held solely responsible. Her husband and the men of the hamlet denounce her, accuse her of trying to obstruct male authority, and kill one of her pigs. Among the Foré as among many other New Guinea societies, men appropriate the best sources of animal protein for themselves. The men argue that women's sources of protein—frogs, small game, and insects—would make men sick. These prejudices can have lethal effects. Throughout New Guinea they are associated with much higher death rates for young girls than for young boys (Buchbinder 1977). The same lethal results are evident in Bangladesh:

> The male child receives preferential nutrition. With his father he eats first, and if there is a choice, luxury foods or scarce foods are given to him rather than to his female siblings. The result is a Bengalese population with a preponderance of males, and a demographic picture in which the mortality rate for females under 5 years of age is in some years 50% higher than that for males. [Lindenbaum 1977:143]

Box 13.3

SEXUAL SYMBOLISM IN BANGLADESH

Men are associated with the right, preferred side of things, women with the left. Village practitioners state that a basic physiological difference between the sexes makes it necessary to register a man's pulse in his right wrist, a woman's in her left, and they invariably examine patients in this way. Most villagers wear amulets to avert illness caused by evil spirits; men tie the amulet to the right upper arm, women to the left. Similarly, palmists and spiritualists read the right hands of men and the left hands of women. In village dramas, where both male and female parts are played by male actors, the audience may identify men gesturing with the right arm, women with the left. During religious celebrations there are separate entrances at such public places as the tombs of Muslim saints or Hindu images, the right avenue being reserved for men and the left for women. In popular belief, girls are said to commence walking by placing the left foot forward first, men the right.

In some instances, this right-left association indicates more than the social recognition of physiological difference, carrying additional connotations of prestige, honour and authority. Women who wish to behave respectfully to their husbands say they should, ideally, remain to the left side while eating, sitting and lying in bed. The same mark of respect should be shown also to all social superiors: to the rich, and in present times to those who are well educated.

Thus, the right-left dichotomy denotes not only male-female but also authority-submission. It also has connotations of good-bad and purity-pollution. Muslims consider the right side to be the side of good augury, believing that angels dwell on the right shoulder to record good deeds in preparation for the Day of Judgment, while on the left side, devils record misdeeds. The left side is also associated with the concept of pollution. Islam decrees that the left hand be reserved for cleansing the anus after defecation. It must never, therefore, be used for conveying food to the mouth, or for rinsing the mouth with water before the proscribed daily prayers.

Source: Lindenbaum 1977:142.

Variations in Gender Hierarchies: Hunter-Gatherers

In the words of Eleanor Leacock (1978:247), we cannot go from the proposition that "women are subordinate as regards political authority in most societies" to "women are subordinate in all respects in all societies." The very notions of "equality" and "inequality" may represent an ethnocentric misunderstanding of the kind of gender roles that exist in many societies. Leacock (1978:225) does not dispute the fact that when "unequal control over resources and subjugation by class and by sex developed," it was women who in general became subjugated to men (recognizing, of course, that the degree of subjugation varied depending on local ecological, economic, and political conditions). But in the absence of classes and the state, Leacock argues that gender roles were merely different, not unequal. There is certainly much evidence to indicate that power of any sort, whether of men over men or men over women, was trivial or nonexistent in many (but not all) band and village societies, for reasons discussed in Chapter 10.

Writing of her fieldwork among the Montagnais-Naskapi foragers of Labrador, Leacock (1983:116) notes that "they gave me insight into a level of respect and consideration for the individuality of others, regardless of sex, that I had never before experienced." In his study of the forest dwelling Mbuti of Zaire, Turnbull (1982) also found a high level of cooperation and mutual understanding between the sexes, with considerable authority and power vested in women. Despite his skills with bow and arrow, the Mbuti male does not see himself as superior to his wife. He "sees himself as the hunter, but then he could not hunt without a wife, and although hunting is more exciting than being a beater or a gatherer, he knows that

the bulk of his diet comes from the foods prepared by the women" (1982:153).

Marjorie Shostak's (1981) biography of Nisa shows the !Kung to be another foraging society in which nearly egalitarian relationships between the sexes prevail. Shostak states that the !Kung do not show any preference for male children over female children. In matters relating to child rearing, both parents guide their offspring, and a mother's word carries about the same weight as the father's. Mothers play a major role in deciding whom their children will marry, and after marriage !Kung couples live near the wife's family as often as the husband's. Women dispose of whatever food they find and bring back to camp as they see fit.

> All in all !Kung women have a striking degree of autonomy over their own and their children's lives. Brought up to respect their own importance in community life, !Kung women become multifaceted adults and are likely to be competent and assertive as well as nurturant and cooperative. [1981:246]

However, one should not lose sight of the fact that many hunter-gatherers do not have equal gender roles. This seems to have been especially true of the Aborigines of Australia (Burbank 1989; Goodale 1971). In Northern Queensland, for example, polygyny was common, some men acquiring as many as four wives. Men discriminated against women in the distribution of food. A man "often keeps the animal food for himself, while the woman has to depend principally upon vegetables for herself and her child." The sexual double standard prevailed: Men beat or killed their wives for adultery, but wives did not have similar recourse. Furthermore, the division of labor between the sexes was anything but equal, with women doing most of the drudge work (D. Harris 1987).

Gender in Matrilineal Societies

While matrilineal, matrilocal societies should not be confused with matriarchies, women in matrilineal societies often dominated domestic life and exercised important prerogatives in political affairs. From their palisaded villages in upstate New York, the matrilocal and matrilineal Iroquois dispatched armies of up to 500 men to raid targets as far away as Quebec and Illinois. Upon returning to his native land, the Iroquois warrior joined his wife and children at their hearth in a village longhouse. The affairs of this communal dwelling were directed by a senior woman who was a close maternal relative of the man's wife. It was this matron who organized the work that the women of the longhouse performed at home and in the fields. She took charge of storing harvested crops and drawing on them as needed. When husbands were not off on some sort of expedition — absences of a year were common — they slept and ate in the female-headed longhouses but had virtually no control over how their wives lived and worked. If a husband was bossy or uncooperative, the matron might at any time order him to pick up his blanket and get out, leaving his children behind to be taken care of by his wife and the other women of the longhouse.

Turning to public life, the formal apex of political power among the Iroquois was the Council of Elders, consisting of elected male chiefs from different villages. The longhouse matrons nominated the members of this council and could prevent the seating of the men they opposed. But they did not serve on the council itself. Instead, they influenced the council's decisions by exercising control over the domestic economy. If a proposed action was not to their liking, the longhouse matrons could withhold the stored foods, wampum belts, feather work, moccasins, skins, and furs under their control. Warriors could not embark on foreign adventures unless the women filled their bearskin pouches with the mixture of dried corn and honey men ate while on the trail. Religious festivals could not take place, either, unless the women agreed to release the necessary stores. Even the Council of Elders did not convene if the women decided to withhold food for the occasion (Brown 1975; Gramby 1977).

Women in West Africa

Favorable female gender relationships among chiefdoms and states occurred in the forested areas of West Africa. Among the Yoruba, Ibo, Igbo, and Dahomey, women had their own fields and grew their own crops. They dominated the local markets and could acquire considerable wealth from trade. To get married, West African men had to pay bride-price — iron hoes, goats, cloth, and, in more recent times, cash — a transaction that in itself indicated that the groom and his family and the bride and her family agreed that the bride was a very valuable person and that her parents and relatives would not "give her away" without being compensated for her economic and reproductive capabilities (Bossen 1988; Schlegel and Eloul 1988). West Africans believed that to have many daughters was to be rich.

Although men practiced polygyny, they could do so only if they consulted their senior wife and obtained her permission. Women, for their part, had considerable freedom of movement to travel to market towns, where they often had extramarital affairs. Furthermore, in many West African chiefdoms and states, women themselves could pay bride-price and "marry" other women. Among the Dahomey (see page 141), a female husband built a house for her "wife" and arranged for a male consort to get her pregnant. By paying bride-price for several such "wives," an ambitious woman could establish control over a busy compound and become rich and powerful.

West African women also achieved high status outside the domestic sphere. They belonged to female clubs and secret societies, participated in village councils, and mobilized en masse to seek redress against mistreatment by men.

Among the Igbo of Nigeria, women met in council to discuss matters that affected their interests as traders, farmers, or wives. A man who violated the woman's market rules, let his goats eat a woman's crops, or persistently mistreated his wife ran the risk of mass retaliation. The miscreant would be awakened in the middle of the night by a crowd of women banging on his hut. They danced lewd dances, sang songs mocking his manhood, and used his backyard as a latrine until he promised to mend his ways. They called it "sitting-on-a-man."

The supreme rulers of these West African chiefdoms and states were almost always males. But their mothers and sisters and other female relatives occupied offices that gave women considerable power over both men and women. In some Yoruba kingdoms, the king's female relatives directed the principal religious cults and managed the royal compounds. Anyone wanting to arrange rituals, hold festivals, or call up communal labor brigades had to deal with these powerful women first before gaining access to the king. Among the Yoruba, women occupied an office known as "mother of all women," a kind of queen over females, who coordinated the voice of women in government, held court, settled quarrels, and decided what position women should take on the opening and maintenance of markets, levying

of taxes and tolls, declarations of war, and other important public issues. And in at least two Yoruba kingdoms, Ijesa and Ondo, the office of queen-over-women may have been as powerful as the office of king-over-men. Every grade of male chief under the king-of-men had a corresponding grade of female chief under the queen-of-women. The king-over-men and the queen-over-women met separately with their respective councils of chiefs to discuss matters of state. They then conferred with each other. No action was taken unless both councils were in agreement.

Women in India

In contrast to couples in West Africa, those in Northern India express a strong preference for sons over daughters. As Barbara Miller (1981, 1987a, 1987b) has shown, women are an "endangered sex" as a result of the high rate of female infant and child death caused by parental neglect. A north Indian man who had many daughters regarded them as an economic calamity rather than an economic bonanza. Instead of receiving bride-price, the north Indian father paid each daughter's husband a dowry (see page 145) consisting of jewelry, cloth, or cash. In recent years, disgruntled or merely avaricious husbands have taken to demanding supplementary dowries. This has led to a spate of "bride-burnings" in which wives who fail to supply additional compensation are doused with kerosene and set on fire by husbands who pretend that the women killed themselves in cooking accidents (Sharma 1983).

Further on the subject of burnings, north Indian culture has always been extremely unfriendly to widows. In the past, a widow was given the opportunity of joining her dead husband on his funeral pyre. Facing a life of seclusion with no hope of remarrying, subject to food taboos that brought them close to starvation, and urged on by the family priest and their husbands' relatives, many women chose fiery death rather than widowhood. The contrast with how widows were treated in West Africa is striking. West African widows often married their deceased husband's brother (the *levirate*; see page 150) and their prospects were seldom as ominous as in Northern India.

Causes of Variations in Gender Hierarchies

The presence and intensity of warfare are a major factor influencing the status of women in bands and villages. Since males in every human population on average have a physical advantage over females (Gray and Wolfe 1980:442; Percival and Quinkert 1987:136) with respect to the force they can exert with a club; the distance they can throw a spear, shoot an arrow, or hurl a stone; and the speed with which they can run short distances (see Table 13.1), males constitute the main fighting force

Table 13.1
WORLD RECORDS

EVENT	MEN (MIN:SEC)	WOMEN (MIN:SEC)
100-meter dash	0:09.92	0:10.49
1 mile	3:46.32	4:15.71
400-meter hurdle	0:47.02	0:52.94[a]
	(FT) (IN)	(FT) (IN)
High jump	8 0	6 10¼

[a] Women's hurdles are set lower than men's.

Source: The World Almanac & Book of Facts 1990, p. 917.

in every known society (see Box 13.4). Males therefore are trained to be fierce and aggressive and to kill with a weapon far more often than women (Figure 13.5). The training, combat experience, and the monopoly that men possess over the weapons of war empower them to dominate women. Thus the gender-equal !Kung and Mbuti seldom if ever engage in warfare, whereas the Australian Aborigines and other hunter-gatherers with marked gender hierarchies do engage in frequent warfare.

Brian Hayden (Hayden et al. 1986) has tested the theory that wherever conditions favored the development of warfare among hunter-gatherers, the political and domestic subordination of women increased. Using a sample of 33 hunter-gatherer societies he found that the correlation between low status for females and deaths due to armed combat was "unexpectedly high."

> The reasons for overwhelming male dominance in societies where warfare is pronounced seem relatively straightforward. The lives of group members depend to a greater degree on males and male assessment of social and political conditions. Male tasks during times of warfare are simply more critical to the survival of everyone than is female work. Moreover, male aggressiveness and the use of force engendered by warfare and fighting renders female opposition to male decisions not only futile but dangerous. [Ibid.:458]

A similar relationship holds between the intensity of warfare and male dominance among village peoples and simple patrilineal chiefdoms. Thus the Yanomami, with their high level of warfare, are well-known for strong male biases and their practice of female infanticide. Eastern Highland New Guinea, noted for its male-centered communal cults

---

Box 13.4

THE BODY AND CULTURE

Like everything else about human beings, the anatomical and physiological differences between men and women that are important for assigning combatant roles to males in preindustrial warfare are a product of the interaction of genetic and cultural influences. Feminist author Anne Oakley (1985:28) has shown that the shape and strength of the human body can be greatly altered by the type of work each sex performs and the quality and quantity of food they consume. In some societies such as Bali where men and women perform similar kinds of work, they are even difficult to tell apart. Indeed, theoretically, the strength and swiftness differences between the sexes could not only be effaced but completely reversed by sufficiently favoring the physical training and diet of women and by drastically curtailing male activities and food consumption (see Figure 13.4). However, the point being made here is that any band or village society that chose to make its women physically better suited for hand-to-hand combat than its men would not survive combat with groups that invested primarily in conditioning its males for combat;

Figure 13.4   Female bodybuilding champion. Gladys Portugese celebrates her victory at Madison Square Garden.

genetic differences still guarantee that a maximum of investment in males will produce a brawnier and swifter combat team than a maximum investment in females.

---

and physical mistreatment of women, is also famous for its incessant warfare. As Daryl Fiel (1987:69) puts it, war was "general, pervasive, and perpetual." The treatment of women by men was proportionately brutal:

> Women were severely punished for adultery by having burning sticks thrust into their vaginas, or they were killed by their husbands; they were whipped with cane if they spoke out of turn or presumed to offer their opinions at public gatherings; and were physically abused in marital arguments. Men could never be seen to be weak or soft in dealings with women. Men do not require specific incidents or rea-

(a)

(b)

(c)

(d)

(e)

Figure 13.5   Aggressive male games.
There is evidence of a close correlation between
warfare and aggressive male sports: (a) Afghan
game requires daring feats of horsemanship; (b) the
sporting life in England—rugby; (c) boxing, the
United States; (d) mock combat in Indonesia; (e) the
gentle art of football, the United States.

sons to abuse or mistreat women; it is part
of the normal course of events; indeed, in
ritual and myth, it is portrayed as the essential order of things. [Ibid.:203]

Finally, as we have seen (page 191), there is
a strong correlation between unbalanced sex
ratios and the practice of warfare (Divale and
Harris 1976) among prestate societies in general. We must remember, however, that the
correlation between intense warfare and female subordination does not hold in the case of
matrilocal and matrilineal societies where warfare is practiced against distant foes, and fore-
stalls rather than encourages male control over
production and domestic life (see page 164).

The correlation between frequency and
intensity of warfare and male dominance also
does not hold for advanced chiefdoms and
states. While stratified societies have bigger
armies and wage war on a much grander scale
than classless societies, the effect of warfare on
women is less direct and generally less severe
than in bands and villages (but not as favorable
as in matrilineal societies). What makes the difference is that in state societies soldiering is a
specialty reserved for professionals. Most
males no longer train from infancy to be killers
of men, even killers of animals (since there are
few large animals left to hunt, except in royal

preserves). Instead they find themselves reduced to being unarmed peasants who are no
less terrified of professional warriors than are
their wives and children. Warfare does create a
demand for suitably macho men to be trained
as warriors, but in state societies most women
do not have to deal with husbands whose capacity for violence has been honed in battle.
Nor does women's survival depend on training
their sons to be cruel and aggressive. Female
status in advanced chiefdoms and states therefore depends less on the intensity, frequency,
and scale of warfare than on whether the anatomical differences between men and women
endow males or females with a decisive advantage in carrying out some crucial phase of
production.

Thus the contrasting gender hierarchies of
West Africa and Northern India are correlated
with two very different forms of agriculture. In
West Africa, the main agricultural implement
was not an ox-drawn plow, as in the plains of
North India, but a short-handled hoe (Goody
1976). The West Africans did not use plows
because in their humid, shady habitat the tsetse
fly made it difficult to rear plow animals. Besides, West African soils do not dry out and
become hard-packed as in the arid plains of
North India, so that women using nothing but
hoes were as capable as men in preparing fields
and had no need for men to grow, harvest, or
market their crops. In North India, on the
other hand, men maintained a monopoly over
the use of ox-drawn plows. These implements
were indispensable for breaking the long dry
season's hard-packed soils. Men achieved this
monopoly for essentially the same reasons that
they achieved a monopoly over the weapons of
hunting and warfare: Their greater bodily
strength enabled them to be 15 to 20 percent
more efficient than women. This advantage
often means the difference between a family's

survival and starvation, especially during prolonged dry spells when every fraction of an inch to which a plowshare penetrates beneath the surface and every minute less it takes a pair of oxen to complete a furrow are crucial for retaining moisture. As Morgan Maclachlan (1983) found in a study of the sexual division of labor in India, the question is not whether peasant women could be trained to manage a plow and a pair of oxen but whether in most families, training men to do it leads to larger and more secure harvests.

Further support for this theory can be found in the more female-favorable gender roles that characterize Southern India and much of Southeast Asia and Indonesia. In these regions, noted for their strong matrifocal and complementary gender relationships, rice rather than wheat is the principal crop, and the principal function of traction animals in agriculture is *puddling* (softening and mixing the mud of rice paddies in preparation for planting) rather than plowing. This operation can be performed as efficiently by women and children as by men. Moreover, the operation of transplanting, which is as crucial as that of plowing or puddling, can also be carried out by women at least as efficiently as by men.

Is a factor as simple as male control over plowing sufficient to explain female infanticide, dowry, and widows throwing themselves onto their husbands' funeral pyres? Not if one thinks only of the direct effects of animal-drawn implements on agriculture itself. But in evolutionary perspective this male specialty was linked to a chain of additional specializations that cumulatively do point to a plausible explanation of many features of the depressed status of women in Northern India as well as in other agrarian state societies with similar forms of agriculture in Europe, Southwest Asia, and

Northern China. Wherever men gained control over the plow, they became the master of large traction animals. Wherever they yoked these animals to the plow, they also yoked them to all sorts of carts and vehicles. Therefore with the invention of the wheel and its diffusion across Eurasia, men yoked animals to the principal means of land transport. This gave them control over the transportation of crops to market, and from there it was a short step to dominating local and long-distance trade and commerce. With the invention of money, men became the first merchants. As trade and commerce increased in importance, records had to be kept, and it was to men active in trade and commerce that the task fell of keeping these records. Therefore, with the invention of writing and arithmetic, men came to the fore as the first scribes and accountants. By extension, men became the literate sex; they did reading, writing, and arithmetic. Therefore men, not women, were the first historically known philosophers, theologians, and mathematicians in the early agrarian states of Europe, Southwest Asia, India, and China.

All of these indirect effects of male control over traction animals acted in concert with the continuing gender role effects of warfare. By dominating the armed forces, men gained control over the highest administrative branches of government, including state religions. And the continuing need to recruit male warriors made the social construction of aggressive manhood a focus of national policy in every known state and empire. It is therefore no wonder that at the dawn of industrial times men dominated politics, religion, art, science, law, industry and commerce, as well as the armed forces, wherever animal-drawn plows had been the basic means of agricultural production.

Gender and Industrialism

During the smokestack phase of industrialism, women had little opportunity to overthrow the heritage of the classic Eurasian gender hierarchy. After an initial period of intense exploitation in factory employment, married women were excluded from industrial work and were confined to domestic tasks in order to assure the reproduction of the working class. Factory-employed male breadwinners collaborated in this effort in order to preserve their privileges while fending off the threat that women posed to the male wage rate. A decisive break came after World War II with the shift in the mode of production to information and service production. This led to a call-up of literate women into low-paid, nonunionized information and service jobs, the feminization of the labor force, a fall in fertility rates to historic lows, and the destruction of the male-breadwinner family (Harris 1981).

Today's hyperindustrial mode of production is almost totally indifferent to the anatomical and physiological differences between men and women (except to the extent that women still may wish to have children). It is no accident that women's rights are rising as the strategic value of masculine brawn declines. Who needs extra muscle power when the decisive processes of production take place in automated factories or while people sit at desks in computerized offices? Men continue to fight for the retention of their old privileges, but they have been routed from one bastion after another as women fill the need for service and information workers by offering competent performance at lower wage rates than males. Even more than the market women of West Africa, women in today's advanced industrial societies have moved toward gender parity based on an ability to earn a living without being dependent on husbands or other males (Figure 13.6). We will return to the subject of modern-day gender roles in Chapter 18.

Figure 13.6   Breaking the gender barrier.
(a) Female M.D.; (b) cowgirl; (c) construction engineer.

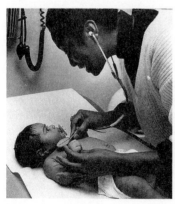

(a)   *(b)*   *(c)*

Human Sexuality

Because of the pervasive effects of culturally constructed gender roles, knowledge about human sexuality that is gained from the study of people living in one culture can never be taken as representative of human sexual behavior in general (Frayser 1985; Gregersen 1982). All aspects of sexual relationships, from infantile experiences through courtship and marriage, exhibit an immense amount of cultural variation. For example, among the Mangaians of Polynesia, according to Donald Marshall (1971), boys and girls never hold hands and husbands and wives never embrace in public. Brothers and sisters must never be seen together. Mothers and daughters and fathers and sons do not discuss sexual matters with one another. And yet both sexes engage in intercourse well before puberty. After puberty, both sexes enjoy an intense premarital sex life. Girls receive varied nightly suitors in the parents' house, and boys compete with their rivals to see how many orgasms they can achieve. Mangaian girls are not interested in romantic protestations, extensive petting, or foreplay. Sex is not a reward for masculine affection; rather, affection is the reward for sexual fulfillment:

> Sexual intimacy is not achieved by first demonstrating personal affection; the reverse is true. The Mangaian . . . girl takes an immediate demonstration of sexual virility and masculinity as the first test of her partner's desire for her and as the reflection of her own desirability. . . . Personal affection may or may not result from acts of sexual intimacy, but the latter are requisite to the former — exactly the reverse of the ideals of western society. [Marshall 1971:118]

According to a consensus reached by Marshall's informants, males sought to reach orgasm at least once every night, and women expected each episode to last at least 15 minutes. They agreed on the data presented in Table 13.2 as indicative of typical male sexual activity.

A very different attitude toward sexual activity appears to be characteristic of Hindu India. There is a widespread belief among Hindu men (and shared by men in many other societies — see page 261) that semen is a source of strength and that it should not be squandered.

> Everyone knew that semen was not easily found; it takes forty days and forty drops of blood to make one drop of semen. . . . Everyone was agreed . . . that the semen is ultimately stored in a reservoir in the head, whose capacity is twenty tolas (6.8 ounces). . . . Celibacy was the first requirement of true fitness, because every sexual orgasm meant the loss of a quantity of semen, laboriously formed. [Carstairs 1967; quoted in Nag 1972:235]

Contrary to popular stereotypes concerning Hindu eroticism (Figure 13.7), there is evi-

Table 13.2
Mangaian Male Sexuality

Approximate Age	Average Number of Orgasms per Night	Average Number of Nights per Week
18	3	7
28	2	5–6
38	1	3–4
48	1	2–3

Source: Marshall 1971:123.

Figure 13.7 Hindu erotic art.
Erotic themes are common in the sacred art of India. Shown, Lord Shiva and Parvati.

Table 13.3

AMERICAN AND HINDU FEMALE
COITAL FREQUENCY

AGE GROUP	WHITE U.S. AVERAGE WEEKLY	HINDU AVERAGE WEEKLY
10–14	—	0.4
15–19	3.7	1.5
20–24	3.0	1.9
25–29	2.6	1.8
30–34	2.3	1.1
35–39	2.0	0.7
40–44	1.7	0.2
Over 44	1.3	0.3

Source: Adapted from Nag 1972:235.

dence that coital frequency among Hindus is considerably less than among U.S. whites in comparable age groups. Moni Nag gives a summary (Table 13.3) of average weekly coital frequency for Hindu and white U.S. women. It is also clear, again contrary to popular impressions, that India's high level of fertility and population growth is not the result of sexual overindulgence caused by "not having anything else to do for entertainment at night."

Male Homosexuality

Attitudes toward homosexuality range from horror to chauvinistic enthusiasm. Knowledge of male homosexuality is more extensive than knowledge of female homosexuality. Several cultures studied by anthropologists incorporate male homosexuality into their systems for developing masculine male personalities. For example, certain men donned female attire and dedicated themselves to providing sexual

favors to great warriors. Known as *berdache*, these homosexuals were regarded as a separate gender and were honored in turn (Figure 13.8). For a warrior to be served by a berdache was proof of manliness (Callender and Kochems 1983; Williams 1986).

Similarly, among the Azande of the Sudan, also renowned for their prowess in warfare, the unmarried warrior-age grade, which lived apart from women for several years, had homosexual

Figure 13.8   Berdache.
Finds-Them-And-Kills-Them, last of the Crow male homosexual transvestites.

relations with the boys of the age grade of warrior apprentices. After their experiences with "boy-wives," the warriors graduated to the next age status, got married, and had many children (Evans-Pritchard 1970).

Male homosexuality was highly ritualized in many New Guinea and Melanesian societies. It was ideologically justified in a manner that has no equivalent in Western notions of sexuality. It was not viewed as a matter of individual preference but as a social obligation. Men were not classifiable as homosexual, heterosexual, or bisexual. All men were obliged to be bisexual as a matter of sacred duty and practical necessity. For example, among the Etoro, who live on the slopes of the central Papua New Guinea highlands, the emics of homosexuality revolve around the belief that semen is the source not only of babies but of manhood as well. Like the men of Hindu India, the Etoro believe that each man has only a limited supply of semen. When the supply is exhausted, a man dies. While coitus with one's wife is necessary to prevent the population from becoming too small, husbands stay away from wives most of the time. Indeed, sex is taboo between husband and wife for over 200 days per year. The Etoro males regard wives who want to break this taboo as witches. To complicate matters, the supply of semen is not something that a man is born with. Semen can be acquired only from another male. Etoro boys get their supply by having oral intercourse with older men. But it is forbidden for young boys to have intercourse with each other and, like the oversexed wife, the oversexed adolescent boy is regarded as a witch and condemned for robbing his agemates of their semen supply. Such wayward youths can be identified by the fact that they grow faster than ordinary boys (Kelly 1976).

Among the Sambia of the southeastern highlands of New Guinea, boys are allowed to play with girls only until age 4 or 5. Subsequently they are strictly regulated and all heterosexual play is forcefully punished. It is normal for young boys to hold hands with each other. Sambia males and females never kiss, hold hands, or hug each other in public. Late in childhood, boys are initiated into the men's secret society and are taught how to act as warriors. Obedience to the male elders is rigidly enforced. Younger men, as among the Etoro, obtain the gift of semen from their seniors. Males must continue to avoid any heterosexual contact until they are married (Herdt 1987).

Homosexuality in New Guinea and Melanesia is closely associated with a heightened level of male-female sexual antagonism, fear of menstrual blood, and exclusive male rituals and dwellings. From an etic perspective, there seems to be a strong association between socially obligatory homosexuality and intense warfare. Warfare justified and rationalized an ethos of masculine prowess that placed men above women as desirable sexual partners. New Guinea societies that have ritualized male homosexuality to the greatest extent appear to be refugees from more densely populated regions (Herdt 1984a:169). As in other warlike village societies (see page 191), their juvenile sex ratios show a marked imbalance favoring males over females, attaining ratios as high as 140:100 (Herdt 1984b:57).

It is difficult to avoid the conclusion, therefore, that ritual homosexuality in New Guinea and Melanesia is part of a population-regulating negative feedback (see page 202) system. As Dennis Werner (1979) has shown, societies that are strongly antinatalist tend to accept or encourage homosexual and other nonreproductive forms of sex. In addition, Melvin Ember (1982) has demonstrated that warfare in New Guinea is correlated with competition for scarce and/or depleted resources.

However, much controversy surrounds these relationships.

Whatever the explanation for obligatory male homosexuality may be, its existence should serve as a warning against equating one's own culturally determined expressions of sexuality with human nature.

Female Homosexuality

Less is known about female homosexuality then about male homosexuality because of the predominance of male-biased ethnographics. Unlike males, females seldom seem to be subjected to initiation rituals that entail homosexual relationships. It is reported, however, that among the Dahomey, adolescent girls prepared for marriage by attending all-female initiation schools where they learned how to "thicken their genitalia" and engaged in sexual intercourse (Blackwood 1986).

Since women seldom bear the brunt of military combat, they have little opportunity to use same-sex erotic apprenticeships to form solidary teams of warriors. Similarly, enforced absence from the classical Greek academies precluded women's participation in homosexual philosophical apprenticeships, and since men regarded women as their sexual "object," the incidence of overt lesbian behavior between women of rank and slave girls or other social inferiors could never be very high. More commonly, women do adopt socially sanctioned "not-man-not-woman" gender roles, dressing like men, performing manly duties such as hunting, trapping, and going to war and using their in-between gender status to establish their credibility as shamans. Thirty-three American Indian societies are reported to have accepted gender transformations in women (Albers 1989:135). Among several western Na-

tive American tribes, female not-men-not-women entered into enduring lesbian relationships with women, whom they formally "married" (Blackwood 1984).

Several reported cases of institutionalized lesbianism are related to the migration of males in search of work. On the Caribbean island of Carriacou, where migrant husbands stay away from home for most of the year, older married women bring younger single women into their households and share the absent husband's remittances in exchange for sexual favors and emotional support. A similar pattern exists in South Africa, where it is known as the "mummy-baby game" (Gay 1986).

One of the most interesting forms of institutionalized lesbianism occurred in mid-nineteenth-century – early twentieth-century China in several of the silk-growing districts of the Pearl River Delta region in southern Kwangtung. Single women provided virtually all of the labor for the silkworm factories. Although poorly paid, they were better off than their prospective husbands. Rather than accept the subordinate status that marriage imposed on Chinese women, the silk workers formed antimarriage sisterhoods that provided economic and emotional support. While not all of the 100,000 sisters formed lesbian relationships, enduring lesbian marriages involving two and sometimes three women were common (Sankar 1986).

It seems clear that even when allowance is made for blind spots in the ethnographic reports of male observers, there are fewer forms of institutionalized female than of male homosexuality. Does this mean that females engage in homosexual behavior less often than males? Probably not. More likely most female homosexuality has simply been driven underground or has been expressed in noninstitutionalized contexts that escape observation. Although seldom reported, adolescence is probably an occasion for a considerable amount of female homosexual experimentation the world over. Only recently, for example, has it come to light that among the Kalahari !Kung, young girls engage in sexual play with other girls before they do so with boys (Shostak 1981:114).

Polygynous marriage is another context in which lesbian relationships probably flourish. The practice seems to have been common in West Africa among the Nupe, Haussa, and Dahomey, and among the Azande and Nyakusa in East Africa. In Middle Eastern harems, where co-wives seldom saw their husbands, many women entered into lesbian relationships despite the dire punishment such male-defying behavior could bring.

Summary

Human sexual identity is mediated by culturally constructed gender roles. The gender roles of Western society in which men are "masculine" and women are "feminine" are not representative of the variations that occur around the world.

In many cultures males believe they are spiritually superior to females and that women are a source of pollution. These beliefs are present in the male-centered religions of Western civilization, which hold that women were created out of a piece of man. Women often do not accept these male versions of gender roles, as illustrated by the examples of the Yurok and Kaliai. Moreover, as demonstrated in the restudy of the Trobriand Islanders, male ethnographers have often underestimated the etic power of women. Nonetheless, men have more frequently dominated women while the mirror image of patriarchy — matriarchy — is unknown. As illustrated by the consequences of

gender roles in Bangladesh and the Foré, anti-female prejudices are often associated with high rates of illness and death among women.

Gender roles among hunter-gatherers are often egalitarian, as among the !Kung, Neskapi, and Mbuti, but in other hunter-gatherers — for example, the Queensland Aborigines — males are dominant. Female-favorable gender roles are also found in many matrilineal societies such as the Iroquois, but perhaps the most powerful women in preindustrial societies lived in West Africa among the Yoruba, Ibo, Igbo, and Dahomey. In contrast, the male-dominant sex roles of Northern India, like those of Bangladesh, endanger the survival and well-being of females, especially when they are very young or very old.

Variations in gender hierarchies among hunter-gatherers and village societies are closely correlated with the frequency and intensity of warfare carried out against nearby groups. By contrast, long-distance warfare between village groups tends to promote matrilocality and a higher status for women. At the advanced chiefdom and state levels only specialist warriors receive training for armed combat; consequently, variations in gender hierarchies depend less on the frequency and intensity of warfare than on the significance of the anatomical differences of men and women for carrying out certain crucial agricultural tasks. Thus, underlying the contrast between West African gender relations and those of Northern India are two different modes of agricultural production: hoe agriculture and plow agriculture, respectively. Women can use hoes as effectively as men, which leads to their controlling their own food supply, being involved in trade and markets, having an equal say in the management of household affairs, and wielding considerable political power. In Northern India men outperform women in the critical task of preparing hard-packed soils for planting by means of ox-drawn plows, leading to the preference for sons, female infanticide, dowry, and the mistreatment of widows in contrast to the preferences for daughters, bride-price, and the levirate in West Africa.

Further consequences of the Eurasian animal-drawn plow complex include male control over trade, accounting, mathematics, literacy, and church and state bureaucracies, as well as continued control over the army. Southern India, Southeast Asia, and Indonesia, with their contrastive use of animals for puddling rather than plowing rice paddies and their more female-favorable gender roles, lend additional support to this theory.

In the smokestack phase of the industrial revolution, married women were excluded from factory work and confined to the home as dependents in male-breadwinner families. But after World War II, male muscular aptitudes were no longer significant in the emerging information and service economy, and women entered the labor force in unprecedented numbers, leading to increased independence from men and radical changes in gender roles, gender hierarchy, and family life.

Cross-cultural variations in gender roles prevent any single culture from serving as the model for what is natural in the realm of sex. Mangaian heterosexual standards contrast with those of Hindu India, which contrast with those of contemporary industrial societies. Homosexuality also defies neat stereotyping, as can be seen in the examples of the Crow and Azande. Ritual male homosexuality, as among the Etoro, Sambia, and other New Guinea and Melanesian societies, is an elaborate, compulsory form of sexuality that has no equivalent in Western societies. It was probably selected for by the need to rear male warriors under conditions of environmental stress and competition.

Female homosexuality is less frequently reported, possibly as a result of male-bias among ethnographers and the suppression of female liberties by dominant males.

Chapter 14

PERSONALITY AND CULTURE

This chapter explores the relationship between personality and culture. It defines personality, discusses Freudian theories of personality formation in the light of cross-cultural studies, and examines the concept of national character and the relationship between culture and mental illness.

Culture and Personality

Culture refers to the patterned ways in which the members of a population think, feel, and behave. *Personality* also refers to patterned ways of thinking, feeling, and behaving, but the focus is on the individual. Personality, as defined by Victor Barnouw (1985:8), "is a more or less enduring organization of forces within the individual associated with a complex of fairly consistent attitudes, values, and modes of perception which account, in part, for the individual's consistency of behavior." More simply, "personality is the tendency to behave in certain ways regardless of the specific setting" (Whiting and Whiting 1978:57).

The concepts employed in describing the thinking, feeling, and behavior of personality types are different from those employed in describing infrastructure, structure, and superstructure. In describing personalities, psychologists use concepts such as aggressive, passive, anxious, obsessive, hysterical, manic, depressed, introverted, extroverted, paranoid, authoritarian, schizoid, masculine, feminine, infantile, repressed, dependent, and so forth. Here is a part of a more extensive list of terms appropriate for the study of personality that appeared in a study of culture and personality in a Mexican village (Fromm and Maccoby 1970:79):

practical	anxious
economical	orderly
steadfast, tenacious	methodical
composed under stress	loyal
careful	unimaginative
reserved	stingy
patient	stubborn
cautious	indolent
imperturbable	inert
suspicious	pedantic
cold	obsessional
lethargic	possessive

If these concepts are employed to describe an entire population, the result will not add up to a description of modes of production and re-production, domestic and political economy, systems of war and peace, or magico-religious rites and institutions. Rather, they will add up to a description of that population's personality type.

Freud's Influence

According to Sigmund Freud, the founder of psychoanalysis, an individual's adult personality is largely shaped by his or her experiences in resolving certain universally recurrent conflicts experienced during infancy and childhood. These conflicts, known as the *Oedipus complex* (Oedipus, according to ancient Greek legend, unwittingly committed incest with his mother), are allegedly caused by biologically determined sexual strivings and jealousies within the nuclear family.

Freud held that the early sexual feelings of a young boy are directed first toward his mother. But the boy soon discovers that mother is the sexual object of his father and that he is in competition with his father for sexual mastery of the same woman. The father, while providing protection, also provides stern discipline (Figure 14.1). He suppresses his son's attempt to express sexual love for the mother. The son is frustrated and fantasizes that he is strong enough to kill his father. This arouses fear and guilt in the young boy: fear, because the father in fact or in fancy threatens to cut off the son's penis; and guilt, because the father is not only hated but also loved. To resolve this conflict successfully, the young boy must redirect his sexuality toward females other than his mother and learn how to overcome his fear and express his hostility in constructive ways.

For the young girl, Freud envisioned a par-

Figure 14.1   Freud's milieu.
A turn-of-the-century middle-class father with his two sons. He is stern but protective.

allel but fundamentally different trauma. A girl's sexuality is also initially directed toward her mother, but she soon makes a fateful discovery: She lacks a penis. She blames her mother for this and redirects her sexual desires away from her mother and toward her father:

Why this takes place depends upon the girl's reaction of disappointment when she discovers that a boy possesses a protruding sex organ, the penis, while she has only a cavity. Several important consequences follow from this traumatic discovery. In the first place she holds her mother responsible for her castrated condition. . . . In the second place, she transfers her love to her father because he has the valued organ which she aspires to share with him. However, her love for the father and for other men as well is mixed with a feeling of envy because they possess something she lacks. Penis envy is the female counterpart of castration anxiety in the boy. [Hall and Lindzey 1967:18]

Girls are supposed to suffer the lifelong trauma of penis envy as a result of their discovery that they are anatomically "incomplete." In this fashion, Freud sought to ground the primacy of males in the unalterable facts of anatomy—hence the Freudian aphorism: "Anatomy is destiny." Freud thought that not having a penis "debases" women and dooms them to a passive and subordinate role, the role of the "second sex." Freud believed the best hope a woman has of overcoming her penis envy is to accept a passive, secondary role in life, develop her charm and sexual attractiveness, marry, and have male babies.

> Her happiness is great if later on this wish for a baby finds fulfillment in reality, and quite especially so if the baby is a little boy who brings the longed-for penis with him. [Freud, in Millet 1970:185]

According to Freud, everyone's personality depends on the severity of the Oedipal conflict they have experienced and the extent to which they have resolved it or not resolved it.

IS THE OEDIPUS COMPLEX UNIVERSAL?

Starting with Bronislaw Malinowski's (1927) research on the avunculocal Trobriand family (see Chapter 9), anthropologists have criticized the concept of the Oedipus complex on the grounds that it imposes on the rest of the world a view of personality development appropriate to nineteenth-century middle-class Vienna, where Freud practiced and developed his theories. According to Malinowski, Trobriand males did not develop the same kind of complex because it was their mother's brother and not their father who exercised authority over them. Thus, Trobriand males grew up without the hate-love feelings toward their fathers that Freud postulated as being universal. Melford Spiro (1982) defends the Freudian position by separating the hate-love engendered by sexual jealousy from the hate-love engendered by authority. The Trobriand male lives with his father and mother until he is an adolescent. While his father is an easygoing and nonauthoritarian figure, there is still plenty of opportunity for father and son to develop feelings of sexual rivalry over the mother and wife. Spiro concludes, therefore, that Malinowski did not prove that the Trobrianders were without any basis for developing the Oedipus complex. It remains true, however, that the intensity and importance of the Oedipus complex must vary in relation to the amount and quality of the control that parents exercise over their children, and such control varies with the structure of the domestic group.

Most anthropologists interested in culture and personality studies reject the idea that the Oedipus complex is a universal (Parsons 1967). Freud's continuing influence, however, can be seen in the idea that personality is formed largely as a result of infant and childhood experiences. What anthropologists have added is the qualification that these experiences vary widely in conformity with the specific forms of family life and gender roles characteristic of particular cultures.

Childhood Training and Personality

Parents in a particular culture tend to follow similar *childhood training practices* involving the feeding, cleaning, and handling of infants and children. These childhood training prac-

(a)

(b)

Figure 14.2   Care of children.
Cultures vary greatly in the amount of body contact between mother and infant. (a) Swazi mother and child.
(b) Arunta mother and child; mother has all-purpose carrying dish on head and digging stick in hand.

tices vary widely from one society to another and are probably responsible for some cross-cultural differences in adult personalities. In many cultures, for example, infants are constrained by swaddling bandages or cradle boards that immobilize their limbs. Elsewhere, freedom of movement is encouraged. Similarly, nursing may occur either on demand at the first cry of hunger or at regular intervals at the convenience of the mother. Nursing at the mother's breast may last for a few months or several years, or may not take place at all. Supplementary foods may be taken in the first few weeks; they may be stuffed into the baby's mouth, prechewed by the mother, played with by the baby, or omitted entirely.

Weaning may take place abruptly, as when the mother's nipples are painted with bitter substances, and it may or may not be associated with the birth of another child. In some cultures infants are kept next to their mother's skin and carried wherever the mother goes (Figure 14.2); elsewhere, they may be left behind in the care of relatives. In some cultures infants are fondled, hugged, kissed, and fussed over by large groups of adoring children and adults; in others they are kept relatively isolated and touched infrequently.

Toilet training may begin as early as 6 weeks or as late as 24 months. The mode of training may involve many different techniques, some based on intense forms of punish-

Figure 14.3 Toilet training, Soviet style.
Soviet children are toilet trained in their nursery schools by their teachers. How might this influence their personalities in comparison with American children who are toilet trained by their parents before they go to nursery school?

Figure 14.4 Javanese girl and brother.
One way to free mother for work in the fields is to turn over the care of infants to a 7-year-old sister.

ment, shame, and ridicule, and others involving suggestion, emulation, and no punishment (Figure 14.3).

Treatment of infant sexuality also varies widely. In many cultures mothers or fathers stroke their babies' genitals to soothe them and stop them from crying; elsewhere, even the baby is prevented from touching its own genitals, and masturbation is severely punished.

Another series of variables relevant to personality formation consists of later childhood and adolescent experiences: numbers of siblings, their relationships and mutual responsibilities (Figure 14.4), patterns of play, opportunities to observe adult intercourse, opportunities to engage in homosexual or heterosexual experimentation, incest restrictions, and type of threat and punishment used against culturally prohibited sexual practices (Weisner and Gilmore 1977).

Figure 14.5 depicts one theory of how these childhood training practices may be related to personality and to other aspects of culture. The basic variables influencing child-rearing patterns are influenced by the nature of the culture's domestic, social, political, and economic institutions. These in turn are influenced by the ecosystem. Child-rearing practices are also constrained by the necessity of satisfying certain biologically determined universal needs, drives, and capacities that all human infants share (e.g., oral, anal, and genital urges). The interaction between the child-

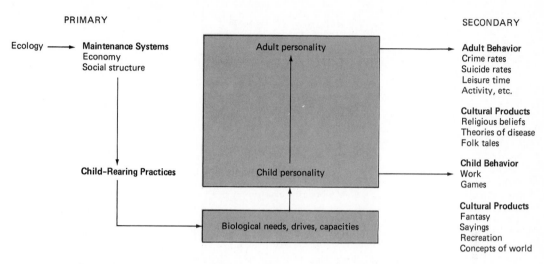

PRIMARY

SECONDARY

Ecology ⟶ **Maintenance Systems**
Economy
Social structure

Adult personality

Adult Behavior
Crime rates
Suicide rates
Leisure time
Activity, etc.

Cultural Products
Religious beliefs
Theories of disease
Folk tales

Child-Rearing Practices

Child personality

Child Behavior
Work
Games

Biological needs, drives, capacities

Cultural Products
Fantasy
Sayings
Recreation
Concepts of world

Figure 14.5   The relationship of basic personality to ecology, child-rearing practices, and secondary and projective institutions.
After LeVine 1973:57.

rearing practices and these biological needs, drives, and capacities molds personality; personality, in turn, expresses itself in *secondary* institutions—that is, roughly what has been called "superstructure" in this book.

Male Initiation and Childhood Training

John Whiting (1969) and his associates have developed an interesting theory relating childhood experiences to the formation of adult personality. Whiting has shown that statistical correlations exist among (1) protein scarcities, (2) nursing of children for 1 year or more, (3) prohibition of sexual relations between husband and wife for 1 year or more after the birth of their child, (4) polygyny, (5) domestic sleeping arrangements in which mother and child sleep together and father sleeps elsewhere, (6)

child training by women, (7) patrilocality, and (8) severe male initiation rites.

> Following our model, the following chain develops: Low protein availability and the risk of Kwashiorkor [a protein-deficiency disease] were correlated with an extended postpartum sex taboo to allow the mother time to nurse the infant through the critical stage before becoming pregnant again. The postpartum sex taboo was significantly correlated with the institution of polygyny, providing alternate sexual outlets for the male. Polygyny, in turn, is associated with mother-child households, child training by women, resultant cross-sex identity, and where patrilocality is also present, with initiation rites to resolve the conflict and properly inculcate male identity. [Harrington and Whiting 1972:491]

"Cross-sex identity" refers to the psychodynamic process by which boys who are reared

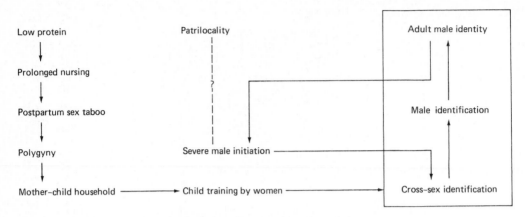

Figure 14.6 Psychodynamic model of relationship between low-protein diet and severe male initiation.

exclusively by their mothers and older women identify themselves with their mothers and other women. Where patrilocality is present, reasons Whiting, functional consistency demands that adult males must make a strong identification with their fathers and other males. Hence there is a conflict between what the male must do and think as an adult and what he is trained to do and think as an infant. Severe male initiation ceremonies involving circumcision or other forms of mutilation, prolonged seclusion, beatings, and trials of courage and stamina are thus required to resolve this conflict by breaking the prepubescent identity. The functional-causal links in Whiting's model are diagramed in Figure 14.6.

Patterns and Themes

Many proposals have been made concerning how to treat the relationship between personality and culture. One popular option acknowledges that culture and personality represent two different ways of looking at the propensity to think, feel, and behave that are characteristic of a given population, and uses psychological terms to characterize both personality and the cultural system. For example, Ruth Benedict, in her famous book *Patterns of Culture* (1934), characterized the institution of the Kwakiutl potlatch (Chapter 7) as a "megalomaniacal" performance—behavior dominated by fantasies of wealth and power. She saw potlatch as part of a Dionysian pattern that was characteristic of all institutions of Kwakiutl culture. By *Dionysian* she meant the desire to achieve emotional excess, as in drunkenness or frenzy. Other cultures, such as that of the Pueblo Indians, she saw as *Apollonian*—given to moderation and the "middle of the road" in all things. Benedict's *patterns* were psychological elements reputedly found throughout a culture, "comparable to the chromosomes found in most of the cells of a body" (Wallace 1970:149). Most anthropologists have rejected such attempts to use one or two psychological terms to describe whole cultures. Even the most simple hunter-gatherer cultures have too many different kinds of personalities to be summed up in such a manner.

Rather than attempt to sum up whole cultures under one or two psychological concepts, some anthropologists point to dominant themes or values that express the essential or main thought and feeling of a particular culture. The "image of limited good" is one such theme (see Chapter 12). Themes and values are readily translatable into personality traits. For example, the image of limited good reputedly produces personalities that are jealous, suspicious, secretive, and fearful. The culture of poverty (see Chapter 12) also has its psychological components—improvidence, lack of future-time orientation, sexual promiscuity. An important theme in Hindu India is the "sacredness of life," and an important theme in the United States is "keeping up with the Joneses." The problem with attempts to portray cultures in terms of a few dominant values and attitudes is that contradictory values and attitudes can usually be identified within the same cultures and even within the same individuals. Thus, although Hindu farmers believe in the sacredness of life (Opler 1968), they also believe in the necessity of having more bullocks than cows (see page 20); and although many people in the United States believe it is alright to flaunt their possessions, there are others who believe that conspicuous consumption is foolish and wasteful.

Basic Personality and National Character

A somewhat different approach to culture and personality postulates that every culture produces a basic or deep personality structure that can be found in virtually every individual member of the culture. When the populations involved are organized into a state, the basic personality is often called *national character*. Little support can be found for this concept.

The notion of basic personality structure has always enjoyed considerable popularity among travelers to foreign lands as well as among scholars (Figure 14.7). One often hears it said that the English are "reserved," the Brazilians "carefree," the French "sexy," the Italians "uninhibited," the Japanese "orderly," the Americans "outgoing," and so forth. Gerardus Mercator, the father of mapmaking, wrote the following descriptions of European basic personalities in the sixteenth century (see if you can guess Mercator's nationality):

Franks: Simple, blockish, furious.

Bavarians: Sumptuous, gluttons, brazen-faced.

Swedes: Light, babblers, boasters.

Saxons: Dissemblers, double-hearted, opinionative.

Spaniards: Disdainful, cautious, greedy.

Belgians: Good horsemen, tender, docile, delicate.

Modern scholarly versions of basic personality structure make use of more sophisticated psychological concepts.

The concept of basic personality type must not be permitted to obscure the fact that there is a great range of personalities in every society and that the more populous, complex, and stratified the society, the greater the variability. In every society many individuals have personalities that deviate widely from the *statistical mode* (most frequent type), and the range of individual personalities produces wide overlaps among different cultures. For example, it would certainly be correct to characterize the basic type of Plains native American male personality as an aggressive, independent, and

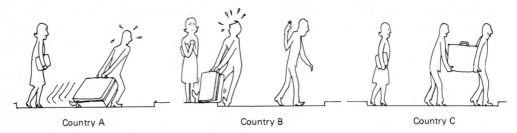

Country A   Country B   Country C

Figure 14.7 National character.

Allen Funt's popular TV show, "Candid Camera," frequently explored national character differences by means of informal cross-cultural experiments. The three scenes represented here show the same young woman in three different countries, standing at a curb with a suitcase filled with 100 pounds of bricks. In each scene, she solicits a male passerby to help her get her suitcase across the street. In Country A, the man tugs and pulls at the suitcase with all his might, finally managing to get it across the street. In Country B, the man tries to move the suitcase, but when he finds it unexpectedly heavy, he gives up and goes on his way. In Country C, on finding the bag too heavy for one person to pick up, the man enlists the aid of another male passerby, and the two of them carry it across with no difficulty. Can you guess which country each scene depicts? In view of recent changes in gender roles, what other scenarios might be likely to occur today?

Answers: (A) England; (B) France; (C) USA.

fearless person. Yet, as we have seen (page 260), there were always some young men who found themselves temperamentally unsuited to the male role.

Very little is actually known about the amount of personality variance in different societies. It is certain, however, that complex state-level populations consisting of millions of people contain an enormous variety of personality types. The more complex the criteria used to define the basic personality, the more likely that the modal type of personality will be found in relatively few individuals. Anthony Wallace (1952) used 21 dimensions to define basic personality among the Iroquois. He found that the modal type was shared by only 37 percent of the total sample.

JAPANESE NATIONAL CHARACTER

Despite the varieties of personality found in a given society, many psychological traits and their associated behaviors may be rare, "strange," or utterly alien to certain societies and not to others. This follows logically from the fact that a society's personality is culture described in psychological terms. Valid interpretations of personality configurations in alien cultures, however, require great familiarity with the language and deep immersion in the context of everyday life. The lived experience of being a member of another society often cannot be adequately represented by simple contrasts and conventional categories.

For example, the Japanese are stereotyped

by Westerners as a people who are deferential, shy, self-effacing, conformist, and dependent on group approval. "Few Japanese," writes one anthropologist, "achieve a sense of self that is independent of the attitude of others" (cited in Kumagai and Kumagai 1986:314, cf. Plath 1983). Examples of exaggerated deference are found in the frequent bowing and elaborate courtesy of Japanese business conferences, and the readiness with which Japanese identify themselves as a work team or a corporation rather than as individuals. Indeed, self-effacement has been linked by many observers to the secret of Japan's industrial success. Japanese management style plays down the difference between executives and workers. Everyone eats in the same company cafeteria and groups of workers regularly join with management to solve problems of mutual interest in a cooperative rather than adversarial manner.

However, there is another side of the Japanese personality that is reserved for private and intimate occasions. For anyone who is not a member of a Japanese family group and who does not interact with family members when there are no guests or outside observers present, it is difficult to witness the strength of individual ego-assertion that is also part of Japanese daily life. In an intimate setting,

> People are relaxed and do not worry about formalities. . . . They can talk and joke about their innermost concerns. . . . Even the most formal of women may be informal with close friends. . . . They even tease each other about the formalities which they notice on other occasions. . . . With close friends, one can argue, criticize, and be stubborn without endangering the relationship. There is inevitably a great deal of laughter mixed with mutual support and respect. . . . It is

> partly the sharp contrast between seeing a close friend and a mere acquaintance that makes contacts with outsiders seem so stiff. . . . The visitor to Japan who does not appreciate the difference in behavior toward friends and acquaintances is likely to consider the Japanese as more formal than they actually are. [Quoted in Sugimoto and Mover 1983:12]

Virtually all Japanese are brought up to be adept at changing back and forth between the assertive private "I" and the formal public concern with "thou." The significance of these different modes of presenting one's self has little if anything to do with the inner psychological strength of the Japanese ego.

Since there is no real equivalent in the West to such a public-formal mode of self-effacement, Japanese personality has often been incorrectly and unfavorably perceived by Westerners. Lacking a Western equivalent, Westerners interpret the posture of self-effacement as indicative of hypocrisy and deviousness. On the other side, the Japanese are equally befuddled by the failure of Westerners to make a distinction between expressions of one's ego in public-formal versus intimate-private situations. As recounted by a Japanese social scientist, being a dinner guest in an American home can be especially perplexing:

> Another thing that made me nervous was the custom whereby an American host will ask a guest, before the meal, whether he would prefer a strong or a soft drink . . . [and after dinner] whether [he takes] coffee or tea, and—in even greater detail—whether one wants it with sugar, and milk, and so on. [Ibid]

While the visitor soon realized that the hosts were trying to be polite, he felt extremely un-

Figure 14.8   Japanese riot.
Police and demonstrators clash during a protest
against expansion of Tokyo airport. No deference
and conformity here.

trial societies. Many public situations do not call for formal deferential behavior. The Japanese can become just as individualistic, aggressive, and assertive in traffic jams and commuter trains and buses as New Yorkers or Parisians. And despite the stereotypes concerning Japanese submission to authority, Japanese political dissidents have mounted violent and prolonged street demonstrations (Figure 14.8). Nor should one forget that the image of the traditional Japanese samurai warrior is that of a fierce and individualistic combatant (Sugimoto and Mouer 1983; Mouer and Sugimoto 1986).

Culture and Mental Illness

Anthropologists do not agree on the role that cultural differences play in the incidence and nature of mental illness. Recent medical research has shown that there are probably important viral, genetic, and chemical-neurological bases for certain classic mental disorders such as schizophrenia (Torrey 1980). This accords with the evidence that the rates of those diseases among groups as diverse as Swedes, Eskimos, the Yoruba of West Africa, and modern Canadians do not show marked differences (Murphy 1976). However, there is no doubt that, while broad symptoms of the same mental diseases can be found cross-culturally, there is considerable variation in the specific symptoms found in different cultures. For example, a comparison of schizophrenic patients of Irish and Italian descent in a New York hospital revealed that substantially different sets of symptoms were associated with each group. The Irish patients tended to be obsessed with sexual guilt and to be much more withdrawn and quiet than the Italian patients, while the Italian

comfortable with having to say what *he* would like, since in the self-effacing "thou" posture appropriate to being a guest in a Japanese home, one avoids expressions of personal preference with respect to what is being served. Guests are dependent on hosts and surrender all vestiges of personal preference. The hosts in turn must avoid embarrassing their guests by asking them to choose their own food. Unlike Americans, Japanese hosts do not discuss how they prepared the main dish. They say, "This may not suit your taste, but it is the best we could do." The guests are not supposed to be interested in knowing any of the details of this effort.

There is a third dimension to Japanese national character that overlaps with personality patterns found in all modern urbanized indus-

patients were sexually aggressive and far more prone to violent fits and tantrums (Opler 1959). Just as Crow Indians have a particular visionary experience based on their cultural expectations (see page 281), so too the specific content of psychotic hallucinations varies from culture to culture.

For example, American patients have delusions about putting Cadillac engines into people's heads or of talking with angels in spacesuits, themes that one does not expect to occur among people who do not own cars or watch rocket lift-offs. Westerners began to have delusions about being controlled by rays of electricity only around the beginning of the century. Similarly, a common delusion of modern schizophrenics is that they have become robots. This delusion did not exist before the word and concept of robot was introduced in 1921 in a play by Karel Čapek (Barnouw 1985:361).

Moreover, as psychiatrist Richard Warner (1985) has shown, the severity of schizophrenia and the prospects of spontaneously recovering from it vary from culture to culture. In preindustrial societies with extended families, small face-to-face communities, and religions that stress the existence of a multitude of ever-present spirit-beings, the schizophrenic individual is not regarded as a shameful and threatening presence or even as a person who has gone crazy. Relatives continue to render physical and emotional support while the community blames the schizophrenic's hallucinations and bizarre behavior on some pesky spirit. In contrast, schizophrenics in industrial societies are often expelled from both family and community, deprived of physical and emotional support, isolated and made to feel worthless and guilty. These culturally defined conditions make the prospects for recovery much poorer

in industrial societies despite the availability of modern medical therapies.

CULTURE-SPECIFIC PSYCHOSES

Evidence for more powerful effects of culture on mental illness can be found in *culture-specific psychoses* — disorders that have a distinctive set of symptoms limited to only one or a few cultures. One of the best known of these culture-specific psychoses is called Arctic hysteria, or *pibloktoq* (Figure 14.9). Unlike classic

Figure 14.9 Arctic hysteria.
The victim is an Eskimo woman from Greenland.

(a)

(b)

psychoses, pibloktoq strikes suddenly. Its victims leap up, tear off their clothes, move their limbs convulsively, and roll about naked in the snow and ice. One explanation for this behavior likens it to a severe case of "cabin fever." Cooped up in their small, crowded dwellings for long periods during which they are unable to vent their feelings of hostility, pibloktoq victims may become hysterical as a means of dealing with their pent-up frustrations. It seems more likely, however, that the underlying cause also lies in the highly carnivorous diet of the Eskimo. Lacking plant foods and solar radiation, the Eskimo are forced to rely on the consumption of sea mammal and polar bear livers for their supply of vitamin A and vitamin D. Eating too much of these livers produces a poisonous excess of vitamin A, but eating too little can result in a deficit of vitamin D, which in turn leads to a deficit of calcium in the bloodstream. Both conditions—too much vitamin A and too little calcium in the blood—are known to be associated with convulsions and psychotic episodes (Landy 1985; Wallace 1972). Thus pibloktoq is probably a consequence of the interaction between culturally determined living conditions and the chemistry of nutrition.

WINDIGO "PSYCHOSIS"

Among the hunter-gatherer northern Ojibwa and Cree of the Canadian subarctic forest, there is a widespread belief that humans can become possessed by the spirit of Windigo, a cannibal monster whose heart is made out of ice. This belief has given rise to the hypothesis that the Cree and Ojibwa are subject to a culture-specific malady called *Windigo psychosis*. Those who are possessed by Windigo are said to experience an overwhelming desire to kill

and eat their campmates. Living in a harsh environment, the Cree and Ojibwa often found themselves snowbound and close to starvation in their isolated winter camps. The likelihood of someone becoming a Windigo is said to have been greatest under such conditions. Various reports verify the fact that famished campmates did sometimes eat the bodies of their deceased companions in order to keep themselves alive. (Similar accounts of "crisis cannibalism" have been reported from many parts of the world, including one about a soccer team whose plane crashed in the Andes Mountains.) Once having experienced human flesh, human Windigos are said to crave more. They lose their taste for ordinary food, their hearts feel like a lump of ice, and the people around them no longer look like people but like deer, moose, or other game animals. Unless the Windigos are killed first, they will kill and devour their companions.

As Louis Marano (1982) has shown, there are many authenticated cases of the killing of people said to be Windigos by their alarmed campmates. Recurrently, Windigo-killers cite evidence that justifies their homicides: The victims looked at them strangely, tossed about and mumbled in their sleep, had saliva dripping from their mouths, or tried to attack and bite their companions. In one instance, the alleged Windigo even seemed to hover off the ground and had to be pulled down by his attackers. Recurrently, the alleged Windigos themselves are said to have asked that they be killed lest they eat their campmates one by one. What is lacking in all of these accounts, however, is any hard data showing that the alleged Windigos thought and acted in the manner described by their executioners. Without such data, the existence of a genuine Windigo psychosis remains in doubt and a much simpler explanation can be offered for the belief in Windigo posses-

Box 14.1

SCAPEGOATING THE WINDIGO

Upon close scrutiny the Windigo psychosis discloses itself not as a culturally isolated anthropophagic (i.e., cannibal) obsession, but instead as a rather predictable — though culturally conditioned — variant of triage homicide and witch hunting typical of societies under stress. In this process, as in all witch hunts, the victims of the aggression are socially redefined as the aggressors. Here the specific form of the redefinition was determined by the constant threat of starvation, a situation in which cannibalism has proved to be a tempting recourse for persons of all cultures throughout history. By attributing society's most salient fear to the scapegoat, the group was able to project its modal anxiety onto the individual, thus generating a rationale for homicide with which everyone could identify.

Source: Marano 1982:385.

sion (Box 14.1). Under conditions of extreme hunger and stress, the northern Ojibwa and Cree accused certain troublesome campmates of being Windigos as a justification for getting rid of them, thereby increasing the chances of survival for the rest of the camp. Thus, the typical executed Windigo was a sickly individual delirious with a high fever, someone who was too ill to walk, a senile old man or woman, or a stranger from another ethnic group. In Marano's words, the Windigo beliefs were not evidence of a psychosis but of a system of

"triage homicide" (i.e., letting some die in order that others might live) in which the fear of being eaten was used to overcome the fear of breaking the taboo on killing a campmate.

The Normal Versus the Abnormal

Personality traits and behavior that appear to be sick or deviant to the outsider may in fact represent a culturally sanctioned pattern for coping with the stresses and tensions of life as far as the insiders are concerned.

This point of view has been defended by anthropologist Mac Marshall (1978) in his study of drinking and brawling among the young men of Truk, an island in the eastern Caroline Islands of Micronesia (Figure 14.10). Virtually all the able-bodied young men between 18 and 35 engage in daily or weekly bouts of drinking, accompanied by frequent outbursts of violent behavior usually directed at youths from other villages. The weekends are especially lively. In getting drunk, the young men sit in the bushes, laugh, sing, swap tales, and plan affairs with young women. Once drunk, they swagger, curse, utter ear-splitting war cries, break down doors, rush after women, intimidate friend and foe alike, and swing at each other with *nanchaku* (two sticks joined by a length of chain). Drunks are called "sardines," because like sardines in the can they have lost their heads.

Drunks are considered to be crazy, like animals, beyond the capacity of reasoning. However, they are seldom blamed for what they do when under the influence. All of this, claims Marshall, is not deviant alcoholism but culturally expected behavior. It is deviant not to get drunk. On Truk, young men should

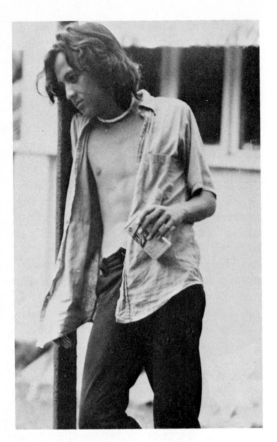

Figure 14.10 Truk.
A weekend warrior.

behave aggressively, they should be preoccupied with proving their manliness, they should take risks, and they should engage in amorous pursuits: "Drinking and flamboyant drunken comportment are expected of young men; in Truk the young man who abstains is 'abnormal' not the other way around" (Marshall 1978:67).

Getting drunk gives expression to the frustrations of not having one's opinions taken seriously and of having to show respect to one's elders. It is a way of venting pent-up aggressions that formerly were expressed in armed combat during military exploits (Box 14.2).

Box 14.2

GETTING DRUNK ON TRUK

Traditionally young men have been viewed as high spirited, irresponsible persons preoccupied with love affairs and image building. Young men are quite literally expected to engage in the proverbial "wine, women and song" in approximately that order. Their opinions are not sought on important lineage or community decisions. . . . Aboriginally, the major outlet through which young men could blow off steam . . . was by waging warfare. . . . Quite fortuitously as this outlet was closed off [after colonial contact] a new outlet was offered in drunkenness.

Source: Marshall 1978:125.

Dreams and Hallucinations

The cultural patterning of mental life affects the content of dreams, visions, and drug-induced hallucinations. For example, a form of individualistic religion (see page 292) common in North and South America involves the acquisition of a personal *guardian* spirit or supernatural protector. Typically this spirit protector is acquired by means of a visionary experience induced by fasting, self-inflicted torture, or hallucinogenic drugs. The Jívaro youth's search for an *arutam* soul (page 463) is one variant of this widespread complex. Although each *arutam* vision is slightly different from the next, they all follow a similar pattern.

For many native North Americans the central experience of life was also an hallucinatory vision (Figure 14.11). Young men needed this hallucinatory experience to be successful in love, warfare, horse stealing, trading, and all other important endeavors. In keeping with their code of personal bravery and endurance, they sought these visions primarily through self-inflicted torture.

Among the Crow, for example, a youth who craved the visionary experience of his elders went alone into the mountains, stripped off his clothes, and abstained from food and drink. If this was not sufficient, he chopped off part of the fourth finger of his left hand. Coached from childhood to expect that a vision would come, most of the Crow vision-

seekers were successful. A buffalo, snake, chicken hawk, thunderbird, dwarf, or mysterious stranger would appear; miraculous events would unfold; and then these strange beings would "adopt" the vision-seeker and disappear.

Although each Crow's vision had some unique elements, Robert Lowie (1948) found that they were usually similar in the following regards: (1) Some revelation of future success in warfare, horse raiding, or other acts of bravery was involved; (2) the visions usually occurred at the end of the fourth day—four being the sacred number of the native North Americans; (3) practically every vision was accompanied by

Figure 14.11 Sioux vision.
Section of pictographic biography done by Rain in the Face. (a) In a dream, the lightning tells him that unless he gives a buffalo feast, the lightning will kill him. He gives the feast, one part of which consists of filling a kettle with red-hot buffalo tongues, of which he eats in order to save his life. (b) He dreams of buffalo again. While dancing, he is shot by an arrow that enters the feathers. In removing it, he soon vomits and, grabbing a handful of earth, rubs it into the wound, healing it rapidly.

(a)   (b)

the acquisition of a sacred song; (4) the friendly spirits in the vision adopted the youth; and (5) trees or rocks often turned into enemies who vainly shot at the invulnerable spirit being. Lowie concludes:

> He sees and hears not merely what any faster, say in British Columbia or South Africa, would see and hear under like conditions of physiological exhaustion and under the urge of generally human desires, but what the social tradition of the Crow tribe imperatively suggests. [1948:14]

Summary

Culture and personality are closely related concepts concerned with the patterning of thoughts, feelings, and behavior. Personality is primarily a characteristic of individuals; culture is primarily a characteristic of groups. Yet it is possible to speak of the personality of a group — of a basic, modal, or typical personality. The two approaches, however, use different technical vocabularies to describe the patterning of thought, feelings, and behavior.

Anthropologists who study personality generally reject the cross-cultural universality of the Oedipus complex but they follow Freud's lead in emphasizing the importance of infant and childhood experiences in the development of adult personality. This has led to an interest in how adults interact with and relate to infants and young children, especially in such matters as toilet training, nursing, weaning, and sexual discipline. In some theories these experiences are seen as determining the nature of "secondary" institutions such as art and religion, or, as John Whiting has shown, the practice of severe male puberty rituals.

Other approaches to culture and personality attempt to characterize whole cultures in terms of central themes, patterns, basic personality, or national character. Care is necessary in order to avoid overgeneralizing the applicability of such concepts. A wide range of personality types is found in any large population.

This is not to deny that profound differences exist between personality patterns in different cultures. The Japanese, for example, have a distinctive disposition to separate ego-effacing from ego-asserting situations. This disposition, however, cannot be reduced to the stereotype that Japanese are hypocritical or devious.

The relationship between culture and mental disease remains problematical. Classic disorders such as schizophrenia and manic-depressive psychosis are somewhat modified by cultural influences, yet they occur in many different societies and probably are the result of interactions among cultural, biochemical, and genetic variables. Culture-specific psychoses such as *pibloktoq* indicate that cultural factors may powerfully influence the state of mental health, but, as the case of Windigo psychosis shows, caution is needed in evaluating allegations concerning the existence of such psychoses.

Caution is also called for in labeling certain patterns of behavior as being abnormal or deviant according to Western preconceptions and categories. Alcohol consumption on Truk, for example, is excessive by Western conventions, but normal by Truk standards.

The pervasive effect of culture on mental life is revealed by the patterning of dreams and hallucinations. As in the vision quests of native North and South Americans, the content of what is seen when under the influence of trance-inducing substances and procedures is specific to each culture's traditions.

Chapter 15

RELIGION

❧❧❧

This chapter begins our study of the realm of super-structure. It examines general aspects of the culturally patterned ideas that are conventionally known as religion, myth, and magic. It also examines the patterns of behavior that are called ritual and that are intended to mediate between human beings and natural forces, on the one hand, and supernatural beings and supernatural forces, on the other. It defines basic concepts such as religion and magic, and sets forth the basic types of religious organizations and rituals. We shall see that although infrastructural and structural conditions provide a means for understanding the origin of specific beliefs and rituals, religion frequently plays a crucial role in organizing the impulses leading toward major transformations of social life.

Animism

What is religion? The earliest anthropological attempt to define religion was that of E. B. Tylor. For Tylor, the essence of religion was belief in the idea of "god." Most Western peoples find such a belief an essential ingredient in their conception of what constitutes religion. The Victorian Age in which Tylor lived, however, tended to regard religion in even narrower terms, often restricting the concept to Christianity. Other peoples' beliefs in gods were relegated to the realm of "superstition" and "paganism." Tylor's principal contribution was to show that the Judeo-Christian concept of god was essentially similar to beliefs about supernatural beings found the world over.

Tylor attempted, with considerable success, to show that the idea of god was an elaboration of the concept of "soul." In his book *Primitive Culture*, Tylor (1871) demonstrated that belief in "the doctrine of souls" occurs to some extent and in one form or another in every society. He gave the name *animism* to the belief that inside ordinary, visible, tangible bodies there is a normally invisible, normally intangible being: the soul. Throughout the world souls are believed to appear in dreams, trances, visions, shadows, and reflections, and to be implicated in fainting, loss of consciousness, birth, and death. Tylor reasoned that the basic idea of soul must have been invented in order to explain all these puzzling phenomena. Once established, the basic idea was embroidered upon and ultimately gave rise to a variety of supernatural beings, including the souls of animals, plants, and material objects, as well as gods, demons, spirits, devils, ghosts, saints, fairies, gnomes, elves, angels, and so forth.

Tylor has been criticized by twentieth-century anthropologists for his suggestion that animism arose merely as a result of the attempt to understand puzzling human and natural phenomena. Today we know that religion is much more than an attempt to explain puzzling phenomena. Like other aspects of superstructure, religion serves a multitude of economic, political, and psychological functions.

Another important criticism of Tylor's

stress on the puzzle-solving function of religion concerns the role of hallucinations in shaping religious beliefs. During drug-induced trances and other forms of hallucinatory experience, people "see" and "hear" extraordinary things that seem even more "real" than ordinary people and animals. One can argue, therefore, that animistic theories are not intellectual attempts to explain trances and dreams, but direct expressions of extraordinary psychological experiences. Nonetheless, it cannot be denied that religion and the doctrine of souls also serve the function of providing people with answers to fundamental questions about the meaning of life and death and the causes of events.

Although certain animistic beliefs are universal, each culture has its own distinctive animistic beings and its own specific elaboration of the soul concept. Some cultures insist that people have two or more souls, while some cultures believe that certain individuals have more souls than others. Among the Jívaro of eastern Ecuador (Harner 1972b), for example, three kinds of souls are recognized: an ordinary, or "true," soul; an *arutam* soul; and a *musiak* soul (Box 15.1). The Dahomey say that women have three souls and men four, while the Fang of Gabon believe they have seven souls each (Rivière 1987).

Animatism and Mana

As Robert Marett (1914) pointed out, Tylor's definition of religion as animism is too narrow. When people attribute lifelike properties to rocks, pots, storms, and volcanoes, they do not necessarily believe that souls are the cause of the lifelike behavior of these objects. Hence there is a need to distinguish a concept of a supernatural force that does not derive its effect from souls. Marett introduced the term *animatism* to designate the belief in such non-soul forces. Possession of concentrated animatistic force can give certain objects, animals, and people extraordinary powers independent of power derived from souls and gods. To label this concentrated form of animatistic force, Marett used the Melanesian word *mana*. An adze that makes intricate carvings, a fishhook that catches large fish, a club that kills many enemies, or a horseshoe that brings "good luck" have large amounts of *mana*. People, too, may be spoken of as having more or less *mana*. A woodcarver whose work is especially intricate and beautiful possesses *mana*, whereas a warrior captured by the enemy has obviously lost his *mana*.

In its broadest range of meaning, *mana* simply indicates belief in a powerful force. Many vernacular relationships not normally recognized as religious beliefs in Western cultures can be regarded as *mana*. For example, vitamin pills are consumed by many millions of people in expectation that they will exert a powerful effect on health and well-being. Soaps and detergents are said to clean because of "cleaning power," gasolines provide engines with "starting power" or "go-power," salespeople are prized for their "selling power," and politicians are said to have *charisma* or "vote-getting power." Many people fervently believe that they are "lucky" or "unlucky," which could easily be translated as a belief that they control varying quantities of *mana*.

Natural and Supernatural

One way to prevent the definition of religion from getting so broad as to include virtually every belief is to distinguish between natural and supernatural forces. It must be emphasized, however, that few cultures neatly and

Box 15.1

THREE SOULS OF THE JÍVARO

The Jívaro believe that the true soul is present from birth inside every living Jívaro, male and female. Upon a person's death, this soul leaves the body and undergoes four additional changes. First it returns to its body's birthplace and relives its former life in an invisible form. Next it changes into a demon, and roams the forest, solitary, hungry, and lonely. The true soul then dies again and becomes a *wampang*, a species of giant moth that is occasionally seen flitting about. It too is perpetually hungry. In its fourth and final phase, the true soul turns to mist:

> After a length of time about which the Jívaro are uncertain, the wampang finally has its wings damaged by raindrops as it flutters through a rainstorm, and falls to die on the ground. The true soul then changes into water vapor amidst the falling rain. All fogs and clouds are believed to be the last form taken by true souls. The true soul undergoes no more transformations and persists eternally in the form of mist. [Harner, 1984:151]

No one is born with the second Jívaro soul. To obtain it, one must fast, bathe in a sacred waterfall, and drink tobacco water or the juice of Datura, a plant that contains an halucinogenic substance. The second soul comes out of the depths of the forest in the form of a pair of giant jaguars or a pair of huge snakes rolling over and over toward the soulseeker. When the apparition gets close, the seeker must run forward and touch it. That night it will then enter the seeker's body.

People who possess a second soul speak and act with great confidence and feel an irresistible craving to kill their enemies. As long as they keep it, they themselves are immortal. Unfortunately, the second soul cannot be kept forever. It will leave its temporary abode just before its possessor kills someone. Eventually, wandering in the forest, it will be recaptured by other soul-seekers brave enough to touch it.

The third Jívaro soul is the avenging soul. The avenging soul comes into existence when people who formerly possessed a second soul are killed by their enemies. The avenging soul develops inside the victim's head and tries to get out and attack the killer. To prevent this from happening, the best thing to do is to cut off the victim's head, "shrink" it, and bring it back home (Figure 15.1). If it is handled properly in various rituals and dances, the avenging soul can make the killer strong and happy. After it has been used to the killer's advantage, a ritual is performed to send it back to the village from which it came. To get it to go back, the women sing this song (Harner 1984:146):

> Now, now, go back to your house
>   where you lived.
> Your wife is there calling from your
>   house.
> You have come here to make us happy.
> Finally we have finished.
> So return.

Figure 15.1   Jívaro trophy head.

Figure 15.2   Gururumba medicine.
This man is inducing vomiting by swallowing a 3-foot length of cane. After he has pushed it all the way into his stomach, he will work it up and down until he vomits. It is thought to be necessary to do this to rid the individual of contaminating influences gotten through contact with women.

conveniently divide their beliefs into natural and supernatural categories. In a culture where people believe ghosts are always present, it is not necessarily either natural or supernatural to provide dead ancestors with food and drink. The culture may simply lack emic categories for "natural" and "supernatural." Similarly, when a shaman blows smoke over a patient and triumphantly removes a sliver of bone allegedly inserted by the patient's enemy, the question of whether the performance is natural or supernatural may have an emic meaning.

Writing of the Gururumba (Figure 15.2) of the highlands of western New Guinea, Philip Newman notes that they "have a series of beliefs postulating the existence of entities and forces we would call supernatural." Yet the contrast between natural and supernatural is not emically relevant to the Gururumba themselves:

It should be mentioned . . . that our use of the notion "supernatural" does not correspond to any Gururumba concept: they do not divide the world into natural and supernatural parts. Certain entities, forces, and processes must be controlled partially through *lusu,* a term denoting rituals relating to growth, curing, or the stimulation of strength, while others need only rarely be controlled in this way. . . . However, *lusu* does not contrast with any term denoting a realm of control where the nature of controls differ from *lusu.* Consequently *lusu* is simply part of all control techniques and what it controls is simply part of all things requiring human control. [1965:83]

Sacred and Profane

Some anthropologists have suggested that beliefs or practices are religious when they produce a special emotional state or "religious experience." Robert Lowie (1948:339) characterized this experience as consisting of "amazement and awe," a feeling that one is in the presence of something extraordinary, weird, sacred, holy, divine. Lowie was even willing to rule that beliefs about gods and souls were not religious beliefs if the existence of these beings was taken for granted and if, in contemplating them, the individual did not experience awe or amazement.

The theoretician who made the greatest contribution to this way of looking at religion was Emile Durkheim. Like many others, Durkheim proposed that the essence of religious belief was that it evoked a mysterious feeling of communion with a sacred realm. Every society has its sacred beliefs, symbols, and rituals, which stand opposed to ordinary or *profane* events (Figure 15.3). Durkheim's distinctive contribution was to relate the realm of the sacred to the control exercised by society and culture over each individual's consciousness. When people feel they are in communion with occult and mysterious forces and supernatural beings, what they are really experiencing is the force of social life. In our awe of the sacred, we express our dependence on society in symbolic form. Thus, according to Durkheim, the idea of "god" is but one form of the worship of society.

Every culture does make a distinction between sacred and profane realms, and there is probably some element of truth in Durkheim's idea that the sacred represents the worship of collective life. As we will see, the ability to appeal to the sacred character of certain beliefs and practices has great practical value in diminishing dissent, compelling conformity, and re-

Figure 15.3 Sacred and profane.
Shoes are left outside the mosque, symbolizing the transition from ordinary, mundane affairs to the realm of the holy and extraordinary.

solving ambiguities (see Rappaport 1971a and 1971b).

Magic and Religion

Sir James Frazer attempted to define religion in his famous book *The Golden Bough.* For Frazer, the question of whether a particular belief was religious centered on the extent to which the participants felt that they could make an entity or force do their bidding. If the attitude of the participants was one of uncertainty, if they felt humble and were inclined to supplicate and request favors and dispensations, their beliefs and actions were essentially religious. If they thought they were in control of the entities and forces governing events, felt no uncertainty about the outcome, and experienced no need for humble supplication, their beliefs and practices were examples of magic rather than of religion.

Frazer regarded prayer as the essence of religious ritual. But prayers are not always rendered in a mood of supplication. For example, prayers among the Navajo must be letter-perfect to be effective. Yet the Navajo do not expect that letter-perfect prayers will always get results. Thus, the line between prayers and "magical spells" is actually hard to draw. Supplication cannot be taken as characteristic of verbal communication between people and their gods. As Ruth Benedict (1938:640) pointed out, "Cajolery and bribery and false pretense are common means of influencing the supernatural." Thus the Kai of New Guinea swindle their ancestral ghosts as they swindle each other. Other cultures try to outwit the spirits by lying to them. The Tsimshian of the Canadian Pacific Coast stamp their feet and shake their fists at the heavens and call their gods "slaves" as a term of reproach. The Manus of the Bismarck Archipelago keep the skulls of their ancestors in a corner of the house and try their best to please "Sir Ghost." However, if someone gets sick, the Manus may angrily threaten to throw Sir Ghost out of the house. This is what they tell Sir Ghost: "This man dies and you rest in no house. You will but wander about the edges of the island" (used for excretory purposes) (Fortune 1965:216).

An additional important part of Frazer's scheme was his attempt to distinguish magic from science. The magician's attitude, he claimed, was precisely that of the scientist. Both magician and scientist believe that if A is

done under the proper set of conditions, B will follow regardless of who the practitioner is or what the attitude toward the outcome may be. A piece of an intended victim's fingernail tossed into the fire, or pins stuck into an effigy doll are believed to accomplish their results with the automatic certainty characteristic of the release of an arrow from a bow or the felling of a tree with an ax. Frazer recognized that if this was going to be the essence of the distinction between magic and religion, then magic differed little from science. Indeed, he called magic "false science" and postulated a universal evolutionary sequence in which magic, with its concern about cause and effect relationships, gave birth to science, whereas religion evolved along completely independent lines.

Frazer's scheme has not withstood the test of fieldwork. The attitudes with which fearful Dobuan magicians dispose of fingernails and confident Zuni priests whip up yucca suds to bring rain do not conform to Frazer's neat compartments. Human religious behavior unfolds as a complex mixture of awe and wonder, boredom and excitement, power and weakness.

The degree of anxiety and supplication associated with any sequence of behavior is probably regulated more by the importance of the outcome to the participants than by their philosophy of cause and effect. Not enough is known about the inner psychological state of priests, magicians, shamans, and scientists to make any firm pronouncements in this field.

The Organization of Religious Beliefs and Practices

As we have just seen, religious beliefs and rituals involve a great variety of thoughts, feelings, and practices. Yet in this domain, as in all others, there are orderly processes. A good way to begin to understand the diversity of religious phenomena is to ask whether there are beliefs and practices associated with particular levels of infrastructural and structural development.

Anthony Wallace (1966) has distinguished four principal varieties of religious "cults" — that is, forms of organization of religious doctrines and activities — that have broad evolutionary implications. The four principal forms are (1) *individualistic cults,* (2) *shamanistic cults,* (3) *communal cults,* and (4) *ecclesiastical cults,* defined as follows:

1. **Individualistic cults.** The most basic form of religious life involves individualistic (but culturally patterned) beliefs and rituals. Each person is a specialist; each individual enters into a relationship with animistic and animatistic beings and forces as each personally experiences the need for control and protection. One might call this "do-it-yourself" religion.

2. **Shamanistic cults.** As Wallace points out, no culture known to anthropology has a religion that is completely individualistic, although the Eskimo and other hunters and gatherers lean heavily in this direction. Every known society also exhibits at least the *shamanistic* level of religious specialization (Figure 15.4). The term *shaman* derives from the word used by the Tungus-speaking peoples of Siberia to designate the part-time religious specialist consulted in times of stress and anxiety. In cross-cultural applications, however, *shaman* may refer to individuals who act as diviners, curers, spirit mediums, and magicians for other people in return for gifts, fees, prestige, and power.

Figure 15.4 San curing. Shaman in trance.

3. **Communal cults.** At a more complex level of political economy, communal forms of beliefs and practices become more elaborate. Groups of nonspecialists organized in terms of age grades, men's societies, clans, or lineages assume responsibility for regular or occasional performance of rituals deemed essential for their own welfare or for the survival of the society. While communal rituals may employ specialists such as shamans, orators, and highly skilled dancers and musicians, once the ritual performance is concluded, the participants revert to a

common daily routine. There are no full-time religious specialists.

4. **Ecclesiastical cults.** The ecclesiastical level of religious organization involves a full-time professional clergy or priesthood. These professionals form a bureaucracy that monopolizes the performance of certain rites on behalf of individuals, groups, and the whole society. Ecclesiastical bureaucracies are usually closely associated with state-level political systems. In many instances the leaders of the ecclesiastical hierarchy are members of the ruling class and, in some cases, a state's political and ecclesiastical hierarchies are indistinguishable.

Wallace notes that the individualistic, shamanistic, communal, and ecclesiastical form of beliefs and rituals constitute a *scale*. That is, each of the more complex levels contains the beliefs and practices of all the less complex levels. Consequently, among societies with ecclesiastical cults, there are also communal cults, shamanistic cults, and strictly individualistic beliefs and rituals (Figure 15.5). In the following sections, examples of each of these forms of religious organization will be given.

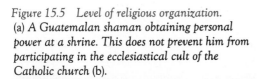

Figure 15.5   Level of religious organization.
(a) *A Guatemalan shaman obtaining personal power at a shrine. This does not prevent him from participating in the ecclesiastical cult of the Catholic church* (b).

(a)

(b)

Individualistic Beliefs and Rituals: The Eskimo

The individualism of much of Eskimo belief and ritual parallels the individualism of the Eskimo mode of production. Hunters alone or in small groups constantly match their wits against the cunning and strength of animal prey, and confront the dangers of travel over the ice and the threats of storms and month-long nights. The Eskimo hunter was equipped with an ingenious array of technological devices that made life possible in the Arctic, but the outcome of the daily struggle remained in doubt. From the Eskimo's point of view, it was not enough to be well equipped with snow goggles, fur parkas, spring-bone traps, detachable barbed harpoon points, and powerful compound bows. One also had to be equipped to handle unseen spirits and forces that lurked in all parts of nature and that, if offended or not properly warded off, could reduce the greatest hunter to a starving wretch. Vigilant individual effort was needed to deal with wandering human and animal souls, place spirits, Sedna the Keeper of the Sea Animals, the Sun, the Moon, and the Spirit of the Air (Wallace 1966:89). Part of each hunter's equipment was his hunting song, a combination of chant, prayer, and magic formula that he inherited from his father or father's brothers or purchased from some famous hunter or shaman. This he would sing under his breath as he prepared himself for the day's activities. Around his neck he wore a little bag filled with tiny animal carvings, bits of claws and fur, pebbles, insects, and other items, each corresponding to some Spirit Helper with whom he maintained a special relationship. In return for protection and hunting success given by his Spirit Helpers, the hunter had to observe certain taboos, refrain from hunting or eating certain species, or avoid trespassing in a particular locale. A hunter should never sleep out on the ice edge. Every evening he had to return to land or to the old firm ice that lies some distance back from the open sea, because the Sea Spirit does not like her creatures to smell human beings while they are not hunting (Rasmussen 1929:76). Care also must be taken not to cook land and sea mammals in the same pot; fresh water must be placed in the mouth of recently killed sea mammals, and fat must be placed in the mouth of slain land mammals (Wallace 1966:90). Note that some of these "superstitions" may have alleviated psychological stress or have had a practical value for hunting or some other aspect of Eskimo life. Not sleeping out on the ice, for example, is a safety precaution.

Shamanistic Cults

Shamans are those who are socially recognized as having special abilities for entering into contact with spirit beings and for controlling supernatural forces. Shamanism usually includes some form of trance experience during which the shaman's powers are increased. *Possession*, the invasion of the human body by a god or spirit, is the most common form of shamanistic trance. The shaman goes into a trance by smoking tobacco, taking drugs, beating on a drum, dancing monotonously, or simply by closing his or her eyes and concentrating. The trance begins with rigidity of the body, sweating, and heavy breathing. While in the trance the shaman may act as a *medium*, transmitting messages from the ancestors. With the help of friendly spirits, shamans predict future events, locate lost objects, identify the cause of illness, prescribe cures, and give advice on how clients can protect themselves against the evil intentions of enemies.

There is a close relationship between shamanistic cults and individualistic vision quests. Shamans are usually personalities who are psychologically predisposed toward hallucinatory experiences. In cultures that use hallucinogenic substances freely in order to penetrate the mysteries of the other world, many people may claim shamanistic status.

Among the Jívaro, one out of every four men is a shaman, since the use of hallucinogenic vines makes it possible for almost everyone to achieve the trance states essential for the practice of shamanism (Harner 1972b:154). Elsewhere, becoming a shaman may be restricted to people who are prone to having auditory and visual hallucinations.

An important part of shamanistic performance in many parts of the world consists of simple tricks of ventriloquism, sleight of hand, and illusion. The Siberian shamans, for example, signaled the arrival of the possessing spirit by secretly shaking the walls of a darkened tent. Throughout South America the standard shamanistic curing ceremony involves the removal of slivers of bone, pebbles, bugs, and other foreign objects from the patient's body. The practice of these tricks should not be regarded as evidence that the shaman has a cynical or disbelieving attitude. Michael Harner (1982), a modern exponent of shamanic practice, insists that there is nothing fraudulent about the sucking cure (see Box 15.3). Shamans put the offending object in their mouths because its presence helps to withdraw the *spiritual* counterpart of such objects that are, in fact, inside the patient's body and causing the illness. And so by spitting or vomiting up the intrusive object, the shamans are merely displaying a material symbol of the spirit-world reality.

Although trance is part of the shamanistic repertory in hundreds of cultures, it is not universal. Many cultures have part-time specialists who do not make use of trance but who diagnose and cure disease, find lost objects, foretell the future, and confer immunity in war and success in love. Such persons may be referred to variously as magicians, seers, sorcerers, witch doctors, medicine men or medicine women, and curers. The full shamanistic complex embodies all these roles.

Among the Tapirapé, a village people of central Brazil (Wagley 1977), shamans (Figure 15.6) derive their powers from dreams in which

Figure 15.6 Tapirapé shaman.
The shaman has fallen into a tobacco-induced trance and cannot walk unaided.

Box 15.2

HOW IKANANCOWI BECAME A SHAMAN

In his dream [Ikanancowi] walked far to the shores of a large lake deep in the jungle. There he heard dogs barking and ran in the direction from which the noise came until he met several forest spirits of the breed called munpí anká. They were tearing a bat out of a tree for food. [The spirits] talked with Ikanancowi and invited him to return to their village, which was situated upon the lake. In the village he saw periquitos [paraqueets] and many socó . . . birds which they kept as pets. [They] had several pots of kauí [porridge] and invited Ikanancowi to eat with them. He refused for he saw that their kauí was made from human blood. Ikanancowi watched one spirit drink of the kauí and saw him vomit blood immediately afterwards: the shaman saw a second spirit drink from another pot and immediately spurt blood from his anus. He saw the munpí anká vomit up their entrails and throw them upon the ground, but he soon saw that this was only a trick; they would not die, for they had more intestines. After this visit the munpí anká caled Ikanancowi father and he called them his sons; he visited them in his dreams frequently and he had munpí anká near him always.

Source: Wagley 1943:66–67.

---

they encounter spirits who become the shaman's helpers. Dreams are caused by souls leaving the body and going on journeys. Frequent dreaming is a sign of shamanistic talent. Mature shamans, with the help of the spirit familiars, can turn into birds or launch themselves through the air in gourd "canoes," visit with ghosts and demons, or travel to distant villages forward and backward through time (Box 15.2).

Tapirapé shamans are frequently called on to cure illness. This they do with sleight of hand and the help of their spirit familiars while in a semitrance condition induced by gulping huge quantities of tobacco smoke, which makes them vomit (Box 15.3). It is interesting to note in conjunction with the widespread use of tobacco in native American rituals that tobacco contains hallucinogenic alkaloids and may have induced visions when consumed in large quantities.

Communal Cults

No culture is completely without communally organized religious beliefs and practices. Even the Eskimos have group rites. Frightened and sick Eskimo individuals under the cross-examinations of shamans publicly confess violations of taboos that have made them ill and that have endangered the rest of the community.

Among the native Americans of the Western Plains there were annual public rites of

Box 15.3

Cure by Vomit

Unless the illness is serious enough to warrant immediate treatment, shamans always cure in the late evening. A shaman comes to his patient, and squats near the patient's hammock; his first act is always to light his pipe. When the patient has a fever or has fallen unconscious from the sight of a ghost, the principal method of treatment is by massage. The shaman blows smoke over the entire body of the patient; then he blows smoke over his own hands, spits into them, and massages the patient slowly and firmly, always toward the extremities of the body. He shows that he is removing a foreign substance by quick movement of his hands as he reaches the end of an arm or leg.

The more frequent method of curing, however, is by the extraction of a malignant object by sucking. The shaman squats alongside the hammock of his patient and begins to "eat smoke" —swallow large gulps of tobacco smoke from his pipe. He forces the smoke with great intakes of breath deep down into his stomach; soon he becomes intoxicated and nauseated; he vomits violently and smoke spews from his stomach. He groans and clears his throat in the manner of a person gagging with nausea but unable to vomit. By sucking back what he vomits he accumulates saliva in his mouth.

In the midst of this process he stops several times to suck on the body of his patient and finally, with one awful heave, he spews all the accumulated material on the ground. He then searches in this mess for the intrusive object that has been causing the illness. Never once did I see a shaman show the intrusive object to observers. At one treatment a Tapirapé [shaman] usually repeats this process of "eating smoke," sucking, and vomiting several times. Sometimes, when a man of prestige is ill, two or even three shamans will cure side by side in this manner and the noise of violent vomiting resounds throughout the village.

Source: Wagley 1943:73–74.

self-torture and vision quest known as the Sun Dance (Figure 15.7). Under the direction of shaman leaders, the sun dancers tied themselves to a pole by means of a cord passed through a slit in their skin. Watched by the assembled group, they walked or danced around the pole and tugged at the cord until they fainted or the skin ripped apart. These public displays of endurance and bravery were part of the intense marauding and warfare complex that developed after the coming of the Europeans.

Communal rites fall into two major categories: (1) *rites of solidarity* and (2) *rites of passage*. In the rites of solidarity, participation in dramatic public rituals enhances the sense of

Figure 15.7   Dakota Sun Dance.
Painted by Short-Bull, chief of the Oglala Dakota (Sioux), this painting represents the Sun Dance of more than 90 years ago. The circle in the center represents a windbreak formed of fresh cottonwood boughs. In the center is the Sun Dance pole and hanging from it is the figure of a man and a buffalo. Outside the Sun Dance enclosure, devotees perform. One of them is dragging four buffalo skulls by cords run through openings in the skin on his back. He will continue to drag these until they tear loose.

group identity, coordinates the actions of the individual members of the group, and prepares the group for immediate or future cooperative action. Rites of passage celebrate the social movement of individuals into and out of groups or into or out of statuses of critical importance to the individual and to the community. Reproduction, the achievement of manhood and womanhood, marriage, and death are the principal worldwide occasions for rites of passage.

COMMUNAL RITES OF SOLIDARITY: TOTEMISM

Rites of solidarity are common among clans and other descent groups. Such groups usually have names and emblems that identify group members and set one group off from another. Animal names and emblems predominate, but insects, plants, and natural phenomena such as rain and clouds also occur. These group-identifying objects are known as *totems*. Many totems such as bear, breadfruit, or kangaroo are useful or edible species, and often there is a stipulated descent relationship between the members of the group and their totemic ancestor. Sometimes the members of the group must refrain from harming or eating their totem. There are many variations in the specific forms of totemic belief, however, and no single totemic complex can be said to exist.

The Arunta of Australia provide one of the classic cases of totemic ritual. Here an individual identifies with the totem of the sacred place near which one's mother passed shortly before becoming pregnant (see page 154). These places contain the stone objects known as *churinga,* which are the visible manifestations of each person's spirit (Figure 15.8). The *churinga* are believed to have been left behind by ancestors as they traveled about the countryside at the beginning of the world. The ancestors later turned into totems. The sacred places of each totem are visited annually during rites known as *Intichiuma.*

These rituals have many meanings and functions. The participants are earnestly concerned with protecting their totems and ensuring their reproduction. But the exclusive membership of the ritual group also indicates that they are acting out the mythological dogma of

Figure 15.8   Bull roarer.
String is tied through hole and used to whirl bull roarer around head. This specimen is from Australia. It is made of stone and is known as a churinga. *It represents a human spirit.*

their common ancestry. The totem ceremonies reaffirm and intensify the sense of common identity of the members of a regional community. The handling of the *churinga* confirms the fact that the totemic group has "stones" or, in a more familiar metaphor, "roots" in a particular land.

COMMUNAL RITUALS: RITES OF PASSAGE

Rites of passage accompany changes in structural position or status that are of general public concern. Why are birth, puberty, marriage, and death (Figure 15.9) so frequently the occasions for rites of passage? Probably because of their public implications: The individual who is born, who reaches adulthood, who takes a spouse, or who dies is not the only one implicated in these events. Many other people must adjust to these momentous changes. Being born not only defines a new life but brings into existence or modifies the positions of parent, grandparent, sibling, heir, age-mate, and many other domestic and political relationships. The main function of rites of passage is to give communal recognition to the entire complex of new or altered relationships and not merely to the changes experienced by the individuals who get born, marry, or die.

Rites of passage conform to a remarkably similar pattern among widely dispersed cultures (Eliade 1958; Schlegel and Barry 1979). First, the principal performers are separated from the routines associated with their earlier lives. Second, decisive physical and symbolic steps are taken to extinguish the old status. Often these steps include the notion of killing the old personality. To promote "death and transfiguration," old clothing and ornaments are exchanged for new, and the body is painted or mutilated. Finally, the participants are ceremoniously returned to normal life.

(a)

Figure 15.9   Religion and life crises.
(a) Dogon funeral dancers. The Crow scaffold
burial (b) shows a common means of disposing of
the dead in sparsely inhabited regions. (c) The
Peruvian mummies show another method, which is
common in arid climates.

(b)

(c)

The pattern of rites of passage can be seen in the male initiation ceremonies of the Ndembu of northern Zambia (Figure 15.10). Here, as among many African and Middle Eastern peoples, the transition from boyhood to manhood involves the rite of circumcision. Young boys are taken from their separate villages and placed in a special bush "school." They are circumcised by their own kinsmen or neighbors, and after their wounds heal, they are returned to normal life.

In many cultures girls are subject to similar rites of separation, seclusion, and return in relationship to their first menses and their eligibility for marriage. Genital surgery is also common for girls, and there is a widely practiced operation known as *clitoridectomy* (Abdallah 1982; Gruebaum 1988). In this operation, the external tip of the clitoris is cut off. Among many Australian groups, both circumcision and clitoridectomy were practiced. In addition, the Australians knocked out the pubescent child's front tooth. Males were subject to the further operation of *subincision*, in which the underside of the penis was slit open to the depth of the urethra. In several parts of Africa, clitoridectomy was followed by a procedure in which the two sides of the vulva are attached to each other by stitching with silk or catgut sutures or by thorns, thus preventing vaginal intercourse until their removal at the time of marriage (Dualeh 1982; Gruenbaum 1988).

Ecclesiastical Cults

As stated above, ecclesiastical cults have in common the existence of a professional clergy or priesthood organized into a bureaucracy. This bureaucracy is usually associated with and under the control of a central temple. At secondary or provincial temple centers, the clergy

Figure 15.10   *Ndembu rites.*
(a) *Although the women are supposed to be terrified of the "monster," they are actually amused and skeptical.* (b) *The circumcision camp—the "place of dying."*

(a)

(b)

Figure 15.11 Ecclesiastical cult.
A Roman Catholic high mass is celebrated.

may exercise a considerable amount of independence. In general, the more highly centralized the political system, the more highly centralized the ecclesiastical bureaucracy.

The ecclesiastic specialists are different from both the Tapirapé shamans and the Ndembu circumcisers and guardians. They are formally designated persons who devote themselves to the rituals of their office (Figure 15.11). These rituals usually include a wide variety of techniques for influencing and controlling animistic beings and animatistic forces. The material support for these full-time specialists is usually closely related to power and privileges of taxation. As among the Inca (page 206), the state and the priesthood may divide up the rent and tribute exacted from the peasants. Under feudalism (see page 205), the ecclesiastical hierarchy derives its earnings from its own estates and from the gifts of powerful princes and kings. High officials in feudal ec-

clesiastical hierarchies are almost always kin or appointees of members of the ruling class.

The presence of ecclesiastical organizations produces a profound split among those who participate in ritual performances. On the one hand, there is an active segment, the priesthood; on the other, the passive "congregation," who are virtual spectators. The members of the priesthood must acquire intricate ritual, historical, calendrical, and astronomical knowledge. Often they are scribes and learned persons. It must be stressed, however, that the "congregation" does not altogether abandon individualistic, shamanistic, and communal beliefs and rituals. These are all continued, sometimes secretly, in neighborhoods, villages, or households, side by side with the "higher" rituals, despite more or less energetic efforts on the part of the ecclesiastical hierarchy to stamp out what it often calls idolatrous, superstitious, pagan, heathen, or heretical beliefs and performances.

THE RELIGION OF THE AZTECS

Many of the principal characteristics of belief and ritual in stratified contexts can be seen in the ecclesiastical organization of the Aztecs of Mexico. The Aztecs held their priests responsible for the maintenance and renewal of the entire universe. By performing annual rituals, priests could obtain the blessing of the Aztec gods, ensure the well-being of the Aztec people, and guard the world against collapse into chaos and darkness. According to Aztec theology, the world had already passed through four ages, each of which ended in cataclysmic destruction. The first age ended when the reigning god, Tezcatlipoca, transformed himself into the sun and all the people of the earth were devoured by jaguars. The second age, ruled over by the feathered serpent Quetzalcoatl

Figure 15.12   Temple of Quetzalcoatl, or the Plumed Serpent.
Teotihuacan.

Figure 15.13   Tenochtitlán.
A reconstructed view of the Aztec capital with its numerous temple-topped pyramids.

(Figure 15.12), was destroyed by hurricanes that changed people into monkeys. The third age, ruled over by Tlaloc, god of rain, was brought to a close when the heavens rained fire. Then came the rule of Chalchihuitlicue, goddess of water, whose time ended with a universal flood, during which people turned into fish. The fifth age is in progress, ruled over by the sun god Tonatiuh, and doomed to destruction sooner or later by earthquakes.

The principal function of the 5000 priests living in the Aztec capital was to make sure that the end of the world came later rather than sooner. This could be assured only by pleasing the legions of gods reputed to govern the world. The best way to please the gods was to give them gifts, the most precious being fresh human hearts. The hearts of war captives were the most esteemed gifts, since they were won only at great expense and risk.

Aztec ceremonial centers were dominated by large pyramidal platforms topped by temples (Figure 15.13). These structures were stages on

which the drama of human sacrifice was enacted at least once a day throughout the year. On especially critical days there were multiple sacrifices. The set pattern for these performances involved first the victim's ascent of the huge staircase to the top of the pyramid; then, at the summit, the victim was seized by four priests, one for each limb, and bent face up, spread-eagled over the sacrificial stone. A fifth priest cut the victim's chest open with an obsidian knife and wrenched out the beating heart. The heart was smeared over the statue of the god and later burned. Finally, the lifeless body was flung over the edge of the pyramid where it was rolled back down the steps. It is believed that during a four-day dedication ceremony of the main Aztec temple in Tenochtitlán, 20,000 prisoners of war were sacrificed in the manner described above. A yearly toll estimated to have been as high as 15,000 people was sent to death to placate the bloodthirsty gods. Most of these victims were prisoners of war, although local youths, maidens, and children were also sacrificed from time to time (Berdan 1982; Coe 1977; Soustelle 1970; Vaillant 1966). The bodies of most of those who were sacrificed were rolled down the pyramid steps, dismembered, and probably cooked and eaten (Harner 1977).

AZTEC CANNIBALISM

Prior to the emergence of the state, many societies practiced human sacrifice and ritually consumed all or part of the bodies of prisoners of war (Harris 1985). Lacking the political means to tax and conscript large populations, chiefdoms had little interest in preserving the lives of their defeated enemies. With the advent of the state, however, these practices tended to disappear. As we have seen (page 202), conquered territories were incorporated into the state and the labor power of defeated populations was tapped through taxation, conscription, and tribute. Thus, the preservation of the lives of defeated peoples became an essential part of the process of state expansion.

The Aztec, however, were an exception to this general trend. Instead of tabooing human sacrifice and cannibalism and encouraging charity and kindness toward defeated enemy peoples, the Aztec state made human sacrifice and cannibalism the main focus of ecclesiastical beliefs and rituals (Figure 15.14). As the Aztec became more powerful, they became more rather than less cannibalistic. Since the skulls of the victims were placed side by side on tall wooden racks after the brains were taken out and eaten, it was possible for members of Cortés's expedition to count at least one cate-

Figure 15.14   Aztec sacrificial knife.

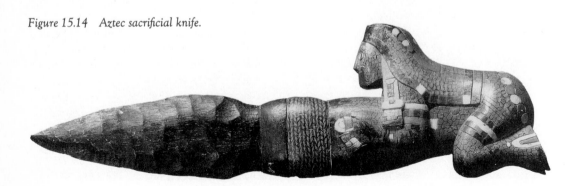

Figure 15.15 Skull rack.
One of the smaller racks in the Aztec capital. The
skulls in the photograph are sculpted in stone;
during Aztec times, real skulls were exhibited on
wooden structures raised on the sculpted base. Part
of the ongoing excavation in Mexico City.

gory of victim (Figure 15.15). They reported
that one of these skull racks at the center of Tenochtitlán held 136,000 heads, but they were
unable to count another group of victims
whose heads were heaped into two tall towers
made entirely of crania and jawbones (Tápia
1971:583), nor did they count the skulls displayed on five smaller racks that were located
in the same central area. According to calcula-
tions performed by Ortiz de Montellano
(1983:404), the principal rack could not have
held more than 60,000 skulls. Even if this lower
figure is more accurate, the amount of human
sacrifice and cannibalism practiced in Tenochtitlán remains unique in human history.

Although it is considered controversial,
Michael Harner's (1977) explanation of the
Aztec state's unique cannibal religion deserves

serious consideration. Harner starts from the
fact that as a result of millennia of intensification and population growth, the central Mexican highlands had lost their best domesticable
animal species. Unlike the Inca, who obtained
animal foods from llama, alpaca, and guinea
pigs—or the Old World states that had sheep,
goats, pigs, and cattle—the Aztec had only
semidomesticated ducks and turkeys, and hair-
less dogs. Wild fauna, such as deer and migrat-
ing waterfowl, were not abundant enough to
provide the Aztecs with more than 1 or 2 grams
of animal protein per capita per day (compared
with over 60 grams in the United States). The
depleted condition of the natural fauna is
shown by the prominence in the Aztec diet of
bugs, worms, and "scum cakes," which were
made out of algae skimmed off the surface of
Lake Texcoco (see Harris 1979c; Sahlins 1978).

Harner's theory implies that the severe depletion of animal resources made it uniquely
difficult for the Aztec state to prohibit the consumption of human flesh in order to facilitate
its expansionist aims. Due to the severe depletion of animal resources, human flesh rather
than animal flesh was redistributed as a means
of rewarding loyalty to the throne and bravery
in combat. Moreover, to have made serfs or
slaves out of captives would only have wor-
sened the animal food shortage. There was
thus much to lose by prohibiting cannibalism
and little to gain.

It cannot be said from an etic perspective
that the Aztecs went to war to obtain prisoners
and meat. Like all states, the Aztec went to war
for reasons that are associated with the inherently expansionist nature of the state (Hassing
1988). From an emic perspective, as reported to
the Spanish by the Aztecs, however, one could
say that the desire to capture prisoners for sacrifice and consumption was an important objective of the participants.

As indicated earlier with reference to game depletion and Yanomamo warfare (page 187), animal foods are an extremely valuable compact package of nutrients essential for human growth, health, and vigor. Meat and other animal products are widely valued by human beings not only for the high-quality proteins they contain but for their fats, minerals, and vitamins.

The perennial shortages of meat were an important source of popular discontent that led to the downfall of the communist systems of the Soviet Union and Poland (see Box 15.4).

Harner's theory cannot be disproved by showing that the Aztecs could have obtained all of the essential amino acids (the nine or ten building blocks of proteins that cannot be synthesized by the human body) from worms and insects, from algae, and from corn and beans and other plant foods (Ortiz de Montellano 1978). Worms and insects are small, dispersed food packages that occupy a position low in the food chain. In conformity with optimal forag-

ing theory (page 77), it is usually more efficient to let higher organisms such as birds, fish, and mammals hunt and collect worms and insects and to eat the higher species instead of their prey. Also it is much more efficient to let fish eat algae and to eat the fish than it is to gather and process the algae and deprive the fish of their food.

A healthy adult can obtain all essential amino acids by eating large quantities of cereals alone (Lieberman 1987; Pellet 1987). But such diets remain deficient in minerals (e.g., iron) and vitamins (e.g., vitamin A). Moreover, the protein levels that are adequate for normal adults and that can be obtained from cereals alone or from combinations such as corn and beans become hazardous when considering the needs of children, pregnant and lactating women, and anybody suffering from parasitical or viral infections or other diseases and body trauma caused by accidents or wounds (Scrimshaw 1977). Hence, the high value that the Aztecs placed on the consumption of human flesh was not an arbitrary consequence of their religious beliefs. Rather, their religious beliefs (i.e., the cravings of their gods for human blood) reflected the importance of animal foods in relation to human dietary needs and the depleted supply of nonhuman animals in their habitat. (Note that most so-called vegetarian cultures are lactovegetarians or ovovegetarians — that is, they spurn meat but eat dairy products and eggs [Harris 1985].)

Box 15.4

MEAT AND POLITICS IN THE SOVIET UNION

"If we could put 80 kilograms [176 pounds] of meat a year on the consumer's table, all other problems we have would not be as acute as they are now. It is no exaggeration to say that the shortage of meat products is a problem that is worrying the whole nation." — Mikhail Gorbachev addressing the Soviet Central Committee.

Source: Gumbel 1988.

Religion and Political Economy: High Gods

Full-time specialists, monumental temples, dramatic processions, and elaborate rites performed for spectator congregations are incompatible with the infrastructure and political economy of hunters and gatherers. Similarly, the complex astronomical and mathematical basis of ecclesiastical beliefs and rituals is never found among band and village peoples.

The level of political economy also influences the way in which gods are thought to relate to each other and to human beings. For example, the idea of a single high god who creates the universe is found among cultures at all levels of economic and political development. These high gods, however, play different kinds of roles in running the universe after they have brought it into existence (Sullivan 1987). Among hunter-gatherers and other prestate peoples, the high gods tend to become inactive after their creation task is done. It is to a host of lesser gods, demons, and ancestor souls that one must turn in order to obtain assistance (cf. Hayden 1987). On the other hand, in stratified societies the high god bosses the lesser gods and tends to be a more active figure to whom priests and commoners address their prayers (Swanson 1960), although the lesser gods may still be revered more actively by ordinary people.

A plausible explanation for this difference is that prestate cultures have no need for the idea of a central or supreme authority. Just as there is an absence of centralized control over people and strategic resources in life, so in religious belief, the inhabitants of the spirit world lack decisive control over each other. They form a more or less egalitarian group. On the other hand, the belief that superordination and subordination characterize relationships among the gods helps to obtain the cooperation of the commoner classes in stratified societies (Figure 15.16).

One way to achieve conformity in stratified societies is to convince commoners that the gods demand obedience to the state. Dis-

Figure 15.16   Religion and stratification. Bishops and other high prelates of the Corpus Christi Cathedral in Cuzco, Peru, are an awe-inspiring sight to an Indian peasant.

obedience and nonconformity result not only in retribution administered through the state's police-military apparatus but also in punishments in present or future life administered by the high gods themselves. In prestate societies, for reasons discussed in Chapter 10, law and order are often rooted in common interest. Consequently, there is little need for high gods to administer punishments for those who have been "bad" and rewards for those who have

Table 15.1

RELIGION, CLASS, AND MORALITY

GOD INTERESTED IN MORALITY	SOCIETIES WITH SOCIAL CLASSES	SOCIETIES WITHOUT SOCIAL CLASSES
Present	25	2
Absent	8	12

Source: Adapted from Guy E. Swanson, 1960, *The Birth of the Gods: The Origin of Primitive Beliefs*, p. 166. Ann Arbor: University of Michigan Press.

been "good." But as Table 15.1 shows, where there are class differences, the gods are believed to take a lively interest in the degree to which each individual's thoughts and behavior are immoral or ethically subversive.

Revitalization

The relationship of religion to structure and infrastructure can also be seen in the process known as *revitalization*. Under the severe stresses associated with colonial conquest and intense class or minority exploitation, religions tend to become movements concerned with achieving a drastic improvement in the immediate conditions of life and/or in the prospects for an afterlife. These movements are sometimes referred to as *nativistic, revivalistic, millenarian*, or *messianic*. The term *revitalization* is intended to embrace all the specific cognitive and ritual variants implied by these terms (see Wallace 1966).

Revitalization is a process of political and religious interaction between a depressed caste, class, minority, or other subordinate so-

cial group and a superordinate group. Some revitalization movements emphasize passive attitudes, the adoption of old rather than new cultural practices, or salvation through rewards after death; others advocate more or less open resistance or aggressive political or military action. These differences largely reflect the extent to which the subordinate groups are prepared to cope with the challenge to their power and authority. Revitalizations that take place under conditions of massive suffering and exploitation sooner or later result in political and even military probes or confrontations, even though both sides may overtly desire to avoid conflict (Worsley 1968). It should be kept in mind that Christianity and Islam began as revitalization movements. Protestantism and many of its subdivisions, such as the Amish, Hutterites, and Pentecostals, also resemble revitalization movements in several important respects, as do many of the current "electronic churches" (see Chapter 18).

NATIVE AMERICAN REVITALIZATIONS

Widespread revitalizations were provoked by the European invasion of the New World and by the conquest and expulsion of the native American peoples and the destruction of their natural resources.

The most famous of the nineteenth-century revitalization movements was the Ghost Dance, also known as the Messiah craze. This movement originated near the California-Nevada border and roughly coincided with the completion of the Union Pacific Railroad. The Paviotso prophet Wodziwob envisioned the return of the dead from the spirit world in a great train whose arrival would be signaled by a huge explosion. Simultaneously the whites would be swept from the land, but their build-

Figure 15.17   Wovoka.
Leader of the Ghost Dance.

ings, machines, and other possessions would be left behind. (The resemblance to the neutron bomb is worth noting.) To hasten the arrival of the ancestors, there was to be ceremonial dancing accompanied by the songs revealed to Wodziwob during his visions.

A second version of the Ghost Dance was begun in 1889 under the inspiration of Wovoka (Figure 15.17). A vision in which all the dead had been brought back to life by the Ghost Dance was again reported. Ostensibly Wovoka's teachings lacked political content, and as the Ghost Dance spread eastward across the Rockies, its political implications remained ambiguous. Yet for the native Americans of the Plains, the return of the dead meant that they

would outnumber the whites and hence be more powerful.

Among the Sioux, there was a version that included the return of all the bison and the extermination of the whites under a huge landslide. The Sioux warriors put on Ghost Dance shirts, which they believed would make them invulnerable to bullets. Clashes between the U.S. Army and the Sioux became more frequent, and the Sioux leader Sitting Bull was arrested and killed. The second Ghost Dance movement came to an end with the massacre of 200 Sioux at Wounded Knee, South Dakota (Figure 15.18), on December 29, 1890 (Mooney 1965).

After all chance of military resistance was crushed, the native American revitalization movement became more introverted and passive. Visions in which all the whites were wiped out ceased to be experienced, confirming the responsiveness of revitalizations to political reality. The development and spread of beliefs and rituals centering on peyote, mescal, and other hallucinogenic drugs are characteristic of many twentieth-century native American religions. Peyote ritual involves a night of praying, singing, peyote eating, and ecstatic contemplation followed by a communal breakfast (Figure 15.19). The peyote eaters are not interested in bringing back the buffalo or making themselves invulnerable to bullets; they seek self-knowledge, personal moral strength, and physical health (La Barre 1938; Stewart 1987). (See Box 15.5.)

Peyotism and similar movements do not, of course, signal the end of political action on the part of the native Americans. With the emergence of the "Red Power" movement, the native Americans are trying to hold on to and regain their stolen lands through protests and political pressure (DeLoria 1969; Josephy 1982; D. Walker 1972).

(a)

(b)

Figure 15.18 Wounded Knee.
In the first battle (a), in 1890, 200 Sioux Indians were killed by the U.S. Army. In the second battle, (b), in 1973, militant Indians occupied the village of Wounded Knee, South Dakota, and exchanged gunfire with U.S. marshals.

Figure 15.19   Peyote ceremony.
Delaware Indians of Oklahoma spend the night in
prayer and meditation. At right, they emerge to
greet the dawn.

CARGO CULTS

In New Guinea and Melanesia, revitalization is associated with the concept of *cargo*. The characteristic vision of the Melanesian revitalization prophets is that of a ship bringing back the ancestors and a cargo of European goods. In recent times airplanes and spaceships have become the favorite means of delivering the cargo (see Worsley 1968).

As a result of the abundance of goods displayed by U.S. military forces during the Pacific island campaigns of World War II, some revitalizations stressed the return of the Ameri-

Box 15.5

PEYOTE RELIGION

The peyote religion is a syncretistic cult, incorporating ancient Indian and modern Christian elements. The Christian theology of love, charity, and forgiveness has been added to the ancient Indian ritual and aboriginal desire to acquire personal power through individual visions. Peyotism has taught a program of accommodation for over 50 years and the peyote religion has succeeded in giving Indians pride in their native culture while adjusting to the dominant civilization of the whites.

Source: Stewart 1968:108.

cans. In Espiritu Santo in 1944, the prophet Tsek urged his people to destroy all trade goods and throw away their clothes in preparation for the return of the mysteriously departed Americans. Some of the American-oriented revitalizations have placed specific American soldiers in the role of cargo deliverers. On the island of Tana in the New Hebrides, the John Frumm cult cherishes an old GI jacket as the relic of one John Frumm, whose identity is not otherwise known (Figure 15.20). The prophets of John Frumm build landing strips, bamboo control towers, and grass-thatched cargo sheds. In some cases beacons are kept ablaze at night and radio operators stand ready with tin-can microphones and earphones to guide the cargo planes to a safe landing.

An important theme is that the cargo planes and ships have been successfully loaded by the ancestors at U.S. ports and are on their

Figure 15.20 John Frumm.
Members of the Tana, New Hebrides, cargo cult.

way, but the local authorities have refused to permit the cargo to be landed. In other versions, the cargo planes are tricked into landing at the wrong airport. In a metaphorical sense these sentiments are applicable to the actual colonial contexts. The peoples of the South Seas have indeed often been tricked out of their lands and resources (Harris 1974).

In 1964 the island of New Hanover became the scene of the Lyndon Johnson cult. Under the leadership of the prophet Bos Malik, cult members demanded that they be permitted to vote for Johnson in the village elections scheduled for them by the Australian administration. Airplanes passing overhead at night were said to be President Johnson's planes searching for a place to land. Bos Malik advised that in order to get Johnson to be their president, they would have to "buy" him. This was to be done by paying the annual head tax to Malik instead of to the Australian tax collectors. When news reached New Hanover that an armed force had been dispatched to suppress the tax revolt, Malik prophesied that the liner *Queen Mary* would soon arrive bearing cargo and U.S. troops to liberate the islanders from the Australian oppressors. When the ship failed to materialize, Malik accused the Australian officials of stealing the cargo.

The confusion of the Melanesian revitalization prophets stems from lack of knowledge of the workings of cultural systems. They do not understand how modern industrial wage-labor societies are organized, nor comprehend how law and order are maintained among state-level peoples. To them, the material abundance of the industrial nations and the penury of others constitute an irrational flaw, a massive contradiction in the structure of the world.

The belief system of the cargo cults vividly demonstrates why the assumption that all people distinguish between natural and supernatural categories is incorrect (see page 287). Cargo prophets who have been taken to see modern Australian stores and factories in the hope that they would give up their beliefs return home more convinced than ever that they are following the best prescription for obtaining cargo. With their own eyes they have observed the fantastic abundance the authorities refuse to let them have (Lawrence 1964).

Taboo, Religion, and Ecology

As we have seen (page 288), religion can be regarded as the concentration of the sense of the sacred. It follows that an appeal to the sacred nature of a rule governing interpersonal relations or of a rule governing the relationship between a population and its environment will be useful in resolving the uncertainties that people may sometimes experience concerning what they ought to do (Flannery, Marcus, and Reynolds 1989).

For example, the prohibition on incest within the nuclear family is widely seen as a sacred obligation. The violation of an incest taboo is looked on as a profane or antisacred act. One plausible explanation for these powerful sentiments is that people are strongly tempted to commit incest, but that the short-run satisfactions they might receive from such acts would have long-run negative consequences for them and for the continuity of social life because of the reduced ability of individuals and local groups to establish adaptive intergroup relationships (see page 148). By surrounding incest prohibitions with the aura of sacredness, the long-term individual and collective interest comes to prevail, and the ambiguities and doubts individuals feel about re-

nouncing the prohibited sexual relationships are resolved more decisively than would otherwise be possible. This does not mean that incest ceases to occur or that all psychological doubts are removed, but merely that such doubts are brought under more effective social control.

A similar tension between short-run and long-run costs and benefits may explain the origin of certain food taboos that are regarded as sacred obligations. For example, it seems likely that the ancient Israelite prohibition on the consumption of pork reflects the contradiction between the temptation to rear pigs and the negative consequences of raising animals that are useful only for meat. Pigs require shade and moisture to regulate their body temperature. With the progressive deforestation and desertification of the Middle East caused by the spread and intensification of agriculture and stock raising and by population growth, habitat zones suitable for pig rearing became scarce. Hence an animal that was at one time reared and consumed as a relatively inexpensive source of fat and protein could no longer be reared and consumed by large numbers of people without reducing the efficiency of the main system of food production (Harris 1985). The temptation to continue the practice of pig raising persisted, however; hence the invocation of sacred commandments in the ancient Hebrew religion. Note that the explanation of the ancient origins of this taboo does not account for its perpetuation into the present. Once in existence, the taboo against pork (and other foods) acquired the function of demarcating or bounding Jewish ethnic minorities from other groups and of increasing their sense of identity and solidarity (see page 233). Outside the Middle East the taboo no longer served an ecological function, but it continued to be useful on the level of structural relationships.

The general ecological adaptiveness of taboos regulating potentially important sources of animal protein in the Amazon Basin has been studied by Eric Ross (1978). Ross holds that certain large animals, such as deer, the tapir, and the white-lipped peccary, are not hunted or eaten by the Achuara, who live on the border of Peru and Ecuador, because to do so would be to misdirect the hunting effort away from gregarious, abundant, relatively accessible, and less costly species such as monkeys, birds, and fish. The costs of obtaining species such as deer and tapir among the Achuara are prohibitive because the Achuara live in very small dispersed villages and cannot form hunting parties with enough men to pursue, kill, and bring back the bigger animals.

It is interesting to note in this connection the origin of the word *taboo*. It is a Polynesian term that denotes the practice followed by Polynesian chiefs in limiting access to certain depleted agricultural lands or overfished portions of the seacoast. Anyone violating such taboos was subject to both natural and supernatural punishment.

THE SACRED COW

The case of the sacred cow of India conforms to the general theory that the flesh of certain animals is made taboo when it becomes very expensive as a result of ecological changes. Like pigs in the Middle East, cattle were sacrificed and eaten quite freely in India during the Neolithic. With the rise of the state and of dense rural and urban populations, however, cattle could no longer be raised in sufficient numbers to be used both as a source of meat and as the principal source of traction power for pulling plows. But as the taboo on cattle use developed, it took a form quite different from the Israelite taboo on the pig. Whereas the pig was valued almost exclusively for its flesh, cattle were also valued for their milk and especially for their traction power. When pigs became too costly to be raised for meat, the whole animal became taboo and an abomination. But as cattle in India became too costly to be raised for meat, their value as a source of traction power increased (the land had to be plowed more intensively as population grew). Therefore, they had to be protected rather than abominated, and so the Hindu religion came to emphasize everyone's sacred duty to refrain from killing cattle or eating beef. Interestingly enough, the Brahmans, who at one time were the caste responsible for ritually slaughtering cattle, later became the caste most concerned with their protection and most opposed to the development of a beef slaughtering industry in India (Harris 1977, 1979a; Simoons 1979).

What about the sacred cow today? Is the religious ban on the slaughter of cattle and the consumption of beef a functionally useful feature of modern Hinduism? Everyone agrees that the human population of India needs more calories and proteins. Yet the Hindu religion bans the slaughter of cattle and taboos the eating of beef. These taboos are often held responsible for the creation of large numbers of aged, decrepit, barren, and useless cattle. Such animals are depicted as roaming aimlessly across the Indian countryside, clogging the roads, stopping the trains, stealing food from the marketplace, and blocking city streets (Figure 15.21). A closer look at some of the details of the ecology and economy of the Indian subcontinent, however, suggests that the taboo in question does not decrease the capacity of the present Indian system of food production to support human life.

The basis of traditional Indian agriculture is the ox-drawn plow. Each peasant farmer

Figure 15.21   Sacred cows.
This resident of Calcutta is not wandering aimlessly. Its owner knows where it is. These cows are "parked," not blocking traffic. In India, cattle are ecologically more valuable than cars.

needs at least two oxen to plow the fields at the proper time of the year. Despite the impression of surplus cattle, the central fact of Indian rural life is that there is a shortage of oxen, since one-third of the peasant households own less than the minimum pair. It is true that many cows are too old, decrepit, and sick to do a proper job of reproducing. At this point the ban on slaughter and beef consumption is thought to exert its harmful effect. For rather than kill dry, barren, and aged cows, the Hindu farmer is depicted as ritually obsessed with preserving the life of each sacred beast, no matter how useless it may become. From the point of view of the poor farmer, however, these relatively undesirable creatures may be quite essential and useful. The farmer would prefer to have more vigorous cows, but is prevented from achieving this goal not by the taboos

against slaughter but by the shortage of land and pasture (Chakravarti 1985a; 1985b).

Even barren cows, however, are by no means a total loss. Their dung makes an essential contribution to the energy system as fertilizer and as cooking fuel. Millions of tons of artificial fertilizer at prices beyond the reach of the small farmer would be required to make up for the loss of dung if substantial numbers of cattle were sent to slaughter. Since cattle dung is also a major source of cooking fuel, the slaughter of substantial numbers of animals would require the purchase of expensive dung substitutes, such as wood, coal, or kerosene. Cattle dung is relatively cheap because the cattle do not eat foods that can be eaten by people. Instead, they eat the stubble left in the fields and the marginal patches of grass on steep hillsides, roadside ditches, railroad embankments, and other nonarable lands. This constant scavenging gives the impression that cows are roaming around aimlessly, devouring everything in sight. But most cows have an owner, and in the cities, after poking about in the market refuse and nibbling on neighbors' lawns, each cow returns to its stall at the end of the day.

In a study of the bioenergetic balances involved in the cattle complex of villages in West Bengal, Stuart Odend'hal (1972) found that "basically, the cattle convert items of little direct human value into products of immediate human utility." Their gross energetic efficiency in supplying useful products was several times greater than that characteristic of agroindustrial beef production. He concludes that "judging the productive value of Indian cattle based on western standards is inappropriate."

Although it might be possible to maintain or exceed the present level of production of oxen and dung with substantially fewer cows of larger and better breeds, the question arises as to how these cows would be distributed among the poor farmers. Are the farmers who have only one or two decrepit animals to be driven from the land?

Aside from the problem of whether present levels of population and productivity could be maintained with fewer cows, there is the theoretically more crucial question of whether it is the taboo on slaughter that accounts for the observed ratio of cattle to people. This seems highly unlikely. Despite the ban on slaughter, Hindu farmers cull their herds and adjust sex ratios to crops, weather, and regional conditions. The cattle are killed by various indirect means equivalent to the forms of neglect discussed in Chapter 6 with respect to human population controls. In the Gangetic plain, one of the most religiously orthodox regions of India, there are over 200 oxen for every 100 cows (Vaidyanathan et al. 1982).

Stepping away from the point of view of the individual farmer, there are a number of additional reasons for concluding that the Hindu taboos have a positive rather than a negative effect on carrying capacity. The ban on slaughter, whatever its consequences for culling the herds, discourages the development of a meat-packing industry. Such an industry would be ecologically disastrous in a land as densely populated as India. In this connection it should be pointed out that the protein output of the existing system is not unimportant. Although the Indian cows are very poor milkers by Western standards, they nonetheless contribute critical if small quantities of protein to the diets of millions of people. Moreover, a considerable amount of beef does get eaten during the course of the year, since animals that die a natural death are consumed by carrion-eating outcastes. Finally, the critical function of the ban on slaughter during fam-ines should be noted. When hunger stalks the Indian countryside, the slaughter taboo helps the peasants to resist the temptation to eat their cattle. If this temptation were to win out over religious scruples, it would be impossible for them to plant new crops when the rains began. Thus the intense resistance among Hindu saints to the slaughter and consumption of beef takes on a new meaning in the context of the Indian infrastructure. In the words of Mahatma Gandhi:

> Why the cow was selected for apotheosis is obvious to me. The cow was in India the best companion. She was the giver of plenty. Not only did she give milk but she also made agriculture possible. [1954:3]

Summary

Edward Tylor defined religion as animism or the doctrine of souls. According to Tylor, from the idea of the soul the idea of all godlike beings arose, while the idea of the soul itself arose as an attempt to explain phenomena such as trances, dreams, shadows, and reflections. Tylor's definition has been criticized for failing to consider the multifunctional nature of religion and for overlooking the compelling reality of direct hallucinatory contact with extraordinary beings.

As the Jívaro belief in three souls demonstrates, each culture uses the basic concepts of animism in its own distinctive fashion.

Tylor's definition of religion was supplemented by Marett's concepts of animatism and *mana*. *Animatism* refers to the belief in an impersonal life force in people, animals, and objects. The concentration of this force gives people, animals, and objects *mana*, or the capacity to be extraordinarily powerful and successful.

It should also be noted that the Western

distinction between natural and supernatural is of limited utility for defining religion emically. As the case of the Gururumba indicates, the need for rituals to control certain entities, processes, or forces does not mean that other entities, processes, or forces can be controlled by a contrastive set of rituals. In other words, in many cultures there are no supernatural versus natural controls, only controls.

The distinction between sacred and profane realms of human experience may have greater universal validity than that between natural and supernatural. According to Durkheim, the feeling that something is sacred expresses the awe in which the hidden force of social consensus is held. Thus, although the content of the realm of the sacred may vary from one culture to another, the contrast between sacred and profane matters probably occurs universally.

Frazer tried to cope with the enormous variety of religious experience by separating religion from magic. Humility, supplication, and doubt characterize religion; routine cause and effect characterize magic. This distinction is difficult to maintain in view of the routine and coercive fashion in which animistic beings are often manipulated. There is no sharp difference between prayers and magic spells. Religion is a mix of awe and wonder, boredom and excitement, power and weakness.

The principal varieties of beliefs and rituals show broad correlations with levels of political economic organization. Four levels of religious organizations or cults can be distinguished: individualistic, shamanistic, communal, and ecclesiastical.

Eskimo religion illustrates the individualistic or do-it-yourself level. Each individual carries out a series of rituals and observes a series of taboos that are deemed essential for survival and well-being, without the help of any part-time or full-time specialist. Do-it-yourself cults, however, are not to be confused with "anything goes." Vision quests, beliefs, and rituals always follow culturally determined patterns. Even dreams are culturally patterned.

No culture is devoid of shamanistic cults, defined by the presence of part-time magico-religious experts, or shamans, who have special talents and knowledge, usually involving sleight of hand, trances, and possession. As the case of Tapirapé shamanism indicates, shamans are frequently employed to cure sick people, as well as to identify and destroy evildoers. Many shamans think they can fly and move backward and forward through time.

Communal cults, involving public rituals deemed essential for the welfare or survival of the entire social group, also occur to some extent at all political-economic levels. Two principal types of communal rituals can be distinguished: rites of solidarity and rites of passage. As illustrated by the Arunta totemic rituals, rites of solidarity reaffirm and intensify a group's sense of common identity and express in symbolic form the group's claims to territory and resources. As illustrated in the Ndembu circumcision rituals, rites of passage symbolically and publicly denote the extinction or "death" of an individual's or group's socially significant status and the acquisition or "birth" of a new socially significant status.

Finally, ecclesiastical cults are those that are dominated by a hierarchy of full-time specialists or "priests" whose knowledge and skills are usually commanded by a state-level ruling class. To preserve and enhance the well-being of the state and of the universe, historical, astronomical, and ritual information must be acquired by the ecclesiastical specialists. Ecclesiastical cults are also characterized by huge investments in buildings, monuments, and personnel and by a split between the specialist performers of ritual and the great mass of more or less passive spectators who constitute the "congregation." With the development of the state, the objective of warfare shifted from that of routing the enemy population to incorporating them within imperial systems. This brought an end to the practice of sacrificing and eating prisoners of war. A theory that explains the unique features of Aztec religion is that the animal resources of central Mexico had been depleted. It was difficult for the Aztec state to refrain from rewarding its armies with the flesh of enemy soldiers in its effort to justify, expand, and consolidate ruling-class power. The depleted nature of Aztec animal resources is shown by the prominence of insects, worms, and algae in their diet. While balanced protein rations can be obtained from such foods as well as from corn and beans, the emphasis on obtaining and consuming vertebrate flesh and dairy products reflects a universal adaptive strategy for maximizing protein, fat, mineral, and vitamin consumption. The Aztecs' consumption of human flesh was an expression of this adaptive strategy; it could not be suppressed because of the depletion of alternative sources of animal foods.

Revitalization is another category of religious phenomena that cannot be understood apart from political-economic conditions. Under political-economic stress, subordinate castes, classes, minorities, and ethnic groups develop beliefs and rituals concerned with achieving a drastic improvement in their immediate well-being and/or their well-being in a life after death. These movements have the latent capacity to attack the dominant group directly or indirectly through political or military action; on the other hand, they may turn inward and accommodate by means of passive doctrines and rituals involving individual guilt, drugs, and contemplation.

Native American revitalizations were initially violent protests against genocide and ethnocide. The Sioux put on Ghost Dance shirts to protect themselves against bullets. After the suppression of the Ghost Dance movement, revitalization returned to contemplative renewal of native traditions, as in the peyote religion. More recently, the struggle of native Americans has become more secular and legalistic.

Melanesian and New Guinea cargo revitalizations foresaw the ancestors returning in ships laden with European trade goods. Later, airplanes and spaceships were substituted for sailing ships and steamboats. Cargo cults reflect a misunderstanding of industrial state systems by peoples who are living on the village level of political evolution when they are brought into the wage-labor system.

Religious beliefs and rituals also exhibit adaptive relationships in the form of taboos. Taboos often take the form of sacred injunctions that resolve ambiguities and control the temptation to engage in behavior, such as incest, that has short-term benefits but is socially disruptive in the long run. Many taboos on animals whose exploitation leads to ambiguous ecological and economic consequences can be seen in the same light. The ancient Israelite pig taboo, for example, can be understood as an adaptation to the changing costs and benefits of pig rearing brought about by population increase, deforestation, and desertification. Similar short-term versus long-term cost-benefits among villages of different sizes in the Amazon tropical forest may also account for the pattern of animal use and nonuse and taboos associated with various intensities of sacredness. A final example of the way in which taboos and whole religions adapt to changing political, economic, and ecological contexts is represented by the sacred cow of India.

Chapter 16

ART

❧❧❧

This chapter is concerned with aspects of super-structure: the thought and behavior associated with painting, music, poetry, sculpture, dance, and other media of artistic creation. It seeks to explain why the specific forms and styles of artistic expression vary from one culture to another. We will see that art is not an isolated sector of human experience. It is intimately connected with and embedded in other aspects of sociocultural systems.

What Is Art?

Alexander Alland (1977:39) defines art as "play with form producing some aesthetically successful transformation-representation." The key ingredients in this definition are "play," "form," "aesthetic," and "transformation." *Play* is an enjoyable, self-rewarding aspect of activity that cannot be accounted for simply by the utilitarian or survival functions of that activity. *Form* designates a set of restrictions on how the art play is to be organized in time and space—the rules of the game of art. *Aesthetic* designates the existence of a universal human capacity for an emotionally charged response of appreciation and pleasure when art is successful. *Transformation-representation* refers to the communicative aspect of art. Art always represents something—communicates information—but this something is never represented in its literal shape, sound, color, movement, or feeling. To be art, as distinct from other forms of communication, the representation must be transformed into some metaphoric or symbolic statement, movement,

image, or object that stands for whatever is being represented. A portrait, for example, no matter how "realistic," can only be a transformation-representation of the individual it depicts.

As Alland points out, play, adherence to form, and an aesthetic sense are found in many nonhuman animals. Chimpanzees, for example, like to play with paints (Figure 16.1). Their adherence to form can be demonstrated by their placement of designs in the center of blank spaces or by their balancing of designs on different parts of a page. (They don't simply paint right off the page.) An aesthetic sense can be inferred by their repeated attempts to copy accurately simple designs such as circles and triangles. Moreover, as we have seen in Chapter 4, the capacity to use symbols and to learn rules of symbolic transformation is not entirely confined to human beings. The 3-year-old chimp Moja drew a bird and gave the sign for it. The trainer tried to make sure that it was a bird rather than a berry, so he asked her to draw a berry, which she promptly did (Hill 1978:98).

Nonetheless, just as grammatical language

(a)

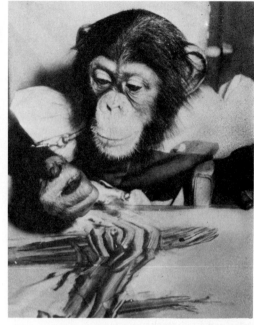

(b)

Figure 16.1   Chimpanzee artists.
(a), (b) *A 2-year-old chimpanzee finger painting at the Baltimore Zoo. Note attempt to center painting. (c) A chimpanzee named Candy exhibits her artwork at the San Francisco Zoo.*

remains rudimentary among apes in nature, so too does their artistry. Although the rudiments of art can be found in our primate heritage, only *Homo sapiens* can justly be called the "artistic animal."

Art as a Cultural Category

Although it is possible to identify art as a category of thought and behavior in all human cultures, an emic distinction between art and

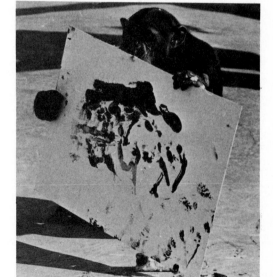

(c)

nonart is not universal (just as the distinction between natural and supernatural is not universal). What Westerners mean by *art* is a particular emic category of activities and products that stands opposed to the category of nonart. In Western civilization a particular performance is deemed artistic if specialists who make or judge art and who control the museums, conservatories, critical journals, and other organizations and institutions devoted to art as a livelihood and style of life judge it to be art (Becker 1982). Most cultures lack any semblance of an art establishment. This does not mean they lack art or artistic standards. A pointed design on a pot or a rock, a carved mask or club, or a song or chant in a puberty ordeal is subject to critical evaluation by both performers and spectators. All cultures distinguish between less satisfactory and more satisfactory aesthetic experiences in decorative, pictorial, and expressive matters.

Basic to the modern Western idea of art versus nonart is the exclusion of designs, stories, and artifacts that have a definite use in day-to-day subsistence activities and that are produced primarily for practical purposes or for commercial sale. Carpenters are distinguished from people who make wooden sculptures, bricklayers from architects, house painters from those who apply paint to canvas, and so forth. A similar opposition between art and practicality is seldom found in other cultures. Many works of art are produced and performed in complete harmony with utilitarian objectives. People everywhere, whether specialists or nonspecialists, derive pleasure from playfully embellishing and transforming the contours and surfaces of pots, fabrics, wood, and metal products (Figure 16.2). All cultures, however, recognize that certain individuals are more skilled than others in making utilitarian objects and in embellishing them

(a)

(b)

(c)

(e)

(d)

(f)

Figure 16.2   Art has many media.
Native American cultures produced these objects. (a) Gold mummy mask with green stone eyes; Chumu, Peru.
(b) Globular basket with coiled weave; Chumash, California. (c) Feathers of blue and yellow form the design
of a Tapirapé mask; Brazil. (d) Painted wooden kero, or beaker, representing ocelot head; Inca, Peru. (e)
Ceramic jar; Nazca, Peru. (f) Blanket, in blue, black, and white, with stripes and frets; Navajo.

with pleasureable designs. Most anthropologists regard skilled wood carvers, basketmakers, potters, weavers, or sandalmakers as artists.

Art and Invention

As Alland (1977:24) suggests, play is a form of exploratory behavior that permits human beings to try out new and possibly useful responses in a controlled and protected context. The playful creative urge that lies behind art, therefore, is probably closely related to the creative urge that lies behind the development of science, technology, and new institutions. Art and technology often interact, and it is difficult to say where technology ends and art begins, or where art ends and technology begins. The beautiful symmetry of nets, baskets, and woven fabrics is essential for their proper functioning. Even in the development of media of musical expression there may be technological benefits. For example, there was probably some kind of feedback between the invention of the bow as a hunting weapon and the twanging of taut strings for musical effect (Figure 16.3). No one can say which came first, but cultures with bows and arrows invariably have musical strings. Wind instruments, blowguns, pistons, and bellows are all related. Similarly, metallurgy and chemistry relate to experimentation with the ornamental shape, texture, and color of ceramic and textile products. Thus, it is practical to encourage craftworkers to experiment with new techniques and materials. Small wonder that many cultures regard technical virtuosity as *mana* (see page 285). Others regard it as the gift of the gods, as in the classical Greek idea of the Muses—goddesses of orators, dancers, and musicians—whose assistance was needed if worthy artistic performances were to occur.

Figure 16.3   !Kung San plays the bow.
Thumb plucks the string; mouth opens and closes, moving along string to control tone and resonance. Which came first: bow for hunting, or bow for making music?

Art and Cultural Patterning

Most artwork is deliberately fashioned in the image of preexisting forms. It is the task of the artist to replicate these forms by original combinations of culturally standardized elements —familiar and pleasing sounds, colors, lines, shapes, movements, and so on. Of course, there must always be some playful and creative ingredient, or it will not be art. On the other hand, if the transformation-representation is to communicate something—and it must communicate something if it is to be a successful work of art—the rules of the game cannot be the artist's own private invention. Complete originality, therefore, is not what most cultures strive after in their art.

It is the repetition of traditional and familiar elements that accounts for the major differences among the artistic products of different cultures. For example, Northwest Coast native American sculpture is well known for its consistent attention to animal and human motifs rendered in such a way as to indicate internal as

Figure 16.4   Masks.
(a) Mask within a mask within a mask. Whale
conceals bird, which conceals human face, which
conceals face of wearer; another Kwakiutl
masterpiece. (b) Mask within a mask. Wearer of the
Kwakiutl mask uses strings to pull eagle apart,
revealing human face.

(a)

well as external organs. These organs are symmetrically arranged within bounded geometri-
cal forms (Figure 16.4). Maori sculpture, on the
other hand, requires that wooden surfaces be
broken into bold but intricate filigrees and
whorls (Figure 16.5). Among the Mochica of
ancient Peru, the sculptural medium was pottery, and the Mochica pots are famous for their
representational realism in portraiture and in
depictions of domestic and sexual behavior
(Figure 16.6). Hundreds of other easily recog-
nizable and distinctive art styles of different
cultures can be identified. The continuity and
integrity of these styles provide the basic con-

(b)

Figure 16.5   Maori canoe prow.
The Maori of New Zealand are among the world's
greatest wood carvers.

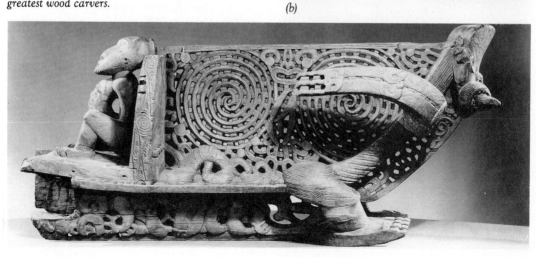

Figure 16.6 Mochica pot.
A pre-Columbian portrait made by the Mochica of
northern Peru.

bility of their audience to appreciate and understand true genius.

Thus the creative, playful, and transformational aspects of modern art have gotten the upper hand over the formal and representational aspects (Figure 16.7). Contemporary Euramerican artists consciously strive to be the originators of entirely new formal rules. They compete to invent new transformations to replace the traditional ones. Modern aesthetic standards hold that originality is more important than intelligibility. Indeed, a work of art that is too easily understood may be condemned. Many art critics more or less consciously take it for granted that novelty must result in a certain amount of obscurity. What accounts for this obsession with being original?

One important influence is the reaction to mass production. Mass production leads to a downgrading of technical virtuosity. It also leads to a downgrading of all artwork that closely resembles the objects or performances others have produced. Another factor to be considered is the involvement of the modern

text for a people's understanding and liking of art (Price 1989).

Establishment art in modern Western culture is unique in its emphasis on formal originality. It is taken as normal that art must be interpreted and explained by experts in order to be understood and appreciated. Since the end of the nineteenth century, the greatest artists of the Western art establishment are those who break with tradition, introduce new formal rules, and at least for a time render their work incomprehensible to a large number of people. Joined to this de-emphasis of tradition is the peculiar and recent Western notion of artists as lonely people struggling in poverty against limitations set by the preexisting capa-

Figure 16.7 What does it mean?
Fur-covered cup, saucer, and spoon. Cup is 4⅜"
diameter, saucer is 9¾" diameter, and spoon is 8"
long. (Méret Oppenheimer, Object [1936].)

artist in a commercial market in which supply perennially exceeds demand. Part-time band- and village-level artists are concerned with being original only to the extent that it enhances the aesthetic enjoyment of their work. Their livelihood does not depend on obtaining an artistic identity and a personal following. Still another factor to be considered is the high rate of cultural change in modern societies. To some extent, the emphasis on artistic originality merely reflects this rate of change. Finally, the alienating and isolating tendencies of modern mass society may also play a role. Much modern art reflects the loneliness, puzzlement, and anxiety of the creative individual in a depersonalized and hostile urban, industrial milieu.

Art and Religion

The history and ethnography of art are inseparable from the history and ethnography of religion. Art is intimately associated with all four organizational levels of religion. For example, at the individualistic level, magical songs are often included among the revelations granted the vision seekers of the Great Plains. Even the preparation of trophy heads among the Jívaro must meet aesthetic standards, and singing and chanting are widely used during shamanistic performances. There are many aesthetic components in the Tapirapé shaman's description (page 294) of how he met the *munpí anká* forest spirits.

On the communal level, puberty rituals, as among the Ndembu (page 299), provide occasions for dancing and myth and storytelling. Body painting is also widely practiced in communal ceremonies, as among the Arunta. Singing, dancing, and the wearing of masks are common at both puberty and funeral rituals.

(a)   (b)

Figure 16.8   Ba Kota funerary figures.
The Ba Kota of the Gabon Republic place the skeletal remains of dead chiefs in bark boxes or baskets surmounted by Mbulu-ngulu guardian figures of wood faced with brass or copper sheets or strips. Although each figure expresses the creative individuality of the artist, they conform to the same stylistic pattern.

Much artistic effort is expended in the preparation of religiously significant funeral equipment such as coffins and graveposts (Figures 16.8 and 16.9). Many cultures include among a deceased person's grave goods ceremonial artifacts such as pottery and clubs, points, and other weapons. Ancestors and gods are often depicted in statues and masks that are kept in men's houses or in shrines (Figure 16.10). *Churingas* (page 297), the Arunta's most sacred objects, are artfully incised with whorls and loops depicting the route followed by the ancestors during the dream time.

Figure 16.9   *Asmat gravepost.*
Around the world, much talent has been lavished
on commemorating the dead, but styles and media
vary enormously.

Figure 16.10   *Art and architecture.*
Brightly painted faces on a men's house in Sepik
River basin, New Guinea.

Finally, on the ecclesiastical level, art and religion are fused in pyramids, monumental avenues, stone statuary, monolithic calendar carvings, temples, altars, priestly garments, and a nearly infinite variety of ritual ornaments and sacred paraphernalia.

It is clear that art, religion, and magic satisfy many similar psychological needs in human beings. They are media for expressing sentiments and emotions not easily expressed in ordinary life. They impart a sense of mastery over or communion with unpredictable events and mysterious, unseen powers. They impose human meanings and values on an indifferent world — a world that has no humanly intelligi-

ble meanings and values of its own. They seek to penetrate behind the façade of ordinary appearance into the true, cosmic significance of things. And they use illusions, dramatic tricks, and sleight of hand to get people to believe in them.

Art and Politics

Art is also intimately related to politics. This is especially clear in the context of state-sponsored art. As we have seen, in stratified societies, religion is a means of social control. The skills of the artist are harnessed by the ruling class to implant religious notions of obedience and to sanctify the status quo (Figure 16.11). Contrary to the popular modern image of the artist as a free spirit disdainful of authority, most state-level art is politically conservative (Pasztory 1984:20). Ecclesiastical art generally interprets the world in conformity with prevailing myths and ideologies justifying inequities and exploitation. Art makes the gods visible as idols. Gazing on massive stone blocks carved as if by superhuman hands, commoners comprehend the necessity for subservience. They are awed by the immense size of pyramids and fascinated and befuddled by processions, prayers, pomp, and the sacrifices of priests in dramatic settings — golden altars, colonnaded temples, great vaulted roofs, huge ramps and stairways, windows through which only the light from heaven passes (Figure 16.12).

The church and state have been the greatest patrons of the arts in all but the last few hundred years of history. With the rise of capitalism, ecclesiastical and civil institutions in the

Figure 16.11 Gold death mask of Tut.
Another example of the interrelationship of art, religion, and politics.

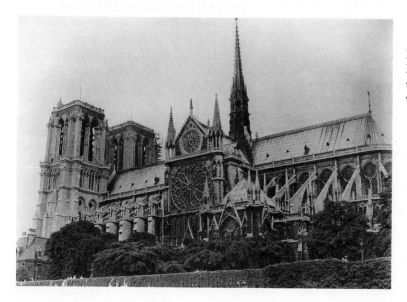

Figure 16.12 Art and religion.
Notre Dame Cathedral, Paris. No one ever had to ask what it means, but how it was built remains a mystery.

West became more decentralized, and wealthy individuals largely replaced church and state as patrons of the arts. Individualized sponsorship promoted greater flexibility and freedom of expression. Politically neutral, secular, and even revolutionary and sacrilegious themes became common. The arts became established as individualistic, secular forms of expression and entertainment. To protect and preserve its newfound autonomy, the art establishment adopted the doctrine of "art for art's sake." But once they were free to express themselves as they saw fit, artists were no longer sure what they wanted to express. They devoted themselves more and more to idiosyncratic and obscure symbols organized into novel and unintelligible patterns, as noted earlier in this chapter. And the patrons of art, concerned less and less with communication, increasingly looked toward the acquisition and sponsorship of art as a prestigious commercial venture that yielded substantial profits, tax deductions, and a hedge against inflation.

The Evolution of Music and Dance

Some anthropologists hold that the influence on art of structural and infrastructural components extends directly into the formal characteristics and aesthetic standards of different cultural styles. According to Allan Lomax and his associates (Lomax 1968; Lomax and Arensberg 1977), for example, certain broad characteristics of song, music, and dance are closely correlated with a culture's level of subsistence. Band and village peoples in general tend to have a different complex of music, song, and dance than do chiefdoms and states. Dividing cultures into those that are low and those that are high on the scale of subsistence technology leads to the following correlations:

Musical intervals. The less advanced subsistence systems employ musical scales in which notes are widely separated — that is, have intervals of a third or more. Advanced subsistence systems employ scales that are marked by more and smaller intervals.

Repetition in song text. The less advanced subsistence cultures employ more repetition in their lyrics — fewer words, over and over again.

Complexity and type of orchestra. Advanced subsistence is correlated with musical performances involving more performers and a greater variety of instruments. Less advanced subsistence systems use only one or two kinds of instruments and small numbers of each.

Dance styles. The advanced subsistence systems are correlated with dance styles in which many body parts — fingers, wrists, arms, torso, legs, feet, toes — have distinctive movements to make or "parts to play." Also, the more advanced the subsistence system the more the dance style tends to emphasize complex curving motions, as opposed to simple up-and-down or side-to-side steps like hopping or shuffling.

Lomax sees these correlations between subsistence and art as resulting from direct and indirect influence of subsistence. Large, complex orchestration, for example, reflects the structural ability of a society to form large, coordinated groups. Dance styles, on the other hand, may simply express the characteristic movements employed in using such implements of production as digging sticks versus plows or complex machines. Some dances can be regarded as training for work, warfare, or self-defense. Obviously, there are many other functions of dance (Box 16.1).

Box 16.1

∽∾✺∾∾

SOME SOCIAL FUNCTIONS OF MUSIC, SONG, AND DANCE

1. Emotes: Lets people "blow off steam," makes them feel good.
2. Socializes: Maintains traditions.
3. Educates: Develops poise and confidence in performance.
4. Bonds: Creates a sense of togetherness among performers.
5. Rallies: Prepares for dangerous situations (e.g., warfare and journeys).
6. Intimidates: Lets people "show their stuff."
7. Worships: Brings people closer to the gods.
8. Seduces: Arouses sexual passions, displays charms.
9. Coordinates: Gets people to work or move together, as in sea chanties or military marches.
10. Entertains: Prevents boredom.

Lomax's correlations have been criticized on technical grounds relating to sampling and coding procedures (see Kaeppler 1978). Nonetheless, Lomax's attempt to measure and compare music and dance styles, and to relate them to social structure and subsistence constitutes an important avenue of approach.

The Complexity of Primitive Art: Campa Rhetoric

Westerners must guard against the notion that art among band and village societies is necessarily more simple or naive than art in modern industrial societies (Titon 1984). Although, as we have just seen, many stylistic aspects of art have undergone an evolution from simple to more complex forms, other aspects may have been as complex among Stone Age hunter-gatherers as they are today. The case of Campa rhetoric illustrates this point.

Rhetoric is the art of persuasive public discourse and is closely related to the theatrical arts. As Gerald Weiss (1977b) has discovered, the preliterate Campa, who live in eastern Peru near the headwaters of the Amazon River, use most of the important rhetorical devices cultivated by the great philosophers and orators of ancient Greece and Rome. Their object in public discourse is not merely to inform, but to persuade and convince. "Campa narration is 'a separate time,' where a spellbinding relationship between narrator and audience is developed, with powerful rhetorical devices employed to create and enhance the quality of that relationship" (1977b:173).

Here are a few examples of these devices, as translated by Weiss from the Campa language, which belongs to the native American family of languages known as Arawak:

Rhetorical questions. The speaker makes the point that the Campa are deficient in their worship of their sky god, the sun, by asking a question that the speaker himself or herself will then answer. *Do we supplicate him, he here, he who lives in the sky, the sun? We do not know how to supplicate him.*

Iterations (effect by repetition). The speaker imparts an emphatic, graphic, cinematic quality to the point by repeating some key words. The enemy comes out of the lake: *And so they emerged in great numbers—he saw them emerge, emerge, emerge, emerge, emerge, emerge, emerge, emerge, emerge, all, all.*

Imagery and metaphor. Death is alluded to in the phrase *The earth will eat him.* The body is described as *The clothing of the soul.*

Appeal to evidence. To prove that the oilbird was formerly human in shape: *Yes, he was formerly human—doesn't he have whiskers?*

Appeal to authority. *They told me long ago, the elders, they who heard these words, long ago, so it was.*

Antithesis (effect by contrast). A hummingbird is about to raise the sky rope, which the other larger creatures have failed to do: *They are all big whereas I am small and chubby.*

In addition, the Campa orator uses a wide variety of gestures, exclamations, sudden calls for attention ("watch out, here it comes"); asides ("imagine it, then"; "careful that you don't believe, now"). Altogether, Weiss lists 19 formal rhetorical devices used by the Campa.

Myth and Binary Contrasts

Anthropologists have found considerable evidence suggesting that certain kinds of formal structures recur in widely different traditions of oral and written literature, including myths and folktales. These structures are characterized by binary contrasts—that is, by two elements or themes that can be viewed as standing in diametric opposition to each other. Many examples of recurrent binary contrasts can be found in Western religion, literature, and mythology: good versus bad, up versus down, male versus female, cultural versus natural, young versus old, and so forth. According to the French anthropologist Lévi-Strauss, the

founder of the research strategy known as structuralism (see Appendix), the reason these binary contrasts recur so often is that the human brain is "wired" in such a way as to make binary contrasts especially appealing, or "good to think." From the structuralist point of view, the main task of the anthropological study of literature, mythology, and folklore is to identify the common, unconscious binary contrasts that lie beneath the surface of human thought and to show how these binary contrasts undergo unconscious transformation-representations.

Consider the familiar tale of Cinderella: A mother has two daughters and one stepdaughter. The two daughters are older, the stepdaughter is younger; the older ones are ugly and mean, while Cinderella is beautiful and kind. The older sisters are aggressive; Cinderella is passive. Through a kind fairy godmother, as opposed to her mean stepmother, Cinderella goes to the ball, dances with the prince, and loses her magical shoe. Her sisters have big feet, she has little feet. Cinderella wins the prince. The unconscious binary oppositions in the deep structure of this story might include:

passive	*aggressive*
younger	*older*
small	*large*
good	*evil*
beautiful	*ugly*
culture	*nature*
fairy godmother	*stepmother*

Structuralists contend that the enjoyment people derive from such tales and their durability across space and time derive mainly from the unconscious oppositions and their familiar yet surprising representations.

Structuralist analyses can be extended from the realm of myth and ritual to the entire fabric of social life. According to David Hicks, who studied the Tetum of Timor in Indonesia, Tetum culture as a whole is structured by the following "binary matrix":

human beings	*ghosts*
secular	*sacred*
secular world	*sacred world*
above	*below*
men	*women*
right	*left*
superior	*inferior*
wife-givers	*wife-takers*
aristocrats	*commoners*
secular authority	*sacred authority*
elder brother	*younger brother*

Any single binary contrast can symbolize any other (Hicks 1976:107) — that is, in contrasting men and women, one could just as readily be contrasting elder brothers with younger brothers (among the Tetum, younger brothers must serve elder brothers just as women must serve men). The secular, above-ground, masculine world contrasts with the ghostly, sacred, below-ground, feminine world. Thus Tetum mythology recounts how the first human emerged from vaginalike holes in the ground and how after leading a secular life on the surface of the earth, humans return to the sacred world below and to the ghostly ancestors. Tetum house architecture also participates in the same set of symbolic oppositions (Figure 16.13). The house has two entrances; the back entrance for the women leads to the "womb" or women's part of the house, which contains the hearth and a sacred house post. The front

Figure 16.13   Tetum house.
Women's entrance is around the back; men's entrance is through the front door.

entrance is for the men and leads to the male living quarters.

Structural analyses of literature, art, myths, rituals, and religion abound in anthropology. However, they are surrounded by considerable controversy, primarily because it is not clear whether the binary matrices discerned by the anthropologists really exist as unconscious realities in the minds of the people being studied. It is always possible to reduce complex and subtle symbols to less complex and gross symbols and then finally to emerge with such flat oppositions as culture versus nature or male versus female (Harris 1979b).

Summary

Creative play, formal structure, aesthetic feelings, and symbolic transformations are the essential ingredients in art. Although the capacity for art is foreshadowed in the behavior of nonhuman primates, only *Homo sapiens* is capable of art involving "transformation-representations." The distinctive human capacity for art is thus closely related to the distinctive human capacity for the symbolic transformation that underlies the semantic universality of human language.

Western emic definitions of art depend on the existence of art authorities and critics who place many examples of play, structured aesthetic, and symbolic transformation into the category of nonart. The distinction between crafts and art is part of this tradition. Anthropologists regard skilled craftspersons as artists.

Art has adaptive functions in relation to creative changes in other sectors of social life. Art and technology influence each other, as in the case of instruments of music and the hunt, or in the search for new shapes, colors, textures, and materials in ceramics and textiles.

Despite the emphasis on creative innovation, most cultures have art traditions or styles that maintain formal continuity through time. This makes it possible to identify the styles of cultures such as the Northwest Coast, Maori, or Mochica. The continuity and integrity of such styles provide the basic context for a people's understanding of and the liking for the artist's creative transformations. Establishment art in modern Western culture is unique in emphasizing structural or formal creativity as well as creative transformations. This results in the isolation of the artist. Lack of communication may be caused by factors such as the reaction to mass production, commercialization of art markets, a rapid rate of cultural change, and the depersonalized milieu of urban industrial life.

Art and religion are closely related. This can be seen in the songs of the vision quest, preparation of shrunken heads, singing and chanting in shamanistic performances, Tapirapé shamanistic myths, Ndembu circumcision, storytelling, singing and dancing, Arunta *churingas*, and many other aspects of individual, shamanistic, communal, and ecclesiastical cults. Art and religion satisfy many similar psychological needs, and it is often difficult to tell them apart.

Art and politics are also closely related. This is clear in state-sponsored ecclesiastical art, much of which functions to keep people in awe of their rulers. It is only in recent times, with the rise of decentralized capitalist states, that art has enjoyed any significant degree of freedom from direct political control. Even today, however, many artists in both capitalist and socialist societies regard art as an important medium of political expression, both conservative and revolutionary.

To the extent that bands, villages, chiefdoms, and states represent evolutionary levels, and to the extent that art is functionally related to technology, economy, politics, religion, and other aspects of the universal cultural pattern, it is clear that there has been an evolution of the content of art. There is evidence that styles of song, music, and dance — including musical intervals, repetition in song texts, complexity and type of orchestra, body part involvement, and amount of curvilinear motion — have also undergone evolutionary changes. The example of Campa rhetoric shows that extreme caution must be exercised in judging the complexity and sophistication of preliterate art styles.

Structuralism attempts to interpret the surface content of myths, rituals, and other expressive performances in terms of a series of unconscious universal binary oppositions. Common binary oppositions can be found in the Cinderella myth and in Tetum cosmology, ritual, and house architecture.

Chapter 17

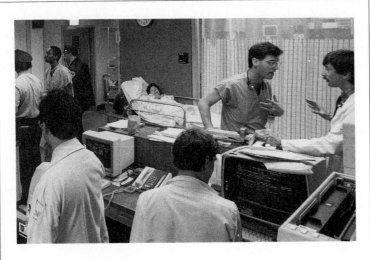

APPLIED
ANTHROPOLOGY

❧❧❧

This chapter explores the relationships between anthropological research and the achievement of practical goals by organizations that sponsor or use such research. A variety of cases illustrating the distinctive strong points of applied anthropology will be set forth and analyzed.

What Is Applied Anthropology?

Since World War II, an increasing number of cultural anthropologists have become involved occasionally or regularly in research that has more or less immediate practical applications. They are known as practitioners of *applied anthropology.*

The core of applied anthropology consists of research commissioned by public or private organizations in the hope of achieving practical goals of interest to those organizations. Such organizations include federal, state, local, and international government bureaus and agencies, such as the U.S. Department of Agriculture, the Department of Defense, the National Park Service, the Agency for International Development, the Bureau of Indian Affairs, the World Bank, the World Health Organization, the Food and Agricultural Organization, various drug abuse agencies, education and urban planning departments of major cities, and municipal hospitals, to mention only a few. In addition, private organizations that have hired or contracted with anthropologists to carry out

practical, goal-oriented research include major industrial corporations, foundations such as Planned Parenthood and the Population Council, and various branches of the Rockefeller and Ford Foundations' International Crops Research Institutes (Chambers 1985; Willigen 1986).

It should be emphasized that cultural anthropologists do not have a monopoly on applied anthropology: Physical anthropology, archaeology, and linguistics also have their applied aspects. But here we shall deal mainly with the applied aspects of cultural anthropology.

Research, Theory, and Action

Although the hallmark of applied anthropology is involvement in research aimed at achieving a special practical result, the extent to which the applied anthropologist actually participates in bringing about the desired result varies from one assignment to another. At one extreme, the applied anthropologist may merely be charged with developing information the sponsoring organization needs in order to make decisions. In other instances, the applied anthropologist may be asked to evaluate the feasibility of a planned program or even to draw up a more or less detailed set of plans for achieving a desired goal (Husain 1976). More rarely, the anthropologist, alone or as a member of a team, may be responsible for planning, implementing, and evaluating a whole program from beginning to end. When anthropologists help to implement a program, they are spoken of as practicing *action anthropology* (see page 355).

Note that the separation of applied from nonapplied anthropology shades off imperceptibly as theoretical and abstract interests come to dominate specific and concrete goals. It is often difficult to draw a line between applied and nonapplied research. Some anthropologists maintain that abstract theorizing can itself be construed as applied anthropology if it provides a general set of principles to which any action program must conform if it is to achieve success. For example, general theories about the causes of peasant backwardness and of urban poverty (see pages 221 and 224) can have important practical consequences even though the research behind these theories may not have been sponsored by organizations with the expressed goal of eliminating (or perpetuating) underdevelopment and urban poverty. Applied anthropology premised on weak or blatantly incorrect theory is misapplied anthropology (R. Cohen 1984b).

Moreover, we must bear in mind that anthropologists who refrain from involvement in sponsored, practical, goal-oriented research may have practical ends in view for their descriptions and theories, but may be unable to obtain the support of suitable organizations for putting their findings to practical use. For example, the author of this book was sponsored by the Ford Foundation to carry out research on the nature of cultural change and race relations in what was then (1956–1957) the Portuguese colony of Moçambique. Although neither I nor the sponsoring foundation was explicitly concerned with a definite set of practical goals, I at least had the hope that the findings would be of some practical use in helping the people of Moçambique to achieve their independence from Portugal. I tried to render this help by publishing materials that documented the severely repressive and exploitative nature of Portugal's colonial system, the hope being that the U.S. State Department would therefore be persuaded to change its policy of endorsing and underwriting the perpetuation of Portuguese rule in Africa (Harris 1958).

Ironically, the founder of the Moçambique liberation movement, Dr. Eduardo Mondlane, was a sociologist-anthropologist who received his Ph.D. from Northwestern University. Mondlane can thus be said to have been involved in a form of action anthropology that has greatly influenced the course of events in southern Africa. He thought of himself both as a social scientist and as a political leader (Mondlane 1969).

What Do Applied Anthropologists Have to Offer?

The effectiveness of applied anthropology is enhanced by three distinctive attributes of general anthropology (see page 4): (1) relative freedom from ethnocentrism and Western biases, (2) concern with holistic sociocultural systems, and (3) concern with ordinary etic behavioral events as well as with the emics of mental life.

DELINEATION OF ETHNOCENTRISM

The applied anthropologist can be of assistance to sponsoring organizations by exposing the ethnocentric, culture-bound assumptions that often characterize cross-cultural contacts and prevent change-oriented programs from achieving their goals. For example, Western-trained agricultural scientists tend to dismiss peasant forms of agriculture as backward and inefficient, thereby overlooking the cumulative wisdom embodied in age-old practices handed down from generation to generation. The attitude of Western experts toward the use of cattle in India is a case in point (see page 313). Anthropologists are more likely to reserve judgment about a traditional practice such as using cattle to plow fields, whereas a narrowly trained specialist might automatically wish to replace the animals with tractors. Again, applied anthropologists are likely to see that the attempt to model a health care delivery system after those with which Western-trained doctors are familiar may represent nothing more than an attempt to replace the culturally unfamiliar with the culturally familiar. Expensive staffs, costly hospitals, and the latest electronic gadgetry, for example, are not necessarily the way to improve the quality of health services (Cattle 1977:38). The American notion that milk is the "perfect food" has led to much grief and dismay throughout the world, since many populations in less developed countries to which tons of surplus milk in powdered form were sent as nutritional supplements lacked the enzyme needed to digest lactose, the predominant form of sugar in milk (Harris 1985). Western notions of hygiene automatically suggest that mothers must be persuaded not to chew food and then put it in their babies' mouths. Yet it was found that in the case of the Pijoan Indians of the U.S.

Southwest, this custom was an effective way to combat the iron-deficiency anemia to which the infants who are fed exclusively on mother's milk are subject (Freedman 1977:8).

A HOLISTIC VIEW

As industrial society becomes increasingly specialized and *technocratic* (that is, dominated by narrowly trained experts who have mastered techniques and the use of machines others do not understand), the need for anthropology's holistic view of social life becomes more urgent. In diverse fields (e.g., education, health, economic development), there has been a convergence toward using narrow sets of easily quantified variables in order to verify objectively the accomplishment or lack of accomplishment of an organization's goals. All too often, however, the gain in verifiability is accomplished at the expense of a loss in "validity" (or "meaningfulness"). Easily quantified variables may represent only a small part of a much bigger system whose larger set of difficult-to-measure variables has the capacity to cancel out the observed effects of the small set of variables (Bernard 1981:5). For example, after World War II the U.S. auto industry found it could earn more money by building heavier and more powerful cars without paying too much attention to the question of how long the cars would function without need of repairs. Other sets of variables — namely, the ecological consequences of auto emission pollution, the political and military conditions that made it possible for the United States to enjoy low oil prices, and the perception by foreign auto producers that there was a market for small, fuel-efficient, reliable, and long-lasting vehicles — were considered irrelevant to the task of maximizing the U.S. auto industry's profits. Hence what ap-

---

Box 17.1

❧

WITHOUT HOLISM: AN ANDEAN FIASCO

Under the auspices of an international development program, experts from Australia tried to get the peasant Indians of Chimborazo Province in Ecuador to substitute high-yield Australian merino sheep for the traditional scrawny breeds the Indians owned. No one wanted the sheep, despite the offer to let the Indians have them free if used for breeding purposes. Finally, one "progressive" Indian accepted the offer and successfully raised a flock of cross-bred merinos that were far woolier and heavier than the traditional Indian flocks. Unfortunately, the Indians of Chimborazo live in a caste-structured society. Non-Indian farmers who live in the lower valleys resented the attention being paid to the Indians; they began to

fear that the Indians would be emboldened to press for additional economic and social gains, which would undermine their own positions. The merinos caught someone's attention, and the whole flock was herded into a truck and stolen. The rustlers were well protected by public opinion, which regarded the animals as "too good for the Indians anyway." The "progressive" innovator was left as the only one in the village without sheep. Variables such as ethnic and class antagonism, opportunities for theft, and the political subservience of peasants are not part of the expertise of sheep breeders, but awareness of these factors nonetheless proved to be essential to the achievement of their goals.

---

peared in a narrow context to be a highly objective measure of success (large profits and domination of the U.S. auto market) turned out in a longer time frame to be devoid of validity.

Thus, in commonsense language, anthropological holism boils down to being aware of the long term as well as the short term, the distant as well as the near, parts other than the one being studied, and the whole as well as the parts. Without these perspectives, even the seemingly straightforward and simple project can end up as a disaster (Box 17.1).

AN ETIC VIEW OF ORGANIZATIONS

Technification and specialization are usually accompanied by the growth of bureaucracy. An essential component of bureaucracy is an emic plan by which the units within an organization are related to each other and according to which the individuals are expected to perform their tasks. As in most sociocultural systems, there is considerable likelihood that the etic behavior of organizations and situations differs from the mental emics of the bureaucratic plan. Anthropologists who are trained to approach social life from the ground up, and who are concerned with everyday events as they actually unfold often can provide a view of organizations and situations that the bureaucracy lacks. Hospitals as studied by applied anthropologists, for example, are a rich source of jarring discrepancies between the emics of various staff specialists and the etics of patient care. From the perspective of the hospital bureaucracy, its various rules and regulations are designed to promote the health and well-being of patients. In fact, numerous studies have shown that the main effect of many rules and regulations is to shock and depersonalize the patients and to create in them a level of apprehension comparable to that which can be observed in an Ndembu boy awaiting the rite of circumcision in the "place of death" (see page 299). On entering the hospital, patients are stripped of their clothing and their money. Each becomes a case in a numbered room wearing a numbered bracelet for identification (the same way newborn babies are numbered). Groups of costumed personnel (some even wearing masks) speak to them in a strange new dialect: "Did you _void_ this morning?" "When was your last B.M.?" (bowel movement). "You're going to have an EEG" (electroencephalogram). Patients are awakened, fed, and put to sleep according to a rigid schedule, and they are kept uninformed about their condition and what is happening to them (Figure 17.1). One is forced to conclude that many hospital rules exist primarily for the convenience of the staff and have an adverse effect on the health and well-being of the patients (Foster and Anderson 1978:170–171).

Figure 17.1   Emergency room of a metropolitan hospital. Where are the patients?

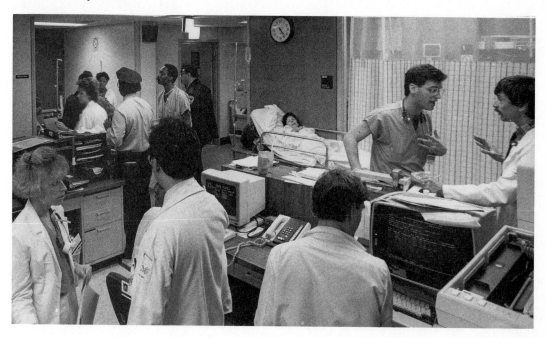

The kind of work being done by applied anthropologists covers a range of cases far too broad to be surveyed in a single chapter. The following examples have been selected to illustrate the great diversity of problems that can benefit from an anthropological approach.

or members of interdisciplinary projects aimed at raising Third World standards of living (Barlett and Brown 1985). More rarely, anthropologists have themselves been appointed to direct, plan, implement, and evaluate development projects from beginning to end.

Agricultural Development

Anthropologists have traditionally carried out field research in less developed countries, not only among remote band and autonomous village peoples but among peasants as well. In fact, as was said in Chapter 12, anthropologists have studied peasants more often than they have studied any other social type. Their knowledge of the conditions and aspirations of peasant life makes anthropologists useful as consultants to

The Vicos Project

A classic example of an anthropological development effort took place in the 1950s under the auspices of the Cornell-Peru Vicos project. Vicos was a *hacienda* (a large farm on which a variety of crops are grown, worked by resident peasants) in the Peruvian highlands inhabited by 1703 serfs (Figure 17.2). Cornell University leased the *hacienda* and turned it over to anthropologist Allan Holmberg with the objec-

Figure 17.2   Vicos.
A community work party begins its potato harvest.

tive of raising the Indians' standard of living and making them economically independent. At the time of intervention, the people of Vicos were unable to grow enough food to feed themselves, their farming lands were broken up into thousands of tiny scattered plots, their potato crop was subject to frequent failure, and they lacked motivation for producing a surplus, since they were constantly in debt or at the beck and call of the landlords.

Under the feudal rules of the *hacienda* system, the peasants were required to labor on the owner's fields for 3 days per week. Holmberg decided to take advantage of this obligation by using it to familiarize the peasants with improved varieties of potatoes, fertilizers, fungicides, and insecticides. After seeing how successful the new seeds and methods were during their obligatory labor on the new boss's plot, the peasants were more willing to do the same on their own plots. This was facilitated by advancing the seeds and other materials through a government-sponsored cooperative credit program. Anthropologists and technicians carefully supervised the use of the new methods to ensure their success.

Meanwhile, other activities were underway: a full-scale educational program; a school hot-lunch program that introduced fruits and eggs, previously not part of the diet; a demonstration garden for growing leafy vegetables; and sewing machine lessons that enabled women and men to make their own clothes. In addition, through frequent communal meetings and discussions, the peasants gradually came to place more trust in one another and to seek cooperative, communal solutions to their problems.

The culmination of all these changes was the purchase of the *hacienda* by the families living on it. Along with higher incomes, better health, and literacy, this event was considered dramatic evidence of the success of the project (Dobyns 1972:201). Most importantly, the people of Vicos continued to improve their standard of living and their social and political status long after all the anthropologist-collaborators had left the community. Studies show that other communities in the same region have had much lower rates of improvement in per capita income, literacy, health conditions, and political representation (Doughty 1987:152).

As a model for developing the entire peasant sector of the Peruvian Andes, however, the project has attracted certain criticisms. The per capita cash outlays were quite modest in comparison with those of other international development efforts, yet there were hidden human inputs that are not likely to be duplicated on a scale large enough to affect a significant portion of the Peruvian peasantry. Vicos benefited from highly trained, honest, and relatively unselfish experts (including Holmberg) who worked diligently to improve the lot of the peasants. They were paid by universities and foundations, and many of them worked for next to nothing as graduate students hoping to be compensated by getting their Ph.D.s and making their careers in anthropology. Although extremely interesting as a demonstration of what can be done by applied anthropologists who had considerable power to manage the people in their charge, the Vicos project fell short of providing a more general solution to the problem of underdevelopment in the Peruvian Andes. But these criticisms fail to take into account the limited goals of the project. The organizers wanted to demonstrate that it was possible for a low-budget, face-to-face collaborative effort by anthropologists, preexisting government agencies, and the people themselves to overcome centuries of poverty, isolation, ignorance, and prejudice. Judged on this basis, the project was eminently successful.

The Haitian Agroforestry Project

If agricultural development is to be meaningful, it cannot be confined to one or two peasant communities. It must use scientific knowledge to ensure that beneficial innovations will be spread rapidly throughout a region or a country by local participants rather than by foreign experts.

The Haitian Agroforestry Project was specifically designed to meet this goal. Planned and directed in its initial phase by anthropologist Gerald Murray, the Agroforestry Project successfully induced Haitian peasants to plant millions of fast-growing trees in steep hillside farmlands threatened by erosion. Depletion of soil as a result of rapid run-off from treeless hillsides has long been recognized as one of Haiti's greatest problems. In addition, trees are needed as a source of charcoal—the principal cooking fuel in poor households—and as a source of building materials. There have been many other reforestation programs in Haiti, but they have met with little or no success either because the funds for planting were squandered or diverted by government bureaucrats or because peasants refused to cooperate and protect the seedlings from hungry goats.

The Haitian Agroforestry Project was designed to avoid both pitfalls. In accepting a $4 million grant from the United States Agency for International Development (USAID), Murray insisted on an unusual stipulation: No funds were to be transferred to the Haitian government or through the Haitian government. Instead, the funds were to be given to local community groups—private voluntary organizations—interested in peasant welfare. In practice, the majority of these groups were grass-roots religious associations formed by Catholic or Protestant priests, pastors, or missionaries. The project provided these groups with seedlings of fast-growing species matched to local ecological conditions and with access to expert advisors. The private voluntary organizations, in turn, undertook to assemble and instruct the local farmers and to distribute the seedlings to them free of charge, provided each farmer agreed to plant a minimum of 500.

It was clear that unless the peasants themselves were motivated to plant the seedlings and to protect them, the project could not succeed. Murray's analysis of why previous projects had been unable to obtain the peasants' cooperation was based on his firsthand knowledge of Haitian peasant life and on certain principles of anthropological theory (see below). Haitian peasants are market-oriented—they produce crops for cash sale. Yet previous attempts to get them to plant trees stipulated that trees should not be sold. Instead the peasants were told that trees are an unmarketable national treasure. Thus, trees were presented as exactly the opposite of the cash crops that the peasants planted on their own behalf.

> One reforestation program after another has come in with the finger-wagging message that the tree should be seen as a sacred soil-conserving, rain-drawing object which the peasant should plant but never cut. Tree-cutting is viewed not as a legitimate economic behavior, but as a type of economic misbehavior. [Murray 1984:154]

Putting himself in the peasants' shoes, Murray realized that previous reforestation projects had created an adverse balance of costs over benefits for the peasants. It was perfectly rational for the peasants to let their goats eat the seedlings instead of donating their labor and land to trees that they would be forbidden to harvest (or could only harvest 30 or 40 years in the future). Accordingly, Murray decided to distribute the seedlings as a cash crop over which the peasants would have complete control. The project merely informed the peasants how to plant the trees and take care of them. They were also shown how to set the seedlings in rows between which other crops could be planted until the trees matured. They were told, too, how fast the trees would grow and how much lumber or charcoal they could expect to get at various stages of growth. Then the peasants were left on their own to decide when it would be in their best interest to cut some or all of them.

> To emphasize this ownership, the Project goes so far as to insist that if, after a year or so, the peasant changes his mind about the trees, he is perfectly free to pull them out. . . . The function of such an unusual message is to remove any fear in the peasant's mind that the Project retains any ownership rights in the trees which the peasant plants on his land. [Ibid.]

The project's goal was to assist 5,000 peasant families to plant 3 million trees in four years. After 6 years (1982–1988), it had in fact assisted 200,000 farmers to plant 35 million trees (Figure 17.3). Considerable numbers of trees have already been used for charcoal and for building purposes. While it remains to be seen how much extra income will eventually be generated and how much erosion has been curtailed, Murray's basic analysis appears to have been correct (Conway 1989).

Murray predicts that cash-oriented *agroforestry* (see Box 17.2) will become a major feature of peasant agriculture throughout the Third World. He interprets cash-oriented agroforestry as a response to a set of infrastructural conditions that are similar to the conditions responsible for the rise of agricultural modes of production out of hunting and gath-

Figure 17.3 Haitian agroforestry project. These trees are of the species Leucaena leucophala *and are about two and one-half years old. Several other species were also being planted.*

ering: widespread depletion of a natural resource and population pressure. Peasants, having depleted the trees on which they depend for soil regeneration, fuel, and building material, will now find it to their advantage to plant trees as one of their basic crops. In Murray's words (personal communication):

> The anthropologically most important element of the model . . . is the diachronic [evolutionary] component in which I am positing a scarcity-and-stress-

---

Box 17.2

CO-OPTING THE "DEMON" BEHIND DEFORESTATION

I propose that we look carefully at the "demon" which is currently blamed for putting the final touches on the environment of Haiti—the market which currently exists for charcoal and construction materials. It is this market, many would argue, which sabotages forever any hopes of preserving the few remaining trees in Haiti.

I would like to argue that it is precisely this market which can restore tree growth to the hills of Haiti. The demon can be "baptized" and joined in wedlock to the ecological imperatives whose major adversary he has been up till now. With creative programming we can turn the tables on history and utilize the awe-inspiring cash-generating energy present throughout Haitian society in a manner which plants trees in the ground faster than they are being cut down. If this is to be done, it must be the peasant who does it. But he will *not* do it voluntarily or spontaneously *unless* tree planting contributes to the flow of desperately needed cash into his home. I propose that the mechanism for achieving this is the introduction of *cash-oriented agroforestry.*

Source: Murray 1984:147.

---

generated readiness for a repeat in the domain of fuel and wood of the transition from foraging to planting which began some 15 millennia ago in the domain of food.

The Not-So-Green Revolution

A more typical role for the applied anthropologist is that of critic-observer of the change process. An important example of this role can be found in the anthropological critique of the "Green Revolution." This critique again illustrates the importance of a holistic perspective for development projects.

The Green Revolution had its origin in the late 1950s in the dwarf varieties of "wonder wheat" developed by Nobel Prize winner and plant geneticist Norman Borlaug at the Rockefeller Foundations's Ciudad Obregon research center in northwest Mexico. Designed to double and triple yields per acre, wonder wheat was soon followed by dwarf varieties of "miracle rice" engineered at a joint Rockefeller and Ford Foundation research center in the Philippines. (The significance of the dwarfed forms is that short, thick stems can bear heavy loads of ripe grain without bending over.) On the basis of initial successes in Mexico and the Philippines, the new seeds were hailed as the solution to the problem of feeding the expanding population of the underdeveloped world and were soon planted in vast areas of Pakistan, India, and Indonesia (Cloud 1973). Although the new seeds have resulted in an increase in output per acre, they have done so only at considerable economic and social cost. Moreover, this rate of increase has not been large enough to offset the rate of population growth and the diversion of land and capital from traditional staples, such as millet and beans, to high-yield crops. As a result, food output per capita between 1960 and 1980 in low-income countries with a combined population of 2.25 billion people fell by 0.3 percent (McNamara 1984:1118). Between 1984 and 1988, world per capita output of grains fell from an all-time high of 345 kilograms to 296 kilograms while year-end grain stocks were back to the level of 1974 (L. Brown 1989:55). The main problem with the miracle seeds is that they were engineered to outperform native varieties of rice and wheat *only* if grown in fields heavily irrigated and treated with large inputs of chemical fertilizers, pesticides, insecticides, and fungicides. Without such inputs, the high-yield varieties perform little better than the native varieties, especially under adverse soil and weather conditions.

The question of how these inputs are to be obtained and how and to whom they are to be distributed immediately presents profound problems. Most peasants in the underdeveloped world not only lack access to irrigation water, but they are unable to pay for expensive chemical fertilizers and other chemical inputs. This means that unless extraordinary efforts are made by the governments of countries switching to miracle seeds, the chief beneficiaries of the Green Revolution will be the wealthy farmers who already occupy the irrigated lands and who are best able to pay for the chemical inputs (Cummings 1978; Glaeser 1987; Mencher 1974a, 1978; Oasa 1985:220).

Anthropologist Richard Franke (1973, 1974) studied the Green Revolution in central Java. Despite the fact that yield increases of up to 70 percent were being obtained, in the village studied by Franke only 20 percent of the farming households had joined the program. The chief beneficiaries were the farmers who were already better off than average, owned the most land, and had adequate supplies of water. The poorest families did not adopt the new seeds. They made ends meet by working part time for well-to-do farmers who lent them money to buy food or who paid them in kind (Figure 17.4). The richer farmers prevented their part-time workers from adopting the new seeds. The wealthier farmers feared they would lose their supply of cheap labor, and the poor farmers feared that if they cut themselves off from their patrons, they would have no one to turn to in case of sickness or drought. Franke concludes that the theories behind the Green Revolution are primarily rationalizations for ruling elites trying to find a way to achieve economic development without the social and political transformation their societies need.

Experts defend the Green Revolution against the criticism that it has primarily benefited well-to-do farmers by pointing out that most of the high-yield wheat farms in the Indian Punjab have less than 4 hectares (about 10 acres) and that Yaqui River Valley wheat farms average only 69 hectares (Plucknett and Smith 1982:217). But throughout the underdeveloped world, any farmer who possesses as much as 2 or 3 hectares of *irrigated* land ranks among the top 10 percent of the rural population.

The authorities and technicians responsible for promoting the Green Revolution originally sought to convert peasant farming into agribusiness systems modeled after high-energy agriculture in the developed countries (Cleaver 1975). It was hoped that by stimulating the development of agribusiness in the tropics, the productivity of agriculture would

(a)

(b)

Figure 17.4   Rice harvest, Java.
(a) *Harvesting is done with a small hand knife, known as the* ani-ani-. *Each stalk is individually cut, but with the large supply of labor, a single morning is enough for all but the very largest plots to be harvested.* (b) *The paddy is bound in bundles and carried to the home of the owner, where a one-tenth portion is divided among the harvesters; no other wage is paid.*

be raised enough to catch up with the rate of population growth. This transformation obviously risks the virtual destruction of small peasant holdings — just as it has meant the destruction of the small family farm in the United States. There are penalties associated with this transformation even in the industrial nations, where the former farm population can be employed as carhops, meat packers, and tractor mechanics (see page 360). But in the underdeveloped countries, where there are few jobs in the manufacturing and service sectors of the economy, migration to the cities cannot result in higher standards of living for hundreds of millions of underemployed peasants (Raj 1977).

The lesson of the Green Revolution is that technological solutions often fail to achieve their intended purpose because they underestimate the effects of pre-existing differences between the affluent and the poor.

Mexico's Second Green Revolution

Between 1965 and 1979, despite the Green Revolution and government subsidies, per capita production of maize, wheat, and beans, Mexico's principal food crops, fell by 40 percent. The reason for this decline has been studied by anthropologist Billie DeWalt (1984:44). As the Mexican government lowered its price supports for maize, wheat, and beans, farmers turned to a new and more lucrative grain: sorghum (Figure 17.5). Prior to 1960, sorghum, which is widely grown in Africa and Asia for human food, was practically unknown in Mexico. In a mere 20 years, sorghum production increased by 2772 percent. Today the amount of land devoted to sorghum production is twice as great as the amount of land devoted to wheat. DeWalt calls this Mexico's "second green revolution," a revolution that has taken place "without the benefit of a government-sponsored program to encourage production, without the sponsorship of any bilateral mutual aid agency, and without the teaching and technical assistance of any extension grants" (ibid.:40). The principal advantage of sorghum over wheat is that although it responds to irrigation, it can also prosper as a rain-fed crop and can survive dry spells.

If one totals up the production of maize, wheat, beans, and sorghum, it seems as if Mexico has solved its food production problems: Per capita grain production in 1980 was double the per capita grain production in 1945. This is exactly what the planners of the first Green Revolution had hoped for. Yet Mexico is now importing more grain than in 1945. The reason — totally unanticipated by the planners of the Green Revolution — is that 100 percent of the sorghum, 14 percent of the maize, and 10 percent of the wheat are being fed to animals and converted into pork, beef, and chicken. This results in a loss of about 4 out of every 5 calories in the grains (see page 83). While increased animal food consumption is desirable, the people most in need of additional calories and proteins cannot afford to eat significant quantities of such foods. About 30 million

Figure 17.5   Sorghum in Mexico.
Only animals will eat this crop when it is harvested.

Box 17.3

DIETARY AFFLUENCE FOR SOME, SCARCITY FOR THE MASSES

Mexico has experienced two Green Revolutions in the past quarter century, yet finds that its agricultural situation is relatively and absolutely in a worse condition than before. In spite of excellent yields of wheat and sorghum, and somewhat better yields of maize and beans, the country is woefully short of meeting its basic grain needs. There are those who would lay the blame for this problem on the Mexican agricultural sector because it is backward and not productive enough. Others would suggest that population growth which is outstripping the productive capacity of the land is the problem. The evidence, however, indicates that Mexico's food problem is not a production problem but that it is simply another symptom of the country's unequal development.

It is unlikely that further technological advances by themselves will eliminate world hunger. . . . As we have seen, by any technical standards, the revolution in wheat and sorghum production would have to be judged as successes. Yet increased production has done little to make any real impact on the plight of the poor and the malnourished. Despite Mexico's heavy investment in building irrigation works, transportation facilities, storage structures, and other parts of the infrastructure; although the government has subsidized the purchase of agricultural machinery, fertilizers, and other inputs, and despite the application of green revolutionary technology, the country is no closer to solving the nutritional needs of a large part of its population than it was in 1940.

Source: DeWalt 1985:44, 54.

Mexicans are too poor ever to eat meat, and 20 million are too poor to eat enough maize, wheat, and beans to satisfy minimum nutritional standards.

In DeWalt's view, the spectacular rise in the amount of land planted in sorghum has had an adverse effect on the welfare of Mexico's poorest classes (Boxes 17.3 and 17.4). Instead of being planted primarily as a rain-fed crop for direct human consumption, the grain is being grown for animal consumption on some of the country's best-irrigated lands. Therefore, not only is it an inefficient source of proteins and

calories because it is converted into meat, but it also has preempted lands for which the government had built irrigation works, roads, and other facilities in order to wipe out hunger and make Mexico self-sufficient in the production of staple grains (DeWalt 1984).

Marijuana in Jamaica

It has long been recognized that the moods, expectations, and personalities of drug users affect their reaction to psychoactive (mind-al-

Box 17.4

A CONTRARY POINT OF VIEW

Stagnation and a dampening of initiative do not serve the interests of the rural or urban poor. Few Third World countries can afford to bypass the opportunity to maximize production in their better lands.

Some critics contend that high-yielding varieties reduce labor demand because of mechanization. But none of the varieties requires machines to produce high yields. Where tractors, mechanical threshers, and harvesters are in use, labor demand usually increases. Animals rather than people are replaced, freeing land for the cultivation of crops for human consumption. By permitting more intensive cropping, machinery can increase the need for labor by 20 to 50 percent.

The increased food supplies generated by the spread of high-yielding varieties have created additional employment opportunities in such service industries as the marketing of crop products and the manufacture, sale, and maintenance of vehicles, fertilizers, herbicides, and pesticides. Furthermore, food prices have been moderated by the increased volume of cereal production—a bonus for the rural and urban poor. (It is not unusual for low-income people to spend three-fourths of their income on food.) In Colombia, for example, the real price of rice dropped after the introduction of high-yielding varieties.

Excessive concern over the distribution of income in rural areas could lead to agricultural policies that extinguish initiative and impede food production. This would be to the detriment of poor people, especially those residing in towns and cities. In many developing countries close to half the population now lives in urban areas.

Source: Plucknett and Smith 1982:218.

tering) drugs as much as the specific chemicals in the drugs themselves. Since culture denotes the total complex of behavioral and mental traditions surrounding individuals, one can expect that marked differences in reactions to psychoactive drugs will be found in different cultures. The study of the cultural component in drug-induced thoughts and behavior is therefore a source of essential information for anyone concerned with formulating or administering drug control policies.

Early in the 1970s a team of anthropologists and other behavioral and medical scientists led by Vera Rubin and Lambros Comitas (1975) undertook a cross-cultural study of marijuana use. Funds for the research were supplied by the National Institute of Mental Health's Center for Studies of Narcotic and Drug Abuse. Because they were interested in examining the long-term effects of marijuana on the health and well-being of chronic users, Rubin and Comitas selected the Caribbean island of Jamaica as the site for their study. Although marijuana is an illegal substance in Ja-

Figure 17.6 Jamaican Rastafarians.
These two men are members of a movement in
which the smoking of marijuana is viewed as a reli-
gious sacrament.

maica, Jamaicans are probably the most inveterate users of marijuana in the Western Hemisphere (Figure 17.6). In the rural areas of the island, the researchers found that between 60 and 70 percent of working-class people use marijuana by smoking it, drinking it in tea, or eating it mixed with food. The most important difference between the marijuana complex in Jamaica and the marijuana complex in the United States is that working-class Jamaicans do not smoke marijuana to "turn on" or to achieve the hedonistic effects valued by middle-class American users. Rather, the Jamaicans are motivated to smoke marijuana because they believe it helps them work better and makes them healthier and stronger than nonusers.

Much of the opposition to the use of marijuana in the United States stems from the belief that marijuana deprives people of ambition and reduces their work drive. Although this may be true in the United States context, the Jamaican

study suggests that apathy is not induced by the chemical, but by the cultural conditions that surround its use. In Jamaica the primary reason given for smoking marijuana is that it helps one perform arduous and dull work. While weeding fields, for example, farmers said they were able to concentrate more on their tasks after smoking. Videotapes of farmers weeding with and without smoking suggested that their work was in fact more thorough and detailed after smoking. No evidence was found that those who smoked on the job worked less rapidly or less efficiently than those who did not. Rubin and Comitas conclude:

> In all Jamaican settings observed, the workers [who smoke] are motivated to carry out difficult tasks with no decrease in heavy physical exertion, and their perception of increased output is a significant factor in bolstering their motivation to work. [1975:75]

Many other aspects of the marijuana complex were studied. To assess the impact of chronic use on the health and personalities of users, a group of 30 smokers and a group of 30 nonsmokers with similar backgrounds and personal attributes were given a broad battery of clinical tests at the University Hospital in Jamaica (participation by both groups was completely voluntary). Aside from impairment of respiratory functions, which may be attributable to the fact that heavy marijuana smokers are also heavy tobacco smokers, the physical health of the Jamaican smokers was not significantly different from that of the nonsmokers. As for psychological states — intelligence, neurological fitness, sensory perception, memory, and attention — "There is no evidence that long-term use of cannabis [marijuana] is related to chronic impairment" (1975:119). It must be emphasized that this finding is not necessarily applicable to other cultures. It may very well be that in other cultural settings, such as the United States, the long-term use of marijuana does lead to impairment—the effects of cultural factors being no less real than those of physical or chemical factors.

Marijuana in Costa Rica

Nonetheless, a second intensive cross-cultural study of marijuana smoking in a cultural setting different from Jamaica has led to conclusions similar to those drawn by Rubin and Comitas. This study was carried out in the Central American country of Costa Rica by a multidisciplinary team whose leaders included anthropologists William Carter (1980) and Paul Doughty. It employed a research design based on "matched pairs"—each of 41 male users was carefully paired with a male nonuser for age, marital status, education, occupation, alcohol consumption, and tobacco consumption. As a result of this design, all the above factors could be ruled out as causes of any of the observed differences in the behavior and physical condition of the users and nonusers.

Initially, the Costa Rican study seemed to corroborate the widely held view that long-term marijuana use leads to lack of motivation for work and economic advancement. It was found that the users tended to have more part-time jobs, more unemployment, more job changes, and fewer material possessions than the nonusers. Yet there was an alternative explanation for these findings. It was possible that the users had become users because they were subject to greater economic and personal stress than the nonusers. If there was indeed a causal relationship leading to economic failure and apathy, corroboration could be found by showing that economic failure and apathy in-

creased in direct proportion to the quantity of marijuana used. When comparisons within the user group were made, the results did not support the hypothesis that higher dose levels were correlated with more marginal economic status. The reverse, in fact, was found to be the case. The more marijuana smoked, the more likely the user was to hold a steady, full-time job. Those who were working were smoking nearly twice as much marijuana per day as those who were unemployed. Those who had the shortest periods of unemployment were the heaviest users (Carter 1980:152ff).

Although some of the users in the Costa Rican study conformed to the stereotype of the unemployed, uncouth, streetwise vagrant, the majority of the users were more like Hector:

> Hector is a laborer in a bakery where he has worked for the last three and a half years. He has a wife and two children for whom he is the only means of support. Hector never smokes at home or in the street or in public places. He does smoke, however, in the bathroom at the bakery, where he works from five in the afternoon until three in the morning. He claims that marijuana makes his work go faster and the night pass more quickly. [Ibid.:156]

Thus we can see that systematic cross-cultural comparisons are essential if we are to distinguish between cultural and physical-chemical aspects of psychoactive substances.

Kuru: The Case of the Laughing Sickness

Applied cultural anthropology has an important role to play in helping physical anthropologists and medical researchers understand the interaction between cultural and natural factors that cause people to become ill. The solution of the mystery of Kuru is a classic instance of how medical knowledge can be advanced by examining the interaction between cultural and natural causes of a deadly disease.

During the late 1950s, reports that a previously unknown disease was rampant among the Foré (see page 247) peoples of highland New Guinea suddenly made headlines around the world. Victims of the disease, called Kuru, were said to be laughing themselves to death. As reliable accounts began to replace rumor, Kuru turned out to be no laughing matter. Its victims progressively lost control over their central nervous systems, including the nerves controlling their facial muscles, so that their faces were often contorted by ghastly grimaces and smiles. The disease was always fatal within a year or two of its first symptoms (Figure 17.7).

Researchers led by D. Carleton Gajdusek found a puzzling *epidemiological* pattern (i.e., distribution and incidence of the disease in the population). Most of the victims were women and girls. Although a few young men came down with it, adult men never did. None of the neighboring tribespeople ever got Kuru, nor was it ever passed on to the Europeans who were in close contact with the Foré.

The first hypothesis was that the disease was genetic and was passed on in family lines from generation to generation. But genetics could not explain the preponderance of female victims plus the occasional young man. Rejecting the genetic explanation, Gajdusek, who was trained as a physical anthropologist and as a virologist (one who studies viruses), began to explore the possibility that Kuru was caused by a type of virus known as a *slow virus*, whose existence in human beings had never been demonstrated but had been long suspected. Beginning in 1963, Gajdusek inoculated chimpanzees with brain extracts of Kuru victims.

Figure 17.7   Young girl with advanced Kuru disease.

After long incubation periods, the chimpanzees began to show the Kuru symptoms. The demonstration that humans could harbor slow viruses has important implication for the study of many puzzling diseases, such as multiple sclerosis, acquired immune deficiency syndrome (AIDS), and certain forms of cancer. For his work, Gajdusek received the Nobel Prize for medicine in 1976.

It was left to two cultural anthropologists, Robert Glasse and Shirley Lindenbaum, however, to complete the explanations for the puzzling epidemiological pattern. Glasse and Lindenbaum drew attention to the fact that in years prior to the outbreak of Kuru, the Foré had begun to practice a form of cannibalism as part of their funeral rituals. Female relatives of the deceased consumed the dead person's brain. Since it was women who were always charged with the task of disposing of the dead, and never men, the Kuru virus never infected adult males. But what about the young men who also occasionally got Kuru? As in many cultures, the Foré's distinction between male and female roles was held less rigidly before puberty than after. Occasionally, therefore, a boy would be permitted to partake of what otherwise was defined as strictly female food. And some years later, this occasional youth would succumb to Kuru along with the much greater number of girls and women (Lindenbaum 1979). Since neither Gajdusek nor Lindenbaum actually witnessed the eating of human flesh by the Foré, the suggestion has been made that the virus was spread merely by contact with the corpse rather than by consumption of infected morsels. Yet Foré women themselves freely told several researchers that they had previously engaged in cannibalism as part of mortuary rituals (Gajdusek 1977; Harris 1985; Steadman and Merbs 1982). Today, since the Foré have given up their cannibalistic rites, Kuru has virtually ceased to exist among them.

The Case of the Vanishing Associations

Villalta is a small town in the Dominican Republic that has all the problems associated with life in an underdeveloped country: poverty, unemployment, illiteracy, and lowered life expectancy. Yet in one respect the town seems to be more "modernized" than others. It has a larger number of voluntary associations (or so-

dalities; see page 182). Such associations are often interpreted as a sign of a community's progress in the direction of development.

But anthropologists Malcolm Walker and Jim Hanson (1978:64–68) found that these associations were disappearing or lapsing into disuse as fast as they were being created. During a short period, the townspeople organized two adult education programs, cooking and sewing classes, a Red Cross chapter, a Youth for Reform association, a Girl Scout troop, a health clinic, a social club, and self-help programs for breeding rabbits, raising chickens, building bridges, and installing water pumps. But none of these projects or associations lasted more than a few days or weeks.

The circumstances surrounding the rise and fall of one of the adult education programs is typical of the rest. Members of the local elite called for a meeting to organize the program. Several outsiders were present, and an official from the Education Department gave a speech about the importance of adult education. The people at the meeting agreed and decided they would ask for volunteer teachers to teach evening classes in the schoolhouse. Another meeting was to be held in two weeks, at which time the teachers and classes would be organized:

> Nothing in fact happened, and the follow up meeting was postponed indefinitely. The official was not heard of again. [Walker and Hanson:66]

"If these associations are doomed to failure almost before the first meeting is over," asked Walker and Hanson, "why do the people of Villalta form them?" Their answer is that they are used by the local elites to give state officials the impression that Villalta is a thriving and forward-looking community responsive to the proposals of influential outsiders from whom the local elites hope to gain favors:

Through associations, the community can give the impression of its responsiveness and progressiveness; the community has its associations on stage, as it were, to put on a convincing performance before the audience of visiting officials. The performance itself is most important, not what happens after its conclusion and the departure of the audience. [Ibid.:67]

This case illustrates the importance of living in a community and gaining a firsthand knowledge of its etic behavioral realities in order to distinguish between what people say they are doing and what they are actually doing. An investigator visiting Villalta for a short time might easily be impressed with the seeming responsiveness of its people to new ideas and its openness to change. While the community has changed, conclude Walker and Hanson, it is not necessarily for the better: "It has learned how to contrive performances and deceive outsiders" (ibid.).

The Case of the Unused Clinic

During the 1970s, a series of community health centers was established by the Department of Health and Hospitals of a large northeastern city. These centers were located in poor neighborhoods and designed to provide health care for the local people. All but one of the centers was used to capacity. Anthropologist Delmos Jones (1976) was charged with the task of discovering why this particular facility was underused.

Jones proceeded on the assumption that the main reasons for the underutilization of the health center would be found not in the characteristics of the population it was designed to serve, but in certain traits of the center itself. Initial investigation showed that many people

in the neighborhood did not know about the center's existence. Unlike the other centers, this one was located inside a hospital and could not be seen from the street. Moreover, among those who had heard about the center, few were aware of where it was or what it did. In addition, many people had tried to use the center but had failed to do so. Probing further, Jones discovered that the neighborhood people had a negative image of the hospital in which the clinic was located. It had the reputation of being very "fancy" and not for poor people. This led them to doubt that somewhere inside the hospital there was a free clinic. Rumor had it that poor people were even turned away from the hospital's emergency room.

People who had persisted in trying to use the clinic reported that they couldn't find it. When they got to the hospital they couldn't find any signs telling them where to go. Even some of the hospital's receptionists didn't know where it was, or refused to say. Jones suspected the latter was the case, because key members of the staff expressed displeasure at having a free clinic in their fancy hospital.

As at the other centers, this one had several neighborhood representatives. But these representatives had developed a defeatist attitude toward the client population and made little effort to contact people in the neighborhood. This apparently pleased the clinic's staff, who let it be known that they preferred to be under- rather than overworked.

Jones set about correcting the situation. First, signs were placed in obvious spots to direct patients to the clinic. Second, receptionists were told where the clinic was. Third, leaflets were printed up and distributed throughout the neighborhood. Finally, new neighborhood representatives were hired who had a more positive attitude toward the neighborhood and the clinic. Attendance rose, but the story does not have a happy ending.

Although the new neighborhood representatives were initially enthusiastic, they began to perceive that the hospital staff continued to frown on having the clinic in the hospital, and they became increasingly hesitant to recommend the clinic to the neighborhood people.

Despite the fact that the reasons for the clinic's underuse seemed rather obvious, the hospital's administration refused to accept Jones's explanation. They preferred to continue to think that the problem lay with the attitudes of the neighborhood people. "I, the researcher," reports Jones, "became an advocate for my own research findings . . . when policy makers don't listen, this could mean we are not telling them what they want to hear" (Jones 1976:227).

Advocacy as Action Anthropology

The fact that the implementation phase of a project is often controlled by administrators or politicians who will not accept the anthropologist's analysis or suggestions has led a number of applied anthropologists like Delmos Jones to adopt the role of advocate. Advocacy anthropologists have fought to improve conditions in women's jails, lobbied in state legislatures for raising welfare allotments, submitted testimony before congressional committees in support of child health care programs, lobbied against the construction of dams and highways that would have an adverse effect on local communities, and engaged in many other consciousness-raising and political activities.

Some anthropologists hold the view that the only legitimate professional function of the applied anthropologist is to provide administrators, politicians, or lawyers with an objective analysis of a situation or organization, and that at most, action should be limited to suggesting but not implementing a plan. In this way it is hoped that anthropology will be able to preserve its scientific standing, since it is clear that an all-out attempt to achieve a practical goal frequently involves rhetorical skills, cajolery, half-truths or outright deceptions, threats, and even violence.

Against this view, advocacy anthropologists insist that the objectivity of anthropology and the other social sciences is illusory and that failure to push for the implementation of a goal represents a form of advocacy in itself. The objectivity is illusory, they argue, because political and personal biases control the commitment to study one situation rather than another (to study the poor rather than the wealthy, for example; see page 366). And refraining from action is itself a form of action and therefore a form of advocacy, because one's inaction assures that someone else's actions will weigh more heavily in the final outcome. Anthropologists who do not actively use their skills and knowledge to bring about what they believe to be a solution simply make it easier for others with opposite beliefs to prevail. Such anthropologists are themselves part of the problem (R. Cohen 1984b).

No consensus exists among anthropologists about how to resolve these different views of the proper relationship between knowledge and the achievement of controversial practical goals. Perhaps the only resolution of this dilemma is the one that now exists: We must search our individual consciences and act accordingly.

In conclusion, it should be emphasized that we have looked at only a few of the many faces of applied anthropology. As Box 17.5 suggests, many other equally important and interesting cases could have been presented.

Box 17.5

PUTTING ANTHROPOLOGY TO PRACTICAL USE

TYPE OF ACTION	ANTHROPOLOGIST
Document the prevalence of hunger; advocacy for the homeless and hungry in New York City	Dehavenon (1984)
Designed and spread inexpensive storage facilities for potatoes in highland Peru and the Philippines	Rhoades (1984); Werge (1979)
Prevented construction of dam that threatened a pre-existing irrigation system in the Southwest	Jacobs (1978)
Evaluated community health projects in Tumaco, Colombia	Buzzard (1982)
Helped mothers to feed babies a life-saving remedy for dehydration resulting from diarrhea in Third World countries	Kendall (1984)
Helped to prepare litigation for a $47 million award to the Pembina Chippewa Indians for the loss of their tribal lands	Feraca (1986)
Helped to get fraud charges against Bannock-Shoshoni women dismissed, on grounds of cultural misunderstanding by English-speaking social workers	Joans (1984)
Developed quality-control procedures for the hotel industry	Glover (1984)
Designed, implemented, and evaluated a community health program in Miami to take account of ethnically diverse medical needs	Weidman (1983)

Summary

Applied anthropology is concerned with research that has practical applications. Its core consists of research sponsored by public and private organizations with an interest in achieving practical goals. The role of the applied cultural anthropologist may consist merely in researching the possible means of attaining such goals; sometimes it includes drawing up plans and helping to implement them, as well as evaluating the results of implementation. Applied anthropologists involved in implementation are known as practitioners of action anthropology.

Beyond that core, other forms of research may also be considered part of applied anthropology. Abstract theorizing often has important practical implications, as in the case of alternative theories about the causes of underdevelopment or urban poverty. Much research that is not sponsored by a particular organization with a definite goal in view may nonetheless be aimed at achieving such a goal, such as the independence of a colony or the development of a newly independent state.

Applied anthropology has three major and distinctive contributions to make to the analysis and solution of urgent practical problems: (1) exposure of ethnocentric biases; (2) a holistic viewpoint stressing the long as well as the short term, the interconnectedness of the parts of a sociocultural system, and the whole of the system as well as its parts; and (3) a commitment to distinguishing etic behavioral events from emic plans and ideologies. All too often the intended effects of an organization's plans and policies differ sharply from their actual everyday etic consequences.

The Cornell-Peru Vicos project illustrates applied anthropology functioning over the entire range of research, planning, implementation, and evaluation. This project substantially improved the standard of living of the serflike peasants who lived on the Vicos *hacienda*. An important ingredient in this success was the use of the authoritarian powers of the new manager to introduce new forms of agriculture and other innovations. While successful in its own sphere, it is doubtful if Vicos provides a model for the development of the Peruvian highlands, because of the hidden costs of the experts who guided the Vicosinos from day to day over a 10-year period. The Haitian Agroforestry Project is another example of anthropological research, planning, implementation, and evaluation—in this case, applied to the goal of getting peasants to plant and protect trees. By appealing to the peasants' self-interest in using trees as a cash crop, this project shows signs of achieving a solution to one of Haiti's most serious problems.

The case of the Not-So-Green Revolution illustrates the importance both of a holistic perspective for development projects and of the role of the applied anthropologist as critic rather than change agent. Anthropologists have recurrently pointed out that high-yield miracle seeds benefit large landowners more than poor small farmers because the seeds require heavy inputs of water and expensive chemicals. The cases of rice in Indonesia and sorghum and wheat in Mexico point up the futility of seeking a purely technical solution to poverty and underdevelopment, since the effects on every technological innovation are modified by the total sociocultural context into which it is introduced.

The studies of marijuana use in Jamaica and Costa Rica illustrate the importance of controlling for ethnocentric biases in research related to problems of health and welfare. Just as technological innovations must be seen in a definite sociocultural context, so too must the use of psychoactive drugs. The Jamaican and Costa Rican studies show that marijuana cannot be seen as a purely chemical-physiological problem. Its effects are different in different cultures. By contrast to the United States, marijuana use in Jamaica and Costa Rica serves to relieve the burden of work rather than to provide relaxation after work.

The case of Kuru illustrates the importance of knowing the cultural context in which diseases occur. Understanding the role of cannibalism in funerary rituals and the development of distinct dietary patterns among men and women provided the key to solving the disease's mysterious epidemiology.

The last two cases emphasize the discontinuity between the emics of bureaucratic plans and the etics of everyday behavior. In Villalta, a town in the Dominican Republic, the local elite enthusiastically sets up one association after another. Members typically meet for one session and then let the association lapse into limbo. From the ground-up etic viewpoint of the applied anthropologist, this behavior becomes intelligible as an effort on the part of the local elite to curry favor with state officials. A similar discontinuity between plans and behavior characterizes the case of the underused urban clinic in the northeastern United States. The administrators in charge of the clinic program either do not recognize or will not admit the discrepancy between their stated plans and their own behavior. In such a situation, the administrators create the chief obstacle to implementation. This means that anthropologists who are committed to implementation — to action anthropology — must often assume an advocacy role. No agreement exists as to whether professional anthropologists can assume an advocacy role as professionals without damaging the claim that anthropology is an objective, scientific discipline.

Chapter 18

THE ANTHROPOLOGY OF AN INDUSTRIAL SOCIETY

This chapter briefly describes some of the principal features of society and culture in the United States. Naturally, it is impossible to cover all aspects of such a complex subject in a single chapter. Thus, the chapter highlights topics that relate to social problems of widespread concern to the people of the United States, such as boredom and alienation in the workplace, poverty, unemployment, the concentration of wealth, ethnic and race relations, crime, drug use, welfare, changing family structure and gender roles, and new forms of religious expression. We shall see that it is the shift in the mode of production from goods to information and services that best accounts for major ongoing changes in U.S. society and culture.

Mode of Production and Political Economy

The United States can be characterized by its mode of production and its political economy. Its mode of production is industrialism. Its political economy is a blend of statism and oligopoly capitalism. Let us clarify these concepts. An industrial society is a society that relies on the *detailed division of labor* in combination with power-driven machinery to achieve mass production of goods and services. *Detailed division of labor* refers to the separation of production tasks into many tiny steps carried out by different workers.

The United States remains the top-ranking industrial manufacturing country in the world. Nonetheless, two-thirds of its work force is no longer engaged in manufacturing, and two-thirds of the gross domestic product consists of non-goods production (Figure 18.1). Three-quarters of all employees produce information and services rather than tangible objects (Howe and Parks 1989:6). Most employed adult Americans work in offices, stores, restaurants, schools, clinics, and moving vehicles rather than on factory assembly lines. They wait on customers, repair broken machines, keep accounts, write letters, transfer funds, and provide grooming, schooling, training, information, counseling, and therapy to students, clients, customers, and patients.

Farming, which once accounted for the vast majority of American workers, now occupies less than 3 percent of the work force. With the industrialization and automation of agriculture, large numbers of workers were displaced. Migration from farm to city provided much of the labor supply for the growth of the manufacturing sector of the economy. But the percentage of workers employed in manufacturing peaked in 1950. With the automation of factories, large numbers of workers were displaced and entered the service and information industries. Also, large numbers of service and information workers were recruited from the ranks of married housewives, with consequences to be discussed below.

The rise of the service and information sectors has led to the characterization of the United States as a "postindustrial society" (Bell 1973). It would seem more appropriate, how-

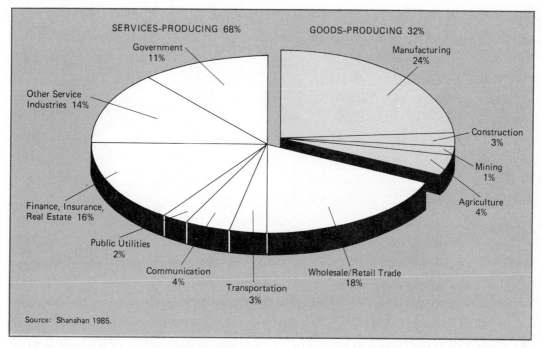

Figure 18.1 Gross domestic product, United States.

ever, to call the United States a hyperindustrial society (*hyper-* means extra strong) rather than a postindustrial society, since the shift to service and information processing has merely resulted in extending the detailed division of labor and the use of mass-production machines into additional kinds of production (M. Harris 1987; Sanderson 1988:451).

The modern office has come to resemble the factory, and the distinction between blue-collar and white-collar workers has become increasingly blurred (Figure 18.2). In the office, as in the factory, the detailed division of labor leads to the separation of mental from physical operations and of management from labor. Separate workers open mail, date and route orders, clear credit, check inventory, type invoices, calculate discounts and shipping fees, and dispatch items for shipment:

Just as in manufacturing processes . . . the work of the office is analyzed and parcelled out among a great many detail workers, who now lose all comprehension of the process as a whole and the policies which underlie it. The special privilege of the clerk of old, that of being witness to the operation of the enterprise as a whole . . . disappears. Each of the activities requiring intervention of policy or contact beyond the department or section becomes the province of a higher functionary. [Braverman 1974:314]

State Socialism

Although Americans think of the United States as being a capitalist country, its economy is actually best characterized as a mixture of

Figure 18.2   Information factory.
Collections department of telephone company. Note the predominance of women.

socialist-like state enterprises and capitalist enterprises. Some 17 million people are directly employed by federal, state, and local governments. Another 36.7 million depend largely on government social security payments. Other forms of state, local, and federal pensions support an additional 5.2 million people. Welfare in the form of aid to dependent children, home relief, and aid to the handicapped supports about 14 million people. There are 2 million people in the armed forces and 2.3 million receiving unemployment benefits (U.S. Bureau of the Census 1989). At least a million farm families depend on federal price supports. Then there are an estimated 6 million people whose jobs in private industry depend on government purchases of military equipment, construction contracts, government "bailout" loans to companies on the verge of bankruptcy, and assorted forms of government subsidies. Adding the dependents of these workers raises

the total in this category to at least 10 million. By conservative estimate, therefore, about 80 million U.S. citizens depend on the redistribution of tax money rather than a share of profits made as a result of capitalist free enterprise. It can be said with a grain of truth that the United States is the third largest "socialist" state in the world after China and the Soviet Union.

Oligopoly Capitalism

The essence of capitalist enterprise is the freedom to buy and sell in competitive price-making markets. Price-making markets exist where there are enough buyers and sellers to enable buyers to compete with buyers, buyers to compete with sellers, and sellers to compete with sellers for the prices that best suit their respective interests. It has long been recognized that in order to preserve the free enterprise system, limitations must be placed on the ability of small groups of powerful buyers or sellers to gain control over a market to the extent that the prices they offer effectively determine the price that must be paid by anyone who wants a particular product or service. Early in this century, the U.S. Congress passed laws against the formation of monopolies and actively pursued the breakup of companies that then dominated the railroad, meat-packing, and petroleum industries. The antimonopoly laws stopped short, however, of prohibiting the formation of semimonopolies or *oligopolies* — that is, companies that control not all, but a major share of the market for a particular product.

The trend toward oligopoly was already well advanced in the earlier part of this century. But after the end of World War II, the pace of acquisitions and expansions quickened. In 1988 there were 3,637 mergers and acquisitions at a cost of 311.4 billion dollars (*World Almanac* 1990:87). As a result of this trend, the 100 largest corporations in the United States own 60 percent of all assets owned by U.S. corporations (Bureau of the Census 1989:536).

Despite the growth of oligopoly, there remain millions of small-scale owner-operated companies in the United States. Many of these, however, are franchise operations in service and retail trades and in the gasoline and fast-food industries. Their policies, prices, and products are controlled by giant parent companies.

Industrial Bureaucracy and Alienation

As a result of the growth of government and oligopolistic corporations and the spread of industrialism to information and service occupations, the majority of Americans work for large-scale organizations governed by bureaucratic rules. These organizations do not reward individual initiative or free enterprise so much as the willingness of workers to perform standardized routine tasks. This has led to the appearance of what has been called "alienation": on factory assembly lines and in offices, stores, hospitals, and shops. Workers in large bureaucratized enterprises, government or private, tend to become bored with their tasks, hostile to management, indifferent to the quality of their product, and uninterested in the welfare of the ultimate consumers of the goods and the services they help to produce.

Some observers claim that automation is eliminating jobs that previously allowed for a considerable amount of individual style and self-expression. For example, as the fast-food chains take over the restaurant business, they do away with the need for qualified cooks and chefs, personalized menus, and knowledgeable waiters, waitresses, and stewards. They use "equipment and products designed to be operated (or sold) by minimally trained, unskilled persons, of whom high turnover rates are expected," whose jobs consist of sorting out boxed, uniform portions of food prepared and frozen off-premises (Job 1980:41).

There is considerable evidence that automation of the service and information sector — the "electronic office" — leads to an increase in the detailed division of labor, the elimination of many interesting and versatile secretarial positions, and a downgrading of skills and wages (Balsham 1988; Glenn and Feldberg 1977; Nelson 1986). Karen Nussbaum, of the National Association of Office Workers, writes:

> Office automation as it is being introduced today requires that a great many people

tediously enter the data, push the right buttons, fill out forms "for the computer" with perfect accuracy, and feed the forms to the computer. Each worker must discipline herself to the system imposed by the machine. Most often, clericals work with computer terminals which have been strictly programmed to perform only one task. [Nussbaum 1980:3]

The new office machines themselves supervise and discipline their operators, virtually eliminating contact and conversation with other workers except those who perform similar functions nearby (Box 18.1).

For typists, telephone operators, cashiers, stock clerks, and mail sorters, automation means progressively less to know and less to think. By using optical scanning machines, file clerks can dispense with knowing the sequence of the alphabet. Supermarket cashiers no longer have to know how to add or subtract. Airline reservationists no longer need to know anything about timetables. Bank tellers, in Harry Braverman's words (1974:340), have become "mere check out clerks at a money supermarket."

On the other hand, some observers contend that as a result of automation, jobs are actually becoming more complex. In the textile industry, for example, those who operate and repair the new generation of automated looms must be able to read and interpret complex manuals. One study predicts that the percentage of jobs that require the highest skill levels will rise from 6 percent in 1984 to 13 percent in 2000 (Storper 1989:159–164; Swasy and Hymowitz 1990).

Box 18.1

MODERN TIMES: WORKING FOR A LARGE OIL COMPANY AS A CUSTOMER SERVICE OPERATOR

The pace is strenuous (an average of 160 calls per day) and automatically set by the computer's automatic call distributor, tasks are repetitive, and workers are isolated in carrels on duty, while their movement is restricted by their headsets and the necessary concentration on the VDT screen. Machine-measured performance statistics are the basis for promotion: for each operator the computer measures the number of calls taken, the length of each call, the number of callers who "abandoned" before being answered, and the amount of time spent off the telephone or away from the work station. In order to monitor performance, supervisors listen in on 10% of each operator's daily call volume (approximately 16 calls) each month, using a telephone pickup that cannot be heard by the operator. More than three errors places the operator below the shop standard for "accuracy." One supervisor and former operator observed, "You can tell when they've been working the phones too long; their voices on the phone get louder and louder without their noticing it."

Source: Nelson 1986:158.

Class Stratification

Like all state-organized societies, the United States is a stratified society and has a complex system of classes, minorities, and other hierarchical groups (cross-cut by gender hierarchies). Emic versions of U.S. stratification hierarchies differ from one class to another and bear little resemblance to etic accounts. James West (1945), who studied class relations in a small Midwestern community he called Plainville, concluded that there were different class hierarchies, depending on whether one took the viewpoint of the "upper crust," "good religious people," "non-church people," "all us good honest working people," Methodists, Baptists, and so on. At the bottom of all these hierarchies there was a category called "people who live like animals."

Lloyd Warner (1949) attempted to study the class structure of Yankee City (pseudonym for Newburyport, Massachusetts) by classifying people according to occupation, source of income, house type, and dwelling area. Warner's picture of Yankee City's classes (Figure 18.3) represents a mixture of emic and etic criteria.

There is no doubt that the United States is

Figure 18.4   Homeless.
This tragic figure haunts the streets of Washington, D.C., capitol of the richest country in the world.

a highly stratified society (Figure 18.4). In terms of income, the poorest 10 percent of U.S. families account for only 1 percent of aggregate family income, while the wealthiest 10 percent account for 33 percent; the poorest 20 percent account for only 4.7 percent of aggregate family income, while the wealthiest 20 percent account for 43 percent (Morehouse and Dembo 1985a:11,19, 1985b; 1988).

Is There a Ruling Class in the United States?

From both a practical and a theoretical point of view, the most important question that can be asked about class in the United States is

Figure 18.3   Class hierarchy, Yankee City.

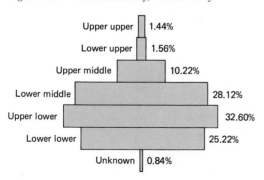

Upper upper	1.44%
Lower upper	1.56%
Upper middle	10.22%
Lower middle	28.12%
Upper lower	32.60%
Lower lower	25.22%
Unknown	0.84%

whether there is a ruling class. Paradoxically, this is a subject about which relatively little is known.

The existence of a ruling class in the United States seems to be negated by the ability of the people as a whole to vote political power holders in or out of office by secret ballot. Yet the fact that only half of the eligible voting-age population votes in presidential elections (Figure 18.5 and Table 18.1) suggests that the majority of citizens distrusts the candidates' promises or doubts that one candidate can do anything more than any other to make life significantly better (Hadley 1978; Ladd 1978). Moreover, the actual selection of political candidates and the financing and conduct of election campaigns are controlled through special-interest groups and political action committees. Small coalitions of powerful individuals working through lobbyists, law firms, legislatures, the courts, executive and administrative agencies, and the mass media can decisively influence the course of elections and of national affairs. The great bulk of the decision-making process consists of responses to pressures exerted by special-interest groups (Drew 1983; Thomas 1986; Sabato 1989). In the campaigns for election to Congress, the candidate who spends the most money usually wins.

Those who deny that there is a ruling class in the United States argue that power is dispersed among many different contending blocs, lobbies, associations, clubs, industries, regions, income groups, ethnic groups, states, cities, age groups, legislatures, courts, and unions, and that no coalition powerful enough to dominate all the others can form (Dahl 1981). In the terminology of the economist John Kenneth Galbraith (1967), there is no ruling class; there is only "countervailing" power. But the crucial question is this: Is there a category of people who share a set of underlying interests in the perpetuation of the status quo and who by virtue of their extreme wealth are able to set limits to the kinds of laws and executive policies that are enacted and followed out? The evidence for the existence of such a category of people consists largely of studies of the

Figure 18.5
Percentage of eligible voters who vote for president is declining.

Candidates	Percent of eligible voters who voted	Number of votes cast
1960 Kennedy—Nixon	63.1%	68,838,000
1964 Johnson—Goldwater	61.8%	70,645,000
1968 Humphrey—Nixon	60.7%	73,212,000
1972 McGovern—Nixon	55.1%	77,625,000
1976 Carter—Ford	53.6%	81,603,000
1980 Carter—Reagan	52.6%	86,497,000
1984 Mondale—Reagan	53.1%	92,631,000
1988 Bush—Dukakis	50.1%	91,584,820

Source: U.S. Bureau of the Census, *Congressional Quarterly*, Jan. 21, 1989.

Table 18.1
PRESIDENTIAL MANDATES?

YEAR	WINNER (PARTY)	PERCENTAGE OF TOTAL POPULAR VOTE	PERCENTAGE OF VOTING-AGE POPULATION
1932	Roosevelt (D)	57.4	30.1
1936	Roosevelt (D)	60.8	34.6
1940	Roosevelt (D)	54.7	32.2
1944	Roosevelt (D)	53.4	29.9
1948	Truman (D)	49.6	25.3
1952	Eisenhower (R)	55.1	34.0
1956	Eisenhower (R)	57.4	34.1
1960	Kennedy (D)	49.7	31.2
1964	Johnson (D)	61.1	37.8
1968	Nixon (R)	43.4	26.4
1972	Nixon (R)	60.7	33.5
1976	Carter (D)	50.1	26.8
1980	Reagan (R)	50.7	26.7
1984	Reagan (R)	58.8	31.2
1988	Bush (R)	53.4	26.8

Even the most "popular" presidents have been elected by only about one-third of the voting-age population.
Source: Cook 1989:137.

extent of interlocking memberships on corporate boards of directors and the concentration of ownership and wealth in giant corporations and well-to-do families. This kind of data alone cannot prove the existence of a ruling class, since there remains the problem of how boards of directors and wealthy families actually influence decisions on crucial matters such as the rate of inflation, unemployment, national health service, energy policy, tax structure, resource depletion, pollution, military spending, urban blight, and so forth (Domhoff 1983, 1987; Schwartz 1987; Useem 1984). As we will see in the next section, the concentration of wealth and economic power in the United States shows at least that there is a real poten-

tial for such influence to be exerted (Roberts and Brintnall 1982:259).

THE CONCENTRATION OF WEALTH

According to the Federal Reserve Board's 1983 "Survey of Consumer Financing," 2 percent of U.S. families owned the following:

20 percent of all real estate

50 percent of all privately held stocks

39 percent of all taxable bonds

70 percent of all nontaxable bonds

33 percent of all business assets

30 percent of all liquid assets

Additional Federal Reserve Board studies show that the top 2 percent of the population hold 28 percent of total net wealth and that the top 10 percent hold 57 percent of total net worth, while the bottom 50 percent hold only 4.5 percent of total net worth (Thurow 1987:30). Other studies show even greater concentration of wealth. The Joint Economic Committee of Congress estimates that 1 percent of Americans in 1986 owned more than 33 percent of total wealth, up from 27 percent in 1974 (Batra 1987; Thurow 1987).

The concentration of economic power is far greater than these statistics suggest. The reason is that for most of the population, the main form of wealth consists of residences and automobiles. These forms of wealth are not capital. They cannot be used to create more capital nor can they be used to control economic decisions. On the other hand, people who own large amounts of business assets — stocks, bonds, and commercial real estate — own capital and can exert control over those who do not. Moreover, the fact that 0.5 percent of the population owns 50 percent of the corporate stock in private hands does not tell us how much capital is actually controlled by these individuals. To control a large corporation, one does not need to own 51 percent of the stock. Since most private investors hold only small quantities of stock, investors who own 15 percent or less of the stock control corporate policy.

According to *Forbes* magazine, the 400 richest people in the United States are members of 82 wealthy families. These individuals and families owned $166 billion of business assets in 1983. But when these assets are broken down into blocks of corporate holdings that comprise 15 percent or more of the stock in such corporation, these people were found to control not $166 billion worth of capital, but

$2213 billion of capital — or 40.2 percent of all fixed nonresidential private capital in the United States (Morehouse and Dembo 1985a:23).

About half of stocks and bonds are owned by institutional investors, who administer pension funds, trust funds, and insurance companies. It is the corporations, families, and people who control these institutional investors that have the greatest economic power.

According to a study carried out on voting rights in major corporations by the U.S. Senate Committee on Governmental Affairs (1978), power to vote stock in 122 of the largest corporations in America was concentrated in 21 institutional investors. These 122 corporations had 2259 subsidiaries and affiliates comprising the largest industrial, financial, transportation, insurance, utility, and retail firms in the country. The 21 top institutional investors consisted mostly of banks and insurance companies such as Morgan Guaranty, Citicorp, Prudential Insurance, Bankamerica, Manufacturers Hanover, Bankers Trust, Equitable Life, and Chase Manhattan. Not only was each of these banks one of the 5 largest stock voters in anywhere from 8 to 56 of the largest corporations, but as a group they were one another's largest stock voters. Morgan Guaranty, which was the top stock voter in 27 of the largest corporations, was also the top stock voter in Citicorp, Manufacturers Hanover, Chemical New York, Bankers Trust, and Bankamerica. But the controllers and the controlled were really one and the same, because the largest institutional stock voters in Morgan Guaranty were none other than Citicorp, Chase Manhattan, Manufacturers Hanover, and Bankers Trust (U.S. Senate Committee on Governmental Affairs 1978:3).

As a result of the wave of buyouts and mergers that took place in the United States during the 1980s (see page 363), the concentration of economic power has continued to increase. It is entirely possible, therefore, that a small group of individuals and families exerts a decisive influence over the policies of an immensely powerful group of corporations. Some of the individuals and families involved are well known. Besides the Mellons, they include Rockefellers, DuPonts, Fords, Hunts, Pews, and Gettys (Figure 18.6). But it is a testament to the ability of the super-rich to live in a world apart that the names of many other powerful families are unknown to the general public. Anthropologists have been remiss in not studying the patterns of thoughts and actions of the super-rich (Nader 1972).

Poverty and Upward Mobility in the United States

Modern industrial democracies attribute great importance to the achievement of mobility from the subordinate to the superordinate classes. In the United States, it was traditionally held that by diligent effort poor people could work their way up from poverty to riches within a lifetime. It is clear, however, that only a tiny fraction of the population can hope to move into the ruling class.

At the lower levels, the U.S. stratification system is fairly open — but not as open as was traditionally believed. The main factor that determines a person's chances of upward mobility is the level at which one starts: "There is much upward mobility in the United States, but most of it involves very short social distances" (Blau and Duncan 1967:420).

According to official government standards 32 million Americans were living below the poverty line in 1986 (Bureau of the Census 1989:434). Twenty percent of the nation's children fall into this group (Bane and Ellwood 1989). The adequacy of the government's definition of poverty remains in doubt, however. At least one-third of a low-income family's budget must be spent on food in order to maintain minimum nutritional standards. Families of four with incomes twice as high as

Figure 18.6   Members of the ruling class?
(a) H. Ross Perot; (b) Donald Trump; (c) David Rockefeller.

(a)   *(b)*   *(c)*

the poverty cutoff do not necessarily enjoy a comfortable standard of living. The costs of housing, education, transportation, and medical attention have risen more rapidly than income, and such families have had to contend with the declining quality of goods, services, utilities, roads, streets, public buildings, parks, and public transportation (Harrington 1980).

What is the reason for the persistence of a large poverty class in the United States? The perennial favorite explanation is that the poor are victims of their own mental, behavioral, and cultural shortcomings. But as we have seen (page 227) values said to be distinctive of the culture of poverty are actually shared by the middle class. Many middle-class Americans seem to believe that the poorer you are, the more you should save, and the harder you should work: "The first principle is that in order to move up, the poor must not only work, they must work harder than the classes above them" (Gilder 1981:256). But isn't this a case of expecting more from those who have least? According to Anthony Leeds, the poor in the United States are not victims of their own values; rather they are the victims

> of certain kinds of labor markets which are structured by the condition of national technology, available capital resources, enterprise location, training institution, relations to foreign and internal markets, balance-of-trade relations, and the nature of the profit system of capitalist societies. . . . These are not independent [characteristics] of some suppressed culture [of poverty] but characteristics or indices of certain kinds of total economic systems. [Leeds 1970:246]

What this boils down to is that due to factors beyond their control, most of the poor are doomed to remain poor, even when they try harder than the people above them (Thurow 1987).

STREETCORNER MEN, WASHINGTON, D.C.

The view that America's poor refuse to work hard and to save because of a culture of poverty fails to take into account the types of work and opportunities that are open to them. In his book *Tally's Corner* (1967), Elliot Liebow, an ethnographer who has studied the black streetcorner men of Washington, D.C., describes the conditions shaping the work patterns of the unskilled black male. The streetcorner men are full of contempt for the menial work they must perform, but this is not a result of any special tradition they acquire from the culture of poverty. Historically, the dregs of the job market in the United States have been left for blacks and other minorities—jobs whose conditions and prospects are the mark of failure, that are demeaned and ridiculed by the rest of the labor force and that pay only the minimum wage or less; jobs that are dull, as in dishwashing or floor polishing; dirty, as in garbage collecting and washroom attending; or backbreaking, as in truck loading or furniture moving (Figure 18.7).

The duller, dirtier, and more exhausting the work, the less likely that extra diligence and effort will be rewarded by anything but more of the same. There is no "track" leading from the night maid who cleans the executive's office to vice-president; from the dishwasher to the restaurant owner; from the unskilled, unapprenticed construction worker to journeyman electrician or bricklayer. These jobs are dead ends from the beginning. As Liebow points out, no one is more explicit in expressing the worth-

Figure 18.7   Dead-end job.
Nonunion employment at a construction site in
Washington, D.C.

lessness of the job than the boss who pays so little for it. The rest of society, contradicting its professed values concerning the dignity of labor, also holds the job of dishwasher or janitor in low esteem.

> So does the streetcorner man. He cannot do otherwise. He cannot draw from a job those social values which other people do not put into it. [Liebow 1967:59]

According to Liebow, an additional mark of the degradation is that wages for menial work in hotels, restaurants, hospitals, and office and apartment buildings take into account the likelihood that the workers will steal food, clothing, or other items in order to bring their take-home pay above subsistence. The employer then sets the wages so low that stealing must take place. Although implicitly acknowledging the need for theft, the employer nonetheless

tries to prevent it and will call the police if someone is caught stealing.

Liebow tells the story of Richard, a black man in his twenties who had tried to support his family with extra jobs ranging from shoveling snow to picking peas and who had won the reputation of being one of the hardest-working men on the street. "I figure you got to get out there and try. You got to try before you can get anything," said Richard. But after five years of trying, Richard pointed to a shabby bed, a sofa, a couple of chairs, and a television set, and gave up:

> I've been scuffling for five years from morning till night. And my children still don't have anything, my wife don't have anything, and I don't have anything. [Ibid.:67]

Liebow sums up the etic conditions regulating the work pattern of the streetcorner men as follows:

> A man's chances for working regularly are good only if he is willing to work for less than he can live on, and sometimes not even then. On some jobs, the wage rate is deceptively higher than others, but the higher the wage rate, the more difficult it is to get the job, and the less the job security. Higher paying construction work tends to be seasonal and, during the season, the amount of work available is highly sensitive to business and weather conditions and to the changing requirements of individual projects. Moreover, high-paying construction jobs are frequently beyond the physical capacity of some of the men, and some of the low-paying jobs are scaled down even lower in accordance with . . . the assumption that the man will steal part of his wages on the job. [Ibid.:50–52]

RACIAL AND ETHNIC CHAUVINISM
VERSUS CLASS CONSCIOUSNESS

The intensity and clarity of racial and ethnic struggles in the United States present a counterpoint to the generally unconscious and confused nature of class relations. Far more than classes, racial and ethnic minorities and majorities are the stratified groups that manifest a sense of their own identity, consciousness of a common destiny, and collective purpose. Why has this been the case? The persecution, segregation, and exploitation of minority enclaves by racial and ethnic majorities, and the activism of minorities on their own behalf can be viewed as forms of political and economic struggle that preserve the overall pattern of class stratification. Instead of uniting to improve schools, neighborhoods, jobs, and health services, ethnic and racial groups seek to achieve their own advancement at one another's expense (Figure 18.8). Ethnic chauvinism thus pits "have-nots" against "have-littles," and thereby allows the "haves" to maintain their wealth and power (see Bottomore 1966; Perlo 1976; Sowell 1983).

Blacks were abandoned (and actively persecuted) by working-class whites and left behind to suffer the worst effects of low wages, unemployment, and exploitation because large numbers of whites, by abandoning blacks, increased (or thought they increased) their own chances of rising to middle-class status. However, it can be argued that working-class whites pay an enormous penalty for failing to unite with black poverty and working-classes. For example, in her study of the working-class neighborhood of Greenpoint-Williamsburg in Brooklyn, New York, Ida Susser (1982:208)

Figure 18.8   Minority against minority.
Victims of prejudice are not necessarily free of prejudice. Here, black youths warn Puerto Ricans to stay out of their club's territory.

found that racial divisions debilitated collective action and allowed elected officials and commercial developers a free hand that benefited middle- and upper-class whites. "So long as racial issues kept white voters loyal, elected officials could ignore the needs of a poor white working-class constituency."

The New Racism

One of the reasons for the limited success of the black power movement in the United States is that it provoked a reactive increase in the solidarist sentiments and activities of the white cultural, racial, and ethnic groups. In response to real or imagined threats to their schools, neighborhoods, and jobs, "white ethnics"—people of Italian, Polish, Irish, and Jewish descent—fought back against black power. They mounted antibusing campaigns and created new private and public school systems based on segregated suburban residence patterns (Glasser 1988; Katz and Taylor 1988; Stein and Hill 1977).

During the 1980s, tensions between whites and blacks increased markedly in many different cities and regions all across the United States. A wave of racially motivated verbal and physical abuse directed against blacks affected not only urban neighborhoods (such as New York's Howard Beach and Bensonhurst) but college campuses as well. This resurgence of overt racism results in part from the fact that Ronald Reagan's administration devalued civil rights, encouraged resentment against affirmative action, and fostered racial polarization by cutting back on critical social programs (Glasser 1989; C. Murray 1984). But there is a deeper level of sociocultural causation that needs to be explored. One must ask why such a political program became viable

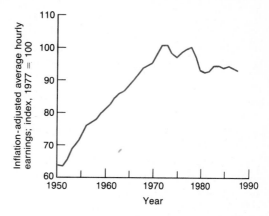

Figure 18.9   The decline in average real earnings.

during the 1980s. It seems likely that the support of political leaders who were indifferent to or vindictive about the plight of the country's minorities was related to the marked deterioration in the economic prospects of the white majority. Polls reveal that many working- and middle-class whites have grown apprehensive about being able to improve or even maintain their socioeconomic well-being. For the first time in history, many young people feel that they will not be able to live as comfortably as their parents (Figure 18.9) (A. Murray 1989). These are not groundless fears. The wave of racial and ethnic unrest coincides with a period during which the average real weekly earnings of production and nonsupervisory wage laborers has declined by 18 percent (Morehouse and Dembo 1988:7) and hourly take-home pay has for the first time slipped well below that of the other major industrial powers (see Table 18.2). Whites, struggling to get a larger piece of a shrinking pie, regard any form of affirmative action as "reverse discrimination," and have lost whatever interest they ever had in extending a helping hand to the poor, especially the black and Hispanic poor. Coming from segre-

Table 18.2

HOURLY PAY LEVELS (FOR PRODUCTION WORKERS,
IN U.S. DOLLARS)

	1985	1986	1987	1988
U.S.	$12.95	$13.19	$13.44	$13.62
Japan	6.47	9.47	11.14	13.80
West Germany	9.56	13.35	16.87	20.19
Italy	7.40	10.01	12.33	14.77
France	7.52	10.27	12.42	14.03
Britain	6.19	7.50	8.96	11.06

Source: Malabre 1989.

gated neighborhoods and largely if not totally segregated schools, blacks and whites seldom form friendships in their youth. They grow up as if they came from entirely different societies. It is no wonder, then, that when blacks are thrown together with whites in predominantly white high schools and colleges, they feel insecure and huddle together for protection against insensitive or openly hateful treatment (Flemming 1984; Hacker 1989).

VALUES AND THE MATRIFOCAL FAMILY: THE FLATS

One of the explanations for poverty in the urban ghettos focuses attention on the problem of so-called fatherless, or *matrifocal*, families (see page 139). (The most common explanation for black poverty continues to be based on notions of racial inferiority. See page 37 for a discussion of this explanation.)

The main structural features of matrifocality are as follows: The domestic unit consists of a mother and her children by several different men. Some of the woman's coresident adult daughters may also have children. The fathers provide only temporary and partial support.

Men who move in and out of the domestic unit are etically "married" to mothers — they act out all the typical husband-father roles. Yet emically the relationship is distinguished from "true marriage" (González 1970).

In 1965, with the release of a report by Daniel P. Moynihan, then U.S. Assistant Secretary of Labor, matrifocality received official recognition as the prime cause of the perpetuation of poverty among blacks in the United States. According to Moynihan, black youths are not properly motivated to take jobs that are actually available because of the absence of a male father figure in their families. They are reared in households where only the women are regularly employed. Adult males drift in and out of these households, and thus black youths grow up without the aid and inspiration of a stable male figure holding a steady job and providing comfort and security for wife and children. Moynihan proposed that matrifocality was a cause not only of poverty but of crime and drug addiction as well (Moynihan 1986).

Explanations of poverty that appeal to enculturation experience within matrifocal households don't explain very much because the phenomenon of matrifocality is itself a response to poverty.

Like all domestic arrangements, the matrifocal family in the United States represents an adjustment to certain conditions that are beyond the control of its members. The conditions in question are these: (1) Both men and women lack access to strategic resources — that is, they own no significant property; (2) wage labor is available to both men and women; (3) women earn as much as or more than men; and (4) a man's wages are insufficient to provide subsistence for a dependent wife and children.

The official welfare policies of the U.S. government greatly strengthen the tendency to form matrifocal families. Households that seek welfare support usually cannot contain able-bodied "fathers." Mothers whose husbands or children's fathers do not earn enough money to support the household can claim Aid to Families with Dependent Children (AFDC) welfare allotments, provided the fathers are not coresident with their children. One of the reasons this expedient is built into the national and state welfare laws is that it is cheaper for the government to provide such payments than to establish a high-quality system of child day-care centers that would free poor mothers to go to work. Since poor fathers cannot stay home with their children and claim AFDC allotments, the law confers upon poor women an extra economic value that makes it inevitable that they will become the center of domestic life as long as the men cannot earn enough to make the AFDC allotments unnecessary. Since it is the woman who is favored for AFDC payments, it is she who gets the lease in public housing projects and who controls (but does not own) the family's dwelling space.

In her study of the Flats, a black ghetto in a midwestern city (Figure 18.10), Carol Stack (1974) provides an account of the strategies that poverty-level families follow in attempting to maximize their security and well-being in the face of the AFDC laws and the inadequate

Figure 18.10   Children of the flats. Area of Carol Stack's study.

wages of the unskilled male. Nuclear families do not exist in the Flats because the material conditions necessary for such families do not exist. Instead, the people of the Flats are organized into large female-centered networks of kinfolk and neighbors. The members of these networks engage in reciprocal economic exchanges, take care of one another's children, provide emergency shelter, and help one another in many ways not characteristic of middle-class domestic groups.

In the Flats the most important single factor that affects interpersonal relationships between men and women is unemployment and the difficulty that men have in finding secure jobs:

> Losing a job, or being unemployed month after month, debilitates one's self-importance and independence, and for men, necessitates that they sacrifice their role in the economic support of their families.

Then they become unable to assume the masculine role as defined by American society. [Stack 1974:112]

Ironically, as Stack points out:

Attempts by those on welfare to formulate nuclear families are efficiently discouraged by welfare policy. In fact, welfare policy encourages the maintenance of non-coresidential cooperative domestic networks. [Ibid.:127]

A woman can be cut off from welfare as soon as her husband gets out of the army or comes home from prison, or if she gets married. Thus, "Women come to realize that welfare benefits and ties with kin networks provide greater security for them and their children" (ibid.:113).

THE CRIME CONNECTION

The United States has one of the highest rates of violent crime found among industrial nations. More than one-fifth of the inhabitants of America's largest cities feel "very unsafe" when they have to go out at night in their own neighborhoods. Women and old people have the greatest fear. Over half of all U.S. women say that they are afraid to go out alone after dark. Senior citizens are afraid to leave their apartments during the day. People also feel insecure indoors: One-third of all U.S. households contain firearms purchased for protection against intruders (U.S. National Criminal Justice Information and Statistics Service 1978). In 1986 there were over 4 million victims of assaults, 1 million victims of personal robberies (not including victims robbed in commercial establishments), 130 thousand victims of rapes or attempted rape, and 163 thousand victims of purse snatchings (*Sourcebook of Criminal Justice Statistics* 1987). According to the FBI's an-

nual *Uniform Crime Reports*, there are about 20,000 homicides per year.

There are 5 times more homicides, 10 times more rapes, and 17 times more robberies in the United States than in Japan; and there are 7 times more homicides, 12 times more rapes, and 8 times more robberies in the United States than in Great Britain. London and Tokyo have far lower incidences of violent crime than do less populous American cities such as Chicago, Philadelphia, or St. Louis. In 1979 there were 279 times as many robberies, 14 times as many rapes, and 12 times as many murders in New York City as in Tokyo (Ross and Benson 1979).

One reason for the higher rate of violent crime in the United States is that U.S. citizens own far more pistols and rifles per capita than the Japanese or British. Fewer than 150 crimes each year in the whole of Japan involve the use of handguns (Chang 1988:143). The right to "bear arms" is guaranteed by the U.S. Constitution. But the failure to pass stricter gun control laws itself reflects, in part at least, the pervasive, realistic fear of being robbed or attacked and the consequent desire to defend person and property. Hence, the cause of the high incidence of violent crimes must be sought at deeper levels of U.S. culture.

Much evidence links the unusually high rate of crime in the United States to the long-term, grinding poverty and economic hopelessness of America's inner-city minorities, especially of blacks and Hispanics. Although suburban crime is also on the rise, the principal locus of violent crime remains the inner cities. The FBI's *Uniform Crime Reports* shows that blacks, who constitute 11 percent of the population, account for about 43 percent of all criminal offenders arrested for violent crimes. In two crucial categories of such crimes—homicides and robberies—black offenders actually outnumber whites on a nationwide basis, rural and urban areas included. But the disproportion is much larger in the cities, where the incidence of violent crime is greatest (Hindelang 1978).

One should note too that proportionately blacks themselves suffer more from violent crimes than do whites. A poor black is 25 times more likely than a wealthy white to be a victim of a robbery resulting in injury, and the ratio of black homicide victims to white homicide victims is 8 to 1. In fact, homicide is the ranking killer of black males between 15 and 24 years of age. More black males die from homicide than from motor vehicle accidents, diabetes, emphysema, or pneumonia. (Two out of five black male children born in an American city in 1980 will not reach age 25.)

The basic reason for all this crime is long-term chronic unemployment and poverty. During and after World War II, U.S. blacks migrated in unprecedented numbers from farms to cities in search of factory jobs just when the economy was in rapid transition from goods production to service and information production. Today over half of America's blacks live in major cities, and over half of these — about 7.5 million people — live in the dirtiest and most dilapidated inner cores of these cities. During the 1970s in the large cities, while the number of central-city whites living in poverty declined by 5 percent, the number of central-city blacks living in poverty increased by 21 percent. Whereas one in eight whites fit the government's definition of poor in 1983, every third black did. "Working one's way out of poverty is not easy when the economy values the average black's labor at 60% of a white's, the same three-fifths ratio that the authors of the U.S. Constitution used to value black slaves for purposes of political representation" (MacDougal 1984).

Figure 18.11   Youth on a stoop.
The alternatives are dishwashing, floor polishing, and truck loading.

Teenagers, both black and white, commit a disproportionate share of violent crimes. Ronald H. Brown of the National Urban League (1978) calculates that over half of all black teenagers are unemployed; and in ghettos like Harlem in New York City, the unemployment rate among black youths may be as high as 86 percent (Figure 18.11).

There is a body of scholarly opinion that claims that poverty in general has little to do with the high rate of criminal violence in the United States and therefore that black unemployment and poverty are not sufficient in themselves to account for the high rates of U.S. crime. If one simply compares crime rates by state or city, those with low per capita incomes do not necessarily have high rates of criminal violence. But the poverty of the black ghetto is different from the poverty of rural whites or of an earlier generation of urban ethnics. Unlike the rural poor, inner-city blacks have the opportunity as well as the motive to commit violent crimes. The city is an ideal setting for finding and surprising victims and successfully eluding the police. Most important, unlike the European immigrants of previous generations, blacks have with the passage of time become more and not less concentrated inside their ghettos (Figure 18.12). Under these conditions, the benefits of criminal behavior outweigh the risks of getting caught and being sent to jail. John Conyers, a member of the black congressional caucus, writes:

(a)

(b)

(c)

Figure 18.12 *Low-cost housing. (a) Pruitt-Igoe-public housing complex in St. Louis; (b) Scudder Homes housing project in Newark; (c) a building in New York City's South Bronx— cheerful decals cover the empty windows.*

When survival is at stake, it should not be surprising that criminal activity begins to resemble an opportunity rather than a cost, work rather than deviance, and a possibly profitable undertaking that is superior to a coerced existence directed by welfare bureaucrats. [1978:678]

THE DRUG CONNECTION

A recognition of high odds against attaining economic success through academic achievement or legitimate business lies behind the decision of many black, Hispanic, and other minority youth to traffic in illicit drugs. A week spent selling crack can bring more wealth than a year of working as a dishwasher or a fast-food server. Ironically, the most successful drug businesses are run by young men who refrain from taking drugs themselves and who display many of the characteristics associated with successful entrepreneurship in legitimate businesses. They break into the trade with a small investment, hire employees, keep careful accounts, strive to establish good relationships with their customers, encourage the consumption of their product, adjust prices to market conditions, and keep careful tabs on what their competitors are doing. Of course, the use of crack and other addictive substances has a devastating effect on the consumers who use it as a means of escape from their squalid reality. The people of the United States pay an enormous price for the drug trade in the form of increased crime, overburdened courts and jails, drug-related health problems such as AIDS, and ruined lives (Massing 1989; Williams 1989).

THE WELFARE CONNECTION

A disproportionate share of violent urban crime in the United States is committed by black and Hispanic juveniles brought up in matrifocal families that receive AFDC allotments. This connection between juvenile delinquency and matrifocality reflects the fact that AFDC benefits are set below poverty-level incomes. Almost all inner-city AFDC women therefore count on supplementary incomes from husbands-in-hiding, coresident male consorts, or former consort fathers of their children.

Anthropologist Jagna Sharff (1981) found that all the mothers in a group of 24 Hispanic AFDC families living in New York City's Lower East Side had some kind of male consort (Figure 18.13). While few of the men in the house held regular full-time jobs, even those who were unemployed chipped in something toward food and rent from selling stolen goods, dealing in marijuana or cocaine, and from an occasional burglary or mugging. Some women had more than one consort, while others picked up money and gifts through more casual relationships.

In their early teens, young inner-city boys

Figure 18.13   Lower east side.
The vicinity of Jagna Sharff's study.

make substantial contributions to their households' economic balance through their involvement in street crime and dope peddling. In addition, they confer an important benefit on their mothers in the form of protection against the risk of rape, mugging, and various kinds of ripoffs to which the ghetto families are perpetually exposed.

Sharff found that AFDC mothers value sons for streetwise *macho* qualities, especially their ability to use knives or guns, which are needed to protect the family against unruly or predatory neighbors. While the AFDC mothers did not actively encourage their sons to enter the drug trade, everyone recognized that a successful drug dealer could become a very rich man. To get ahead in the drug business, one needs the same *macho* qualities that are useful in defending one's family. When young men bring home their first drug profits, mothers have mixed feelings of pride and ap-prehension. Since young ghetto males have a 40 percent chance of dying by age 25, a ghetto mother has to have more than one son if she hopes to enjoy the protection of a streetwise male. In her sample of AFDC families, Sharff compiled a record of male homicides (see Table 18.3).

One must be careful not to conclude that every family on AFDC conforms to this pattern. For many mothers, AFDC represents a one-time emergency source of funds used in the aftermath of divorce or separation until they can find jobs and arrange for child care. Also one must be careful not to conclude that there is something special about Hispanic or black culture that leads their young men and mothers to behave in the manner depicted by Sharff. A very similar pattern exists, for example, among Irish welfare recipients in the D-Street projects of South Boston (personal communication, Nancy Scheper-Hughes).

Table 18.3

MALE HOMICIDES IN 24 AFDC FAMILIES,
1976–1979

VICTIM'S AGE	IMMEDIATE CAUSE OF DEATH
25	Shot in drug-related incident
19	Shot in dispute in grocery store
21	Shot in drug-related incident
28	Stabbed in drug-related incident
32	"Suicide" in a police precinct house
30	Stabbed in drug-related incident
28	Poisoned by adulterated heroin
30	Arson victim
24	Shot in drug-related incident
19	Tortured and stabbed in drug-related incident

Source: Sharff 1980.

Hyperindustrial Family and Gender Roles

The rise of the information and service economy was dependent on and has contributed to a dramatic shift in the sexual composition of the U.S. labor force and to a rise in the cost of rearing children (see page 96); these changes in turn are responsible for other notable shifts at the structural and ideological levels of U.S. social life.

Since World War II, two out of three new jobs have been taken by calling up a "reserve army" of married women. Concurrently, partially as a result of the premium placed on education for upward mobility in a service and information economy, and partially as a result of the call-up of married women, middle-income families with only one wage earner no longer can afford to rear even one or two children. These infrastructural changes account for other changes on the structural and super-structural levels, affecting marriage patterns, family organization, and behavioral and ideological aspects of gender roles and sexuality, such as the post–World War II rise of feminist doctrines and the politics of female liberation (Margolis 1984).

Four major categories of effects can be traced to the shifting sexual composition of the work force and the increased cost of rearing children: (1) declining rates of fertility, (2) falling marriage and rising divorce rates, (3) new forms of family structures, and (4) new gender roles and new forms of sexuality.

FERTILITY

After World War II, U.S. fertility rates rose rapidly, producing the phenomenon of the "baby boom" that reached its peak in 1957. Subsequently, the completed fertility rate fell to levels that are still at a historic low, a full 50 percent from the peak of the baby boom — from 3.69 to 1.81. While it is true that the crude birthrate per 1000 women has risen slightly since 1975, the all-important completed fertility rate has remained unchanged at its historic low. The reason the crude birth rate per 1000 women has risen slightly is due entirely to the fact that the age cohort of baby boom children has been in its prime reproductive years, and there is no indication that the completed fertility rate is about to rise (Newitt 1985; Westoff 1986). The upper, middle, and low projections of the U.S. Census Bureau are 2.1, 1.9, and 1.6 births respectively, to the end of the century.

There are many ideological expressions of the trend toward smaller numbers of children per woman. Surveys show that the number of women between age 18 and 34 who say that they do not expect to have children has quintupled since 1967; 11 percent of the women in this age group say they want no children at all. Among those who want children, the number of offspring desired dropped from four to two during the decade 1970–1980. In 1970, 53 percent of women cited motherhood as "one of the best parts of being a woman"; in 1983, only 26 percent did (Dowd 1983).

MARRIAGE AND DIVORCE RATES

One out of three U.S. marriages now ends in divorce, a threefold increase since 1960. Among couples under 30 years old, the rate of divorce is rapidly approaching one out of two marriages, four times higher than it was in 1960. (These figures represent the number of *current* marriages divided by the number of *current* divorces. They do not reflect the total number of past marriages and past divorces.)

This has been accompanied by a great deal of remarriage. Over one-fifth of all marriages are remarriages involving at least one previously divorced partner. Fifty percent of divorced women remarry within 2 years (Sachs 1985:761). Today there are more marriages per 1000 people than in 1960 — almost as many as in 1900. But among single women aged 15 – 44, marriage rates per 1000 have fallen by 30 percent since 1960. Americans are waiting longer to get married. The percentage of women aged 20 – 24 who are unmarried rose from 36 percent to 53 percent between 1970 and 1982; for men in the same age group, the change was from 55 to 72 percent (*The New York Times*, 27 May 1985). Moreover, the probability of divorce increases with remarriage: 33 percent overall for the first time, 50 percent for the second (Sachs 1985:761). So marriage itself as an institution is not in decline. What is in decline is monogamous marriages that last until one of the partners dies.

FAMILY STRUCTURE

At the beginning of the century, most marriages were entered into for life, and families were headed by male breadwinners. Each married pair had on the average three or more children, and the children were brought up by their natural parents unless the marriage was terminated through death.

Today, matrifocal domestic groups are the fastest-growing form of family, up by 80 percent since 1960. There are over 8 million such domestic groups in the United States. Currently 20.5 percent of all children under age 18 live in households headed by divorced, never-married, separated, or widowed women. As we have seen (page 374), matrifocality is especially common among blacks: 47 percent of black households with children present are headed

by women, five times more than in 1950. But this kind of family is growing even faster among whites and constitutes over 15 percent of all white households with children present. Largely as a result of divorce, separation, and growth of female-headed families, 50 percent of all children born today in the United States can expect to live with only one parent for some period before they reach the age of 18 (Bane and Ellwood 1989:1051). Or to look at it slightly differently, 33 percent of all children are already living either with only one natural parent or one with natural parent and a stepparent. Very little is known as yet about how parents, stepparents, stepsiblings, children, and stepchildren are dealing with each other — what kinds of bonds they form, what kinds of responsibilities they accept, and what kinds of conflicts they experience (Weitzman 1985). It seems likely, however, that higher divorce rates for second and third marriages are linked to the strains of coping with the nation's 6.5 million stepchildren under age 18 (Collins 1985:15).

NEW GENDER ROLES AND FORMS OF SEXUALITY

Surveys show that a profound change has taken place in the United States with respect to attitudes toward premarital and extramarital intercourse. The number of adults who in response to questionnaire surveys say that they sanction or accept premarital and extramarital intercourse rose from 20 percent of adults to over 50 in the period from 1960 to 1980. During the same period, the number of unmarried couples who say they are living together increased almost as fast as the number of female-headed families. While this trend seems to have slowed between 1980 and 1985, the increase in the number of young adults, aged 25 to 34, who say they are living alone—already up from 1 out of 20 in 1950 to 1 out of 3 in 1980—continued between 1980 and 1985 (Herbers 1985). The relevant point is that people in this age bracket who are living alone are unlikely to be sleeping alone.

Considerable evidence points to an increase in premarital sexual activity among unwed juveniles and young adults. Planned Parenthood studies show that one-half of the teenagers graduating from high school have an active sex life. Given the absence of intensive, publicly supported contraceptive programs for teenagers, it is not surprising that the rate of teenage pregnancies has doubled since 1965 and that the United States now finds itself with the highest rate in the industrial world. This distinction is partially attributable to the very high rate of pregnancies among U.S. black teenagers, but the rate for white teenagers (83 per 1000) is double that of England and quadruple that of the Netherlands. Four out of ten American women will have become pregnant by the time they reach 20 years (Brozan 1985).

The basic shift in U.S. attitudes toward sexuality can be described in terms of an ever-widening separation of the hedonistic from the reproductive aspects of sexual relations. One derivative of this trend is the increased production and consumption of pornographic materials, including "adult" books, *Playboy*, *Hustler*, and *Penthouse*-type magazines (Figure 18.14), and pornographic videocassettes. "What would have been off-limits even in a

Figure 18.14   Porn.
Making money out of sex is a big industry in the United States.

red-light district a few years ago is now available for people to see in their living rooms" (Lindsey 1985:9).

The relaxation of U.S. laws against homosexuality can also be viewed as an expression of the same trend. As we have seen (page 261), societies that interdict homosexuality are strongly pronatalist and tend to condemn all forms of sex that do not lead to childbirth and parenting. Heterosexual couples committed to the separation of sex from reproduction do not differ from homosexual couples in this regard. The increase in the numbers of self-identified homosexuals testifies to the general liberalization of sexual rules of conduct since World War II (Figure 18.15). It remains to be seen, however, how far the fear of AIDS (acquired immune deficiency syndrome) will force homosexuals "back into the closet" (Figure 18.16). Since heterosexuals can contract AIDS from bisexual partners, sexual promiscuity is in decline throughout the population. If no vaccine or cure for AIDS is found, will marriage rates increase? Possibly. But fertility rates will probably remain unaffected.

A Theory of Culture Change in the United States

All of the changes we have described can be related to the hyperindustrial mode of production. The trend away from factory employment required and facilitated the call-up of female

Figure 18.15   Out of the closet.
A gay rights march in New York City.

Figure 18.16   Aids march.
There are early indications that the AIDS epidemic is reducing sexual promiscuity among homosexuals and heterosexuals.

labor previously locked up in child care; concurrently the premium placed on education for employment in nonmanufacturing jobs, together with the increase in the "opportunity costs" of pregnancy and parenting (that is, the

amount of income foregone when women stop working to bear and raise children), inflated the costs of rearing children, weakened the marriage bond, depressed the fertility rate, and furthered the separation of the reproductive from the hedonistic components of sexuality (Harris 1981).

The principal change that has occurred in the labor force is not only an increase in the proportion of women who are employed (see Table 18.4), but a growth in the proportion of employed women who are married and have children. Prior to World War II, only 15 percent of women living with husbands worked outside the home. In 1985, 59 percent of married women with children 6 years and under and 65.8 percent of all women with children aged 6–17 were in the labor force (Hayghe 1985:31). What do these women do? Over 83 percent of them hold nonmanufacturing, service- and information-producing jobs — mostly low-level jobs that pay on the average less than 70 percent of the wages earned by males (Serrin 1984:1).

The link between feminization and the information and service economy is reciprocal: Women, especially married women, had for-

Table 18.4

LABOR FORCE PARTICIPATION RATES OF WOMEN
BY AGE, SELECTED YEARS, 1948–1987

	PARTICIPATION RATE IN			
AGE	1948	1967	1977	1987
Total, 16 years and over	32.7	41.1	48.4	56.0
16 to 19 years	42.0	41.9	51.2	53.3
20 to 24 years	45.3	53.3	66.5	73.0
25 to 34 years	33.2	41.9	59.7	72.4
35 to 44 years	36.9	48.1	55.8	74.5
45 to 54 years	35.0	51.8	55.8	67.1

Source: Jacobs et al. 1989:16.

merly been barred from unionized, male-dominated manufacturing jobs in which they were seen by husbands and unions as a threat to the wage scale. In the nonunionized and traditionally feminine information and service occupations — secretaries, schoolteachers, health workers, saleswomen, and so on — there was less resistance. Seen from the perspective of capital investment, the reserve army of housewives constituted a source of cheap, docile labor that made the processing of information and people a profitable alternative to investment in factories devoted to goods production (Figure 18.17). In fact, U.S. firms were able to find an equivalent class of cheap labor for manufacturing enterprises only by transferring a considerable share of their goods production facilities to less developed countries, especially to Asia and Latin America. Thus the feminization of the labor force and the decline of goods manufacturing are closely related phenomena, although, as we have seen (page 257), this relationship has nothing to do with the inherent capacities of the sexes for physical labor and factory work.

Why did U.S. women respond in such large numbers to the service and information call-up? Ironically their primary motivation was to strengthen the traditional multichild, male breadwinner family in the face of rising costs of food, housing, and education. The real costs of these goods and services have risen faster than has the average male breadwinner's take-home pay. After 1965, family income in the United States was able to keep up with inflation only because of the contribution from working wives. The incomes of families in the age group 25–34 has dropped steadily since 1965 when compared with all family households, from the peak in 1965 at 96 percent of all family incomes to 86 percent in 1983, despite the prevalence of two-earner households (Mariano 1984).

Despite their lower rate of remuneration, married women's wages became critical for maintaining or achieving middle-class status, especially, as shown by Valery Oppenheimer in her book *Work and the Family* (1982), during "life-cycle squeezes" when young couples are just starting out and when older couples have to face the costs of sending children to college. To raise a child to age 18 at middle-class standards of consumption now costs over $100,000 — some estimates put it at over $300,000 — for a child born in 1981 (Espenshade 1984). Thereafter, a 4-year college education costs from $15,000 to $60,000 per child (Belkin 1985). The more the economy shifts toward services, information, and high-tech jobs, the greater the amount of schooling needed to achieve or maintain middle-class status. In other words, "higher-quality" children cost more. In this respect the current costs of rearing children represent the climax of the long-term shift from agricultural to industrial modes of production and from rural to urban ways of life associated with the demographic transition (see page 102). It is this substitution of quality for quantity that underlies the decade-by-decade drop in U.S. fertility prior to the baby boom, and the historic low fertility rate achieved in the decade 1975–1985. These lower fertility rates also reflect a decline in the counterflow of economic benefits from children to parents as children work apart from parents, establish separate households, and are no longer capable of paying the medical and housing costs of their aged fathers and mothers.

While the average U.S. family cannot rear more than one or two "high-quality" children without a second income, wives are incapable of providing that second income if they have to raise more than one or two children (given the virtually total absence of adequate subsidized day-care facilities in the nation). It is this con-

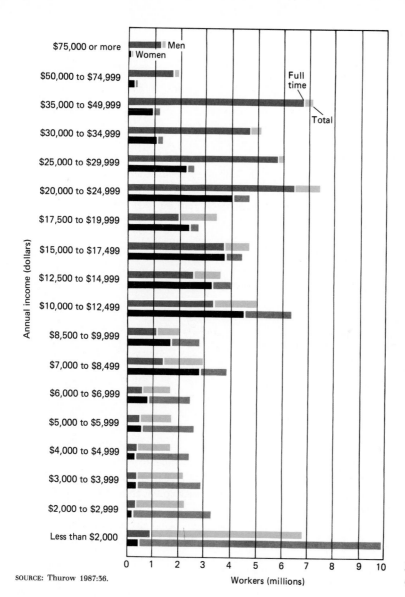

SOURCE: Thurow 1987:36.

Workers (millions)

Figure 18.17   Women as cheap labor.

tradition that explains why married women accept low-paying and dead-end jobs. But this situation is changing. There is a positive feedback effect (page 202) between working in the labor force, staying in it, and paying the cost of raising children. The more a woman puts into a

job, the more she earns and the more it costs her in the form of "forgone income" if she quits. As forgone income increases, so does the cost of staying home to rear children—and the likelihood that fewer children will be born.

Attitudes about motherhood have

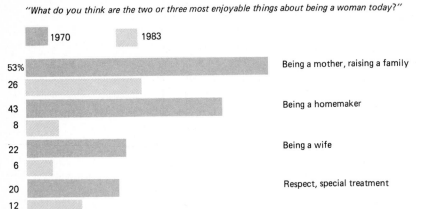

"What do you think are the two or three most enjoyable things about being a woman today?"

☐ 1970   ☐ 1983

53%	Being a mother, raising a family
26	
43	Being a homemaker
8	
22	Being a wife
6	
20	Respect, special treatment
12	
9	Career, jobs, pay
26	
14	General rights and freedoms
32	

1970 data from a Virginia Slims poll conducted by Louis Harris and Associates.
1983 data from a New York Times poll of 927 women conducted Nov. 11-20, 1983.

SOURCE: *The New York Times,* 4 December 1983.

Figure 18.18   Women on womanhood, United States.

changed accordingly. In 1970, when North American women were asked to name the most enjoyable things in life, 53 percent mentioned being a mother and raising a family, while only 9 percent mentioned career, jobs, or pay. In 1983, 26 percent mentioned being a mother and raising a family, 26 percent mentioned career, jobs, and pay, but only 6 percent mentioned being a wife, down from 22 percent in 1970 (Figure 18.18).

A common misunderstanding of declining U.S. fertility rates should be discussed. Many people hold that it is due to the introduction of birth control pills. This is incorrect, since the decline began in 1957 and it was not until 1963–1964 that the pill was widely adopted.

Beyond that, many contraceptive devices and practices were available in the 1930s, as demonstrated by the fact that the fertility rate in the 1930s was much lower than it became immediately after World War II. Moreover, as we have seen (Chapter 6), even preindustrial populations have effective means of limiting family size in relation to the costs and benefits of rearing children.

Divorce rates obviously reflect the falling fertility rate as well as married women's participation in the work force. Not having children tends to facilitate divorce; conversely, having large numbers of children makes divorce extremely difficult. And the more a married woman becomes involved in the labor force, the more independent she becomes of the male income, the more likely she is to accept the idea that she can get along without having a husband, and so the more likely she is to get divorced.

Finally, the feminization of the work force, mediated by declining fertility, higher divorce rates, and the demise of the male breadwinner family, is implicated in the separation of the reproductive from the hedonistic aspects of sexuality. The marital and procreative imperative of Victorian and early twentieth-century times, which stated that all sex was to take place within marriage and that all sex within marriage was to lead to reproduction, cannot appeal to men and women who are either not married or who, if married, are not having children. This, as already pointed out, places the structure of the households of many middle-class heterosexual couples on the continuum with that of homosexual couples, while simultaneously explaining the overt acceptance of casual sexual encounters (prior to the AIDS epidemic) and the rapid expansion of commerce in pornography.

As we have seen (Chapters 8 and 9), family structure is closely correlated with demographic, technological, economic, and environmental variables. It is impossible in the present case to mistake the direction of causality. While multiple and complex feedbacks have operated at all stages of the process, the main thrust emanated from changes occurring at the infrastructural level — the shift from goods production to service and information production. Alterations at the structural level — marriage and the organization of the family — did not show up until a substantial commitment to the new mode of production had taken place. For example, the number of women who had husbands present and who were participating in the work force had al-

ready risen from 15 percent to 30 percent by 1958. Yet it was not until 1970 that the feminist movement attained a level of national consciousness, when women shed their bras, held crockery-smashing parties, and marched down New York's Fifth Avenue shouting slogans like "Starve a rat tonight; don't feed your husband." These antics expressed the pent-up frustration of wives who were already in the labor force and experiencing the contradictions of the old and new gender roles. As noted by Maxine Margolis in her book *Mothers and Such:*

> While the media devoted much space to "bra-burning" and other supposed actrocities of the women's movement, little attention was paid to the reality of women's work which had set the stage for the revival of feminism. [1984:231]

Writing from an sociologist's perspective, Valerie Oppenheimer, in her book *Work and the Family,* makes the same point:

> There is no evidence that these substantial shifts in women's labor force participation were precipitated by prior changes in sex-role attitudes. On the contrary, they [change in sex role attitudes] lagged behind behavioral changes, indicating that changes in behavior have gradually brought about changes in sex role norms rather than the reverse. Moreover, the evidence clearly indicates that the start of the rapid changes in women's labor force behavior greatly preceded the rebirth of the feminist movement. [1982:30]

As Oppenheimer explains further, this is not to say that "more equalitarian sex-role attitudes and a feminist ideological perspective are not major motivating forces," but "that these attitudes reinforce or provide an ideological rationale (or normative justification)" (ibid.).

To identify the infrastructural conditions of a social movement and to assign them a causal priority over values and ideas is not to diminish the role of values and ideas or of volition in the dynamism of history. We have seen (page 306) that the extent to which action is mobilized under ideological and sentimental auspices alters the odds favoring the fulfillment of a particular infrastructural potential. Nonetheless, it is essential in this case, as well as in other controversial social movements, that both those who favor and those who oppose a particular change comprehend that some outcomes are more probable than others. In the present instance, for example, it seems highly improbable that women in the United States can be restored to their former situation as housewives. In order to resurrect the male breadwinner family and put women back behind the sink, the nation would have to revert to a more primitive phase of capitalism and industrialization, a course that even the most conservative antifeminists do not propose to take.

Religion

It might be supposed that as one of the world's technologically most advanced industrial societies, the United States would also be one of the societies in which the majority of citizens reject traditional forms of animism and animatism (see Chapter 15). Science is the principal source of modern technology, which in turn underlies the industrial mass production and consumption of goods, services, and information. While science is not necessarily opposed to a belief in souls, gods, or luck, scientific principles of knowledge do require that propositions based on faith, tradition, hunches, or visions be subjected to systematic logical and empirical tests. One might expect, therefore, that in a society in which science and scientific technology play a prominent role, most people would be agnostics, neither believing nor disbelieving in animism or animatism, if not outright atheists.

Yet 94 percent of U.S. citizens profess a belief in God or a universal spirit, 89 percent say they pray, and 78 percent say they belong to some organized religious group (Princeton Religious Research Center 1980:17). True, only 57 percent say that their religious beliefs are "very important" to them, and only 41 percent attend church during an average week (down from 49 percent in 1955). Nonetheless, this degree of belief and practice is far higher than in the noncommunist industrial societies of Western Europe and Japan (Princeton Religious Research Center 1979). Moreover, there are signs that while the established U.S. churches are having difficulty holding their own (or are slowly losing influence), many novel forms of religious belief and practice seem to be taking their place.

Some observers detect signs of a large-scale religious "awakening." This awakening involves more than a reaffirmed belief in an active, personal deity. The forms of awakening range from weekend encounter groups to messianic prophets. As seen by sociologist Robert Bellah (1976), the most representative aspect of this awakening is the acceptance of "Asian spirituality" as an antidote for Western "utilitarian individualism." According to Bellah, aspects of Zen, Taoism, Buddhism, Hinduism, Sufism, and other Oriental religions first began to strike a responsive chord in the counterculture of the late 1960s, as many Americans began to feel that the struggle to achieve material gains by and for individuals was hollow and meaningless. Helped along by drugs and meditation, the counterculture generation realized the "illusoriness of worldly striving." "Careerism and status-seeking, the sacrifice of present fulfillment for some ever-receding future goal, no longer seemed worthwhile" (Bellah 1976:341).

Recognizing that the United States had many unsolved material problems such as racism and poverty, Bellah nonetheless insists that the religious awakening was brought on as much by "the success of the society" and by the "realization that education and affluence did not bring happiness or fulfillment" as by its failures. Following this line of reasoning to its logical outcome, we are led to conclude that the basic cause of the religious awakening in the United States is a crisis of spirit and meaning rather than a crisis of practical material needs. Writes Bellah: "The deepest cause, no matter what particular factors contributed to the actual timing, was, in my opinion, the inability of utilitarian individualism to provide a meaningful pattern of personal and social existence" (ibid.:339).

It can be argued against this view, however, that the deepest and most characteristic impulse of America's religious awakening is not the search for ultimate meaning but the search for solutions to America's unsolved economic and social problems. The role of "Asian" spirituality in the formation and propagation of new religious groups and rituals in the United States is easily exaggerated. The number of people involved in new individualistic, shamanic, communal, and ecclesiastical cults and revitalization movements that have as their principal concern contemplation, withdrawal from worldly affairs, and other supposedly "Asian" motifs is actually quite small. Much more prominent are cults and move-

ments that have a definite "Western" program for mastering worldly problems and enhancing individual material welfare (Figure 18.19).

The point seems self-evident for those Americans who want to predict the future from horoscopes (like Nancy Reagan), cure illness through shamanistic trances, or disable their boss or teacher by sticking pins in dolls. These are all techniques for mastering the world rather than retreating from it.

Utilitarian motives are also self-evident in the seemingly endless varieties of weekend encounter groups and mind-body therapies that are part of the "human-potential movement." Executives prescribe encounter groups and sensitivity training courses to improve relationships among employees and to step up sales.

Figure 18.19   Reverend Robert Schuler in his Crystal Cathedral.
Ten thousand one-way mirrors set in filigreed steel, Orange, California.

In the more etherealized and spiritualized "trainings," the predominant, recurring theme is that of mind over matter. Not only do participants expect to control others by improving their control over themselves, but they expect to control physical happenings by the imposition of their thoughts on matter. Erhard Seminars Training (est), for example, claims that "nobody has to die unless he chooses to; all deaths are suicides, and there are no accidents. And you can fly if you allow yourself to know how" (Conway and Siegelman 1978:169). Similar extreme forms of mentalism — belief in the omnipotence of thought — characterize the principles and goals of the more "meditative" human potential disciplines. Scientology, for example, holds forth the promise of "not worrying and bogging myself down with a burden of problems," "freedom from my compulsions," "no longer feel[ing] afraid of anything," "ability to change body size," "ability to see through walls," and "ability to hear other people's thoughts" (Wallis 1977:121). Even cults such as the "Moonies" (The Unification Church), the Hare Krishnas (Figure 18.20), and the Divine Light Mission have a definite worldly commitment — a yearning for control — contradicting the notion that the current religious awakening in the United States is best understood as an Asian-inspired "critique of the expansion of wealth and power." Former "Moonie" Barbara Underwood, for example, confessed that she wanted to make "millions of dollars" to purchase and maintain hotels, resorts, palatial residences from Chicago to New Orleans, training and living centers, college

Figure 18.20   Hare Krishna.
One of the Asian-derived cults that offer a life-style opposed to mainstream U.S. culture.

campuses, yachts, and even the Empire State and Pan Am buildings. "Instilled in us was the firm belief that Moon must reclaim all ownership of money and land from Satan's stockpile." "Christians think that the Messiah must be poor and miserable," says a Unification Church training manual. "He did not come for this. Messiah must be the richest. Only He is qualified to have dominion over things. Otherwise, neither God nor Messiah can by happy" (Underwood and Underwood 1979:76; Welles 1978:255).

THE ELECTRONIC CHURCH

Whatever the balance may be between worldly and otherworldly themes in the cults that have adopted aspects of Asian religions, such cults are not representative of the main thrust of religious change in the United States today. Far more powerful are Protestant fundamentalism and the various born-again Christian revitalization movements that have been able to use television to expand membership and raise funds. These so-called electronic churches, or TV cults, to a large extent recruit their membership through a personal "gospel of wealth" — they promise material success and physical well-being to the true believer. Their message appeals especially to people who are sick, old, or isolated, impoverished by illness, bewildered by the changes in sex mores and the family, and frightened by crime in the streets. According to TV preacher Jim Bakker: "The scripture says, 'Delight yourself in the Lord and he'll give you the desire of your heart'. . . . Give and it shall be given unto you." Bakker tells how one man prayed for a Winnebago mobile home, color brown, and got just that. Says Bakker: "Diamonds and gold aren't just for Satan—they're for Christians, too" (Bakker 1976).Unfortunately, Bakker's

appetite for diamonds and gold led him to sell lifetime vacations in nonexistent condos. In 1989 he was sentenced to jail for 5 years for fraud and embezzlement.

On his "Old Time Gospel Hour," Moral Majority leader Jerry Falwell (Figure 18.21) asks the faithful to turn over one-tenth of their income: "Christ has not captured a man's heart until He has your pocketbook." Two million potential contributors whose names and addresses are kept in a computer data bank receive frequent requests for money, one of which reads: "Maybe your financial situation seems impossible. Put Jesus first in your stewardship and allow him to bless you financially" (*Time*, 1 October 1979:68).

Finding himself $50 million short of the funds needed to complete his City of Faith hospital complex near Tulsa, Oklahoma, video evangelist Oral Roberts raised money with the aid of swatches from a "miracle cloth." "My hands feel as if there is a supernatural heat in them," he declared. "My right hand is especially hot right now." Following God's instructions, Roberts began to turn out millions of swatches imprinted with his right hand. In return, those who acquire the cloth are promised "special miracles" (*Newsweek*, 10 September 1979). Another TV evangelist, Pat Robertson, recruits followers and raises funds through what he calls the Kingdom Principles: The Bible says the more you give to Jesus the more you will get back in return. And the harder it is to give, the greater will be the increase. Thus, as described in Rifkind and Howard (1979:108), a woman in California who was on a limited income and in poor health

decided to trust God and to step out in faith on the Kingdom Principles. She was already giving half her disability money to the 700 Club to spread the gospel of Jesus Christ. But just last week, she decided to

Figure 18.21   The electronic church.
Jerry Falwell's "Old Time Gospel Hour" being televised live from Lynchburg, Virginia, to a network of 391 television stations. Cameras can be seen on the balcony and in the center of the audience.

go all the way, and give God the money she spends for cancer medicine—$120 a month. And three days later—get this!—from an entirely unexpected source, she got a check for three thousand dollars!

Since all the other aspects of U.S. culture are in flux, it is not surprising that religious beliefs and practices are going through a period of change and ferment (Beckford 1986, 1989; Beckford and Luckman 1989). The experience of other cultures and historical epochs demonstrates that stresses brought on by rapid cultural change usually find expression in spiritual yearning, questing, and experimenting that lead to an expansion and intensification of religious activity, broadly defined.

All the major world religions were born during times of rapid cultural transformations. Buddhism and Hinduism arose in the Ganges Valley of northern India during an epoch of deforestation, population increase, and state formation. Judaism arose during the prolonged migrations of the ancient Israelites. Christianity arose in conjunction with attempts to break the yoke of Roman imperialism. Islam arose during the transition from a life of pastoral nomadism to that of trade and empires in Arabia and North Africa. Protestants split from Catholicism as feudalism gave way to capitalism. As we have seen (page 307), messianic and millenarian cults swept across the Great Plains as the American Indians lost their lands and hunting grounds, while in the wake of the European colonization of New Guinea and Melanesia, hundreds of cargo cults, devoted to acquiring worldly wealth with the assistance of ancestors returned from the dead, spread from island to island.

There is reason to believe, therefore, that the rising intensity of religious activity in the United States constitutes an attempt to solve or to escape from the problems of malfunctioning consumerism, unemployment, the upending of sex roles, the breakup of the breadwinner family, alienation from work, oppressive government and corporate bureaucracies, feelings of isolation and loneliness, fear of crime, and bewilderment about the root cause of so many changes happening at once.

Summary

As a result of the recent expansion of the service and information sectors, the United States is best described as a hyperindustrial society, since virtually all forms of economic activity now involve mass production, the detailed division of labor, and mechanical or electronic machinery.

Although from an emic perspective the political economy of the United States is said to be capitalism, from an etic perspective it is a mixture of socialism and capitalism. Again, from an emic perspective, the capitalist sector of the economy is viewed as being based on free enterprise price competition; etically, however, the degree of concentration of economic resources in the largest conglomerate corporations creates a situation of oligopoly that precludes the setting of prices through competitive market supply and demand.

The majority of Americans work for bureaucratized organizations that do not reward individual initiative so much as they reward the willingness of people to carry out routine, standarized tasks. As a consequence, there is widespread alienation not only on the assembly line but in information and service jobs as well. While some observers look to the automation of information and services as a means of overcoming the problem, there is evidence that the electronic office of the future will further routinize and de-skill the labor force.

The emics and etics of the system of social stratification in the United States offer sharply contrasting views. Emic versions downgrade the degree of separation between the classes and deny the existence of a ruling class. From an etic perspective, however, there is considerable evidence that, despite countervailing sources of political influence, there is a ruling elite that decisively influences the overall shape of U.S. social, economic, and military policies. This evidence consists of the concentration of wealth in super-rich families and in the interlocking stock voting powers of a handful of top institutional investors. In contrast to the many studies of the poor, however, very little is known about the super-rich; anthropologists have been remiss in not studying "up" as well as "down."

The persistence of a large poverty class again points to a serious split between emic and etic versions of U.S. life. Upward mobility is not as rapid or extensive as most Americans believe. There is a tendency to blame the perpetuation of the poverty class on the victims of poverty, as seen in the notion of a "culture of poverty" and in the demand that the poor must work harder than the affluent. The poor, however, share most values with the middle class, and there is little evidence that by trying harder the poor can overcome the structural conditions that lead to unemployment and underemployment. Evidence to the contrary can be seen in Elliot Liebow's account of Washington's streetcorner men.

In contrast to the emic blurring of class lines in the United States, racial and ethnic minorities and majorities consciously conceive of themselves as sharply defined and competitive groups. Ethnic and social chauvinism pits black "have-nots" against white "have-littles" and thereby helps the "have-lots" maintain wealth and power. The black power movement has further entrapped the majority of blacks in the nation's urban ghettos. The worsening plight of America's black underclass is often attributed to the allegedly pathological nature of the black matrifocal family. But matrifocality is itself a family form produced by poverty, unemployment, and the rules of the AFDC welfare program, as shown in Carol Stack's study of the Flats.

The United States pays a huge hidden cost for its failure to ameliorate the situation in which the black underclass finds itself. The long-term high unemployment of black and Hispanic ghetto males has created a situation of hopelessness and envy that has led a disproportionate percentage of blacks and Hispanics to make a career of crime, especially the sale of drugs. America's racial and ethnic dilemma accounts to a large extent for the marked difference between rates of violent crime in the United States and in the Western industrial nations and Japan. AFDC is also implicated in the high rates of violent crime in America's inner cities. As Jagna Sharff's study of Hispanic women on AFDC in New York shows, the AFDC stipends are set too low for families to live on, thereby encouraging young men to resort to criminal behavior to fill the gap in family budgets.

The development of the United States's hyperindustrial service and information economy has had a powerful effect on middle-class family life. After World War II, married women entered the labor force in unprecedented numbers, taking the rapidly expanding lower-paying service and information jobs. As inflation wiped out the possibility of achieving or maintaining middle-class status on their husbands' incomes, married women became locked into the labor force. Their role as wage earners conflicted with their role as mothers, subverted the traditional marital and procreative imperative and undermined the male breadwinner family. It has also led to the separation of sex from reproduction, the spread of single-parent families, consensual trial unions, declining first-time marriage rates, and historically low fertility rates. The separation of sex from reproduction in turn has encouraged the expression of once-prohibited forms of sexuality, including homosexuality and pornographic movies, books, and videotapes.

The rapid pace of change and the problems induced by inflation; the bureaucratization, oligopolization, alienation, and feminization of the economy and the labor force; the challenge to the marital and procreative imperative; the prevalence of crime; and the persistence of poverty and sharp inequalities in wealth and power may supply the basic reasons for America's current religious awakening. The history of other cultures demonstrates that stresses brought on by rapid cultural change and social unrest usually find expression in spiritual yearning, questing, and experimenting that lead to an expansion and intensification of religious activity. Although some aspects of America's religious awakening can be attributed to an attempt to reject the material world, the center of religious ferment as seen in the video cults and human potential movement consists of attempts to overcome practical and mundane problems.

Appendix

A HISTORY OF
THEORIES OF CULTURE

This appendix serves as a brief outline of the history of the development of anthropological theories. It also presents the main research strategies employed by contemporary anthropologists.

The impulse lying behind the development of cultural anthropology is probably as old as our species. Members of different human groups have always been curious about the customs and traditions of strangers. The fact that people who live in different societies build different kinds of shelters, wear different kinds of clothing, practice different kinds of marriages, worship different spirits and gods, and speak different languages has always been a source of puzzlement. The most ancient and still most common approach to these differences is to assume that one's own beliefs and practices are normal expressions of the true or right way of life, as justified by the teachings of one's ancestors and the commandments or instructions of supernatural beings. Most cultures have origin myths that set forth the sequence of events leading to the beginning of the world and of humanity, and to the adoption of the group's way of life. The failure of other groups to share the same way of life can then often be attributed to their failure to be true, real, or normal human beings.

The Enlightenment

As Europe entered the age of exploration and mercantile expansion, interest in describing and explaining cultural diversity increased. The discovery and exploration of a whole "New World" — the Americas — opened the eyes of philosophers, political leaders, theologians, and scientists to astonishing contrasts in the human condition.

Toward the middle of the eighteenth century, during the period known as the Enlightenment, the first systematic attempts to offer scientific theories of cultural differences began to emerge. The common theme of these theories was the idea of progress. It was held by scholars such as Adam Smith, Adam Ferguson, Jean Turgot, and Denis Diderot that cultures were different not because they expressed innate differences in human capacities or preferences, but because they manifested different levels of rational knowledge and achievement. It was believed that humankind, including Europe's ancestors, had at one time lived in an "uncivilized" condition, lacking knowledge of farming and animal husbandry, laws and governments. Gradually, however, guided by the ever-expanding role of reason in human affairs, humankind progressed from a "state of nature" to a state of enlightened civilization. Cultural differences were thus largely a result of the different degrees of intellectual and moral progress achieved by different peoples.

Nineteenth-Century Evolutionism

The idea of cultural progress was the forerunner of the concept of cultural evolution that dominated theories of culture during the nineteenth century. Cultures were usually seen as moving through various stages of development, ending up with something resembling nineteenth-century Euramerican life-styles. Auguste Comte postulated a progression from theological to metaphysical to positivistic (scientific) modes of thought. Georg Wilhelm Friedrich Hegel saw a movement from a time when only one man was free (the Asiatic tyrant) to a time when some were free (Greek city-states), to a time when all would be free (European constitutional monarchies). Others wrote of an evolution from status (such as slave, noble, or commoner) to contract (employee and employer, buyer and seller); from small communities of people who knew each other's faces to large, impersonal societies; from slave to military to industrial societies; from animism to polytheism to monotheism; from magic to science; from female-dominated horticultural societies to male-dominated agricultural societies; and from many other hypothetical earlier and simpler stages to later and more complex ones.

One of the most influential schemes was

that proposed by the American anthropologist Lewis Henry Morgan in his book *Ancient Society*. Morgan divided the evolution of culture into three main stages: savagery, barbarism, and civilization. These stages had figured in evolutionary schemes as early as the sixteenth century, but Morgan subdivided them and filled them out in greater detail and with greater reference to ethnographic evidence than had anyone else. (Morgan himself carried out a lifelong study of the Iroquois, who lived near his hometown of Rochester, New York.) Morgan held that "lower savagery" subsistence had been gained exclusively by gathering wild foods, that people mated promiscuously, and that the basic unit of society was the small nomadic "horde" that owned its resources communally. By the period of "upper savagery," the bow and arrow had been invented, brother-sister marriage was prohibited, and descent was reckoned primarily through women. With the invention of pottery and the beginning of farming came the transition to barbarism. Incest prohibitions were extended to include all descendants in the female line, and clan and village became the basic social units.

The development of metallurgy marked the upper phase of barbarism; descent shifted from the female to the male line, men married several women at one time (polygyny), and private property appeared. The invention of writing, the development of civil government, and the emergence of the monogamous family marked the beginning of "civilization."

Social Darwinism

In addition to the greater complexity and detail of the nineteenth-century evolutionary schemes, there was one fundamental difference between them and the eighteenth-century notions of universal progress. Almost all the nineteenth-century schemes (with the conspicuous exception of Marxism) postulated that cultures evolved in conjunction with the evolution of human biological types and races. Not only were the cultures of modern-day Europe and America seen as the pinnacle of cultural progress, but the white race (especially its male half) was seen as the epitome of biological progress.

This fusion of biological evolutionism with cultural evolutionism is often but incorrectly attributed to the influence of Charles Darwin. In fact, the development of biological interpretations of cultural evolution preceded the appearance of Darwin's *Origin of Species*, and Darwin was himself greatly influenced by social philosophers such as Thomas Malthus and Herbert Spencer. Malthus's notion that population growth led to an inevitable "struggle for existence" had been elaborated by Spencer into the idea of the "survival of the fittest" before Darwin published his theories of biological evolution.

The success of Darwin's theory of the survival of the fittest (he called it "natural selection") greatly enhanced the popularity of the view that cultural evolution depended on biological evolution. After the publication of Darwin's *Origin of Species*, there appeared a movement known as Social Darwinism, based on the belief that cultural and biological progress depended on the free play of competitive forces in the struggle of individual against individual, nation against nation, and race against race. The most influential Social Darwinist was Herbert Spencer, who went so far as to advocate the end of all attempts to provide charity and relief for the unemployed and impoverished classes and the so-called "backward races" on the grounds that such assistance interfered with the operation of the "law of the survival of the fittest" and merely prolonged the agony and deepened the misery of those who were "unfit." Spencer used Social Darwinism to justify the capitalist free enterprise system, and his influence continues to be felt among advocates of unrestrained capitalism as well as among advocates of white supremacy.

Marxist Evolutionism

It is important to realize that while the writings and thoughts of Karl Marx were diametrically opposed to Social Darwinism, Marxism was also heavily influenced by the prevailing nineteenth-century notions of cultural evolution and progress. Marx saw cultures passing through the stages of primitive communism, slave society, feudalism, capitalism, and communism. Also, like many of his contemporaries, Marx stressed the importance of the role of struggle in achieving cultural evolution and progress. All history, according to Marx, was the outcome of the struggle between social classes for control over the means of production. The proletarian class, brought into existence by capitalism, was destined to abolish private property and bring about the final stage of history: communism. Upon reading Morgan's *Ancient Society*, Marx and his associate, Friedrich Engels, thought they had found a confirmation of their idea that during the first stage of cultural evolution there was no private property and that the successive stages of cultural progress had been brought about by changes in the "mode of production" — as, for example, in the co-occurrence of the development of agriculture and the transition between savagery and barbarism in Morgan's scheme. Morgan's *Ancient Society* provided the basis for Engels's *Origin of the Family, Private Property and the State*, which, until the middle of the twentieth century, served as a cornerstone of Marxist anthropology.

The Reaction to Nineteenth-Century Evolutionism

Early in the twentieth century, anthropologists took the lead in challenging the evolutionary schemes and doctrines of both the Social Darwinists and the Marxist Communists. In the United States, the dominant theoretical position was developed by Franz Boas and his students and is known as *historical particularism.* According to Boas, nineteenth-century attempts to discover the laws of cultural evolution and to schematize the stages of cultural progress were founded on insufficient empirical evidence. Boas argued that each culture has its own long and unique history. To understand or explain a particular culture, the best one can do is to reconstruct the unique path it had followed. The emphasis on the uniqueness of each culture amounted to a denial of the prospects for a generalizing science of culture. Another important feature of historical particularism is the notion of *cultural relativism,* which holds that there are no higher or lower forms of culture. Such terms as *savagery, barbarism,* and *civilization* merely express the ethnocentrism of people who think that their way of life is more normal than those of other peoples.

To counter the speculative "armchair" theories and ethnocentrism of the evolutionists, Boas and his students also stressed the importance of carrying out ethnographic fieldwork among non-Western peoples. As the ethnographic reports and monographs produced by the historical particularists multiplied, it became clear that the evolutionists had indeed misrepresented or overlooked the complexities of so-called primitive cultures and that they had grossly underestimated the intelligence and ingenuity of the non-Caucasoid, non-European peoples of the world.

Boas's most important achievement was his demonstration that race, language, and culture were independent aspects of the human condition. Since both similar and dissimilar cultures and languages are found among people of the same race, there was no basis for the Social Darwinist notion that biological and cultural evolution were part of a single process.

Diffusionism

Another early twentieth-century reaction to nineteenth-century evolutionism is known as *diffusionism.* According to its advocates, the principal source of cultural differences and similarities is not the inventiveness of the human mind, but the tendency of humans to imitate one another. Diffusionists see cultures as a patchwork of elements derived from a haphazard series of borrowings among near and distant peoples. In the critical case of the origin of American Indian civilizations, for example, diffusionists argued that the technology and architecture of the Inca of Peru and the Aztecs of Mexico were diffused from Egypt or from Southeast Asia, rather than invented independently (see page 15 for a critique of diffusionism).

British Functionalism and Structural-Functionalism

In Great Britain, the dominant early twentieth-century research strategies are known as *functionalism* and *structural-functionalism.* According to the functionalists, the main task of cultural anthropology is to describe the recurrent *functions* of customs and institutions, rather than to explain the origins of cultural differences and similarities. According to one of the leading functionalists, Bronislaw Malinowski, the attempt to discover the origins of cultural elements was doomed to be speculative and unscientific because of the absence of written records. Once we have understood the function of an institution, argued Malinowski, then we have understood all we will ever understand about its origins.

A. R. Radcliffe-Brown was the principal advocate of structural-functionalism. According to Radcliffe-Brown, the main task of cultural anthropology was even narrower than that proposed by Malinowski. Whereas Malinowski emphasized the contribution of cultural elements to the biological and psychological welfare of individuals, Radcliffe-Brown and the structural-functionalists stressed the contribution of the biological and psychological welfare of individuals to the maintenance of the social system. For the structural-functionalists, the function of maintaining the system took precedence over all others. But like Malinowski, the structural-functionalists labeled all attempts to find origins as speculative history.

Thus, the functionalists and structural-functionalists evaded the question of the general, recurrent causes of cultural differences, while emphasizing the general, recurrent functional reasons for similarities. This set the functionalists and structural-functionalists apart from the diffusionists as much as from the nineteenth-century evolutionists. Nor were the functionalists and structural-functionalists sympathetic to Boas's historical particularism. But like Boas and his students, the British functionalists and structural-functionalists stressed the importance of carrying out fieldwork, insisting that only after two or more years of immersion in the language, thoughts, and events of another culture could anthropologists provide valid and reliable ethnographic descriptions.

Culture and Personality

In turning away from the nineteenth-century notions of causality and evolution, many anthropologists, influenced by the writings of Sigmund Freud, attempted to interpret cultures in psychological terms. The writings of Freud and the anti-evolutionism of Boas set the stage for the development of the approach known as *culture and personality*. Two of Boas's most famous students, Ruth Benedict and Margaret Mead, pioneered in the development of culture and personality theories. Such theories in general may be described as psychological forms of functionalism that relate cultural beliefs and practices to individual personality and individual personality to cultural beliefs and practices. As we saw in Chapter 14, many advocates of the culture and personality approach stress the importance of early childhood experiences such as toilet training, breast feeding, and sex training in the formation of a basic or modal type of adult personality or national character. Some culture and personality theories attempt to explain cultural differences and similarities as a consequence of basic or modal personality. In general, however, culture and personality advocates do not deal with the problem of why the beliefs and practices that mold particular personality types or national characters occur in some cultures but not in others.

The New Evolutionism

After World War II, increasing numbers of anthropologists became dissatisfied with the anti-evolutionism and lack of broad generalizations and causal explanations characteristic of the first half of the century. Under the influence of Leslie White, an effort was launched to reexamine the works of the nineteenth-century evolutionists such as Lewis Henry Morgan, to correct their ethnographic errors, and to identify their positive contribution to the development of a science of culture. White pioneered in postulating that the overall direction of cultural evolution was largely determined by the quantities of energy that could be captured and put to work per capita per year (see page 84).

At the same time (about 1940 to 1950), Julian Steward laid the basis for the development of the approach known as *cultural ecology*, which stressed the role of the interaction of natural conditions such as soils, rainfall, and temperature with cultural factors such as technology and economy as the cause of both cultural differences and similarities.

The return to broad evolutionary points of view in the second half of the twentieth century among American cultural anthropologists was stimulated by archaeological evidence that diffusion could not account for the remarkable similarities between the development of states and empires in the New and Old Worlds (see page 206). The step-by-step process by which native American peoples in the Andean and Mesoamerican regions independently developed their own elaborate civilizations is now fairly well known, thanks to modern archaeological research.

Julian Steward was especially impressed with the parallels in the evolution of the ancient civilizations of Peru, Mexico, Egypt, Mesopotamia, and China, and called for a renewed effort on the part of anthropologists to examine and explain these remarkable uniformities. Yet Steward was careful to distin-guish his scheme of cultural evolution from the more extreme versions of nineteenth-century evolutionism. According to Steward, the problem with these earlier evolutionists was that they postulated a single or "unilinear" set of stages for all cultures, whereas there are actually many, or "multilinear," paths of development depending on initial environmental, technological, and other conditions.

Dialectical Materialism

Both White and Steward were influenced by Marx and Engels's emphasis on changes in the material aspects of modes of reproduction as the mainspring of cultural evolution. However, neither accepted the full set of Marxist propositions embodied in the point of view known as *dialectical materialism*, which gained considerable popularity among Western anthropologists for the first time in the 1960s and 1970s. Dialectical materialists hold that history has a determined direction — namely, that of the emergence of communism and of classless society. The sources of this movement are the internal contradictions of sociocultural systems. To understand the causes of sociocultural differences and similarities, social scientists must not only study these contradictions but must also take part in the "dialectical" resolutions that lead to progress toward communism. The most important contradiction in all societies is that between the means of production (roughly, the technology) and the relations of production (who owns the means of production). In the words of Karl Marx: "The mode of production in material life determines the general character of the social, political, and spiritual process of life. It is not the consciousness of men that determines their existence, but on the contrary, their social existence determines their consciousness" (1970 [1859]:21).

Cultural Materialism

Further elaboration of the theoretical perspectives of Marx, White, and Steward has led to the appearance of the point of view known as *cultural materialism*. This research strategy holds that the primary task of anthropology is to give causal explanations for the differences and similarities in thought and behavior found among human groups. Like dialectical materialists, cultural materialists hold that this task can best be carried out by studying the material constraints to which human existence is subjected. These constraints arise from the need to produce food, shelter, tools, and machines, and to reproduce human populations within limits set by biology and the environment. These are called *material* constraints or conditions in order to distinguish them from constraints or conditions imposed by ideas and other mental or spiritual aspects of human life such as values, religion, and art. For cultural materialists, the most likely causes of major variation in the mental or spiritual aspects of human life are the differences in the material costs and benefits of satisfying basic needs in a particular habitat.

Cultural materialists differ from dialectical materialists mainly in rejecting the notion that anthropology must become part of a political movement aimed at destroying capitalism and at furthering the interests of the proletariat. Cultural materialists allow for a diversity of political motivation among anthropologists united by a common commitment to the devel-

opment of a science of culture. In addition, cultural materialists reject the notion that all important cultural changes result from the playing out of dialectical contradictions, holding that much of cultural evolution has resulted from the gradual accumulation of useful traits through a process of trial and error.

Sociobiology

We have seen (page 40) that sociobiology is a research strategy that attempts to explain some sociocultural differences and similarities in terms of natural selection, and that it is based on a refinement of natural selection known as the principle of inclusive fitness. According to sociobiology, selection does not necessarily bring about a one-to-one correlation between genes and behavior, but between genes and tendencies to behave in certain ways rather than others. For example, sociobiologists hold that the tendency for humans to forage in a manner that optimizes energy produced per unit of time is selected because it maximizes reproductive success (Lewontin et al. 1984; Wilson 1975, 1978).

From a cultural materialist perspective it is not necessary to posit that useful traits are always selected because they maximize reproductive success. In the case of optimal foraging theory (see page 77), for example, the favorable balance of energetic benefits over costs in satisfying an individual's nutritional needs is sufficient to understand why certain animals are captured and others are not, without reference to its effects on reproductive success. Moreover, it is clear, contrary to sociobiological principle, that humans do not always seek to maximize reproductive success. The most glaring discrepancy is the low rate of reproductive success characteristic of the affluent classes in industrial society. The behavior of one-child American families scarcely seems to be dominated by the urge to have as many children as possible.

Structuralism

Not all post–World War II approaches to cultural theory are aimed at explaining the origin of cultural differences and similarities.

In France, under the leadership of Claude Lévi-Strauss, the point of view known as *structuralism* has been widely accepted. Structuralism is concerned only with the psychological uniformities that underlly apparent differences in thought and behavior. According to Lévi-Strauss, these uniformities arise from the structure of the human brain and of unconscious thought processes. The most important structural feature of the human mind is the tendency to dichotomize, or to think in terms of binary oppositions, and then, to attempt to mediate this opposition by a third concept, which may serve as the basis for yet another opposition. A recurrent opposition present in many myths, for example, is culture versus nature. From the structuralist point of view, the more cultures change, the more they remain the same, since they are all merely variations on the theme of recurrent oppositions and their resolutions. Structuralism, therefore, is concerned with explaining the similarities among cultures, but not with explaining the differences. See the section "Myth and Binary Contrasts" in Chapter 16 for examples of structuralist analysis.

Particularizing Approaches

Mention must also be made of the fact that many anthropologists continue to reject all general causal viewpoints, holding that the chief aim of ethnography ought to be the study and interpretation of the emics of different cultures — their world views, symbols, values, religions, philosophies, and systems of meanings. During the 1980s, these approaches grew in popularity and were characterized by rejection of the distinction between observer and observed, etics and emics, and science and nonscience. Extreme relativism (see page 11) and anti-evolutionism reminiscent of Franz Boas's historical particularism also characterize recent approaches. For many contemporary cultural anthropologists the main task of ethnography is to become familiar with a culture in the same way one becomes familiar with a book or a poem, and then to "read" or interpret it as if one were a literary critic. The goal of these anthropologists is not to discover the scientific truth about a culture but to compose interpretations about the "other" — the other culture — that are elegant and convincing.

One recent manifestation of this line of development is called *deconstructionism*. It focuses on the hidden intentions and unexpressed biases of the author of an ethnography rather than on the question of what the culture being described is really like.

Although deconstructionists make valid points about the need to expose biases and prejudices in scientific descriptions (remember Malinowski), their flat rejection of scientific truth as a goal of ethnography results in fragmented, contradictory, and essentially nihilistic notions about the human condition.

BIBLIOGRAPHY

In the citation system used in this text, the names in parentheses are the authors of the publications mentioned, or of publications that support the descriptions or interpretations of matters being discussed. The year following the names is the year of publication and should be used to identify specific sources when more than one publication of the author is included. Letters following a date (e.g., 1972a) distinguish different publications of one author for the same year. "See" is used to refer to points of view opposed to those given in the text. Specific page numbers are provided only for direct quotes or controversial points.

ABRUZZI, WILLIAM
1982 "Ecological Theory and Ethnic Differentiation Among Human Populations." *Current Anthropology* 23:13–35.

ACHESON, JAMES M.
1972 "Limited Good or Limited Goods: Response to Economic Opportunity in a Tarascan Pueblo." *American Anthropologist* 74:1152–1169.

1974 "Reply to George Foster." *American Anthropologist* 76:57–62.

ADAMS, M., AND J. V. NEIL
1967 "The Children of Incest." *Pediatrics* 40:55–62.

ADAMS, RICHARD N.
1968 "An Inquiry into the Nature of the Family." In *Selected Studies in Marriage and Family*, R. F. Winch and L. W. Goodman, eds., pp. 45–57. New York: Holt, Rinehart and Winston.

ALBERS, PATRICIA
1989 "From Illusion to Illumination: Anthropological Studies of American Indian Women." In *Gender and Anthropology*, Sandra Morgen, ed., pp. 132–170. Washington, D.C.: American Anthropological Association.

ALEXANDER, RICHARD
1974 "Evolution of Social Behavior." *Annual Review of Ecological Systems* 5:325–383.
1976 "Evolution: Human Behavior and Determinism." *PSA* 2:3–21.

1977 "Natural Selection and the Analysis of Human Sociology." In *The Changing Scenes in the Natural Sciences, 1776–1976*, C. E. Goulden, ed., pp. 283–337. Academy of Natural Science. Special Publication 12.

ALLAND, ALEXANDER
1977 *The Artistic Animal: An Inquiry into the Biological Roots of Art.* Garden City: N.Y.: Doubleday (Anchor Books).

Anglo Saxon Chronicle
1962 New Brunswick, N.J.: Rutgers University Press.

ARMELAGOS, GEORGE, AND A. MCARDLE
1975 "Population, Disease, and Evolution." *American Antiquity* 40:1–10.

BAKKER, JIM
1976 *Move That Mountain.* Plainfield, N.J.: Logos International.

BAKSH, MICHAEL
1985 "Faunal Food as a 'Limiting Factor' on Amazonian Cultural Behavior: A Machiguenga Example." *Research in Economic Anthropology* 7:145–175.

BALEE, WILLIAM
1984 "The Ecology of Ancient Tupi Warfare." In *Warfare, Culture and Environment*, Brian Ferguson, ed., pp. 241–265. Orlando, Fla.: Academic Press.

BELSHEM, MARTHA
1988 "The Clerical Worker's Boss: An Agent of Job Stress." *Human Organization* 47:361–367.

BANE, MARY, AND DAVID ELLWOOD
1989 "One Fifth of the Nation's Children: Why Are They Poor?" *Science* 245:1047–1053.

BARASH, DAVID
1977 *Sociobiology and Behavior.* New York: Elsevier.

BARBER, BERNARD
1968 "Social Mobility in Hindu India." In *Social Mobility in the Caste System*, J. Silverberg, ed., pp. 18–35. The Hague: Mouton.

BARLETT, PEGGY, AND PETER BROWN
1985 "Agricultural Development and the Quality of Life: An Anthropological View." *Agriculture and Human Values* 2:28–35.

BARNOUW, VICTOR
1985 *Culture and Personality.* Homewood, Ill.: Dorsey Press.

BARNES, J. A.
1960 "Marriage and Residential Continuity." *American Anthropologist* 62:850–866.

BAYLISS-SMITH, TIMOTHY
1977 "Human Ecology and Island Populations: The Problems of Change." In *Subsistence and Survival: Rural Ecology in the Pacific*, T. Bayliss-Smith and R. Feachem, eds., pp. 11–20. New York: Academic Press.

BATRA, RAVI
1987 "Are the Rich Getting Richer?" *The New York Times*, May 3, Section 3:2.

BEATTIE, JOHN
1960 *Bunyoro: An African Kingdom.* New York: Holt, Rinehart and Winston.

BECKER, HOWARD
1982 *Art Worlds.* Berkeley: University of California Press.

BECKFORD, JAMES A.
1986 *New Religious Movements and Rapid Social Change.* London: Sage.

1989 *Religion and Advanced Industrial Society.* London: Unwin Hyman.

BECKFORD, JAMES, AND THOMAS LUCKMAN, EDS.
1989 *The Changing Face of Religion.* Newberry Park, Calif.: Sage.

BELKIN, LISA
1985 "Parents Weigh Costs of Children." *The New York Times,* May 23:19, 21.

BELL, DANIEL
1973 *The Coming of Post-Industrial Society: A Venture in Social Forecasting.* New York: Basic Books.

BELLAH, ROBERT
1976 "New Religious Consciousness and the Crisis in Modernity." In *The New Religious Consciousness,* Robert Bellah and Charles Clock, eds., pp. 333–352. Berkeley: University of California Press.

BELMONTE, THOMAS
1989 *The Broken Fountain,* 2nd ed. New York: Columbia University Press.

BENDER, DONALD R.
1967 "A Refinement of the Concept of Household: Families, Co-residence, and Domestic Functions." *American Anthropologist* 69:493–503.

BENDIX, REINHARD, AND S. M. LIPSET, EDS.
1966 *Class, Status and Power: Social Stratification in Comparative Perspective.* New York: Free Press.

BENEDICT, RUTH
1934 *Patterns of Culture.* Boston: Houghton Mifflin.
1938 "Religion." In *General Anthropology,* F. Boas, ed., pp. 627–665. New York: Columbia University Press.

BERDAN, FRANCES
1982 *Aztecs of Central Mexico.* New York: Holt, Rinehart and Winston.

BEREITER, CARL, AND S. ENGELMAN
1966 *Teaching Disadvantaged Students in Pre-School.* Englewood Cliffs, N.J.: Prentice-Hall.

BERNARD, H. RUSSELL
1981 "Issues in Training in Applied Anthropology." *Practicing Anthropology* 3 (Winter).

BERNARDI, BERNARDO
1985 *Age Class Systems: Social Institutions and Politics Based on Age.* New York: Cambridge University Press.

BERREMAN, GERALD D.
1966 "Caste in Cross-cultural Perspective." In *Japan's Invisible Race: Caste in Culture and Personality,* G. De Vos and H. Wagatsuma, eds., pp. 275–324. Berkeley: University of California Press.
1975 "Bazar Behavior: Social Identity and Social Interaction in Urban India." In *Ethnic Identity: Cultural Continuity and Change,* L. Romanucci-Ross and G. De Vos, eds., pp. 71–105. Palo Alto, Calif.: Mayfield.

BERREMAN, GERALD, ED.
1981 *Social Inequality: Comparative and Developmental Approaches.* New York: Academic Press.

BICKERTON, DEREK
1984 "The Language Biogram Hypothesis." *Behavioral and Brain Sciences* 7:173–221.

BINFORD, LEWIS R.
1988 "Fact and Fiction About the Zinjanthropus Floor: Data, Arguments and Interpretations." *Current Anthropology* 29:123–151.

BINFORD, LEWIS R., AND NANCY STONE
1986 "Zhou Kou dian: A Closer Look." *Current Anthropology* 27:453–475.

BIOLSI, THOMAS
1984 "Ecological and Cultural Factors in Plains Indian Warfare." In *Warfare, Culture and Environment*, Brian Ferguson, ed., pp. 141–168. Orlando, Fla.: Academic Press.

BIXLER, RAY
1981 "Incest Avoidance as a Function of Environment and Heredity." *Current Anthropology* 22:639–654.
1982 "Comment on the Incidence and Purpose of Royal Sibling Incest." *American Ethnologist* 9:580–582.

BLACK, FRANCIS
1961 *Family Structure in Jamaica: The Social Context of Reproduction*. New York: Free Press.
1975 "Infectious Disease in Primitive Societies." *Science* 187:515–518.

BLACKWOOD, EVELYN
1984 "Sexuality and Gender in Certain North American Indian Tribes: The Case of Cross-Gender Females." *Signs* 10:27–42.
1986 "Breaking the Mirror: The Construction of Lesbianism and the Anthropological Discourse on Homosexuality." In *Anthropology and Homosexual Behavior*, Evelyn Blackwood, ed., pp. 1–18. New York: Haworth Press.

BLAKE, JUDITH
1961 *Family Structure in Jamaica: The Social Context of Production*. New York: Free Press.

BLAU, PETER, AND O. D. DUNCAN
1967 *The American Occupational Structure*. New York: Wiley.

BLOCH, MARC
1964 "Feudalism as a Type of Society." In *Sociology and History: Theory and Research*, W. J. Cahnman and A. Boskoff, eds., pp. 163–170. New York: Free Press.

BODLEY, JOHN
1989 *Victims of Progress*, 3rd ed. Menlo Park, Calif.: Cummings.

BOLLES, A., AND D. D'AMICO-SAMUELS
1989 "Anthropological Scholarship on Gender in the English-Speaking Caribbean." In *Gender and Anthropology*, Sandra Morgen, ed., pp. 171–188. Washington, D.C.: American Anthropological Association.

BONGAARTS, JOHN
1980 "Does Malnutrition Affect Fertility? A Summary of the Evidence." *Science* 208:564–569.
1982 "Malnutrition and Fertility." (Reply to Rose Frisch.) *Science* 215:1273–1274.

BONGAARTS, JOHN, AND F. ODILE
1984 "The Proximate Determinants of Fertility in Sub-Saharan Africa." *Population and Development Review* 10:511–537.

BOSERUP, ESTER
1965 *The Condition of Agricultural Growth: The Economics of Agrarian Change under Population Pressure*. Chicago: Aldine.

BOSSEN, LAUREL
1988 "Toward a Theory of Marriage: The Economic Anthropology of Marriage Transactions." *Ethnology* 27:127–144.

BOTTOMORE, T. B.
1966 *Classes in Modern Society*. New York: Random House (Vintage Books).

BOULDING, KENNETH E.
1973 *The Economy of Love and Fear*. Belmont, Calif.: Wadsworth.

Bowles, S., and H. Gintis
1976 *Schooling in Capitalist America.* New York: Basic Books.

Braverman, Harry
1974 *Labor and Monopoly Capital: The Degradation of Work in the Twentieth Century.* New York: Monthly Review Press.

Brown, Judith K.
1975 "Iroquois Women: An Ethnohistoric Note." In *Toward an Anthropology of Women,* Rayna Reiter, ed., pp. 235–251. New York: Monthly Review Press.

Brown, Lester
1978 *The Global Economic Prospect: New Sources of Economic Stress.* Washington, D.C.: Worldwatch Institute. Worldwatch Paper 20.

1989 "Reexamining the World Food Prospect." In *State of the World,* Lester Brown et al., eds., pp. 41–58. New York: Norton.

Brown, Peter
1985 "Microparasites and Macroparasites." Paper read at the 1985 annual meeting of the American Anthropological Association, Washington, D.C.

Brown, Ronald
1978 Testimony: Hearings Before the Subcommittee on Crime, House of Representatives. Ninety-Fifth Congress, Serial No. 47, Washington, D.C.: U.S. Government Printing Office.

Brozan, Nadine
1985 "U.S. Leads Industrialized Nations in Teen Age Births and Abortions." *The New York Times,* March 13, pp. 1, 22.

Brunton, Ron
1975 "Why Do the Trobriands Have Chiefs?" *Man* 10(4):545–550.

Buchbinder, Georgeda
1977 "Nutritional Stress and Population Decline among the Maring of New Guinea." In *Malnutrition, Behavior, and Social Organization,* Lawrence S. Greene, ed., pp. 109–141. New York: Academic Press.

Buckley, Thomas
1982 "Menstruation and the Power of Yurok Women." *American Ethnologist* 9:47–90.

Burbank, Victoria
1989 "Gender and the Anthropology Curriculum: Aboriginal Australia." In *Gender and Anthropology,* Sandra Morgen, ed., pp. 116–131. Washington, D.C.: American Anthropological Association.

Burton, Michael, Lilyan Brudner, and Douglas White
1977 "A Model of the Sexual Division of Labor." *American Ethnologist* 4(2):227–251.

Burton, Michael, and D. White
1987 "Sexual Division of Labor in Agriculture." In *Household Economies,* M. Machlachlan, ed. Lanham, Md.: University Press of America.

Buzzard, Shirley
1982 *The PLAN Primary Health Care Project, Tumaco, Colombia: A Case Study.* Warwick, R.I.: Foster Parents Plan International.

Cain, Meade
1977 "The Economic Activities of Children in a Village in Bangladesh." *Population and Development Review* 3:201–227.

CALDWELL, JOHN
1982 *Theory of Fertility Decline.* New York: Academic Press.

CALDWELL, JOHN, P. H. REDDY, AND PAT CALDWELL
1983 "The Causes of Demographic Change in Rural South India: A Micro Approach." *Population and Development Review* 8:689–727.

CALLENDAR, CHARLES, AND L. KOCHEMS
1983 "The North American Berdache." *Current Anthropology* 24:443–470.

CAMPBELL, SHIRLEY
1983 "Kula in Vakuta: The Mechanics of *keda*." In *The Kula: New Perspectives on Massim Exchange*, J. Leach and E. Leach, eds., pp. 201–227. Cambridge: Cambridge University Press.

CARLSTEIN, TONY
1983 *Time Resources, Society and Ecology.* London: George Allen & Unwin.

CARNEIRO, ROBERT
1960 "Slash-and-Burn Agriculture: A Closer Look at Its Implications for Settlement Patterns." In *Men and Cultures: Selected Papers of the International Congress of Anthropological and Ethnological Sciences*, A. Wallace, ed., pp. 229–234. Philadelphia: University of Pennsylvania Press.
1970 "A Theory of the Origin of the State." *Science* 169:733–738.
1978 "Political Expansion as an Expression of the Principle of Competitive Exclusion." In *Origins of the State*, Ronald Cohen and E. Service, eds., pp. 205–223. Philadelphia: ISHI.
1981 "Chiefdom: Precursor of the State." In *The Transition to Statehood in the New World*, Grant Jones and Robert Kautz,

eds., pp. 37–75. New York: Cambridge University Press.
1988 "The Circumscription Theory: Challenge and Response." *American Behavioral Scientist* 31:497–511.

CARPENTER, C. R.
1940 "A Field Study in Siam of the Behavior and Social Relations of the Gibbons, Hylobateslar." *Comparative Psychological Monographs* 16:1–212.

CARROLL, LUCY
1977 " 'Sanskritization,' 'Westernization,' and 'Social Mobility': A Reappraisal of the Relevance of Anthropological Concepts to the Social Historian of Modern India." *Journal of Anthropological Research* 33(4):355–371.

CARSTAIRS, G. M.
1967 *The Twice-born.* Bloomington: Indiana University Press.

CARTER, WILLIAM, ED.
1980 *Cannabis in Costa Rica: A Study of Chronic Marihuana Use.* Philadelphia: ISHI.

CATTLE, DOROTHY
1977 "An Alternative to Nutritional Particularism." In *Nutrition and Anthropology in Action*, Thomas Fitzgerald, ed., pp. 35–45. Amsterdam: Van Gorcum.

CHAGNON, NAPOLEON
1974 *Studying the Yanomamö.* New York: Holt, Rinehart and Winston.
1977 *Yanomamö: The Fierce People*, 2nd ed. New York: Holt, Rinehart and Winston.

CHAGNON, NAPOLEON, AND RAYMOND HAMES
1979 "Protein Deficiency and Tribal Warfare in Amazonia: New Data." *Science* 203:910–913.

CHAKRAVARTI, A. K.

1985a "Cattle Development Problems and Programs in India: A Regional Analysis." *Geo Journal* 10(1):21–45.

1985b "The Question of Surplus Cattle in India: A Spatial View." *Geografiska Annaler* 67B:121–130.

CHAMBERS, ERVE

1985 *Applied Anthropology: A Professional Guide.* Englewood Cliffs, N.J.: Prentice-Hall.

CHAMPION, TIMOTHY, ET AL., EDS.

1984 *Prehistoric Europe.* New York: Academic Press.

CHANG, DAE

1988 "Crime and Delinquency Control Strategy in Japan: A Comparative Note." *International Journal of Applied Criminal Justice* 12:139–149.

CHARNOV, ERIC

1976 "Optimal Foraging: The Marginal Value Theorem." *Theoretical Population Biology* 9:129–136.

CHILD, ALICE, AND J. CHILD

1985 "Biology, Ethnocentrism, and Sex Differences." *American Anthropologist* 87:125–128.

CHOMSKY, NOAM

1973 "The General Properties of Language." In *Explorations in Anthropology: Readings in Culture, Man and Nature,* Morton Fried, ed., pp. 115–123, New York: Crowell.

CICCHETTI, DANTE, AND VICKI CARLSON, EDS.

1989 *Child Maltreatment: Theory and Research on the Causes and Consequences of Child Abuse and Neglect.* New York: Cambridge University Press.

CIOCHON, RUSSEL

1985 "Hominoid Cladistics and the Ancestry of Modern Apes and Humans." In *Primate Evolution and Human Origins,* R. Ciochon and J. Fleagle, eds., pp. 345–362. Menlo Park, Calif.: Benjamin/Cummings.

CLARKE, WILLIAM

1976 "Maintenance of Agriculture and Human Habitats within the Tropical Forest Ecosystem." *Human Ecology* 4(3):247–259.

CLEAVER, HARRY

1975 "Will the Green Revolution Turn Red?" In *The Trojan Horse: A Radical Look at Foreign Aid,* Steve Weisman, ed., pp. 171–200. New York: Monthly Review Press.

CLOUD, WALLACE

1973 "After the Green Revolution." *The Sciences* 13(8):6–12.

COCKBURN, T. A.

1971 "Infectious Diseases in Ancient Populations." *Current Anthropology* 12:45–62.

COE, MICHAEL

1977 *Mexico,* 2nd ed. New York: Praeger.

COHEN, MARK N.

1977 *The Food Crisis in Prehistory.* New Haven, Conn.: Yale University Press.

1986 "The Significance of Long Term Changes in Human Diet and Food Economy." In *Food and Evolution: Toward a Theory of Human Food Habits,* M. Harris and E. Ross, eds., pp. 261–283. Philadelphia: Temple University Press.

COHEN, MARK, AND G. ARMELAGOS, EDS.

1984 *Paleopathology and the Origin of Agriculture.* New York: Academic Press.

COHEN, MYRON

1976 *House United, House Divided.* New York: Columbia University Press.

COHEN, RONALD

1978a "State Origins: A Reappraisal." In *The Early State,* H. Claessen and P. Skalnik, eds., pp. 31–75. The Hague: Mouton.

1978b "Ethnicity." *Annual Review of Anthropology* 7:379–403.

1984a "Warfare and State Foundation: Wars Make States and States Make Wars." In *Warfare, Culture and Environment.* ›Brian Ferguson, ed., pp. 329–355. Orlando, Fla.: Academic Press.

1984b "Approaches to Applied Anthropology." *Communication and Cognition* 17:135–162.

COHEN, YEHUDI

1978 "The Disappearance of the Incest Taboo." *Human Nature* 1(7):72–78.

COHN, BERNARD

1955 "Changing Status of a Depressed Caste." In *Village India: Studies in the Little Community,* M. Mariott, ed., 83:55–77. American Anthropological Memoirs.

COLE, JOHN, AND L. GODFREY

1985 "The Paluxy River Footprint Mystery Solved." *Creation/Evolution* 15:5(1). Special Issue.

COLLINS, GLENN

1985 "Remarriage: Bigger Ready-Made Families." *The New York Times,* May 13, p. 15.

CONDOMINAS, GEORGE

1957 *Nous avons mangé la foret de la Pérre-Genie Goo.* Paris.

1972 "From the Rice Field to the Miir." *Social Science Information* 11:41–62.

Congressional Quarterly

1989 47(3)(June 21):136–138.

CONWAY, FLO, AND JIM SIEGELMAN

1978 *Snapping: America's Epidemic of Sudden Personality Change.* Philadelphia: Lippincott.

CONWAY, FREDERICK

1989 "The Agroforestry Outreach Project in Haiti: A Case Study for Project Design." Unpublished paper prepared for the Pan American Development Fund.

CONYERS, JOHN

1978 "Unemployment Is Cruel and Unusual Punishment." In Hearings Before the Subcommittee on Crime, House of Representatives. Ninety-Fifth Congress, Serial No. 47. Washington: D.C.: U.S. Government Printing Office, 674–679.

COOK, R.

1989 "Turnout Hits 64-Year Low in Presidential Race." *Congressional Quarterly Weekly Report* 47 (Jan. 21):135–138.

COUNTS, DOROTHY

1985 "Tamparonga: The Big Women of Kaliai (Papua New Guinea)." In *In Her Prime: A New View of Middle-Aged Women,* J. Brown and V. Kerns, eds., pp. 49–64. South Hadley, Mass.: Bergin and Garvey.

CRAIG, DANIEL

1979 "Immortality through Kinship: The Vertical Transmission of Substance and Symbolic Estate." *American Anthropologist* 81:94–96.

CROSBY, ALFRED

1986 *Ecological Imperialism: The Biological Expansion of Europe 900–1900.* New York: Cambridge University Press.

CUMMINGS, R. C.
1978 "Agriculture Change in Vietnam's Floating Rice Region." *Human Organization* 37:235–245.

CURVIN, ROBERT, AND BRUCE PORTER
1978 "The Myth of Blackout Looters. . . ." *The New York Times*, July 13, p. 21.

DAHL, ROBERT
1981 *Democracy in the United States*, 4th ed. Boston: Houghton Mifflin.

DALTON, GEORGE
1965 "Primitive Money." *American Anthropologist* 67:44–65.
1969 "Theoretical Issues in Economic Anthropology." *Current Anthropology* 10:63–102.
1972 "Peasantries in Anthropology and History." *Current Anthropology* 13:385–416.
1974 "How Exactly Are Peasants Exploited?" *American Anthropologist* 76:553–561.

D'ALTROY, T., AND T. K. EARLE
1985 "Staple Finance, Wealth Finance, and Storage in Inca Political Economy." *Current Anthropology* 26:187–206.

DAS GUPTA, MONICA
1978 "Production Relations and Population: Rampur." *Journal of Development Studies* 14(4):177–185.

DAVIS, SHELTON
1977 *Victims of the Miracle: Development and the Indians of Brazil*. New York: Cambridge University Press.

DEHAVENON, A. L.
1984 "The Tyranny of Indifference and the Re-Institutionalization of Hunger, Homelessness and Poor Health." New York: The East Harlem Interfaith Welfare Committee. (See "Talk of the Town." *The New Yorker*, May 13, 1985.)

DE LAGUNA, FREDERICA
1968 "Presidential Address: 1967." *American Anthropologist* 70:469–476.

DE LORIA, VINE
1969 *Custer Died for Your Sins*. London: Collier-Macmillan.

DEMAREST, WILLIAM
1977 "Incest Avoidance among Human and Non-Human Primates." In *Primate Bio-Social Development: Biological, Social and Ecological Determinants*, S. Chevalier-Skolinikoff and F. Poirer, eds., pp. 323–342. New York: Garland.

DE MOTT, BENJAMIN
1980 "The Pro-Incest Lobby." *Psychology Today*, March, pp. 11–16.

DENTAN, ROBERT
1968 *The Semai: A Non-Violent People of Malaya*. New York: Holt, Rinehart and Winston.

DESPRES, LEO
1975 "Ethnicity and Resource Competition in Guyanese Society." In *Ethnicity and Resource Competition in Plural Societies*, L. Despres, ed., pp. 87–117. The Hague: Mouton.

DEVEREUX, GEORGE
1967 "A Typological Study of Abortion in 350 Primitive, Ancient, and Pre-Industrial Societies." In *Abortion in America*, H. Rosen, ed., pp. 95–152. Boston: Beacon Press.

DE WAAL, F.
1983 *Chimpanzee Poltics*. New York: Harper & Row.

DeWalt, Billie

1984 "Mexico's Second Green Revolution: Food for Feed." *Mexican Studies/Estudios Mexicanos* 1:29–60.

Dillingham, Beth, and B. Isaac

1975 "Defining Marriage Cross-culturally." In *Being Female: Reproduction, Power and Change*, D. Raphael, ed., pp. 55–63. The Hague: Mouton.

Divale, William

1972 "Systematic Population Control in the Middle and Upper Paleolithic: Inferences Based on Contemporary Hunters and Gatherers." *World Archeology* 4:221–243.

1974 "Migration, External Warfare, and Matrilocal Residence." *Behavior Science Research* 9:75–133.

Divale, William, and Marvin Harris

1976 "Population, Warfare and the Male Supremacist Complex." *American Anthropologist* 78:521–538.

1978a "Reply to Lancaster and Lancaster." *American Anthropologist* 80:117–118.

1978b "The Male Supremacist Complex: Discovery of a Cultural Invention." *American Anthropologist* 80:668–671.

Divale, William, M. Harris, and D. Williams

1978 "On the Misuse of Statistics: A Reply to Hirschfield et al." *American Anthropologist* 80:379–386.

Dobyns, Henry

1972 "The Cornell-Peru Project: Experimental Intervention in Vicos." In *Contemporary Societies and Cultures of Latin America*, Dwight Heath, ed., pp. 201–210. New York: Random House.

1983 *Their Numbers Became Thinned: Native American Population Dynamics in Eastern North America.* Knoxville: University of Tennessee Press.

Dole, Gertrude

1966 "Anarchy without Chaos: Alternatives to Political Authority among the Kuikuru." In *Political Anthropology*, M. J. Swartz, V. W. Turner and A. Tuden, eds., pp. 73–88. Chicago: Aldine.

Domhoff, G. William

1983 *Who Rules America Now?* Englewood Cliffs, N.J.: Prentice-Hall.

Domhoff, G. W., and T. R. Dye, eds.

1987 *Power Elites and Organizations.* Newberry Park, Calif.: Sage.

Doughty, Paul

1987 "Against the Odds: Collaboration and Development at Vicos." In *Collaborative Research and Social Change: Applied Anthropology in Action*, Donald Stull and J. Schensul, eds., pp. 129–157. Boulder, Colo.: Westview Press.

Dowd, Maureen

1983 "Many Women in Poll Equate Value of Job and Family Life." *The New York Times*, December 4, I-3.

Drew, Elizabeth

1983 *Politics and Money: The New Road to Corruption.* New York: Macmillan.

Dualeh, Raqiya

1982 *Sisters in Affliction: Circumcision and Infibulation of Women in Africa.* London: Zed Press.

Dumond, Don

1975 "The Limitation of Human Population: A Natural History." *Science* 187:713–721.

DUMONT, LOUIS
1970 *Homo Hierarchicus: The Caste System and Its Implications.* Trans. Mark Sainsbury. Chicago: University of Chicago Press.

EARLE, TIMOTHY
1977 "A Reappraisal of Redistribution in Complex Hawaiian Chiefdoms." In *Exchange Systems in Prehistory,* Timothy Earle and Jonathan Ericson, eds., pp. 213–232. New York: Academic Press.
1989 "The Evolution of Chiefdoms." *Current Anthropology* 30:84–88.

EHRENBERG, MARGARET
1989 *Women in Prehistory.* Norman: University of Oklahoma Press.

ELIADE, M.
1958 *Birth and Rebirth: The Religious Meaning of Initiation in Human Culture.* New York: Harper & Row.

EMBER, CAROL, M. EMBER, AND B. PASTERNAK
1974 "On the Development of Unilineal Descent." *Journal of Anthropological Research* 30:69–94.

EMBER, MELVIN
1982 "Statistical Evidence for an Ecological Explanation of Warfare." *American Anthropologist* 84:645–649.

EMBER, MELVIN, AND CAROL R. EMBER
1971 "The Conditions Favoring Matrifocal Versus Patrifocal Residence." *American Anthropologist* 73:571–594.

EPSTEIN, T. SCARLETT
1968 *Capitalism, Primitive and Modern: Some Aspects of Tolai Economic Growth.* East Lansing: Michigan State University Press.

ERRINGTON, FREDRICK, AND D. GEWERTZ
1987 *Cultural Alternatives and a Feminist Anthropology: An Analysis of Culturally Constructed Gender Interest in Papua, New Guinea.* New York: Cambridge University Press.

ESPENSHADE, THOMAS
1984 *Investing in Children: New Estimates of Parental Expenditures.* Washington, D.C.: Thomas J. Espenshade.

EVANS-PRITCHARD, E. E.
1940 *The Nuer, A Description of the Modes of Livelihood and Political Institutions of a Nilotic People.* Oxford: Clarendon Press.
1970 "Sexual Inversion among the Azande." *American Anthropologist* 72:1428–1433.

FALLERS, LLOYD
1977 "Equality and Inequality in Human Societies." In *Horizons of Anthropology,* 2nd ed., S. Tax and L. Freeman, eds., pp. 257–268. Chicago: Aldine.

FEI, HSIAO-T'UNG, AND CHANG CHIH-I
1947 *Earthbound China: A Study of Rural Economy in Yunnan.* Chicago: University of Chicago Press.

FEIL, DARYL
1987 *The Evolution of Highland Papua New Guinea Societies.* New York: Cambridge University Press.

FEINMAN, G., AND J. NEITZEL
1984 "Too Many Types: An Overview of Sedentary Prestate Societies in the Americas." In *Advances in Archaeological Method and Theory,* M. B. Schiffer, ed., pp. 39–102. New York: Academic Press.

FERACA, STEPHEN
1986 Personal Communication (see Pl. 97–403, 97th Congress, Second Session, 1982).

FERGUSON, BRIAN
1984 "Introduction: Studying War." In *Warfare, Culture and Environment,* Brian Ferguson, ed., pp. 1–61. Orlando, Fla.: Academic Press.
1989 "Game Wars: Ecology and Conflict in Amazonia." *Journal of Anthropological Research* 45:179–206.

FINKELHOR, D.
1979 *Sexually Victimized Children.* New York: Free Press.

FIRTH, RAYMOND
1957 *We, The Tikopia: A Sociological Study of Kinship in Primitive Polynesia.* Boston: Beacon Press.

FITTKAU, E. J., AND H. KLINGE
1973 "On Biomass and Tropic Structure of the Central Amazon Rain Forest Ecosystem." *Biotropica* 5:1–14.

FLANNERY, KENT
1972 "The Origin of the Village as a Settlement Type in Mesoamerica and the Near East: A Comparative Study." In *Man, Settlement and Urbanism,* P. J. Ucko, R. Tringham, and G. W. Dimbleby, eds., pp. 23–53. Cambridge, Mass.: Schenkman.

FLANNERY, K., J. MARCUS, AND R. REYNOLDS
1989 *The Flocks of the Wamani.* San Diego: Academic Press.

FLEMING, STUART
1977 Dating in Archaeology: A Guide to Scientific Techniques. New York: St. Martins Press.

FORTES, MEYER
1969 *Kinship and the Social Order: The Legacy of Lewis Henry Morgan.* Chicago: Aldine.

FORTUNE, REO
1965 *Manus Religion.* Lincoln: University of Nebraska Press.

FOSTER, GEORGE M.
1967 *Tzintzuntzan: Mexican Peasants in a Changing World.* Boston: Little, Brown.
1974 "Limited Good or Limited Goods: Observations on Acheson." *American Anthropologist* 76:53–57.

FOSTER, GEORGE, AND BARBARA ANDERSON
1978 *Medical Anthropology.* New York: Wiley.

FOUTS, R., AND D. FOUTS
1985 "Signs of Conversation in Chimpanzees." In *Sign Language of the Great Apes,* B. Gardner, R. Gardner, and T. van Cantforts, eds. New York: State University of New York Press.

FRANKE, RICHARD W.
1973 "The Green Revolution in a Javanese Village." Ph.D. dissertation, Harvard University.
1974 "Miracle Seeds and Shattered Dreams." *Natural History* 83(1):10ff.

FRAYSER, SUZANNE
1985 *Varieties of Sexual Experience: An Anthropological Perspective on Human Sexuality.* New Haven, Conn.: HRAF.

FRAZER, JAMES
1911–1915 *The Golden Bough,* 3rd ed. London: Macmillan.

FREDRICK, J., AND P. ADELSTEIN
1973 "Influence of Pregnancy Spacing on Outcome of Pregnancy." *British Medical Journal* 4:(5895):753–756.

FREEDMAN, ROBERT
1977 "Nutritional Anthropology: An Overview." In *Nutrition and Anthropology in Action,* Thomas Fitzgerald, ed., pp. 1–23. Amsterdam: Van Gorcum.

FRIED, MORTON H.

1967 *The Evolution of Political Society: An Essay in Political Anthropology.* New York: Random House.

1975 *The Notion of Tribe.* Menlo Park, Calif.: Cummings.

1978 "The State, the Chicken, and the Egg: Or What Came First?" In *Origins of the State,* Ronald Cohen and Elman Service, eds., pp. 35–47. Philadelphia: Institute for the Study of Human Issues.

FRISANCHO, A. R., J. MATOS, AND P. FLEGEL

1983 "Maternal Nutritional Status and Adolescent Pregnancy Outcome." *American Journal of Clinical Nutrition* 38:739–746.

FRISCH, ROSE

1984 "Body Fat, Puberty, and Fertility." *Science* 199:22–30.

FROMM, ERICH, AND M. MACCOBY

1970 *A Mexican Village: A Sociopsychoanalytic Study.* Englewood Cliffs, N.J.: Prentice-Hall.

FURSTENBERG, FRANK, THEODORE HERSHBERG, AND JOHN MEDELL

1975 "The Origins of the Female-Headed Black Family: The Impact of the Urban Experience." *Journal of Interdisciplinary History* 6(2):211–233.

GAJDUSEK, D. C.

1977 "Unconventional Viruses and the Origin and Disappearance of Kuru." *Science* 197:943–960.

GALBRAITH, JOHN K.

1967 *The New Industrial State.* Boston: Houghton Mifflin.

GANDHI, MOHANDAS K.

1954 *How to Serve the Cow: Ahmedabad.* Navajivan Publishing House.

GARDNER, B. T., AND R. A. GARDNER

1971 "Two-Way Communication with a Chimpanzee." In *Behavior of Non-Human Primates,* A. Schrier and F. Stollnitz, eds., vol. 4, pp. 117–184. New York: Academic Press.

GARDNER, R. A., AND B. T. GARDNER

1975 "Early Signs of Language in Child and Chimpanzee." *Science* 187:752–753.

GAY, JUDITH

1986 "'Mummies and Babies' and Friends and Lovers in Lesotho." In *Anthropology and Homosexual Behavior,* Evelyn Blackwood ed., pp. 97–116. New York: Haworth Press.

GILDER, GEORGE

1981 *Wealth and Poverty.* New York: Basic Books.

GILMORE, DAVID

1990 *Manhood in the Making: Cultural Concepts of Masculinity.* New Haven, Conn.: Yale University Press.

GIVENS, DAVID

1989 *Careers in Anthropology.* Washington, D.C.: American Anthropological Association.

GLAESER, BERNHARD, ED.

1987 *The Green Revolution Revisited: Critique and Alternatives.* Boston: Allen and Unwin.

GLASER, DANYA, AND S. FROSH

1988 *Child Sexual Abuse.* Chicago: Dorsey.

GLASSER, IRA

1989 "How Long America." *Civil Liberties,* Summer, 12ff.

GLASSOW, MICHAEL

1978 "The Concept of Carrying Capacity in the Study of Cultural Process." In *Advances in Archaeological Theory and*

Method, Michael Schiffler, ed., pp. 31–48. New York: Academic Press.

GLENN, EVELYN, AND ROSLYN FELDBERG
1977 "Degraded and Deskilled: The Proletarianization of Clerical Work." *Social Problems* 25:52–64.

GLOVER, G., ET AL.
1984 "Making Quality Count: Boca Raton's Approach to Quality Assurance." *The Cornell Hotel and Restaurant Administration Quarterly*, November, pp. 39–45.

GLUCKMAN, MAX
1955 *Custom and Conflict in Africa*. Oxford: Blackwell.

GODFREY, LAURIE
1981 "The Flood of Anti-evolutionism." *Natural History*, June, pp. 4–10.

GONZALEZ, NANCY L.
1970 "Towards a Definition of Matrilocality." In *Afro-American Anthropology: Contemporary Perspectives*, N. E. Whitten and J. F. Szwed, eds., pp. 231–243. New York: Free Press.

GOOD, KENNETH
1987 "Limiting Factors in Amazonian Ecology." In *Food and Evolution: Toward a Theory of Human Food Habits*, M. Harris and E. Ross, eds., pp. 407–426. Philadelphia: Temple University Press.
1989 Yanomami Hunting Patterns: Trekking and Garden Relocation as an Adaptation to Game Availability in Amazonia, Venezuela. Ph.D. Dissertation. The University of Florida.

GOODALE, JANE
1971 *Tiwi Wives*. Seattle: University of Washington Press.

GOODY, JACK
1976 *Production and Reproduction*. New York: Cambridge University Press.

GOUGH, E. KATHLEEN
1959 "Criterion of Caste Ranking in South India." *Man in India* 39:115–126.
1968 "The Nayars and the Definition of Marriage." In *Marriage, Family, and Residence*, P. Bohannan and J. Middleton, eds., pp. 49–71. Garden City, N.Y.: Natural History Press.

GOULD, HAROLD
1971 "Caste and Class: A Comparative View." *Module* 11:1–24. Reading, Mass.: Addison-Wesley.

GOULD, RICHARD
1982 "To Have and Not to Have: The Ecology of Sharing Among Hunter-Gatherers." In *Resource Managers: North American and Australian Hunter-Gatherers*, Nancy Williams and Eugene Hunn, eds., pp. 69–91. Boulder, Colo.: Westview Press.

GRAMBY, RICHARD
1977 "Deerskins and Hunting Territories: Competition for a Scarce Resource of the Northeastern Woodlands." *American Antiquity* 42:601–605.

GRAVES, THEODORE
1974 "Urban Indian Personality and the Culture of Poverty." *American Ethnologist* 1:65–86.

GRAY, PATRICK, AND LINDA WOLFE
1980 "Height and Sexual Dimorphism and Stature Among Human Societies." *American Journal of Physical Anthropology* 53:441–456.

GREENBERG, JOSEPH
1968 *Anthropological Linguistics: An Introduction*. New York: Random House.

GREGERSON, EDGAR
1982 *Sexual Practices: The Story of Human Sexuality*. London: Mitchell Beazley.

GREGOR, THOMAS A.
1969 "Social Relations in a Small Society: A Study of the Mehinacu Indians of Central Brazil." Ph.D. dissertation. Columbia University.
1985 *Anxious Pleasures: The Sexual Lives of an Amazonian People*. Chicago: University of Chicago Press.

GROSS, DANIEL R.
1975 "Protein Capture and Cultural Development in the Amazon Basin." *American Anthropologist* 77:526–549.
1981 "Reply to Beckerman." Mss.
1984 "Time Allocation: A Tool for the Study of Cultural Behavior." *Annual Review of Anthropology* 13:519–558.

GRUENBAUM, ELLEN
1988 "Reproductive Ritual and Social Reproduction: Female Circumcision and the Subordination of Women in Sudan." In *Economy and Class in Sudan*, Norman O'Neill and Jay O'Brien, eds., pp. 308–323. Brookfield, Vt.: Gower.

GUMBEL, PETER
1988 "Down on the Farm: Soviets Try Once More to Straighten Out Old Agricultural Mess." *The Wall Street Journal*, Dec. 2, p. 1.

HAAS, JOHNATHAN
1982 *The Evolution of the Prehistoric State*. New York: Columbia University Press.

HACKER, ANDREW
1989 "Affirmative Action: The New Look." *The New York Review of Books*, Oct. 12, pp. 63–68.

HADLEY, ARTHUR
1978 *The Empty Polling Booth*. Englewood Cliffs, N.J.: Prentice-Hall.

HALL, CALVIN, AND G. LINDZEY
1967 "Freud's Psychoanalytic Theory of Personality." In *Personalities and Cultures: Readings in Psychological Anthropology*, Robert Hunt, ed., pp. 3–29. Garden City, N.Y.: Natural History Press.

HALLER, JOHN S.
1971 *Outcasts from Evolution*. Urbana: University of Illinois Press.

HAMILTON, SAHNI, B. POPKIN, AND D. SPICE
1984 *Women and Nutrition in Third World Countries*. South Hadley, Mass.: Bergin and Garvey.

HANDWERKER, W. P.
1983 "The First Demographic Transition: An Analysis of Subsistence Choices and Reproductive Consequences." *American Anthropologist* 85:5–27.
1986 "The Modern Demographic Transition." *American Anthropologist* 88:400–417.

HARNER, MICHAEL J.
1970 "Population Pressure and the Social Evolution of Agriculturalists." *Southwestern Journal of Anthropology* 26:67–86.
1977 "The Ecological Basis for Aztec Sacrifice." *American Ethnologist* 4:117–135.
1978 "Reply to Ortiz de Montallano." Paper read at the New York Academy of Sciences, November 17, 1978.
1982 *The Way of the Shaman: A Guide to Power and Healing*. New York: Bantam Books.
1984 *The Jívaro: People of the Sacred Waterfall*, 3rd ed. Berkeley: University of California Press.

HARRINGTON, CHARLES, AND J. WHITING
1972 "Socialization Process and Personality."
In *Psychological Anthropology*, Francis
Hsu, ed., pp. 469–507. Cambridge,
Mass.: Schenkman.

HARRINGTON, MICHAEL
1980 *Decade of Decision*. New York: Simon
& Schuster.

HARRIS, DAVID
1987 "Aboriginal Subsistence in a Tropical
Rain Forest Environment: Food Pro-
curement, Cannibalism and Population
Regulation in Northeastern Australia."
In *Food and Evolution: Toward a Theory
of Human Food Habits*, M. Harris and E.
Ross, eds., pp. 357–385. Philadelphia:
Temple University Press.

HARRIS, MARVIN
1958 *Portugal's African "Wards": A First
Hand Report on Labour and Education
in Mozambique*. New York: American
Committee on Africa.
1968 *The Rise of Anthropological Theory*.
New York: Crowell.
1971 *Culture, Man, and Nature*, 1st ed. New
York: Crowell.
1977 *Cannibals and Kings: The Origins of
Cultures*. New York: Random House.
1979a "Comments on Simoons' Questions in
the Sacred Cow Controversy." *Current
Anthropology* 20:479–482.
1979b *Cultural Materialism: The Struggle for
a Science of Culture*. New York: Random House.
1979c "Reply to Sahlins." *The New York
Review of Books*, June 28, pp. 52–53.
1981 *America Now: The Anthropology of a
Changing Culture*. New York: Simon &
Schuster.
1984 "Animal Capture and Yanomamö
Warfare: Retrospective and New

Evidence." *Journal of Anthropological
Research* 40:183–201.
1985 *Good to Eat*. New York: Simon &
Schuster.
1987a *Why Nothing Works* (originally
published as *America Now*). New York:
Touchstone.
1987b "Reply to Sebring." *Journal of
Anthropological Research* 43:320–322.
1989 *Our Kind: Who We Are, Where We
Came From, Where We Are Going*. New
York: Harper & Row.

HARRIS, MARVIN, AND ERIC ROSS, EDS.
1987 *Food and Evolution: Toward A Theory
of Human Food Habits*. Philadelphia:
Temple University Press.

HARRIS, MARVIN, AND E. O. WILSON
1978 "The Envelope and the Twig." *The
Sciences* 18(8):10–15, 27.

HART, C. W. M., AND A. R. PILLING
1960 *The Tiwi of North Australia*. New
York: Holt, Rinehart and Winston.

HARTUNG, JOHN
1985 Review of *Incest: A Biosocial View* by
J. Shepher. *American Journal of Physical
Anthropology* 67:169–171.

HASSAN, FEKRI
1973 "On Mechanisms of Population
Growth During the Neolithic." *Current
Anthropology* 14:535–540.
1981 *Demographic Archaeology*. New York:
Academic Press.

HASSIG, ROSS
1988 *Aztec Warfare*. Norman: University of
Oklahoma Press.

HAUGEN, EINAR
1977 "Linguistic Relativity: Myths and
Methods." In *Language and Thought:
Anthropological Issues*, W. C. McCor-

mack and S. A. Worm, eds., pp. 11–28. The Hague: Mouton.

HAWKES, KRISTEN, KIM HILL, AND J. O'CONNELL
1982 "Why Hunters Gather: Optimal Foraging and the Aché of Eastern Paraguay." *American Ethnologist* 9:379–398.

HAYDEN, BRIAN
1986 "Resources, Rivalry and Reproduction: The Influence of Basic Resource Characteristics on Reproductive Behavior." In *Culture and Reproduction: An Anthropological Critique of Demographic Transition Theory*, W. P. Handwerker, ed., pp. 176–195. Boulder, Colo.: Westview Press.

HAYDEN, BRIAN, ET AL.
1986 "Women's Status Among Hunter Gatherers." *Human Evolution* 1:449–474.

HAYGHE, L.
1984 "Working Mothers Reach Record Numbers in 1984." Bureau of Labor Statistics, *Monthly Labor Review*, December, p. 31.

HEADLAND, THOMAS
1990 "Introduction: A Dialogue Between Kenneth Pike and Marvin Harris on Emics and Etics." In *Emics and Etics*, Thomas Headland, ed. Troy, N.Y.: Sage.

HECHINGER, FRED
1979 "Further Proof That I.Q. Data Were Fraudulent." *The New York Times*, January 30, p. C-4.

HEIDER, KARL G.
1969 "Visiting Trading Institutions." *American Anthropologist* 71:462–471.
1972 *The Dani of West Irian*. Reading, Mass.: Addison-Wesley.

HENRY, JULES
1963 *Culture Against Man*. New York: Random House.

HERBERS, J.
1985 "Non-Relatives and Solitary People Make Up Half of New Households." *The New York Times*, November 20, p. 1.

HERDT, GILBERT
1984a "Semen Transactions in Sambia Cultures." In *Ritual Homosexuality in Melanesia*, Gilbert Herdt, ed., pp. 167–210. Berkeley: University of California Press.
1984b "Ritualized Homosexuality Behavior in the Male Cults of Melanesia 1862–1983: An Introduction." In *Ritual Homosexuality in Melanesia*, Gilbert Herdt, ed., pp. 1–81. Berkeley: University of California Press.
1987 *The Sambia: Ritual and Custom in New Guinea*. New York: Holt, Rinehart and Winston.

HERSKOVITS, MELVILLE J.
1938 *Dahomey, An Ancient West African Kingdom*. New York: J. J. Augustin.

HERTZLER, JOYCE O.
1965 *A Sociology of Language*. New York: Random House.

HICKS, DAVID
1976 *Tetum Ghosts and Kin*. Palo Alto, Calif.: Mayfield.

HILL, JANE
1978 "Apes and Language." *Annual Review of Anthropology* 7:89–112.

HINDELANG, MICHAEL
1978 "Race and Involvement in Common Law Personal Crimes." *American Sociological Review* 43:93–109.

HIRSCHFELD, LAWRENCE, J. HOWE, AND B. LEVIN
1978 "Warfare, Infanticide and Statistical Inference: A Comment on Divale and

Harris." *American Anthropologist*
80:110–115.

HOCKETT, CHARLES, AND R. ASCHER
1964 "The Human Revolution." *Current Anthropology* 5:135–147.

HOGBIN, H. IAN
1964 *A Guadalcanal Society: The Kaoka Speakers*. New York: Holt, Rinehart and Winston.

HOMMON, ROBERT
1986 "Social Evolution in Ancient Hawaii." In *Island Societies: Archaeological Approaches to Evolution and Transformation*, Patrick Kirch, ed., pp. 55–69. New York: Cambridge University Press.

HOWE, JAMES
1978 "Ninety-two Mythical Populations: A Reply to Divale et al." *American Anthropologist* 80:671–673.

HOWELL, NANCY
1976 "Toward a Uniformitarian Theory of Human Paleodemography." In *The Demographic Evolution of Human Populations*, R. H. Ward and K. M. Weiss, eds., pp. 25–40. New York: Academic Press.

HUNT, ROBERT
1988 "Size and Structure of Authority in Canal Irrigation Systems." *Journal of Anthropological Research* 44:335–355.

HUSAIN, TARIQ
1976 "The Use of Anthropologists in Project Appraisal by the World Bank." In *Development from Below: Anthropologists and Development Situations*, David Pitt, ed., pp. 71–81. The Hague: Mouton.

HYMES, DELL
1971 "Introduction." In *The Origin and Diversification of Language*, M. Swadesh and J. F. Sherzer, eds. Chicago: Aldine.

IRWIN, GEOFFREY
1983 "Chieftanship, Kula and Trade in Massim Prehistory." In *The Kula: New Perspectives on Massim Exchange*, J. Leach and E. Leach, eds., pp. 29–72. Cambridge: Cambridge University Press.

ISAAC, BARRY
1988 "Introduction." In *Prehistoric Economies of the Pacific Northwest Coast*, Barry Isaac, ed., pp. 1–16. Greenwich, Conn.: JAI Press.

ITANI, JUN'ICHIRO
1961 "The Society of Japanese Monkeys." *Japan Quarterly* 8:421–430.

ITANI, J., AND A. NISHIMURA
1973 "The Study of Infra-Human Culture in Japan." In *Precultural Primate Behavior*, E. W. Menzell, ed., pp. 26–50. Basel: S. Karjer.

JACOBS, EVA, S. SHIPP, AND G. BROWN
1989 "Families of Working Wives Spending More on Services and Nondurables." *Monthly Labor Review* 117(Feb.):15–23.

JACOBS, SUE
1978 "Top-down Planning: Analysis of Obstacles to Community Development in an Economically Poor Region of the Southwestern United States." *Human Organization* 37(3):246–256.

JACOBS, SUE, AND C. ROBERTS
1989 "Sex, Sexuality, Gender, and Gender Variance." In *Gender and Anthropology*, Sandra Morgen, ed., pp. 438–462. Washington, D.C.: American Anthropological Association.

JANZEN, DANIEL
1973 "Tropical Agroecosystems." *Science* 182:1212–1219.

JELLIFFE, D. B., AND E. F. JELLIFFE
1978 "The Volume and Composition of Human Milk in Poorly Nourished

Communities: A Review." *American Journal of Clinical Nutrition* 31:492–515.

JENSEN, NEAL
1978 "Limits to Growth in World Food Production." *Science* 201:317–320.

JOANS, BARBARA
1984 "Problems in Pocatello in Linguistic Misunderstanding." *Practicing Anthropology* 6(3, 4):6ff.

JOB, BARBARA COTTMAN
1980 "Employment and Pay Trends in the Retail Trade Industry." *Monthly Labor Review*, March, pp. 40–43.

JOHNSON, ALLEN W.
1975 "Time Allocation in a Machiguenga Community." *Ethnology* 14:301–310.

JOHNSON, ALLEN, AND TIMOTHY EARLE
1987 *The Evolution of Human Societies from Foraging Groups to Agrarian States.* Stanford, Calif.: Stanford University Press.

JONES, DELMOS
1976 "Applied Anthropology and the Application of Anthropological Knowledge." *Human Organization* 35:221–229.

JORGENSON, JOSEPH
1971 "On Ethics and Anthropology." *Current Anthropology* 12(3):321–334.

JOSEPHIDES, LISETTE
1985 *The Production of Inequality: Gender and Exchange Among the Kewa.* New York: Tavistock.

JOSEPHY, ALVIN
1982 *Now That the Buffalo's Gone: A Study of Today's American Indians.* New York: Knopf.

JUNOD, HENRI
1912 *Life of a South African Tribe.* Neuchatel, Switz.: Imprimerie Attinger Fréres.

KABERRY, PHYLLIS
1970 (1939) *Aboriginal Woman, Sacred and Profane.* London: Routledge.

KAEPPLER, ADRIENNE
1978 "Dance in Anthropological Perspective." *Annual Review of Anthropology* 7:31–49.

KAFFMAN, M.
1977 "Sexual Standards and Behavior of the Kibbutz Adolescent." *American Journal of Orthopsychology* 47:207–217.

KAHZANOV, A. M.
1984 *Nomads and the Outside World.* Cambridge, Eng.: University of Cambridge Press.

KANG, ELIZABETH
1979 "Exogamy and Peace Relations of Social Units: A Cross-Cultural Test." *Ethnology* 18:85–99.

KATZ, JEROLD
1971 *The Underlying Reality of Language and Its Philosophical Import.* New York: Harper & Row (Torchbooks).

KATZ, PHYLLIS, AND S. A. TAYLOR
1988 *Eliminating Racism: Profiles in a Controversy.* New York: Plenum.

KAY, PAUL, AND W. KEMPTON
1984 "What Is the Sapir-Whorf Hypothesis?" *American Anthropologist* 86:65–79.

KEEGAN, WILLIAM, AND MORGAN MACLACHLAN
1989 "The Evolution of Avunculocal Chiefdoms." *American Anthropologist* 91:613–630.

KEELY, LAWRENCE
1988 "Hunter-Gatherer Economic Complexity and 'Population Pressure': A Cross-

Cultural Analysis." *Journal of Anthropological Archaeology* 7:373–411.

KELLY, RAYMOND
1976 "Witchcraft and Sexual Relations." In *Man and Woman in the New Guinea Highlands*, P. Brown and G. Buchbinder, eds., pp. 36–53. Washington, D.C.: Special Publication No. 8, American Anthropological Association.

KENDALL, CARL
1984 "Ethnomedicine and Oral Rehydration Therapy: A Case Study of Ethnomedical Investigation and Program Planning." *Social Science and Medicine* 19(3):253–260.

KERTZER, DAVID
1978 "Theoretical Developments in the Study of Age Group Systems." *American Ethnologist* 5(2):368–374.

KHARE, RAVINDRA
1984 *The Untouchable as Himself: Identity and Pragmatism Among the Lucknow Chamars*. New York: Cambridge University Press.

KHAZANOV, K. M.
1984 *Nomads and the Outside World*. Cambridge: Cambridge University Press.

KIRCH, PATRICK
1984 *The Evolution of Polynesian Chiefdoms*. New York: Cambridge University Press.

KLASS, MORTON
1979 *Caste: The Emergence of the South Asian Social System*. Philadelphia: ISHI.

KLUEGEL, JAMES, AND E. R. SMITH
1981 "Beliefs about Stratification." *Annual Review of Sociology* 7:29–56.

KNIGHT, ROLF
1974 "Grey Owl's Return: Cultural Ecology and Canadian Indigenous Peoples." *Reviews in Anthropology* 1:349–359.

KORTLAND, A.
1967 "Experimentation with Chimpanzees in the Wild." In *Progress in Primatology*, D. Starck, R. Schneider, and H. Kuhn, eds., pp. 185–194. Stuttgart: Gustav Fischer.

KOTTAK, CONRAD
1990 *Prime Time Society: An Anthropological Analysis of Television and Culture*. Ann Arbor: University of Michigan Press.

KROEBER, ALFRED L.
1948 *Anthropology*. New York: Harcourt Brace.

KUMAGAÍ, HISA, AND ARNO KUMAGAÍ
1986 "The Hidden 'I' in Amae: Passive Love and Japanese Social Perception." *Ethos* 14:305–320.

LA BARRE, WESTON
1938 *The Peyote Cult*. New Haven, Conn.: Yale University Press. Yale University Publications in Anthropology, No. 19.

LABOV, WILLIAM
1972a *Language in the Inner City*. Philadelphia: University of Pennsylvania Press.
1972b *Sociolinguistic Patterns*. Philadelphia: University of Pennsylvania Press.

LADD, EVERETT, JR.
1978 *Where Have All the Voters Gone?* New York: Norton.

LAKOFF, R.
1973 "Language and Woman's Place." *Language in Society* 2:45–79.

LANCASTER, CHET, AND J. B. LANCASTER
1978 "On the Male Supremacist Complex: A

Reply to Divale and Harris." *American Anthropologist* 80:115–117.

LANDY, DAVID
1985 "Pibloktok and Inuit Nutrition: Possible Implications of Hypervitaminosis A." *Social Science and Medicine* 21:173–185.

LANG, H., AND R. GÖHLEN
1985 "Completed Fertility of the Hutterites: A Revision." *Current Anthropology* 26(3):395.

LANGDON, STEVE
1979 "Comparative Tlingit and Haida Adaptation to the West Coast of the Prince of Wales Archipelago." *Ethnology* 18:101–119.

LATTIMORE, OWEN
1962 *Inner Asian Frontiers of China.* Boston: Beacon Press.

LAWRENCE, PETER
1964 *Road Belong Cargo: A Study of the Cargo Movement in the Southern Madang District, New Guinea.* Manchester: University of Manchester.

LEACH, EDMUND R.
1968 "Polyandry, Inheritance, and the Definition of Marriage, with Particular Reference to Sinhalese Customary Law." In *Marriage, Family, and Residence,* P. Bohannan and J. Middleton, eds., pp. 73–83. Garden City, N.Y.: Natural History Press.

LEACOCK, ELEANOR B.
1973 "The Montagnais-Naskapi Band." In *Cultural Ecology: Readings on the Canadian Indians and Eskimos,* B. Cox, ed., pp. 81–100. Toronto: McClelland & Stewart.

1978 "Woman's Status in Egalitarian Society: Implication for Social Evolution." *Current Anthropology* 19:247–275.
1981 *Myths of Male Dominance.* New York: Monthly Review Press.
1983 "Ideologies of Male Dominance as Divide and Rule Politics: An Anthropologist's View." In *Women's Nature,* Marian Lowe and Ruth Hubbard, eds., pp. 111–121. New York: Pergamon Press.

LEAVITT, GREGORY
1989 "Disappearance of the Incest Taboo." *American Anthropologist* 91:116–131.

LEE, RICHARD B.
1968 "What Hunters Do for a Living, or How to Make Out on Scarce Resources." In *Man the Hunter,* R. B. Lee and I. DeVore, eds., pp. 30–43. Chicago: Aldine.
1969 "!Kung Bushman Subsistence: An Input-Output Analysis." In *Environment and Cultural Behavior: Ecological Studies in Cultural Anthropology,* A. P. Vayda, ed., pp. 47–79. Garden City, N.Y.: Natural History Press.
1979 *The !Kung San: Men, Women and Work in a Foraging Society.* New York: Cambridge University Press.

LEE, R., AND M. HURLICH
1982 "From Forager to Fighters: South Africa's Militarization of the Namibian San." In *Politics and History in Band Society,* Eleanor Leacock and Richard Lee, eds., pp. 327–345. Cambridge: Cambridge University Press.

LEEDS, ANTHONY
1970 "The Concept of the Culture of Poverty: Conceptual, Logical, and Empirical Problems, with Perspectives from

Brazil and Peru." In *The Culture of Poverty: A Critique*, E. Leacock, ed., pp. 226–284. New York: Simon & Schuster.

LEES, SUSAN, AND D. BATES
1974 "The Origins of Specialized Nomadic Pastoralism: A Systemic Model." *American Antiquity* 39:187–193.

LEONARD, KAREN I.
1978 *Social History of an Indian Caste*. Berkeley: University of California Press.

LESSER, ALEXANDER
1968 "War and the State." In *War, The Anthropology of Armed Conflict and Aggression*, M. Fried, M. Harris, and R. Murphy, eds., pp. 92–96. Garden City, N.Y.: Natural History Press.

LÉVI-STRAUSS, CLAUDE
1963 *Tristes Tropiques*. New York: Atheneum.

LEWIS, OSCAR
1961 *The Children of Sanchez: Autobiography of a Mexican Family*. New York: Random House.
1964 *Pedro Martinez: A Mexican Peasant and His Family*. New York: Random House.
1966 *La Vida: A Puerto Rican Family in the Culture of Poverty—San Juan and New York*. New York: Random House.

LEWONTIN, R., S. ROSE, AND L. KAMIN
1984 *Not in Our Genes: Biology, Ideology and Human Nature*. New York: Pantheon.

LICK, JOHN
1983 "Ranked Exchange in Yela (Rossel Island)." In *The Kula: New Perspectives on Massim Exchange*, J. Leach and E. Leach, eds., pp. 503–528. Cambridge: Cambridge University Press.

LIEBERMAN, LESLIE
1987 "Biocultural Consequences of Animals Versus Plants as Sources of Fats, Proteins, and Other Nutrients." In *Food and Evolution: Toward a Theory of Human Food Habits*, M. Harris and E. Ross, eds., pp. 225–258. Philadelphia: Temple University Press.

LIEBOW, ELLIOT
1967 *Tally's Corner: A Study of Negro Street-Corner Men*. Boston: Little, Brown.

LINDENBAUM, SHIRLEY
1977 "The Last Course: Nutrition and Anthropology in Asia." In *Nutrition and Anthropology in Action*, Thomas Fitzgerald, ed., pp. 141–155. Atlantic Highlands, N.J.: Humanities Press.
1979 *Kuru Sorcery*. Palo Alto, Calif.: Mayfield.

LINDSEY, ROBERT
1985 "Official Challenges Outlets That Offer Explicit Videotapes." *The New York Times*, June 3, pp. 1, 9.

LINTON, RALPH
1959 "The Natural History of the Family." In *The Family: Its Function and Destiny*, R. Anshen, ed., pp. 30–52. New York: Harper & Row.

LIVINGSTONE, FRANK B.
1968 "The Effects of Warfare on the Biology of the Human Species." In *War: The Anthropology of Armed Conflict and Aggression*, M. Fried, M. Harris, and R. Murphy, eds., pp. 3–15. Garden City, N.Y.: Doubleday.
1969 "Genetics, Ecology, and the Origins of Incest and Exogamy." *Current Anthropology* 10:45–62.
1981 "Comments on Bixler 1981." *Current Anthropology* 22:645–656.

LIZOT, JAQUES
1977 "Population, Resources and Warfare among the Yanomami." *Man* 12:497–517.
1979 "On Food Taboos and Amazon Cultural Ecology." *Current Anthropology* 20:150–151.

LOCHLIN, J. C., AND R. C. NICHOLS
1976 *Heredity, Environment and Personality.* Austin: University of Texas Press.

LOMAX, ALAN, ED.
1968 *Folksong Style and Culture.* Washington, D.C.: American Association for the Advancement of Science, Publication 88.

LOMAX, ALAN, AND CONRAD ARENSBERG
1977 "A Worldwide Evolutionary Classification of Cultures by Subsistence Systems." *Current Anthropology* 18:659–708.

LONG, BRUCE
1987 "Reincarnation." *Encyclopedia of Religion*, Vol. 12, pp. 265–269. New York: Macmillan.
1948 (1924) *Primitive Religion.* New York: Liveright.

MCASKIE, M., AND A. M. CLARKE
1976 "Parent-Offspring Resemblances in Intelligence: Theories and Evidence." *British Journal of Psychology* 67:243–273.

MCCALL, DAVID
1980 "The Dominant Dyad: Mother-Right and the Iroquois Case." In *Theory and Practice*, Stanley Diamond, ed., pp. 221–261. The Hague: Mouton.

MACCORMACK, CAROL P.
1982 "Adaptation in Human Fertility and Birth." In *Ethnography of Fertility and Birth*, Carol P. MacCormack, ed., pp. 1–23. New York: Academic Press.

MACDOUGAL, A.
1984 "Gap Between Rich, Poor Is Widening." *Los Angeles Times*, October 21.

MCGREW, W. C.
1977 "Socialization and Object Manipulation of Wild Chimpanzees." In *Primate Bio-Social Development*, Susan Chevalier-Skolinkoff and Frank Poirier, eds., pp. 261–288. New York: Garland.

MACLACHLAN, MORGAN
1983 *Why They Did Not Starve: Biocultural Adaptation in a South Indian Village.* Philadelphia: Institute for the Study of Human Issues.

MACLEISH, KENNETH
1972 "The Tasadays: The Stone Age Cavemen of Mindanao." *National Geographic* 142:219–248.

MCNAMARA, ROBERT
1984 "Time Bomb or Myth: The Population Problem." *Foreign Affairs* 62:1107–1131.

MACNEISH, RICHARD
1981 "The Transition to Statehood as Seen from the Mouth of a Cave." In *The Transition to Statehood in the New World*, Grant Jones and Paul Kautz, eds., pp. 123–154. New York: Cambridge University Press.

MAIR, LUCY
1969 *Witchcraft.* New York: McGraw-Hill.

MALABRE, ALFRED
1989 "Is the Bill Arriving for the Free Lunch?" *The Wall Street Journal*, January 9, A1ff.

MALINOWSKI, BRONISLAW
1920 "War and Weapons among the Natives of the Trobriand Islands." *Man* 20:10–12.

1922 *Argonauts of the Western Pacific.* New York: Dutton.

1927 *Sex and Repression in Savage Society.* London: Routledge & Kegan Paul.

1935 *Coral Gardens and Their Magic* (2 vols.). London: Allen & Unwin.

MALONEY, WILLIAM
1987a "Dharma." *Encyclopedia of Religion,* Vol. 4, pp. 239–332. New York: Macmillan.

1987b "Karman." *Encyclopedia of Religion,* Vol. 8, pp. 261–266. New York: Macmillan.

MAMDANI, MAHMOOD
1973 *The Myth of Population Control: Family, Caste and Class in an Indian Village.* New York: Monthly Review Press.

MARANO, LOU
1982 "Windigo Psychosis: The Anatomy of an Emic-Etic Confusion." *Current Anthropology* 23:385–412.

MARETT, ROBERT R.
1914 *The Threshold of Religion.* London: Methuen.

MARIANO, ANN
1984 "Baby Boomers Face Housing and Job Market Bummers." *Salt Lake Tribune,* September 23, F7 (orig. *Washington Post*).

MARGOLIS, MAXINE
1984 *Mothers and Such.* Berkeley: University of California Press.

MARSHALL, DONALD
1971 "Sexual Behavior on Mangaia." In *Human Sexual Behavior,* D. Marshall and R. Suggs, eds., pp. 103–162. Englewood Cliffs, N.J.: Prentice-Hall.

MARSHALL, MAC
1978 *Weekend Warriors: An Interpretation of Drunkenness in Micronesia.* Palo Alto, Calif.: Mayfield.

MARTIN, PAUL
1984 "Prehistoric Overkill: The Global Model." In *Quaternary Extinctions: A Prehistoric Revolution,* Paul S. Martin and R. Klein, eds., pp. 354–403. Tucson: The University of Arizona Press.

MARX, KARL
1970 (1859) *A Contribution to the Critique of Political Economy.* New York: International Publishers.

MASON, CAROL
1964 "Natchez Class Structure." *Ethnohistory* 11:120–133.

MASON, J. ALDEN
1957 *The Ancient Civilizations of Peru.* Harmondsworth, Eng.: Penguin.

MASSING, MICHAEL
1989 "Crack's Destructive Sprint Across America." *The New York Times Magazine,* Oct. 1, pp. 38ff.

MATHEWS, HOLLY
1985 "We Are Mayordomo: A Reinterpretation of Women's Roles in the Mexican Cargo System." *American Ethnologist* 12:285–301.

MATTHEWS, MERVYN
1978 *Privilege in the Soviet Union: A Study of Elite Life-Styles Under Communism.* London: George Allen & Unwin.

MATHUR, HARI
1977 *Anthropology in the Development Process.* New Delhi: Vikas.

MEAD, MARGARET
1950 *Sex and Temperament in Three Primitive Societies.* New York: Mentor.
1970 *Culture and Commitment.* Garden City, N.Y.: Natural History Press.

MENCHER, JOAN
1974a "Conflicts and Contradictions in the Green Revolution: The Case of Tamil Nadu." *Economic and Political Weekly* 9:309–323.
1974b "The Caste System Upside Down: Or, the Not So Mysterious East." *Current Anthropology* 15:469–478.
1978 *Agricultural and Social Structure in Tamil Nadu.* New Delhi: Allied Publishers.

MILLER, BARBARA
1981 *The Endangered Sex: Neglect of Female Children in Rural North India.* Ithaca, N.Y.: Cornell University Press.
1987a "Female Infanticide and Child Neglect in Rural North India." In *Child Survival,* Nancy Scheper-Hughes, ed., pp. 95–112. Boston: D. Reidel.
1987b "Wife-beating in India: Variations and Theme." Paper read at the annual meetings of the American Anthropological Association, November 1987.

MILLET, KATE
1970 *Sexual Politics.* Garden City, N.Y.: Doubleday.

MINGE-KALMAN, WANDA
1978a "Household Economy during the Peasant-to-Worker Transition in the Swiss Alps." *Ethnology* 17(2):183–196.
1978b "The Institutionalization of the European Family: The Institutionalization of 'Childhood' as a Market for Family Labor." *Comparative Studies in Society and History* 20:454–468.

MINTURN, LEIGH, AND JOHN T. HITCHCOCK
1963 "The Rajputs of Khalapur, India." In *Six Cultures, Studies of Child Rearing,* B. B. Whiting, ed., pp. 203–361. New York: Wiley.

MINTURN, LEIGH, AND J. STASHAK
1982 "Infanticide as a Terminal Abortion Procedure." *Behavior Science Research* 17:70–90.

MITCHELL, D., AND L. DONALD
1988 "Archaeology and the Study of Northwest Coast Economies." In *Prehistoric Economies of the Pacific Northwest Coast,* Barry Isaac, ed., pp. 293–351. Greenwich, Conn.: JAI Press.

MIYADI, D.
1967 "The Differences in Social Behavior among Japanese Macaque Troops." In *Progress in Primatology,* D. Starck, R. Schneider, and H. Kuhn, eds. Stuttgart: Gustav Fischer.

MONDLANE, EDUARDO
1969 *The Struggle for Mozambique.* Baltimore: Penguin.

MOONEY, JAMES
1965 (1896) *The Ghost Dance Religion.* Chicago: University of Chicago Press.

MORAN, EMILIO
1982 *Human Adaptability: An Introduction to Ecological Anthropology.* Boulder, Colo.: Westview Press.

MOREHOUSE, WARD, AND DAVID DEMBO
1985a *The Underbelly of the U.S. Economy: Joblessness and Pauperization of Work in America.* Special Report No. 2 (February). New York: Council on International and Public Affairs.
1985b *The Underbelly of the U.S. Economy:*

Joblessness and Pauperization of Work in America. Special Report No. 4 (August). New York: Council on International and Public Affairs.

1988 *Background Paper. Joblessness and the Pauperization of Work in America.* New York: Council on International and Public Affairs.

MORREN, GEORGE
1984 "Warfare in the Highland Fringe of New Guinea: The Case of the Mountain Ok." In *Warfare, Culture and Environment,* Brian Ferguson, ed., pp. 169–208. Orlando, Fla.: Academic Press.

MORRIS, C.
1976 "Master Design of the Inca." *Natural History* 85:(10):58–67.

MORRIS, JOHN, ED.
1974a *Scientific Creationism for Public Schools.* San Diego: Institute for Creation Research.
1974b *The Troubled Waters of Evolution.* San Diego: Creation Life.
1986 "The Paluxy River Mystery." *Impact* 151:i–iv. El Cajon, Calif.: Institute for Creation Research.

MOSKOWITZ, BREYNE
1978 "The Acquisition of Language." *Scientific American* 239(5):92–108.

MOUER, ROSS, AND YOSHI SUGIMOTO
1986 *Images of Japanese Society: A Study in the Structure of Social Reality.* London: Routledge and Kegan Paul.

MOYNIHAN, DANIEL P.
1965 *The Negro Family, the Case for National Action.* Washington, D.C.: U.S. Department of Labor.
1986 *Family and Nation.* San Diego: Harcourt Brace Jovanovich.

MÜNZEL, MARK
1973 *The Aché Indians: Genocide in Paraguay.* International Work Group for Indigenous Affairs (IWGIA), 11.

MURDOCK, GEORGE P.
1949 *Social Structure.* New York: Macmillan.
1967 *Ethnographic Atlas.* Pittsburgh: University of Pittsburgh Press.

MURDOCK, GEORGE, AND C. PROVOST
1973 "Factors in the Division of Labor by Sex." *Ethnology* 12:203–225.

MURPHY, ROBERT
1956 "Matrilocality and Patrilineality in Mundurucu Society." *American Anthropologist* 58:414–434.
1976 "Man's Culture and Woman's Nature." *Annals of the New York Academy of Sciences* 293:15–24.

MURRAY, ALAN
1989 "Many Americans Fear U.S. Living Standards Have Stopped Rising." *The Wall Street Journal,* May 1, A1.

MURRAY, CHARLES
1984 *Losing Ground: American Social Policy 1950–1980.* New York: Basic Books.

MURRAY, GERALD
1984 "The Wood Tree as a Peasant Cash Crop: An Anthropological Strategy for the Domestication of Energy." In *Haiti — Today and Tomorrow: An Interdisciplinary Study,* Charles Fost and A. Valdman, eds., pp. 141–160. Lanham, Md.: University Press of America.

NADER, LAURA
1972 "Up the Anthropologist — Perspectives Gained from Studying Up." In *Reinventing Anthropology,* Dell Hymes, ed., pp. 284–311. New York: Random House.

NAG, MONI
1972 "Sex, Culture, and Human Fertility: India and the United States." *Current Anthropology* 13:231–238.
1983 "The Impact of Sociocultural Factors on Breastfeeding and Social Behavior." In *Determinants of Fertility in Developing Countries* 1:163–198. New York: Academic Press.

NAG, MONI, AND N. KAK
1984 "Demographic Transition in the Punjab Village." *Population and Development Review* 10:661–678.

NAG, MONI, B. WHITE, AND R. PEET
1978 "An Anthropological Approach to the Study of the Economic Value of Children in Java and Nepal." *Current Anthropology* 19:293–306.

NARDI, BONNIE
1983 "Reply to Harbison's Comments on Nardi's Modes of Explanation in Anthropological Population Theory." *American Anthropologist* 85:662–664.

NAROLL, RAOUL
1973 "Introduction" to *Main Currents in Anthropology*, R. Naroll and F. Naroll, eds., pp. 1–23. Englewood Cliffs, N.J.: Prentice-Hall.

NASH, JIL
1974 *Matriliny and Modernization: The Nagovisi of South Bougainville*. New Guinea Research Bulletin.

NELSON, KRISTEN
1986 "Labor Demand, Labor Supply, and the Suburbanization of Low-Wage Office Work." In *Production, Work, Territory: The Geographical Anatomy of Industrial Capitalism*, A. Scott and M. Storper, eds., pp. 149–171. Boston: Allen and Unwin.

NEVILLE, GWEN
1979 "Community Form and Ceremonial Life in Three Regions of Scotland." *American Ethnologist* 6:93–109.

NEWCOMER, PETER
1977 "Toward a Scientific Treatment of Exploitation: A Critique of Dalton." *American Anthropologist* 79:115–119.

NEWITT, JANE
1985 "How to Forecast Births." *American Demographics*, January, pp. 30–33, 51.

NEWMAN, PHILIP L.
1965 *Knowing the Gururumba*. New York: Holt, Rinehart and Winston.

NEWMEYER, FREDERICK
1978 "Prescriptive Grammar: A Reappraisal." In *Approaches to Language: Anthropological Issues*, W. C. McCormack and S. A. Wurm, eds., pp. 581–593. The Hague: Mouton.

New York Times, The
1989 "Women in Parliaments," August 25, p. A7.

NISHIDA, T.
1973 "The Ant-Gathering Behavior by the Use of Tools among Wild Chimpanzees of the Mahali Mountains." *Journal of Human Evolution* 2:357–370.

NUSSBAUM, KAREN
1980 *Race Against Time*. Cleveland: National Association of Office Workers.

OASA, EDMUND
1985 "Farming Systems Research: A Change in Form But Not in Content." *Human Organization* 44:219–227.

ODEND'HAL, STUART
1972 "Energetics of Indian Cattle in Their Environment." *Journal of Human Ecology* 1:3–22.

OLIVER, DOUGLAS
1955 *A Solomon Island Society: Kinship and Leadership among the Siuai of Bougainville.* Cambridge, Mass.: Harvard University Press.

OPLER, MORRIS
1959 "Cultural Differences in Mental Disorders: An Italian and Irish Contrast in the Schizophrenias — U.S.A." In *Culture and Mental Health,* Morris Opler, ed., pp. 425–442. New York: Atherton.

OPPENHEIMER, VALERIE
1982 *Work and the Family: A Study in Social Demography.* New York: Academic Press.

ORANS, MARTIN
1968 "Maximizing in Jajmaniland: A Model of Caste Relations." *American Anthropologist* 70:875–897.

ORTIZ DE MONTELLANO, B. R.
1978 "Aztec Cannibalism: An Ecological Necessity?" *Science* 200:611–617.
1983 "Counting Skulls: Comments on the Aztec Cannibalism Theory of Harner-Harris." *American Anthropologist* 85:403–406.

ORTNER, SHERRY, AND H. WHITEHEAD, EDS.
1981 *The Cultural Construction of Gender and Sexuality.* Cambridge: Cambridge University Press.

OSBERG, LARS
1984 *Economic Inequality in the United States.* New York: M. E. Sharpe.

OSBORNE, R. T.
1978 "Race and Sex Differences in Heritability of Mental Test Performance: A Study of Negroid and Caucasoid Twins." In *Human Variation: The Biopsychology of Age, Race, and Sex,* R. T. Osborne, C.

Noble, and N. Weyl, eds., pp. 137–169. New York: Academic Press.

OTTENHEIMER, MARTIN
1984 "Some Problems and Prospects in Residence and Marriage." *American Anthropologist* 86:351–358.

OTTERBEIN, KEITH
1973 "The Anthropology of War." In *The Handbook of Social and Cultural Anthropology,* J. Honigman, ed., pp. 923–958. Chicago: Rand McNally.

PAOLISSO, MICHAEL, AND ROSS SACKETT
1982 "Hunting Productivity Among the Yukpa Indians of Venezuela." Paper read at the annual meeting of the American Anthropological Association, Washington, D.C.

PARENTI, MICHAEL
1986 *Inventing Reality: The Politics of the Mass Media.* New York: St. Martin's Press.

PARKER, SUE
1985 "A Social-Technological Model for the Evolution of Languages." *Current Anthropology* 26:617–639.

PARSON, TALCOTT
1970 "Equality and Inequality in Modern Society, or Social Stratification Revisited." In *Social Stratification: Research and Theory for the 1970's,* Edward Laumann, ed., pp. 13–72. New York: Bobbs-Merrill.

PASTERNAK, BURTON, CAROL EMBER, AND MELVIN EMBER
1976 "On the Conditions Favoring Extended Family Households." *Journal of Anthropological Research* 32(2):109–123.

PASZTORY, ESTHER
1984 "The Function of Art in Mesoamerica."

Archeology, January – February, pp. 18 – 25.

PATTERSON, FRANCES
1981 *The Education of Koko.* New York: Holt, Rinehart and Winston.

PATTERSON, ORLANDO
1977 *Ethnic Chauvinism: The Reactionary Impulse.* New York: Stein and Day.

PELLET, PETER
1987 "Problems and Pitfalls in the Assessment of Human Nutritional Status." In *Food and Evolution: Toward a Theory of Human Food Habits*, M. Harris and E. Ross, eds., pp. 163 – 179. Philadelphia: Temple University Press.

PELTO, PERTTIE, AND GRETL PELTO
1973 "Ethnography: The Fieldwork Enterprise." In *Handbook of Social and Cultural Anthropology*, J. Honigman, ed., pp. 241 – 248. Chicago: Rand McNally.
1976 *The Human Adventure: An Introduction to Anthropology.* New York: Macmillan.

PERCIVAL, L., AND K. QUINKERT
1987 "Anthropometric Factors." In *Sex Differences in Human Performance*, Mary Baker, ed., pp. 121 – 139. New York: Wiley.

PERLO, VICTOR
1976 *Economics of Racism U.S.A.: Roots of Black Inequality.* New York: International Press.

PHILIPS, SUSAN
1980 "Sex Differences and Language." *Annual Review of Anthropology* 9:523 – 544.

PIDDOCK, STUART
1965 "The Potlatch System of the Southern Kwakiutl: A New Perspective." *South-* *western Journal of Anthropology* 21:244 – 264.

PIGGOTT, STUART
1966 *Ancient Europe.* Chicago: Aldine.

PILBEAM, DAVID
1985 "Patterns of Hominoid Evolution." In *Ancestors: The Hard Evidence*, Eric Delson, ed., pp. 51 – 59. New York: Alan R. Liss.
1986 "Hominoid Evolution and Hominoid Origins." *American Anthropologist* 88(2):295 – 312.

PIMENTEL, DAVID, ET AL.
1973 "Food Production and Energy Crisis." *Science* 182:443 – 449.
1975 "Energy and Land Constraints in Food Protein Production." *Science* 190:754 – 761.

PIMENTEL, D., AND M. PIMENTEL
1985 "Energy Use for Food Processing for Nutrition and Development." *Food and Nutrition Bulletin* 7(2):36 – 45.

PIVEN, FRANCES, AND R. CLOWARD
1971 *Regulating the Poor: The Functions of Public Welfare.* New York: Random House (Vintage).

PLATH, DAVID, ED.
1983 *Work and Life Course in Japan.* Albany, N.Y.: State University of New York Press.

PLUCKNETT, D., AND N. SMITH
1982 "Agricultural Research and Third World Food Production." *Science* 217:215 – 219.

PODOLEFSKY, AARON
1984 "Contemporary Warfare in the New Guinea Highlands." *Ethnology* 23:73 – 87.

POLANYI, KARL
1957 *The Great Transformation.* Boston: Beacon Press.

POLGAR, STEVEN
1972 "Population History and Population Policies from an Anthropological Perspective." *Current Anthropology* 13:203–215.

PORAT, MARC
1979 "The Information Economy." Ph.D. dissertation, Stanford University.

POSPISIL, LEOPOLD
1963 *The Kapauku Papuans of West New Guinea.* New York: Holt, Rinehart and Winston.
1968 "Law and Order." In *Introduction to Cultural Anthropology,* J. Clifton, ed., pp. 200–224. Boston: Houghton Mifflin.

POST, JOHN
1985 *Food Shortage, Climatic Variability, and Epidemic Disease in Pre-Industrial Europe.* Ithaca, N.Y.: Cornell University Press.

PREMACK, DAVID
1971 "On the Assessment of Language Competence in the Chimpanzee." In *The Behavior of Nonhuman Primates,* vol. 4, A. M. Schrier and F. Stollnitz, eds., pp. 185–228. New York: Academic Press.
1976 *Intelligence in Ape and Man.* Hillsdale, N.J.: Erlbaum.

PRICE, BARBARA
1979 "Turning States' Evidence: Problems in the Theory of State Formation." In *New Directions in Political Economy: An Approach from Anthropology,* M. B. Léons and F. Rothstein, eds., pp. 269–306. Westport, Conn.: Greenwood Press.

PRICE, SALLY
1989 *Primitive Art in Civilized Places.* Chicago: University of Chicago Press.

PRINCETON RELIGIOUS RESEARCH CENTER
1979 *Emerging Trends.* Princeton, N.J.: 1 (March).
1980 *Religion in America 1979–1980.* Princeton, N.J.: Princeton Religious Research Institute.

RAJ, K. N.
1977 "Poverty, Politics and Development." *Economic and Political Weekly* (Bombay), annual number, February, pp. 185–204.

RAMIREZ, F., AND J. MEYER
1980 "Comparative Education: The Social Construction of the Modern World System." *Annual Review of Sociology* 6:369–399.

RAPPAPORT, ROY
1971a "Ritual, Sanctity, and Cybernetics." *American Anthropologist* 73:59–76.
1971b "The Sacred in Human Evolution." In *Explorations in Anthropology,* Morton Fried, ed., pp. 403–420. New York: Crowell.
1984 *Pigs for the Ancestors: Ritual in the Ecology of a Papua New Guinea People,* 2nd ed. New Haven, Conn.: Yale University Press.

RASMUSSEN, KNUD
1929 *The Intellectual Culture of the Iglulik Eskimos.* Report of the 5th Thule Expedition, 1921–1924, vol. 7, no. 1. Translated by W. Worster. Copenhagen: Glydendal.

REED, C. M.
1984 "Maritime Traders in the Archaic Greek World." *The Ancient World* 10:31–43.

RENFREW, COLLIN
1973 *Before Civilization: The Radiocarbon Revolution and Prehistoric Europe.* New York: Knopf.

RHOADES, ROBERT
1984 *Breaking New Ground: Agricultural Anthropology.* Lima, Peru: International Potato Center.

RIBEIRO, DARCY
1971 *The Americas and Civilization.* New York: Dutton.

RICHARDS, PAUL
1973 "The Tropical Rain Forest." *Scientific American* 229:58–68.

RIFKIND, JEREMY, AND TED HOWARD
1979 *The Emerging Order: God in the Age of Scarcity.* New York: Putnam.

RIVIÈRE, C.
1987 "Soul: Concepts in Primitive Religions." In *The Encyclopedia of Religion*, pp. 426–430. New York: Macmillan and Free Press.

ROBERTS, PAUL
1964 *English Syntax.* New York: Harcourt Brace Jovanovich.

ROBERTS, RON, AND D. BRINTNALL
1982 *Reinventing Inequality.* Boston: Schenkman.

ROHNER, RONALD
1969 *The Ethnography of Franz Boas.* Chicago: University of Chicago Press.

ROHRLICH-LEAVITT, RUBY
1977 "Women in Transition: Crete and Sumer." In *Becoming Visible: Women in European History*, Renate Bridenthal and C. Koonz, eds., pp. 38–59. Boston: Houghton Mifflin.

ROSALDO, MICHELLE, AND LOUISE LAMPHERE, EDS.
1974 *Women, Culture, and Society.* Stanford: Stanford University Press.

ROSS, ERIC
1978 "Food Taboos, Diet, and Hunting Strategy: The Adaptation of Animals in Amazon Cultural Ecology." *Current Anthropology* 19:1–36.
1979 "Reply to Lizot." *Current Anthropology* 20:151–155.

ROSS, JANE
1984 "Effects of Contact on Revenge Hostilities Among Achuarä Jívaro." In *Warfare, Culture, and Environment*, Brian Ferguson, ed., pp. 83–109. Orlando, Fla.: Academic Press.

ROSS, RUTH, AND G. BENSON
1979 "Criminal Justice from East to West." *Crime and Delinquency* 25:76–86.

ROSZAK, THEODORE
1975 *Unfinished Animal: The Aquarian Frontier and the Evolution of Consciousness.* New York: Harper & Row.

RUBIN, VERA, AND LAMBROS COMITAS
1975 *Ganja In Jamaica: A Medical Anthropological Study of Chronic Marihuana Use.* The Hague: Mouton.

RUMBAUGH, D. M.
1988 "Comparative Psychology and the Great Apes: Their Competence in Learning, Language, and Numbers." Address presented at the annual meeting of the American Pyschological Association, Atlanta.

RUYLE, EUGENE E.
1973 "Slavery, Surplus, and Stratification on the Northwest Coast: The Ethnoenerge-

tics of an Incipient Stratification System." *Current Anthropology* 14:603–631.
1975 "Mode of Production and Mode of Exploitation: The Mechanical and the Dialectical." *Dialectical Anthropology* 1:7–23.

RYAN, WILLIAM
1982 *Equality.* New York: Vintage.

SABATO, LARRY
1989 *Paying for Elections: The Campaign Finance Thicket.* New York: Priority Press.

SACHS, BERNICE
1985 *Vital Speeches of the Day* 50(4):757–762.

SACKS, KAREN B.
1971 "Economic Bases of Sexual Equality: A Comparative Study of Four African Societies." Ph.D. dissertation, University of Michigan.

SAHLINS, MARSHALL
1972 *Stone Age Economics.* Chicago: Aldine.
1978 "Culture as Protein and Profit." *The New York Review of Books,* November 23, pp. 45–53.

SALZMAN, PHILIP, ED.
1971 "Comparative Studies of Nomadism and Pastoralism." *Anthropological Quarterly* 44(3):104–210.

SANDAY, PEGGY
1981 *Female Power and Male Dominance: On the Origins of Sexual Inequality.* New York: Cambridge University Press.

SANDERSON, STEPHEN
1988 *Macrosociology: An Introduction to Human Societies.* New York: Harper & Row.

SANJEK, ROGER
1977 "Cognitive Maps of the Ethnic Domain in Urban Ghana: Reflections on Varia-

bility and Change." *American Ethnologist* 4:603–622.

SANKAR, ANDREA
1986 "Sisters and Brothers, Lovers and Enemies: Marriage Resistance in Southern Kuangtung." In *Anthropology and Homosexual Behavior,* Evelyn Blackwood, ed., pp. 69–81. New York: Haworth Press.

SAPIR, EDWARD
1921 *Language.* New York: Harcourt Brace.

SCHEFFLER, HAROLD
1973 "Kinship, Descent, and Alliance." In *Handbook of Social and Cultural Anthropology,* J. Honigman, ed., pp. 747–793. Chicago: Rand McNally.

SCHEPER-HUGHES, NANCY
1984 "Infant Mortality and Infant Care: Cultural and Economic Constraints on Nurturing in Northeast Brazil." *Social Science and Medicine* 19(5):535–546.

SCHERMERHORN, R. A.
1978 *Comparative Ethnic Relations.* Chicago: University of Chicago Press.

SCHLEGEL, ALICE
1972 *Male Dominance and Female Autonomy.* New Haven, Conn.: Human Relations Area Files.

SCHLEGEL, ALICE, AND H. BARRY
1979 "Adolescent Initiation Ceremonies: A Cross-Cultural Code." *Ethnology* 18:199–210.
1986 "The Cultural Consequences of Female Contribution to Subsistence." *American Anthropologist* 88:142–150.

SCHLEGEL, ALICE, AND R. ELOUL
1988 "Marriage Transactions: Labor, Prop-

erty and Status." *American Anthropologist* 90:291–309.

SCHWARTZ, MICHAEL
1987 *The Structure of Power in America: The Corporate Elite as a Ruling Class.* New York: Holmes and Meier.

SCODITTI, G.
1983 "Kula on Kitava." In *The Kula: New Perspectives in Massim Exchange,* J. Leach and E. Leach, eds., pp. 249–273. New York: Cambridge University Press.

SCOTT, EUGENIE
1984 "Anthropology and 'Scientific Creationism.'" Washington, D.C.: American Anthropological Association.

SCOTT, JAMES
1985 *Weapons of the Weak: Everyday Forms of Peasant Resistance.* New Haven, Conn.: Yale University Press.

SCRIMSHAW, NEVIN
1977 "Through a Glass Darkly: Discerning the Practical Implications of Human Dietary Protein-Energy Interrelationships." *Nutrition Reviews* 35:321–337.

SCRIMSHAW, SUSAN
1983 "Infanticide as Deliberate Fertility Control." In *Determinants of Fertility in Developing Countries: Fertility Regulation and Institutional Influences,* R. Bulatao and R. Lee, eds., vol. 2, pp. 245–266. New York: Academic Press.

SERRIN, WILLIAM
1984 "Experts Say Job Bias Against Women Persists." *The New York Times,* November 25, pp. 1, 18.

SERVICE, ELMAN R.
1975 *Origins of the State and Civilization: The Processes of Cultural Evolution.* New York: Norton.

1978 "Classical and Modern Theories of the Origin of Government." In *Origins of the State: The Anthropology of Political Evolution,* R. Cohen and E. Service, eds., pp. 21–34. Philadelphia: ISHI.

SHANAHAN, EILEEN
1985 "Measuring the Service Economy." *The New York Times,* Sunday, October 27, p. 4.

SHARFF, JAGNA
1980 *Life on Dolittle Street: How Poor People Purchase Immortality.* Final Report, Hispanic Study Project N. 9, Department of Anthropology, Columbia University.

1981 "Free Enterprise and the Ghetto Family." *Psychology Today,* March.

SHARMA, URSULA
1983 "Dowry in North India: Its Consequences for Women." In *Women and Property, Women as Property,* Renee Hirschon, ed., pp. 62–74. London: Croom Helm.

SHEPHER, J.
1971 "Mate Selection among Second Generation Kibbutz Adolescents and Adults." *Archives of Sexual Behavior* 1:293–307.

1983 *Incest: A Biosocial View.* New York: Academic Press.

SHORT, RICHARD
1984 "On Placing the Child Before Marriage, Reply to Birdsell." *Population and Development Review* 9:124–135.

SHOSTAK, MARJORIE
1981 *Nisa, The Life and Words of a !Kung Woman.* Cambridge, Mass.: Harvard University Press.

SILVERSTEIN, MICHAEL
1972 "Linguistic Theory: Syntax, Semantics,

Pragmatics." *Annual Review of Anthropology* 3:349–382.

SILK, LEONARD
1985 "The Peril Behind the Takeover Boom." *The New York Times*, December 29, sec. 3, p. 1.

SIMOONS, FREDERICH
1979 "Questions in the Sacred Cow Controversy." *Current Anthropology* 20:467–493.

SIMPSON, GEORGE, AND J. M. YINGER
1985 *Racial and Cultural Minorities: An Analysis of Prejudice and Discrimination,* 5th ed. New York: Plenum.

SMITH, C. T.
1970 "Depopulation of the Central Andes in the 16th Century." *Current Anthropology* 11:453–460.

SMITH, E. A.
1983 "Anthropological Applications of Optimal Foraging Theory: A Critical Review." *Current Anthropology* 24:625–651.

SMITH, M. G.
1966 "A Survey of West Indian Family Studies." In *Man, Settlement, and Urbanism: West Indian Perspectives,* L. Comitas and D. Lowenthal, eds., pp. 365–408. Garden City, N.Y.: Anchor Books, 1973.
1968 "Secondary Marriage among Kadera and Kagoro." In *Marriage, Family, and Residence,* P. Bohannan and J. Middleton, eds., pp. 109–130. Garden City, N.Y.: Natural History Press.

SMITH, RAYMOND T.
1973 "The Matrifocal Family." In *The Character of Kinship,* Jack Goody, ed., pp. 121–144. London: Cambridge University Press.

SOLZHENITSYN, ALEXANDER
1974 *Gulag Archipelago.* New York: Harper & Row.

SORENSON, RICHARD
1972 "Socio-Ecological Change among the Foré of New Guinea." *Current Anthropology* 13:349–383.

SORENSON, RICHARD, AND P. E. KENMORE
1974 "Proto-Agricultural Movement in the Eastern Highlands of New Guinea." *Current Anthropology* 15:67–72.

SOUSTELLE, JACQUES
1970 *Daily Life of the Aztecs.* Stanford: Stanford University Press.

SOUTHWORTH, FRANKLIN
1974 "Linguistic Masks for Power: Some Relationships Between Semantic and Social Change." *Journal of Anthropological Linguistics* 16:177–191.

SOWELL, THOMAS
1983 *The Economics and Politics of Race.* New York: Morrow.

SPECK, FRANK
1915 "The Family Hunting Band as the Basis of the Algonkian Social Organization." *American Anthropologist* 17:289–305.

SPENCER, P.
1965 *The Samburu: A Study of Gerontocracy in a Nomadic Tribe.* Berkeley: University of California Press.

SPENGLER, JOSEPH
1974 *Population Change, Modernization, and Welfare.* Englewood Cliffs, N.J.: Prentice-Hall.

SPIRO, MELFORD
1954 "Is the Family Universal?" *American Anthropologist* 56:839–846.

1982 *Oedipus in the Trobriands.* Chicago: University of Chicago Press.

SPONSEL, LESLIE
1986 "Amazon Ecology and Adaptation." *Annual Review of Anthropology* 15:67–97.

SPUHLER, JAMES
1985 "Anthropology, Evolution, and Scientific Creationism." *Annual Review of Anthropology* 14:103–133.

SRINIVAS, M. N.
1955 "The Social System of a Mysore Village." In *Village India: Studies in the Little Community,* M. Marriott, ed., pp. 1–35. Memoir 83, American Anthropological Association.

STACK, CAROL
1974 *All Our Kin: Strategies for Survival in a Black Community.* New York: Harper & Row.

STEADMAN, LYLE, AND C. MERBS
1982 "Kuru: Early Letters and Field-Notes from the Collection of D. Carleton Gajdusek." *American Anthropologist* 84:611–627.

STEIN, HOWARD, AND R. F. HILL
1977 *The Ethnic Imperative: Examining the New White Ethnic Movement.* University Park: Pennsylvania State University Press.

STEINHART, JOHN, AND CAROL STEINHART
1974 "Energy Use in the U.S. Food System." *Science* 184:307–317.

STEWART, OMER C.
1948 *Ute Peyotism.* University of Colorado Studies, Series in Anthropology, No. 1. Boulder: University of Colorado Press.
1968 "Lorenz/Margolin on the Ute." In *Man and Aggression,* M. F. Ashley Montagu, ed., pp. 103–110. New York: Oxford University Press.
1987 *Peyote Religion: A History.* Norman: University of Oklahoma Press.

STORPER, MICHAEL
1989 *The Capitalist Imperative: Territory, Technology, and Industrial Growth.* New York: Basil Blackwell.

STREET, JOHN
1969 "An Evaluation of the Concept of Carrying Capacity." *Professional Geographer* 21(2):104–107.

STURTEVANT, EDGAR H.
1964 *An Introduction to Linguistic Science.* New Haven, Conn.: Yale University Press.

SUGIMOTO, Y., AND R. MOUER
1983 *Japanese Society: A Study in Social Reconstruction.* London: Routledge & Kegan Paul.
1986 *Images of Japanese Society: A Study in the Structure of Social Reality.* London: Kegan Paul.

SUGIYAMA, YUKIMARU
1969 "Social Behavior of Chimpanzees in the Budongo Forest, Uganda." *Primates* 10:197–225.

SULLIVAN, LAWRENCE
1987 "Supreme Beings." In *The Encyclopedia of Religion,* vol. 14, pp. 166–181. New York: Macmillan and Free Press.

SUSSER, IDA
1982 *Norman Street.* New York: Oxford University Press.

SUTTLES, WAYNE
1960 "Affinal Ties, Subsistence, and Prestige among the Coast Salish." *American Anthropologist* 62:296–305.

SWANSON, GUY E.
1960 *The Birth of the Gods: The Origin of Primitive Beliefs.* Ann Arbor: University of Michigan Press.

SWASY, ALECIA, AND C. HYMOWITZ
1990 "The Workplace Revolution." *The Wall Street Journal Reports,* February 9, R6–R8.

TANNER, NANCY
1974 "Matrifocality in Indonesia and Africa and among Black Americans." In *Woman, Culture and Society,* M. Rosaldo and L. Lamphere, eds., pp. 129–156. Stanford: Stanford University Press.

TAPIA, ANDRÉS DE
1971 "Relación Hecha por El Señor Andrés de Tapia Sobre la Conquista de México." In *Colección de Documentos para la Historia de México,* vol. 2, J. G. Icazbalceta, ed., pp. 554–594. Nendeln/Liechtenstein: Kaus Reprint.

TAYLOR, PAUL
1985 "Notice Regarding the Motion Picture, 'Footprints in Stone.'" Mesa, Ariz.: Films for Christ Association.

TAX, SOL
1953 *Penny Capitalism: A Guatemalan Indian Economy.* Washington, D.C.: Smithsonian Institution.

TEFFT, STANTON
1975 "Warfare Regulation: A Cross-Cultural Test of Hypotheses." In *War: Its Causes and Correlations,* M. Nettleship, R. D. Givens, and A. Nettleship, eds., pp. 693–712. The Hague: Mouton.

TERRACE, HERBERT
1979 "Is Problem Solving Language?" Journal of the Experimental Analysis of Behavior 31:161–175.

TESTART, A.
1982 "The Significance of Food Storage Among Hunter-Gatherers." *Current Anthropology* 23:523–537.

THOMAS, LEWIS
1986 "Peddling Influence." *Time,* March 3, pp. 26–36.

THUROW, LESTER
1987 "A Surge in Inequality." *Scientific American* 256(5):30–35.

TILAKARATNE, M. W.
1978 "Economic Change, Social Differentiation, and Fertility: Aluthgana." In *Population and Development: High and Low Fertility in Poorer Countries,* G. Hawthorn, ed., pp. 186–197. London: Frank Cass.

TORREY, E. F.
1980 *Schizophrenia and Civilization.* New York: Jason Aronson.

TRIGGER, BRUCE
1978 "Iroquois Matriliny." *Pennsylvania Archaeologist* 48:55–65.

TRUSSELL, JAMES, AND ANNE PEBLY
1984 "The Potential Impact of Changes in Fertility on Infant, Child, and Maternal Mortality." *Studies in Family Planning* 15:267–280.

TURNBULL, COLIN M.
1982 "The Ritualization of Potential Conflict Between the Sexes Among the Mbuti." In *Politics and History in Band Societies,* Eleanor Leacock and Richard Lee, eds., pp. 133–155. Cambridge: Cambridge University Press.

TURNER, VICTOR W.
1967 *The Forest of Symbols: Aspects of Ndembu Ritual.* Ithaca, N.Y.: Cornell University Press.

TYLOR, EDWARD B.
1871 *Primitive Culture.* London: J. Murray.

UNDERWOOD, BARBARA, AND BETTY UNDERWOOD
1979 *Hostage to Heaven.* New York: Clarkson W. Potter.

U.S. BUREAU OF THE CENSUS
1989 *Statistical Abstract, 1989.* Washington, D.C.: U.S. Government Printing Office.

U.S. NATIONAL CRIMINAL JUSTICE INFORMATION AND STATISTICS SERVICE
1978 *Myths and Realities about Crime.* Washington, D.C.: U.S. Government Printing Office.

U.S. SENATE COMMITTEE ON GOVERNMENTAL AFFAIRS
1978 *Voting Rights in Major Corporations.* 95th Congress, 1st Session. Washington, D.C.: U.S. Government Printing Office.

USEEM, MICHAEL
1984 *The Inner Circle: Large Corporations and the Rise of Business Political Activity in the U.S. and U.K.* New York: Oxford University Press.

VAIDYANATHAN, A., N. NAIR, AND M. HARRIS
1982 "Bovine Sex and Age Ratios in India." *Current Anthropology* 23:365–383.

VAILLANT, GEORGE C.
1966 (1941) *The Aztecs of Mexico.* Baltimore: Penguin.

VALENTINE, CHARLES
1970 *Culture and Poverty: Critique and Counterproposals.* Chicago: University of Chicago Press.

VAN DEN BERGHE, P.
1980 "Royal Incest and Inclusive Fitness." *American Ethnologist* 7:300–317.

VAN LAWICK-GOODALL, JANE
1986 *The Chimpanzees of Gombe.* Cambridge, Mass.: Harvard University Press.

VERDON, MICHAEL
1982 "Where Have All the Lineages Gone? Cattle and Descent Among the Nuer." *American Anthropologist* 84:566–579.

VICKERS, WILLIAM
1980 "An Analysis of Amazonian Hunting Yields as a Function of Settlement Age." In *Working Papers on South American Indians*, no. 2, Spring, Raymond H. Hames, ed., pp. 7–30. Bennington, Vt.: Bennington College Press.
1988 "Game Depletion Hypothesis of Amazonian Adaptation: Data from a Native Community." *Science* 239:1521–1522.

VILLA, PAOLA, ET AL.
1986 "Cannibalism in the Neolithic." *Science* 233:431–437.

WADEL, CATO
1973 *Now, Whose Fault Is That?: The Struggle for Self-Esteem in the Face of Chronic Unemployment.* Institute of Social and Economic Research, Memorial University of Newfoundland.

WAGLEY, CHARLES
1943 "Tapirapé Shamanism." Boletim Do Museu Nacional (Rio De Janiero), *Antropología* 3:1–94.
1977 *Welcome of Tears: The Tapirapé Indians of Central Brazil.* New York: Columbia University Press.

WAGLEY, CHARLES, AND M. HARRIS
1958 *Minorities in the New World.* New York: Columbia University Press.

WALKER, DEWARD
1972 *The Emergent Native Americans.*
Boston: Little, Brown.

WALKER, MALCOM, AND JIM HANSON
1978 "The Voluntary Associations of
Villalta." *Human Organization* 37:64–68.

WALLACE, ANTHONY F. C.
1952 *The Modal Personality Structure of the
Tuscarora Indians, as Revealed by the
Rorschach Test.* Bulletin 150, Bureau of
American Ethnology. Washington, D.C.:
U.S. Government Printing Office.
1966 *Religion: An Anthropological View.* New
York: Random House.
1970 *Culture and Personality,* 2nd ed. New
York: Random House.
1972 "Mental Illness, Biology and Culture."
In *Psychological Anthropology,* Francis
Hsu, ed., pp. 363–402. Cambridge:
Shankman.

WALLIS, ROY
1977 *The Road to Total Freedom: A Sociological Analysis of Scientology.* New York:
Columbia University Press.

WARNER, RICHARD
1985 *Recovery from Schizophrenia: Psychiatry
and Political Economy.* London: Routledge & Kegan Paul.

WARNER, W. LLOYD, ED.
1963 *Yankee City.* New Haven, Conn.: Yale
University Press.

WATSON, JAMES
1977 "Pigs, Fodder, and the Jones Effect in
Postipomean New Guinea." *Ethnology*
16:57–70.

WEATHERFORD, JACK
1988 *Indian Givers: How the Indians of the
Americas Transformed the World.* New
York: Crown.

WEIDMAN, HELEN
1983 "Research, Service, and Training
Aspects of Clinical Anthropology." In
Clinical Anthropology, D. Shimkin and P.
Golde, eds., pp. 119–153. Washington,
D.C.: University Press of America.

WEIL, PETER
1986 "Agricultural Intensification and
Fertility in the Gambia (West Africa)."
In *Culture and Reproduction: An
Anthropological Critique of Demographic
Transition Theory,* W. P. Handwerker,
ed., pp. 294–320. Boulder, Colo.:
Westview Press.

WEINER, ANNETTE
1976 *Women of Value, Men of Renown.*
Austin: University of Texas Press.

WEISMAN, STEVEN
1978 "City Constructs Statistical Profile in
Looting Cases." *The New York Times,*
August 14, p. 1.

WEISNER, THOMAS, AND RONALD GILMORE
1977 "My Brother's Keeper: Child and
Sibling Caretaking." *Current Anthropology* 18:169–190.

WEISS, GERALD
1977a "The Problem of Development in the
Non-Western World." *American
Anthropologist* 79:887–893.
1977b "Rhetoric in Campa Narrative."
Journal of Latin American Lore 3:169–
182.

WEITZMAN, LENORE
1985 *The Divorce Revolution: Consequences
for Women and Children in America.*
New York: Free Press.

WELLES, CHRIS
1978 "The Eclipse of Sun Myung Moon." In
Science, Sin and Scholarship, Irving

Horowitz, ed., pp. 243–258. Cambridge, Mass.: MIT Press.

WERGE, R.
1979 "Potato Processing in the Central Highlands of Peru." *Ecology of Food and Nutrition* 7:229–234.

WERNER, DENNIS
1979 "A Cross-Cultural Perspective on Theory and Research on Male Homosexuality." *Journal of Homosexuality* 4:345–362.

WEST, JAMES
1945 *Plainville, U.S.A.* New York: Columbia University Press.

WESTERMARK, E.
1894 *The History of Human Marriage.* New York: Macmillan.

WESTOFF, CHARLES
1978 "Marriage and Fertility in the Developed Countries." *Scientific American* 239(6):51–57.
1986 "Fertility in the United States." *Science* 234:544–559.

WHITE, BENJAMIN
1976 "Production and Reproduction in a Javanese Village." Ph.D. dissertation, Columbia University.
1983 "Agricultural Innovation and Its Critics: Twenty Years after Clifford Geertz." Institute of Social Studies Working Papers, Series No. 6, The Hague.

WHITE, LESLIE
1949 *The Science of Culture.* New York: Grove Press.

WHITING, JOHN M.
1969 "Effects of Climate on Certain Cultural Practices." In *Environment and Cultural Behavior: Ecological Studies in Cultural Anthropology,* A. P. Vayda, ed., pp. 416–455. Garden City, N.Y.: Natural History Press.

WHITING, JOHN, AND BEATRICE WHITING
1978 "Strategy for Psychocultural Research." In *The Making of Psychological Anthropology,* George Spindler, ed., pp. 41–61. Berkeley: University of California Press.

WHORF, BENJAMIN
1956 *Language, Thought and Reality.* New York: Wiley.

WILKINSON, CHARLES
1987 *American Indians, Time, and the Law.* New Haven, Conn.: Yale University Press.

WILLIAMS, TERRY
1989 *The Cocaine Kids: The Inside Story of a Teenage Drug Ring.* Reading, Mass.: Addison-Wesley.

WILLIAMS, WALTER
1986 *The Spirit and the Flesh: Sexual Diversity in American Indian Culture.* Boston: Beacon.

WILLIGEN, JOHN VAN
1986 *Applied Anthropology: An Introduction.* South Hadley, Mass.: Bergin and Gawey.
1982 "Biological Variables in Forager Fertility Performance: A Critique of Bongaarts Model." Working Paper 60, African Studies Center, Boston University.

WILMSEN, EDWIN
1982 "Biological Variables in Forager Fertility Performance: A Critique of Bongaarts Model." Working Paper No. 60, African Study Center, Boston University.

WILSON, E. O.
1975 *Sociobiology: The New Synthesis.*

Cambridge, Mass.: Harvard University Press.

1977 "Biology and the Social Sciences." *Daedalus* 106(4):127–140.

1978 *Human Nature*. Cambridge, Mass.: Harvard University Press.

WILSON, MONICA

1963 *Good Company: A Study of Nyakyusa Age-Villages*. Boston: Little, Brown.

WIRSING, ROLF

1985 "The Health of Traditional Societies and the Effects of Acculturation." *Current Anthropology* 26:303–322.

WITOWSKI, STANLEY, AND CECIL A. BROWN

1978 "Lexical Universals." *Annual Review of Anthropology* 7:427–451.

1985 "Climate, Clothing, and Body-Part Nomenclature." *Ethnology* 24:197–214.

WITTFOGEL, KARL A.

1957 *Oriental Despotism: A Comparative Study of Total Power*. New Haven, Conn.: Yale University Press.

1960 "A Stronger Oriental Despotism." *China Quarterly*, January–March, pp. 32ff.

WOLF, ARTHUR P.

1968 "Adopt a Daughter-in-Law, Marry a Sister: A Chinese Solution to the Problem of the Incest Taboo." *American Anthropologist* 70:864–874.

WOLF, A., AND C. S. HAUNG

1980 *Marriage and Adoption in China, 1845–1945*. Stanford: Stanford University Press.

WOLF, ERIC R.

1966 *Peasants*. Englewood Cliffs, N.J.: Prentice-Hall.

1969 *Peasant Wars of the Twentieth Century*. New York: Harper & Row.

WOOD, CORINNE

1975 "New Evidence for the Late Introduction of Malaria into the New World." *Current Anthropology* 16:93–104.

WOODBURN, JAMES

1982 "Egalitarian Societies." *Man* 17:431–451.

The World Almanac and Book of Facts, 1990. New York: Press Publishing Co.

WORSLEY, PETER

1968 *The Trumpet Shall Sound: A Study of "Cargo" Cults in Melanesia*. New York: Schocken.

CREDITS

We gratefully acknowledge the use of the following material.*

TEXT

Chapter 1   Page 7, Frederica De Laguna, "Presidential address: 1967." Reproduced by permission of the American Anthropological Association from *American Anthropologist* 70:3 (June 1968), 475. Not for sale or further reproduction.

Chapter 2   Page 13, Margaret Mead, *Culture and Government*, pp. 77–78. Published 1970 by Natural History Press/Doubleday.

Chapter 4   Pages 61–62, excerpt from Alfred L. Kroeber, *Anthropology*, new revised edition, p. 245. Copyright © 1948 by Harcourt Brace Jovanovich, Inc., and renewed 1976 by Theodore Kroeber Quinn. Reprinted by permission of the publisher.

Chapter 6   Page 97, reprinted with permission of the Population Council from Meade Cain, "The economic activities of children in a village in Bangladesh," *Population and Development Review* 3:3 (September 1977), 225. / pp. 100–101, Nancy Scheper-Hughes, "Infant mortality and infant care: Cultural and economic constraints on nurturing in northeast Brazil," *Social Science and Medicine* 19:5 (1984), 535–546.

Chapter 7   Pages 114, 179, excerpts from Robert Dentan, *The Semai: A Non-Violent People of Malaya*. Copyright © 1968 by Holt, Rinehart and Winston, Inc. Reprinted by permission of the publisher. / p. 123, excerpts from Leopold Pospisil, *The Kapauku Papuans of West New Guinea*. Copyright © 1963 by Holt, Rinehart and Winston, Inc. Reprinted by permission of the publisher.

Chapter 8   Page 140, E. Kathleen Gough, "The Nayars and the definition of marriage," p. 68 in *Marriage, Family, and Residence*, Paul Bohannan and John Middleton, eds. Published 1968 by Natural History Press/Doubleday. / p. 143, M. G. Smith, "Secondary marriage among Kadara and Kagoro," p. 113 in *Marriage, Family, and Residence*, Paul Bohannan and John Middleton, eds. Published 1968 by Natural History Press/Doubleday. / p. 143, Edmund Leach, "Polyandry, inheritance, and the definition of marriage," p. 76 in *Marriage, Family, and Residence*, Paul Bohannan and John Middleton, eds. Published 1968 by Natural History Press/Doubleday.

Chapter 10   Pages 176–177, 178, Gertrude Dole, "Anarchy without chaos: Alternatives to political authority among the Kuikuru," pp. 74 and 76 in *Political Anthropology*, M. J. Swartz, V. W. Turner, and A. Tuden, eds. Published 1966 by Aldine, Chicago. / p. 179, Claude Lévi-Strauss, *Tristes Tropiques*, p. 303. Copyright © 1955 by Librarie Plon. English translation ©

* An attempt has been made to obtain permission from all suppliers of photographs used in this edition. Some sources have not been located, but permission will be requested on notification to us of their ownership of the material.

1973 by Jonathan Cape, Ltd. Reprinted with permission of Macmillan Publishing Company. / pp. 179-181, Leopold Pospisil, "Law and order," p. 221 in *Introduction to Cultural Anthropology*, J. Clifton, ed. Published 1968 by Houghton Mifflin. Reprinted with permission of the author. / pp. 184, 185, C. W. M. Hart and Arnold R. Pilling, *The Tiwi of North Australia*, p. 84. Copyright © 1960 by Holt, Rinehart and Winston, Inc. Reprinted by permission of the publisher.

Chapter 11 Pages 196, 197, Douglas Oliver, *A Solomon Island Society: Kinship and Leadership Among the Sivai of Bougainville*, pp. 399, 411, 415. Published 1955 by Harvard University Press. / pp. 198-199, Bartram in Collin Renfrew, *Before Civilization: The Radiocarbon Revolution and Prehistoric Europe*, p. 234. Published 1973 by Alfred Knopf. Reprinted with permission of Random House, Inc. / p. 200, Raymond Firth, *We, the Tikopia: A Sociological Study of Kinship in Primitive Polynesia*, pp. 176-177. Published 1957 by Standford University Press. / p. 210, Jules Henry, *Culture Against Man*, pp. 287-288. Published 1963 by Random House, Inc. Reprinted with permission of the publisher.

Chapter 12 Page 227, Oscar Lewis, *La Vida: A Puerto Rican Family in the Culture of Poverty—San Juan and New York*, p. 21. Published 1966 by Random House, Inc. Reprinted with permission of the publisher.

Chapter 13 Page 245, Annette Weiner, *Women of Value, Men of Renown*, pp. 118 and 228. Published 1976 by the University of Texas Press. Reprinted by permission of the author and the publisher. / p. 247, Shirley Lindenbaum, *Kuru Society*, p. 129. Published 1979 by Mayfield, Palo Alto, California. Reprinted with permission. / p. 252, Brian Hayden, "Resources, rivalry and reproduction: The influence of basic resource characteristics on reproductive behavior," p. 458 in *Culture and Reproduction: An Anthropological Critique of Demographic Transition Theory*, W. P. Handwerker, ed. Published 1986 by Westview Press, Boulder, Colorado. / pp. 253-255, Daryl Feil, *The Evolution of Highland Papua New Guinea Societies*, pp. 69, 203. Published 1987 by Cambridge University Press, New York. / pp. 381-382, extract from G. Morris Carstairs, *The Twice-born*. Published 1967 by Chatto & Windus/The Hogarth Press. Reprinted by permission of the publisher.

Chapter 14 Pages 267-268, Calvin S. Hall and Gardner Lindzey, "Freud's psychoanalytic theory of personality," p. 18 in *Personalities and Cultures: Readings in Psychological Anthropology*, Robert C. Hunt, ed. Published 1967 by Natural History Press/Doubleday.

Chapter 15 Page 287, excerpt from Philip L. Newman, *Knowing the Gururumba*, p. 83. Copyright © 1965 by Holt, Rinehart and Winston, Inc. Reprinted by permission of the publisher.

Chapter 16 Page 331, David Hicks, *Tetum Ghosts and Kin*, p. 107. Copyright © 1976, reissued 1988 by Waveland Press, Inc., Prospect Heights, Illinois. Used with permission.

Chapter 17 Pages 353-354, Malcolm Walker and Jim Hanson, "The voluntary associations of Villalta," pp. 66-67 in *Human Organization* 37 (1978). Reproduced by permission of the Society for Applied Anthropology.

Chapter 18 Page 361, Harry Braverman, *Labor and Monopoly Capital: The Degradation of Work in the Twentieth Century*, pp. 314 and 340. Copyright © 1974 by Harry Braverman. Reprinted by permission of Monthly Review Press. / p. 370, Anthony Leeds, "The concept of the culture of poverty: Conceptual, logical and empirical problems, with perspectives from Brazil and Peru," p. 246 in *The Culture of Poverty: A Critique*. Copyright © 1971 by Simon & Schuster, Inc. Reprinted by permission of the publisher. / p. 371, Elliot Liebow, *Tally's Corner: A Study of Negro Street Corner Men*, pp. 50-52, 59, 67. Published 1967 by Little, Brown, / pp. 390-391, Robert Bellah, "New religious consciousness and the crisis in modernity," pp. 339 and 341 in *The New Religious Consciousness*, Charles Glock and Robert Bellah, eds. Copyright © 1976 The Regents of the University of California. / pp. 393-394, Jeremy Rifkind with Ted Howard, *The Emerging Order: God in the Age of Scarcity*, p. 108. Copyright © 1979 by Putnam Publishing Group.

BOXES AND TABLES

Chapter 1 Box 1.2, David Givens, *Careers in Anthropology*. Published 1989 by the American Anthropological Association. Reprinted with permission. Not for further reproduction.

Chapter 4 Boxes 4.1 and 4.2, William Labov, *Language in the Inner City*, pp. 214-225, 229. Published 1972 by the University of Pennsylvania Press. Reprinted with permission. / Box 4.4, *The Anglo-Saxon Chronicle*, translated by Dorothy Whitelock. Published by Eyre & Spottiswoode. Reprinted by permission of Methuen Ltd., London.

Chapter 7 Box 7.1, Richard Lee, "!Kung bushman subsistence: An input-output analysis," p. 58 in *Environment and Cultural Behavior: Ecological Studies in Cultural Anthropology*, A. P. Vayda, ed. Published 1969 by Natural History Press/Doubleday. / Box 7.2, Richard Lee, "What hunters do for a living, or how to make out on scarce resources," p. 62 in *Man the Hunter*, R. B. Lee and I. Devore, eds. Published 1968 by Aldine, Chicago.

Chapter 10 Box 10.1, Knud Rasmussen, *The Intellectual Culture of the Iglulik Eskimos*, Report of the Fifth Thule Expedition, 1921-1924, vol. 7, no. 1, pp. 231-232. Translated by W. Worster. Published 1929 by Gylendalske Boghandel,

Copenhagen. / Box 10.3, E. E. Evans-Pritchard, *The Nuer, A Description of the Modes of Livelihood and Political Institutions of a Nilotic People*, pp. 181–182. Published 1940 by Clarendon Press, Oxford. / Box 10.4, Brian Ferguson, "Introduction: Studying war," p. 12 in *Warfare, Culture and Environment*, Brian Ferguson, ed. Copyright © 1984 by Academic Press. Reprinted with permission.

Chapter 11 Box 11.3, R. Lee and M. Hurlich, "From forager to fighters: South Africa's militarization of the Namibian San," pp. 335–336 in *Politics and History in Band Society*, Eleanor Leacock and Richard Lee, eds. Published 1982 by Cambridge University Press. / Box 11.4, Gerald Weiss, "The problem of development in the non-Western world," in *American Anthropologist* 79:4 (December 1977). Reproduced by permission of the American Anthropological Association. Not for sale or further reproduction.

Chapter 12 Box 12.1, George M. Foster, *Tzintzuntzan: Mexican Peasants in a Changing World*, pp. 150–151. Published 1967 by Little, Brown. / Boxes 12.2 and 12.3, Thomas Belmonte, *The Broken Fountain*, second edition, pp. 141–143, 144. Copyright © 1989 Columbia University Press. Used by permission.

Chapter 13 Table 13.1, *The World Almanac and Book of Facts*, 1990 edition, p. 917. Copyright © 1989 Newspaper Enterprise Association, Inc., New York, New York 10166. / Table 13.2, Donald S. Marshall, "Sexual behavior in Mangaia," p. 123 in *Human Sexual Behavior*, Donald S. Marshall and Robert Suggs, eds. Copyright © 1971 Prentice-Hall, Inc., Englewood Cliffs, New Jersey. Reprinted by permission of the publisher. / Box 13.1, Alice Child and J. Child, "Biology, ethnocentrism, and sex differences," in *American Anthropologist* 87:1 (March 1985), 127. Reproduced by permission of the American Anthropological Association. Not for further sale or reproduction. / Box 13.2, Marjorie Shostak, *Nisa, The Life and Words of a !Kung Woman*. Published 1981 by Harvard University Press. / Box 13.3, Shirley Lindenbaum, "The last course: Nutrition and anthropology in Asia," p. 142 in *Nutrition and Anthropology in Action*, Thomas Fitzgerald, ed. Published 1977 by Van Gorcum BV, Assen, The Netherlands.

Chapter 14 Box 14.2, Mac Marshall, *Weekend Warriors: An Interpretation of Drunkenness in Micronesia*, p. 125. Published 1978 by Mayfield, Palo Alto, California. Reprinted with permission.

Chapter 15 Table 15.1, Guy E. Swanson, *The Birth of the Gods: The Origin of Primitive Beliefs*, p. 166. Published 1960 by the University of Michigan Press. / Box 15.1, Michael J. Harner, *The Jívaro: People of the Sacred Waterfalls*, pp. 146, 151. Published 1972 by Natural History Press/Doubleday. / Boxes 15.2 and 15.3, Charles Wagley, "Tapirapé Shamanism," in Boletim Do Museu Nacional, *Anthropologia* 3 (1943), 66–67, 73–74. Reprinted by permission of the Museu Nacional, Rio de Janiero. / Box 15.4, Peter Gumbel, "Down on the farm: Soviets try once more to straighten out old agricultural mess," in *The Wall Street Journal*, December 2, 1988, p. 1. Reprinted by permission of *The Wall Street Journal*. Copyright © 1988 Dow Jones & Company, Inc. All rights reserved worldwide. / Box 15.5, Omer C. Stewart, "Larenz/Margolin on the Ute," p. 108 in *Man and Aggression*, M. F. Ashley Montagu, ed. Published 1968 by Oxford University Press, New York. Reprinted by permission of the editor and publisher.

Chapter 17 Box 17.2, Gerald Murray, "The wood tree as a peasant cash crop: An anthropological strategy for the domestication of energy," p. 147 in *Haiti—Today and Tomorrow: An Interdisciplinary Study*, Charles Fost and A. Valdman, eds. Published 1984 by University Press of America. Reprinted with permission. / Box 17.3, Billie DeWalt, "Mexico's green revolution: Food for feed," in *Mexican Studies/Estudios Mexicanos* 1 (1985), 44, 54. Reprinted by permission of the author. / Box 17.4, D. Plucknett and N. Smith, "Agricultural research and third world food production," p. 218 in *Science* 217. Copyright © 1982 by the American Association for the Advancement of Science.

Chapter 18 Box 18.1, extract taken from Kristen Nelson, "Labor demand, labor supply, and the suburbanization of low-wage office work," p. 158 in *Production, Work, Territory: The Geographical Anatomy of Industrial Capitalism*, A. Scott and M. Storper, eds. Published 1986 by Allen & Unwin, Boston. / Table 18.2, Alfred Malabre, "Is the bill arriving for the free lunch?" *The Wall Street Journal*, January 9, 1989, p. A1. Reprinted by permission of *The Wall Street Journal*. Copyright © 1989 Dow Jones & Company, Inc. All rights reserved worldwide.

CHAPTER OPENER PHOTOS

Chapter 1 Institute of Human Origins / **Chapter 2** Mimi Forsyth, Monkmeyer Press / **Chapter 3** Michael K. Nichols, Magnum Photos / **Chapter 4** Michael Grecco, Stock Boston (left); Patrick Ward, Stock Boston (right) / **Chapter 5** Peter Menzel, Stock Boston / **Chapter 6** Courtesy of Moni Nag / **Chapter 7** Stacy Pick, Stock Boston / **Chapter 8** J. P. Laffont, Sygma / **Chapter 9** Mark Antman, The Image Works / **Chapter 10** Kenneth R. Good / **Chapter 11** William Stevens, Gamma Liaison / **Chapter 12** Navosti, Sygma / **Chapter 13** Vivienne Della Grota, Photo Researchers / **Chapter 14** Reuters, Bettmann / **Chapter 15** Mexican National Tourist Council / **Chapter 16** Wide World Photos / **Chapter 17** Steve Goldberg, Monkmeyer Press / **Chapter 18** C. Thatcher, Woodfin Camp & Associates.

FIGURES AND ILLUSTRATIONS

Chapter 1   Figure 1.1a, University of Florida, Information Services / 1.1b, Irven Devore, Anthro-Photo / 1.1c, Institute of Human Origins / 1.1d, AP, Wide World Photos / p. 5, "The Far Side," cartoon by Gary Larson, is reprinted by permission of Chronicle Features, San Francisco.

Chapter 2   Figure 2.1a, Mimi Forsyth, Monkmeyer Press / 2.1b, Alan Carey, The Image Works / 2.1c, FAO / 2.2a, UPI, Bettmann / 2.2b, Michael Grecco, Stock Boston / 2.2c, Spencer Grant, Photo Researchers / 2.2d, Ira Kirschenbaum, Stock Boston / 2.3a, Barbara Alper, Stock Boston / 2.3b, Jacques Henri Lartique, *Beach at Villerville*, 1908. Museum of Modern Art, Photo Researchers / 2.4a, Max Goldstein, Star File / 2.4b, Wide World Photos / 2.5a, AP, Wide World Photos / 2.5b, Russel Dian, Monkmeyer Press / 2.6a, Irven Devore, Anthro-Photo / 2.6b, Cartier-Bresson, Magnum Photos / 2.6c, UPI, Bettmann / 2.7a, Mike Kagan, Monkmeyer Press / 2.7b, Rob Nelson, Black Star / 2.7c, Patricia Hollander Gross, Stock Boston / 2.7d, Albertson, Stock Boston.

Chapter 3   Figure 3.1, Masao Kawai / 3.2a, Masao Kawai / 3.2b, Mitsuo Iwamoto / 3.3, by Baron Hugh Van Lawick. © National Geographic Society / 3.4, by Baron Hugh Van Lawick. © National Geographic Society / 3.5, National Museums of Kenya / 3.6 Anthro-Photo / 3.8, H. S. Terrace, Anthro-Photo / 3.9, Elizabeth Rupert, Yerkes Regional Primate Research Center / 3.10, © Ronald H. Cohn, The Gorilla Foundation / 3.11, © 1983 Michal Heron, Woodfin Camp & Associates / 3.12, John R. Cole.

Chapter 4   Figure 4.2a, Michael Grecco, Stock Boston / 4.2b, Patrick Ward, Stock Boston / 4.3, John Running, Stock Boston / 4.5, The Bettmann Archive.

Chapter 5   Figure 5.1, AP, Wide World Photos / 5.2, Robert L. Carneiro / 5.3a, photo by Harold C. Conklin, Yale University. From *Ethnography Atlas of Ifugao*, 1980, Yales University Press / 5.3b, Blair Seitz, Photo Researchers / 5.3c, United Nations / 5.3d, China Pictures, Eastfoto / 5.4, Robert Harding Associates / 5.5a, Owen Frankin, Sygma / 5.5b, Paul Fortin, Stock Boston / 5.7, Richard B. Lee, Anthro-Photo / 5.8a & b, Kevin T. Jones, University of Utah Aché Project / 5.9, Roy Rappaport / 5.10, Cherry Lowman / 5.11, Roland and Sabrina Michaud, Woodfin Camp & Associates / 5.12, Peter Menzel, Stock Boston.

Chapter 6   Figure 6.1, Mel Konner, Anthro-Photo / 6.2, J. P. Laffont, Sygma / 6.3, J. P. Laffont, Sygma / 6.4, courtesy of Moni Nag / 6.5a & b, Jennifer Scheper-Hughes.

Chapter 7   Figure 7.1, Kenneth R. Good / 7.2, United Nations / 7.3, Leopold Pospisil / 7.4, AP, Wide World Photos / 7.5, courtesy Department Library Services, American Museum of Natural History / 7.6, Neg. no. 42298. Photo by Edward Dossetter. Courtesy Department Library Services, American Museum of Natural History / 7.7, Neg. no. 336116. Photo by Dr. Frang. Courtesy Department Library Services, American Museum of Natural History / 7.8, Stacy Pick, Stock Boston / 7.9, *Financial Times*, Gamma Liaison / 7.10, Allen and Orna Johnson / 7.11, AP, Wide World Photos / 7.12, J. P. Laffont, Sygma.

Chapter 8   Figure 8.1, J. P. Laffont, Sygma / 8.2, Stuart Smucker, Anthro-Photo / 8.3a, © 1984 Eugene Gordon / 8.3b, © 1985 Eugene Gordon / 8.4a, United Nations / 8.4b, Museum of the American Indian, Heye Foundation, New York / 8.5, Sid Schuler, Anthro-Photo / 8.6, The Bettmann Archive / 8.7, Myron L. Cohen / 8.8, Leopold Pospisil / 8.9, © 1978 Thomas Hopker, Woodfin Camp & Associates / 8.10, The Granger Collection, New York / 8.11, © Mike Goldberg–Neve Ilan, Stock Boston.

Chapter 9   Figure 9.1, Mark Antman, The Image Works.

Chapter 10   Figure 10.1, Napoleon Chagnon / 10.2, Courtesy of Royal Danish Ministry of Foreign Affairs / 10.3, Robert L. Carneiro / 10.4, Thomas Gregor / 10.5, Pitt Rivers Museum, University of Oxford / 10.6, Australian Information Service / 10.7, Kenneth R. Good / 10.8, Kenneth R. Good.

Chapter 11   Figure 11.1, © 1984 Eugene Gordon / 11.2, The Granger Collection, New York / 11.3a & b, © 1984 Eugene Gordon / 11.4, from a photo by the late Dr. A. T. Schofield, in *The Uganda Journal*, courtesy of Dr. J. Beattie. / 11.5, The Bettmann Archive / 11.6, Malcolm Kirk, Peter Arnold / 11.7, UPI, Bettmann / 11.8, Henle, Monkmeyer Press / 11.9, Stuart Franklin, Magnum Photos / 11.10, William Stevens, Gamma Liaison / 11.11a, UPI, Bettmann / 11.11b, Jim Stratford, Black Star.

Chapter 12   Figure 12.1, © Charles Gatewood, The Image Works / 12.2a, Sovfoto from *Tass* / 12.2b, Navosti, Sygma / 12.3a & b, Eastfoto / 12.3c, Walter Aguiar / 12.4, United Nations / 12.5a, Irene B. Meyer, Monkmeyer Press / 12.5b, Ira Kirschenbaum, Stock Boston / 12.6, UPI, Bettmann / 12.7, Paul Conklin, Monkmeyer Press / 12.8, Fujihira, Monkmeyer Press / 12.9, Richard Farley, Topham, The Image Works / 12.10a, © Charles Gatewood, The Image Works / 12.10b, © 1979 Kroll, Taurus / 12.10c, © Owen Franken, Stock Boston / 12.10d, © 1981 Sarah Putnam, The Picture Cube / 12.11, P. Durand, Sygma / 12.12, UPI, Bettmann.

Chapter 13   Figure 13.1, Neg. no. 125283. Photo by Captain Frank Hurley. Courtesy Department Library Services. American Museum of Natural History / 13.2a (left), The Granger Collection, New York / 13.3, Annette B. Weiner, New York University / 13.4, Christopher Morrow, Black Star / 13.5a, © 1982 Eugene Gordon / 13.5b, George Gardner, Photo

Researchers / 13.5c, UPI, Bettmann / 13.5d, © 1984 Eugene Gordon / 13.5e, UPI, Bettmann / 13.6a, Vivienne Della Grotta, Photo Researchers / 13.6b, Beryl Goldberg / 13.6c, Bruce Roberts, Photo Researchers / 13.7, Sharma, DPI / 13.8, Museum of the American Indian, Heye Foundation, New York.

Chapter 14 Figure 14.1, The Bettmann Archive / 14.2a, Courtesy Department Library Services, American Museum of Natural History / 14.2b, Neg. no. 122772. Courtesy Department Library Services, American Museum of Natural History / 14.3, Neil Goldstein, Stock Boston / 14.4, United Nations / 14.8, Reuters, Bettmann / 14.9a & b, Neg. nos. 232188 and 232202. Photos by D. B. MacMillan. Courtesy Department Library Services, American Museum of Natural History / 14.10, Media Class, Xavier High School, Truk. Photo courtesy of Keith Marshall / 14.11 a & b, Museum of the American Indian, Heye Foundation, New York.

Chapter 15 Figure 15.1, Hector Aceves, Photo Researchers / 15.2, Neg. no. 328284. Photo by Philip L. Newman. Courtesy Department Library Services, American Museum of Natural History / 15.3, UPI, Bettmann / 15.4, Irven Devore, Anthro-Photo / 15.5a, © 1982 Eugene Gordon / 15.5b, United Nations / 15.6, Charles Wagley / 15.7, Neg. no. 326848. Photo by Rota. Courtesy Department Library Services, American Museum of Natural History / 15.8, Neg. no. 324767. Photo by A. J. Rota. Courtesy Department Library Services, American Museum of Natural History / 15.9a, © 1989 Eugene Gordon / 15.9b, Museum of the American Indian, Heye Foundation, New York / 15.9c, Neg. no. 31592. Photo by J. Otis Wheelock. Courtesy Department Library Services, American Museum of Natural History / 15.10 a & b, From Victor Turner, *The Forest of Symbols: Aspects of Ndembu Ritual.* © 1967 by Cornell University. Used by permission of the publisher, Cornell University Press / 15.11, Laimute Druskis, Photo Researchers / 15.12, Mexican National Tourist Council / 15.13, Neg. no. 326597. Photo by Rota. Courtesy Department Library Services, American Museum of Natural History / 15.14, Neg. no. 37704. Courtesy Department Library Services, American Museum of Natural History / 15.15, © 1983 Peter Menzel, Stock Boston / 15.16, Sergio Larrain, Magnum Photos / 15.17, Nevada Historical Society / 15.18a, Museum of the American Indian, Heye Foundation, New York / 15.18b, AP, Wide World Photos / 15.19, Painting by Ernest Spybuck. Museum of the American Indian, Heye Foundation, New York / 15.20, © 1982 Kal Muller, Woodfin Camp & Associates / 15.21, Courtesy of Moni Nag.

Chapter 16 Figure 16.1a–c, Wide World Photos / 16.2a–f, Museum of the American Indian, Heye Foundation, New York / 16.3, Richard Lee, Anthro-Photo / 16.4a, Neg. no. 31198. Photo by R. Weber. Courtesy Department Library Services, American Museum of Natural History / 16.4b, Neg. no. 331865. Photo by Rota. Courtesy Department Library Services, American Museum of Natural History / 16.5, Neg. no. 334177. Photo by Rota. Courtesy Department Library Services, American Museum of Natural History / 16.6, Neg. no. 332624. Photo by Rota. Courtesy Department Library Services, American Museum of Natural History / 16.7, Meret Oppenheim, *Object* (1936). Fur-covered cup, saucer, and spoon: cup, 4-3/8″ diameter; saucer 9-3/8″ diameter; spoon, 8″ long; overall height 2-7/8″. Collection, The Museum of Modern Art, New York. Purchase. / 16.8a & b, de Havenon Collection / 16.9, © 1982 Eugene Gordon / 16.10, UPI, Bettmann / 16.11, photograph by Egyptian Expedition, The Metropolitan Museum of Art. All rights reserved. / 16.12, French Government Tourist Office / 16.13, Maxine Hicks.

Chapter 17 Figure 17.1, Steve Goldberg, Monkmeyer Press / 17.2, Paul L. Doughty / 17.3, Michael Bannister, Department of Forestry, University of Florida / 17.4a & b, Richard W. Franke / 17.5, Photo by Billie R. DeWalt / 17.6, © Peter Simon, Peter Arnold / 17.7, From *Edge of the Forest: Sand, Childhood and Change in a New Guinea Protoagricultural Society,* Smithsonian Institution Press, 1976. Photo by Dr. E. R. Sorenson.

Chapter 18 Figure 18.2, Gerard Fritz, Monkmeyer Press / 18.6a, C. Thatcher, Woodfin Camp & Associates / 18.6b, Ted Thai, Sygma / 18.6c, UPI, Bettmann / 18.7, Richard Kalvar, Magnum Photos / 18.9, Alan Murray, "Many Americans fear U.S. living standards have stopped rising," *The Wall Street Journal,* May 1, 1989, p. A1. Reprinted by permission of *The Wall Street Journal.* © 1989 Dow Jones & Company, Inc. All rights reserved worldwide. / 18.8, UPI, Bettmann / 18.10, Carol Stack / 18.11, Kirk Edwards, Monkmeyer Press / 18.12a, *St. Louis Post-Dispatch* / 18.12b, UPI, Bettmann / 18.12c, Keith Meyers, NYT Pictures / 18.13, Hispanic Study Project, J. W. Sharff, Director. Photo by Jennifer Benepe. / 18.14, Johnson, DeWys / 18.15, Eagan, Woodfin Camp & Associates / 18.16, © Patsy Davidson, The Image Works / 18.19, David Burnett, Contact Press Images / 18.20, T. Lopker, Woodfin Camp & Associates / 18.21, Wide World Photos.

NAME INDEX

SUBJECT INDEX

Warfare *(Continued)*
  class, 220
  defined, 183
  and division of labor, 124
  functions of, 187
  and homosexuality, 261–262
  and human sacrifice, 303–304, 316
  in hunting and gathering societies, 183–185
  impact on gender roles, 246–247, 252–253, 255, 263
  and marriage alliances, 149
  and martrilineality, 164
  and patrilineality, 163, 164, 170
  and population control, 190–191, 193
  and potlatch, 118
  and power, 217
  and religious revitalization, 306
  and sex ratio, 191
  as sport, 186–187
Wealth, concentration of, 367–369
Weaning, 269
Weapons, 118
  and division of labor, 124

  primate use of, 32
  in the United States, 376
Welfare system
  and crime, 379–380, 396
  and matrifocality, 375–376
  and state socialism, 362
West Africa, 134, 250–251, 255, 263
West Indies, 140
White-collar workers, 361, 363–364
White's law, 84–85
Whorf's hypothesis, 58–59
Widows
  in India, 251–252
  levirate, 150, 151, 252
Wife stealing, 175–176
Windigo psychosis, 278–279, 282
Witch hunting, 279
Wodziwob, 306–307
Work, patterns of, 125. *See also* Division of Labor
Work and Family (Oppenheimer), 386, 389
Work force. *See also* Unemployment
  child labor in, 96–98
  feminization of, 257, 385–386, 389

  in information/service sector, 13, 360, 361, 363–364
  married women in, 9–10, 360, 381, 385, 396
  migrant, 224, 233
  unskilled, 370–371
  white-collar, 361, 363–364
World Almanac, 363
Wovoka, 307

Xingu National Park, 179

Yahgan, 183
Yams, 198, 199, 244
Yanomamo, 92, 185, 187–189, 193
Yellow fever, 94
Yoruba, 251
Yupka, 190
Yurok, 243

Zaire, Mbuti of, 109, 249
Zambia
  Barotse of, 139
  Ndembu of, 299